Revival and Awakening

Revival and Awakening

American Evangelical Missionaries in Iran and the Origins of Assyrian Nationalism

ADAM H. BECKER

The University of Chicago Press
Chicago and London

Adam H. Becker is associate professor of religious studies and classics at New York University. He is the author of *Fear of God and the Beginning of Wisdom.*

The University of Chicago Press, Chicago 60637
The University of Chicago Press, Ltd., London
© 2015 by The University of Chicago
All rights reserved. Published 2015.
Printed in the United States of America

24 23 22 21 20 19 18 17 16 15   1 2 3 4 5

ISBN-13: 978-0-226-14528-0 (cloth)
ISBN-13: 978-0-226-14531-0 (paper)
ISBN-13: 978-0-226-14545-7 (e-book)
DOI: 10.7208/chicago/9780226145457.001.0001

Library of Congress Cataloging-in-Publication Data

Becker, Adam H., 1972– author.
Revival and awakening : American evangelical missionaries in Iran and the origins of Assyrian nationalism / Adam H. Becker.
pages ; cm
Includes bibliographical references and index.
ISBN 978-0-226-14528-0 (cloth : alk. paper) — ISBN 978-0-226-14531-0 (pbk. : alk. paper) — ISBN 978-0-226-14545-7 (e-book) 1. Missions to Assyrian Church of the East members—History—19th century. 2. Protestant churches—Missions—Iran—History—19th century. 3. Missionaries—United States—History—19th century. 4. Evangelistic work—Iran—History—19th century. 5. Syriac Christians—Iran—Religion—History—19th century. 6. Assyrian Church of the East members—History—19th century. 7. Nationalism—Religious aspects—Christianity—History—19th century. I. Title.
BV2628.N4B43 2015
266'.02373055—dc23   2014019847

♾ This paper meets the requirements of ANSI/NISO Z39.48-1992 (Permanence of Paper).

Patri Matrique (hac in serie, Michael).

Contents

Prelude: A Song of Assyria

I have a music video to thank for the origins of this project. Around the year 2000 I discovered Juliana Jendo's "Alap Bet," a song and video that aim to teach the Christian Aramaic alphabet.[1] Jendo, an Assyrian pop singer, originally hails from Tel Tamer, a village north of Hassake in Syria. Assyrian Christians settled in this part of eastern Syria in the 1930s after many were expelled from the new state of Iraq. Some of those expelled were already refugees from what is now Turkey due to the expulsion of Assyrians during World War I, an event simultaneous with and related to the better-known Armenian genocide. In 1980 Jendo and her family came to Chicago, where a large Assyrian community remains today.

The lyrics of the song, which I translate here from Neo-Aramaic, begin: "*alap*: Assyria is our mother / *bet*: Mesopotamia is our country. We have one language and these are our letters." The first lines have an alliterative acrostic play: the word for "Assyria," *ator*, begins with *alap*, the first letter of the Assyrian alphabet, whereas *bet*, the second letter, is part of the word for "Mesopotamia," *bet nahrain* (lit. "the place of the rivers," originally meaning "between the rivers"). The twenty-two letters of the alphabet are then chanted, a series that is repeated in the song's refrain. Each individual letter of the alphabet receives special attention in the song as a series of words that begin with that letter are listed—*alap alaha ata* (*alap*: then the words for "God," "flag"), *bet baba bruna brata* (*bet*: "father," "son," "daughter")—and the lyrics continue through the whole alphabet alliteratively listing words from the mundane ("world" and "wealth") to abstractions, practices, and social figures relevant to the community ("love," "freedom," "fasts," "prayers," "teachers," and "martyrs"). During the introductory credits of the accompanying video, which include Jendo's name in English and Aramaic, a winged ancient Assyrian bull flies across the screen. These creatures, familiar to those who have visited the Metropolitan Museum of Art in New York or the British Museum, are commonly found in contemporary Assyrian national iconography.

The bulk of the video consists of an alternation between images of the Aramaic alphabet in the Assyrian national colors of red, white, and blue and images relevant to the words listed after each letter of the alphabet. Superimposed over the letter *ṣad*, which begins the words for "prayer" and "cross," is a crucifix, and on the side are the profiles in bright pink and blue, respectively, of a young girl and boy praying with yellow halos over their heads; the letter *semkat*, which begins the word for "martyrs," has a baby behind it and a cross next to it. In the center of the cross is an Assyrian national star, and on the top of it is a soldier's helmet. Interspersed among all these images is footage of children on a sports field. They are dressed in the national colors, and as the song proceeds, they collectively form the letters with their bodies and also spell out *ator*, Assyria. Jendo sings and dances among them. At points in the video, images of ancient Assyrian architecture appear, as well as photographs of the rebuilt walls and gate of ancient Nineveh, today across the Tigris from Mosul in northern Iraq, and by the end Jendo flies over these stone structures.

At the song's conclusion, Jendo adds a final verse: "Come, let us be like the vowels in our lovely letters." This exhortation requires explanation because in Aramaic, as in other Semitic languages, vowels are not treated as letters. Written texts in Semitic languages often do not include vowels, which are diacritical marks written around the consonants. Today, in Hebrew and Arabic, for example, most writing does not require these vowel marks because readers know the languages well enough to read without them. It is as if I were to write "Kck th dg," assuming you would understand "Kick the dog." (In English, ambiguities in such a system of shorthand would be more common than they are in Semitic languages.) The word for "vowel" in Aramaic, *zoʻa*, literally means "movement," and so Jendo's call to "be like the vowels" implies the animation of the letters and provides a sense absent from a simple English translation. Her invitation to enliven the letters fits with the football-halftime-like performance of the children in the video, forming the letters with their bodies. Furthermore, "movement" in Neo-Aramaic has the same political sense as it does in English: like its Arabic equivalent, *haraka*, the word for political movement is also *zoʻa*, and the main Assyrian nationalist organization in Iraq, the Assyrian Democratic Movement, is often simply referred to as "the movement" (*zoʻa*).

The tune itself is singsongy and repetitive. Its saccharine sound and sentimental politics inspired the original questions of this project, and the close identification it draws between nationality and language, including the very embodiment of the letters of the alphabet by the children performing in the video, has fascinated me as both typical of nationalism but also particular to the church tradition of Assyrian Christians. Large human maneuvers on the field are characteristic of national performances, from Nazi Germany to modern Turkey and the United States, but such a focus on the alphabet is rare. As is common in the ancient Mediterranean and Near Eastern worlds, the alphabet in Classical Christian Aramaic—or Syriac, as the dialect is referred to by scholars—has traditionally been understood to have certain inherent powers. For many Jews and Christians in antiquity (and later Muslims), the alphabet was not an arbitrary system of signs: the letters of the alphabet were considered no less than the very building blocks of creation. In one late sixth-century Syriac text, composed in a city in southeastern Turkey, on the border with Syria and not far from northern Iraq, God's act of creating the world is described as a reading lesson in which God put together letters to spell out words for the angels. As he subsequently read each word aloud, each respective entity came into being and the angels then repeated the name of the entity before him. The alphabet could serve as a magical tool in antiquity, one even used in nonsense abracadabra word formations. In the Jendo video the alphabet remains special, but it depends upon and represents a national ontology, not a divine one: the letters now represent a national culture, albeit one that is sacralized and linked to Christianity. In the video the nation is embodied by the letters, which are in turn animated by the children on the field, moving as "vowels" do. This nationalizing of the letters fits with shifts in the basic usage of terms. Words, such as "freedom" (*heruta*), which in Classical Syriac is used to refer to theological "free will," are used here for political freedom, and the "martyr" (*sahda*) is now represented by the soldier martyr of the battlefield of nations.

*

Most of my scholarly work has been on the history of what is known as Syriac Christianity. Syriac, a Christian dialect of Aramaic, remains today the liturgical language of several Christian communities in the Middle East and in diaspora. My work has focused on late antiquity and the early Islamic period (fourth through seventh centuries), examining texts composed in Mesopotamia, in a region now straddling Iraq, Iran, Turkey, and Syria. While immersing myself more and more in Syriac studies as a student, I gradually learned bits and pieces about the modern Christian communities who participate in the Syriac heritage. In graduate school, in order to better understand a collection of ancient Syriac medical texts published in 1913, I began to examine the memoir of E. A. Wallis Budge, the famous orientalist and editor of these

texts. Reading his account of collecting manuscripts in Mesopotamia introduced me to the complex multireligious, multiethnic, and multilingual world
of upper Mesopotamia in the late nineteenth century. Later, while working
on my dissertation, I was compelled to engage with the modern struggles of
the Syriac communities and the violence they suffered: one of the primary
sources for my dissertation was edited by Mar Addai Sher, the bishop of Siirt,
a city in southeastern Turkey, and published in 1907 ("Mar," lit. "lord," is a title
of respect in Aramaic). I had some questions about the original manuscripts
upon which Sher based his edition, but then I learned that several of these
were burned in 1915 and that Sher was hunted down and murdered during the
Armenian and Assyrian/Syriac Christian genocide.

Modern Syriac Christian history mediates the ancient Syriac past, and
therefore, as a scholar, I was drawn into this modern history. Furthermore, it
seems to me to be disingenuous and selfish to intellectually and professionally
benefit from a tradition and ignore the contemporary inheritors of that tradition. To be sure, many changes have occurred since antiquity—a major one
is the topic of this book—but for me "objective" scholarship does not absolve
me of a responsibility to those communities whose history I study. Rather, it
behooves me to understand the complex mediation of my sources from their
authors' pens in the early Middle Ages to my desk as I study them. However,
this does not imply an obligation to toe the line of Assyrian nationalist discourse, and this raises an ethical difficulty for me in this project.

The implications of this book may understandably trouble some members of the Assyrian community. Many people would prefer not to read that
aspects of their ethnic identity are part of a recent historical composition
and cannot be traced back into the heroic past. Furthermore, it is clear that
even rarefied academic discussions of the constructedness of national identity can at times function outside of academic contexts to disparage national
discourse as "unauthentic."[2] My response is only that I am a historian who
wants to understand the present through the alterity of the past. I have no
need to squabble about the foundations of Assyrian identity, nor do I desire to
antagonize members of the Assyrian community. In fact, despite the possible
implications of this present project, I have devoted most of my research career
heretofore to the study of Syriac Christianity, the tradition to which Assyrians
also lay claim, and I hope that my work has helped to bring deserved attention to this important religious and cultural tradition. Concerning this issue,
one Assyrian interlocutor wrote to me: "I really do believe that both scholars
and the people they study can benefit from cooperation and exchanges. But
you should understand that Assyrians are sensitive to questions about their
identity. We have endured tremendous suffering over the past 100 years at the

hands of those who seek to end our very existence as a distinct group, so when it *appears* that a foreigner is trying to deny our identity, we find it hard to distinguish between someone who does so conscientiously and someone that does so to harm us (e.g. the Baath regime in Iraq)." I hope that in this project I have demonstrated the conscientiousness to which my interlocutor refers.

On reflection it is evident how my own identity has—inevitably—contributed to guiding my interest in the material and the questions I have asked of it. I myself come from an ethnoreligious community that, like the Assyrians, is regularly in contention about hyphenated ideas of community—is Judaism a religion or an ethnicity or both?—in contrast to the universalizing of certain forms of Christianity and Islam. I am willing to acknowledge the inventions of my own background and tradition, and yet that does not mean that my identity is something I treat as completely arbitrary. Just because something is constructed does not mean we do not experience it as real. Think of love: there is a time before we know the beloved, but love is no less real because it comes about in time.

Despite my own ambivalence about the historical stability of identity, I am sympathetic to the ongoing debates within the Assyrian community and Syriac Christian communities in general about the limits and criteria of what defines the broader community. Judaism and the Church of the East were both deeply affected by the development of nationalism within their respective communities in the early twentieth century, and members of both traditions have suffered greatly due to the volatile combination of historic communal frictions, modern competing nationalisms, and the capacity to dislocate and kill human beings offered by modern technologies and forms of knowledge. However, the two communities took different paths: Jewish nationalism succeeded in creating a viable state, whereas Assyrian nationalism, in its territorial form, has failed. It is perhaps also my own ambivalence about the "success" of Jewish nationalism and my embrace of diasporic Jewish identity that have been the background for my thinking about Assyrianism and my desire to examine the process by which it came into being. Despite many claims about the impending decline of the nation-state and its sovereignty, nationalism does not seem to be going anywhere. However, like many others, I stand intellectually and emotionally outside of it, unable to engage in its festivity and always aware of its potential violence and record of bloodshed. And yet it would be disingenuous, even unethical, to imply that I do not have my own myths, ones that can make my blood boil. Fortunately and unfortunately, most of life is not as dispassionate as scholars' abstractions or historians' inventions.

Acknowledgments

Many people have helped me in this project in a variety of ways. They include Nicholas Al-Jeloo, Talal Asad, the late Youel Baaba, Varuni Bhatia, Sebastian Brock, Peter Brown, Elizabeth Castelli, Damian Chalmers, Chip Coakley, Kati Curts, Mark Elmore, Khaled Fahmy, Jonathan Goldman, Bruce Grant, Philip Hamburger, Kristian Heal, Joseph N. Hermiz, Adam McCollum, Alessandro Mengozzi, Turi Munthe and Muzia Sforza, David Owen, Janine Paolucci, Leslie Peirce, Todor Petev, Bridget Purcell, Rafael Sanchez, Noah Silverman, Benjamin Sommer, Fr. Gewargis Sulaiman, Jack Tannous, David Taylor, Joel Walker, G. Carol Woodall, İpek Yosmaoğlu, and various members of the *Hugoye* Syriac Studies e-mail discussion group. I apologize to those I have forgotten. Gabriele Yonan kindly sent me portions of her archive, and Shawqi Talia saved me from errors in my reading of Neo-Aramaic poetry. Daniel Wolk generously shared his work with me at the beginning of this project. David Malick was an immeasurable help at various points and ever supportive. Furthermore, this project would have been impossible without his work and the work of Heleen Murre-van den Berg, who turned out to be an extremely helpful anonymous reader. I also thank the other anonymous reader. It has been a pleasure to work with the University of Chicago Press: I thank in particular executive editor T. David Brent and associate editor Priya Nelson for their support and for escorting me through the process and Susan J. Cohan for her detailed copyediting. I enjoyed a year of leave as a fellow at the Straus Institute for the Advanced Study of Law and Justice, where I was able to move toward the completion of this project. I thank the staff for their support throughout that year. I also thank the staff at various libraries where I did my archival research: the British Library, Michael Hopper at Widener Library at Harvard, Houghton Library at Harvard, the Presbyterian Historical

Society, and the Rare Book and Manuscript Library at Columbia University. Joy Connolly, NYU's dean for the humanities, generously provided financial subvention for publication from her discretionary fund. I thank the Kevorkian Center at NYU, especially Michael Gilsenan and Greta Scharnweber, for the opportunity I was given to present my work, as well as Ellen Muehlberger, who invited me to speak on one of my chapters at the University of Michigan. In the fall of 2011 I shared several rough drafts of chapters with my graduate seminar, and I thank them for their feedback. My colleague at the time, Anthony Petro, also sat in on the seminar, and his feedback then as well as on a number of other occasions was immensely helpful, as were the numerous suggestions Geoffrey Pollick, another Americanist colleague, has offered. Kerem Öktem offered two months of wonderful hospitality in Istanbul at the beginning of the writing process, and my aunt Judith Posner provided the same in Jerusalem at its end, in addition to various editorial comments. Patsy Speyer provided excellent feedback at the halfway point. Markus Dressler has been an important interlocutor and friend, and the similarities of our two recent projects attest to the fruits of our friendship. Arang Keshavarzian has long supported my intellectual efforts as a friend and a learned resource on the modern Middle East. Ra'anan Boustan invited me to UCLA to present one of the chapters and has always been a source of feedback and both intellectual and emotional support. Two scholars whom I greatly respect, both ever supportive friends, Tamer el-Leithy and Omri Elisha, have served as models of learning and thinking for me. I would not be the intellectual that I am without the friendship, mentoring, and collegiality of Angela Zito.

As always, I acknowledge the love and support of my sisters, Rachel Petev and Danielle Speckhart, and their respective families. Toward the latter part of this project, I met Therese, my *bashert*, and since then she has not ceased to challenge me, both intellectually and in general. Nonetheless, I thank her. Now she can stop nagging me, "Come on, babe, finish that book already!" After a frenzy of labor, the final draft of the manuscript was sent to the press ten days before the birth of my son, Solomon Louis Spock Becker. I thank him for the incentive he provided to get it done. Finally, I thank my parents, Katherine A. Becker and Michael L. Becker, to whom this book is dedicated. If this book is about an encounter between different worlds and the creativity it engenders over three generations, then it can be read as an allegory for the world in microcosm my parents have created in the three generations of our family. It is only the amorous bond that has kept them together that can make full sense of the familial and professional success they and their children have enjoyed.

Note on Transliteration and Names

In transliterating Classical Syriac and Neo-Aramaic words, I have aimed at clarity, not linguistic exactitude. It is enough that those who read Neo-Aramaic or other relevant languages with cognate terms (Hebrew, Arabic, Persian, Turkish, Kurdish) be able to recognize the words to which I am referring. I generally do not use macrons or other diacritics commonly used for phonetic transcription. However, I do distinguish Semitic letters in transliteration: *ḥ* for *Ḥeth* (voiceless pharyngeal fricative), *ṭ* for *Ṭeth* (emphatic *t*), *ṣ* for *Ṣadhe* (emphatic *s* or *ts* sound), ' for *'Ayn* or *'E* (voiced pharyngeal fricative), and *š* for *Šin* (similar to English *sh*). I only mark the aleph (') when it is medial, frontal without a full vowel, or in the few instances where it is necessary for the specific discussion. Spirantization of plosive/fricative allophones, the so-called begadkephat letters, has been marked in Classical Syriac words with the letter *h*; thus, following the tendency to Hebraize Syriac pronunciation in academic settings, *bh* is pronounced *v*. Various distinctions exist between the pronunciation and orthography of Neo-Aramaic, but my purpose has been to demonstrate the terms that are important for my argument, not to make them phonetically transparent. For example, the Neo-Aramaic digraph *ay* is pronounced *ê*, but I do not mark this. Nor do I mark all the fricative phonemes that derive from the historical allophonic system, with the exception of the letter *bet* as *w* in its fricative form (e.g., Syriac *kthabha* becomes *ktawa*). For what would be represented as *aw* or *abh* in Classical Syriac, I provide the Neo-Aramaic *o* (e.g., *tawditha* becomes *todita*). I have used doubled consonants in Neo-Aramaic words derived from Classical Syriac ones that are formed upon the D-stem (gemination of the second radical; e.g., the *pa'el* form of the verb). On occasion I render words to fit the standard spelling used in Literary Urmia Aramaic. For example, in some early mission tracts there are variations in spelling (e.g., 'ahwale for 'ahwale). Disparities occasionally arise in transliteration. For example, the term *malik* ("chief") I spell in a way that reflects the more common Arabic vocalization, but *Malek, Malech,* and *Malick* appear in some names. In Turkish words I distinguish between the vowels ı (close or high back unrounded) and i (close or high front unrounded).

I usually employ the English form of first names when it is a very common English name, *David* for *Dawid* or *George* for *Gewargis.* However, in order to avoid confusion, some names have remained in their Neo-Aramaic form, but without diacritical marks. I use *kh* to mark the *ḥeth* in names, sometimes following the more common spelling of the mission sources (e.g., Dunkha for Denḥa). For ease of pronunciation I occasionally add an *e* to a word instead of marking the half vowel schwa. I have also used the spelling conventionally found in the sources for some names (e.g., the town Geogtapa, which is better rendered *Gög Tapa* or *Gök Tepe*). In referring to communities, I try to use terms that have less political baggage. *East Syrians* and *Church of the East* are superior to *Nestorians; West Syrians* and *Syrian Orthodox* to *Monophysites* or *Jacobites,* the theological enemies of the East Syrians since the fifth century. Contradictions can be found in any appellation if one looks closely enough, because it is impossible to encapsulate the complexities of human history and social life in delimiting categories. Moreover, naming is a particularly fraught issue with regard to the various communities of the Syriac heritage, as this book will in part explain.[1] Similarly, place names are politically charged: for example, most of the town and village names I mention in what is today the Republic of Turkey have been changed, thus further erasing the history of the Assyrian Christian population of the region.

Introduction

Religious Reform, Nationalism, and Christian Mission

Wake up, wake up, Assyria, and tear down the walls of folly.
—first line of a poem in Classical Syriac, published in New York in 1920[1]

In 1906 in Urmia, Iran, a group of indigenous Christians, most of whom were educated at the American Presbyterian mission in the city, began to publish a nationalist newspaper, the *Star* (*Kokhwa*), for their fellow "Syrians," as members of their community commonly called themselves at the time. The Syrians belonged to the ancient Church of the East and had for over a thousand years been known as "Syrians," not because of an inherent connection to what is now modern Syria. They had used the Christian dialect of Classical Aramaic, Syriac (Syr. *suryaya*), in their liturgy since antiquity, and the name *Syrian* helped to differentiate them from the Armenian and Greek church communities. The prologue of the first issue of this Neo-Aramaic periodical, which was printed at the American mission press, spells out the reasons for its publication.

> An anxious wish of the sons of our nation [*melatan*] over the past years has been that we might have a newspaper [*ruznama*] of our own, in which we might make our pains known, encourage one another, and be encouraged by one another. More than anything else today we need a bond which will bind the scattered sons of our nation to one another, a Syrian [*suraya*] bond, not a foreign one, Eastern, not Western, adhering to the country and homeland [*watan*] of our father and grandfather. There is great fear that by migration and by estrangement people are alienated from one another, they "forget Jerusalem" [Ps 137:5], and deny their mother who produced them.[2]

The purpose of the newspaper, we are told, is "to bind the nation [*melat*] together by letters, speeches, and news," because sectarian diversity has led to a lack of "national sympathy [*sumpatiya umtanayta*]." "Our nation is now scattered in Turkey, Iran, Russia, and America. There are signs that this diaspora will increase. Year after year it decreases the number of those who still live in the region of their homeland [*watan*]."³

Anxiety about social centrifuge, the modern fear that society could dissipate into anomie or amnesiac loss of group identity, requires a notion that the collective, whether it be society or the nation, is composed of numerous parts, each potentially extricable from the whole. The social is imagined as a constituency of various members of a body bound together. Such a concern for the bonds needed to maintain the "nation" and its "unity," as we see in this article, persisted among the "Syrians," and from the 1920s onward, when the name *Assyrian* became the dominant appellation for this ethnoreligious community, unity remained an ongoing concern of Assyrian nationalists. This anxiety about the nation and its imminent demise was a response to the real struggles and oppressions endured by the Assyrian people, especially in the early twentieth century. However, the idea of the social itself, that the nation is a composition of individuals existing in synchronicity, was, as I argue in this book, the result of a decades-long encounter between the Syrians and foreign missionaries.

The *Star* continues, "We are the sons of one nation, we are the flesh and blood of one another," who share one language. This unity is threatened by the two dangers of tribalism and sectarianism, which are then equated: "The primary purpose of this newspaper is and ought to be the establishment of ethics [*etiqonuta*] in the nation [*melat*], to inform the nation about those foundational structures of religious confession [*todita*], which all of us accept without any debate. The *Star* will not be without religion [*mazhab*] but it will not be an organ of tribalism [*qabilayuta*]."⁴ Thus, the ethical reform of the nation will take place in the religious sphere, but this sphere will be limited, a shared ethical space of overlapping consensus. In line with the Protestant backgrounds of most of those involved in the paper's production, shared beliefs take priority over shared practices. The theological disputes of the past and the religious diversity stimulated by foreign missions are to be transcended, whereas Syrian nationality is treated as irreducible.

Indigenous writers had expressed similar sentiments about nationality and its relationship to religion already for several years in the pages of the American mission periodical *Rays of Light* (*Zahrire d-bahra*). Religion, some Syrians had begun to argue, was divisive, whereas a self-conscious knowledge of their own culture, which included their language and history, would unite them as a people. In "The Preservation of the Syrian Nation and Its Language," an 1899 article in the Catholic mission periodical *Voice of Truth* (*Qala d-šrara*), Mirza Mesroph Khan Karam (1862–1943), an associate of the American mission, sets religion's capacity to divide next to the history, language, and national identity shared by the Syrians. Mesroph begins by noting how newspapers (*ruzname*), such as *Rays of Light*, are the principal means for elevating and perfecting the spoken language. He then singles out *Voice of Truth*, which had only first appeared in 1897, for its manifest concern for the Syrian nation (*umta*) and its language.

> It teaches reform [*turraṣa*] of language and the composition of sentences, as much as possible, according to the spirit of the true and pure Syrian language, and it heralds love, peace, and unity [*ḥuyyada*]. We hope that both these newspapers will be faithful, as much as they have it in them, to us Syrians and to our language. Although they differ in confession [*todita*] from one another, nevertheless in national sentiment [*umtanayuta*] they are one. However, both are for Syrians and both ought to trust in the seed of Shem, that is, in our Syrian nation [*umta*], which has drawn its descent from Shem. Both ought to honor Laban the Syrian, Abraham the Chaldean, Aram, and Ashur [*ator*], the progenitors of the Syrian nation, and remember that we Syrians are the seed of Nimrod the mighty and of Nebuchadnezzar, Tiglathpileser, Ninos, Senacherib and Queen Shamiram, etc., remember that the Syrian nation has given the world mighty and famous men who introduced culture [*marduta*] and the arts and sciences into the world; it has given other men in great number who spilled their blood mightily for the faith, like Mar Shemʿon Barsabbaʿe, the victorious martyr, and other fathers who received the crown of martyrdom with him, as well as other numberless martyrs, and others who ascended to the lofty rank of angelic sanctity, and others who shined like stars in the firmament of the church, like Mar Ephrem, Mar Jacob, Mar Narsai, and the rest of the teachers. Allow both these newspapers to come and pass through with us to examine the ruins of Nineveh and Babylon, that we may see with our own eyes the columns of the temples of Syrianism [*suryayuta*] broken and fallen to the ground, and let us gaze at the environs of our Zion and let us count its towers and think about its beginning and see its end, so that we can talk about it to the generations to come (Ps 48) and repeat with the king, the Psalmist, "If I forget you, Jerusalem, if I forget my mother . . ." [Ps 137:5].[5]

The links Mesroph draws among language, history, archeology, nationality, and reform echo similar nationalist configurations elsewhere. Nationalist movements have often advocated the purification of the national language and the ethical reform of the nation. Although the disparate list of characters—the mythical Shamiram, the ancient Assyrian king Tiglathpileser, and the fourth-century Christian poet Ephrem—and the archeology of ancient Assyria and Babylon are particular to Assyrian nationalism, such a plumbing of the past for historical figures and material culture to link to the contemporary nation is also a common nationalist intellectual practice. Moreover, the language of

Zion, which we also find in the above article from the *Star*, as well as an emphasis on martyrs, often appears in other nationalist cultures. Mesroph's article is only a step away from the full-blown Assyrian nationalism of the 1920s, when, after the dislocation and massacres of World War I, many began to claim that they were "Assyrians," some even making territorial demands for their nation now in exile, longing for a state in what they deemed to be their ancestral homeland of Assyria in northern Iraq.

Another trait common to a variety of nationalist cultures is the use of the motif of "waking up" from sleep to characterize national mobilization and the raising of national consciousness (e.g., "Deutschland erwacht"). "Wake up!" is a standard nationalist imperative, just as it has also been used elsewhere in calls for social and political awareness. By the 1910s and 1920s, Assyrians were calling for a national "awakening," whether in Neo-Aramaic (*mar'ašta*), Classical Syriac (*'irutha*), or Ottoman (*intibah*). The so-called Arab awakening, the Nahda, of the nineteenth and early twentieth centuries employed similar terms. What is noteworthy about the Assyrian awakening is that the Neo-Aramaic terminology itself, *mar'ašta* and its cognates (e.g., the imperative *r'uš*, "Wake up!"), was often used by American evangelical missionaries from the 1830s onward to refer to Christian "revival" and the coming to consciousness of one's own and one's nation's sinful condition, an integral part of evangelical conversion. Personal awakening from sin is a metaphor that already appears in the Classical Syriac tradition, but the increased focus by the late nineteenth century on awakening as a personal and communal goal was a result of the missionary encounter. This book will articulate the relationship between Christian "revival" and national "awakening," one and the same term in Neo-Aramaic.

Focus of This Book

Western missions played an important role in the political, cultural, and social history of Ottoman Anatolia, Syria, Lebanon, and Egypt in the long nineteenth century.[6] Moreover, missions had significant effects even after World War I in, for example, British Mandate Palestine and republican Egypt.[7] The history of American missions in particular is an important early part of the longer story of American relations with the Middle East, a recently popular topic due to current political circumstances.[8]

This is a study of how the presence of American evangelical missionaries in the borderlands between Qajar Iran and the Ottoman Empire in the nineteenth century contributed to the development of a secularized (but *not* desacralized) national identity among the indigenous Christian population of the region. The Americans, primarily Congregationalists and Presbyterians, aimed to "reform" and "revive" the ancient Church of the East by establishing schools, publishing and distributing literature in the vernacular, and preaching a penitential return to "biblical Christianity," but their interventions in the region helped rather to lay the groundwork for a new identity and communal understanding articulated by the East Syrians, many of whom began to call themselves "Assyrians." This book is about families, fellow villagers and tribesmen, and nearby coreligionists, and how through a creative engagement with foreign missionaries they made a new name for themselves.

When the American mission was established in Urmia, Iran, in the 1830s, the Church of the East was an ancient ecclesial community in what is now northwestern Iran, southeastern Turkey, and northern Iraq. The "Nestorians" (or "Syrians" as they usually called themselves) often lived intermingled with a number of other religious and linguistic groups and spoke a variety of dialects of Neo-Aramaic. At the time of the arrival of the missionaries, this ethnoreligious community was loosely joined under several competing patriarchs, and tribal affiliation or village of origin seem to have been the predominant basis of self-identification. However, by the turn of the twentieth century, a national consciousness had developed whereby many Assyrians understood themselves to be descendants of an ancient Near Eastern nation, even race. Living today in Iran and Iraq, as well as scattered in a worldwide diaspora, the Assyrians are part of a larger Syriac (Christian Aramaic) community that numbers perhaps as many as three million (and this does not include the large Syriac Christian communities in South India).

This book will examine the impact the missionary encounter had on this social and communal transformation, which is the central turning point in the modern history of the Church of the East. In doing so, it will describe a local articulation of modernity, including its various internal "tensions that relate to each other asymptomatically."[9] The missionaries introduced innovations in media, collective ritual, and epistemology, as well as new notions of self and community. In addition to examining the introduction of such new forms of thinking and knowing, I also focus on affect, sentimentality, and ways of being both together and alone, all of which were cultivated by the mission for evangelical purposes, but which ultimately contributed to a national self-understanding. The affect, sentiment, and piety I examine became part of a particular configuration of modernity belonging to a visceral realm often unrecognized in characterizations of secularism and the Enlightenment. As I will demonstrate, only after a national consciousness and national ways of relating to one another and others had come into being did the East Syrians then take up the name *Assyrian*. By the turn of the twentieth century, some Syrian nationalists responded *autoethnographically* to the orientalist and biblical archeological knowledge, which was disseminated by the missions in vernacular publications, by locating their origins historically in the ancient Near East: they linked the national consciousness that had been developing through the nineteenth century to the name and history of the Assyrians. This identification persists in the community today, and over the last century many people have been born, lived their lives, and died as Assyrians, some of them fiercely proud of their ancient ancestors and with a hopeful expectation that their nation will be reunited someday under an autonomous government in their imagined ancestral homeland.

With only a few exceptions, no scholars have looked closely at missions to the Church of the East.[10] The book covers primarily the period from 1834 to 1918—that is, from the arrival in Iran of Justin Perkins, the director of the American mission for thirty-five years, to the early years of Assyrian nationalism and the cataclysm of World War I. The sources consist primarily of Neo-Aramaic literature published by the missionaries (including Bibles, commentaries, tracts, Christian novellas, textbooks, almanacs, and a monthly newspaper published from 1849 to 1918), missionaries' memoirs and other publications for American domestic readership, and material from the mission archive. Most of the book focuses on the American mission, but other missions (Catholic, Anglican, Orthodox, and Lutheran) are also addressed, especially in the last two chapters. Few scholars have examined *any* of this archive. Moreover, only a handful of scholars read Neo-Aramaic, and those who do are primarily linguists and not historians.

Through a close reading of the sources, this book reconstructs the social and intellectual world of the American mission, and in doing so tells the story of how Protestant religious (devotional, creedal, epistemological, and moral) reform and the new practices, ideas, and affects the missionaries aimed to cultivate in it helped foster a new secular national identity. What began as an intra-Christian dialogue in the mid-nineteenth century in the environs of the American mission, a protonationalism evolving out of a Christian discourse, was eventually parallel to, and even took inspiration from, similar movements we see in Iran and across the Ottoman Empire by the turn of the twentieth century. The veracity of national claims became self-evident to many East Syrians, or Assyrians as they are now more commonly called, and this book is an attempt to provide a history of the development of that self-evidence.

I have in the course of research had to acquire a historical grasp of the American Christians who traveled across the globe to spread their Gospel. Americanists do not have access to a large part of my sources due to linguistic limitations. Missionaries printed an abundance of literature in the languages of those they were missionizing, and Americanists are unable to read these often obscure languages. For this reason Americanists may find this study of interest: in examining the American mission, I have sketched out certain trends in the Christian culture of the nineteenth-century United States. In the latter chapters I address missionaries working within the progressive Protestantism of the turn of the twentieth century, but the majority of the book covers the interaction between the East Syrians and American missionaries in the antebellum period. These missionaries were primarily well-educated New England and Mid-Atlantic middle-class white evangelicals from the Reformed tradition (Congregationalist and Presbyterian). Openly reviling figures such as Rousseau and Voltaire, they were women and men who embraced the Enlightenment in a particular mode. In fact, light was a key metaphor in much of their preaching. Note even the title of the Neo-Aramaic monthly published by the mission: *Rays of Light*. They saw no contradiction between scientific learning and Scripture nor between the ordered rationality of the universe and a deep need for a sentimental relationship with God and their fellow Christians. They approached the world with a philosophy of common sense and the mechanistic physics of Newton, even if they were able to perceive Satan's wiles woven throughout our lives. They were anxious about the ills introduced by American market culture, and yet they were certain that American republicanism was the highest form of Christian civilization and they relied on the tools of modern business to organize their work.

Protestant missions had a disproportionate influence on liberal political movements around the world in the nineteenth and early twentieth centuries, and this was no less the case in Urmia: at the turn of the twentieth century, the American mission was at the forefront of advocating liberal political reform in Iran.[11] However, one of the arguments of this book is that the liberalism of the American mission is apparent from its origins in the 1830s. In attempting to introduce the "nominal" Christians of the Middle East to the creed, morality, natural science, and correct worship characteristic of what they deemed true Christianity, these evangelical missionaries in the antebellum period set the stage for the development of a racialized and liberal ethnic nationalism that would at times reject ecclesial identity.

The Nation Is a Montage, Not a Church

An 1898 article in *Rays of Light* entitled "The Nation's Reputation" (*Šema d-melat*, lit. "name of the nation") begins:

> Sometimes pictures are taken by photographers in this way: first they take a
> picture of one person, then on that same glass they take a picture of another
> person, and again a picture of another person. A picture of this sort is not
> simply a picture of one person, but rather a mixed picture of all of them. This
> is called a composite picture. So the reputation of a nation is a composite
> reputation, which is formed by the reputations of the different people of that
> nation.[12]

The article that follows describes the spread of Syrians all over the world,
some in search of work, but others for less respectable reasons. The good
reputation of a nation depends on the deeds of all of its members, and, so the
article warns, all Syrians must behave well wherever their travels take them.
Such a concern for the good name of the nation was common in early Assyrian nationalist literature. National reputation was the focus in objections to
the "Thieves of the Cross," those Syrians who traveled the globe in the nineteenth and early twentieth centuries under the pretext of collecting funds for
the suffering Christians of the Middle East, but who in reality were charlatans
bilking sentimental Christians in Europe and the United States (and even
South Africa and farther afield) out of their charity.[13]

"The Nation's Reputation" employs relatively recent technology to describe the nation. Photo montage, although it had been developed by the
1850s, was popular at the turn of the twentieth century. In this figurative usage, the nation is on display as in a photograph, but because its members are
scattered, they must be combined in one frame. Implicit in this imag(in)-
ing of the nation is the notion that each of its members is an autonomous
participant in a horizontal society of equals. No one member of the nation
represents the rest: each represents all. Like the analogous composite photograph, the nation has no center, no hierarchy, and the group is a collection of
individuals. One of the primary arguments of this book is that nationalism,
at least in the case of the East Syrians, emerged within the context of a new
social formation consisting of sets of social practices and ideas of the social
introduced by the American mission, and this emergent nationalism then
received further impetus from the breakdown in traditional East Syrian social
relations due to the genocide: Assyrian nationalism does not represent simply
the continuity of a past social group under a different name, but a new configuration, one that was imagined as consisting of individuals, a "body" with
various "members."

Let us compare the imagined composite photograph of the nation to
the traditional image of the church. The Church of the East, as the Syriac
churches in general, inherited from the Classical Syriac tradition an ornate
ecclesiology that set the church within a stratified temporal and ontological

frame.[14] As Israel prefigured the church, so the church as a potentially escha-
tological community looks forward to the kingdom of heaven. With ancient
Israel as its type and the heavenly kingdom as its prototype, the church, we
might say, is a prefigured prefiguration. Existing always in a higher frame outside of earthly time, it moves through this world as a ship on a voyage to its
haven.[15] However, the church, as opposed to the synagogue, was a people from
the peoples, a composition of various nations ('amme), in contrast to the Jews,
who, often with disdain, are referred to in Syriac sources as simply "the nation" ('amma). "The Church of the Nations came to be / where the Temple of
the Nation was destroyed," claims Saint Ephrem (d. 373), the most influential
of the Syriac Fathers.[16] This new people of God were prefigured in Scripture
by carnal Israel, a people who have now been superseded.

The church is also the body of Christ, especially through the Eucharist, as
Saint Ephrem states:

> In a new way his body
> has been fused with our bodies,
> and his pure blood
> has been poured into our veins.
> His voice, too, is in [our] ears
> and his splendor in [our] eyes.
> The whole of him with the whole of us
> is fused by his mercy.
> And because he loved his Church greatly,
> he did not give her the manna of her rival;
> He became the Bread of Life
> for her to eat him.[17]

The need for a unified church is often articulated in the tradition, especially in
the face of the heretical dissensions or disobedience that threaten to separate
Christ, its head, from the ecclesial body, but the metaphorical potential of the
Pauline notion of the church as the body of Christ, its members his limbs,
is not as productive in the Syriac tradition as it is in Western Christianity.
Rather, Christians are at times thought to have their own individual journeys
as pilots of ships upon a stormy sea, and thus they are microcosms of the
divine head and body of Christ.

Despite the occasional corporate imagery of the church and the appearance of the notion that Christians make up the body of Christ, there are essential differences from the montage imagery of the 1898 article. In the classical
ecclesial tradition, Christians are not imagined as isolated and isolatable constituents of the body of Christ. The only distinction that does arise between

them is in the occasional reference to the bishop as the head or spouse of the church, which thus marks him as hierarchically superior, a shepherd to his flock. However, the church is not imagined as a machine in motion with its various parts conceptually isolatable. There is a difference in temporality: the montage image works with the premise that at any moment, if we could freeze time, we would be able to examine each of the constituent parts of the nation wherever they are. The nation of the montage is a multipart entity re-forming itself in the world through time. In contrast, the church is not of this world, it belongs to an underlying and fundamental reality and stands outside of earthly time, its fulfillment will take place in the kingdom, and its members include all who have ever participated in the body: the patriarchs and prophets, the apostles, the saints, the clergy, and all Christians living and dead.[18] As I shall demonstrate, the origins of Assyrian nationalism and of a social imaginary in which the nation could be conceptualized as a montage must be understood within the East Syrians' encounter with foreign missionaries, especially American evangelicals. The emergence of Assyrian national consciousness was concomitant with the development of a new secular culture, albeit one spurred on by Protestant piety and manifesting characteristics of East Syrian Christianity as it was being reconfigured in the context of the mission. In this new secular national discourse, Syrian nationalists juxtaposed parts of the ecclesial tradition in creative ways in the process of articulating the nation.[19]

Religion as a Product of Discursive Processes

The Christianity of the American missionaries was not simply an alternative Christian tradition, a variation on shared themes. It closely corresponded with the discourse of modernity, and it is often difficult in analyzing the sources to draw a line between the one and the other. While examining the American evangelical mission, it is necessary to observe how the missionaries introduced the modern category of "religion" and how their Christianity resonated with the ideas, practices, and affects of modernity. In their focus on "true Christianity," the American missionaries helped the Syrians to articulate their own discourse on religion.

It has become commonplace in religious studies to maintain that religion is itself a modern phenomenon, an entity constituted within (and constitutive of) secular modernity (which itself should not be treated as a culmination or end of history but rather scrutinized as a historically contingent product). However, scholarship working with the assumptions of the secularization thesis tends to treat religion, when it does persist publicly, as an irregularity, a hangover, a hybrid, or a "fundamentalist" reaction. The very notion of secularization requires a definition of religion: secularization heuristically entails a delimitation of religion in order to describe its differentiation, privatization, and eclipse. Instead of pushing us to examine the transmogrification of a concept and the formulation of a new set of ideas, practices, and affects, as well as changes in communal formation over time, "religion" in this case functions as the exception that proves the rule, a recalcitrant substance that is either precipitated out of the analysis, or isolated and reified for discrete examination.

However, "religion" is not a stable entity nor category. The term has a long, complex history from its origins in ancient Roman *religio*, its later Christian usage, and more significantly the proliferation of the term during the Reformation and in the colonial encounter as a category for addressing difference. The term was pluralized, making it possible for there to be numerous religions due to the Christian sectarianism of the Reformation and the variety of religious practices and beliefs "discovered" by Europeans as they began to cross and colonize the globe.[20] Part of this process included the development, especially in European and American philological, orientalist, and theological scholarship, of a discourse of "world religions" and a science of comparative religion.[21] In social scientific fields as well as elsewhere, religion came about as part of an intellectual response to modernity, a tool for understanding those parts of human life that were deemed irrational or difficult to subordinate to progress.[22] However, although it is part of modernity, it is important to remain aware of how religion has long been part of an internal Christian conversation.

> Religion, in other words, is the result of a tradition and of a name, which Christianity gave itself, part of a style of thought, which it elaborated over centuries in order to achieve some degree of unity—much like "the West" was described as doing earlier. It is not so much that the concept makes the object, but rather that the concept is part of the object—here "Christianity" or "religion"—and participates in determining its *potential* boundaries.[23]

In this sense, religion—perhaps paradoxically—is the process itself of naming religion more than any coherent object or thing in itself. Religion has involuted origins within Christianity, and this means that it continues even today to slide in and out of normative, often Christian, claims about the world.

The work of Talal Asad, as well as more recent work on secularism, points the way to what we might call a "post-secular historiography of religion."[24] What I mean by this is the following: the critical turn in religious studies understands the category of religion as itself a product of discursive processes, a result of numerous modern events, conversations, and contestations. To be

sure, ideas, practices, and affects we often label "religious" have existed almost anywhere we look in human history, but religion as a category came
into being in modernity and is constituted by various political, legal, social,
and economic discourses, while being the mutual constituent of the "secular."
The secular is "a concept that brings together certain behaviors, knowledges,
and sensibilities in modern life" and "is neither singular in origin nor stable
in its historical identity, although it works through a series of particular op-
positions."[25] The secular is a specific set of conditions in which religion is
constituted: what began as a theological idea—that is, the Christian notion
of the *saeculum* ("the world")—unfolded and embraced the object it isolated
as religion. At the same time, what we heuristically understand as religion in
the premodern period was reconfigured in the process of naming religion.
This means that religion cannot be universally defined except as a node of
contestation and definition. There is no transhistorical and transcultural phenomenon "religion."[26]

Extending this analysis, scholars have begun to examine what we may
call "religionization"—that is, the process whereby the discourse of religion
is taken up in different cultures, or "religion-making," as one recent volume
terms it.[27] The notion of religionization offers a new perspective on the effects
of Western expansion through colonialism and mission. In the study of South
Asia, the question of the "invention" of Hinduism has spurred a debate going
back over twenty years: were Western colonial administrators, missionaries,
and orientalist scholars the culprits, or does Hinduism as a coherent religious system derive from internal developments of devotion and reform?[28]
Regardless of origins, the colonial and missionary encounter led to further
reifications, and the religionizing process is apparent in academic discourse
as well as national politics: Hinduism as a coherent and systematic religion
of scholarly purview corresponds with the further development of a formal
Hindu religious community from the nineteenth century onward.[29] The same
process is apparent in noncolonial contexts—for example, among the Alevis
in Turkey.[30] Sectarianism and its heightened tensions therefore are no longer
to be seen simply as age-old phenomena, but modern articulations, which
derive in part from colonial rule and missionary education.

Religionization as a process often entails the isolation, codification, and
naming of a "tradition," or traditionalization, which itself plays an important
role in the mythologizing origins of nations. Religion and nation are not discontinuous from each other nor inherently linked as reductive equivalents,
but two related instances of the reifications of modernity. As with tradition,
we should not understand religion as preceding modernity or as opposed
to it, but rather as constituted within it, and this is consistent with the play

of categories in both the colonial and missionary encounter. Both colonizer and colonized, missionary and missionized, have often strategically employed "religion," "tradition," "magic," and the other representations of difference that play a fundamental role in the discourse of modernity.[31]

This critical stance on religion has also provided an impetus to look at the indigenous categories of the past.[32] If religion is not eternal, then how were relations between heaven and earth, between self and other, and between manifestations of power in the world and human social groups construed in the past? Such a conceptual history corresponds with Talal Asad's vision of anthropology as a tool for the interrogation of Western concepts. One of Asad's motivations for his work in *Genealogies of Religion* was a concern to demonstrate the pitfalls of allowing a normalizing concept of religion to be employed uncritically in the study of Islam. He demonstrates how instead of the modern emphasis on meaning or belief, embodied forms of piety and discipline should be taken into account when we address Islam and medieval Christianity. He posits that when religion "was gradually compelled to concede the domain of public power to the constitutional state, and of public truth to natural science," it was constructed "as a new historical object: anchored in personal experience, expressible as belief-statements, dependent on private institutions, and practiced in one's spare time."[33] In *Formations of the Secular* he recasts the discussion as part of the anthropology of the secular and an attempt to think beyond the "evacuation thesis," or "subtraction stories," as Charles Taylor puts it.[34] The evacuation thesis is the idea that "secular" refers to simply the absence of religion and that therefore "secularization" is the general disappearance of religion from the world.

> I am arguing that "the secular" should not be thought of as a space in which *real* human life gradually emancipates itself from the controlling power of "religion" and thus achieves the latter's relocation. It is this assumption that allows us to think of religion as "infecting" the secular domain or as replicating within it the structure of theological concepts. The concept of "the secular" today is part of a doctrine called secularism. Secularism doesn't simply insist that religious practice and belief be confined to a space where they cannot threaten political stability or the liberties of "free-thinking" citizens. Secularism builds on a particular conception of the world ("natural" and "social") and of the problems generated by that world.[35]

Relying upon Asad's formulation of the secular, several scholars have provided examples of illiberal piety that resists being bounded by the limitations of a secular regime.[36] Such work is useful for historians because contemporary illiberal forms of piety can serve as a heuristic tool for thinking about premodernity and what a difference the secular makes. I do not mean to suggest that contemporary illiberal forms of piety ("fundamentalism") provide examples of past phenomena. They are essentially modern. However, they help us to parochialize the secular modern and think outside of it, as does the work of contemporary Christian thinkers such as Stanley Hauerwas and those associated with Radical Orthodoxy.[37]

Christ and Culture: Christian Mission and the Invention of Religion

> Go ye therefore, and teach all nations, baptizing them in the name of the Father, and of the Son, and of the Holy Ghost: Teaching them to observe all things whatsoever I have commanded you: and, lo, I am with you alway, even unto the end of the world.
> —MATTHEW 28:19–20 (King James Version)

The problem of "Christ and culture," which goes back to the apologists of the second century onward, or even to Paul (1 Cor 1:26–31), played itself out in nineteenth-century debates among missionaries about how best to approach their audiences. This intra-Christian theological question resulted in American missionaries deliberating over where to draw the line in differentiating religion as distinct from ethnicity, nationality, and culture. At the same time American missions often stumbled upon the contradiction between spreading a universal Christianity and the exceptional role Americans and their culture played in this.[38] The most significant factor in the evolution of the Jesus movement, a Jewish messianic sect, into Christianity was the decision to preach the good news of the life and death and resurrection of Jesus Christ to the "nations" ("Gentiles," Hebr. *goyim*, Gr. *éthne*). Since its origins, Christianity has remained, at least discursively, a proselytizing tradition. This question with which modern missionaries grappled, the relationship between Christianity and culture, was already a problem for Christians in late antiquity and the early Middle Ages.[39] In fact, some of the conceptual tools Christians developed in their negotiation with the "pagan" traditions of classical antiquity were recycled in the early modern period.[40]

With European expansion in the "age of discovery" and the subsequent social, political, and economic interminglings of the colonial period, Christianity's universalist message went truly global. Catholic missions in the sixteenth and seventeenth centuries and large Catholic and Protestant missionary organizations from the late eighteenth century onward spread Christianity and Euro-American culture around the world. Some missions were highly successful, whereas others, at least in their explicit aims, failed. The modern mission's project of Christianization, however, also brought with it unintended consequences, such as the sparking of secular ideas and ethnic nationalism among the missionaries' audiences.[41]

At first glance, the secular effects of modern missions could be interpreted as suggesting that while intending to promote religion, missionaries were subverting it. However, implicit in such an understanding is the evacuation thesis. Missions did not simply remove religion from the world by accident. The secularism promoted at missions was the flip side of religionization—that is, the spread of "religion" as a distinct social, intellectual, and experiential category in human life, a discourse in which the secular is relationally implicit. In this way, Christian missions had a significant impact on the global process of religionization. In the Christian missionary encounter, religion itself was repackaged and defined by the missionaries in order that it might be exported, or rather translated, across cultural boundaries, and in modern missions this has often had secularizing effects. Christian missions frequently provided an impetus to the discursive process whereby religion was named, defined, and delimited; certain traditions, both Christian and non-Christian, were reified; and spaces of legitimate religiosity were created. Christianity had in fact long played a role in this process.[42] In order to convey Christianity to others, to convert the "nations," that which was to be promulgated had to be defined: a conversionary ethos demands the definition of religion. This is true in the history of Christianity in general, but the need to define became more acute in the modern period, such that this ethos and its effects were qualitatively different.

Nineteenth-century American missions could be large, often businesslike organizations specifically designed for promulgating the Gospel, and their at times shrill calls for the conversion of the world raised massive amounts of money and mobilized thousands of people. Whereas Christian thinkers have always had to determine what it was that they wanted to impart, modern missionaries have often engaged in explicit conversations about what the essence of Christianity is, to what extent it relates to culture, and what parts of their own culture they need not include in their proselytizing message. In modern missions "Christianity" is more easily identifiable as an object distinct from culture.

Protestant reform promoted a purer form of religion, an intensified "true Christianity," and in the process of identifying and naming this true Christianity, it compartmentalized religion. This was an ideological component of the so-called structural differentiation of spheres, which is commonly thought to be constitutive of modernity.[43] In other words, within the intensified piety of Protestant reform, particularly at Christian missions, religion and its identification as "religion" led to a certain configuration of modernity.

In the laboratory of mission, religion as a category, modernity as a way of being, and nationality as an irreducible identity were concocted in a manner reminiscent of what occurred in the colonial encounter. Moreover, the contradictions of secularism are also built into the missionizing process. Missionaries must draw an unstable distinction between the sacred and the secular, but this boundary is not a natural one, and it creates contradictions, loopholes, and paradoxes.

The Secularization of Mission

One of the paradoxes of the American mission was that despite their earnest millennial form of Christianity, the missionaries' work had secular effects within the East Syrian community. Justin Perkins (1805–69) opened the first mission school in Urmia in 1836. Under the auspices of the American Board of Commissioners for Foreign Missions (ABCFM), which was founded in 1810 and consisted primarily of Congregationalists and Presbyterians, Perkins and others like him had been sent to the Middle East to reinvigorate the "oriental" churches, which were understood by Western Protestants to be in decline. The primary purpose of their missionary work was to reform indigenous Christians so that they might revive their own past authentic Christianity. They in turn, as orientals, who knew oriental ways, would have a beneficial effect on the region as a whole by aiding in the conversion of Muslims to Christianity. Ottoman and Qajar authorities as well as local custom restricted direct proselytism of Muslims, and it was hoped that through their neighbors, Muslims would hear the message of the Gospel.

By the time Perkins left for Persia in 1832, the ABCFM, which was the largest American missionary society of the nineteenth century, was already entering its second generation, and criticisms had begun to arise within the board concerning the correct methods for missionary work. By the late 1830s there was a debate within the ABCFM around the question of the relationship between evangelizing and civilizing, or Christianity and culture. The early representative of a new, more wary position concerning this relationship was Rufus Anderson (1796–1880), who played a dominant role in the ABCFM through the mid-nineteenth century. Concerning "Whether Savages Must Be Civilized before They Can Be Christianized,"[44] Anderson came out in strong opposition. He deemed a failure ABCFM attempts to civilize in India and the Middle East and among Native Americans. Anderson noted, "The pupils were faithfully instructed in the Scriptures; but it was found, that the tendency of their training, on the whole, was to make them foreign in their manners,

foreign in their habits, foreign in their sympathies; in other words, to dena-
tionalize them."[45] Such denationalization would especially be a problem if,
as in the case of the indigenous Christians of the Middle East, the purpose
of conversion was to create true Christians who yet maintained their local
customs.[46] A domestic catalyst for the articulating of the binary of Christ and
culture, or Christianity and civilization, was the abolitionism of the ABCFM.
Some, including Anderson, argued that slaveholding was a social problem
and not an individual sin—that is, it was part of culture.[47] Anderson's missionary philosophy, though he argued that it was based upon his own missionary experience, corresponds with a Protestant focus on salvation by faith
in Christ alone.

Anderson's ideas had a strong influence on the missionary movement,
even if missionary ideology shifted in the opposite direction in the latter
part of the century. He "articulated an ideology that appeared respectful of
other cultures while remaining fundamentally Eurocentric in its orientation,
and he propounded a theory that sought to foster native agency by suppress-
ing indigenous aspirations."[48] Although they often maintained a position at
variance from Anderson's, missionaries after him continued to engage with
the problem of discerning the right relationship between Christianity and
civilization.

However, by the late nineteenth century, a shift had again occurred in the
missionary approach, from a focus on conversion alone to an effort at "civilizational" transformation.[49]

> In many missions in the Middle East, British, American and German, a trend
> towards secularization of missionary activities can be detected. This may
> probably be explained from the converging of two developments: the grow-
> ing wish to attract more Muslims, which encouraged downplaying the role of
> overt evangelization, and the world-wide trend towards developing sophisti-
> cated institutions of higher education (universities) and medical care (hospi-
> tals). This required a different type of missionary, a woman or man who had
> been educated as a doctor or teacher, not as a minister or evangelist. However,
> alongside these somewhat secularized and often liberal types of missions, mis-
> sions with explicitly conversionist aims were continually re-introduced into
> the region.[50]

The shift toward the progressive Social Gospel among the Americans by the
turn of the twentieth century had a significant impact on the development
of Assyrian nationalism, as did the growing presence of other missions. As
we will see, competition among various missions allowed for a picking and

choosing of ecclesial identity, a denominationalism that functioned to relativize "religion" while leaving "Syrianness" intact. Orientalism, archeology, and
biblical studies all contributed to this process by offering the "Assyrians" a
name and a history and inviting them into the wider contemporary conversation about nations that was often inflected through the sciences of language
and history.

The final result of the process I am examining, like modernity itself (however we choose to define it), was not singular in cause. However, one of the
main arguments of this book, the focus through chapter 6, is that the secularism promoted by the mission was not due to a secularization of mission
but was a result of the evangelical secularism of the mission from the very
beginning, especially as it was mediated through the contradictions of the
missionary encounter. The development of national sentiment is documented
in antebellum sources—that is, *before* the 1870 accession of the mission to
the Presbyterian Church and the emergence of the Social Gospel in the late
nineteenth century. By the late 1860s a separate evangelical church had been
formed, but, as has been noted by other scholars, if we focus on numbers, we
miss the historical relevance of Christian missions.[51] The pre-1870 mission
was *not* particularly successful at making converts to evangelical Christianity.
The "Mission to the Nestorians" created new social relationships and introduced new affects, concepts, and practices, with which many East Syrians
were compelled to engage, even if they often failed to or rejected the calls to
convert. In other words, just as not all capitalists were Calvinists, according
to Weber's famous thesis in *The Protestant Ethic and the Spirit of Capitalism*
(1905), so also not all East Syrians became evangelical Christians, but the
presence of some and the work of the mission transformed the East Syrian
community in Urmia before the liberal and modernizing mission of the turn
of the twentieth century. Millennial evangelicalism in the antebellum period
had its own secular effects.

Missionary Modernity and Christian Reform

The relegation of "religion" to its own distinct sphere, this differentiation constitutive of modernity, was not advocated only by thinkers and politicians
who aimed both to demote certain institutions that they deemed too powerful
and to immunize society against divisive social differences. Rather, an intensification of piety has at times functioned to reduce the presence of religion
in everyday life. In the intellectual sphere, this is attested in *On Religion*,
Friedrich Schleiermacher's 1799 attempt to separate religion from metaphys-

ics (rational speculation about the world) and morality (ethics) and to define it as an immediate affective response, a deep intuition or feeling. American evangelical missionaries shared Schleiermacher's sentiments. Religion was foremost a feeling, one of dependence upon the creator, and not an ethical or intellectual system. They also agreed with John Locke, the forbearer of the separation of church and state and their cousin in Calvinism, that true religion is something internal to the heart and that it does not in its essence consist of practices. The Reformed (Calvinist) tradition resonated on several levels with a secularized notion of religion, and was in a reciprocal relationship with capitalism as a progenitor of the modern order.

Scholars have long recognized these overlaps, correspondences, and genealogical links between Christianity, especially Protestantism, and the secular, and this has been highlighted more recently within American Christianity in the antebellum period in John Modern's work on "evangelical secularism."[52] In the antebellum missionary encounter, evangelical secularism went abroad and contributed to what we might call a broader "missionary modernity."[53] Such an expression, "missionary modernity" (like "evangelical secularism"), may have paradoxical significance to some, because configurations of modernity often include the relegation of religion to the private sphere and even its eventual wished-for total disappearance as it is eclipsed by reason and enlightened self-awareness. According to such a logic, Christian missions are retrograde and unmodern because they disseminate "religion." However, as a term of inquiry, missionary modernity pushes us to better understand the religious foundation of secular modernity, including secularity's other, religion, both as a historic artifact and as a continuing quandary.[54]

Missions were an important part of the globalization of certain forms of Christianity and both directly and through colonial rule participated in the global history of modernity, promoting its "shared imaginary."[55] Despite the fact that they were religious institutions—or perhaps because they were!— Christian missions were vehicles of certain styles of modernity.[56] They often failed to "reform" or convert, especially in the Middle East, but they unintentionally aided in the transformation of their audiences by drawing them into the discursive nexus of modernity. Nineteenth-century missions were voluntary, international organizations with a universalist tendency that while spreading the Gospel advocated ideas of liberty, progress, and Enlightenment.[57]

Protestant missionaries were aware of the novelty of their endeavors and appreciated the political, economic, and technological conditions that allowed for them. Rufus Anderson claimed in "The Time for the World's Conversion" in 1837:

> The Protestant form of association—free, open, responsible, embracing all
> classes, both sexes, all ages, the masses of the people—is peculiar to modern
> times, and almost to our age. Like our own form of government, working with
> perfect freedom over a broad continent, it is among the great results of the
> progress of Christian civilization in this "fullness of time" for the world's con-
> version. Such great and extended associations could not possibly have been
> worked, they could not have been created, or kept in existence, without the
> present degree of civil and religious liberty and social security, or without the
> present extended habits of readings and the consequent wide-spread intel-
> ligence among the people; nor could they exist on a sufficiently broad scale,
> nor act with sufficient energy for the conversion of the world, under despotic
> governments, or without the present amazing facilities for communication on
> the land, and the world-wide commerce on the seas. Never till now, did the
> social condition of mankind render it possible to organize the armies requisite
> for the world's spiritual conquest.[58]

Anderson offers us a perspective on the complex imbrication of mission and
modernity: each promotes the other. And yet the missionaries' purpose was
not simply to promote modernity or "civilization," especially in the pre-1870
mission at Urmia, but to reform Christians. In fact, what many missionaries
abhorred about their own contemporary homelands they hoped to avoid in
the field, even if unknowingly they were spreading a Gospel that served as a
Trojan horse for some of the same domestic phenomena that worried them.

One example of how evangelical projects had modernizing and secular
effects is offered in the case of the spread of individualism. The doctrine of
salvation by faith "presupposes the independence of individual judgment and
the primacy of individual will."[59]

> The individual is set free, and his judgment is declared under God, supreme.
> Suppose then the individual takes a further step and affirms that he is indeed
> free and that his judgment is, without any qualification, supreme. The inevi-
> table happens: Secularism and Protestantism merge into one another; and the
> doctrine of salvation by grace, which was a means of attaining the Life Eternal,
> becomes an alluring instrument for the building of Heaven on Earth; Nation-
> alism is begotten.

A fuller version of the story Elie Kedourie sketches out in this rapid succession of effects from individual judgment to nationalism has been told in more
recent work on Levantine Arab culture, as well as for the Armenian and Alevi
communities.[60]

Although, in their scale and practice, missions are modern institutions,
they clearly fit into the wide-ranging Christian discursive tradition, which
demonstrates a number of characteristics common to most instantiations of

Christianity.[61] Included among these characteristics are the idea of conversion; the problem of inculturation (Christianity and culture); the notion of the imitation of Christ, which is best attested in martyrdom; and the regular epistemological, experiential, and ontological distinction between imminence and transcendence. The notion of reform, which is intensified in missionary modernity, is another characteristic of this discursive tradition. Multiple strains of Christianity commonly posit the possibility of transforming our mortality, of recreating from its fallen state that human being created in the beginning in the image of God. Accordingly, Christianization has always entailed a notion of reform (as well as the delimitation of Christianity, through creed and practices, an objectification instrumental to proselytism). In fact, missionaries' calls for renewal may have been familiar to East Syrians, whose own tradition held that human beings received a renewal (Syr. ḥuddatha) by the coming of Christ. Missionaries and indigenous Christians at times spoke a similar Christian idiom.

Reform means a return: the dissidents of the Reformation saw themselves as merely returning to the authentic apostolic church, although reform is a wider phenomenon in Christian history and precedes the Reformation.[62] Shifts in devotion in the high Middle Ages, including an emphasis on personal and inner forms of piety, were the beginning of a trend that would culminate in the radical claim made during the Reformation that salvation comes by faith alone. Grander historiographies would even posit reform as part of a process going back to the so-called axial age.[63] In any case, it is clear that in Western churches in the post-Reformation period, "reform" became a focus, motivating many and playing itself out in the missionary field. In fact, the competing Western missions of the nineteenth century may be understood as divergent versions of reform: a concern for reform persisted also within the Catholic Church in the Counter-Reformation, encouraging greater discipline and piety.

Reform includes an epistemological aspect: it is a return to true knowledge, even if the ultimate object of evangelical reform is the heart. Epistemological reform is not simply an intellectual matter. It is also ethically incumbent upon all human beings. In this way Christian reform lies behind, and is imbricated in, the "moral narrative of modernity," which, according to Webb Keane, reflects a set of intuitions that "center on the idea that modernity is, or ought to be, a story of human liberation from a host of false beliefs and fetishisms that undermine freedom."[64] In order to liberate their audience, nineteenth-century missions introduced Western science and empiricism, which in turn required a transformation of the senses. Just as Protestantism should not be understood as only an interiorization of religion and a shift from the social to the individual, it is important to remain aware of "just how the senses were implicated in different ways in Protestant traditions."[65] The world was to be experienced in Newtonian terms, as a mechanism distinct from ourselves, a series of objects subject to human beings and God the creator of all. This is why the American missionaries understood the East Syrians' rejection of images in their worship as a sign of their proto-Protestant character: Protestantism was a rejection of the fetish and the embrace of a "commonsense" philosophy of the world.

This epistemological reform and its promotion of a strict empirical regime contributed to the phenomenon commonly referred to as "disenchantment." This disenchantment should not be understood as a total deadening of the world, a stripping of all possibility of transcendence, but rather in the Weberian etymological sense of "demagicification."[66] By disenchantment, I am not referring to the utter eradication from the world of its capacity to entice us by suggesting that there is something else beyond our eyes. The self is still affected by the world, but it is now "buffered," and yet it seeks what it has lost.[67] This self is fixed in the world through sensibilities that yearn for "meaning" and senses that now serve as the gateways to knowledge. The experience of nature's beauty and of love; an awareness of divine majesty, providence, and mystery; a sense of our place in mundane history; and a capacity to read Scripture in a spiritual way—all of which provide "meaning"—come to the fore in the midst of this disenchantment. Within this culture of sentimentality certain affects were to be cultivated, and this in turn corresponds with the evangelical configurations of gender typical of nineteenth- and early twentieth-century American missions: women could offer special sentiments like maternal warmth.

In introducing new epistemologies and different configurations of the senses and sentiments, missions, like other religious institutions, also helped to spread the disciplinary society characteristic of Western modernity.[68] Christian mission motivated an ordering both of bodies and minds and of time and space, like that of contemporary military and imperial bureaucratic reform in the Middle East (and of course like that of the prison, as Michel Foucault addresses in *Discipline and Punish* [1975]). As at the mission in Urmia, missions in South Asia and Egypt used the Lancastrian system of education, which employed a panoptic approach to authority, an all-seeing gaze that is internalized in and by the subject him- or herself: students were responsible for themselves but also for the students below them, while teachers observed from above.[69] These mission projects were akin to calls for reform, often originating in a concern for military competitiveness, among elites in the Ottoman Empire,[70] Khedival Egypt,[71] and Qajar Iran.[72]

Christian institutions, like state reformers, often attempted to relegate religion to distinct spheres of life: although evangelical piety envisioned an expansion of Christianity into everyday life, it also held that some parts of life are more markedly "religious." For example, respect for Sunday as the Lord's Sabbath was a common evangelical concern, and implicit in the repeated claim that true religion is based upon faith alone is a notion that the day-to-day world of practical action is secular. Religious reform itself therefore can relegate religion to certain spaces, if not privatize it. As Muhammad Qasim Zaman has noted regarding modern Islamic education, "The initiatives towards reform, no less than the opposition to them, have fostered views of religion as occupying a distinct sphere in society."[73]

The disciplinary power of the mission, as well as its capacity to relegate religion to certain spaces, was dependent on specific practices characteristic of evangelical modernity. Evangelical missionaries introduced new social practices and sentiments about sociality, which should be set next to the more commonly identified Protestant individualism and interiorization of religion. One of the goals of this study is to go beyond the simplistic dichotomy between traditional relationalism and modern individualism in the study of Christian missions and to examine the new social practices and ideas introduced by missionaries at the same time that they put so much emphasis on the individual.[74] Just as nationalism is not only an abstraction but also a visceral set of social relations, so evangelical modernity should not be reduced to a Protestant version of autonomous Enlightenment reason or an abstract individualism.

Religious Community and the Origins of Nationalism

Taking a critical perspective on religion and its development in modernity challenges us also to rethink the relationship between religion and the origins of nationalism. Asad aptly notes:

> To insist that nationalism should be seen as religion, or even as having been "shaped" by religion is, in my view, to miss the nature and consequence of the revolution brought about by modern doctrines and practices of the secular in the structure of collective representations. Of course modern nationalism draws on preexisting languages and practices—including those that we call, anachronistically, "religious." How could it be otherwise? Yet it doesn't follow from this that religion forms nationalism.[75]

If we eschew the static notion of religion employed by most scholars of nationalism, the story of the relationship between religion and nationalism becomes more complex. In fact, one of the aims of this book is to serve as a corrective for how religion and the origins of nationalism are often treated. I will maintain an awareness throughout that religion itself is an entity that came into being within and as part of modernity. By incorporating an awareness of "religionization" into the historiography of nationalism, I would like to avoid making a (Durkheimian) functionalist equivalence between religion and nation. Not only are there discontinuities between the two, but both came into being simultaneously and often help to constitute each other in their differences. To be sure, in the development of nationalism among the East Syrians, certain parts of the ecclesial tradition were renegotiated and mediated into the developing nation. However, the Christianity itself of the East Syrians changed in this process of translation.

Nationalism has enjoyed consistent scholarly attention since the 1980s and a consensus has developed concerning the constructedness of nations, even if these constructions depended at times on earlier communal formations.[76] This book focuses on the emergence of nationalism among an ethnoreligious community that straddled Qajar Iran and the Ottoman Empire, regions that witnessed radical transformations, including the development of several nationalisms and liberal politics, at the turn of the twentieth century. Qajar Iran and the Ottoman Empire were Muslim-dominated polities consisting of multiethnic and multireligious populations, and from within these heterogeneous populations, several national identities emerged by the early twentieth century. The growth of sectarianism in the Ottoman Empire in particular set the stage for the future nationalisms in the region. It is a commonplace in scholarship on the later Ottoman Empire to note the shift in meaning in the Ottoman term *millet*, from designating recognized religious community to national community. A *millet* was a "protected" non-Sunni religious community sanctioned by the Ottoman authorities.[77] In the nineteenth century, the Ottoman *millets* were "hierarchically organized religious bodies with a decidedly political function."[78] However, *millet* came to be used for distinct ethnic or national communities. Today, the word and its cognates mean "nation" in several languages, including Turkish, Persian, and Neo-Aramaic.

> In contrast to the Muslim ideal of the indivisible *umma*, the evolution of the non-Muslim religious communities of the Ottoman Empire into officially recognized religio-political bodies (*millets*) with powers of taxation and collective representation in the eighteenth century provided opportunities for the empire's non-Muslims to create Anderson's "imagined communities."[79]

The development of these "religio-political bodies" was a complex process involving the policies of the imperial court; the politics of the various churches, including their leaders' attempts to centralize their own power; and the arrival of European merchants and missionaries, who privileged certain religious communities over others. By the nineteenth century, a period of dissonance had set in, which would continue even after the breakup of the empire into the numerous nation-states that exist in the same territory today. The outbreaks of sectarian violence from the mid-nineteenth century onward in the empire's Arab domains, and the even greater violence of the late nineteenth century in Anatolia, were all precursors to the ongoing sectarian problems of the twentieth century. In fact, the slow development of hardened communal identities among the different religious groups in Lebanon in the nineteenth century dispels the myth that primordial communal hatreds lay behind the Lebanese civil war of the 1970s and early 1980s.[80] Broadly speaking, the situation was similar for the East Syrians, who suffered from sectarian violence from the mid-nineteenth century onward and for whom a national consciousness developed by the end of the century. Their political, social, economic, and religious relations were multiplex, and especially for those East Syrians who were nominal Ottoman subjects, their position became more and more precarious through the nineteenth century.

The shift in understanding of *millet* raises larger questions that hark back to the primordialist/constructivist debate about the origins of nations. In other words, the *millet* as ethnoreligious community, or *ethnie*, to use Anthony Smith's term, seems to have anticipated the nation in some way, and this continuity demands an examination of what it was that changed in the shift to national identity. This shift was not simply a renaming but entailed a fundamental social and epistemological transformation, and yet these new national identities often include exclusions based upon their religious past: Turkish national identity still suffers contradictions due to its Sunni foundations, just as the Greek nation remains in ways fundamentally Orthodox. A modern Assyrian would have trouble converting to Islam, because this would suggest she or he were an Arab. Instabilities are inherent to national identity, and the complex and dialectical relationship between religion and nation and the failures of Assyrian nationalism, I would suggest, attest to this. The bifurcation of ethnoreligion, promoted by secularism, is not permanent, and this is so because of the instabilities of the secular itself.

The transformation of the *millet* from religious community to nation and the emergence of the nation from the missionary encounter in particular both challenge radical claims about the discontinuity between religion and nationalism. However, a critical perspective on religion itself is required lest we fall into a primordialism or simplistic Durkheimian functionalism. In *Imagined Communities* (1983), a work that has been generative in several fields, Benedict Anderson maintains a fundamental difference between religion and nationalism: "The most messianic nationalists do not dream of a day when all the members of the human race will join their nation in the way that it was possible, in certain epochs, for, say, Christians to dream of a wholly Christian planet."[81] According to Anderson, the universalism of religion, or at least that of a number of religious traditions, means that religion does not fit one of the primary features of his definition of the nation: "It is an imagined political community—and imagined as both inherently *limited* and sovereign."[82]

While maintaining the distinction between religion and nationalism, Anderson later explicitly denies a clear link between secularization and nationalism, "that somehow nationalism historically 'supersedes' religion."[83] However, despite its discontinuity with the religious past, nationalism is not for him a political ideology and must be understood "by aligning it . . . with the large cultural systems that preceded it, out of which—as well as against which—it came into being."[84] The preceding cultural systems, which, like nationalism, had their own "self-evident plausibility," were the "dynastic realm" and "religious community," the latter of which he addresses only with regard to the way in which sacred languages (e.g., Latin, Arabic, and Chinese) linked classical religious communities together through the notion of "the non-arbitrariness of the sign."[85] The "gradual demotion of the sacred language" was concomitant with a "relativization" and "territorialization" spurred on by European exploration. In conjunction with the rise of what we might refer to as "semiotic ideology," to use Webb Keane's coinage, there was a decline in the dynastic centripetal politics of kingship, which had been typical of most states until the twentieth century.[86]

Anderson notes: "Beneath the decline of sacred communities, languages and lineages, a fundamental change was taking place in the modes of apprehending the world, which, more than anything else, made it possible to 'think' the nation."[87] This fundamental change was the shift from an experience of time as linked, "a simultaneity of past and future in an instantaneous present,"[88] to a notion he famously borrows from Walter Benjamin, "an idea of 'homogeneous, empty time,' in which simultaneity is, as it were, transverse, cross-time, marked not by prefiguring and fulfillment, but by temporal co-incidence, and measured by clock and calendar."[89] As Charles Taylor states, "The modern notion of simultaneity comes to be, in which events utterly unrelated in cause or meaning are held together simply by their co-occurrence at the same point in this simple profane time line."[90]

It is within the space of this empty time, according to Anderson, that the nation is imagined. "The idea of a sociological organism moving calendrically through homogeneous, empty time is a precise analogue of the idea of the nation, which also is conceived as a solid community moving steadily down (or up) history."[91] One of the modern rituals in which this sense of simultaneity in time originates is reading the daily newspaper.

> The significance of this mass ceremony—Hegel observed that newspapers serve modern man as a substitute for morning prayers—is paradoxical. It is performed in silent privacy, in the lair of the skull. Yet each communicant is well aware that the ceremony he performs is being replicated simultaneously by thousands (or millions) of others of whose existence he is confident, yet whose identity he has not the slightest notion. Furthermore, this ceremony is incessantly repeated at daily or half-daily intervals throughout the calendar. What more vivid figure for the secular, historically clocked imagined community can be envisioned?[92]

This is part of Anderson's well-known thesis that print capitalism provided a significant impetus for the origins of nationalism—in other words, that nationalism came about as part of a media revolution.

Although Anderson delinks the rise of nationalism from the supposed decline of religion in modernity, he works nonetheless with a model of secularization in which religion is an entity of static character that decreases over time, and many scholars have maintained such an approach for the past thirty years since the publication of his classic work. Some have understood religion to be an important protoform of a later national entity, whereas others have emphasized the gap of discontinuity between the religious past and the nationalism of secular modernity.[93] Despite this difference, both take religion for granted as a static entity always already there at any moment in nationalism's development. It is presupposed that the nation came into being while religion was simultaneously displaced, demoted, built on, or continued under a different name.

Although my project relies on Anderson's touchstone work, there are aspects of the origins of Assyrian nationalism that point to the limits of his formulation, and these are especially apparent in the impetus religious reform offered to the emergence of national culture. The two apparently contradictory sides in Anderson's comparison of the nation as "limited" and the Christian dreaming of a "wholly Christian planet," a particularism opposed to a universalism, are folded together in the Christian theology of nations we find at the American mission: depending ultimately on a Protestant reading of Paul, the missionaries advocated a universal Christian mission specifically aimed at each and every nation. Christianity's universalism thus instigated an ethnic particularism.

Furthermore, in the case of the Assyrians, where exactly does the "sociological organism" to which Anderson refers come from? Anderson's analysis, including the emphasis he puts on reading practices, corresponds with the notion of the development of the public sphere, that extrapolitical "metatopical space, in which members of society could exchange ideas and come to a common mind."[94] It is metatopical in that it does not exist simply in space but is constituted by various mediations: conversation, newspaper, and public ritual. In the late Ottoman and Qajar contexts, nations (*millets*) became aware of themselves through the development of a public sphere, one that in the case of the East Syrians, as well as many Armenians, Arabs, and Copts, had an evangelical basis.

Anderson's "newspapers" in the case of the East Syrians were missionary pamphlets and monthlies. This is significant: the public sphere in which nationalism emerged belonged to the context of Christian reform. This was the case elsewhere in the nineteenth century, when voluntary religious societies "were instrumental in creating a modern public sphere on which the nation-state could be built."[95] In fact, national reform itself, a common notion in the ideology of nationalism, often derives from the reformist language of religious institutions. Peter van der Veer notes, "Reform is certainly, to a considerable extent, an 'invented tradition' in response to colonial modernity, but it is as much a product of religious discursive traditions of longue duree."[96] Van der Veer later adds, "Religion is a major source of rational, moral subjects and a central organizational aspect of the public spheres they create."[97] If Anderson's argument is in the end about media and the practices of its consumption, in this case the media and its consumption are introduced by Christian missionaries. With regard to Assyrian nationalism, "The task of accounting for the social processes that engender reified conceptions of nation and nationhood" entails a close study of Christian mission.[98]

However, I am referring here to more than just a "public sphere." "Homogeneous, empty time" was promoted at the mission in Urmia through Protestant piety—that is, through both rituals of collective prayer and exhortations for moral and epistemological reform, including the cultivation of a semiotic ideology. The missionaries encouraged new forms of sociality, making an abstract social sphere outside the family more easily recognizable, and this sphere was eventually named the "nation." This introduction of innovative forms of embodied engagement counters scholarly presuppositions about the privatizing and individualizing of religious life built into Protestantism. To be sure, the missionaries introduced religious rituals that were to be "performed in silent privacy, in the lair of the skull," but the solitary self came about at the American mission in a simultaneous social world. The "sociological organism" Anderson refers to emerged through a set of religious practices, such as new rituals of collective prayer, and intimate rhetoric encouraging epistemological and moral reform. East Syrians preached, prayed, and studied together in new ways at the American mission, and these new social practices, correlative with "homogeneous, empty time," allowed for the disembedding of the social: "What we now retrospectively call *the social*, that all-inclusive secular space that we distinguish conceptually from variables like 'religion,' 'state,' 'national economy,' and so forth, *and on which the latter can be constructed, reformed, and plotted*, didn't exist prior to the nineteenth century."[99] This new idea of the social, performed through the activities of everyday life at the mission, contributed to sentiments of national belonging and was part of a "new kind of collective agency . . . one with which its members identify, typically as the realization/bulwark of their freedom and/or locus of their national/cultural expression (or most often, some combination of the two)."[100]

Social Agency, Race, and the Absence of Colonialism

Missionaries prepared the ground for the introduction of new hegemonies.[101] Like colonialism, the worldwide missions of the nineteenth century had multiple local effects, one of which was the development of a discursive framework in which nationalism had a coherent logic. Furthermore, we can triangulate Christian mission, imperialism, and liberalism: although at times in tension, the three often resonated with one another.[102] In addition to their underlying links, it is clear that religion sometimes "provided essential cultural justification for imperial expansion."[103] In some cases, such as in South Africa and South Asia, it set the stage discursively for colonial rule, and yet also for resistance to it. Whereas many books on missions in the nineteenth and early twentieth centuries examine "colonial evangelism," usually in the context of the British Empire, missions to the Ottoman Empire and Qajar Iran are noteworthy because of the absence of a concomitant colonial authority.[104] Despite their ability to bring in diplomatic pressure when needed—in the early decades primarily only against other missions—and their abundant material resources, the American missionaries in Urmia did not have a colonial political arm.

Postcolonial theory is applicable to missions in the Middle East, however, even when the missions were not empowered by colonial rule. At the American mission in Urmia, two different strains of the Christian tradition encountered each other, however unevenly and under conditions wherein one of them enjoyed material and structural advantages over the other. Due to the missionaries' superior access to financial, cultural, and other forms of capital, the same processes of symbolic and cultural dominance unfolded in effect at the mission, even if political power was absent. In fact, the absence of colonialism may have at times made missionary impacts more prominent as the missionaries had the "ability to borrow and build on certain constructions of imperial ideology without being burdened by the exigencies and compromises inherent in colonial rule."[105] Resistance can be more difficult to muster against what is voluntary, whereas missions in India and South Africa at times were obstructed by the colonial authorities themselves.

Contradiction is built into colonial rule: whereas colonial rulers often aim to reform the colonized, fixed notions of race or cultural difference make it impossible for the colonized ever to become like the colonial models set before them. According to Partha Chatterjee, this "rule of colonial difference" leads to a bifurcation between the material and spiritual domains, the former dominated by the colonizer, the latter autonomous and ordered by the colonized. A nationalist critique of colonial rule then develops within this private realm.

> The nationalist response was to constitute a new sphere of the private in a domain marked by cultural difference: the domain of the "national" was defined as one that was different from the "Western." The new subjectivity that was constructed here was premised not on a conception of universal humanity, but rather on particularity and difference: the identity of the "national" community as against other communities.[106]

Chatterjee's formulation sheds light on the East Syrian / Assyrian material in several ways.

His approach is part of a critique of the so-called modular nation form in Anderson's work—that is, the notion that European versions of the nation provided the blueprint for possible national iterations elsewhere, that colonial rule unilaterally introduced the language of resistance to the colonized.[107] One of Chatterjee's concerns is the erasure of indigenous agency in such accounts, but this leads to a conundrum in examining the East Syrians' encounter with the missionaries: our own heuristic concern for agency is genealogically related to a similar concern held by the missionaries themselves. The *Annual Report for the Mission to the Nestorians* in 1845 declares: "The rearing of a native agency, and the employment of that agency,—not only as a means of influence, but also of disciplining and improving the agency itself,—enters deeply into the plan of the missions prosecuted by the Board."[108] Our historiography is imbricated with the aims of the missionaries.

My argument in this book is not simply that foreign missionaries introduced ideas of nationality in their encounter with the East Syrians and that out of this Assyrian nationalism grew. This was indeed true, but there is more to the story. Furthermore, it would be easy to point out that secular nationalist ideas were "in the air" throughout the Middle East in the nineteenth century, which would be an additional "modular" argument. The East Syrians lived on the margins of two empires becoming, slowly and with difficulty, modern nation-states. By the end of the century, the East Syrian diaspora was far-flung, and it had become common for young men to travel to Europe and the United States for more advanced education before returning home to work, often at the missions. Labor migration was also common. Citing such historical factors, one could discount the novelty of Assyrian nationalism and attribute it to vague "broader cultural trends."

However, such "in the air" transmission, whether from missionaries or from the nationalisms of the surrounding region, does not sufficiently explain the early development of Assyrian nationalism nor address the conditions of its growth. It also fails to take into account the social agency of the Syrians themselves. The number of formal converts to American Protestantism was low throughout the history of the American mission, especially relative to the number of East Syrians who interacted with, and were educated by, the mission. East Syrians therefore often had a complex, even ambivalent, relationship with this institution. Furthermore, early nationalist organizing came out of the direct initiative of East Syrians themselves, even if most were associated with the American mission. They were acting according to a national consciousness that preceded their nationalism, a social sentiment, "a structure of feeling," stimulated by Protestant reform.[109]

The "rule of colonial difference" was in effect at the American mission in Urmia. The Syrians were regularly exhorted to a higher, purer form of Christianity, and yet their national, even racial difference, often articulated in a critique of their religious difference, their "sinful condition," kept them under suspicion. This racialization frequently played on themes deriving from the Western Christian discourse on Jewish difference, and in this there is some irony: the Syriac tradition, which had its own strong trend of anti-Judaism, was recast as a Semitic, ethnic, nonuniversal other against Western Christianity (just as the Reformation turned Christian anti-Judaism against the Catholic Church).[110] As had been the case in North America for some time, the "ethnoreligion" of white Protestantism, although accommodating of a variety of Protestantisms, was "restrictive enough to demarcate the ethnic, racial and class boundaries of the Christianity it defined as normative."[111]

Through the nineteenth century, American and European ideas of race helped to prompt a racialization of the East Syrians. To be sure, an ecclesial notion of peoplehood had already existed among them as an inheritance from the ancient Near East through the Hebrew Bible. This was intensified by a Protestant emphasis on such biblical themes, especially when combined with nineteenth-century American biological theories about race and the racializing effects of culture, which were distinct from local notions of race or genus.[112] By the 1890s, within this field of racial difference, the East Syrians asserted a new national identity, one that derived from the late nineteenth-century Euro-American fascination with ancient Assyria. In the context of theological and soteriological uncertainty brought about by evangelical reform, national identity, framed within a Protestant ecumenism, seemed to offer an irreducible and worldly stability.

In nineteenth-century colonial and missionary encounters, such racializations resonated with the nationalization of religion, the textualization of tradition, and the articulation of new religious sentiments, as well as the notion that enlightened religion could be based upon reason.[113] Simultaneous with these developments, the colonized and/or missionized engaged in an appropriation of the learned culture of the colonizer. For example, in the nineteenth and early twentieth centuries, Europeans used a fictive India and the Aryan myth to "discover" their own past.[114] In time the indigenous took up this myth as mediated through colonial rule, and for reformers the idealized past served as a model for the future of the nation. East Syrian assertions of difference through the further elevation of the patriarch and a close engagement with Syriac and ancient Near Eastern history and literature belong to a self-conscious articulation of tradition, one that could not be as easily "colonized" by foreign missions.

This process may be understood as a retrieval, recovery, or reformation of indigenous culture. For example, in the late nineteenth century, educated Bengalis, the *Bhadralok* ("respectable people"), engaged in a nationalizing "recovery" of Gaudiya Vaishnavism, a devotional tradition (*bhakti*) deriving from the sixteenth century.[115] Such a recovery was in response to a sense of loss instigated by English education and reformed religiosity, both introduced within a colonial context. However, there are meaningful differences in this case from that of Assyrian nationalism. In the case of South Asia, the spiritual developed as a realm autonomous of the colonial authorities, and religion as it was construed by middle-class reformers provided an impetus for national reform. In contrast, at the mission in Urmia, Protestant reform served as an engine for three related processes: the reification of tradition, the compartmentalization of "religion," and the dialogic emergence of a national discourse. The evangelical demand for reform led to the distinction between nation—even race—and religion, the former of which was often treated as irreducible.

The proliferation of foreign missions by the turn of the twentieth century led to the further development of the notion that Syrian nationality was distinct from religion. This ethnoreligious binary was built into the universalism preached by each of the various missions. If, as Charles Taylor notes, "a denominational identity tends to separate religion from the state," we could say the same about the effect of denominationalism on national identity.[116] Thus, in this case religionization goes hand in hand with the emergence of national consciousness. Early Syrian nationalists promoted the patriarch as a leader of the nation while expressing an antipathy toward those aspects of religion that they understood to be divisive. These thinkers tended to embrace a liberal, transdenominational form of Christianity, which advocated the centrality of Christ and ethical reform for the whole "nation" regardless of church.

It has become a truism in postcolonial scholarship to emphasize the two-way relationship, the circuit of mutual effects, that exists between the colonized and the colonizer.[117] However, this is not a study in which I examine how "both colonizer and colonized were intimately connected and transformed through a shared process of colonization."[118] An "interactional perspective" on the study of missions takes into account the effects upon, and function within, the Christian culture at home that the missionary discourse and bureaucratic apparatus had.[119] A staggering number of mission publications was produced, such as memoirs and periodicals, and missionaries when home often traveled giving lectures on their work in the field and taking up collections. East Syrians educated at the mission acted as intermediaries themselves of the Orient: many published for an American audience and traveled the United States at the turn of the century lecturing on Persia and their own community. The missionary encounter did not leave the missionary culture untouched, but this is not the concern of this project.

Brief Summary of the Book

The first two chapters compare the two worlds of those involved in the missionary encounter. Chapter 1 sets the stage for the arrival of the American missionaries in the 1830s by providing a basic geographic, social, linguistic, economic, and political survey of the "Nestorians" and the region in which they lived in the early nineteenth century, primarily Urmia, Iran, and the mountainous region of Hakkari, which was nominally under Ottoman control. In the end I question the effect secularism and our own liberal political assumptions about tolerance, religious freedom, and equality have on our ability to understand the heterogeneous social worlds of premodernity.

Chapter 2 juxtaposes the social and religious world of Urmia with the American Protestant background of the first missionaries through an analysis of the early life and missionary career of Justin Perkins, who led the mission in Urmia for thirty-five years under the aegis of the American Board of Commissioners for Foreign Missions (ABCFM). Much of the chapter consists of a comparison of Perkins's 1834 arrival with a trip he made back to the United States in 1842 accompanied by an East Syrian bishop. This chapter focuses particularly on how the media culture of the mission fit with an evangelical notion of "true Christianity." Implicit in Perkins's evangelical emphasis on faith was the idea that religion should be disembedded from the world of social and economic relations, and it thereby resonated with a discourse of secularism.

The two chapters after this address the new ideas and practices introduced by the mission. Chapter 3 examines a number of concepts and terms, as well as the morality and epistemology, promoted by the American mission, through an analysis of the Neo-Aramaic literature printed there, including *Rays of Light*. The mission promoted nineteenth-century science as a form of natural theology and, along with this naturalistic view of the world, new ideas about health, time, religion, culture, race, and nationality. The chapter demonstrates how the missionaries unintentionally helped to create a discursive framework within which new ideas of community could emerge and in the long run nationalist claims would make sense. Millennialist Christian exhortation created a conceptual grammar for the nation in the antebellum period, a Christian liberalism long before the Social Gospel and the supposed secularization of mission in the late nineteenth century.

Chapter 4 describes new social practices and forms of social interaction cultivated at the mission, particularly at its educational institutions. It provides a broad survey of these new practices, which included preaching, moral exhortation, Bible study, classroom discipline, and public prayer at events where the audience at times ran into the hundreds. This chapter also addresses the mission's ideas of family and its negotiation of gender roles. By the end of the period covered, an autonomous Syrian Evangelical Church had been founded, and some Syrians imagined themselves as part of a Christian nation in decline. One of my goals is to make an intervention in the historiography of Protestantism and modernity by examining what is fundamentally social about Protestant reform (which thus belies the common assumption that Protestantism has primarily individualizing effects).

The next two chapters address some of the immediate consequences of the early missionary encounter with the East Syrians. Chapter 5 looks at how the American mission introduced new ideas of death and mourning, while rejecting the indigenous culture's understanding of the possible relationships that could exist between the dead and the living. For the Americans, the dead could only serve as moral examples and nothing more. This critique of the East Syrian culture of death also fit with the missionaries' prioritization of the self as isolated and solitary and the interiorization of religion. The chapter ends with a description of the various revivals experienced almost yearly at the mission from 1846 into the 1860s. These were ritual events that responded to the gospel of dread the Americans preached and that reveal the social anxieties existing within the mission community due to the contradictory, even impossible, demands made by the Americans. These same demands contributed to the emergence of a racialized Syrian national identity.

Chapter 6 demonstrates how the American message of reform was taken up by examining documents composed by East Syrians in the mid-nineteenth century. It first describes two journals composed by native assistants recounting their preaching tours outside of Urmia. In their travels in the mountains of Hakkari as well as south to Mosul and west to Bohtan, they addressed other East Syrians as members of a common nation in order to draw them into the Reformed Gospel. The chapter then examines the evangelical interiority manifested in the letters of a native assistant imprisoned by the Ottoman authorities, and finally an evangelical memoir from the end of the century. The documents in this chapter attest to evangelical conversion as well as the debates the mission inspired among Syrians.

In the last two chapters, I turn to the developments of the late nineteenth and early twentieth centuries. Chapter 7 describes the development of a progressive Social Gospel at the American mission, the growth of the Syrian Evangelical Church, and the proliferation of a variety of European and American missions later in the century. The intensification and expansion of missionary work at this time created a pluralism in which a secularized ethnic discourse emerged. Among others, the Chaldeans (Uniate Catholics), Anglicans, and Russian Orthodox focused their efforts on Urmia. The demands put upon the Syrians by different missions at times led to a back-and-forth maneuvering by the patriarch, and in 1897 there was a failed attempt at mass conversion to Orthodoxy for what seem to be primarily political purposes. It was at this time that the earliest explicit nationalism appeared. In defense of the patriarch and the Old Church, Syrian men primarily with an American educational background and often evangelical church membership began to organize within the community, eventually creating the nationalist newspaper, the *Star*, in 1906. Chapter 8 examines the European and American orientalist and biblical archeological background to, and the local intellectual context for, the earliest claims that the East Syrians were the descendants of

the ancient Assyrians. It sets these claims within the context of early nationalist debates about the Aramaic language, history, and the ethnonym *Assyrian*,
and the promotion of the new idea of "Syrian" literature.

Finally, the epilogue discusses the life and works of David George Malik,
an early Assyrian nationalist, using the events of the 1910s and 1920s as a
frame. His poetry, composed by someone whose family had long been associated with the American mission, demonstrates a particular type of secularity.
I then briefly address developments in the history of the community and the
Assyrian Church of the East, as the church was later renamed, in the period
after World War I.

The Church of the East before the Modern Missionary Encounter: Historicizing Religion before "Religion"

Since ancient times the nation [*melat*] of the Syrians, who are called the Christians of Mar Thomas, have lived in India; they resided on the coast of the Sea of Malabar. Whether they are natives of India and came to believe in the preaching of Mar Thomas, or they went there from the land of Palestine and increased, this is not known because there are no histories. They themselves say that their church was there in the year 200 after Christ and that 1300 years after that time bishops were established by the patriarch of Antioch.

Some years ago I heard Priest John of Kosi, who read in an ancient book on the topic of these Syrians, say, "They were a part of our nation [*melatan*], to whom our bishops went and one of whose letters they read." In addition to these things he also said that the book that this report is written in is in Shirabad. After the death of Priest John I sought that book and here we will write some of that report so that you may read it and enthusiastically take as examples the patience, instruction, and fear of God that existed among your ancestors.[1]

So writes Justin Perkins, the founder of the American "Mission to the Nestorians," in the December 1849 issue of the mission monthly, *Rays of Light* (*Zahrire d-bahra*). Perkins then provides the first part of his translation from Classical Syriac to Neo-Aramaic of a document describing events from almost 350 years earlier.[2]

The document tells the following story: at the turn of the sixteenth century, the Christian church in India sent three men, one of whom died en route, to Mesopotamia to bring ordained clergy back to their own country with them. The Patriarch Shem'on V (1497–1502) ordained the two emissaries, George and Joseph, at his seat in Gazarta (Cizre, Jizre), a city on the Tigris, today in southeastern Turkey, not far from the point where Turkey, Syria, and Iraq meet.[3] The two men then visited the monastery of Mar Awgen (Eugene), part of an almost one-thousand-year-old monastic center approximately one hundred kilometers to the west. There they met two monks named Joseph, whom the patriarch then ordained as Mar Thomas and Mar John. All four then traveled to India. John remained there, but Thomas returned to find that the patriarch had died and that Eliya V (1502–4) had succeeded him in office. Eliya ordained three more members of the Mar Awgen community at the

nearby monastery of Mar John the Egyptian in the Tigris valley, not far from
Gazarta. The newly ordained metropolitan of India, Yahballaha, and two new
bishops, traveled with Thomas to India and sent back a letter, dated to 1504
and cosigned by John, reporting the events that transpired after their arrival.

The letter reached the patriarchal see after Eliya's death, when Shemʿon VI
(1504–38) had taken office. It describes their healthy and happy arrival in India, including the joyous welcome they received, as well as the great number
of Christians they found there and the diverse geography of the community.
It then provides an account of the arrival of European Christians (*frangaye*)
in well-equipped ships and the animosities that spread against the foreigners, both among the infidels (*kapore*) and Muslims (lit. "Ishmaelites"). The
Muslims claimed before one of the local kings in Calcutta that the European
Christians wanted to wrest his kingdom from him in order to hand it over to
their own king. Such claims were not wrong: these "Franks" were Vasco da
Gama (d. 1524) and his crew, and the Portuguese were there to stay. According
to the letter, battles were fought, which included attacks on the local Christian
population by neighboring non-Christians, an all-too-common phenomenon
in the history of the Christians of the Middle East and Asia after European
power began to expand around the world. The strangers also established a
trading colony in a neighboring kingdom on the Malabar coast. At the end of
the letter, the authors describe a pleasant visit at this colony with their fellow
Christians from the West and how "fear and distress [concerning the foreign
Christians] fell upon all the idolaters and Ishmaelites who are in these lands."[4]

As this story suggests, the Church of the East was a widely dispersed ecclesial community, a global congregation, long before the world was sliced up
by national boundaries. At the same time that Columbus was "discovering"
America in an attempt to reach India, East Syrians from a region currently
in southeastern Turkey were traveling back and forth to India in order to
minister to a church that had long been established there. The church had for
centuries in fact sent out its apostles from its Mesopotamian center, which
ran from what is now southern Iraq to southeastern Turkey. The movement of
East Syrians across the continent of Asia, fostering their particular Christian
culture and interacting openly and assuredly with a heterogeneous, premodern world, is repeatedly attested, whether in the church's spread through the
Sasanian Empire in late antiquity, its continuing success in the Arab caliphate,
its move into Central Asia and China, or its wide dispersal within the Mongol Empire. In the thirteenth century East Syrians made up the numerous
Christians associated with the Mongol court, such as Sorghaghtani Bekhi,
the mother of Kublai Khan (d. 1294), and Dokuz Khatun, the Christian wife
of Hulagu (d. 1265), the sacker of Baghdad in 1258 (who happens to be buried

on one of the islands of Lake Urmia, as Justin Perkins himself notes[5]). At the time of Marco Polo, Rabban Barsauma (ca. 1220–94), born near Beijing of a Uighur family, traveled across Asia twice and eventually was sent at the suggestion of his student, who had become Patriarch Yahballaha III (1245–1317), to the pope to attempt to broker an alliance between the Franks and the Mongols (*rabban*, "our master," is a title of respect).[6] As an old man in Baghdad, he composed a long account in Syriac of his itinerant life, a book that attests to the worldliness that existed in the Church of the East at the time when Western Christians' enthusiasm for crusading had only recently waned. However, over time the church contracted from within its widest limits, receiving a particular blow in the disarray caused by the violent campaigns of Tamerlane (1336–1405).

Although the nineteenth-century missionaries promoted the myth of a lost tribe of mountain Christians, they also brought with them an awareness of the global past of the Church of the East, a past that they themselves sought to invoke as part of their effort to spread the Gospel again across Asia. The links that Perkins wanted to recall by his translation of the sixteenth-century document had never been fully severed and were later to become stronger through the modern East Syrian diaspora. I emphasize this long-term relationship with the Indian community because, when approaching the East Syrians in the early nineteenth century, just before the arrival of the missionaries, it is easy to fall into the fallacy of treating them as a little tradition, a particularistic subcommunity living primarily in an obscure region, in contrast to the worldly Euro-Americans whose global vision corresponded with the lengths they had traveled to missionize these "oriental" Christians. This would be a mistake.

The Church of the East, at least on the elite and ecclesial level, was an institution that had long engaged in mobility far and wide. The world of the majority of the laity was small, consisting of village agricultural life or seminomadic pasturing in the mountains, but elites within the community had a long history of imagining the "Church of the East," as it was called, as a Christian city that extended east to India and deep into the formative era of Christian history. The patriarch, or Catholicos, as he was called, was based for centuries in Ctesiphon, the winter residence of the Shahs of Sasanian (pre-Islamic) Iran, and later in Baghdad. The church's institutions, such as monasteries and schools, were important cultural and economic centers, and the learned elites of the church played significant roles in the intellectual culture of Mesopotamia. The renown of the School of Nisibis (modern Nusaybin), the Church of the East's most important center of learning in the sixth and seventh centuries, reached Constantinople and early medieval Italy. Later, in

the 'Abbasid period, East Syrians played an important role in the early translation movement, rendering Greek philosophical and medical literature into
Arabic.

Elites in the church, with links both to the region in which they lived
and to the broader ecclesial hierarchy—and imaginatively to heaven—were
cosmopolitans with local attachments, or "local cosmopolitans," to borrow
Engseng Ho's term for the Hadrami Yemeni diaspora.[7] East Syrians, wherever they might be, were not a religious or ethnic minority in the modern
sense of such terms, but members of a church they imagined to be linked to
the biblical and apostolic past, whereas their Muslim neighbors considered
them "people of the book" (ahl al-kitab) and therefore participants in sacred
history.

This was a historically transregional and multiethnic ecclesial community
with a long history of interacting with other religious and ethnic communities. This is especially important to emphasize because not long after the
events described in the document published by Perkins, the Franks would
cause havoc in the church both in the Middle East and in India. Only a few
decades later, in 1553, the church in the Middle East would be split by a fracture that has remained to the present, when missionaries sent from Rome
created a Catholic Uniate church (a secondary and ultimately more successful Uniate church was founded to the northwest in Diyarbakır in 1681). At
the same time, the church in India was compelled by the Portuguese colonial
power to take on the Latin rite, and Syriac manuscripts were burned in an
attempt to eradicate the "heresy" of "Nestorianism" from the Indian Christian community. Long before the American missionaries arrived in the 1830s,
members of the Church of the East had been traveling across the globe, and
the church had already almost three centuries of experience with what many
would understand to be the meddling of Western Christians.

The breadth of East Syrian history and the church's cosmopolitan past
provide a broader framework upon which to fit the geographic, social, economic, linguistic, political, and cultural survey of East Syrian life presented
in this chapter. My aim in the following is to set the stage for the arrival of
American missionaries in the 1830s. Before examining the American mission,
it is necessary that we acquire some sense of the complex social and religious
world the "Nestorians" occupied, surrounded by and living among Muslim,
Jewish, and other Christian communities. This mixed world entailed various
forms of religious intermingling and shared practices that the missionaries
frowned upon and attempted to eradicate. The diversity and heterogeneity
that we find within the East Syrian community, a decentered and loosely connected ethnoreligious group living primarily in the region that is now divided

among Iran, Turkey, and Iraq, will serve as a foil for the unified identity imagined after the emergence of Assyrian nationalism at the end of the nineteenth century.

Geography

The plain of Urmia lies west of Lake Urmia in what is now the province of West Azerbaijan in contemporary Iran.[8] The lake, which runs approximately 140 kilometers north to south, is highly saline, thus resembling the Dead Sea: due to its inhospitable chemistry, it lacks any aquatic animal life except the tiny brine shrimp, which feed the storks, gulls, and pelicans that migrate along the lake's small craggy islands. The region west of the lake is divided by low mountains that press in close, through which there is a pass that leads to the Salmas plain on the northwest corner of the lake. Rivers run eastward into the lake from the mountains farther west, irrigating and forming alluvial valleys and plains in which villagers have practiced agriculture since antiquity. The elevated yet well-watered plain of Urmia, with its easy access to irrigation, is an oasis compared to the relatively dry climate of much of the rest of Iran and the Middle East as a whole.

The Nazlu and its tributaries flow toward the lake, rendering green the widest part of the plain, which bulges eastward into the lake, forming its narrowest central point (Today it is from this point that a bridge runs across the lake to its east bank). "This plain is almost perfectly level, extremely fertile, highly cultivated, amply irrigated by canals from several small rivers, and enlivened by almost countless gardens, vineyards, orchards and villages," Perkins wrote on his first visit there in 1834.[9] In contrast to much of Iran, where along with small domestic gardens villagers would maintain larger tracts of agricultural land farther away from town centers, the plain of Urmia was noteworthy for its abundant gardens and groves.[10]

Through the center of the plain there also flows the Shahar, or "City," River. It receives its name from the city it flows past, Urmia, from which the eponymous region and lake derive their name. *Urmia* as a local appellation is attested in cuneiform, but East Syrians later developed their own etymologies for the name, the most popular being "place of water," and another that links it to Ur of the Chaldees, the biblical homeland of the patriarch Abraham. A wide agricultural plain runs south and east of the city along the coast of the lake and is further watered by the Baranduz River to the south. On the southeast corner of the lake begins the Sulduz plain, an area that was occupied historically by Sunni Kurds, as opposed to the Shi'ite Azeri Turkish speakers of the Salmas and Urmia plains.[11]

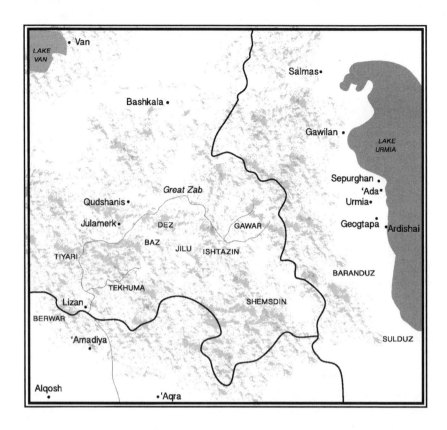

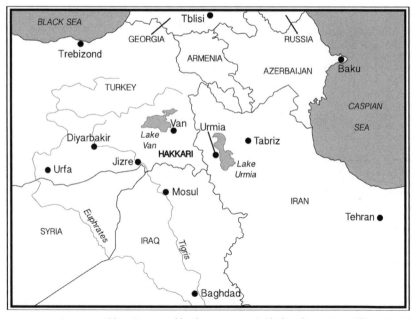

FIGURE 1. Maps. *A*, Hakkari, Urmia, and bordering regions. *B*, The broader region. Modern political boundaries are included on both maps.

North from Salmas, beyond the lake, the next city is Khoy, after which the road splits, its prongs pointing to the two nearest political and cultural powers. To the east it leads to Tabriz, the renowned city of both ancient and modern Iranian history. A political, economic, and cultural center, Tabriz was the seat of the crown prince of the Qajar dynasty (1794–1925) (though the first Qajar ruler, Agha Muhammad Khan, was crowned in Urmia in 1795), and, as it was the capital of the most populous province of the country, it was also a transit center for goods coming from the Black Sea.[12] It was in Tabriz in 1811 that Iran's first printing house was opened, and the city was later the focus of events in Iran's Constitutional Revolution (1905–11).

From Khoy the road also runs northward into Armenia and the Caucasus and beyond that to Russia. Tbilisi (Tiflis), Georgia, the Russian imperial center in the region in the nineteenth century, was increasingly the destination of Syrian Christians seeking work, and by 1900 a substantial community had settled there. From the north the Russian imperial presence could be felt in Urmia throughout the nineteenth century: the city was occupied by Russian troops in 1828 before the Treaty of Turkmenchai ended the hostilities of the last Russo-Persian War (1826–28) and much of what is now modern-day Armenia was ceded to Russia. The Russians occupied Urmia again in 1911 until the city changed hands back and forth during World War I, at which time much of the local Christian population was killed or fled. Heading west from Armenia, one could also take the road to Trebizond and then sail along the Black Sea coast to Constantinople and the world beyond. American missionaries traveled this route on their way to and from Urmia, passing on the south side of the massive dormant volcano of Mount Ararat (5,137 meters / 16,854 feet high), the reputed resting place of the biblical ark, and, according to Perkins, "an object of such impressive sublimity," which "rises from a majestic curve, in the great range, a sublime corner boundary of the three empires of Persia, Turkey, and Russia, and full worthy to be the bridge between the antediluvian and postdiluvian worlds."[13]

On its west side, the Urmia plain becomes mountainous, with river valleys winding into the heights of Baradost and Tergawar, the regions that formed the porous boundary with the Ottoman Empire. Aside from the elevated river valley of Gawar, these heights continue to grow, until Hakkari and the wider mountainous region south and east of Lake Van. This elevated, often rough terrain, with numerous inhabitable valleys and wide pasturage, is the meeting point of the two extensive mountain ranges of the Middle East: the Zagros Mountains, which begin at the Straits of Hormuz at the bottom of the Persian Gulf and form the boundary to the Iranian plateau, and the Taurus

Mountains, which latitudinally separate Turkey's Mediterranean coast from the Anatolian plateau.

Some geographies are impossible to control, and Hakkari is one of them. Only in the mid-nineteenth century did the Ottoman state attempt to impose its suzerainty over the region, often relying on local Kurdish tribes as its arm and playing local powers off of one another. Yet even until recently, the ability of the Kurdish Workers Party (PKK) to maintain its decades-long resistance to the Turkish state within Hakkari and the mountains of southeastern Turkey suggests the political centrifuge that existed in the region in the past. Though nominally Ottoman, Hakkari functioned as a kind of buffer state between the Ottomans and the Qajars.[14] Carriage roads did not come until the 1930s, and this impermeability may explain why Catholic missionary inroads in the nineteenth century remained limited.[15] The caravan traffic that is attested in the Armenian plateau to the north and in the plains of Mesopotamia to the south was absent from Hakkari, with the exception of the tobacco trade that came out of Shemsdin (modern Şemdinli) to the southeast.[16] In contrast to the agricultural village and larger town life of the plains west of Lake Urmia, Hakkari was occupied by seminomadic pastoralists as well as some small-scale terrace farmers. The population consisted of a mix of Kurds and East Syrians.

West of Hakkari the land remains rugged but levels out, as the mountains continue in a northwest direction. This is the Gazarta region, roughly the modern Turkish Şırnak province, the northern part of which was known as Bohtan. The city of Gazarta lies on the bank of the Tigris, which flows southeast, working its way down from distant mountains, passing Diyarbakır, today the second largest city in southeastern Turkey. Farther to the west lies the Tur ʿAbdin ("Mountain of the Servants [of God]"), an elevated plateau with a microclimate reminiscent of the Mediterranean, although it is hundreds of kilometers from the sea. Today the Tur ʿAbdin, part of contemporary Mardin province, is considered the spiritual homeland of the Syrian Orthodox (West Syrians, Süryani), the East Syrians' centuries-long rivals, most of whom now live in Istanbul or scattered across northern Europe and elsewhere. From the enchanting heights of Mardin, the city on the southwest corner of the Tur ʿAbdin, one looks south into the flat plains of Syria. North of the Tur ʿAbdin are the cities of Siirt and Bitlis, and eventually Lake Van—all places hit hard by the Armenian genocide—whereas directly to the west, about 170 kilometers from Mardin, is Urfa (Şanlıurfa), ancient Edessa. Another city "cleansed" of much of its Christian population in 1915, it is the place of origin of Classical Syriac and Syriac Christianity and a city that has become central to the modern imagining of the Syriac past among both East and West Syrians.

South of Hakkari the terrain remains mountainous until it flattens out into the level plains of Mesopotamia and one arrives at Mosul on the Tigris River, the capital of the Ottoman *vilayet* (administrative division) of the same name. This region was occupied historically by a diversity of religious and ethnic groups. East and West Syrians, Jews, Sunni and Shi'ite Arabs and Kurds, Yezidis (adherents of a Kurdish religious community with its holy center at the shrine of Shaykh 'Adi in Lalish in northern Iraq), as well as even small pockets of Turkmen and others. Before modern urban sprawl, Mosul occupied the west bank of the river, whereas on the east bank were located the mounds covering the massive ruins of Nineveh, which would be unearthed in the mid-nineteenth century and later offer fodder for the East Syrian historical imagination. Among the ruins, in the remains of what was a Christian church, was (until its destruction in July 2014) the Mosque of Nabi Yunis, the Prophet Jonah, whom, according to the Bible, God sent to Nineveh to preach against the wickedness of its inhabitants. This event was memorialized each year by the Church of the East in the Fast of the Ninevites, one of the few instances in which an Assyrian past was imagined prior to the arrival of the missionaries. From Mosul, one could make a smooth downstream trip to Baghdad and cities farther south. In contrast, upstream travel was slow: once boats sailing south reached their destination, they had to be dragged back north overland by pack animals. Foreign steamboats were only slowly introduced onto the Tigris in the nineteenth century and, due to its turns and shallows, with much difficulty.

Contrasting Hakkari and Urmia

Urmia and Hakkari are the two regions of primary interest in this book. They were the centers of East Syrian life and also the focus of American missionary efforts. The third major area of East Syrian life, Mosul and its environs, played an important part in the modern history of the Church of the East, but despite missionary efforts there, Mosul as well as most of the area south of Hakkari were already heavily Catholicized by the nineteenth century. This third area was dominated by the Chaldean Church, the local East Syrian church that was Uniate (joined with the Catholic Church). This was also the case for the Salmas plain, with its capital of Khosrowa (Khosrowabad), and Bohtan, west of Hakkari. The East Syrian population figures for the nineteenth century vary.[17] At the time of the arrival of the American mission, the total number of non-Uniate Syrians probably did not exceed one hundred thousand. There were between twenty-five thousand and forty thousand on the Urmia plain, but the population in the city of Urmia itself was small.

In their dispersal across the wider region, the East Syrians lived at times in social interpenetration with other linguistic, religious, and ethnic groups. They were scattered, with some pockets denser than others, throughout the region, with exceptions here and there of dialects and local tradition. Aside from certain villages, they were not the majority in any one area. Historically, the local elite of the Urmia plain were Afshars, a Turkic tribe originally from Central Asia, who settled the region in the seventeenth century and spoke a form of Azeri Turkish. The rest of the Muslim population were Azeri Turks combined with some Kurds as well as the local Persian administrators. The Muslim population was primarily Shi'ite. There were also Armenians and a small Jewish population. East Syrians were a minority in the city of Urmia itself, occupying a quarter near the Church of Mart Maryam, whereas most lived interspersed in their own villages as well as in mixed villages through-out the region west of Lake Urmia.[18] In contrast, the East Syrians of Hakkari tended to live independently of other ethnic and religious groups.

An important social and political distinction between the East Syrians of Urmia and Hakkari was that between those who belonged to independent tribes (*'aširat*) and those who were part of the subject population (*ra'yat*). This distinction was mapped onto the geography: the tribes lived in the moun-tains, and the subject population lived on the plains. As with much of Iran, land on the plain often belonged to the crown or local lords, who as absentees were able to tax the proceeds of their landed possessions.[19] The Christians in the Urmia region were subjects of and tenants (*ra'yat*) to a local Muslim aristocracy. They lived in towns and villages, often as a minority, engaging in small crafts and farming.[20] Fully Christian villages had their own equivalent of the regional village chief (*kethkhoda*): the Christian *koḥa* or *koḥaya* was usually the most prosperous man in the village and monopolized the honor of offering hospitality to visitors of note.[21]

In contrast to the feudal-like system of the plain, the Christians in the "wild west" of Hakkari belonged to a complex tribal (*'aširat*) system of semi-nomadic pastoralists. Different tribes controlled their own portions of this mountainous region.[22] Hakkari in the early nineteenth century was an au-tonomous region, far too rugged and recalcitrant for the Ottomans to con-trol, despite its being technically in their territory. As Hakkari came more and more into the European consciousness in the later nineteenth century, it became a locale of the romantic imagination: fictional tales were published of the exotic Christian nomads of the mountains.[23] Even Karl May (1842–1912), the prolific German writer most known for his adventure stories of the American West, made his contribution, *Durchs wilde Kurdistan* (*Through Wild Kurdistan*). The open world of Hakkari and the frontier region between the Ottomans and Qajar Iran were under new pressures in the nineteenth century. The delimitation and demarcation of a border between the two states was part of the contemporary trend of centralization promoted by foreign intervention.[24] Through the nineteenth century, Hakkari, a region with no historic metropole, was made subject to the late Ottoman state while attempts were made to close its porous boundaries.

Despite its greater social segregation as compared to the plains, Hakkari had a mixed population of Kurds and East Syrians, with the two groups sometimes intermingling in the same villages.[25] In contrast, the rare appearances the Ottomans make in the sources are as representatives of the distant state. With only a few significant differences, Kurds and East Syrians in the region shared a similar social structure and way of life.[26] The tribes maintained a feud and vendetta system of controlled violence, which functioned to maintain order in a region without a state.[27] The pastoralism practiced by the Hakkari tribes entailed a transhumant, seminomadic system of pasturage. The cold season was spent in the village and the summer in the *zuma*, or summer camp (Kurdish, *zozan*). Unlike Kurdish pastoralists, the East Syrian *zuma* was a stationary camp, a place apparently stinking of excrement where vermin proliferated.[28] The one noteworthy link to the growing world economy was the trade in gall nuts, the insect-infected sacs on oak trees that served to produce ink.[29]

The primary Christian tribal groups of Hakkari were the Jilu, the Dez, the Baz, the Tkhuma (Ṭhuma), and the Upper and Lower Tiyari (Ṭyare). We know little about these translocal religious, social, political, and economic organizations before the arrival of the missions and the Ottoman attempt to impose their rule from the 1840s onward. The tribes were economically and politically autonomous from the Ottoman state, belonging to a complex and fluid system of relations with one another and with neighboring Kurdish tribes. Before Ottoman domination, East Syrian tribes at times paid tribute to Kurdish emirs or served as armed contingents for them.[30] Neighboring subtribal groups were on occasion subject to larger tribes. For example, the people of Tal were subject (*ra'yat*) to the Tkhuma tribe and accordingly could not bear arms, nor could their sons marry the daughters from an autonomous tribe.[31] At times Kurdish villages were vassals to these Christian tribes.

The chiefs (*maliks*) were often chosen by the patriarch, who lived in the precarious setting of Qudshanis, a mountain town, semiautonomous from the Ottomans, but ethnically mixed with Kurds and Armenians. The city nearest to Qudshanis was Julamerk (modern Hakkari city), which had a similar mix of surrounding Kurdish and Armenian villages.[32] Encircling the inner core of independent Hakkari tribes there were nontribal groups (*ra'yat*), who were subject to Kurdish *aghas* (tribal chiefs) and sometimes to the Ottomans. These groups, often tied more closely to the land, were identified by their village rather than tribe. To the east, in the mountain region making up the frontier zone between the Ottomans and the Qajars, many East Syrians lived independently, but not as distinct tribes.[33]

The nineteenth century witnessed the beginning of East Syrian migration from their ancestral regions, a precursor of the mass movement that would occur during and after World War I.[34] Labor migration into Georgia and elsewhere in the Caucasus created new communities in the north. Movement north into Georgia also reflects the ease Christians felt living under a Christian empire, just as there were parallel migrations of Muslim populations, such as the Laz and the Abkhazians, from the Caucasus into the Ottoman Empire in response to Russian imperial expansion. The members of the Jilu tribe were known in particular for their tendency to travel. Historically, in the winter they would migrate from the cold fastness of the mountains to work as basket makers in the south. The tribe established rules for where migrants from different Jilu villages could go, with villagers from Mar Zay'a, the holy center of Jilu, being given special permission to travel anywhere. Jilu labor migrations corresponded with the migration of "holy beggars" from the region. These religious mendicants—at times charlatans—from Jilu, which I address further in chapter 6, traveled far and wide, as did those Armenians who engaged in a similar practice. By the late nineteenth century, religious beggars from Jilu were known to travel far beyond Hakkari for their "trade," even to North America.

"Syrians," Syriac, and Neo-Aramaic

The broader region, running from the Tur 'Abdin in the west to Lake Urmia in the east, from the region of Lake Van in the north and south to Mosul, contained in the nineteenth century (as it does today, but far less so) a complex, heterogeneous population of different languages, ethnicities, and religious traditions. Language, self-appellation, and religion were often imbricated with one another, and yet the social promiscuity and heterogeneity of the region reveal exceptions anytime we try to make a rule. The "Syrians" (*suryaye*), as they generally called themselves, *when it was necessary to make a clear distinction from all other ethnoreligious groups*, or "Nestorians," as the missionaries called them, did not refer to themselves as "Assyrians." Village or tribal affiliation would have been more common in the day-to-day usage among one another, whereas if they needed to differentiate themselves from other Syriac Christians, they called themselves "Easterners."

It is difficult to reconstruct precisely what languages and dialects the Syrians spoke in late antiquity and the Middle Ages. It is clear that a variety of

Aramaic dialects were spoken by members of the church as well as others in the region, and that after the Arab conquest in the seventh century, there was a progressive Arabicization of the church in certain areas, which by the modern period often went hand in hand with Catholicization.[35] Such a correlation was in part due to differences in accessibility: with the important exception of the Urmia plain, Aramaic was preserved in the mountainous regions in the same way that the non-Uniate church was. However, most East Syrians by the 1800s still spoke some form of Aramaic.

Scholars divide modern Aramaic into four dialect groups: western dialects, spoken, for example, in Syria in the town of Ma'lula, north of Damascus; the dialect of the Mandaeans in southern Iraq and southwestern Iran; the dialect of the Christians in the Tur 'Abdin, now spoken primarily by the Syrian Orthodox both in Turkey and in diaspora; and finally what scholars refer to as North Eastern Neo-Aramaic (NENA), the language of the East Syrians, also spoken by the Jewish communities of Kurdistan (who have mostly emigrated to Israel). Dialectal variation across the East Syrian community was wide, and NENA was not mutually comprehensible along its whole range of local variations. Furthermore, some East Syrians spoke Armenian, Kurdish, Turkish, Arabic, and Persian, depending on the linguistic history of the particular regions in which they lived.[36]

The written language, which was used in the liturgy and as a form of communication and literary expression by elite men within the church, was Syriac, the Classical dialect of Aramaic first attested in Edessa, about 200 CE, but which spread through the Christian communities of Mesopotamia and the Levant in the following centuries. The laity would have had access to this language primarily through the liturgy, and on account of this, it is likely many had some basic comprehension of it.[37] However, literacy in Classical Syriac seems to have existed mostly among clergy. Syriac was "the language with a long communal history and a sanctified religious tradition, . . . a language charged with symbolic meaning, the use of which underlined the religious unity of the community."[38] Furthermore, the Syriac script itself was flexible, having been used in the past in Central Asia to render Soghdian (from which it is the source of the Old Uyghur and Mongolian scripts) and Kyrgyz (a Turkic language). On occasion modern dialects of Aramaic, such as that of Alqosh in what is now northern Iraq, were written in Classical Syriac script, whereas those communities where Aramaic was no longer the dominant tongue sometimes used Garshuni (Syriac script for a non-Aramaic language) to write in Arabic, Turkish, and other languages. In fact, the Syriac script seems to have functioned as a marker of community, perhaps even more so than the language itself did.

Political Authority, the Status of *Dhimmis*, and "Rough Tolerance"

In both Hakkari and Urmia, the East Syrians lived technically as *dhimmis*—
that is, as an Islamically sanctioned "protected" non-Muslim community—
but this status would have had little bearing on their lives in the autonomous
parts of Hakkari.[39] In Urmia, Christians lived subject to a local Muslim elite
and a governor who served as a representative of the Shah. Many of the limitations and sanctions put upon *dhimmis* in other Muslim-dominated societies
existed, as well as the communal autonomy that went with this. For example,
Christian testimony was worth less in a Muslim court of law, but most Christian communal disputes were settled within the Christian community and
outside of the jurisdiction of Muslim judges. Muslim rule provided Christians with legal autonomy, in which canon law developed into a separate civil
law for Christians. Marriage, for example, was regulated among Christians
according to their own law, and yet Christians were restricted by Muslim
norms, for example, in the public consumption of alcohol.

It is important to emphasize the social historical complexity of life in Urmia (and in many premodern Islamic empires): a strictly legal perspective
alone misconstrues how Christians fit into Islamic society, because law was
not as powerful in the past as it is for us today. Christians certainly suffered
penalties as *dhimmis* and occasionally had difficulty with legal redress. The
Qajar governor would meddle in local affairs once in a while, and Christians
at times lacked certain privileges due to their *dhimmi* status, as the missionaries were always eager to point out, but their lives were more often occupied
with local issues and local authorities. At the same time, that they paid a small
tithe suggests they considered themselves subjects of the patriarch across the
frontier in Hakkari.

Commonly known as the "*millet* system," later Ottoman rule was characterized by communal autonomy and representation for several of the non-
Sunni Muslim religious communities of the empire. The term *millet* came
into use in the seventeenth century, but was not regularly used until the early
nineteenth and not all religious communities received this status. There was a
proliferation of Christian *millets* in the nineteenth century, including a Uniate
Armenian *millet* in 1831, to which Syriac Catholics were joined, and a separate Chaldean *millet* in 1846. An Armenian Protestant *millet* was recognized
in 1850. An attempt was made to create a *Nasturi* ("Nestorian") *millet* in 1864,
but this failed. By this time the majority of Ottoman East Syrians, aside from
those in the unruly mountains, were Chaldean.[40] Scholars generally agree
that *millet* status contributed to the emergence of national identities in the
later Ottoman Empire. For example, in the Ottoman Arab world, religious

communal identities slowly increased in significance over the seventeenth and eighteenth centuries, and this led to clearly defined *millets* by the early nineteenth century.

Such a system was not in effect in the politically acephalous mountains of Hakkari.[41] With the Ottoman authorities far off, insecurity due to the more powerful Kurdish tribes was often a normal part of Christian life.[42] Scholarly assessments of communal relations run the span from negative to hesitantly optimistic (in the same way that the arrival of Americans and Europeans has been understood as a significant cause of anti-Christian violence in the region or as a buffering restraint against it).[43] The matrix of Kurdish tribal politics within which the East Syrians lived was probably more important as a local framework with an immediate impact on the Christian population of Hakkari. This framework was destabilized during the nineteenth century as the Ottomans gradually penetrated the region and Kurdish power declined. As also in Urmia, local powers were needed for the distant state to negotiate its claims, and a pragmatic silence, an absence of codification, continued where the state was either weak or even absent.

In earlier periods, Kurdish tribes were occasionally able to impose their suzerainty over regions wider than their own local territory. One late and extreme example is the case of Badr Khan Bey (1803–68), who became emir of Bohtan in the early 1820s.[44] Long depicted (inaccurately) as an early Kurdish nationalist, he extended his dominion over the region of Bohtan and far beyond. His recalcitrance to Ottoman rule only increased when Ibrahim Pasha, the son of Muhammad Ali, the renegade Ottoman governor in Egypt, defeated the Ottoman army in 1838. In expanding his realm, he killed many Christians, particularly in the massacres of 1843. By 1845 Badr Khan Bey controlled the region from Diyarbakır south to Mosul and east to the Persian frontier. However, in 1847 he was toppled by an Ottoman army that had been sent in part due to British and French insistence that he be prevented from massacring more local Christians. In the end, Badr Khan Bey was the last of the Kurdish emirs to possess extensive power. The Ottoman state was now able to prevent such broad tribal alliances.

The massacres of 1843 were spurred on by the Ottoman attempt to impose external political authority over the region and thus were not instances of traditional violence but rather disruptions caused by the breakdown of the prior political order. As stated above, through the nineteenth century, the frontier between the Ottomans and the Qajars was being turned into a border and the frontier zone was being pacified. On occasion certain Kurdish forces would make forays across this solidifying boundary into the Urmia region, as happened, for example, in Shaykh Ubaydullah's invasion of the area in

1880.[45] However, events such as this, or Simko's Revolt, during which East
Syrians in Salmas were massacred and the patriarch Mar Shem'on XXI Benyamin was assassinated (March 1918), were revolts against crystallizing central
state structures, which have today become permanent entities, even if resistance has continued.[46]

The position of the East Syrians in Hakkari and particularly Urmia—or
dhimmis in general in an Islamic empire—is misunderstood if we rely too
heavily on a notion of tolerance in our historical reconstruction. According
to Bruce Masters, the hardening of religious identities in the later Ottoman
Empire was slow in coming and should not determine our understanding of
earlier periods. "There is no question that religion, as a signifier of identity,
had become more overtly political in the nineteenth century than it had been
in the earlier Ottoman centuries. That does not mean that religious identity
had not been important before, but it now intruded into almost every issue."[47]
"An emphasis on religion as a social category in the historical discourse
might distort our understanding of the Ottoman past," even if the presectar-
ian period was no Shangri-la of tolerance: the *dhimmi* system, at least in the
cities, entailed clear distinctions among Ottoman subjects, and "the question
of who constituted the majority and the minority was thus transparent within
the Ottoman Empire in the early modern period."[48] However, sectarian hatred
was not the norm. Rather, "indifference and an abiding sense of the moral
superiority of one's own community as God's true people were more commonly the reigning attitudes toward those outside it."[49] Such would apply all
the more so in Qajar Urmia, where communal negotiation and representation
were less formalized than in the Ottoman realm, and in Hakkari, which was
under limited, if any, Ottoman control.

In an attempt to get beyond a paradigm of liberal tolerance, Christopher
MacEvitt conceptualizes religious interaction in the Latin crusader states of
the Middle Ages as "rough tolerance," which "is not the equivalent of modern
concepts of multiculturalism, in part because it was not an ideology but a
practice."[50] Unlike the famed Convivencia of Muslim Spain, which entailed
disputation and debate, and worked within the strictures of the *dhimmi* system, what is particularly characteristic of rough tolerance is its silence about
difference.[51] There was a deliberate obfuscation of Christian difference and a
deemphasis on the problem of heresy in this social, religious, and political
context complexly consisting of Greek Orthodox, Arab Melkites, Armenians,
Syriac- and Arabic-speaking Syrian Orthodox, and Catholic Franks.[52] The
Franks arrived in the eleventh century to find a deeply fragmented society:
they and the local elites—sometimes including Muslims—pragmatically negotiated politics; the theological problem of Christian diversity was gener-

ally ignored, as Christians divided since the fifth century prayed together, ordained and baptized one another, and patronized one another's institutions.

Presumably such conditions would be common to any premodern empire, where policing is difficult and political hegemony requires negotiation and compromise. Rough tolerance, or tolerance in practice, is what we find among the Ottomans and Qajars in those areas where they were able to maintain their authority. For example, according to Ussama Makdisi, coexistence between different religious groups in Ottoman Lebanon was compelled from above. "Tolerance was an ineluctable expression of imperial policy. It was a unilateral dispensation rather than a way of life, and its impulse was to discriminate in the literal sense of the term between Muslim and non-Muslim in order to uphold an imperial logic that defined the Ottoman Empire as an *already achieved* Islamic order."[53] However, in the period before the arrival of the mission, the Ottoman presence in Hakkari was limited, if existent, and in Urmia the Qajar "state—if it can be called that—hovered above rather than controlled and penetrated into society."[54] As we will see, American sentiments chafed against the lax yet explicitly ranked communal order of Urmia and the seemingly anarchic Christian tribal system of Hakkari, both of which "fundamentally contradicted the idea of a voluntary, conscious embrace of faith at the heart of American Protestantism."[55]

Imagining Differences

It is difficult to ascertain the attitude most East Syrians had toward members of other religious communities because the sources until the nineteenth century are primarily elite church documents. The few references we find in East Syrian sources to other groups do not help us to fully grasp actual social relations. Jews, for example, are treated with a standard Syriac Christian anti-Jewish vitriol that goes back over a thousand years, whereas sources will refer to some heretics, such as Manicheans, who had disappeared many centuries before.[56] Vernacular sources from the Alqosh region show an antipathy toward Muslims, especially Muslim rulers.[57] There was a general fear of apostasy, and Muslim rule was understood as a punishment from God, a notion also going back centuries in the church's history.[58] Furthermore, apocalyptic hopes for the end of Muslim rule, which are also attested in medieval texts, persisted in the modern period.[59] Reflecting its long-standing concern for communal boundaries, the Church of the East treated the Syrian Orthodox as the proximate Other. Although "Nestorians" and "Jacobites" are often depicted as mortal enemies, rebaptism was not needed for those who moved into the Church of the East from the Syrian Orthodox community.[60] Such permitted proximity existed also with the growing rival Catholic Uniate community, who were not understood as absolutely outside of the church.[61]

In Classical East Syrian texts, we find a particular configuration of the boundaries between political and ecclesial authorities. The most distinctive aspect of East Syrian political theology is its correspondence with a world politically dominated by Muslims. This was a Christian culture that had developed its own distinct modus operandi for dealing with religious and social difference. The East Syrians were Christians who had never enjoyed the Constantinian revolution, the legitimation and patronage of a convert king. Rather, they went from Sasanian (pre-Islamic Iranian) rule to living as *dhimmi* subjects under the various kingdoms that arose after the Arab conquest. For them the age of the martyrs did not come to a triumphant conclusion with Christian empire. They conceived of the church (*'edta*) and the king (*malka*) as distinct authorities (unlike an Augustinian and Calvinist perspective, which envisions a distinction between these institutions, but the ultimate need for them to work together because of our fallen state).[62] In East Syrian martyr texts—a genre in which a major focus is the boundary between heavenly and earthly authority—it is clear that the absence of a Constantinian revolution in the history of the Church of the East led to a political theology holding that Christians are subject to worldly rulers only in body, whereas spiritual authority—or rather, the authority over matters pertaining to the soul—remained with the church, whose representative was the patriarch. A distinction between two worlds (*'alme*), the present one and the world to come, was mapped onto this political theological topography. The Shah in one early martyr text is described as having only "worldly authority" (*šulṭana 'almanaya*). In the traditional schema whereby the church is a ship that moves through this temporal world on its way to the port of salvation, the secular authorities were at worst obstructing storms, which on occasion tested the quality of Christians' devotion.

Ecclesial Authority

Within this mixed social and political world, the Church of the East itself had its own complex ecclesiastical hierarchy. This separate hierarchy derived originally from the divisions that occurred in the early church due to the Christological disputes of the fifth century. By the sixth century, this autonomous church paralleled the expanse of the administrative structure of the Sasanian Empire. At the same time, a separate "Monophysite" (Miaphysite) church hierarchy formed, the Syrian Orthodox, who would remain the sibling rivals of the Church of the East into the modern period. After its medieval acme, the boundaries of the Church of the East slowly contracted over several centuries. In the eighteenth century, there were three different patriarchal lines, and by the early nineteenth century, Catholic efforts had produced a schism in the community, with many East Syrians—most in the Mosul region, which was the most accessible of the three—having become Catholic Uniates under the patriarch supported by Rome.

The patriarch of the non-Uniate party had since the seventeenth century held his dynastic position, which passed from uncle to nephew, at the patriarchal see in Qudshanis in the mountains of Hakkari.[63] As with other high clergy, he was not permitted to eat animal products except eggs and dairy, nor was his sister during her pregnancy when she was carrying the *natar kursya*, the "guardian of the throne," his nephew-successor. This patriarchal line, which is that of the contemporary patriarchal office of the Assyrian Church of the East (held by Mar Dinkha IV since 1976), was originally itself Uniate but later asserted its independence to form a non-Uniate line of patriarchs, a result of the confusion and back-and-forth movement of many East Syrians into and out of the Catholic fold from the seventeenth through the nineteenth centuries. This dynastic line is commonly referred to as the Mar Shem'on line because on succession of office, the new patriarch would commonly take on the name *Shem'on*. In time East Syrians attributed this name change to the fact that the patriarch was thought to be the successor of Shem'on Kepha— that is, the apostle Peter. By the early nineteenth century, East Syrians from the Urmia region paid tithes to this patriarch, even though his authority was often weak and difficult to maintain.

Perhaps due to the absence of formal state authority, the patriarch, despite the precariousness of his position, combined political with religious authority in a manner that many today would be surprised to find in a church leader.[64] From Qudshanis, he served as a virtual transtribal chieftain over the mountain tribes as well as the local subject (*ra'yat*) population. His relationship with the Ottomans is not clear. He collected taxes on occasion for them and was also able to demand tribute for himself, even from the population living in Iran.[65] At certain times he received an Ottoman pension, whereas at other times it seems he was compelled to pay tribute.[66] The patriarch's appearance in the nineteenth century fit with the social position he held: he dressed like a Kurdish *bey* ("lord").[67] Some even compared his court to a circle of bandits.[68] His administration resembled a family business, in part because the patriarchal line had become a hereditary succession. The familial links surrounding his office meant that his brothers often served as his emissaries. Moreover, this also led to the elevation of certain women in the patriarch's family: his sister, the potential mother of the future patriarch, held a special position. In

FIGURE 2. "Mountain Nestorians": Ishai (Jesse), the father of the patriarch Mar Shem'on XXI Benyamin, along with his retinue, during his 1897–98 visit to Urmia. He had contracted yellow fever and come to Urmia for treatment, but he died soon after. (Library of Congress.)

the 1920s, for example, Surma Khanum (1883–1975), the sister of the two preceding patriarchs and aunt of the new one, virtually led the church because her nephew was only a child at the time.

Bishops' lines were also dynastic. Like the patriarch, who always took the name of *Shem'on*, some bishoprics had customarily designated names that officeholders took upon their consecration, such as *Gabriel* for Ardishai, a city in Urmia, *Sargis* for the Jilu region, and *Sliwa* for Gawar.[69] Bishops' dress, like that of the patriarch, resembled that of Kurdish chiefs, and those in the mountains often had a low level of education, if they were literate at all.[70] Mountain clergy in general had little, if any, education, and some sources mockingly suggest that they were far more capable with guns than with books.[71] Like the patriarch, bishops were treated with deep respect: a standard practice mentioned in the sources is the kissing of their hands, a common gesture still performed in the region today to honor a superior.[72] In contrast to the high clergy, priests were abundant in the church, perhaps because it was an office that also passed from father to son.[73] They wore no formal garb, aside from at times a turban, and in their informal position they often served as local judges. They too were often uneducated and also worked as farmers, artisans, or in some other trade.

Traditional Learning and Manuscript Production

The Church of the East had a long tradition of learning, going back to the origins of Christianity in Mesopotamia. The evidence for the continuity of this intellectual tradition from the seventeenth century onward tends to come from those parts of the church that were not under the jurisdiction of the Mar Shemʿon / Qudshanis patriarchal line. Learned churchmen, including patriarchs, tended to belong to the Catholicizing church in the south, such as the Chaldean patriarch Joseph II (d. 1731), who, after studying at a Muslim school, composed a pro-Catholic polemical work, a treatise on the sacraments, a book on spiritual transformation entitled *The Magnet*, and various poems, as well as translations from Latin into Syriac and Arabic.[74] By the early nineteenth century, some Uniates were visiting Rome to study at the Sacred Congregation for the Propagation of the Faith (Sacra congregatio de propaganda fide), which had been founded in 1622 to promote Christianity among the lands newly "discovered" by Europeans. Moreover, learned volumes printed in Rome, such as J. S. Assemani's *Bibliotheca Orientalis* (1719–28), a polymathic compilation of Syriac literary, theological, and historical sources, could be found in the region. However, although the Uniates tended to be more learned, the traditional intellectual culture persisted in the non-Uniate church. Furthermore, it would be wrong to assume a precise and hermetic division between Uniates and non-Uniates. The sources attest a movement back and forth between the different churches, and so Uniate intellectual culture was not distinct from that of the non-Uniate community.

In Hakkari and Urmia, opportunities for education were limited, and the few schools there were (if that is the correct term for what were often informal study circles) taught only basic literacy and some introductory lessons on exegesis and church liturgy.[75] Clergy in Urmia were generally better educated than those in Hakkari, due in some cases to Catholic influence.[76] More often than through formal institutions, literacy was passed from father to son, as were scribal skills. Highly learned and literate individuals appear on occasion in the sources, but these tend to be anomalous figures who acquired their education through informal networks and private study of manuscripts. In any case, by the early nineteenth century, literary composition does not seem to have been common, although the copying of manuscripts continued in some villages.

The contents of the manuscripts copied demonstrate the contours of the intellectual life of those people, primarily men, who were literate and had access to them. The most commonly copied works were liturgical and biblical. The vast majority of manuscripts copied consist of the former: these liturgical works, which were the texts to which the nonliterate public had access through their ritual performance, varied greatly. There were several anaphoras (the regular Eucharistic service) in use within the church, including the Liturgy of the Holy Apostles Addai and Mari, the oldest still in use among Christians anywhere, as well as long liturgical collections covering the whole regular year and the various festivals and holy days. In addition to these, there are extant diverse collections of hymns, often bringing together works by the early Syriac Fathers, Ephrem (d. 373) and Narsai (d. ca. 500), and later liturgical poets. Other genres include lectionaries (collections of regular scriptural readings according to the liturgical cycle), liturgical psalters, and funeral services. There are also several collections of church canons, the most important being the *Nomocanon* of 'Abdisho' of Nisibis (d. 1318) and the massive composite collection associated with the Catholicos Eliya I (d. 1049).

Of biblical works, the New Testament is more common than the Old. Among the biblical books copied, we also find apocryphal texts, such as the obscure Apocalypse of Paul, the History of the Virgin Mary, and the Vision of Ezra the Scribe, the last a revelatory text describing the future eradication of Muslims. Along with biblical works, there are numerous commentaries on all or parts of Scripture, as well as works like the *Gannat Bussame* (Garden of delights), an extensive homiletical commentary on the lectionary cycle.

The Church of the East transmitted the stories of holy men both well known throughout the broader Christian community, such as Saint George and Saints Sergius and Bacchus, and many of its own saints. There are dozens of these lives, some long and detailed, others formulaic and hardly distinguishable from other works of the same genre. The church also preserved various chronicles and other historical works, such as the *Book of Chastity* of Isho'denaḥ of Basra (mid-ninth century), a series of short lives of famous monks. Other copied works include those by the great seventh- and eighth-century monastic authors, who provided a science of spiritual contemplation and ethical self-analysis aiming at revelatory vision. East Syrians also copied translations of ancient Greek medical texts, as well as works of medical practice we might label as "magic," sometimes preserving these apparently contradictory sciences in the same manuscripts.[77] Other technical literature consists of theological works; philosophical works, including introductions to Aristotelian logic; and works on grammar and lexicography; as well as the lengthy catalog of Syriac authors, composed in meter by 'Abdisho' of Nisibis.

Almost half of the extant manuscripts produced from the thirteenth century onward were copied at Alqosh and the nearby monasteries of Rabban Hormizd and Notre Dame des Semences, and this region became the dominant center of manuscript production from the seventeenth century onward in tandem with progressive Catholicization.[78] East Syrian scribes belonged primarily to the clergy, whether they were deacons, priests, monks, or even bishops and metropolitans.[79] Copying at monasteries declined rapidly as monasteries disappeared by the end of the seventeenth century, but simultaneously there was the growth of scribal families, especially those associated with Alqosh.[80] Copying was a practice handed down between individuals, often within a family, and scribes were often those learned in the church tradition, and "certainly most of the learned also served as scribes."[81]

By the nineteenth century, an even higher percentage of manuscripts was produced in Catholic Uniate centers, such as Alqosh and Telkepe. In the nineteenth century, manuscripts were also copied in Hakkari, such as at Ashita and the village of Mazra'a, and the patriarch was known to have a large collection of manuscripts, yet the quantity of manuscripts produced in Hakkari lags far behind that of Alqosh.[82] In contrast, Urmia was not a major center of manuscript production until the later nineteenth century. The increase in copying in the area around Alqosh in part has to do with the commissioning of manuscripts by foreigners, as does the increase in Urmia, which was also affected by the movement of scribes from Hakkari to the Urmia plain due to political instability in the mountains.

The majority of original compositions in Classical Syriac in the early modern period, mostly of a liturgical nature, derive from the Mosul region, and the influence of Catholic expansion into the region is apparent in this literature.[83] Although the ability to compose in Classical Syriac seems to have become more limited, some knowledge of the language perhaps persisted even beyond the clergy.[84] Furthermore, despite the continued preference for composing in Classical Syriac, vernacular literature also developed.[85] Extant vernacular poetry varies from stanzaic poems with Christian themes to wedding and drinking songs to dispute poems, a genre that goes back deep into ancient Near Eastern history. There were also translations of lectionary readings into the vernacular.[86] Theological poems in the vernacular are associated with the so-called school of Alqosh, which was characterized also by increased literary production in Classical Syriac, as well as the boom in manuscript production at Alqosh and in its environs, mentioned above. This increased literary production and use of the vernacular, it has been speculated, were a result of the Catholic presence in the region.[87] Hakkari and Urmia did not witness anything like the small renaissance that took place in the south.

Scribes were not the only ones involved in producing manuscripts. The donors, who are often mentioned in colophons, commissioned and paid for their production. Most extant manuscripts derive from 1500 onward, the period of renewal after the destruction caused by Tamerlane (d. 1405), and most commissioned works are again from the Alqosh region. This may have to do with the Pax Ottomanica, which would not have been felt in the mountains of Hakkari. Commissions were typically for liturgical works for specific churches or monasteries. Commissioning a manuscript was a devotional act that also benefited the donor, who could receive honor and respect within the community for such an act of piety. This is something that should be kept in mind when we address the introduction of printed books and printing in Urmia in the following chapter. In the prior manuscript culture, books were artifacts, objects that could be piously donated like buildings or public fountains. They were part of a culture of philanthropy and material devotion disrupted by the arrival of missionaries with boxes full of books to distribute, and later a printing press. Moreover, contrary to the assumptions of evangelical missionaries about female agency in the Orient, women too commissioned and sponsored manuscripts in the centuries preceding the missionaries' arrival.[88]

The colophons of manuscripts demonstrate that their production was in itself a pious act.[89] They include doxologies, prayers, and invocations of protection upon the scribe, his village, and the donors. Locating the completion of the work at a specific time and place, the colophon links the manuscript, its content, which was often devotional, and all those involved in its production in a sacral network. This network, extending out from the material object of the manuscript, belonged to a world where the sacred had a greater tendency to overflow, where its boundaries were more mobile than those to which the American missionaries were accustomed.

The Plural Locations of the Holy

The East Syrian literary tradition, the contents of the manuscripts copied and the social circles in which such copying took place, attests to an often closed, internally coherent intellectual world, one encouraging pious self-examination and envisioning the social world of the church as singular and unified. This world to which the literate had access was part of a discursive tradition that tended to see people outside the church as idolaters, heretics, or Jews. In contrast to this elite, primarily ecclesial realm, the world of lived religious practice was diverse, socially promiscuous, multilocational, interconfessional, and nonliterate. The holy and its power could be found in a variety of places on the popular level, both in the church and outside its confines.

Most East Syrian villages had a church. Those in Hakkari were simple stone buildings, unrecognizable as churches from the outside. In Urmia churches were more formal structures.[90] Churches were holy places, sometimes even housing the powerful relics of holy men. It is difficult to determine what the actual experience of the illiterate laity was when they went to church and heard the liturgy and lections in a language most of them would have understood only poorly. The church service was a source of power, and the hierarchy of the church—even if there were two, at times three, competing patriarchal lines—received the respect due to an institution linked to heaven and engaged in the performance of the acts necessary for those weighty issues of baptism, forgiveness, and death.

However, the church hierarchy and its claims over parts of life, although powerful, did not have a monopoly on the devotion and care of the Christian community. The heterogeneity of the wider social world found its correlation in the existence of a diverse geography of holy sites, a world of scattered places of power, some even shared with non-Christians. Each church or holy site had its own local practices, traditions, and relationship to the local population: the Church of Mart Maryam (Saint Mary) of Walto, north of Tkhuma, received a sort of brigandage tithe from the local bandits.[91] Of the numerous holy places and shrines, some were linked to the biblical past. Urmia was, according to tradition, the birthplace of Zoroaster, the ancient prophet and wise man of the religious tradition that dominated Iran until the Arab conquest of the seventh century. The local Christian population had their own "Zoroastrian" tradition: the three magi (*magi* was originally a term for Zoroastrian priests), the eastern wise men of the Gospel of Matthew who saw the savior's star and traveled to Bethlehem with gifts, were said to have introduced Christianity to Urmia. Until World War I, the tombstones of these mythical figures could be visited in the Church of Mart Maryam in Urmia, which, tradition held, they themselves built.[92] Similarly, Qudshanis, where the patriarch held his see, was near the Greater Zab River, which was thought to be the Pison River in Genesis's description of the Garden of Eden. On account of this, the patriarch at times signed documents "from my cell on the River of the Garden of Eden," thus fitting his residence into a sacred geography.[93]

Holy sites and sanctuaries were often centers of local pilgrimage. These included the sanctuary of Mar Bisho (Mar Behisho) in the mountains on the Ottoman-Qajar frontier and the cave sanctuary of Mar Addai, the mythical apostolic evangelizer of the region, located south of Hakkari near Zakho.[94] In the Mosul region, the monasteries of Mar Eliya (Dayr Sa'id) and Alqosh were also pilgrimage sites.[95] The supposed tomb of the prophet Nahum was maintained at the latter. Ex-voto offerings would be made by visitors, sometimes leaving the sanctuary a baroque mélange of gifts from far and wide, as in the case of the Church of Mar Zay'a (chapter 6).[96] Some East Syrians made pilgrimages farther afield, even if sporadically, to Jerusalem and Bethlehem.[97]

Perkins describes visiting the church of Mar Sargis (Saint Sergius), which lay on the side of a mountain just a few miles outside Urmia, not far from Sire (Mount Seir), where the mission would set up its retreat and to where the male seminary would be removed in 1847.[98] This centuries-old stone church, "much venerated by both Nestorians and Muhammadans, . . . has the reputation of possessing the rare power of restoring lunatics. And to-day, on entering it, we found several Mussulmâns of both sexes within, who had, this morning, placed a delirious relative in a dark vault of the church and were waiting in expectation of seeing him come forth cured."[99] The cure took twenty-four hours, the family told Perkins, who was outraged that "followers of the False Prophet" are "not satisfied with the endless labyrinth of follies furnished by their dark system" and resorted to the practices of "nominal Christians," whom the Muslims regularly cursed as "infidels and dogs." The visiting Muslims even "employed a *Nestorian deacon* to read prayers over him." This deacon confirmed that it was a regular practice for Muslims to visit the church, and then further outraged Perkins by glibly explaining that he did not understand the Classical Syriac words he chanted. At sanctuaries such as this, it was not uncommon to make a *qurbana*, or "sacrifice," of a lamb, which would then serve as food for a collective meal.[100] Later, when the mission had its retreat at Sire, Perkins mentions Muslims who had been healed at Mar Sargis coming to visit and then later Christian guests, who, after visiting the church, invited Perkins to preach to them.[101]

It was not uncommon for Muslims to visit East Syrian holy sites, and there were some that drew crowds from the various communities of the whole region. Twenty kilometers east of Gazarta and north of Zakho in what is now Şırnak province, Kurds, Christians, Jews, and Yezidis would gather in August at Mount Judi (Cudi Dağ, or Mount Qardu) at a shrine that had been transformed from a Christian sanctuary to a Jewish synagogue, and finally to a Muslim pilgrimage site (*ziyaret*).[102] Local tradition held that the ark landed there and that the remains of Noah lay in the shrine. Shared holy sites such as Mar Sargis or Mount Judi are often deemed dangerous by religious elites, especially in modernity. They suggest a hybrid, even syncretic world that orthodox and systematized pieties disdain. Nonetheless, the kind of religious flexibility attested at such shrines has continued up to the present at some sites in the region, as well as farther north in the Caucasus, where they were preserved even through the forced secularism of the Soviet era.[103] These sites do not attest a simple shared universalism, but rather serve as spaces where sectarian difference is complexly negotiated. The tolerance performed at these sites is one of noninterference, as opposed to one entailing an embrace of the Other. In fact, shared holy sites often are maintained by, and maintain, religious communal hierarchies. For example, at the tomb of Haider Shaykh in Malerkotla (Punjab), which is visited by Sikhs, Hindus, and Muslims (as well as Jains and Christians), sectarian difference is not rejected: rather, a system of differences is constituted within a specific political sphere.

> The sharing of a sacred center by multiple religious traditions necessitates politics, negotiation, strategy, and compromise. These are "signifying sites" at which and through which various identities are projected and received between and within religious and social groups. As such, they are "intertextual" and subject to potentially "conflictual readings." The daily use of the site and the choreography of its use create at least partially observable traces of interweaving, overlapping discourses of bodies, practices, and imaginations.[104]

Shared holy sites are places where the negotiation of multiplicity allows for a true system of differences through a particular "spatial attunement," and newcomers like Perkins, to continue the metaphor, were out of tune.[105]

The East Syrians celebrated a number of festivals, some of which were also attended by members of other religious communities, such as that of the discovery of the true cross, which was celebrated in a number of Eastern churches.[106] A yearly procession was held by the banks of Lake Urmia commemorating the tradition that the apostle Thomas walked across the lake.[107] Another holiday specific to the East Syrians is Nusardil ("Sunday of the Twelve Apostles"), a festival in July celebrating the baptismal rite but often declining into a frolicking public water fight. At 'Ada, a city on the Urmia plain, there was a Church of the Prophet Daniel, which housed a purported relic of the biblical holy man, a bone that would bleed and had special powers. Local tradition held that Daniel was martyred in the spot by fire worshippers, and Jews, Christians, and Muslims would gather each year for the festival to commemorate this event.[108] Such religious intermingling even led to irregular social relations: at Oramur in southern Hakkari, Kurds, although Muslim, permitted certain Christian families to remain so that the local church could continue to operate.[109]

Christian religious authorities themselves enjoyed at times a certain prestige, even aura, among Muslims. For example, Edward L. Cutts, who visited Hakkari in 1876, was told the following story: Once while the learned East Syrian holy man Rabban Yonan was traveling along the road, a Muslim forced him to carry his sack of flour. When some "Nestorians" met the two on the road, they proceeded to beat the Muslim for treating Yonan so shamefully.

"The Mussulman protested that he did not know his sacred character, or he should not have done it, begged his pardon, and would have resumed his sack," but Yonan stopped the men from beating the Muslim and, following a dominical saying (Mt 5:42), continued to carry his burden.[110] The anecdote suggests that Christian holy men were normally recognized as deserving respect even by Muslims. In general, sectarian hatred was not the motivating force of social life, and just as complex alliances and relations existed, so the aura of holiness could be pandemic.

The patriarch had a particular charisma that transcended the Christian community. According to tradition, he held a decree (*firman*) as well as a special knife, both granted to his distant predecessor by the prophet Muhammad, and, as the story goes, Badr Khan Bey cursed Nurullah Bey, the emir of Hakkari, for inciting him to attack the Christians when he found out that the patriarch possessed such protections. Moreover, even pious Muslims, those who would never eat an animal slaughtered by a Christian, would eat what was slaughtered by a member of the patriarchal family.[111]

In the world of social and religious miscegenation I have been describing, there were various practices and technologies we commonly refer to as "magic."[112] Amulets were worn, dreams were sought and interpreted, and books of spells were produced. Surma Khanum explained in 1920:

> Then there are ways of telling fortunes, usually by means of the letters of the name. With us, every letter of the alphabet has its numerical value, and if you write down the value of each letter of a name, add them up, and then divide by some number which is thought mystical, then you can draw omens about the life of the person from either the quotient or from the remainder.[113]

In this politically and socially decentered setting, the possibilities and sources of power were difficult to limit and commonly found.

Several prayer or charm collections, referred to as books of "protection" (*naṭurya*) or books of "anathemas" (*ḥerme*), are extant from the eighteenth and nineteenth centuries.[114] These formulaic texts consist of various prayers, each to a different power for help with a different problem. Prayers address physical ailments and pains, fear of speaking in front of authorities, hunting, wealth, pestilence among livestock, dangerous serpents and scorpions, the evil eye, protection of the household and its prosperity, women in labor, sorcery, travel, and dangerous weapons. Among these prayers are included "anathemas" associated with specific saints or holy figures. That of Mar Thomas protects from the "spirit of the daughter of the moon" (insomnia), whereas that of Mar Hormizd wards off rabid dogs. The manuscripts include vivid illustrations of the different referenced holy persons conquering a diversity of

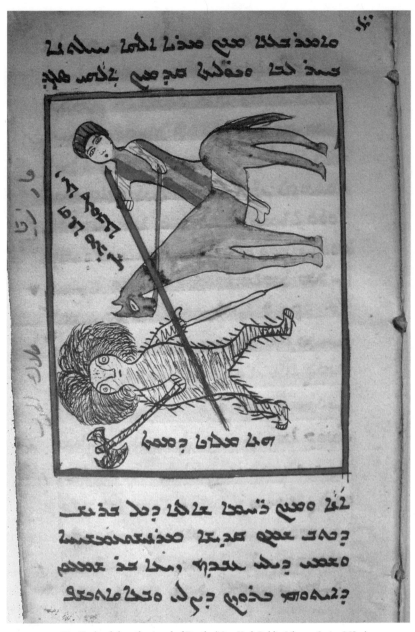

FIGURE 3. Mar Zay'a subdues the Angel of Death. (New York Public Library, Syriac MS 3.)

demons. Such magic, if we should call it that, was not a subversive, alternative practice, but rather the proliferation of the already plural power of the cult of the saints, and was the inverse of the plurality of malignant powers attested in the local demonology.[115]

Conclusion: Secular Liberalism and the History of "Religion" and/or Religion

Despite the occasional violence the East Syrians in Hakkari suffered from neighboring Kurdish tribes and the subject state, with its legal and economic penalties, in which they lived in Urmia and the region north of Mosul, communal relations for the East Syrians were complex and are likely to be misunderstood if we approach them with historically flattening political ideas of tolerance/intolerance, religious freedom/persecution, and equality/inequality. In imagining this heterogeneous world, we should avoid these liberal binaries, which imply the benefits provided by the democratic state. This is difficult to do because many of us can only imagine a world without these explicit democratic protections as a political and social nightmare. We have trouble thinking historically without liberalism and its ideas about politics, religion, and tolerance. I should specify that I use *liberalism* in the broader sense of the term. By it I refer to the political, philosophical, and ethical formation consisting of a concern for moral autonomy, political agency, epistemological independence from tradition, and the preservation of the rights of property, as well as a clear distinction between persons and things. The emphasis on the "modern" typical of much liberal thought has implied a certain "moral narrative" whereby it behooves all humans inasmuch as they *are* human to free themselves from tyranny, ignorance, and enthrallment to the fetish.[116] By "fetish" I refer to the idea that human beings ignorantly attribute agency to what is deemed a trifle, often of a religious nature, such as an idol, and subject themselves to it. In contrast to the Other's imagined fetish, liberalism prioritizes human agency and reason.

Although not necessarily antireligious, liberalism often advocates a rejection of ecclesial forms of authority and the removal of religion from the (supposed) public sphere, a removal that constitutes religion as a distinct and private realm of human life. The liberal model of politics takes for granted a distinction between religion and politics, sometimes even a (utopian) separation of church and state, purportedly in order that all citizens may enjoy equal rights under the law. Occasionally, as in many European countries, liberal politics includes an official or state religion, but the possibility of inequitable treatment of citizens is reduced by the "tolerance" and even special privileges granted to "minorities." Theocracy, in fact a rare institution historically, remains a lurking fear in liberal politics. This is manifested in anxieties about the imagined hegemony of the pope and, like similar concerns motivating politics today, the supposed fanaticism of "the Turk," which is a cousin to the specter of "oriental despotism."

Our contemporary liberal presuppositions result in an implicitly liberal historiographical method.[117] To better grasp social formations and worlds discontinuous from our own, it is necessary to avoid the trap of thinking only about the "problems" of religious diversity, tolerance, and intercommunal violence. Otherwise, the religious diversity of premodern states is rendered in "minoritized" terms, which reflect the history of those excluded from the promise of majoritarian nation-states.[118] It was with the rise of nation-states that diasporic communities, such as the East Syrians, became "minorities" and thereby an acute political problem. A liberal historiographical model has difficulty grasping other, nonliberal ways of being in the world, lifestyles in which the criteria for flourishing are not based upon autonomy and individualism.

The domains we commonly label as the religious and the political are mutually imbricated and have been historically constituted in diverse ways. The two often function in like manner: religion and politics are both activities constituted by the production of social imaginaries around which communities are organized, and both often establish the well-being of the community as the good. In fact, we could understand "politics" in modernity as simply a deracinated form of religion, or "religion" as a more blatantly metaphysical politics. Historically in Europe the political imagination was constituted by and within the theological, and only in modernity set itself up as in opposition to it.[119] This imagination is potentially pluralized because of the internal diversity in any religious community and because different communities in a given society may construe their positions through different conceptual configurations: in other words, Christian communities living under Muslim rule do not understand Muslim rule in the same way Muslims do.

One historiographical question is how to step outside of the very terms *religion* and *politics*, both of which have liberalism, more broadly defined, built into them. It is not enough to compare, for example, how for some moderns religion is—or should be—subject to politics, whereas, in contrast, in other periods and places this relationship is understood differently. Such a comparison fails to take into account how the range of these conceptual categories changes over time and how they are often constituted within a variety

of overlapping discursive fields. For example, religion in modernity is constituted variously, such as in the triad "magic, science, religion," the contemporary contrast between "religion" and "spirituality," or "religion" and "politics."

Instead of tracing the slow liberation of politics from religion, we need to
think not only about how in every time and place religion and politics may relate or differ, but also how each of these entities themselves are produced and
how the realms we commonly label as religious and political often participate
in a wider conceptual field. What is the benefit of this? We can see then that
the very notion of "church-state relations," of "politics and religion," has a
history. We can also better understand the present and how secularism in its
various forms is not simply the removal of religion from the public sphere, the
absence of religion, the evacuation of the sacred, but a specific formation, an
imposed (yet contested) order where the limits of certain spheres are defined
in distinct ways. That is, secularism promotes certain kinds of religiosity; it
produces certain kinds of religion and restricts others.[120] The ideology of secularism, which prescribes the privatization of religion, and the secularization
thesis, the historical model that describes a progressive decline in religion,
both treat religion as an epiphenomenal part of human social life, a secondary
effect that obscures and even misdirects human action in the "real" world of
political and economic life.[121]

In contrasting the premodern to the modern world, scholars at times
point out that religion was embedded in the past, whereas in modernity "religion" is a category that has come into being as a result of specific discursive
processes. However, to say that religion was embedded in antiquity can be
misleading. Such a proposition does not necessarily address the complexity
of the problem it creates. Accordingly, we risk failing to engage with the difficult task of defining the limits of the object of analysis when we purport to
be looking at what is commonly labeled religion.[122] An embedded entity is
different from a disembedded one and may be no entity at all: the process
of disembedding is constitutive. Not engaging with this problem is to imply
that religion is the same in premodernity but just intermingled in the broader
world, like marbles dropped into a stack of hay, remaining the same despite
their chaffy covering.

The Church of the East, as part of Christian tradition and existing within a
complex Muslim, Jewish, and Christian world, participated in some of the important developments in the long-term process of the unfolding of "religion"
as we now know it in our world—that is, as a discursive category, a name and
label that does things. Therefore, the complex world of multiple centers of
power that I have described, where religion, ethnicity, politics, and economics were not delineated as they are in our own (at least by aspiration), was not

a world without religion, but one where "religion" had not been distinctly identified as the private and ultimately secular form of religiosity of the heart that the American (and other) missionaries would hope to introduce.

In the complex political and religious world I have described—one consisting of various churches, holy days, holy men, sacred manuscripts, shrines, magic scrolls, and festivals—the sacred, expansively unfolding, simultaneously separated and intermingled the East Syrians and communities adjacent to them. As it is treated in Christianity and Western religion in general, "the sacred" is constituted by a mobile boundary that changes its position at different times and places and in each society. The sacred has often been treated as a constitutive difference, a heterogeneity that at times expands and contracts.[123] This I take as a sign of its inexorable instability: the boundary between the sacred and the profane is always liable to move under the constant pressure of countervailing forces, especially in premodern settings where "religion" has not yet been formulated within the discursive processes of secular modernity. In other words, in a setting where the "sacred" has not been essentialized and localized, "there was as yet no unitary domain in social life and thought that the concept of 'the sacred' organized. Instead there were disparate places, objects, and times, each with its qualities, and each requiring conduct and words appropriate to it."[124]

In *our* terms, the Ottoman Empire and Qajar Iran were political *and* religious entities, as was the Church of the East. The mutual constitution of religion and the secular, the isolation of the former that functioned to create a space for the latter, had not yet occurred. The question for us is how to conceptualize this without, on the one hand, using all the recognizable terms and categories of our own society and, on the other, saying simply that everything had fuzzy, blurred boundaries. Furthermore, in such nonmodern, illiberal formations, communal diversity is variously negotiated, both by the politically dominant community and by those who are dominated. In contrast to the clearer divisions the American missionaries drew between the sacred and the profane and what allegiances were due to each, the political theology of the East Syrians of Hakkari and Urmia was decentered and disparate: Christians could owe obedience to family members, village elders, local Muslim elites, tribal chiefs, priests, bishops, the patriarch, chiefs of other tribes, the Ottoman sultan, the Qajar governor, or the Shah for what from our perspective is a mixture of religious and political reasons. The East Syrians lived under a wholly different political theological configuration: Muslim rule meant Muslim political theology in which the problem of religious and secular authority was conceived and practiced differently than in the Christian West. Furthermore, the historical mobility of the East Syrians, their capacity to move across regions now divided by national boundaries, corresponds with the different boundaries that constituted the sacred in the premodern world. Imminent nonhuman power with a transcendent source was broadly dispersed and decentered, differently structured and less regulated: terrestrial yet from beyond this world, it was encountered in multiple places in the East Syrians' lives.

The American missionaries rejected this multicentered world of the holy as a miscegenation, a socially confused, intellectually incoherent, and spiritually empty, if not destructive, mess. The reform they brought, with its intensification and interiorization of spiritual concerns, was a form of liberalism, inasmuch as it introduced many of the same concepts that I have been criticizing as restrictive of our own historiographical perspective. In fact, their liberal ideas were genealogically akin to our own, even if the first generation of missionaries were millennialists of the Second Great Awakening. Although they were adamant Christians, they unknowingly introduced liberal notions that had secular effects.

Just as we share certain concerns—for example, about agency—with the American missionaries, so also they cultivated in their audience practices that were already part of the East Syrian tradition, such as intellectual consistency, literacy, spiritual self-reflection, and an experiential approach to the divine. The elite intellectual and religious practice we find reflected in the manuscript tradition of the church, whereby a Christian self was created and nourished, certain feelings of sin and shame were cultivated, and a correct understanding of God's relationship to the world was advocated, is mirrored in what the missionaries promoted for all East Syrians. From a wider historical perspective on reform, one that risks teleologically treating Protestantism as a more advanced form in the evolution of Christianity, we could posit that the Americans were furthering the process of conversion to the Christian life that had begun in antiquity. Through mass literacy and printing, the Americans were democratizing the Christian tradition while transforming it. To be sure, new exclusions and hierarchies were established, especially in their own relations with the indigenous community, but their notion of Christianity was a liberal one that assumed the absence of all intermediaries, and, like liberalism, it failed to see the exclusions it created and maintained. This is apparent in the missionaries' relationship to media. The American mission introduced new forms of media, as we will see in the following chapter, even while a discourse against mediation guided much of their criticism of the indigenous church and its way of life.

A Residence of Eight Years in Persia (1843):
Mr. Perkins of West Springfield, Massachusetts,
meets Mar Yokhannan of Gawilan, Persia

The villagers gathered around us and we entertained them with some account of the New World, of which they had before heard nothing. We make *Yengy Dunia*, (New World,) the rallying theme among the Persians; and their curiosity thus becoming excited, it is easy to lead them into conversation on other subjects. I told the villagers here that a *liar* is, in my country, classed with the dregs of society. They replied that their countrymen are all liars and rascals, the inhabitants of their own village excepted. I asked them what report I should then make of the Persians when I write home. "Report them just as you find them," they answered. They immediately proceeded to apologize, however, for the prevailing vices of their countrymen, referring them all to their civil oppression.

—JUSTIN PERKINS, October 16, 1834[1]

In this chapter I examine episodes in Justin Perkins's memoir from his early years in Iran, in addition to several other sources for the early American "Mission to the Nestorians," in order to understand the encounter and exchange between Perkins, who led the ABCFM (American Board of Commissioners for Foreign Missions) mission in Urmia, Iran, for thirty-five years, and Mar Yokhannan (John), the bishop of the Anzel diocese in the northeastern part of the Urmia plain.[2] I hope to demonstrate the early correspondences and cleavages between two forms of Christianity in the "contact zone" of the American mission.[3] I begin by comparing the trip Perkins made back to the United States in 1842 with his 1834 arrival in Iran. On his visit home, Perkins brought the bishop with him, and the two spent over a year together in the United States before returning to Iran. On his first tour of the region, Perkins distributed books printed in Classical Syriac and in doing so disrupted the prior economy and culture of books that had existed among the local Christian community. Consistent with a Reformed theology of the free gift, Perkins misrecognized the process of gift exchange in which he was engaged with his East Syrian hosts. The episodes presented here illustrate the relationships that can exist between media and language ideology, systems of gift exchange and the theology of the free gift, and a sense of gratitude and that of wonder. Ultimately, this chapter demonstrates how Protestant religious reform stimulated a secular understanding, and thus a further reification, of "religion," which in turn would contribute to the development of national consciousness.

Mar Yokhannan in America

On January 11, 1842, Mar Yokhannan "left the long prison of the cabin of the Magoun and sallied forth into Broadway, ranged over the great commercial metropolis of the New World and gazed upon its wonders."[4] Yokhannan; his companion, Justin Perkins; and, though she is not mentioned in the account, Perkins's wife, Charlotte; along with their precocious daughter Judith had left Urmia in northwestern Iran in early July 1841. They had traveled northwest over hundreds of miles of mountains and rough terrain through the Ottoman city of Erzerum to Trebizond on the Black Sea, then sailed through Constantinople to Smyrna (İzmir), where they boarded a ship for Gibraltar and from there made the long transatlantic voyage. Their arrival in New York is one of the concluding events in Perkins's long memoir, *A Residence of Eight Years in Persia among the Nestorian Christians with Notices of the Muhammedans* (1843), which is based primarily on Perkins's journal accounts and letters from the years described and belongs to a contemporary genre of "residence" memoirs, at times composed by missionaries.[5]

Upon their arrival in New York, Perkins wrote in an unpublished letter: "The bishop is also well. He had about concluded that Eastern travelling is superior to western sailing for comfort & even speed; but the wonders he sees & the kindness he meets on his arrival, have changed his mind; & the rail road travelling will do yet more in this way."[6] The early sources for the American "Mission to the Nestorians" suggest that wonder was an affective response cultivated by the missionaries, and one special source of such wonder was the New World itself, a distant land that had already piqued the interest of many in the East even before the arrival of the missionaries. The New World was not just a hitherto unfamiliar pair of continents, but a strange place full of wonder, "Yengidunya," as Perkins commonly refers to it (equivalent to modern Turkish *yeni dünya*, lit. "new world"). Years before, in 1834, on the boat to Trebizond, on his way to begin his stay in Iran, Perkins first witnessed the wonder the New World could provoke. When his Armenian servant and guide told some Turks that Perkins was from the New World, "They stared at me with amazement, and said it was a day favored beyond any they had ever anticipated, that they were permitted to behold an inhabitant of the New World." When Perkins asked them where they thought the New World was, the Turks pointed upward. The captain of the ship then explained to Perkins that some Persians on a previous trip had "told him, that their countrymen, who know of the existence of the New World, suppose it to be located in the skies, and hold that the English discovered it by the aid of a very large telescope!"[7]

Early in Perkins's stay in Iran, one of his hosts explained to him that he knew nothing of the New World, but "when one has wandered from his home, he said, and is supposed to be dead, on his ultimate return, the inquiry is made, 'Where have you been—to the new world?'"[8] "Everything is superlative that comes from the *new world*," Perkins was told by the governor of the province.[9] Some even thought that Perkins and other missionaries had come to Urmia to abduct local children and transport them to the New World.[10] At the mission Perkins would establish in Urmia, the New World was linked to the wonders of science, like the telescope that supposedly discovered it: it was common to entertain guests at the mission, both Christian and Muslim, with microscopes; maps; globes; descriptions of modern architecture; and a machine that gave off an electrical charge, which was even brought as entertainment to a local wedding.[11] Moreover, the missionaries themselves were treated as a source of wonder: when it was announced that "they come from the new world to preach," the tone was more akin to an announcement of Martian visitors than people who had traveled over land and sea.[12]

This focus on wonder is readily apparent in *Rays of Light*, the Neo-Aramaic monthly that began publication in November 1849. The most common sources of wonder in the pages of *Rays of Light* are described in the "science" (*'ilm*) section. For example, an article on the telegraph states, "The great wonder [*'ajebuta*] of science is this: that people find the means to send information from one city to another distant city as fast as lightning on a wire elevated upon posts."[13] Scientific knowledge is framed, especially in the early years of *Rays of Light*, as a source of wonder and a sign by which one can infer the creator of the universe—that is, as a source of natural theology.[14] The focus on wonder in *Rays of Light* usually leads in the end to an affirmation of God's power, which is so great that, for example, according to one article, there may be people living on the moon, if God chose to make it so.[15] This scientific wonder corresponds with the deeply sentimental descriptions of sublime landscapes found in Perkins's writings. His notion of wonder is both Romantic and Christian, and at the same time often civilizational: modern science is a sign of Western progress, as it is implicit in the sources that such knowledge comes from Europe and the United States.

Yokhannan wondered in America, but he himself was also a source of wonder. After their arrival in the lower Manhattan of Bartleby the Scrivener, Perkins and Yokhannan went on a tour, visiting various prayer meetings, temperance associations, and other Christian assemblies in New England.

Perkins would preach, discuss the Syriac Bible, and provide an ethnographic description of "Persia," hoping to inspire a missionary zeal in some of his audience. Aside from being a wonder, Yokhannan was a moral force: "He captivates everybody, & administers many a salutary rebuke in a very proper way." Perkins even sent an article to the *New York Observer* describing how Yokhannan, affected by evangelical ideas of temperance, would enter taverns and reprimand the proprietors for serving alcohol.[16] The pair also made a speaking tour through New Brunswick, Princeton, including its seminary, Philadelphia, and Washington. Perkins writes, "The next day we went to the capital. The bishop's turban soon arrested the attention of the members of the house (the Senate were not in session), who invited us in—& it was amusing to see them flock around the stranger—(the patriarch—[John Quincy] Adams among the rest)—bringing their scraps of paper to him & to me to obtain our autographs, with all the eagerness of little boys."[17]

Throughout their travels, Perkins was anxious to prevent Episcopalians from turning Yokhannan into one of their agents. He complains of the "officiousness which we everywhere meet from the good Episcopalians."[18] They regularly flocked around the bishop and even cited him as an example of the value of the High Church tradition. This anxiety about Episcopalians, whom Perkins saw as dangerously close to the false Christianity of Catholicism, stemmed in part from the origins of Yokhannan's visit to the United States. It was he who had expressed an interest in making the trip, and when the members of the mission attempted to dissuade him and refused to provide financial support, he threatened that he would then make a trip to England to find help for his people from the Anglicans.[19] Toward the end of their visit, in January 1843, Perkins laments: "No mortal, however, will ever know the anxiety & trials I have passed through during the past year, to keep an artless oriental from being 'caught' by designing churchmen."[20]

Already by June 1842 the visit to the United States had begun to truly sour. Perkins complains of "the extreme fickleness—caprice and weakness of Asiatic character."[21] His letters become dramatically self-pitying as he describes how much he suffered from being the moody bishop's sole intimate in America, and how, because he was the only "object of his spleen," it came with "concentrated violence."[22] By October the bishop was left to travel on his own, and Perkins made plans for him to study at Andover, in part so he himself could have a reprieve from his difficult guest. In arranging for the publication of his memoir, Perkins worried about using a picture of Yokhannan as the frontispiece because it would flatter the bishop too much. In the end he decided to use an image of the Qajar ruler, Mohammad Shah.[23]

Anticipating the kind of strategic manipulation of missions that the East

FIGURE 4. Silhouette of Justin Perkins and Mar Yokhannan by Auguste Edouart (1788–1861), Saratoga Springs, New York, August 27, 1842. The inscription above is Mar Yokhannan's autograph (National Portrait Gallery, Smithsonian Institution; gift of Robert L. McNeil Jr.)

Syrians, especially the clergy, would practice later in the century, Yokhannan regularly threatened during his stay to leave for England to seek Anglican aid, which Perkins thought was only a ploy in order to grift greater benefits from the Americans.[24] Yokhannan was able to capitalize on his exotic appearance by having daguerreotypes made of himself, which he sold for fifty cents each. This, combined with the many donations he received, gave him a certain financial independence during his stay (and also made him resemble the so-called Thieves of the Cross, traveling East Syrian charlatans who used stories of their people's suffering to manipulate naïve Western Christians into opening up their wallets). Perkins himself distributed these portraits of Yokhannan in his own endeavor to draw attention to the mission, but he specifically aimed to reimburse the bishop for the copies he received from him: "I do not intend, at any rate, to be in his debt."[25]

In his correspondence Perkins complains often of Yokhannan's "unreasonable" behavior and especially his lack of gratitude. Not long before setting sail back to Iran, Perkins, who was anxious that Yokhannan should return with him, grumbled: "Asiatics are so little susceptible of gratitude, that I hope little from him on that score. I have never seen any thing like gratitude in him, for all that I have done for him." Perkins even looks forward to Yokhannan's humbling upon his return:

> He will doubtless be unreasonable on the way; but that we can put up with; & when he reaches Persia he will again be a rayah [ra'yat, a subject] — & not that magnus Apollo, which he has been, during the year, in this country. That dependent, subject state is the one best befitting him & many others of his people, for some time to come. Providence, we trust, will order all things well, concerning him & them.[26]

"Magnus Apollo" ("Great Apollo") is a figure from Virgil's third eclogue, and the expression was used in the nineteenth century, often sarcastically, for self-important advisers and authorities.[27] In the same letter Perkins frets about helping Yokhannan find the right gifts for his return, including a "striking clock," and worries about the bishop's possible extravagance.[28] Later, just before their arrival in Smyrna in April 1843, Perkins writes that Yokhannan was "quiet & docile on the passage" and fortunately, being prone to seasickness, would probably not attempt to make the voyage in either direction again.[29]

According to Perkins's letters, Yokhannan demanded too much during his visit and demonstrated a typical "oriental" lack of gratitude. Gratitude for Perkins was the correct response to gifts, just as the free gift of Christ's salvific sacrifice required, and could only be responded to with, gratitude. Perkins does not demonstrate in his letters an awareness of the possible debts that he may have had to Yokhannan from their prior years together in Iran, such as for the hospitable aid Yokhannan gave Perkins when he first arrived and in the years following. For example, in the spring of 1839, when the missionaries decided that they needed a health retreat, a place to withdraw to from the

FIGURE 5. Portrait of Yokhannan from his visit to the United States in 1842. (Courtesy of Allen Richardson.)

city of Urmia, especially during the miasmatic heat of summer, they thought to construct such a retreat in Gawilan, Yokhannan's hometown. (The village of Sire would eventually serve as this retreat.)[30] Perkins and Yokhannan went to Gawilan to begin the project, but a local Muslim big man became anxious about meddling foreign Christians coming to the town, which was primarily

Christian.[31] His son and some ruffians tied Yokhannan to a cart and beat him. They then extorted money from him before untying him. Perkins, who witnessed the attack but was not harmed in any way, gave "earnest remonstrance." They then kidnapped Yokhannan's father and extorted more money before freeing him. After the governor and then the Russian consul were unable to compel remuneration, the money was returned when the local prince, Malik Kasim Mirza, a supporter of the mission, persuaded the Shah to intercede. Perkins describes this episode as an example of the resistance the mission met and of the friends it had in high places. He thus places himself within this story as a passive onlooker, the "seeing-man," as Mary Louise Pratt refers to this "white male subject of European landscape discourse." In the text he becomes one of those who "seek to secure their innocence in the same moment as they assert European hegemony."[32] Perkins fails to acknowledge the benefits he received from Yokhannan and what Yokhannan had suffered for him. Rather, in his account of their relationship, he tends to identify just the benefits he offered Yokhannan, which could only be repaid with gratitude. However, gratitude is not, in Perkins's understanding, equivalent to something that is returned in an exchange. It is rather a correct affective response to gifts conferred combined with an awareness that they *cannot* be reciprocated.

This makes gratitude not unlike wonder. The awe of wonder resembles the warm feeling of gratitude. It is an acknowledgment that something has been granted, which we neither deserve nor would ourselves be able to accomplish alone. These passive virtues, or dispositions rather, of wonder and gratitude are not simply structurally parallel. They relate to each other as Christian virtues inasmuch as we ought to feel gratitude at God's wonders. The Syriac Christian tradition had its own similar discourse, involving notions of wonder, the need to acknowledge God's power, and natural theology, and to be sure, Perkins and Yokhannan's problems reflect the personal idiosyncrasies of two people stuck traveling together. However, Perkins's ideas and the frictions that arose during their stay in America have to do fundamentally with his understanding of religion itself as something loftier than this world, a transcendent truth that was not part of the workaday world of economics and exchange. Aside from being akin to European and American imperial arrogance, Perkins's failure to acknowledge exchange relations is due to his notion of "pure religion" as something existing outside of them.[33] However, before delving further into the aneconomic dynamic of gratitude, wonder, and "pure religion," we need to address why a New England Congregationalist had traveled to Iran in 1834 and how he came to know this Christian bishop from "Persia."

Justin Perkins and His Mission

Justin Perkins was born on March 5, 1805, in West Springfield, Massachusetts.[34] In the late eighteenth century, tensions with the city proper, which lay on the east bank of the Connecticut River, led to the secession and incorporation of West Springfield as a separate town. The Industrial Revolution would later transform West Springfield, but not until Perkins was already on his way out. Perkins attended a local primary school and spent his youth employed in farming on his family's land.[35] According to the biography written by his son, "At the age of eighteen and during the progress of a revival, serious thoughts were awakened in his mind." With a desire to serve and to bring others to repentance, in April 1823 he began preparatory study for college.[36] He also "made a public profession of religion and united with the Congregational Church in July, 1825," before entering Amherst College on September 21, 1825. After graduating in 1829, he taught at the Amherst Academy and then entered the Andover Theological Seminary, which was founded in 1807 by conservative Calvinists who had left Harvard because of the appointment of a Unitarian to a prominent professorship. After studying there for two years, he returned to Amherst to work as a tutor. Henry Ward Beecher (1813–87), the famous Brooklyn-based abolitionist reformer, brother of Harriet Beecher Stowe, was among his students.[37] By January 1833 Perkins had accepted a commission to go as a missionary to Persia. After he married Charlotte Bass of Middlebury, Vermont, on July 21, 1833, the two departed from Boston on September 21.[38] By the time Perkins left for Iran at the age of twenty-eight, he had probably traveled only as far from his hometown of West Springfield as Mar Yokhannan, who had visited Urmia and Tabriz, the two major cities near his hometown of Gawilan. However, Perkins came from a far less ethnically, religiously, and linguistically diverse world than Yokhannan.

Perkins was of the second generation of missionaries who went out into the world under the aegis of the American Board of Commissioners for Foreign Missions (ABCFM). Missions were already founded in Smyrna in 1820, Beirut in 1823, and Constantinople in 1830. Inspired by the enthusiasm for revival of the period commonly known as the Second Great Awakening, Perkins and other Amherst graduates of the day looked to their missionary predecessors who had begun to proselytize Native Americans as well as peoples across the globe as models for the life they would lead. Inspired like their Romantic contemporaries, they were enthusiastic volunteers who trembled before the power of nature, behind which they saw the hand of a provident God. For Perkins and others, the millennium was coming and they could

actively participate in the worldly transformations that were expected to an-
ticipate it.[39]

The story of the origins and founding of the ABCFM itself has been told
before, as well as that of the work of its members in the Middle East. Modern
missionary work, especially as large-scale as the ABCFM's, was fundamentally different from prior Christian efforts at spreading the Gospel: this was an
organized, systematic undertaking, which combined fund-raising, new printing technology, business accounting, and modern disciplines of knowledge
from comparative philology to ethnography. In turn, modern missions also
contributed to these modern fields and sciences.

Although Perkins's was a late ABCFM arrival to the Middle East, the mission to Qajar Iran was new. In the prior generation, the Anglican Henry Martyn (1781–1812), the member of the Church Missionary Society (CMS) well
known for his translations of Scripture into Urdu and Persian, had famously
passed through Persia, openly disputing with local religious elites.[40] His death
by disease in the Ottoman East was treated as that of a martyr, and his name
was often evoked at the American mission in Urmia. Perkins even named one
of his sons, Henry Martyn Perkins, after the early missionary martyr. The CMS
press on Malta printed books in Syriac for a possible mission to Syriac Christians, and there were some initial forays: George Percy Badger (1815–88), the
Anglican known for his contentiousness, who grew up partly on Malta, visited Hakkari in the 1840s and later composed *The Nestorians and Their Rituals*
(1852), still an important source today.[41] However, his and others' attempts to
persuade the archbishop of Canterbury to send a mission took decades to reach
fruition. There had been long-standing Catholic contacts with the region, but
no operations as large as what the Americans were about to establish.

Rufus Anderson, who supervised the ABCFM's overseas labors for more
than thirty years (1832–66) and to whom many of Perkins's letters are addressed, provided Perkins with instructions upon his leaving for the field,
and these are reproduced at the beginning of *A Residence*.[42] Anderson describes the board itself as "an *educating society, a translating society, a society
for printing and distributing books*, and preëminently, *a society for preaching
the gospel*."[43] Furthermore, because "the condition of the world must be as-
certained, before it can be improved," it is also "*a society for observation*."
However, this does not make the board like other organizations "prompted
by mere secular motives" such as geography or politics. Even before mission
work, this inquiry into the "condition of the heathen world" is required in
order "that the *whole world* be laid open to the view of the church—that all its
abominations and miseries be seen, and all its cries of distress be heard; which
indicate a world diseased and perishing for lack of the gospel."[44]

Anderson notes that Perkins will also be "in the very centre of Mŭham-medism, and on the dividing line between the two great sects of that false religion" (i.e., Sunni and Shiʻa Islam). He also reminds Perkins of the missions of the Church of the East into Central and East Asia in earlier centuries and requests that he try to learn more about their history. Because "almost all we know, concerning that sect, in modern times, is derived from Papal writ-ers," Perkins is to make careful observations.[45] He must also demonstrate that they all share the common ground of Jesus Christ and the New Testament in order to persuade the Nestorians that the American Christians do not want to be dominant over them. The purportedly stripped-down Christianity of Protestantism would be presented as a shared space, but of course such a delimited version of Christianity brought with it Protestant notions of read-ing, the rejection of tradition, and a panoply of innovations hidden within an ecumenical common ground. Perkins's main object, according to Anderson, was "to enable the Nestorian church, through the grace of God, to exert a com-manding influence in the spiritual regeneration of Asia."[46] This would be done through the cultivation of indigenous preachers, the establishment of schools, and the distribution of books. Anderson concludes his remarks by reminding Perkins that he will always be remembered at Andover Theological Seminary, "in these halls of sacred science" at "this holy hill of Zion." "And the church will remember you; for the church has awoke, and is putting on the beautiful garments of her priesthood unto God, and never more will she cease to pray, for the spiritual renovation of the world."[47]

One of the major practical and immediate goals of the mission was to prevent more Nestorians from joining the Chaldean Church. As in other regions where Catholics and Protestants competed with each other for souls, the missionary field served as an expanded battleground for their ongoing conflict. Perkins and his colleagues were thoroughly anti-Catholic in their preaching and publications, and the sources show a far greater anxiety about Catholicism and its malignant spread than about Islam, which was thought to be hamstrung and about to submit.[48] Nonetheless, especially in its work in the Middle East, the ABCFM as well as the broader American and European missionary endeavor aimed at a confrontation with the religion of the "false Prophet," whether through direct assault or through the circuitous route of converting the indigenous Jewish and Christian populations, who could then witness to their Muslim neighbors.

The conflict with Catholicism led Western Protestants to see the "Nestori-ans" as the "Protestants of Asia," a small, solitary church that had maintained its autonomy against Catholic aggression since antiquity. That the East Syrians lacked auricular confession, did not have a strong tradition of iconography—

even eschewed images—and rejected Mariolatry since the time of Nestorius, the namesake of the church, added fodder to this myth.[49] Furthermore, as orientals, the "Nestorians" were thought to be perfect instruments for spreading the Gospel. They knew the local languages and ways, and the prior history of the Church of the East and its medieval missionary expansion through Central Asia were thought by the missionaries to suggest their future potential for spreading the Gospel.

Perkins arrived in Iran with the common American evangelical understanding of salvation as based upon faith alone and an aim to create New England–style revivals among the indigenous Christian population.[50] Such revivals required the long-term work of religious and moral reform. This evangelical concern for reform, which was central to the mission's efforts, is well characterized in Webb Keane's *Christian Moderns: Freedom and Fetish in the Mission Encounter* (2007). Keane's subjects, Dutch Reformed missionaries in Indonesia, were engaged in religious and moral reform that in many ways corresponds with the American missionary project: they shared a similar "moral narrative of modernity." As Keane puts it, "In this narrative, progress is not only a matter of improvements in technology, economic well-being, or health but is also, and perhaps above all, about human emancipation and self-mastery." Reform belongs to the project of discovering human agency, and moral progress is linked "to practices of detachment from and reevaluation of materiality."[51] This moral narrative relates to what Keane calls a "semiotic ideology"—that is, the representational economy that links notions of language, signifying practices, and materiality. Keane's work points to the deep links between missionaries' ideas about faith, language, and ritual, and even their anxieties about lying and their concern for spontaneity in prayer "varied according to our feelings, wants, and circumstances."[52] Although the mission's millennialism would give way by the end of the century to the Social Gospel, the "moral narrative of modernity" persisted through the mission's history and was instrumental as a discursive frame for Assyrian nationalism.

Missionary reform attempted to both intensify and yet disembed religion as a distinct part of human experience. As God is transcendent, so also religion was to be something that, although it should guide the heart of the Christian and all of his or her actions all of the time, was not of this world. This disembedding was promoted further at the mission by, among other things, the need to translate "true Christianity" across cultures. Mission required a streamlined and clear definition of what Christianity was in order to package and promote it among its audience.

Perkins Meets Yokhannan

Perkins and Yokhannan met at Gawilan, a town on the northwest side of Lake Urmia, about forty miles from the city of Urmia, on October 18, 1834.[53] North from Gawilan runs the road along a pass through low mountains and hills to the Salmas plain, which lies on the northwest corner of the lake. Perkins had only recently arrived in the region after spending the winter months of the previous year in Constantinople. On a visit the day before to Salmas, his "ear was first delighted with the sound of Syriac,—or rather, a modern dialect of it,—as a vernacular language." In the town of Khosrowa, Perkins received hospitality in the house of a Georgian prince who was in exile due to the Russian accession of his land. The prince himself was in Tabriz, but his servants and the villagers welcomed the party into his home. When the *ketkhodeh* ("lord of the village") asked them what he could give them, "We replied that we had provisions with us, and needed nothing." A meal of "chickens, butter, yogóord and fruit" was sent, and the visitors and the *ketkhodeh* as well as his brother sat down for a meal. "They ate in eastern style, with their fingers, and we with knives and forks." The following day, a Saturday, the party continued their tour of Khosrowa but decided, after a visit to the town of Salmas itself, to head south through the pass that led to the Urmia plain. For the East Syrians of the Salmas plain had been under Catholic influence, and Perkins preferred to spend the impending Sabbath with "Nestorians." In Khosrowa a Catholic monk, who had studied at the Propaganda Fide in Rome, "stood by the road-side, as we were passing to the gardens; but knowing us to be Lütrâns, (Protestants,) and seeing a number of villagers accompanying us in a friendly manner, he turned his back upon us and retained that attitude until we had passed by. We little regretted the loss of his acquaintance."[54]

That evening, as they ascended the heights of the pass, the moon was full, and "a very amiable-looking young man, on horseback, overtook us, announced himself a "Nestorian," and requested permission to join our party." In conversation it was discovered that, while working as a porter in Tbilisi a few years before, this young man had met Eli Smith and H. G. O. Dwight, who had been dispatched by Rufus Anderson to do reconnaissance of the region (1829–31). In fact, Smith and Dwight's optimistic report of their weeklong visit to Urmia in 1831 served as an impetus for Perkins's mission. The young man had taken a cup from the visitors' bag purportedly by accident, and began a relationship with them after seeking them out to return the missing possession. What Perkins takes to be "a very interesting coincidence" may in fact have been no coincidence at all: New Englanders were rare and wondrous birds in Iran.[55]

Perkins's party arrived in Gawilan at four in the morning. Smith and Dwight had also met Mar Yokhannan in March 1831, when he served as an important source for the account they would compose of the Church of the East.[56] Yokhannan, who was the son of George (Gewargis), the local priest of Gawilan, had become the East Syrian bishop of Urmia through the customary hereditary succession of the church, which passed from uncle to nephew. Perkins sent his Armenian servant to announce their late-night arrival. On hearing that Perkins was a friend of Smith and Dwight, the bishop "seemed to recognize in me an old acquaintance, rose quickly, came out and very cordially welcomed us to his country and dwelling."[57] Perkins took this meeting to be a sign of "the good hand of the Lord."[58]

> His recollections of Messrs. S. and D. were so vividly associated with a Syriac New Testament which they had left him, and with their conversations about schools and Bibles for his people, that, before he had received an intimation of my object or been informed that I had a book with me,—indeed, before the first salutation of welcome had fairly dropped from his lips,—with an animated tone he artlessly inquired, "how can you make books for us, in your country, when you do not know our language?"

The bishop then conducted them back to his house and gave them accommodation. The following morning, he, his father, and a number of villagers came to visit Perkins's room. Perkins explained that he had come to circulate Scriptures and set up schools, and they simultaneously acclaimed that he was welcome and that this was "just what we have been hoping and praying for; the Lord has indeed heard and answered our prayers." "I showed them copies of the Syriac books which I had with me,—the gospels, prepared by the British and Foreign Bible Society, and the Nestorian Spelling Book, which was lithographed for me at the press of the Church Missionary Society at Malta. All kissed the books and pronounced them excellent."[59] Yokhannan then showed Perkins the copy of the New Testament Smith and Dwight had given him, pointing to their signature on an empty page. The book "had been kept enveloped in a shawl as a choice treasure." Yokhannan's father then stated that he had compared it to his own New Testament manuscript and found that it had the exact same number of letters, which Perkins explains is typical of the "wanton and painful exaggeration" of Persians. In fact, Yokhannan's father was perhaps doing the standard work of a *muṣaḥḥiḥ*, a corrector of manuscripts: he was treating a printed book as a manuscript and checking it for textual corruption or lacunae, textual defects less likely to appear in a printed book.

After a day of conversation about the differences between their two churches as well as feeling each other out for their respective positions on Catholicism, Perkins, seeing their meeting as a sign of providence, invited Yokhannan to live with him in Tabriz so they could learn each other's languages.[60] Perkins had been living in the city, which was the political, economic, and cultural center of the region, while he perfected his Azeri Turkish and made local contacts. Yokhannan stated that he was not "a secular man" and therefore needed no pay. The next day, however, Yokhannan performed an oracular reading: "The Book of Daniel, an old Ms. [manuscript] copy, was brought forward; the finger of my servant was placed at random on a figured card; the page of the book thus indicated was consulted and the result was soon announced, which was, that he 'must not be *hasty*, but *deliberate*' [Dn 2:15]." Perkins, thinking "the result was accommodated entirely to the will of the experimenter," told his servant to offer a clearly stipulated amount of money to Yokhannan and then left the room. This episode typifies Perkins's inability to see his own participation in transactions of exchange. He describes Yokhannan as disingenuous, and whereas it seems that Yokhannan conjured up the ritual with the biblical manuscript in order to obscure the transparency of the exchange, Perkins is the one who crassly offered him money. That evening Perkins witnessed his first "Nestorian" church service. "The forms were simple. Crossings were frequent, but we saw no images nor pictures. The whole service, however, performed in a dead, obsolete tongue, seemed heartless and painfully void of even the appearance of devotion." When they left Gawilan the next day, Yokhannan's parents were distraught, his mother weeping. "Their simple overflowing of grief reminded me of Jacob of old when bereft of his children."[61] Perhaps as a form of compensation, before leaving, Perkins "gave away a considerable number of books to the priest and two of his sons and one or two others in the village who could read."

The Gift of Books and the Emptiness of Forms

Yokhannan accompanied Perkins's party as they traveled south, the long way around the lake on its west side, on their way back to Tabriz. On this journey Perkins continued to engage with local clergy through the distribution of books. In the city of Urmia, Perkins met with Mar Gabriel (1810–71), the bishop of Ardishai, a town to the southeast near to the lake.[62] His office made him the metropolitan of the wider region, including the city of Urmia itself. Gabriel, who had become bishop at age thirteen, would later become a regional power broker, negotiating among several missions at once. At the close of their meeting, which included Gabriel complaining about the local clergy's disobedience and the woes of living under Muslim rule, Perkins gave him copies of printed Syriac Gospels as well as some spelling books.

In Geogtapa, a town near Urmia where the mission would focus its efforts in years to come, Perkins met someone whom he identifies as "Patriarch Elias." On the way to the town, Perkins notes how the "Nestorians" on the road would approach Yokhannan and kiss his hand. Yokhannan showed the same obeisance to the "patriarch." Perkins's naïve interaction with "Patriarch Elias" demonstrates his ignorance of the complexities of local ecclesiastical politics. For this man was no patriarch at all. He was Mansur Sefaro, the nephew of the Chaldean patriarch, John (Yokhannan) VIII Hormizd (1830–38).[63] The patriarch had sent his nephew to the Qudshanis patriarch, Shem'on XVII Abraham, to be consecrated by him metropolitan of 'Aqra, upon which he took the name *Eliya* (Elias). Hormizd, who had a contentious career and was in conflict with Rome, was the last of the Eliya line of patriarchs at Alqosh. It seems he wanted to put his nephew in a ready position to succeed him in the patriarchal office upon his death, in the traditional manner of succession.[64] The Vatican rejected this and disciplined the newly designated Eliya.[65] The behavior of Eliya, his uncle, the Qudshanis patriarch, and even that of Yokhannan, who kissed Eliya's hand, points to the complex politics of parry and lunge, and at times embrace, that the East Syrians, even longtime Uniate Chaldeans, played with the Catholic Church. Perkins had no knowledge of any of this.

Perkins had his audience with the "patriarch" in the large abode where he was holding—or rather, playing—court, sitting on a pile of luxurious cushions. In a conversation through three translators, from Neo-Aramaic to Azeri Turkish to Armenian to English, Perkins described his interest in bringing books and schools, and the "patriarch" became enthusiastic and requested a printing press. "During our conversation, the great room was nearly filled with listening Nestorians, who seemed to be enraptured at the idea of having the Scriptures and school-books printed in their language. Printed books were a wonder that few of them had ever heard of, and less had ever seen." The chief of the village took up one of Perkins's spelling books and began to teach his child how to read, whereupon everyone in the village became engrossed in the topic of books and schools. Then during a dinner, "which we ate in Asiatic style with our fingers," the fake patriarch told Perkins that many Catholics in the Alqosh region were willing to come back to the Church of the East, while not informing him that he himself was in fact one of them.[66]

In general, Perkins's account in *A Residence of Eight Years in Persia* provides us with a perspective on the local book culture and its difference from the new print culture introduced by the missionaries. Printing and distributing books was one of the primary directives Anderson had given him, in addition to seeking out "Nestorian" manuscripts and examining their history.[67] Throughout his travels, people requested books from him and authorities demanded their further distribution. Books, schools, and manuscripts were a common conversation piece in most of the villages he visited.[68] Printing was for him a sign of European enlightenment: "All this shows that the light of Europe is fast breaking in upon Persia."[69] Moreover, the acute interest that people he met in Tehran showed in copies of the New Testament translated into Persian was a sign for Perkins that "Muhammadism in Persia [was] on the wane."[70]

Despite their robust literary past, which Perkins acknowledges, the East Syrians he met possessed few books. Assuming that books are rare artifacts crafted by hand and pen, Perkins's interlocutors were often impressed by even a mere few. Asahel Grant, the mission physician, had found about sixty books in the patriarch's library in Qudshanis during an October 1839 visit, and some of these were duplicates, whereas villages sometimes had, if any, only a handful, at most as many as ten.[71] Most of these books were Bibles, service books, and the *Sunhados* (a book of canon law and conciliar decisions).[72] These books were treated with a reverence that included kissing, a common practice with copies of the Gospel during the church service and also, as we have seen, upon receiving a gift of books.[73] In one village he visited, Perkins wanted to borrow a manuscript of the New Testament to show to people in America, but the village's Muslim master would not let him take such a sacred object lest, according to him, calamity befall the village.[74] Local Muslims and Christians, Perkins was told, swore oaths on this manuscript before doing business, a practice that further attests to the shared religious world of the region.

Even before his arrival in Urmia, Perkins regularly handed out Bibles, ever aware of their absence in the East and how the classical versions are like "Egyptian hieroglyphics" to the locals.[75] Disembarking from the ship on which he first crossed the Atlantic, he gave Bibles to the crew.[76] This gift giving led to a problem of cargo: he describes the drudgery of carrying cases of books on horses, whereas he had a dispute at the border of Russia about shipping such subversive items, and some books were stolen in transit.[77] Later, after the mission was established, books were used on preaching tours as implements to impress locals, and the native assistant John, son of Hormizd, even describes taking a book out upon coming to a village in order to attract attention.[78] After the press was set up, printed copies of the New Testament were often sold, or given away, to those who could not afford them.[79] Furthermore, once the mission's male and female seminaries were established, New Testaments were regularly handed out as prizes for students who passed special exams. For example, in 1847 students who memorized a biblical catechism consisting of a series of twelve hundred scriptural verses received New Testament prizes.[80]

Perkins expended much energy in bringing these rare objects to Iran because of their content, not because of what they were as objects. But, in his view, Persians, whether Christian or Muslim, had a superficial concern with the materiality of books. Whereas he acknowledges the great beauty of Persian manuscripts and the craftsmanship required to produce Syriac ones, he quotes approvingly Edward Breath, the mission's printer, who told him, "So you see, there is an occasional article that Asiatics value above money."[81] Thus, oriental fetishism trumped decadent oriental greed. Such a perceived love of manuscripts may help to explain the tendency, especially in the earliest printed works at the mission, to imitate the style of a handwritten book. Perkins states that a rubricated printed version of the Psalter was produced to satisfy native taste, and this fits with the mission's use of Classical Syriac orthography to represent the spoken language.[82] Both of these are instances of what we might call co-optive mimicry.

Such an attempt to equate the printed books produced at the mission with local manuscripts appears in descriptions of the preaching tours undertaken by the missionaries and later the native assistants. In a village on the Urmia plain in March 1841, William R. Stocking (mission: 1837–53) preached, "holding up to their view in one hand a manuscript copy of the New Testament belonging to the church and said to be eight hundred years old, and in the other a small pocket Testament in the English language, and observed to them that the contents of that ancient book were all written in the small Testament."[83]

Such criticism of the apparently superficial concerns for the exterior form of books corresponds with the anecdotes Perkins relished sharing with his readers about how "Nestorians" pride themselves on being able to read when in fact they did not know the meaning of the words they read. Thus, Perkins describes a visit with Gabriel, bishop of Ardishai, whom he characterizes as preferring hunting and drink to study, dubbing him sarcastically "the mighty hunter" in reference to Nimrod of Genesis 10:9.[84] According to Perkins, Gabriel would regularly perform his minimal literacy for all those who visited him. Taking up a spelling book "to impress them with his acquisitions," he "as gravely as magnifically recites his lesson, selecting always the second page, and rapidly going through." He would pronounce each line in the syllabary, "ba—be—bi—bo—etc., affording one of the most comical exhibitions that can well be conceived."[85]

The missionaries' anxiety about what they thought to be a native focus on external forms also corresponds with their concern with the emptiness of Nestorian ritual as well as their criticism of local magical practices. Gabriel pretending to read resembled the Nestorian church service as well as the magical incantations practiced by members of the various local religious communities. This adherence to the magic of words and the power of their exterior form was counter to the correct relationship to language advocated by the mission. Beginning with their critique of the recitation of Classical Syriac liturgy, which many East Syrians did not understand, the mission often emphasized the importance of knowing what words actually meant. This critique derives from Protestant attacks on the "mummery" and emptiness of Catholic ritual.[86] For example, one article in *Rays of Light* from October 1851 raises the question of whether an old woman who could not read Scripture was simply a pagan, although she professed to be a Christian.[87] This concern appears also in articles exhorting students to try to understand what they read, whether in the vernacular or in the classical language.[88] The missionaries' ongoing anxiety about lying is consistent with this focus on the correct correspondence between words and things. If words expressed the inner meaning of the heart as the words on the scriptural page expressed God's intimations to man, then lying disrupted the transparency of words, dissociating the inner feeling from the outer expression and denying a coherence between words and the heart. It was not the words themselves that mattered, but rather what they conveyed. Language was "an objective cipher of metaphysical truth."[89]

The Critique of the Traditional Learning of the "*Malpanas*"

Reflecting upon the literature of this "ignorant, degraded people," Perkins mentions his visit with a local village priest in December 1838. "In conversation on the severity of the winter, he produced an old book, which professes to prognosticate the state of the weather and casual events for indefinite future periods." Perkins describes some of the passages the priest read, including one that explained when to "expect a famine, wars in Turkey and the birth of many children."

> This book is a large volume, in the ancient Syriac language; and it appeared to be made up of matter of the same general character with that which I have quoted. The copy that I saw was written about a century ago, and the work is said to have existed from time immemorial. It is regarded by the people, somewhat in the light of an oracle, exerts much influence on their habits of thinking and does not a little to satisfy them of their ignorance. There is no lack of *such* literature in the ancient language of the Nestorians.[90]

The book culture Perkins found in Iran and what he understands as a fe-
tishizing of form over content corresponded in his mind with the false learning of the tradition that the "Nestorians" blindly followed. On his original
visit to Urmia, Perkins met Elias (Eliya, or Elijah) (d. 1863), the bishop of
Geogtapa, at morning services at the church in Urmia, where Perkins had
been spending the night.[91] The bishop had originally acted strangely toward
Perkins's servant when he announced the stranger's arrival in the city. Mar
Yokhannan explained, "We know him very well; he is a little warped in the
brain."[92] It turned out, however, that Elias's abrasiveness was due to his suspicion that Perkins was a Catholic. Moreover, Elias and Yokhannan seemed
to Perkins to have animosity against each other, which Perkins explains was
a result of Elias's vanity being insulted that it was Yokhannan who would
instruct Perkins in their language. However, the two had been acquainted for
some time.

Both Elias and Yokhannan were associated with a school in the village of
Geogtapa, which would be instrumental to the early history of the American
mission. It was Elias who administered this indigenous institution. In fact,
although it is not made explicit in the sources, most of the circle of East Syrian men who worked early on with the mission were associated in some way
with this school. On his original tour of the plain, Perkins met Hormizd "the
pilgrim" (*muqdasi*) of Geogtapa, the founder of the school, and became acquainted with its members. Hormizd, who was approximately seventy when
the two met in 1834, had gone alone on pilgrimage to Jerusalem in the late
1790s (hence his designation *muqdasi*).[93] Hormizd associated himself with
the mission from early on, attending its various events, even after losing his
sight. He died of cholera in his nineties in 1852.[94] Although he himself never
learned to read, he traveled north to Salmas when he was about sixty to find
a teacher for his nephew, Abraham. The teacher, who was possibly Chaldean,
considering the predominance of Catholicism in the Salmas region, was dis-
dainful of traveling to another city to teach only one child. In response, Hormizd set up a school for him where others, including Mar Yokhannan, would
also study. After four years Hormizd then hired Dunkha (Denḥa) of Tiyari,
a learned priest from the Hakkari region, to take over for the priest from
Salmas. Elias, who was the bishop of Geogtapa, was a patron of the school,
which is referred to in the sources as the School of Elias. Another Yokhannan (later known as John), a child Hormizd had with Khanumjan, his second
wife, had also started studying there by the time of Perkins's arrival.

When he first got there, according to Perkins, students from this school
came seeking books.[95] He obliged them with spelling books, which they kissed
as they carried them off. Eventually the School of Elias became that of Per-

kins. Hormizd's nephew, Abraham (d. 1871), who was a priest about twenty years of age when he met Perkins, had studied at this school for seven years. He joined Perkins in Tabriz before he finally settled in Urmia, becoming Perkins's scholarly right-hand man and teacher for years to come. Dunkha and his family, whom I discuss in chapter 5, also joined the mission. When Perkins moved to Urmia for good in November 1835, Hormizd brought his young son Yokhannan to him. "'This child,' said the old man (putting the boy's hand into mine), 'is no longer mine; he is yours; he is no longer Nestorian; he is English; his name is no longer Yokhannan; it is John.'"[96] This John would grow up to be an important native assistant and member of the mission until his death in 1870. The name change in this anecdote was maintained through his life: both the English and the Aramaic sources refer to him as John (*jan* in Aramaic), and not Yokhannan.

Despite Perkins's and the other missionaries' criticisms of the East Syrian system of learning, the School of Elias made an invaluable contribution to the mission's work in printing, formalizing a written form of Neo-Aramaic, and translating the Bible and numerous other texts. (With a few exceptions, before the arrival of missionaries, the Bible was generally read in Classical Syriac and not translated into the vernacular.)[97] The early scholarly work at the mission would not have been possible if Perkins had not co-opted this local institution. Elias, Abraham, Yokhannan, Dunkha, and John are some of the most commonly referenced East Syrians associated with the American mission in the early sources. Despite their importance for the origins of the mission, missionary sources cite these men not as models of learning but rather as examples of the intellectual and spiritual backwardness the mission was there to reform. Perkins appropriated the local system of learning and simultaneously subverted it.

The East Syrian clergy's initial interest in the American mission derived from a desire for books and the establishment of schools. It was the educational part of the potential mission that they recognized and demanded. Moral and religious reform based upon an American evangelical understanding of "true Christianity" would have meant little to this proud, ancient church. They were open to the mission rather because they saw in it the possibility of developing practices that were long part of their own tradition: since antiquity Syriac Christians had employed a language of learning to understand the place of Christianity in the world, and at points in their history they developed complex institutions of study.[98] The memory of this scholastic past combined with the ongoing metaphors and language of learning within the tradition would have made the men in the School of Elias especially receptive to what they thought Perkins was offering.

Perkins notes that Elias was considered "the most *learned* bishop in the province."[99] However, this compliment to Elias's learning was backhanded.

> A copy of my spelling-book was brought, and turning to the alphabet, after entertaining his own people present for some time, he addressed himself to us. "It would be extremely instructive and entertaining for us," he said, "if we only had time to sit down with him and be instructed into the profound meaning of each letter of the Syriac alphabet—alif (a) for instance," he said, "for Allaha (God), and for Adam (man,) and so on." His own people present seemed astonished at such marvellous displays of learning.[100]

Elias's display of learning, which in fact demonstrates a traditional Syriac Christian understanding of the power of letters and their nonarbitrary nature, represented for Perkins the indigenous fetishism he had come to eradicate. According to Perkins's notion of language, which was part of a broader semiotic ideology, letters do not mean anything in themselves: they are arbitrary signs that serve to convey words, which in turn serve as bearers of meaning. This is in contrast to, for example, the traditional Syriac Christian notion that the letters have a mystical connection to the elements that served as the building blocks God used at the time of creation, a notion familiar to those acquainted with Jewish mysticism.[101] This episode attests to the neutral valence of wonder: it must be rightly directed. Whereas wonder at God's creation or the technologies of the "New World" is an appropriate response, a potential opening to transformation, in this case the astonishment of those around Elias points to the closure of their minds.[102]

Elias appears a number of times in Perkins's work as representative of traditional East Syrian learning. When Yokhannan and Abraham of Geogtapa began to study geography with Perkins—"They appear, indeed, to be just waking up from the dreams of infancy"—Abraham asked of what the sky consisted.[103] In his response Perkins explained that he only knew heavenly bodies through optical instruments, because "no body has ever been up far to examine."[104] According to Abraham, Mar Elias "had read to him, from one of their old books, a statement that the sky is formed of ice," a notion that appears in the Syriac exegetical tradition.

At one point Perkins got into a debate with Priest Dunkha about the chronology of the antediluvian era.[105] The two of them both used the Bible for their calculations, but their accounts differed on how many years there were between the creation of the world and the Flood. "'Your Bible,' they replied, 'must then differ from ours; and we shall not allow that our other books, which assign three thousand years to that period are mistaken, until *our Bible* proves them to be so.'" Perkins added the years up again, but this time using "their Bible." Priest Abraham acknowledged the accuracy of the new account, while the rest were amazed at Perkins's reckoning, but then Dunkha suggested that there could be another, mysterious form of counting that Moses himself had used. The next day, after admitting that he was wrong, Dunkha pointed out a geographical problem: Arabia was not the largest country in the world, as their books stated. Dunkha, who himself had traveled to Russia, then admitted that "their old writers" contradict one another.

> These cases are interesting, as they render the errors in the old books of the Nestorians palpable, and on points which cannot be considered as *sectarian.* The people venerate their ancient writers as all but inspired, while they, at the same time, in theory at least, hold that the Bible must be the ultimate standard. The work being fairly commenced, in such instances as I have named, the way may soon be opened, to prove to them the errors of many of their religious *traditions.*[106]

Such anecdotes make clear how the missionaries were setting themselves up against the tradition of the Church of the East and attempting to establish the Bible as the irrefutable standard of spiritual truth.

Perkins describes how Abraham at one point lapsed back into the traditional exegesis in his reading of the Parable of the Leaven (Mt 13:33 and Lk 13:20–21).

> On the parable of the leaven, forgetting himself for the moment, he started upon one of the old stereotyped interpretations, according to which, *every sentence* and every *word* must have a specific, figurative application. "Why," said he, "did the woman hide the leaven in the three measures of meal? I will tell you why; it was because Noah had three sons, from whom the whole world was peopled. The meal is the world; and the three sons are the three races of men."[107]

This episode demonstrates Perkins's ongoing concern about what he deems "mystic interpretations."[108] However, it also provides a good example of how strongly such a tradition of interpretation persisted: the ninth-century Syriac biblical exegete Isho'dad of Merv actually attributes Abraham's same interpretation to, among others, Henana of Adiabene, the head of the School of Nisibis at the turn of the seventh century.[109]

The American critique of East Syrian interpretive practice was not hermeneutically sound, as are most simple Protestant arguments for *sola scriptura.* Scripture, as any text, is not a static entity with a clear and transparent meaning for each syntactical construction of words. Furthermore, although there is certainly a Syriac exegetical tradition of standard explanations of certain scriptural passages, Syriac biblical hermeneutics is more sophisticated than the missionaries, who deemed it obscurantist mysticizing, were aware of or willing to admit. For example, the theological poetry of Saint Ephrem of Nisibis (d. 373), which has been incorporated at points into the liturgy, holds Scripture to be a text of unlimited mysteries, which are revealed to those who meditate upon it, and the later monastic writers exhort their readers to wonder at the unending fullness of the biblical text.[110] In the Syriac tradition the mysteries of the Bible have no end.

The exegetical tradition the Americans rejected was transmitted through the learned men of the community, who were part of a chain of tradition going back to the great teachers of the past. The respect given to figures such as Elias was due to their knowledge not of the Bible per se, but rather of the Syriac exegetical tradition, specifically the books of the "teachers" (Syr. *malphane*). *Malphana*, or *malpana* as it is pronounced in Neo-Aramaic, is the generic Syriac term for "teacher" in the Classical sources. The term was commonly applied to the great theologians and poets of the Classical tradition, such as Saint Ephrem or Narsai (d. ca. 505), the first head of the School of Nisibis. Not unlike the "Fathers" of the Western churches, the *malphane* represented the standard tradition of the church, and their authority was not to be challenged.

Albert Holladay, one of the early missionaries, noted in 1839 that although the Syrians exhibited a new focus on scriptural accuracy, "They are still, however, prone to attach importance to trifles, and to pry into things which are not revealed. This is owing to the superstitious reverence with which they regard the writings of their 'malpanas' or religious teachers, who have professed to give much information on such subjects."[111] After William Stocking preached at Geogtapa in November 1841, Abraham of Geogtapa got into a debate with those who complained Stocking had in his preaching aimed to attack the *malpanas*.[112]

Understanding them to be in thrall to their own tradition, the missionaries also projected onto the East Syrians a desire to defend the *malpanas* and their teachings. At a gathering in Geogtapa with Elias and others in July 1837, Perkins described the origin of dew, that it is deposited from the atmosphere.[113] It is likely that he was responding to the biblical notion that it comes down from the firmament (a position that is openly contested some years later in an article in *Rays of Light*).[114] The conversation then turned to the stars. "The galaxy caught the philosophic eye of Mar Elias, and he proceeded to offer an explanation. 'At the time of the flood,' said he 'we read that the windows of heaven were opened. That light streak is one of those windows which has never been again closed up. So our *Melpánas* (ancient teachers) say.'"[115] In its republication in his memoir, Perkins specifically rendered this episode as about the native tradition of learning: the original manuscript of his journal lacks Elias's final sentence about the *malpanas*.[116] According to Perkins, after Elias gave his explanation, John, the boy who had been given to Perkins to raise, "caught the inspiration of the theme" and rose up and sang a hymn in English about God, who "made the stars and made the comets, / Made the moon and *milky way*; / Made the sun and all the planets, / Light for night and light for day." The audience were riveted by the beauty of his singing and asked him to translate it. They generally agreed that it was just as probable that the Milky Way "is made up of myriads of twinkling stars." Again, several years later, an article in *Rays of Light* describing the "milky way" or "path of thieves," as it was also known, refers to this very episode and conversation.[117]

Perkins describes the reverence for the *malpanas* as a habit difficult to remove. On translating a standard children's geography book, Perkins was surprised when his assistants questioned him about the book's author:

> On one occasion, they soberly asked me, whether Peter Parley is not one of the *American saints*, supposing that such boundless knowledge as his book displays, could be possessed by no mortal less than a saint; and they were much surprised, when I told them that the author of this book is not only not canonized, but is still living and not yet a very old man.[118]

Perkins explained that American Christians had no saints, no man was master, and Parley (Samuel Griswold Goodrich [1793–1860]) was simply the author, under a pseudonym, of a useful textbook.

For Perkins and the other missionaries, the East Syrians clung to books, learned men, teachers of the past, and even the tradition of their own church in a fetish relationship. The fetish, a cultural category for thinking about the Other, depends upon misplaced value, the trifle. To understand others as engaged in a fetish relationship is to posit that true value is not in things themselves, but in their meaning. The East Syrians treated books as objects with an inherent value, and this is a fetish. According to William Pietz, the fetish discourse belongs "to a cross-cultural situation formed by the ongoing encounter of the value codes of radically different social orders."[119] "The discourse of the fetish has always been a critical discourse about the false objective values of a culture from which the speaker is personally distanced."[120] To render it in Keane's terms, the existence of the fetish is a failure or absence of semiotic ideology: "The fetish is precisely *not* a material signifier referring beyond itself, but acts as a material space gathering an otherwise unconnected multiplicity into the unity of its enduring singularity."[121] The missionaries often commented upon the tendency of their audience to kiss books as well as authoritative men, a kiss that, for the missionaries, represented blind submission—in other words, fetishism. In one of the many instances in the sources where the narrator assumes the reader is laughing or cringing with him or her, we are told how Hormizd, the enthusiastic illiterate who founded the School of Elias, kissed the *Edinburgh Encyclopedia*, thinking it to be the Holy Scripture.[122]

In contrast to the East Syrians' docility before manuscripts and teachers, Perkins is glad to describe what he deems to be the correct relationship to books. One of the concluding high points of *A Residence* takes place on March 13, 1841, not long before Perkins returned to America for his visit with Yokhannan in tow.

> The proof-sheets of our *first* tract in the Nestorian language was brought into my study for correction. This is indeed the *first sheet*, ever printed in that language and character. As it was laid upon my table, before our translators, priest Abraham and Dunk[h]a, they were struck with mute astonishment and rapture, to see *their* language in *print*; though they themselves assisted me, a few days before, in preparing the same matter for the press. As soon as recovery from their surprise allowed them utterance, "it is time to give glory to God," they mutually exclaimed, "that our eyes are permitted to behold the commencement of *printing books* for our people!" No wonder that the priests are this interested, pointing, as this tract does, to an era of light and hope for their people. In the evening, I held a meeting with about twenty of the young men and boys, connected with our seminary and printing office, to converse with them on the concerns of their souls. I found several of them very serious and tender in their feelings.[123]

Wonder and gratitude before the printed text reflect the relationship Perkins deems appropriate between the human being and God. Note the absence of the missionaries and their own agency from this anecdote, which ignores the labor of those who brought a printing press over thousands of miles of land and sea, as well as that of Perkins, who edited the aforementioned tract (*Teachings from the Words of God*, which includes the Lord's Prayer, the Ten Commandments, and selections from the Bible).[124]

Against tradition Perkins poses printed Scripture, but Scripture is *mediatorially* different from tradition, as well as from *malpanas* and manuscripts: it is the unmediated word of God. The word of God, when offered to human beings, can transform them, and this may explain why Perkins decided to include mention of the evening meeting immediately after this event. Seriousness and tenderness in feelings are standard motifs in narratives of revival. They point to the opening of human hearts that occurs before conversion. This emotional calm before the storm appears commonly in the descriptions of the revivals that would begin to take place at the mission in 1846.

Conclusion: Books without Media, Commodities without Exchange

After their visit to the United States, Perkins and Yokhannan seem to have worked things out. Yokhannan continued his association with the mission for years to come, both preaching and helping to establish village schools.[125] Following the model of his Protestant colleagues, he even went against his church's practice for men of his rank by taking a wife.[126] However, he never joined the Syrian Evangelical Church, which was founded in the 1860s, and later in life he joined others in petitioning the Russian Orthodox and Anglicans for aid.[127] He died three and a half years after Perkins, on May 28, 1874, and was buried with prestige in the Church of Mart Maryam in Urmia.[128]

This chapter began to tell the story of the ongoing encounter between American missionaries and the Church of the East. To state the obvious, in 1834 Perkins arrived to a world geographically, economically, ethnically, linguistically, and religiously different from his own, one more complex in a number of ways than the life he had known on the Connecticut River. The printed books, and eventually the press, he brought with him were alien technology that for him represented a different relationship to the written word, one that corresponded with his clearly defined and stark notion of Christianity as a religion of nonexchange. From the disparate material I have presented, we can draw certain correlations: the new form of media he introduced, his more reified notion of Christianity, the rejection of East Syrian tradition, the theology of the free gift, and his inability to recognize his own participation in reciprocal gift exchange all reflect the mission's larger project of religious reform.

For Perkins the medium of the printed book went with a particular epistemology, language ideology, and theology. The printed book did not simply take the place of the manuscript, because it did not structurally fit into a religious system in which manuscripts and holy men (and holy places) were revered and the learning of the *malpanas* was authoritative. It represented a different kind of Christianity, a religion of the heart based upon the unmediated truth of Scripture (though in reality mediated by Perkins and his numerous "gifts"). This Christianity did not entail sacrifice at saints' tombs, fasting, or any other ritual, which for Perkins represented a form of exchange, but rather only each individual's recognition of an awesome God and acknowledgment of his or her debt to him. Perkins's distribution of books, and the American mission as a whole, were not only an educational effort, an attempt to increase biblical literacy, but also the performance of the free gift, aneconomic behavior par excellence, as well as a demand for the reevaluation of materiality itself. Perkins was engaged in a pious act of reform that reconstrued the relationship between human beings and things. Knowledge of God was the gift he offered, unmediated access to the creator of the universe who had been hidden by the accretions of East Syrian tradition, which was on the verge of declining into Catholic error.

Religious reform entails dematerialization, or *purification*, a term Webb Keane borrows from Bruno Latour.[129] A semiotic ideology maintaining that there are signifiers and signifieds and that it is the signified that is of value leads to a stripping away of ritual, language, and materiality for a posited ontologically stable and true inner meaning of things. Purification is an "effort to correct what appears to the missionary to be an illicit conflation of words, things, and persons."[130] As the episodes in this chapter suggest, the purification, or dematerialization, of reformed religion obscures relations of exchange and its materiality, even if the bearers of this reform have a greater capital investment and are more socially organized and economically astute than their predecessors in evangelism. The anxieties Perkins expresses about Yokhannan's "oriental" ingratitude and acquisitiveness correspond with his failure to recognize exchange relations as he traveled through Iran for the first time. In contrast, Yokhannan, acting like a guest, had expectations during his stay in America that Perkins was not willing to fulfill. Purification is never completely successful, and hybrids can result: this is apparent in the short term in the frictions of Perkins's relationship with Yokhannan and in the long term in the emergence of national identity among the Syrians within the missionary encounter. National identity was a hybrid resulting from the failure in the translation of reform.

Perkins distributed books freely as gifts. This giving, as well as the practice of mission itself, was a performance of the free gift, the notion of which is essential to Perkins's Calvinist theology. Implicit in this theology is the idea that true religion is not done *for* anything. It is not even *done*. True religion is rather a correct state that leads to evangelical action. Our service may benefit others, but it is an imitation of Christ that does not demand an always corresponding response from those whom we serve. "Religion as doing" would imply works righteousness, that one can work for salvation, specifically by giving to God through prayer and good deeds, and that the evangelist can expect an automatic response from his or her audience. This would be, however, a theological error. We work for others' salvation, but it is grace that brings forth fruits. True religion is a response to God's grace, a response of gratitude, whereas exchange is something of this world and not part of religion. The grateful response to grace—and in fact to all gifts, including that of our salvation—is akin to a sense of wonder in that it is one-sided. It is not a reciprocal action, but simply recognition and acknowledgment. In their at times contentious relationship, we can discern a slide in Perkins's gripes against Yokhannan between God as the correct recipient of gratitude and Perkins himself, as well as American "civilization" more broadly. Perkins expected Yokhannan to feel grateful for his visit to America and to wonder at its Christian civilization, and this is in harmony with the millennialism that inspired Perkins and other members of the ABCFM. America was part of God's plan.

Perkins's denial of exchange, which is also a denial of religion's participation in a realm of commodities, must be set within the context of the world from which he came. First, it is part of "disinterested benevolence," the idea advocated by Samuel Hopkins (1721–1803) that one could in fact give without expecting to receive.[131] This idea, which lay behind much of the American missionary effort, led to an ethic holding that private interests were to be subject to the public good. Second, Perkins was engaged in an evangelical negotiation of market culture: he notes the difficulty of setting up a mission when Europeans are in the vicinity and complains about the importation of rum to the East and the other corrupting influences from Europe and America.[132] He was performing resistance to the ills of his own society, and yet it is the very mechanism of organization introduced by capitalism that allowed him to engage in this endeavor. It is ironic—or perhaps makes sense—that Perkins came from a world where exchange relations were far more explicit and the tendency was stronger to see all things as exchangeable, even though he reacted so coldly to exchange among his audience and even attributed it to their oriental character.

Perkins decries the system of gift exchange in Persia and the obligation of reciprocity placed upon the recipient, and yet describes his own practice of distributing books as gifts and receiving favors in return during his travels. At one point he complains about the local governor attempting to create a gift relationship with him: "In the course of the afternoon the governor sent us presents of tea, sugar, fresh fish, and bushels of grapes and melons. Such presents we are always sorry to receive, in Persia, as an extravagant return is universally expected; and in value corresponding to the rank of the Persian donor."[133] These gifts came after Perkins had already discussed distributing books with the governor, who expressed annoyance that Perkins did not bring printed material in Persian with him.[134] Perkins failed to recognize his own side in this exchange. In fact, instead of a language of exchange, a common metaphor he uses for his labors, including the distribution of books, is one of scattering seed for a future harvest, thus avoiding the notion of reciprocal gift giving.[135] The harvest in this metaphor would be the later Christian revivals from 1846 onward, which are also described in agricultural terms.

Gift and commodity exchange coexist in many societies, and I am not positing a radical alterity between Iran and the United States in the mid-nineteenth century. Humans engage in exchange, especially in the burgeoning capitalist society from which Perkins came, yet Urmia had its own culture of exchange. Rather, what is significant here is that true religion for Perkins was something outside of this world of exchange, a nonmaterial relation belonging to a wholly different sphere. Perkins was not rejecting all exchange, but rather the possibility of exchange existing within religion, and this is an example of the further elevation (and thereby reification) of "religion" through its isolation, a component of the larger project of reform. Just as true Christianity was not of this world, and just as it entailed a unidirectional relationship with God, so also Perkins was trying to engage in true gift giving, and the mission itself, which was funded by contributions from America, was an institution based upon the free gift. Learning to give freely was an important part of being Christian for the missionaries.

For Perkins the distribution of printed books dematerialized the Bible, rendering the meaning more important than the stereotyped, industrially produced object. In contrast to the manuscript, whose auratic presence, in a Benjaminian sense, allows for it to serve as a sacred object, a holy relic upon which, for example, locals could swear oaths, the printed book was not important for Perkins as an object in itself. In mass-produced copies, the material substance loses its enchanted quality and books are more easily treated as commodities for exchange. The content, or rather, the meaning lying beyond the words of the content, is what counts, and this meaning was even more accessible due to Protestant literalist hermeneutics in which the meaning of language was thought to be immediately apparent. However, against this trend in which printed books circulated like commodities in a free market, the free giving of the book rendered it no longer a commodity, but a mere receptacle of something that was of infinite value yet free. This is an instance of "the mutability of things in recontextualization": distributing Bibles transforms them into noncommodities, into pure spirit, their words floating above the bustle of material and economic life.[136]

The shift from manuscripts to books did not result in an immediate reformulation in media practice or phenomenology. The aura of the manuscript could be taken over, at least for a time, by the printed book. The appropriation and transformation of the indigenous media of manuscripts through the introduction of the printed book left an auratic remnant. One type of book displaced another, and the differences between these media were small enough that one could take over the role of the other. In asking to preach from local manuscripts although they had their own printed copies, the missionaries appropriated through their own learned performance the power of local books.

The missionaries' awareness of the power of the book as a visual object is demonstrated by the episodes when printed books were taken out in public simply to draw the attention of the crowd. This was an attempt at media hegemony through mimicry. The objects were self-consciously "fetishized" while at the same time demoted in significance.

A number of scholars have recently suggested that the sphere of human life we commonly identify as "religion" is a form of mediation—that is, a method of accessing a posited transcendent, which is constituted by its very absence and therefore by the process of mediation itself; changes in forms of mediation therefore correspond with transformations in religion and its object.[137] Inasmuch as media, such as sacred texts, provide access to the transcendent, shifts in media can then entail shifts in the nature of that transcendent. The evangelical media practices advocated by Perkins were "premised on the wholly ironic concept of non-mediating mediation . . . a vision of autonomy or autonomous meaning achieved through linguistic incorporation, of consciousness merging with the natural or spiritual 'facts' that words signified."[138] This represented a new and indeed competing "aesthetic formation," or regime of the senses, sensation, and experience. And the printed book constituted a radically disruptive "sensational form" within this regime.[139]

To be sure, new technology does not determine the religious imagination, but "is embedded in the latter through an often complicated negotiation process in which established authority structures may be challenged and transformed."[140] I do not mean to suggest we think according to the "myth of modern media as agents of secularization," as if modern media inevitably make us modern people or lead to the privatization of religion.[141] In other words, "There is nothing inherent in the technology or institutional organization of the print medium that leads to a dispelling of religious authority or the fragmentation of religious sources of knowledge or identity."[142] However, myths can be powerful, and the introduction of printing in Urmia was embedded within the myth of its liberatory effect and the numerous practices that came with it.[143] Perkins was a Christian republican of his time. For him the free access to information through printing had an almost "talismanic importance" in serving as a "natural resistance to imperial sovereignty."[144] This "theory of print" belonged to a broader framework of ideas, many of which the mission would introduce through its numerous publications, as we will see in the following chapter.[145]

Printing the Living Word:
Moral Reform and the Awakening of
Nation and Self (1841–70)

The press has sometimes been called *the modern gift of tongues*. It is so; but is also much more. It is the gift of tongues stereotyped. Instead of the ephemeral unction of a Pentecostal occasion, by which every man was made to hear the wonderful works of God in his own language, it gives to them all the permanent record of those wonderful works, to be read and re-read, and transmitted to successive generations. And instead of being limited to Jerusalem, or carried to their respective countries, by the living voice of all those Parthians and Medes and dwellers of Mesopotamia, as was the gospel originally conveyed, the press has the power of *ubiquity*.

—JUSTIN PERKINS, *A Residence of Eight Years in Persia* (1843)[1]

The ubiquity of printed matter, its capacity to travel far and wide, increased the potential for the effects of the American mission to reach its Syrian Christian audience on the Urmia plain and beyond. The gift of tongues, the multiplication of the Gospel into various languages at Pentecost, as described in the book of Acts (2:1–13), was manifested at Urmia as a stereotype, a printing plate with which numerous copies could be produced. Literacy was slowly increasing due to mission education, as well as Catholic and indigenous initiatives, and through their press, the missionaries broadly disseminated a Christian message with affinities to contemporary liberal, republican, and naturalistic thought. This was an evangelical conceptual system in which Assyrian national thinking would emerge, and, as we will see in the following chapter, this system served as a correlate to the new social formation and social practices developed at the mission.

In this chapter I examine several terms and concepts promoted by the mission, as well as the moral and epistemological framework to which they belong, through an analysis of the Neo-Aramaic literature printed at the press. I hope to demonstrate how the missionaries unintentionally helped to create a discursive framework in which national consciousness and new ideas about community came into being. The basic concepts the missionaries introduced in their attempt to reform and revive the "Nestorian" community, both as individuals and as a group, contributed to the development among the East

Syrians of a sense of themselves as a *national* community and the emergence of a language constitutive of this. This literature addresses its readers both as a subjective reading audience and as the very objects it describes, and the transformation of self and collectivity demanded later by the early nationalists not only recalls this same project of moral reform but often employs its terminology.

The rise of evangelical culture in the United States at the turn of the nineteenth century occurred at the same time as major changes in American publishing. Of course, watersheds in the history of Christianity are often linked to developments in media. Christianity in the Roman Empire, for example, may have spurred on the spread of the codex, which displaced the scroll as the standard form of book, whereas the Reformation is commonly understood in the context of the development of printing. So also evangelicalism is linked to the origins of the modern publishing industry, which has only changed in the last twenty years with the development of digital technology and the Internet. Furthermore, just as nineteenth-century missionaries relied increasingly upon the tools of modern business, evangelical publishing grew into a corporate bureaucracy.[2] Evangelical print culture created a textual community through a canon of authors, and a similar phenomenon occurred, if in microcosm, at the American mission in Urmia.[3] Moreover, the literature from the mission's early years offers us a glimpse of the kind of oral instruction provided during that period.

With some exceptions, the focus in this chapter is on literature printed from 1841 through the 1850s. Significant changes occurred at the mission in the 1860s, such as the development of an autonomous evangelical church. Furthermore, at the end of 1870, not long after Justin Perkins's death, the Presbyterian Church took over responsibility for the mission from the ABCFM. The earlier period is of greater interest because the missionaries still held to the millennial hopes of the Second Great Awakening, and yet many of the ideas in the literature from this period continue to appear in mission sources in the following decades, even into the supposedly more secularized period of the mission's history at the turn of the twentieth century, when the Social Gospel and an explicitly liberal form of Christianity became predominant.

The Mission Press and *Rays of Light*

The American mission press in Urmia published approximately one hundred different works between 1841 and 1871.[4] Edward Breath, who managed the press, left his career as a printer in Illinois to join the mission in 1839.[5] The

first printing press had only been introduced to Iran by Muhammad Shah
(1834–48) in 1836. Breath created several typefaces over the years, until his
death at the mission in 1861. The mission's press was in working order by
November 1840.[6] While learning to speak Neo-Aramaic during his first years
in Iran, Perkins also developed a written form of the language based upon
Classical Syriac and began from early on to translate portions of Scripture
into it.[7] The native assistants, several of whom appeared in the prior chapter,
such as Priest Dunkha of Tiyari, worked closely with Perkins in creating this
new literary language and in running the mission schools.[8]

The press's volume of output was at times over a million pages per year,
with several hundred copies produced of each publication.[9] The breadth of
publications was wide, but we can categorize the numerous works in the following way (with the number of individual publications in parentheses): Old
and New Testaments (whole or portions thereof) (16); hymnals (7); Bible
commentaries and study aids (10); books on arithmetic, geography, medicine, and music (8); books on language, ranging from spelling books and
verb paradigms to a grammar of modern Persian (8); anti-Catholic works (5);
tracts and guides to moral reform of varying lengths (20); Christian narrative
literature by authors popular with the evangelical press, such as John Bunyan
(1628–88), Legh Richmond (1772–1827), and Hannah More (1745–1833), as
well as a study guide to *Pilgrim's Progress* (5); works on the catechism, longer
theological works, and devotional manuals, including evangelical favorites
by Richard Baxter (1615–91), Isaac Watts (1674–1748), and Philip Doddridge
(1702–51) (16); an almanac for 1863 and calendars for 1868 and 1870, which
include miscellaneous articles on history and culture; a church history; and
a history of the mission to Tahiti. Not all of these books fall into simple categories. For example, the elementary reading books include passages from
Scripture combined with specific catechetical lessons, such as in the elementary reader of 1854, which quotes 2 Thessalonians 2:3–12 under the section
title "The Antichrist, in other words, the Pope."[10] In many mission publications, even if only in the introduction, there is an emphasis on the religious
and moral awakening the missionaries hoped to instigate.

Although it did not begin publication until 1849, after almost three dozen
other publications had already appeared, the press's most significant production, aside from perhaps the Bible, was *Rays of Light* (*Zahrire d-bahra*), the
monthly periodical, which continued to be published until 1918, when the
press was destroyed.[11] *Rays of Light* was widely disseminated. We have anecdotes about it being read in the mountains of Hakkari and in the Caucasus,
and there were subscriptions in the United States.[12] By the second issue it had
the basic format that would be maintained for years to come: it was divided

FIGURE 6. Cover of *Rays of Light* from June 1869 with a portrait of Justin Perkins upon his retirement from the American mission. (British Library.)

into the subsections of "True Religion" or "Piety" (*deḥlat alaha*, lit. "fear of God"), "Education" (*marduta*), "Science" (*'ilm*, from the Arabic), and "Miscellanies" (*šuḥlape*). By September 1850 a final song, usually a translation of an evangelical hymn, was added. In the fourth year, the paper began to run an "Evangelism" (*mašḥadta*) section, which often included missionary tales from around the world, and "Youth" (ṭalyuta), which contained moral tales about young children and was sometimes printed in a larger font. By the late 1860s the periodical began to divide the news (ḥabra) between foreign and local (i.e., Urmia).

The decision to call the first section "Fear of God" is significant because the expression has a long history in Classical Syriac, and "fear" at times functioned in the Syriac tradition not wholly unlike our own category, "religion."[13] In contrast to the usage of "Fear of God," the early mission sources refer to what was deemed sectarian or false religion as mazhab, from the Arabic word maḏhab, which typically means "sect" or "school."[14] Religion that was not true Christianity was irredeemably false, an "idle religion" (mazhab baṭil).[15] In contrast, to denote religion as a form of faith, the missionaries often used todita (Classical Syriac, tawditha), which means "acknowledgment" or "confession," but usually has a devotional sense, "religious confession," in Classical Syriac.[16] The term for "education," marduta, also has a Classical Syriac pedigree and is similar to the Arabic adab in that both had an original sense of disciplining through force and then began to connote literate cultivation. Considering the general absence of interest in the indigenous tradition among the early American missionaries, it is striking that they decided to appropriate and employ these Classical Syriac terms so prominently.

Education as a Focus of Mission

Education (marduta) is one of the most common concerns of articles in Rays of Light. This appears both in the section specifically designated for the topic and throughout the periodical. The first issue, of November 1849, contains a programmatic statement about education: "Among all nations [melate], schools are extremely useful [mare payda]. All nations in which they are established want them and give attention to them. Where schools are abandoned, learning is usually at a low level, evil increases, children grow up ignorant and disobedient, and all of the nation's business [šula d-melat] is diminished." Such a state of affairs is especially common, according to the article, when the clergy are uneducated, in which case by reading only the letters in texts but not the meaning, they do harm when they teach others. In general, human beings need "schools, books, and instruction" to exercise their reason and understanding. Schools should be established in every village, because "the lamp of the word of God expels darkness and enlightens [ke bahrena] the mind." In contrast to Persia, parents elsewhere regard education as important and take care of its costs.[17]

In antiquity, the article continues, the "Syrian Fathers" showed a concern for education. In a passage clearly dependent upon "On Schools and Literary Studies" (*De scholis & literarum studiis*) from the Maronite scholar J. S. Assemani's *Bibliotheca Orientalis* (Rome, 1719–28), the article describes ancient and medieval Syriac institutions of learning. These include the famous School of the Persians in Edessa, which the article associates with Saint Ephrem (d. 373), and the School of Nisibis, where "much attention was given to the study of the Old and New Testament, but they also studied grammar, rhetoric, poetics, arithmetic, gematriya, music, astronomy, and medicine."[18] In referring to the School of the Persians and the School of Nisibis, the article outlines an "educated" Christian past for the East Syrians, a lost time of enlightenment to which they should aspire to return. It invites them to reclaim the learning of antiquity and to emend a fallen state, thus promoting both an Enlightenment and a Protestant view of history. This is precisely what by the end of the nineteenth century the first nationalists would advocate, making reference to the same renowned learning and schools of the Syriac past, as I address in chapter 8. It is a commonplace even today in Assyrian and other Syriac nationalist literature to cite the Schools of Edessa and Nisibis as ancient institutions of secular learning, just as Assemani and Perkins cite them as offering forms of learning in accord with their respective eighteenth- and nineteenth-century notions of education.

Later in the same issue of *Rays of Light* the question is asked, "What is the purpose of this paper?" "For it to become truly clear, our readers should be enlightened [*payši buhrene*] by the pages of *Rays of Light* as this paper appears month after month." There are, it is explained, numerous periodicals in Europe and America with a variety of purposes. Sometimes people just want to hear something new, "like in ancient Athens" (Acts 17:21), whereas some publications are for commercial purposes. "Other writers have a higher and more useful purpose, that is, to increase the knowledge of human beings, bringing to them writing that helps to sharpen their thoughts and cleanse their hearts. This, we declare, is our purpose, too." Readers are encouraged to save issues, especially because the aim will be to fill them "with writing that is worth keeping."[19]

The January 1850 issue of *Rays of Light* contains an article on "Instruction" (*taʿlamta*), which also provides a programmatic statement about education as an ongoing historical and national project. The "benefit [*payda*] and value of instruction" is in allowing the human being, who is generally weaker "by nature" (*aṣlanaʾit*), to rule over the beasts. It also helps the "blind pagan" to see God and therefore saves souls, whereas those without it have unhappy lives.

The human being who is not instructed in learning, his mind will not increase. Rather, he will remain precisely in one place, like the mind of an animal, and people grow up as fools and without understanding, and as cowards in some things, and because of this they seize upon empty religions [*mazhabe*] and foundationless hopes, those which are spurned by an enlightened nation [*melat buhrenta*]. If in these next fifteen years schools are not opened among our people [*tayepa*], they will bend to whatever degree of foolishness you may think of.

The article then turns to antiquity and the success of the Persian Empire.

At the time of King Cyrus the Persians had schools and many houses of learning [*madrase w-bet yulpane*] for the instruction of children in various sciences and forms of knowledge. Because of this their kingdom was highly renowned, and sometimes their dominion spread over many parts of Asia, even to Egypt and to Assyria. However, when their mind became enamored of money and luxuries, and they did not supply the expenses for schools [*madrase*] and they abandoned instruction, also their kingdom slowly waned.

Cyrus, one of the few Gentiles depicted positively in the Hebrew Bible, is referred to in Isaiah 45:1 as God's "anointed." He serves here as a model for the good ruler, one whose imperial efforts are appropriate to his enlightened rule. The rise and fall of a nation, in this case ancient Persia, is directly linked to its support for education. However, the end of this passage points to something new, the project of reform going global by means of print, which is likened to an angel: "Thanks be to God that true Christianity is taking deep root in people's hearts throughout the whole world. Printing is causing the streams of knowledge to gush forth. The Gospel's message is transmitted throughout the land, as if upon the shoulder of an angel."[20] The article is followed by one that describes how schools have become widely dispersed, each like the sun, rendering all students like rays of light. Education, as it is addressed in *Rays of Light*, lies at the base of the mission's efforts, providing a foundation for the terms and concepts addressed below.

The Social Group: People (*Tayepa*) and Nation (*Melat*)

Education's collective benefits were to be enjoyed by the object of the missionaries' collective address: the *tayepa* and *melat*, which for heuristic purposes I will gloss here as "people" and "nation." The former was the more common term in the early mission literature, but was eventually displaced by the late nineteenth century by the latter. Neither of these terms has a Classical Syriac pedigree, and in lieu of them turn-of-the-century nationalist literature often uses the Classical terms *'amma* and *umtha*, translated respectively as "people" and "nation."

The term *tayepa*, "people," derives from the Arabic *tâ'ifa*, which appears in both Ottoman Turkish and Modern Persian, and "was liberally assigned to almost any collective social or economic group: craft organization, merchants, tribals, residents of a particular quarter, or even foreigners."[21] *Tâ'ifa* (pl. *tevâ'if*; Arabic *tawâ'if*) appears early in Ottoman sources. The Orthodox Christian community of the empire was originally referred to as a number of *tevâ'if*, but in time as one *tâ'ifa*, and then eventually as a *millet*, a formally recognized religious community.[22] The meaning of *tâ'ifa* was not always clearly differentiated from *millet*, and the term was applied to religious as well as other social groups formally recognized by local government as having certain rules and regulations. For example, in eighteenth-century Aleppo, *tâ'ifa* was used for Christian sects recognized by the state.[23] Living on the margins of the Ottoman Empire and in a province not of primary importance to the Qajars (despite their early dynastic history there), the East Syrians were not formally recognized as a religious community by either kingdom.

The American missionaries brought with them their own ideas of nationality and peoplehood, which lie behind the particular usage of *tayepa* in the mission literature. The variety of terms we find in the Hebrew Bible and the New Testament typically translated into English as "people" or "nation" are most often rendered in the missionary Bible translations with *tayepa* (in contrast to *melat*). In fact, *tayepa* is far more common in the Neo-Aramaic Bible (as *'amma* is in Classical Syriac) than any one term in the original Hebrew because of the paucity of corresponding Aramaic vocabulary. In other words, mission Bible translations in effect rendered *tayepa* a more commonplace word than it had been.

In examining the early issues of *Rays of Light*, we can see how often *tayepa* is used and how it may best be translated by the English "people," although at points it has a wider range. In an article on grace and how it "enlightens the soul and causes it to rejoice," we are told that "our hearts ought to be fervid with prayers for ourselves [or: our souls] and for our poor *tayepa* for the great grace of God."[24] Those whom God saves at the final judgment are "his *tayepa*."[25] The ancient Israelites in exile in Babylon were the "*tayepa* of God," "a prisoner *tayepa*," and a "fallen *tayepa*," whereas George Washington was "the father of a *tayepa*."[26]

In the introduction and chapter 1, I addressed the term *millet* and how the "*millet* system" has come to be used by scholars to talk about the political position of non-Muslim communities of the later Ottoman Empire. Sunni Islam was the religion of the dominant community, whereas others were relegated to *dhimmi* status. In Persian, in contrast, *millet* did not denote a formally recognized community as it did in Turkish. The Qajars did not have a *millet* system, although it is clear that while Iran was loosely controlled from Tabriz, various tribal, religious, and ethnic forces were negotiated through local intermediaries. However, by the mid-nineteenth century, *millet* began to connote a national community in Persian.[27] *Melat*, the derivative Neo-Aramaic cognate term, became an important word in the development of Assyrian nationalism, but it was less popular in the early decades of the American mission specifically because it was understood to be religiously sectarian. It is important to emphasize that *melat* continued to connote "religious community" *even as it was taken up in nationalist discourse*. In fact, the word's complex history correlates to the slow and complex emergence of Syrian national identity as distinct from the church. This was not a significant term before the arrival of the missionaries, but by the end of the nineteenth century, it had become a term, even a social category, of ongoing assessment and debate.

At times in the early mission sources, *melat* is used in what are clearly attempts at rendering the English word *nation*—for example, in the passages on education in the November 1849 and January 1850 issues of *Rays of Light* quoted above. However, sometimes, particularly when used by native speakers, it continues to denote "religious community," its earlier meaning. The wider embrace of *tayepa* as opposed to the perceived divisiveness of *melat* appears in a letter an East Syrian wrote to Joseph P. Cochran from Smyrna about his travels. Cochran's correspondent describes the love he has for "all those who toil to set our poor *tayepa* standing on a strong foundation."[28] He felt joy upon finding a community of Christians in Aintab (Gaziantep), who were also under American missionary influence. They had "renounced their former churches and separated from their *melat*."

In a first-person account of a missionizing tour made by both American missionaries and East Syrian assistants, the author claims, "We spoke with them, whether they were papists or from our *melat*."[29] In the same journey, which went to the Mosul region in the south and west to Bohtan, the missionaries' ultimate goal, we are told, was "to bring the *tayepa* of the Syrians out from under the rule of Satan." The local Christian population in these regions, where the missionaries had trouble communicating because the Neo-Aramaic spoken there was so different from the Urmia and Hakkari dialects, were all thought to be part of the same *tayepa* but not the same *melat*. In this instance the *tayepa* is the broader category of Syriac Christians, even those who spoke different dialects of Aramaic, whereas the *melat* is only the Church of the East. This explains the missionaries' preference for the term *tayepa*. They wanted to blur the ecclesial boundaries that existed among Syriac Christians and reform them into a true church of God. *Tayepa* indicated a wider range than *melat*, which in its earlier meaning was understood to be limited and sectarian, although this connotation was eventually lost as the term was used at the turn of the twentieth century, after the proliferation of foreign missions in Urmia, for the whole "nation" of the East Syrians, whether Old Church, Chaldean, Orthodox, or Protestant.

In some sources it is not clear exactly how *tayepa* and *melat* are thought to relate to each other. An article on evangelism states, "This gift of blessed evangelism in which there is life and salvation, was transmitted to human beings, to the *tayepa* of God, through whom it comes to all the world."[30] However, the article continues, "Every *melat* that sits in the dark either has no light [*bahra*] or has concealed the light of the word of God under a bushel [cf. Mt 5:14–15]." The distinction here seems to be between the Israelites as the singular "people of God" and the Gentiles as the "nations," but this is a distinction deriving from the same term in the Hebrew Bible, *goy*, "nation." The Syrians are referred to in this article as the audience's "*tayepa* who are on the plain and in the mountains."

The idea that the *tayepa* of the Syrians was a distinct ethnoreligious group was often part of the mission's calls for moral and educational reform. An 1852 article, "The Education of Women," provides a good example of how reform was cast as a national project (and how this was linked to "republican motherhood," a notion I will address in the following chapter).

> If someone should ask me why it is that this church of the Syrians is so fallen, why this people [*tayepa*] is so foolish and scorned and oppressed, I would speak about many reasons, but one notable reason is that the mothers in this people are not able to read the words of God. It was not thus in the past. When this church was pure and full of glory, they would send its sons to all of the lands as conquering soldiers, taking prisoners for Christ. Then mothers were able to read and they raised their children in the fear of God. Why is it not thus now? Because the Syrians have abandoned the customs [*'adate*] of the nations [*melate*] of the Christians and sought the church of the pagans. Go to the lands of the Christians, the lands of light, of joy, and of blessings; go to the lands of the pagans, the lands of the darkness of oppression and curses. Why are they so different? Because the mothers in those lands of the Christians are educated and honored, and the mothers in the lands of the pagans are foolish and scorned.[31]

The "church of the pagans" is a reference to Catholicism, and therefore, there is an ambiguity in the meaning of *melate* in this text. It refers to "nations," which have particular "customs," but these customs, which render these nations Christian, are abandoned by those who Catholicize. *Melat* here does not mean "nation" exactly but continues to have a religious communal connotation, whereas *tayepa*, the Syrian "people," is irreducible, thus pointing to the later racialization of the Syrians.

The Individual Self: Heart (*Lebba*) and Soul (*Gan*)

Just as missionaries' direct address to the "people" and the "nation" contributed to the development of a popular self-consciousness, their focus on the heart, the soul, and the self contributed to an individualism consistent with the ideas about community promoted by the mission. This may seem paradoxical at first, but a corollary to the articulation of the Syrian people or nation and the evangelical church as social imaginaries was the notion that each person was an autonomous constituent of these collectivities. Whereas all Syrians were part of the nation, a personal transformation was required for entry into the church. This inner transformation occurred in the heart (*lebba*) and had a bearing on how one related to his or her "self" (*gan*), which also means "soul" (*gan*) in Neo-Aramaic. Both words, *lebba* and *gan*, have complex histories. The range of the former, cognate with a similar Classical Syriac word, varies from the English term in a number of ways, being used to express a broader spectrum of emotions as well as being physically linked to the stomach.[32] This in part derives from the complexities of the equivalent Hebrew term in the Bible. In contrast, *gan* is originally a Persian word, which was taken up in Turkish and tends to displace the Classical Syriac *naphsa* ("self," "soul"), which has a variety of Semitic cognates. The meaning of *gan* can be ambiguous because, like *naphsa*, it is used for the self in a reflexive sense, but also refers to the soul.

This is not the place to review the process of evangelical conversion, which will be addressed further in chapter 5. However, it is important to lay out some of the basic ideas as they appear in the mission literature in order to appreciate the notion of the self fostered by the mission. The conversion process requires work upon oneself, and an important component of this is education, which not only entails instruction by parents and teachers.[33] Rather, "It is necessary that every person by himself [*b- ganuh(y)*] do much for the instruction of himself [*ganuh(y)*]."[34] This work upon oneself is applied to the body, the mind, and the heart. "The instruction of the body and the mind are very beneficial [*mare payda*] for this world, but the instruction of the heart is for eternity."[35]

In the numerous homiletical articles in *Rays of Light* and the tracts published by the mission, the heart is the primary object of the mission's efforts.

It is the special locus of transformation: "God, also in giving his command-ments and laws to his people [*tayepa*] . . . in not one place do we hear a state-ment come from his mouth, 'Torture yourselves in various ways.' Rather, we hear that he wants the heart of a person; he does not want forms of tribute."[36] Having a "broken heart" (*lebba šmiṭa*) is a special step in our transformation, and this comes about not through worldly, external affairs, but by an aware-ness of our own sinfulness.[37]

Integral to this work upon ourselves is semiology, the art of reading the signs that inform us about our present condition. Semiology is a hermeneutics of the inner and outer: we read the outer signs to know the inner condition. "Signs" (*nišanqe*, from Persian *nišan*) are a necessary tool in the introspection required by moral reform. The tract *Second Existence or New Birth* (1844) inquires, "What are the signs of the second existence?"[38] whereas *Words on the Subject of Repentance* (1842) differentiates between the exterior "sign of repentance" and the genuine thing.[39] An article in *Rays of Light* entitled "What Are the Signs of the True Christian?" describes the various virtues a Chris-tian should demonstrate.[40] These are not requirements—for making such de-mands would represent works righteousness—but rather ways we can infer if someone is a Christian. The mission's translation of Isaac Watts's *Preservative from the Sins and Follies of Childhood and Youth* (1842) provided a manual on inquiring into the sinful nature of the self through a science of signs.[41] Philip Dodderidge's *The Rise and Progress of Religion in the Soul* (1857) was another work of self-investigation translated at the mission.[42] Manuals such as these are reminiscent of the monastic literature East Syrian monks had studied for centuries. However, these modern texts are aimed at everyone, even children, and not just monks. This practice of reading signs, both those of the self's sin-ful nature and those that suggest that a transformation has occurred, served as a tool for self-analysis, especially during the various revivals at the mission. The anxieties of those who would convert as well as the anxiety expressed by the missionaries as to whether someone had truly been transformed in his or her heart stem from the uncertainty built into any semiotic system.

Semiology functions to bifurcate entities into the seen and the unseen, often pushing this division deeper and deeper to a self hidden below. The tract *On the Subject of Faith or Some Signs of Saving Faith* (1842) argues that there are two types of faith, the living and vivifying one, and the dead and lazy one.[43] To the question "What is true faith?" the tract succinctly responds, "To believe in the world to come."[44] The world to come, however, is neither like the sun and stars nor like the city of Urmia through which we can stroll about. True faith is to believe in what we are unable to see. Although it is based on an argument found in the Gospel of John, this heightened notion of faith, faith based upon nothing sensible, reflects a Lockean empiricism and corresponds with Perkins's ideas about true religion and exchange, which I addressed in chapter 2: faith is not dependent upon this world. The text then compares God to the Qajar Shah: "If the king of this land, Muhammad Shah, sent his son to this region with a royal decree saying, 'This is my beloved son. Listen to whatever he commands,' would not people listen to his royal decree?"[45] Therefore, the text asks, are people not sinful who do not listen to the son of God? God has sent a similar royal decree, and yet those who obey Muhammad Shah fear a human being, of dust like themselves, more than God and his son.

The ongoing distinction in this text between true and false faith corresponds with a context of intra-Christian exhortation. The missionaries needed to remind their audience that simply being "Christian" does not suffice: in order to be salvific, faith had to be "true." The text pushes its audience to find a deeper self, one beyond superficial faith in exterior things, which it equates with the city of Urmia and its king, Muhammad Shah. Implicit in this analogy is also a secularization of politics: there is the Shah, on the one hand, and the otherworldly God in whom Christians put their faith, on the other. Furthermore, in line with the mission's other literature, the tract maintains a polemic against "works righteousness," the idea that one can be saved by good deeds. Because "works" are more social than faith, in that they entail ritual and good deeds, which are social practices that are often performed socially, the self evoked in the moral exhortation of this text is private, one characterized by self-consciousness rather than its sociality. Such a turning inward transcends religious and local ethnic differences and leads to a flattening out and isolation of the self, yet that resulting abstracted self, when multiplied, would constitute the nation.

Conditionality and Change: Condition (*Ahwal*), Light (*Bahra*), and Awakening (*Mar'ašta*)

Reform involves the transformation from one condition to another, from a state of decline to a state of repair. We should not take for granted that such notions of modality or conditionality are universal or always encompass the same discursive range. In the American mission literature, a term that appears often to describe the "condition" or "state" of both individuals and communities, as well as entities in nature, is *ahwal* (from Arabic *aḥwal*, plural of *ḥal*). The use of *ahwal* in the mission literature connotes the need for transformation, a need to test oneself, to inquire into the depths of the heart in order to determine if one is in the right "state" to be saved. Often the state or condition is a negative one, and the term suggests an anxious need for self-transformation, to move from present uncertainty to a future stability. The use of *ahwal* suggests therefore the capacity to change over time, as well as the very need to do so, especially before the certainty of death. Early nationalist literature follows this mission usage: *ahwal* serves as a term to decry the poor spiritual and material state of the nation and its members.

Generally, *ahwal* is used for the state of the individual's soul or heart, the state of the group, and worldly material conditions. The condition of the individual soul or heart is the most common usage. An exhortatory article from 1849 concludes, "Oh you who are reading this article, in what manner is your condition [*ahwal*]? . . . If you do not care for yourself [or, your soul], know that in truth your condition is rotten and it is greatly feared that you will be lost."[46] An article on God's capacity to see all things emphasizes how he even "knows the condition of the heart."[47] The term is used more often for a negative state than a positive one. The homiletical "Words of Advice" addresses the "eternal condition" of people's souls, which can be in a "condition of danger" and a "condition of sin."[48] The speaker repeatedly explains that his exhortation aims to "awaken" (*mar'eš*) his audience. "Wake up [*r'uš*] to the wretched state [*ahwal*] which you are in, how far you are from Christ!" the author commands. In one homily we are told of a dying sinner crying out, "Alas, if I had done the bidding of my mother and not my own, I would not have arrived at this state [*ahwal*]."[49] The term is also used to refer to the state of the soul after death. One tract from 1842 states: "O reader, you have an immortal soul which after some time must live in heaven or will reside in Gehenna. Do you make no thought of this? Do you have no idea of this in the heaviness of your heart? For which of these two states [*ahwale*] has your soul been prepared? To which of these two states does it hasten?"[50]

Parallel to its use for individuals, the term can also be used collectively for the condition of a group. A letter in *Rays of Light* from "so-in-so the priest to so-in-so the deacon" expresses enthusiasm for the deacon's plan to missionize the "Syrians" among the villages and suburbs of Urmia.[51] The author is concerned because "if they die in this condition [*ahwal*] certainly they will be lost forever." They are "lying upon the edge of the lake of fire. . . . But go, my friend, to them, your heart filled with love, and wake [*mar'eš*] them about their condition and inform them about the way of life." Due to missionary schools, "Now the people of the Sandwich Islands have made much progress [*ḥiše (i)na l-qamay*] in their knowledge and condition [*ahwal*]." In its discussion of Matthew 10:42 ("whoever gives even a cup of cold water to one of these little ones"), one article begins: "It is appropriate, very appropriate to their condition [*ahwal*], that the people [*tayepa*] of God be called those little ones."[52] The term describes also political conditions—for example, a people's "condition of freedom" (ahwal d-azaduta).[53]

Ahwal also denotes physical and material conditions, including our mortal state.[54] One article describes how immigrants from Europe come to the United States because the "condition of the land" (ahwal ar'anayta) is better for farming.[55] In a story of a needy child who seeks work from a generous woman in New York, the woman asks the child, "What does your situation [ahwalok] demand?"[56] This material state sometimes overlaps with the moral one. This is apparent in the question of raising children: the "state" (ahwal) of children without books is terrible, whereas we must be quick to preach and not turn a blind eye to a youth's "rotten state."[57] A fictive dialogue, published in Rays of Light, between a master and a student concludes with the master explaining that people must use their learning "at all times and in all types of condition; otherwise their knowledge will be of no benefit [mare payda] to them."[58] This more specifically material sense seems to increase in time. In later issues of Rays of Light, the word is used to describe the wretched state of the ancient Israelites, the difference in condition between "us" and "pagans," the political situation in Europe, and the sociopolitical condition of certain people (tayepa) in the mountains.[59]

"Penitence" (Syriac tyabhutha, Neo-Aramaic tyawuta) was the response the missionaries wanted from their audience, but this process of transformation was most often characterized as a process of enlightenment and awakening. The word bahra ("light") and its cognates have appeared already above. The title of Rays of Light itself contains this word, which in the missionary literature connotes both ideas of the Enlightenment, such as maturation, reason, and progress, and the older Christian usage of "light" as an attribute of God. Inversely, Perkins uses the word benighted almost two dozen times in his memoir to describe the East. This metaphor of light is often a complement to the common focus on "waking up" (mar'ašta), a word and its cognates we have also already seen above. The verb for "to wake up" or "to awaken" (intransitive ra'eš, transitive mar'eš) lies behind the word for Christian "revival" in the sources, the noun mar'ašta. This word has a different nuance than the English term revival, which at first suggests a return to life, an enlivening of something that was dead. Rather, mar'ašta means to wake up from sleep.[60] Waking and light are often combined. A person's condition can be transformed through the Gospel: the study of it "awakens [mare'ša] people to the desire for knowledge," and without it they "cannot be enlightened [buhrene] Christians and beneficial [mare payda] in the teaching of the Gospel to others."[61]

The word mar'ašta (root: r-'-š) is distantly cognate with the word for the "senses," regše, which derives from Classical Syriac, the root r-g-š being used in the verbal form for "to feel," "to become angry," "to sense," "to perceive," and even "to understand."[62] The root *r-ʿ-š*, which is a dialectical variant of *r-g-š*, continues to bear the meaning of "sense" in Neo-Aramaic.[63] "Waking up," then, can also be an opening up to sensation, whether to pain or some other feeling. Therefore, in contrast to English, a call for revival in Neo-Aramaic is not only a demand to wake up and rub the sand from one's eyes, but a demand to feel, to sense, to be open to what is occurring in one's heart. One who is woken in this way is goaded on, transformed, and inspired to act, like King Cyrus in the Bible, when he was woken up by God.[64] However, the feeling one is to wake up to during revival is not one that comes through the senses. It was not a sensation of taste or touch, but a spiritual sensation of the consciousness, a moving of the heart at the core of the self. In this way, the cultivation of an internal religious feeling was the aim of the mission, a training of the heart that it might find a private intimacy with God combined with a training of the senses that they be accommodated to the materiality of this world.[65]

The transformation the missionaries wanted to catalyze among the East Syrians was an ontological one, the coming into being of a "new creation." The tract *Second Existence or New Creation* (1844) emphasizes the need for a "great spiritual transformation" (*šaḥlapta*).[66] The heart "must come into being anew from the spirit of holiness," and in Pauline terms the "old man" must be replaced by the "new man."[67] The "second existence" is "the works of the spirit in the heart" or in "the soul of the human being."[68] It entails a "purification of the heart."[69] It is a "new existence."[70] The tract asks that "the Lord may enlighten [*bahren*] our understanding so we will understand his word and that with the humility of a small child we will receive it."[71]

The Reform of Manners: Custom and Habit (ʿAdat)

A common term in the mission sources, *ʿadat* (pl. *ʿadate*) can be variously translated as "custom," "regular practice," or "habit." It derives from the Arabic, but is cognate with a similar Classical Syriac term, *ʿyadha*. The expression "*ayk ʿadat*" means "usually" or "according to one's general practice."[72] *ʿAdate* are commonly "habits," and these can be contrasted to "nature," when, for example, we are told that eight hours of sleep each night is due to "habit" (*ʿadat*), because "nature" (*aṣla*) only demands six.[73] When applied to ethnic groups, *ʿadat* denotes something closer to "custom." In China, we are told, women have a custom of storing away bottles of tears to employ "if one of them goes to the judge to make an appeal."[74] Certain groups of people, as well as even species of animals, have their particular *ʿadate*.[75]

The term is more commonly used for habits that are "ruinously bad" and have the capacity to make people "subject."[76] These are habits that need to be changed or reformed. Locking bad children in the cellar is an "oppressive practice" (*'adat zalim*), whereas the presumed student audience of an article on a naughty boy who liked to eavesdrop and was "lacking in good manners [*be adab*]" are advised to "remain far from a habit [*'adat*] that is such a shame in the eyes of men and a great sin before God."[77] That habit tends to be something with a negative valence reflects Protestant anxieties about ritual. For example, an article on acceptable prayer states: "There are many who pray who do not hope to receive spiritual blessings from God. They pray from habit [*'adat*]; they think that prayer is a service that God seeks from them and whenever they have done this service they think it is enough."[78] However, habits can serve also as examples for imitation and further inculcation. Such an interest in imitation is appropriate in a context where the Lancaster system, a monitorial, peer approach to education popular at the time, was used in the schools. Despite a concern to avoid works righteousness, habituation is part of the process of moral reform because Christians must learn to guard the laws and commandments of God, which their ancestors, Adam and Eve, failed to do.[79]

The positive or negative effects of habit are even apparent in human physiology. The consumption of alcohol is a bad *'adat*. In an article in the "Science" section, a person is told to avoid the "habit of drinking wine and arak [liquor]" if he wants to be healthy.[80] In an article that begins "Education [*marduta*] is something that guides the body as it also does the mind," members of the young audience are instructed to stand up straight, "because if not, they will take hold of a habit of humped back-ness, and after they grow up they will not be able to stand up straight again."[81]

An early tract, *On the Subject of Sunday* (1842), demonstrates the variety in the usage of *'adat*. "The observation of a holy day of rest is not like the many customs [*'adate*] based upon different human authorities, but it derives from the commandment of God. It is not like the customs which are necessary for one nation [*melat*], or for one land, or for one generation; rather, it is for all nations [*melate*], lands, and generations."[82] Paul and his colleagues, we are told later, had a habit (*'adat*) of preaching and teaching on Sundays.[83] Because fulfilling our own needs expends so much time and there is a "tendency" (*'adat*) for our minds to be distracted by these needs, the tract explains, "It is necessary that a portion of time be devoted to God and separated off. And if it is not thus, people day by day, little by little, become more worldly [*'almaye*] in their minds and in their desires, and all the more do they forget God, until they are like infidels who do not know God at all."[84] All Christians come together at once and participate in prayer on Sunday.[85] "This is not a new practice ['adat] introduced by Christians of today. Rather, all the earlier Christians of the past maintained this observance of Sunday."

The usage of 'adat in this tract implies both a relativization of culture and an inculturation of Christianity. Nations differ in their "customs," but the observance of the Sabbath is a "habit" that applies to all Christians. In general, the critique of 'adate is part of an ongoing critique of culture: the missionaries had culture, but in the case of the natives, culture had them.[86] Regarding the use of a similar word derived from Arabic among missionaries in Indonesia, Webb Keane claims that we can see in it "a sociological version of the logic by which Christian missionaries elsewhere attempted to define what is cultural and what is religious, to distinguish them from one another, in order to operate upon one without disturbing the other."[87] In their articulation of a notion of cultural habit, the missionaries borrowed from the indigenous discourse on "habits" and "customs" ('adate, 'yadhe), two words in prior use. This helped them to draw out notions of habituation in their ethical exhortation and also to distinguish pure religion from the dross of human custom.

Habit and Political Reform: *Drunkenness and the Gluttony of Wine* (1842)

A concern for temperance was standard in evangelical reform. The missionaries regularly identified wine drinking as one of the bad habits of the East Syrian population.[88] Perkins describes preaching before a group of drunkards, who exclaimed, "Let God give us some money to pay taxes and we will serve him."[89] When challenged, some locals even blamed their poor morality, such as their habit of lying, on Muslim rule.[90] This link between morality and Muslim rule that, at least according to the mission sources, the locals themselves made when the missionaries censured their habits, was taken up in one of the early tracts printed by the mission, *Drunkenness and the Gluttony of Wine* (1842).[91] This tract employs several of the terms and concepts I have discussed so far in this chapter while articulating the missionaries' response to the East Syrians' claims about Muslim rule. Its argument, which demonstrates the parallels the missionaries drew between self and community in their calls for reform, is that Christians who drink alcohol must pay fines, and therefore their immorality invites the intervention of the Muslim authorities in the East Syrian community.[92] One of its intriguing features is that it describes the contemporary social and political position of the East Syrians within Urmia, which it uses for rhetorical purposes, while alluding to the local reception of the missionaries.

The tract maintains a stark distinction between the life of sin and the preservation of the body as an abode for the Holy Spirit. Human beings are like both angels and animals: they have a weak and corruptible nature (*aṣla*) and a spiritual one. Accordingly, wine and the Holy Spirit have distinct yet parallel powers: one destroys, whereas the other gives life, and we should only be filled with the latter of the two. The tract addresses a possible controversial aspect of its complete rejection of wine:

> We know that there are some who will send the people [*tayepa*] into an upheaval and will shout like the Israelites, "Help! (Acts 21:28) These men proclaim words that are contrary to us and teach habits [*'adate*] contrary to our law, because we are Syrians"; or as the citizens of Ephesus, who were members of the guilds of Ephesus, they will shout, "Great is Artemis of Ephesus" [Acts 19:28], that is, "Wine is good for the Syrians."[93]

In its use of these two passages from the book of Acts, the tract compares the traditionalists, who rejected the missionaries' demands for total abstinence from alcohol, to the Jews and pagans who rejected Paul's message in Ephesus.

Wine is destructive to the Syrian "nation" (*melat*), according to the tract, and the source of many evils to the church, the priesthood, and the people (*tayepa*). By drinking, one rejects Christ and salvation. "Oh Syrians, wake up from the sleep of sin and death, and save yourselves from your enemy Satan and from the desires of the body. Flee from the rule of drink. Be free from this yoke of the body."[94] In America, the tract explains, many used to die from consuming alcohol. However, evangelists promoted sobriety and thereupon God greatly blessed the land and sent his Holy Spirit, purifying many people's hearts of sin. Demonstrating the missionaries' common concern for frugality, the tract argues that wine impoverishes people (*tayepa*) due to the laziness it produces: youths do not learn their trade, while members of households give up their responsibilities, sell their possessions and flocks, and leave their plows. They become lazy servants to wine, exalting it like a king or as their tribal chief (*agha*), beautifying it with various colors, and giving it all kinds of honors. They waste their time in empty speech, playing, singing, and other pastimes.

Wine is further a source of poverty because of the penalties it brings, and in this it both resembles and provokes Muslim oppression. When a Syrian gets in trouble or someone is killed, it is usually due to wine, and wine is often involved when people make accusations against Christians. Nevertheless, Syrians willingly give their hearts to this source of oppression, and not to God. On account of wine they go to prison and Muslims take their wages. They are drawn into forced labor, becoming servants of desire.

One excuse wine drinkers use is that it is a custom (*'adat*) to drink. The tract counters this by arguing that this custom comes from humans, not God, and that humans have many bad customs. Another excuse is that the clergy drink. In response, the tract quotes "Mar Isho'yahb the teacher (*malpana*)," most likely patriarch Isho'yahb III (d. 659), on the topic of the priesthood: "From the laziness of the farmers the fields are tread upon."[95] This is understood to mean that those who turn a blind eye to the misdeeds of priests and sin alongside them will be destroyed with them. The tract quotes a saying of another *malpana*, John of Dalyatha, an eighth-century East Syrian monastic writer, about the dangers of wine: "The beginning of wine drinking is like a fox; the middle of it is like an elephant; the end is a simpleton, a fool, and not different from a swine, or a donkey."[96]

The two quotations from Classical Syriac authors, Mar Isho'yahb and John of Dalyatha, are surprising. The American missionaries rarely showed interest in using the indigenous tradition to support their evangelical claims. Albert L. Holladay's journal entry for December 11, 1838, explains the origin of the latter of these quotations: in a discussion with Holladay about intemperance, Mar Elias "opened a book written in the ancient Syriac, and read a long paragraph to prove to me that the 'malpanas' or teachers of his people, understood this subject, and had written much on the evils of wine drinking."[97] Holladay then quotes the fuller passage from which the animal analogy derives. The 1842 tract incorporates the bishop's response that temperance is part of the East Syrian tradition by quoting from that tradition. It also implicitly rejects Elias's reading of the text as about moderation rather than total abstinence. As Holladay notes in his journal, the bishop who quoted this passage "makes free use of wine on feast days."[98]

The material addressing Muslim oppression appears in the portion of the tract that treats how alcohol consumption impoverishes people and harms their bodies. Muslim rule is therefore an external problem, one having to do with the body and the community, as opposed to the heart and the soul. Muslim rule leads to the various social, economic, and political humiliations the Syrians must endure in the world, but it is also treated as a metaphor when it is analogized to the domination alcohol has over the person. People who drink live "under the government [*hukma*] of wine."[99] The East Syrians' *dhimmi* status is thus analogous to their subjection to poor morality.

This evangelical interest in political status reflects a worry that in countries without political freedom, people were restricted from freely following after their own salvation. Inversely, implicit in the Gospel, according to the missionaries, were republican values. One of the few exceptions to the general absence of American politics from *Rays of Light* is an account of the Emancipation Proclamation, which is described in December 1862. (President Lincoln had announced the executive order on September 22, 1862, but it did not go into effect until January 1, 1863.)[100] Many American evangelicals were at the forefront of the abolitionist movement, and slavery for them was a universal moral issue. In fact, the only tract by Justin Perkins published in English back home in the United States was *Our Country's Sin*, which is a sermon Perkins gave in Urmia on July 3, 1853, on the topic of slavery. According to him, it sent the wrong message to the nations of the world about "pure Protestant Christianity" and "republican freedom." (The publication was dedicated to Leonard Bacon [1802–81], whose writings against slavery influenced Lincoln. Bacon was a member of the mission's board and, along with his son, the later controversial clergyman Leonard W. Bacon [1830–1907], visited Mosul in 1851 with the intention of going to Urmia, but their trip was cut short when their party was robbed.)[101] Christianity and republican values went hand in hand.

Utilitarian Argument: Benefit (*Payda*)

The use of the term *payda*, "profit" or "benefit," from the Arabic *fayḍ*, and cognate expressions like *mare payda* ("beneficial," lit. "possessing benefit"), is consistent with the utilitarian discourse employed by the missionaries. Arguments based upon the notion of utility reflect an economic mode of thinking that subjects all decisions and actions to the consideration of cost and benefit. Like the notion of "habit" or "custom," the logic of utility can rhetorically diminish certain practices and thereby subordinate life to specific aims or goals. For the missionaries, Christianity was aneconomic and free of exchange, and yet their notion of true religion, as is often the case in the discourse of modernity, was subject to the language of utility borrowed from the marketplace. Everything had to have its own benefit or utility.

Types of benefit can vary. An article in *Rays of Light* on how the world is round concludes with a discussion of the "benefit of the roundness of the earth," explaining that Columbus would never otherwise have made his discovery, and sailing and astronomy would be different.[102] Another article, "The Benefit of *Rays of Light*," describes how some students returning to the mountains from Urmia were about to be robbed by Kurds.[103] They said, "We are associates of the gentlemen [lit. "people of the *sahabe*"]," but the Kurds asked for proof. When they showed them a copy of *Rays of Light*, the Kurds let them go. This anecdote, which suggests the reputation the mission enjoyed in the mountains of Hakkari, provides a simple example of the language of utility the missionaries regularly employed. The primary benefit, according to the sources, is one that leads to "salvation" (*purqana*). A biblical passage commonly quoted is Matthew 16:26: "For what is a man profited, if he shall gain the whole world, and lose his own soul?"[104] which is at times referred to as the

"Great Question."[105] One early tract on this theme, translated from an English original, is titled *The Great Question That Is Profitable for Mortal Human Beings* (1842).[106] What is beneficial for our salvation can be unexpected: the observation of the growth of plants is "beneficial" (*mare payda*) because it helps us contemplate the perfect world created by God.[107]

Benefits can also be multiple. Astronomy has both a bodily and a spiritual benefit: longitude and latitude aid in travel, but astronomy also shows us the power and wonder of God.[108] As education is the primary tool of missionary reform, so it is the most common topic in discussions of what is beneficial. One article, "The Benefit of Instruction," explains that a "people" (*tayepa*) with learning is "always in a better condition [*ahwal*]."[109] Another benefit offered by instruction is that it contributes to "the increase of the fear of God in the heart of a person. Our hope for this nation [*melat*] is this: that we may situate their young men and daughters that they may be instructed and thus be obedient to God." Elsewhere in *Rays of Light*, the "benefit of learning" is divided into that which is for "this world" and that which is "for eternity." "In this world learning is the cause of elevating a person from a low nature [*aṣla*] to a higher nature. Where there is no learning the mind of that people [*tayepa*] or that person is little different from that of an animal." Readers are asked to "compare the condition [*ahwal*] of one who you see is foreign to learning with the condition of one who is learned, and you will understand the benefit of learning." Without learning, people make mistakes, such as losing money. In reference to Ishmael in Genesis 16:12 and thus equating the East Syrians with Arabs, the author—most likely Perkins—claims, "I have seen a wild nation [*melat*], who was unable to be at peace with one another" due to their lack of learning. Biblical learning in particular "is beneficial [*mare payda*] for eternity," and when it is attained, "the condition of that people [*tayepa*] is blessed."[110] Another article answers the question "What is the benefit from the Holy Scriptures?" by telling the story of the young illiterate boy John who inquires into the "benefit" of the Bible.[111] His father takes him to visit a dying woman whose forbearance provides them with a lesson about how the Bible gives us encouragement in times of suffering.

Natural Theology and the Epistemic Shift: Science (*'Ilm*)

The utilitarian and conditional world of the missionaries was mechanistic yet holy. It was ordered according to Newtonian science, and this pointed to its logical and loving creator. As Sujit Sivasundaram observes with regard to scientific discourse at similar missions in the Pacific, "Nature allowed faith to become real by linking the unseen spiritual realm to the observed." It was "an important avenue through which evangelicals could contemplate the hand of God."[112] The Neo-Aramaic word '*ilm* is derived from Arabic, and as we find in missionary translations into Arabic from Syria and Egypt, the word was reoriented at the mission from its earlier sense of sacred knowledge to something akin to the English *science*.[113] However, the missionaries' use of '*ilm* as "science" did not simply render it a secular form of knowledge. "Missionary science . . . was a popular and religious view of nature, a way of seeing as much as an exercise in theoretical speculation."[114] The missionaries linked science to the divine through natural theology, the notion that one can infer the creator from creation, which, as was discussed in chapter 2, was part of the missionary cultivation of wonder ('*ajebuta*). Natural theology and natural science, which held that the material world had consistent physical laws about which we could learn through our senses, were two forms of knowledge that mutually supported each other.

Over the years, *Rays of Light* published articles describing much of European and American science as it stood in the mid-nineteenth century. In the first year of publication alone (November 1849–October 1850), the "Science" section of the periodical covered the following topics: astronomy; botany, including the work of Linnaeus; zoology; the difference between the speed of light and that of sound; electricity (examples of it, its discovery, and the peculiarity of electric eels); air; humidity; the movement of sound through air; volcanoes, in particular Mount Vesuvius; irrigation; the Milky Way; Isaac Newton; eclipses; gravity, including the famous story of Newton and the apple; dew; rain; snow; hail; warm air and convection; winds; comets; alcohol and its effects; alchemy and its falsehood; the medical use of leeches; the growth of plants; the elements; the bones of the human body; and arsenic mines. Articles in question-and-answer format address, among other things, flowers, natural philosophy as a science of bodies, and inertia and the laws of motion.

Science articles sometimes make explicit the local views they aim to refute. An article on eclipses explains how they occur, but then refers to the "various crazy fears about eclipses among foolish people."[115] Some Persians, we are told, become anxious at the eclipse of the sun because it is the "sign" of their kingdom, whereas Ottomans become anxious at the eclipse of the moon because it is a "sign" of theirs. However, there is nothing to fear: "learned men" can predict eclipses.[116] Not only does this article treat eclipses as part of a natural world, but it also ignores the Near Eastern astronomical sciences that had already predicted them, thus presenting Western science as superior to local tradition. (Maragha, on the other side of Lake Urmia, was an important center of medieval astronomy.)

In contrast, the mission provided science with an ancient biblical pedigree. One article begins, "Perhaps some Syrians will think and say, 'science ['ilm] is something new.' However, listen to what is said about the science of king Solomon."[117] The text then describes Solomon's account of the natural world, citing 1 Kings 4:33, and suggests that although approaches have improved, earlier generations had science. An 1851 article on astronomy suggests that this science, which discusses the firmament, demonstrates the power of God and then cites Job 9:9 on the constellation Arcturus as evidence of science's antiquity.[118] The article concludes with a quotation it attributes to Isaac Newton: "If you teach or learn [science] and do not fear God then you are crazy."

Science is also often justified by its utility. An article on the benefits of science acknowledges that, although some may have seen the wonders of science performed at the mission, they nonetheless do not understand its usefulness because it does not help them to feed or clothe their families.[119] However, without science, long-distance travel, the movement of information, and commerce would not be possible. Science, the article explains, is a benefit (*payda*) to the people of Urmia in various ways, whether it be through chemistry or inventions such as the telegraph. According to this article, the sciences of astronomy and chemistry came originally to Europe from Arab lands, but the Arabs believed in alchemy, and they learned from chemistry to make liquor (*arak*). "Those nations [*melate*] that learn to use the sciences much are greater; other nations and those who do not know them remain inferior."[120] The Arab contribution to Western science is acknowledged in this article, but its significance is diminished inasmuch as the Arabs misused science. In the same issue of *Rays of Light*, in the "Science" section, there is also a short article on the remains of a woman found in America that had not yet decomposed: "Science teaches us how this happened. If this thing had happened earlier, many people would have been scared and thought that it was a sign that a calamity was about to come."[121] Thus, science does away with the anomalies that lead to superstitious fear. It puts things in order, and so, for example, the comet, or "star with a fringe," should not be taken as a sign from heaven of famine or other catastrophes, as it is by foolish people, but like the sun and the moon as a sign of the creator.[122]

Science at the mission included the promotion of empiricism and an awareness of the senses as the only source of knowledge, with the exception of God's revelation in Scripture. An 1852 article in *Rays of Light* describes the five senses (*regše*), which "inform us about things that are outside of us."[123] Our thinking is done in the brain, but the senses serve as "doors by which knowledge of exterior things enter the mind." Detailed articles on touch, taste, and smell follow this one. The missionaries, like their spiritual predecessor Jonathan Edwards (1703–58), who in turn was influenced by John Locke's *Essay Concerning Human Understanding*, thought the human being to be sensorially closed off from the spiritual world. As we saw above, evangelical "awakening" was not based upon sensory experience, but was conceived of as internal to the heart. This new epistemology fit the idea that each person should engage in evangelical self-analysis to discover an inner self that was essentially (and not contingently) sinful. This self, which required conversion, was *buffered*, to use Charles Taylor's term, inasmuch as it was no longer porous to the world's affects.

The mission's reception of Lockean empiricism is in accord with the understanding of dreams we find in the mission literature, as well as with the further limitations on access to the divine implicit in the mission's presentation of modern science. Dreams, we are told in one article in *Rays of Light*, are about the past and do not foretell the future.[124] This rejection of the divinatory capacity of dreams corresponds with what we find in the preface to the mission's translation of John Bunyan's *Pilgrim's Progress* (1848).[125] Possibly the most translated book of all time aside from the Bible, *Pilgrim's Progress* was well received within the East Syrian community and continued to be read, retranslated, and republished in Neo-Aramaic into the twentieth century (even finding a later Neo-Aramaic imitator). In its parable form, it was considered "eminently adapted to the tastes of this primitive, oriental people."[126] The short preface to the translation reveals the concern the missionaries had about the misuse of Bunyan's text.

> When John Bunyan was in prison he composed this book to bear witness to Christ. It is composed in a parable [*masala*] of a dream, but, oh readers, do not think that this book was composed in a vision or in sleep. Its author was quite awake when he composed it and he passed much time and used much thinking in it. Let us not say that this book is from the Holy Spirit, as are the Holy Scriptures of God, the Torah and the New Testament. Nevertheless, we think that it is very much in accord with the words of God.[127]

The missionaries wanted Bunyan's work to serve as a model for each person to use in thinking about his or her own life and "Christian," its hero, to be an example for all. His "plight" (*ahwal*) is similar to our own (*plight* in the English original).[128] Bunyan himself, however, was not to become the center of attention, as if he truly dreamed the dream described in the text. It is a wakefulness to light and reason that the missionaries advocated, and their demotion of dreams was an attempt to excise a possible source of false belief, because dreams were commonly taken to be a source of knowledge from beyond the sensory realm. The awakened and enlightened self is an isolated one, and divinatory dreams are a threat to that goal and to modern science.

Science, Habits, and the Health of the National Body: Race and *The Book of Medicine* (1863)

The material world of science and the notion of "habit" or "custom" resonate with each other in how the mission literature addresses race and hygiene. According to an 1850 "Science" article, there are five races of human being: European, Asian, American, African, and Australian. Of these, Europeans, who were probably the first, are certainly the most beautiful. The article describes the Caucasian thesis popular at the time, which held that the white race came out of the Caucasus. Although not every human has all the various characteristics that exist among them in total, the Bible says that we are all created from one blood. If so, the article asks, how it is that we differ "in beauties, in colors, in families, and among different nations [*melate*]"?[129] The primary differences among human beings derive from several factors: weather and food, both of which determine skin color; "habits and way of life . . . in which there is much authority over form and appearance, and also over the minds and characters of human beings"; and "diseases which children inherit from their parents." The article continues:

> If true Christianity ruled over all the world and all the people were subject to its teaching, there would be many wondrous and good changes of body. True Christianity would make everyone brothers and then walls between colors, families, and peoples [*tayepe*] would be pulled down. It is from descent that many of the differences among human beings derive. There are very many diseases, such as gangrene, consumption, scales, leprosy, and insanity, which children inherit from their parents. Moreover, children inherit from their parents [different] beauties, colors, forms, and also ways of thinking and character.[130]

The text then addresses intellectual differences more closely. "But, moreover, the mind, much more than the body, is able to make progress by education and instruction. If the mind of one generation is used well, this will have a great effect on the mind of the generation that comes after it." This is different from the hardened biological notions of race that became more prominent later in the century.

> The European races' minds are loftier than those of the other races for several reasons. The greatest reason of all is true Christianity, which has so awakened and sharpened the mind of white people. But it is necessary that we sow seeds of Christianity in the hearts of all nations [*melate*], as much as we are able to

do so, and then grey people, red people, and black people will mix with one another and also with white people, who have more abundant [mental] gifts, until all of them learn and confess that God created all the nations of human beings from one blood.[131]

Not only are habits and manner of life mutable, but so are those determining factors that lead to skin color and physical appearance. The material human being can be transformed—as others also argued at this time—and yet the superiority of the white race is repeatedly affirmed. The "ambivalence of colonial discourse" led to such apparent contradictions: race was fixed and yet fluid. For built into what we might call the mission's theology of nations were a Christian universalism and a notion of racial difference that coexisted in tension but not in contradiction.

The reform of habit and its link to race is exemplified in the development of hygiene at the mission, as is attested by the *Book of Medicine* (1863), composed by Frank N. H. Young (1832–68), who served as a doctor for the mission from 1860 to 1863.[132] The *Book of Medicine* advocates civilizational reform through the eradication of bad habits and obsolete superstition. This work, which focuses on the biology and hygiene of the individual, the family, and the nation, demonstrates the trend of addressing the "Syrians" as a nation with organic relations and a biological history, a trend that was further articulated at the mission by the end of the nineteenth century. In the preface, Perkins introduces the volume, demonstrating his customary concern for frugality:

This is a book about keeping a healthy body and maintaining it from disease. If people keep the rules and pieces of advice which Dr. Young gives to them in this book, which are very easy to understand and observe, they will have health a great part of their lives, they will live additional years, they will be more blessed and happy, they will be a greater good to others, and they will prepare their households in a much more frugal way. Also we think that so many of their children will not die in childhood. Certainly the soul is of greater value than the body and its salvation is a greater affair by far, but the body too is a work of the hand of God and it is the more refined of his works which are from dust. . . . We can not expect a clean soul to reside in an unclean and corrupted body. It is very difficult, for example, for a drunkard or a glutton to repent and loosen his hand from sin. Lusts, which are lower than animals, subdue the soul. We hope that many of the Syrians will take pleasure in reading and studying this book and a part of them will receive much benefit from it.[133]

Most of the book consists of a list of medical problems and prescriptions for their cure. However, there is an underlying focus on maintaining a "healthy habit" (*'adat ṣaḥ*). Young explains that medicine is not simply about administering drugs, but requires that one "be able to discern what is wrong with people," which includes semiology.[134] He addresses what seem to be indigenous forms of healing, some of which ultimately go back to Hippocratic medicine and its notion of balance, when he states:

> A great mistake which you make is this: you think that disease comes to heal a force contrary to the rules of the habit of nature [qanone d-'adat d-aṣla]. I do not now speak about fools nor soothsayers [lit. "knowers"], but about those of you who are clever because I have no doubt that those fools think that medicine is a science of sorcery ['ilm d-remeldaruta] or of astrology and they look upon a doctor as they look upon a sorcerer.[135]

Beneath the book's treatment of diverse ailments lies a civilizational discourse, one holding that science requires a true understanding that only comes through the reform of culture.[136] Whereas the Syrians are described as a "people" (tayepa) without doctors, the reader is told, "Remember: 'A doctor who is good is taught and instructed in Europe or in America.'"[137] Lack of cleanliness, often a concern of the missionaries, is a sign of the backwardness of the Syrians on the civilizational scale:

> The first rule of care for the ill is this: to keep them, their bed, their place, etc. very clean. This is the first great difference we see between an enlightened people [tayepa buhrena] and a foolish and barbaric [barbraya] one. The former is clean, whereas the latter is always filthy. Certainly there are many degrees between these two poles. The people [tayepa] that is more clean in its habits [b-'adatu(hy)], its dress, its houses, and its cities is so much more enlightened [buhrena], clever, and blessed. On the other hand, the people that is more filthy is so much more foolish and barbaric. I myself have not seen a people whose condition [ahwalu(hy)] is opposed to this information, although I have seen some from many parts of the peoples [tayepe] of the whole world.[138]

The text further addresses the need for healthy air and clean water, and then health and cleanliness are explicitly linked to Christianity: "Remember that cleanliness is a thing second after holiness and it is not at all necessary for a Christian to have the reproach against him that he is a filthy person. A filthy Christian! How strange is that! (Phil 4:8)."[139] The tract even addresses the importance of the layout of homes: "Bad houses are a major reason for the fallen state [ahwal] of your people [tayepa]."[140] If the Syrians were a "great people," they would set their houses in order.[141]

Health was not distinguished from sanctity through most of Christian history. To describe the body as a temple did not mean that the body was something to be taken care of as a biological entity. 1 Corinthians 6:19 ("Your body is a temple of the Holy Spirit") in its original Pauline context and as it was received in the Syriac monastic and exegetical tradition is not a passage about the need to maintain the health of the body, but rather about avoiding fornication and the capacity for the spirit of God to enter human beings. Health was, to be sure, concomitant with a holy life, but it was not disembedded from that life as its "benefit." In contrast—ironically if we consider the missionaries' claims about their own deeper approach to Scripture and faith—the Christian body for the missionaries was something more literal: the material, biological body, which could be fostered or harmed by correct habits of health and cleanliness. This body was also a national body, a collection of individuals who shared the same poor habits and yet could participate in a collective transformation. In this, the biologizing of the Christian body contributed to a racialization of the Syrians.

The Spatialization of Linear Time and the Idea of Progress (*Mantayta*)

Nature, God's creation, exists in time, and the evangelical transformation of self and community was to occur in it. Mission publications promoted an awareness of this linear time, whether through a focus on biblical chronology and historicism or an emphasis on the calendar in *Rays of Light*. The mission's temporal regime, which we will discuss in the following chapter with regard to the social practices introduced by the mission, reflected the capitalist culture of the United States, but was also part of an evangelical project of temporal reform.[142]

The missionaries attempted to downplay the complex indigenous tradition of festival and fast days in the calendrical year, which they linked rather to the temporality of the natural world. Their use of the Gregorian rather than the Julian calendar made this easier because it meant their liturgical year was different from the Church of the East's. In the 1860s and early 1870s, the January issue of *Rays of Light* began with a special New Year's greeting, which emphasized the transitory nature of time. While looking back at the blessings, failings, and losses of the prior year, albeit abstractly and with few details, wishes were made for blessings in the New Year.[143] These articles, which also include poems on the passage of time or the "year past," are often highly rhetorical, sometimes personifying and directly addressing the new and passing years.[144] *Rays of Light* also printed a chart on the moon cycle for the respective month, as well as times for the rising and setting of the sun, relying on "the reckoning of Europe which is used by all the Christians who are in the world."[145] In accord with this interest in natural, calendrical time, the mission published the *1863 Almanac* (1862) and similar volumes, so-called calendars, for 1868 and 1870 (published in 1867 and 1869, respectively).

The March 1850 issue of *Rays of Light* provides a translation of "What Is Time?" This often-reprinted sentimental poem by Methodist minister and missionary Joshua Marsden (ca. 1777[?]–1837) describes the various answers given to the question posed in its title.[146] After responses from an old man, the dead, a dying sinner, the sun and planets, the seasons, a lost spirit, a sundial, and a Bible, Father Time, without answering, speeds by on his chariot, a common metaphor most famously used in Andrew Marvell's "To His Coy Mistress." The poem concludes (in the more eloquent English rendering): "I ask'd the mighty angel, who shall stand / One foot on sea, and one on solid land; / 'By Heaven,' he cried, 'I swear the mystery's o'er'; / 'Time was,' he cried, 'but Time shall be no more!'" The angel with "one foot on sea, and one on solid land" (Rv 10:2) attests to the millennialism implicit in the missionaries' notion of linear time: The Book of Revelation was not part of the East Syrian canon, whereas this apocalyptic text was central to the missionaries' eschatology. Time moves ever forward, but it will also come to a stop. This terminality applies to the world and each of us as mortals. Furthermore, time and death are linked numerically in an article on the "residents of the grave": statistics are provided for how many people have died since the time of Christ.[147] Death and the millennium are also linked through time: now is a special time (2 Cor 6:2), and we should board the ark of Jesus before the flood of fire comes.[148]

Time was configured by the missionaries in spatial terms. In a piece entitled "Near Home," time is compared to a chariot that moves along bringing us closer and closer each day to our home. "Years, weeks, and days are the stopping places of our life; we are approaching the end."[149] Birgit Meyer describes the "spatialization" of time in the iconography and literature German Pietists brought with them in their missions to Ghana.[150] She includes in her discussion *Pilgrim's Progress*, which renders the course of human life a journey through various lands. The Neo-Aramaic title of the translation of the work, "The Journey of a Pilgrim" (*sapar d-ḥa muqdusi*), suggests this same spatialization of time. An article from 1863 begins by asking how far heaven is from us. The response plays on the dual meaning of distance when both space and time are understood in linear terms: heaven is not far at all, we are told, because death can occur at any moment.[151]

The tract *On the Subject of Sunday* (1842) points to another aspect of the missionaries' emphasis on time. Ignoring the various East Syrian fast days and festivals, the missionaries hoped promoting Sunday as the Lord's Sabbath would displace what they deemed the irregularity of the East Syrian calendar. The Sabbath was to be observed by remembering Christ's resurrection, sanctifying the day, and resting on it. On Sunday neither bodily labor nor "lazy and worldly thoughts" were appropriate, neither talk of worldly things

nor visiting any "house of conversation."[152] Thus, the forward movement of
secular time was staggered each week by Sunday, but through this division
the six profane days were further articulated as part of secular time. However,
despite Sunday's sanctity, every day was thought to deserve its own specific
sanctification. The translation of the devotional book *Green Pastures; or, Daily
Food for the Lord's Flock* (1855), by James Smith (1802–62), consists of scriptural meditations for every day of the year.[153] This book was the favorite of
Mar Elias, bishop of Geogtapa, such that it was placed upon his chest during
the procession carrying him to his grave in December 1863.[154]

The emphasis on linear time led to a new focus on progress, the notion
that in time a person or entity, even a nation, can develop and eventually
prosper. One common expression denoting "to make progress" or "to prosper" literally means "to go in front of oneself" (*azel l-qa[d]mu[hy]*) and therefore connotes the spatialization of time. Progress takes different forms in the
sources. Over time "the work of salvation," one article claims, "made progress" in a number of ways.[155] This usage can be applied to institutions, such
as schools, which "have made progress,"[156] and to individuals: "It is certain to
me that your conscience is awakened to the necessary deeds. You are able to
venture and make progress in the course of your habits without difficulty."[157]
Progress is also civilizational: descriptions of the great inventions of Europe
and the United States and their application are found throughout *Rays of
Light*. For example, that newspapers did not exist in England 150 years before
is presented not only as a fact about the English past, but as demonstrative of
the East Syrian future.[158]

This idea of progress becomes more common and explicit in publications
from the 1860s onward. In these works the term *mantayta*, meaning "prosperity," "success," or "progress," becomes prevalent. For example, one text in
which the idea of "progress" is linked to national temporality as well as the
biblical narrative is *The Rules of Music* (1860), which is a primer to Western
music beginning with do re me and the rule of octaves followed by an extensive offering of translated American songs with notation.[159] In its introduction
this book links the use of music to the varying "states" of ancient Israel.

> Whenever the family of Israel was in a state of prosperity [*ahwal d-mantayta*]
> the blessing of the Lord rested upon it, and her sons gathered produce with
> shouts of a fruitful harvest and her women sang, while grinding with a hand
> mill. However, in a state [*ahwal*] of enmity and imprisonment she hung her
> harps on willows and was reluctant to sing one of the songs of Zion in a for-
> eign land. The power of music, whenever it was well composed by the sons of
> God, relieved oppressions, sang forth sounds of victory over the enemy, and
> awakened tunes which drove out the evil spirit, invited the spirit of prophecy,

increased the glory of God at the establishment of his holy temple, and sanctified the sound of praise, while her faithful worshiped before him in the beauty of holiness. But why is the sound of music not heard from this people [*tayepa*] within whom the special glory and mercy of God rests![160]

The variable condition of ancient Israel serves as a template for the history of nations and their ongoing progress and decline. Time is the space in which the Israelite nation prospered or failed: progress, a national equivalent of reform, occurs in this space.

Conclusion: Evangelical Liberalism and the Nation

The mission's moral exhortative message to the East Syrian community was fundamentally Christian, and the mission was a pious venture to transform the hearts of individual East Syrians and to awaken the East Syrian "nation." As part of this project of reform, however, the missionaries disseminated ideas about: education, peoplehood, nationality, individuality, and conditionality; personal and national transformation as forms of enlightenment and self-awakening; customs (or habits) and their reform; utility, science, empiricism, and natural theology; race, civilization, time, and progress. These ideas were the content of an evangelical discourse, one that was millenarian in its enthusiasm and modern in its implementation.

Despite the missionaries' goal of saving souls, many of the ideas they promoted were in accord with nineteenth-century liberalism. At first glance, John Stuart Mill (1806–73) and Justin Perkins (1805–69) have little in common aside from approximately shared life spans, but a comparison of the two may illuminate the resonances that exist between evangelicalism and liberal thought. Mill was raised in an elite, intensely intellectual atmosphere that was worldly and actively not Christian. He spent his life as a civil servant at the center of a world empire, writing on a variety of topics from economics to ethical philosophy, and remains today a thinker with whom anyone seriously engaged with liberal thought must grapple. Perkins, on the other hand, grew up in a marginal farming village with little education, and only eventually through Christian institutions became a learned if slightly parochial thinker. He then spent the rest of his life on the other side of the globe in a different backwater from his hometown.

In their writings both men are concerned with liberty and the problem of coercion, and both in addressing these issues maintain a distinction between public and private goods. For Perkins a concern for "freedom" (*azaduta* in Neo-Aramaic) is not in itself about politics. Rather, it is a requirement for true Christianity to prosper. Fundamental to and consistent with both men's respective profession of freedom is a colonial attitude compatible with and supportive of imperialism.[161] The two are also suspicious of custom and, in this, of Catholicism as well: they understood both as coercive. Their concern for liberty, one political and the other theological, also corresponds with their libertarian views of business and free trade. Both encourage the maintenance of individualism through the classic liberal argument concerning harm: that which does not harm us should not be restricted.

The liberty with which both are concerned is one in which people are free to excel, whether it be for Mill in various practices or for Perkins in piety. This liberty is not one of simple neglect, but for Mill a "disinterested exertion to promote the good of others."[162] He even refers to this as "disinterested benevolence," a phrase coined already in the American evangelical context by Samuel Hopkins to describe the form of Christian social ethics, which would serve as a motivating force behind Christian missions. For both, the elevation of the status of women is a central goal, but this concern is secular for one, evangelical for the other. This focus on women corresponds with their mutual colonial attitude: the status of women is especially poor among nonwhite civilizations, who need help to improve their condition. Moreover, both men share an anxiety, perhaps best characterized as Romantic, about the condition of the contemporary world and the potential it has to affect people in negative ways. Finally, in the understanding of civilization, progress, and enlightenment articulated in their respective works, nations are thought to be the constituent units of civilization.

Of course, Justin Perkins is no John Stuart Mill (the former's ideas are representative of his day, whereas the latter's are also generative). Any detailed comparison of the two would demonstrate how superficial these similarities are. Moreover, the resonances between the two men's ideas derive in part from a shared genealogy. Mill's political thought harks back to John Locke's, who, in turn, as a Puritan depends ultimately on Reformation ideas concerning religious freedom. Locke's work maintains religious trappings, which are completely absent from Mill's. Perkins's political ideas are evangelical, but he combines an early American republicanism with a Protestant concern for freedom, both political and religious.

Mill's thought was founded on the more radical utilitarianism of his father and of Jeremy Bentham and therefore at its base had different presuppositions than Perkins's evangelical piety. Perkins was deeply Calvinist, whereas Mill, who explicitly criticizes Calvinism, places religion in general in the category of custom or tradition, which according to him tends to limit people's excellence because it coerces them at worst and at best encourages them to sink into thoughtless routines (which would be "ritualism" for Perkins). Despite the obvious differences, the superficial overlaps between the two men's ideas—Mill I use in part only as an example of a classical liberal thinker—suggest how evangelical piety and liberalism resonate with each other. The transition from the evangelical piety of the early mission to the secular nationalism of the end of the nineteenth century did not entail a significant ideological break. This transition would be all the more easy in the late nineteenth century within the growing liberal Christian culture of the American mission and the secularized discourse that emerged due to the proliferation of foreign missions, both of which I address in chapter 7.

Before the arrival of missions, whether in Urmia city, in the villages on the plain, or among the seminomadic tribes in the mountains, the East Syrians lived in a world of diverse social and religious powers; of various holy places, books, and men; and of divination and magical incantations. Clergy performed the powerful Eucharistic ritual. Diverse local authorities held political sway, and the patriarch sat upon his ecclesiastical throne high in the mountains. Some of the ideas the missionaries introduced were foreign to the East Syrians, but others were alternative articulations of concepts they previously held. Despite this world's often different notions of, for example, sacred space and time, which are attested in the colophons of East Syrian manuscripts, many indigenous ideas shared an affinity with those introduced by the mission because of a shared Christian heritage.[163] The mission did not simply displace indigenous East Syrian ideas, but rather drew distinctions and mapped out territories that were at times already there within the East Syrian tradition. Take, for example, the standard distinction we find in Classical Syriac literature between the body and the soul: the mission literature develops a distinction between the bodily and the spiritual, this world and the next, rearticulating it in several areas. Although the East Syrians had their own tradition of prioritizing the spiritual over the corporeal, Calvinist anxiety about works righteousness challenged the possibility of any act being in itself pious, thus rendering "true religion," the realm of the spiritual, as something fundamentally interior. Another example of how the mission rearticulated indigenous terms is apparent in the transformation of the Classical Syriac term for "race" (*gensa*, from Gr. *génos*) into a physiologically oriented term, a materialist and naturalistic notion, which would be further biologized by the end of the nineteenth century.

In their articulation of Christianity, the missionaries redrew conceptual boundaries and defined piety in more precise terms, distinguishing it from culture. (At the same time, foreign diplomats were defining the border between Qajar Iran and the Ottoman Empire, thus splitting the sprawling East Syrian community, and the Ottomans were trying to impose their rule over the historically recalcitrant Hakkari region.) The new boundaries drawn by the mission created the conceptual space in which a nation could be imagined as a civilization that exists in time and space in a "natural" world, a collective of individuals who must be awakened to their poor condition and knowingly be changed through the reform of habits. Religion itself is one of these boundaries or limiting categories: appropriating indigenous terms (*dehlat alaha, todita, mazhab*), the missionaries introduced the Protestant understanding of "true religion" as a private form of devotion that pertained to the spiritual part of the human being (as opposed to the sectarian, divisive, idolatrous, and intrusive forms of "empty religion"). The missionaries' ideas of personhood, nation, progress, and race, as well as their millennial ideas about the civilizing and Christianizing of the world, were all part of their evangelical project, but their notion of religion was so elevated that parts of the project took on a life of their own, and in the delimited space of Christian liberal thought, the nation was imagined.

4

Being Together in the Living Word:
The Mission and Evangelical Sociality (1834–70)

For where two or three are gathered together in my name, there am I in the midst of them.
—MATTHEW 18:20

Our people are thus learning the power of union at the throne of grace. When threatened with being devastated by locusts last year, in many of the villages our congregations met, and by prayer and fasting plead for the removal of the impending judgment; and why should they not believe that the partial lifting up of God's hand, about to rest so strongly upon them, was in answer to prayer? Thus we trust they will learn, as a nation, in all their national troubles to come to God. Thus national feeling will be inspired, and the bonds of national union be created and strengthened.
—SAMUEL RHEA, January 2, 1864[1]

According to the American missionaries, the "Nestorians" were an almost fallen nation, one about to decline from their already nominal Christianity into an idolatry equivalent to Catholicism. The missionaries often addressed the East Syrians as a nation and presupposed that national thinking would be to their spiritual and material benefit. They believed that by education, preaching, and prayer, this nation would be transformed and its ancient Christianity revived. To spur on this revival, the Americans fostered new social practices and forms of social interaction among their East Syrian audience and in doing so contributed to their transformation into a community gripped by national self-consciousness and a longing for unity.

The Social Constitution of the Mission

From what was originally only Justin and Charlotte Bass Perkins, the "Mission to the Nestorians" had grown by 1843 to over thirty members: eighteen Americans and twelve "native helpers," or "assistants," as they were called. Most missionaries arrived with a spouse, and these couples often had children while in the field. The men usually had college degrees and some seminary training, whereas in the pre-1870 period only four women had college degrees, which they all received at Mount Holyoke.[2] In the first ten years, the mission established various outstations; numerous village schools; and a male and a female seminary, both of which offered elementary education through high school. The native assistants, who were usually from either the plain or nontribal communities in the mountains (despite the preponderance of wild mountain folk in American domestic mission publications), were an important social and intellectual link between the missionaries and the East Syrian community. As cultural mediators, they provided access to the East Syrian tradition and the community at large while often enjoying special privileges at the mission.

Soon after Perkins returned to Urmia in April 1843 after almost two years away in America, the mission experienced several setbacks.[3] Badr Khan Bey, the emir of Bohtan, and his ally Nurullah Bey, the emir of Hakkari, assaulted numerous villages in Hakkari, massacring many Christians and driving the patriarch from Qudshanis to Mosul. This put a stop to missionary efforts in the mountains for several years. The first open dispute with the nearby Catholic mission broke out also at this time over the Catholic seizure of an East Syrian church, which the local bishop, Gabriel of Ardishai, wanted the Americans to help renovate.[4] The affair resulted in outraged French diplomats making accusations before the authorities in the capital that the Americans were proselytizing Muslims.[5]

Asahel Grant (b. 1807) of Utica, New York, who had arrived with his wife, Judith, in 1835 to serve as the mission's medical doctor, died in Mosul on April 24, 1844, of typhus. Surrounded by the American missionaries there and visited regularly by the French archaeologist and consul Paul-Émile Botta, as well as the patriarch Shem'on himself, who was there in temporary exile, he died a slow death of delirium and diarrhea.[6] Judith had preceded him in death on January 14, 1839, most likely of malaria.[7] Grant was well known for the claims he had made about the origins of the "Nestorians," who he attempted to demonstrate were the descendants of the lost tribes of Israel.

The summer of 1844 also witnessed a feud between the mission and the patriarchal family, who were upset that they did not receive a stipend from the mission like that provided to the four bishops of the plain, Gabriel of Ardishai, Elias of Geogtapa, Yokhannan of Gawilan, and Joseph of 'Ada, all of whom worked with the mission.[8] This issue was exacerbated by the mission's publication of an anti-Catholic tract that seemed to be aimed implicitly at the Church of the East as well. That fall a dispute also occurred within the mission community itself over the issue of proselytizing Muslims and accommodating the indigenous church.[9]

The doldrums of 1843–45 would soon be forgotten in 1846 and the years to follow as the mission witnessed several hoped-for revivals. Furthermore, despite the various setbacks that began in 1843, that year also saw the arrival of two of the most important members of the mission, Fidelia Fiske (1816–64) and David Tappan Stoddard (1818–57), who became the respective heads of the female and male seminaries. Fiske belonged to the first graduating class of Mount Holyoke, which had only been opened by Mary Lyon in 1837. She was a close associate of Lyon, and the female seminary, which she took charge of not long after her arrival, was referred to as the "Holyoke of Oroomiah" or the "Holyoke of Persia."[10] Fiske was in fact the first female missionary to enter the field from Holyoke: Perkins had met her in January 1843 when he visited the college seeking volunteers (she was the niece of Pliny Fisk [1792–1825], the early ABCFM missionary who died in Beirut).[11] Stoddard, who had studied at Bowdoin and Yale and was ordained in 1843, would take charge of the male seminary, but also played an important role as a scholar at the mission.

The number of American members of the mission dipped through the 1840s. In 1851 there were sixteen. At this time the mission also set up a station in the village of Memekkan, across the Qajar-Ottoman frontier in Gawar, which was an entry point to Hakkari. This station, which was established for future forays into the mountains, was maintained until 1860.[12] Through the 1850s the number of Americans was on average nineteen, increasing into the low twenties in the early 1860s. This dipped again to fifteen or sixteen each year until 1869. Several families served at the mission for more than one generation. The native assistants, who were usually lower clergy, often introduced their own families into the mission community as well.

In time the mission projected its influence widely across the Urmia plain and beyond through its numerous village schools and mission outstations. Village schools were generally taught by clergy who had been educated or were still studying at the mission. Annual reports provide the number of schools and students: in 1842, there were forty schools with 763 students; in 1852, sixty schools with 1,038 students; and in 1866, sixty-two schools with 1,163 students.[13] Geogtapa had two schools by 1841 and a separate school for girls by 1845. The number of students at each school varied greatly: in 1839 there were 50 students in the school at Geogtapa and 33 at 'Ada.[14] Furthermore, by the early 1850s, the mission began to establish its outstations, which were posts administered by East Syrian preachers and teachers. The earliest outstations were in the larger villages near the city of Urmia, such as Geogtapa and Ardishai (1852), Sepurghan and Dizataka (1854), and 'Ada (1856). By 1857 there were stations in Gawar and in the Tkhuma tribal area in Hakkari. The number of outstations remained in the thirties until 1865, when it jumped to over sixty, and by the mid-1860s there were outstations in all the major districts: Urmia, Salmas, different parts of Hakkari, Tergawar, Sulduz, and as far away as 'Amadiya on the southwestern side of Hakkari.

Whereas the number of village schools and outstations varied by the year, the core of the mission, its personnel and its institutions, remained stable. Although the mission was a formal organization for the purpose of evangelism, we should also understand it as a circle of friends, family members, and peers, a voluntary association independent of formal political attachments and advocating a transformation of all East Syrians, one heart at a time. This was an intimate group: the parents and even grandparents of many of the missionaries and assistants at the turn of the twentieth century had known one another. However, despite this social proximity, the peculiar exceptions, distinctions, and exclusions that existed between the Americans and East Syrians led to a heterogeneity of social relations, one that always reminded the East Syrians that they were "Syrians," and not white Americans.

Financing the Mission

Missions required money. The ABCFM trained people, equipped them, put them on ships, and sent them to the other side of the world. Once they arrived, the missionaries bought and built houses, dormitories, classrooms, and churches. They set up a printing press and ran it. They supported themselves (between fifteen and twenty-five Americans as well as their numerous children) and subsidized the work of native assistants. They managed a variety of schools, ranging from boarding school seminaries to small village schools, which were dispersed across Urmia and beyond. All of this required money.

Belonging to the second generation of ABCFM missionaries, the members of the mission were able to travel to Iran and do what they did because they had the backing of an institution funded by donations and run like a modern business. As one scholar of missions notes, "American religious culture had no *inhibitions* about money."[15] The archival sources for the mission are thick with references to its expenses. Modern forms of accounting were employed to make sure every dollar was spent wisely and all expenses were justified. A large part of the mission archive, which is, however, less often published in the annual report or in the *Missionary Herald*, consists of repetitive letters seeking further funding by engaging in that act, familiar to many nonprofit organizations, of finding a balance between boasting of success and lamenting the need for more funds.

The sources of the money that supported the mission usually remained anonymous. Funds were simply provided by the domestic organization in the United States, which owed its own success in fund-raising to specific trends in American religious and civic life. However, at times the donors and recipients were directly linked, making the transaction more transparent. Several native assistants received direct financial support from charitable donations abroad: Yonan of 'Ada, while studying at the male seminary and helping Perkins with translation, was supported by a woman who worked in a factory in Lowell, Massachusetts; John, son of Hormizd, by a special fund supplied by a women's church organization in Malden, Massachusetts, and later by the First Presbyterian Church of Hudson, New York; and Sarah, daughter of Priest Abraham of Geogtapa, by a Sunday school in Owego, New York.[16]

To reverse the old adage, money is time—that is, money provided the leisure required for the numerous collective activities introduced by the mission. Students at the male and female seminaries received room and board, and in the early years, day students received a stipend to compensate for the work their families lost due to their absence from the agricultural and other labors required of them at home.[17] This removal of children from their families to educate them was socially transformative, and it was only possible because of hard cash. Furthermore, money allowed for greater access to the local population. This is exemplified in the case of Samuel Rhea (mission: 1851–65), who distributed bread to passing travelers at the mission station in Gawar in order to find an opportunity to read and explain Scripture to them.[18]

The economic practices of the mission, such as fund-raising and strict bookkeeping, were in turn introduced to the East Syrian community. The mission promoted self-sufficiency as well as the collection of funds from among the East Syrian community to support local and foreign missions. One missionary goal was that the East Syrians would develop their own institutions, which they themselves would support out of their own pockets. Such concerns increased in the 1860s and 1870s as an independent evangelical church came into being. The new relationship to money at the mission was later instrumental to the development of national consciousness: the leisure made possible by foreign capital combined with the ideas advocated in the mission's publications, such as the importance of thriftiness for individuals and the community, helped to create the sphere of public debate, in which this national consciousness was fostered.

Historicizing the Social and Identifying the Emergent

A notion of society in the abstract, an "imagined community," developed at the mission. However, looking solely at such abstractions ignores the social practices and visceral forms of social interaction within which such abstractions emerged. The abstracting process whereby national consciousness came into being was preceded by an embodied experience of community. "Imaginations" only become "tangible . . . by creating a social environment that materializes through the structuring of space, architecture, [and] ritual performance, and by inducing bodily sensations."[19] Therefore, an awareness of the evolution of the idea of national community needs to be supplemented with an appreciation for the embodied collective practices promoted at the mission. For what religion and nationalism share is also, to use Émile Durkheim's famous expression, "collective effervescence," the electric charge felt by merely being within the group. At the mission, collective religious practices helped to create the social body that would be named and experienced as the nation.

Social interaction, according to the classical sociologist Georg Simmel, inevitably takes on a life of its own, beyond the specific and various interests that bring people together in the first place. For heuristic purposes, in his well-known discussion Simmel distinguishes between on the one hand the content or material that leads people to "sociate" (to associate with one another), including human drives, needs, and inclinations, and on the other hand sociation itself, which "is the form (realized in innumerable, different ways) in which individuals grow together into units that satisfy their interests."[20]

> Here, "society," properly speaking, is that being with one another, for one another, against one another which, through the vehicle of drives and purposes, forms and develops material or individual contents and interests. The forms in which this process results gain their own life. It is freed from all ties with contents. It exists for its own sake and for the sake of the fascination which, in its own liberation from these ties, it diffuses. It is precisely the phenomenon that we call sociability [*Geselligkeit*].[21]

Viewed from this perspective as autonomous of its particular aims, this pure form of social interaction is comparable to "the numerous phenomena that we lump together under the category of *play*."[22] For "in both art and play, forms that were originally developed by the realities of life, have created spheres that preserve their autonomy in the face of these realities."[23] The purest form of this social play is conversation, which is "talk for the sake of talking."[24]

In Simmel's analysis, society is better understood as "sociation" (*Vergesell-schaftung*), a process, a being in flux that eventually crystallizes "as permanent fields, as autonomous phenomena."[25]

> As they crystallize, they attain their own existence and their own laws, and may even confront or oppose spontaneous interaction itself. At the same time, society, as its life is constantly being realized, always signifies that individuals are connected by mutual influence and determination. It is, hence, something functional, something individuals do and suffer. . . . In accordance with it, society certainly is not a "substance," nothing concrete, but an *event*: it is the function of receiving and effecting the fate and development of one individual by the other.[26]

In what may be understood as a lowest-common-denominator notion of the social, Simmel emphasizes that what members of a group, especially a large one, have most in common is the group itself. They are all participants in the *event* of the social gathering.[27]

At points there are contradictions in Simmel's discussion. He wants to preserve pure sociality as a locus of analysis and yet examine it as something manifested through the concrete details of life, those phenomena that are not irreducibly social. This leads to a confusion of the heuristic type with reality. Furthermore, the consciousness of the group that develops in pure sociality becomes a collective drive and motivation, and therefore the heuristic distinction he draws between the context that drives people to sociate and sociation itself collapses. However, Simmel pushes us to think about sociality in the abstract, to consider the dynamic of groups while bracketing a concern for the content of their gatherings. Being together, especially in new contexts, can take on a life of its own and lead to new forms of sociation.

By highlighting collective practices and the experience of the collective, we are able to witness new feelings and ideas emerging from the collective and the formation of new identities, but such an analysis is limited by several factors. First, the category of experience itself, especially as something we can historically reconstruct, is problematic: getting into other people's heads is impossible enough when we know them firsthand, and so the experiences of persons we meet in the archive are that much more inaccessible.[28] Second, we are limited by our sources. We do not have detailed first-person East Syrian accounts of most of the events described in this chapter. We have sources from which we can *infer* that new experiences of the social were fostered at the mission: a unitary experience of Christianity and an exclusionary one of racial ambivalence, which worked according to the "rule of colonial difference."

A third, more complex factor limiting my analysis is that the object I am examining is emergent and therefore difficult to identify before it has full substance. In an attempt to grapple with the emergence of new cultural forms, Raymond Williams famously developed the concept of "structures of feeling." New developments in the social world commonly appear at first as "a pre-emergence, active and pressing but not yet fully articulated."[29] The problem for Williams is that analysis tends to convert human experience into "finished products," and the focus tends to be on "formed wholes rather than forming and formative processes."[30] This "slide towards a past tense and a fixed form" limits our ability to think about social processes as entities in flux and not as definitive and specific.[31] Against this reduction to static fixedness, Williams claims that "social forms are then often admitted for generalities but debarred, contemptuously, from any possible relevance to this immediate and

actual significance of being." The various social forms are in themselves not
representative of social consciousness.

> For they become social consciousness only when they are lived, actively, in
> real relationships, and moreover in relationships which are more than sys-
> tematic exchanges between fixed units. Indeed just because all consciousness
> is social, its processes occur not only between but within the relationship and
> the related. And this practical consciousness is always more than a handling
> of fixed forms and units.[32]

Practical consciousness is different from a theoretical perspective, which
gazes at social processes from the outside and defines the inchoate as a specific entity, thereby reifying what is transitory.

According to Williams, "Practical consciousness is what is actually being
lived, and not only what it is thought is being lived."[33] Therefore, in contrast
to the social as something static, formal, and identifiable, Williams suggests
"a kind of feeling and thinking which is indeed social and material, but each
in an embryonic phase before it can become fully articulate and defined exchange."[34] Williams introduces language and then manners and dress as examples of practices that slowly change in style but not necessarily epiphenom-
enally due to specific institutional transformations. Such changes affect social
experience and yet do not first require "definition, classification, or rationalization" to do so.[35] The sense of presence, nontheorized consciousness, experience as it occurs, is transformed over time through changes in "structures of
feeling." "We are talking about characteristic elements of impulse, restraint,
and tone: specifically affective elements of consciousness and relationships;
not feeling against thought, but thought as felt and feeling as thought: practical consciousness of a present kind, in a living and interrelating community."
Williams qualifies "structure of feeling" as a "cultural hypothesis," which must
depend closely upon the evidence, because as something emergent, it is by
definition difficult for us to disembed from the evidence as a specific entity.
"For structures of feeling can be defined as social experiences *in solution*, as
distinct from other social semantic formations which have been *precipitated*
and are more evidently and more immediately available."[36]

Christian Intimacy, Speaking, and Reform

Emergent social experiences, new forms of community, are more difficult to
identify in evangelical culture because evangelicalism often acknowledges
and cultivates sociality while simultaneously masking and denying its central place in human life. The relationality of the mission, the way that social

relationships were imagined and fostered, is therefore important to consider because so often evangelical conversionary discourse and its common focus on the individual are taken at face value. Omri Elisha makes an intervention in the ongoing scholarly conversation about the individuating effects of evangelical piety in his book *Moral Ambition: Mobilization and Social Outreach in Evangelical Megachurches* (2011). His argument is important because, considering the Protestant roots of Western modernity, scholars at times make generalized and often reductive remarks about the inherent individualism of Protestantism. In evangelical culture, Elisha finds rather a "comparable stress on the importance of human social relationships as vehicles of redemption," thus giving the lie to the simple equation of evangelicalism with individualism. In contrast, Elisha argues that for evangelicals a sense of intimacy with the divine is "effectively facilitated and mediated by human intersubjectivity."[37] In fact, social relationships, especially among Elisha's subjects, who are socially engaged evangelicals working with the poor, are understood to help trigger religious conversion.

Elisha's analysis breaks down the simple dichotomy of individualist and relationalist paradigms, whereby communities are understood to promote either a focus on the self or a focus on the group, either individual morality or a morality bound within the limits of collective needs. To do this, he develops the concept of "moral ambition," which he argues will help us "to assess a particular style of religious subjectivity, one that manifests in moments of concerted action and mobilization and yet reflects a range of personal desires, theological and cultural norms, historical circumstances, and social opportunities."[38] "Moral ambition" provides us with a language to address the practice of certain virtues and the conditional limits imposed by people's lives and lived religious worlds. In his study, Elisha wishes to "draw attention to the intrinsic sociality of such aspirations, that is, their inexorable orientation toward other people and their inalienability from social networks and institutions in which standards of personhood are constructed."[39] Central to moral ambition is the desire to provide examples for others, to inspire others to adopt certain moral dispositions and to be motivated to follow the models of one's peers. At the same time, such stimulation is understood to be based upon relations that exist between individuals, and this evangelical focus on one-to-one relationships is often blind to its own social engagement and how such engagements are social practices performed in relation to others.

We can borrow from Elisha's work this emphasis on the significance of relationships in evangelical Christianity. The social relationality we find at the American mission, the ways of relating to others, created the kind of intimacy that exists between those who challenge others to do their best. This intimacy brought with it a notion of Jesus Christ that had not existed before among the East Syrians: Christ as *dost*, or "friend." The carpenter Usta Badal, we are told, exclaimed upon his deathbed, "I have no suffering; Christ is my friend."[40] Mission preachers, while cultivating an intimate relationship with their audience, invoked an intimacy with Christ. "Sinner, do you want to possess this Messiah as your friend, or do you prefer him to be your enemy?" an article in *Rays of Light* entitled "The Beauty of the Messiah" asks.[41] Sentimental intimacy rendered the Christian community a circle of friends with Jesus as *the* Friend, and this is all part of a sentimentalization, or feminization, as Ann Douglas termed it, typical of the American Christianity of the day.[42] At the same time, it is possible that the missionaries were unintentionally building on a notion of the spiritual friend in local Islamic tradition: God is the *dost*, or beloved friend, in Persian Sufi literature. Heleen Murre-van den Berg has noted that in letters to Fidelia Fiske from students who developed evangelical sentiments while studying with her, we do not find a focus on the educational or civilizing effects of the mission, but on Fiske herself as an evangelizing spiritual mother.[43] These young women note the spiritual family they discovered, not the learning they acquired.[44] In these converts' letters there is an "emphasis on the conversion experience over against civilizing activities," and "a personal one-to-one relationship with the missionary seems to have been the overriding factor in the converts' spiritual development."[45] Similarly, in Yonan of 'Ada's encomiastic 1870 obituary for Justin Perkins, spiritual fatherhood is a major motif, whereas a letter from one East Syrian to Perkins describes him as "my chief [*agha*] and my brother."[46]

Such an intimacy is also akin to "the conceptualization of Christian spirituality as an intimate experience," which James S. Bielo examines in his book *Words upon the Word: An Ethnography of Evangelical Group Bible Study* (2009).[47] Bielo wants to examine the "problem of presence," asking the question "How do Christians respond to this dilemma of making a metaphysical God available, visible, and communicable in the physical world?"[48] Ultimately, the cultivation of intimacy with God corresponds with Christians' intimacy with one another. "Evangelicals seek to imitate the close, intimate bond they desire with God in their expectations for relating with each other and with those outside their community of faith."[49] The Bible study session becomes a place to cultivate this intimacy.[50] Among other things, Bielo looks at new practices of collective reading that entail direct address and dialogue, both of which create new forms of intimacy.

Language is obviously an important medium in most social events, especially ones that evoke intimacy and demand specific kinds of personal transformation. Language is a bridge, a medium through which those listening to preaching or witnessing may be drawn to conversion.[51] Inasmuch as language is shared, we can also share experience, and this opens up the possibility of transforming the listener. I take this view of language for granted here, although the issue of conversion will come up more explicitly in chapter 5. In this chapter I look at the variety of spaces in which language could take place, so to speak, in the early history of the mission. I am not looking at language itself, even if it is necessary to describe the exhortatory tone employed in these spaces. Rather, I examine certain episodes of social, and therefore linguistic, interaction, as well as the physical locations and collective settings in which conversionary language occurred. The conceptual content of that language I addressed in the previous chapter, although some of it will inevitably come up again here.

My analysis requires that we blur our often too sharp distinction between words and ideas, on the one hand, and bodies and practices, on the other. Social gatherings are embodied events, and audiences listen, or sometimes must be taught to listen, in specifically embodied ways. The mission's numerous collective gatherings occurred in linguistic spaces mediated not just through words but through bodies *being together*. In turn, being together always means inhabiting a shared linguistic space, especially in Christian ritual settings, where speech is an essential part of the service: "There is no true administration of the sacrament without the word," John Calvin admonishes in the *Institutes*.[52]

The encounter and relationship between Yokhannan and Perkins, which was addressed in chapter 2, was the simplest of the new forms of social interaction introduced by the mission, all of which also entailed new ethical claims. Such claims form community, as exhortation in any shared linguistic space is socially constitutive: to make ethical demands of someone is to create a conversation that one is not always able to exit without difficulty. The key evangelical questions, such as "What shall we do to be saved?" a refrain found throughout the sources, created problems that needed solving and called interlocutors into being. Furthermore, new forms of social interaction introduce new types of hierarchy, new forms of intimacy, not just new words, but new ways of being together and relating to one another. This obviously pertains to education, both in its formal sense, because the missionary encounter often occurred in schools, and in a broader sense, inasmuch as the missionaries' approach was often pedagogical. Education has content, but it is also an ideal and a social process, a way of relating to others that entails certain demands, as all social interaction requires some form of reciprocity.

Preaching, bearing witness to Christ, was a basic building block of social interaction at the mission. By preaching I do not refer simply to the formal act of exhorting a group, but also to the life of bearing witness and "conversational preaching"—that is, informal social interactions, often in domestic settings, where missionaries would introduce evangelical topics of conversation.[53] In fact, mission itself is a form of preaching. Missionaries are witnesses to the Gospel, and not just what they say but how they act through their whole life is a didactic performance of the Gospel. The missionary's life is on display, just as all Christians should ultimately attest to the transformative power of the Gospel. This attitudinal stance, the relation to others as ethical challenge, is different from the social relations that would be performed in traditional East Syrian ecclesial settings, such as the Eucharistic service or a saint's festival. The relation between speaker and audience, or even between two members in a conversation, was highly charged by one interlocutor's intention to enlighten another, to eradicate bad habits, such as stealing, lying, gossiping, and drinking, and to inculcate virtue.

The rhetorical stance of ethical preaching introduced by the missionaries demanded a transformation, a reform of habit, and thus was similar to Norbert Elias's notion of the "civilizing process."[54] It can also be understood as part of an ongoing homiletical process of Christianization, the idealized purification of Christianity from the dross of culture and preconversion sentiment, a process going back to Christian origins and long exemplified in the monastery. Reform means Christians can always be better: preaching in Ardishai, Fidelia Fiske told a loud and rowdy crowd of several hundred women that she would not speak "unless you will all put your fingers upon your lips, and not say one word."[55] The crowd eventually quieted down after she told them that she had a story to tell. It was about an old woman, one, as Fiske stated, she herself did not know, nor did her parents, nor even her grandfather. "Here they began to inquire after my grandfather, and I was obliged again to get all the fingers on the lips, and tell them that they would not hear any more about the woman if they talked about my grandfather."[56] The story Fiske told was of a woman who was unable to keep silent at church meetings despite repeated warnings. Fiske then turned to her audience: "Now, you are very much like that woman. I do not think you can stop talking, so I must stop." This silenced the crowd, who kept their fingers "now closely pressed to their lips."[57] Fiske then "read to them of Mary, and told them I was sure that she never talked in meeting, and that if she had, Jesus would not have loved her so much." The rhetorical posture of preaching consists of directly addressing an audience as potential Christians with the explicit purpose of exhorting them to transform themselves, and in this case Fiske was able to render her boisterous audience unified in silent listening.

Mission literature, no matter what the genre, is primarily framed as exhortation. Many of the ethical essays published in *Rays of Light*, written as second-person addresses and ending with the word *amen*, provide examples of the mission's homiletical approach. They combine the mantra of "by faith in Christ alone" with calls for reform in all parts of life. The success of such preaching is difficult to judge, but, according to the sources, the message sometimes hit home. During a preaching tour in Baranduz, Perkins was approached by a local chief after he had addressed the whole village. "The chief man occasionally drew a deep sigh, and soliloquized in a strain like the following: 'Our faces are black (we are very guilty); we lie, swear, get drunk, and our hearts are full of iniquity.'"[58] According to Perkins, everyone else concurred, and the chief asked to come live with Perkins, which he rejected, suggesting that the chief and his people should rather make habitual the prayer "Lead me not into temptation, but deliver me from evil" (Mt 6:13). The chief and one or two others then accompanied Perkins through the rain two miles to the next village.

Schools

The missionaries established four types of schools: the male seminary, which opened on January 18, 1836; the female seminary, which opened on March 12, 1838, and took in boarders in 1843; the various village and Sunday schools, which often did not have their own structures; and the Muslim school, which began with ten students on January 1, 1840, and continued for several years, but was controversial, underfunded, and established only as an accommodation to local demands.[59]

Both the male and female seminaries, as they were called, were established on the Lancaster system.[60] Named after Joseph Lancaster (1778–1838), the English Quaker educational reformer, who was rejected later in his career by his own constituency when it was revealed that he had been beating students, the Lancaster system was a species of the monitorial method of education whereby senior students served as instructors and aides to junior ones. Students passed from level to level as they learned, while more senior students perfected their own knowledge by teaching their peers. This method, similar to what we now refer to as peer education, was financially less burdensome than the standard classroom and was especially useful in a missionary context where labor was limited. This system of education was common both in England and overseas in the early to mid-nineteenth century, especially for the laboring classes: Emily Brontë seems to have a monitorial system in mind when she describes Lowood, the school where Jane Eyre spends eight years after being pushed out by her cruel aunt. At the American mission the purpose of this system was also to help to raise up native teachers who then would go on to create their own schools.

Several historians have discussed the introduction of the Lancaster system to the Middle East in the nineteenth century. Whereas Timothy Mitchell links it to the emergence of a new political discipline and social order in Khedive Egypt (1867–1914), Paul Sedra addresses how this important part of the Egyptian state apparatus and Egyptian modernity was first brought by British missionaries.[61] Sedra describes how the Lancaster system functioned as a "monitorial machine" in which "missionaries saw their ideal world in microcosm, a world in which all people, and all peoples, understood the fact of their exposure to the eyes of God—that is to say, understood the fact of their common, Christian subordination."[62] The system offered control but at the same time was able "to render networks of power imperceptible."[63] According to Sedra, the Lancaster system also fit the needs of the modern state because it aided in the cultivation of the virtues of industry, discipline, and order.

On January 16, 1836, two days before the male seminary officially opened, Perkins led a religious service in the newly constructed schoolroom.[64] He preached on 1 Kings 8:27 and 9:3, both of which are passages about God finding a dwelling on earth in Solomon's temple. The seminary began as a simple two-room structure, one room to serve for study and prayer, the other as a dormitory.[65] The classroom had enough benches to accommodate eighty students, as well as a pulpit for when it was used as a chapel.[66] The layout of the classroom would have been unfamiliar to many of the students: Perkins mentions constructing desks and chairs, pieces of furniture that were not found in all East Syrian homes. In fact, in a culture in which sitting on the floor was common, the layout of the classroom was innovative: it offered some of the students their first opportunity to sit in a chair. In comparison, we can consider the cultural effects of the introduction of the chair to China in the Tang period as part of the spread of Buddhist monasticism from India: this new technology, which became common between the Late Tang and the Northern Song periods (eighth and eleventh centuries), stimulated a transformation in household life and bodily deportment.[67] The age-old practice in the Middle East had been to sit at the master's feet, such as is represented in the well-known rabbinic expression "to sit at the feet of," meaning "to study under." At the seminary one sat before the master on a bench and eventually at a desk, an individualized place of rest below the master but above the floor, the common space of sitting. One was elevated and observable, and yet because the system was monitorial, a superior position could also be attained.

Observation was not only spatial but also temporal: "The complex clockwork of the mutual improvement school," as Michel Foucault describes the

Lancaster system, this "machine for learning" was organized through a disciplining of time.[68] Perkins at first fixed a bell in the original cellar classroom and attached it to a string that ran upstairs to his workroom "by which I could announce the hours of the day, and in some measure regulate the exercises of the school."[69] Perkins also used the bell to silence the students, who would often all "study aloud at the same time" in the "oriental" manner. This disciplining also entailed social integration. Students came from all over the plain and the frontier region and eventually began to arrive from the tribal areas of Hakkari: like the mission press, education at mission schools encouraged a standardization of language and a leveling of Syrians from diverse backgrounds.

Perkins established schools, in particular the male seminary, rapidly, although he needed to learn the local Aramaic dialect, create pedagogical tools, and produce vernacular translations of the Bible and other books for teaching. He had only arrived in Urmia in November 1835, and began his translation of the Bible on February 16, 1836. However small it was, Perkins wanted the seminary opened that same year. Many of its early personnel, both teachers and students, were originally members of Perkins's first study sessions upon his arrival. The student body grew quickly: there were fifty-five students at the end of 1843, including a number of priests, deacons, and the patriarch's teenage relative who was designated to be a bishop.[70] Most of the students were in their teens, although some in the early years were clergy in their sixties. In June 1847 the seminary was moved from the city of Urmia to Sire, where the mission kept its summer retreat.

The purpose of the schools, with the exception of the Muslim one, was moral and religious reform, especially through the study of Scripture. The male seminary aimed to reform the East Syrian clergy as well as others, rendering them evangelical workers, through whom the people as a whole could be enlightened. Secular sciences were taught as tools for understanding Scripture, whereas Christianity was thought to be based upon and supportive of the sound principles of secular learning. Although the curriculum shifted at times, in the early years it consisted of arithmetic, Neo-Aramaic and Classical Syriac, English, writing, and Bible study.[71] Instruction in natural philosophy— that is, science—included experimental demonstrations. The missionaries saw no contradiction between faith and reason, or religion and science. Such contradictions, raised within the Enlightenment, had passed them by, and the Darwinist disputes of the later nineteenth century had not yet begun.[72] Religion, science, and morality contributed to one another and were considered distinct intellectual spheres neither in human life nor in the educational process. Similarly, reading itself was considered a devotional act and a part of moral formation. Parna Sengupta's claim about missionary education in South Asia may be made also about school practices in Urmia: "The process of reading became a way in which the moral (evangelical) self could be monitored and improved, and was thus constitutive of the new Christian subject. The 'conversion of the individual' was made possible through literacy."[73]

Fidelia Fiske and Her "Daughters": The Female Seminary and the Evangelical Sentimentality of Womanhood

> The design of the school is to so educate Nestorian girls that they may be better daughters and sisters, wives and mothers, than are those usually found among the people. Unless a change, and a very great change, can be wrought in the females here, all the efforts in behalf of the other sex will fail of producing permanent good. We aim to give the members of the school such a training, physical, mental, and moral, as shall best fit them for a happy and useful life among their own people.[74]

Fidelia Fiske wrote this in a letter to the British consul in Tehran in May 1855. Her life and work are exemplary of the missionary role of women and the emphasis on an instrumental femininity at American evangelical missions.[75] Missions were compelled to address gender head-on because of the different norms that existed between the missionaries and their audience, whereas in the United States "missionary work enabled women to break into public life, expand educational opportunities for themselves and other women, and acquire professional competence as teachers."[76]

The attitude of the missionaries was not unlike what Antoinette Burton describes in her study of British feminists and their imperial relationship to Indian women. In general, women were understood to be "the vessels through which the moral improvement of society could be achieved."[77] According to Burton, this was thought to be even more true for British women because, being Christian, they belonged to "a religion superior itself in part because of the special place it accorded to women."[78] Missionaries were "motivated to action by what one might call 'evangelical Orientalism.'"[79] They were concerned to ameliorate what they deemed the absence of the essential qualities of motherhood among orientals. As Lisa Joy Pruitt states, "For early nineteenth-century evangelicals, the status of women meant neither political rights nor legal privileges, but rather social and spiritual equality manifested in a woman's educational level, her position as a cherished partner in a companionate marriage, and her usefulness as a Christian, a wife, and a mother."[80] Sentimentalism was the guide, and beyond politics and economics, affective relations between individuals, whether it be husband and wife, friend and

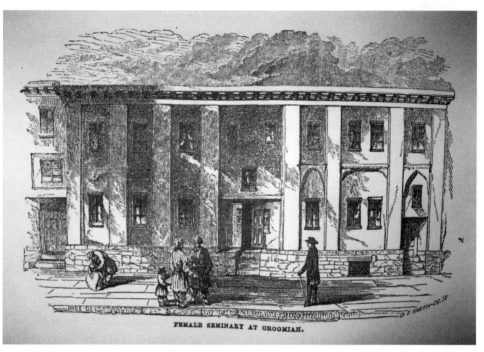

FEMALE SEMINARY AT OROOMIAH.

FIGURE 7. The female seminary in the mid-nineteenth century. (Thomas Laurie, *Woman and Her Saviour in Persia*, 1863.)

friend, or Christian and God, were the irreducible links around which community would be constructed. In this way the notions of gender introduced by the missionaries are directly related to the new ideas and practices of sociality at the mission.

The female seminary in Urmia was on the mission grounds and played an active role in developments within the mission community, including serving as a center of enthusiasm during the revivals that took place from 1846 onward. Regarding the shared life together in prayer, eating, study, domestic work, and caring for one another when ill, Fiske herself would state, "The school is in every sense a family."[81] As stated above, some young women at the institution attributed their own conversions to the special maternal role Fiske played. The sources describe the many tears shed when the students, of which there were twenty-two in 1843, were compelled to part temporarily during a closure of the mission schools in 1844 due to a conflict with the patriarch and his family.[82]

Industry, self-denial, benevolence, and an awareness of time were cultivated at the seminary, as were supposedly feminine virtues, such as modesty. The day was regimented with continuous monitoring and by the use of bells to denote the transition of hours.[83] Personal cleanliness was essential.[84] Public shaming was used to maintain discipline and weed out bad habits. In the morning Fiske would ask all the girls in the classroom to stand up and those who had done their duty of combing their hair that morning were permitted to sit, leaving the others standing, "mortified and ashamed, . . . but if one of them tried to sit down, a glance of the eye detected her."[85] On one occasion when Fiske discovered that some pins had been purloined, she calmly interrogated the students as a group and then, after explaining that God sees all deeds, had them get on their knees to pray, whereupon, before letting them rise, she checked their cloth caps.[86] Fiske was assertive and composed: an angry East Syrian woman once challenged her, saying "Why do you thus speak? Do you think I am a heathen, going to hell, with the Mussulmen? I am a Christian." Fiske asked her, "Do you not believe the words of Jesus Christ?" The woman agreed that she did, and "I then repeated to her some texts of Scripture, showing her that not all bearing the Christian name are Christians indeed. She seemed quieted, and listened with attention."[87]

Aside from an academic curriculum, labors thought to be feminine were taught. Instead of working in the field, which was not uncommon for East Syrian women living in agricultural areas, the girls learned what were deemed the more appropriate crafts of knitting and sewing (and in doing so began to compete with the local embroidering industry).[88] Such retraining clearly reflects the missionaries' bourgeois assumptions about women and labor. Singing was also part of the young women's education. Despite the existence of an indigenous tradition of chanting the Psalter, Perkins spent years attempting to inspire an appreciation for American devotional singing among the East Syrians (a perhaps futile effort driven by the excessive zeal of a young missionary, he later lamented).[89]

If the mission and its schools cultivated new forms of social interaction among the East Syrians, this was all the more so at the female seminary, which was founded and guided according to an aggressive evangelical renegotiation of gender roles. Contemporary publications on the mission played up its role in liberating women (e.g., Thomas Laurie's 1863 *Woman and Her Saviour in Persia*), and the "backwardness" of the lives of East Syrian women is a refrain in the sources. It is commonly noted that Helene, the sister of the patriarch, was the only East Syrian woman who could read at the time of the arrival of the missionaries, whereas the marriage age for girls was often as young as twelve and many parents were reluctant to send their daughters to school.[90] However, a wider examination of the long term skews too sharp a contrast between pre- and postmission gender relations in East Syrian history, because

"the developments of the nineteenth century build upon earlier social and religious patterns in East Syriac society, re-interpreting them and adapting them
to the new times, at the same time leaving intact many of the older structures
and ideas."[91] The missionary sources tend to depict East Syrian women as religiously excluded and socially subject, but some East Syrian women acted
as financial patrons of the church, especially through manuscript donations,
some freely chose a life of virginity, and others had facility at reading, some
even at copying manuscripts. The mission encouraged further participation
in religious life while simultaneously changing these young women's relation
to it: "A new type of religious agency became available, an agency that was
based on the combination of considerable biblical knowledge that enabled
individual interpretation, with highly personal conversion trajectories that
encouraged these young women to share these insights with others."[92] The
missionaries were radical in their advocacy for female education, but prior to
their arrival, women enjoyed other forms of devotional agency.

> In many respects, not much changed with the coming of the foreign mission-
> aries, be they Catholic or Protestant: they too operated from patriarchal as-
> sumptions, they too saw the primary tasks of the women in the household,
> and they too saw the ultimate importance of Christianity in securing life after
> death. And while earlier literature may have been inclined to attribute the
> introduction of female agency to western missionaries, this overview suggests
> that missionaries merely enabled a new kind of agency to evolve, an agency
> of the intellect and the emotions rather than of money, rituals and sacred
> objects.[93]

It is correct to erase the stark distinction the missionaries drew between
their liberated view of women and the traditions of the church. However, the
majority of the cases suggest that those spaces for an autonomous religious
life that did exist for East Syrian women before the arrival of the mission
tended to belong to women with elite standing. Furthermore, the missionaries did not introduce simply a new form of agency, but also a Protestant
concern about agency itself. For the devotional acts involving "money, rituals
and sacred objects" were from the missionaries' perspective a form of ritualism, an enthrallment to objects that recused itself from human agency. The
"agency of the intellect and the emotions" was a self-conscious one, and this
was innovative, even if it is ultimately akin to earlier Christian instantiations
of the discourse on free will, which was historically a concern in East Syrian
theology. At the female seminary, young Christian women were compelled to
interact with, and were addressed *as*, young Christian laywomen, regardless

of family, tribe, or village, and were exhorted to lead the ethical life that was incumbent upon them, to succumb to "the moral narrative of modernity" by acting as free agents. This was something new.

Although the American mission participated in what might be called an evangelical feminist discourse, one genealogically related to later feminism, its aims were often not subversive of, but in harmony with, the patriarchal norms of East Syrian society. The missionaries worked according to an ideology of republican motherhood—that is, the notion that women's most important contribution to the nation was through their maternal role.[94] The focus was not on women being more independent but more useful and self-reliant.[95] This located women's position primarily within the family and therefore does not contradict the East Syrian religious system in which women were responsible for domestic piety and, for example, the complex maintenance of East Syrian dietary practices during times of fasts.[96] Although she never had any children herself, by the 1850s Fiske even began the Maternal Association, a group with which she would meet on Fridays "to instruct them in regard to their duties."[97]

Despite its emphasis on liberation, the gender politics of the missionaries worked according to a different logic and norms from what many today would take to be feminism: self-sacrifice being an important Christian virtue, submission to husbands was considered all the more important for a Christian wife, but affection between the couple and a feeling of mutuality and companionship were promoted in a way that altered marriage from the East Syrian tradition.

In this way, the project of helping Syrian women was closely linked to fitting them into what was understood as a more appropriate place in the home, and this was part of the mission's attempt to reform marriage and, from the missionaries' perspective, Christianize the family. Traditional East Syrian weddings were weeklong events with numerous rituals and customs, in contrast to the American Protestant practice, which astounded the East Syrians in its brevity. One commonly repeated anecdote is of Mar Yokhannan asking Perkins if people in America marry on trains, because the ceremony seemed to him so succinct.[98] Concomitant with the slow development of the indigenous church, Protestant marriage was taken up by some East Syrians (for example, we have a Neo-Aramaic *Rules of Marriage* published in 1858, which consists primarily of a Protestant marriage ceremony).[99] Similarly, the missionaries aimed to promote what they thought were more Christian ideas of family. It is repeatedly pointed out that the East Syrians had no word for "home," only *bayta*, which the missionaries were quick to add only meant "house."[100] The mission even published a *Book of the Family; That Is, for Par-*

ents to Teach to Their Children (1864), which consists of a basic catechism for children in a question-and-answer format.[101]

The effectiveness of missionary discourse on the household is unclear, although there were instances of some East Syrians expressing a new desire to maintain "Christian" homes. The most powerful example of the success of reformed marriage and the new relations advocated for wives and husbands is the several native assistant couples well attested in the sources, such as Sanam and Joseph, whom I will address in chapter 5; or Moressa (d. 1892) and Jacob Yauvre (Yore) (1827–97), who married in 1850 after the two had completed their studies at the female and male seminaries, respectively. The latter couple worked for the mission for over forty years, Jacob, who was well versed in Classical Syriac, contributing to *Rays of Light* into his old age.[102]

Female education was one of the more radical parts of the missionary project, but also one of the parts of that project that received the most fanfare, just as the liberation of Middle Eastern women continues to be an obsession in the Euro-American relationship to the region. Missions elsewhere in the Middle East in the nineteenth century had a similar emphasis.[103] We are told that at a public examination at the girls school in Geogtapa, with over six hundred people in attendance, many parents joyously exclaimed, "Our daughters can learn as well as our sons."[104] The seminary, which was later renamed the Fiske Seminary, continued to play an important role at the mission through the end of the nineteenth century and was only finally closed down in 1933, years after the rest of the mission had ceased.

Village and Sabbath Schools

The village schools, or "free schools" as they were also called, were local institutions administered by native assistants. William R. Stocking and his wife, Jerusha, were responsible for the village schools from their arrival in 1837 until they left in 1853. As superintendent, he would regularly travel from village to village and preach at each, as would other members of the mission, including Perkins, who always maintained a paternal eye on administration. The school at Geogtapa was run by Murad Khan (d. 1897), an early assistant to the mission, whereas the one at Ardishai was in the house of Bishop Gabriel.[105] Some village schools were established in imitation of the mission schools and were only then incorporated into the mission's system, which is an example of the mission's co-option of indigenous initiative.[106] Schools were usually self-supporting but received material aid, such as books, from the mission, and on occasion ad hoc aid, such as clothing for poor students.[107]

Some schools were more developed than others, particularly those of larger towns, such as Geogtapa, where there were male and female schools and the curriculum included "ancient and modern Syriac, geography, arithmetic, biblical history, natural history, some portions of ecclesiastical and secular history, reading and spelling."[108] The curriculum at most schools, however, was primarily Bible study, including the memorization of various passages of Scripture.

> Many of the more advanced pupils have committed to memory about a thousand proof texts on the various doctrines and duties of the Christian religion; and received in return a New Testament, which is highly prized. All are also required to be able to repeat the Ten Commandments, and Watt's shorter and longer catechisms, together with three series of Scripture questions, recently translated and printed, relating to the principal facts of the Old and New Testament history.[109]

The pupils gathered on Sundays at Sabbath school to recite what they had learned.

> On the Sabbath they all meet together in the capacity of Sabbath schools, and recite to their teachers those portions of the Bible which they have learned; on these occasions their friends are invited to be present. The last Sabbath I met, in the church at Geog Tapa, one hundred and forty-five children and youth, connected with the village schools in that place, and was much gratified with the correctness and promptitude with which they answered the Scripture questions, as also with the quiet and serious behavior of the whole youth assembly.[110]

Of course, the success of this practice, especially in the smaller or more distant villages, is difficult to confirm. The purpose of the village schools, more so than that of the male seminary, was to help raise up young men who could preach the Gospel on the local level, and their teachers were often evangelists trained at the male seminary. This was the Lancaster system writ large: teachers from the male seminary taught their peers in the villages.

Aside from the content of study, the schools' emphasis was also on the teaching of discipline itself. For example, in a letter dated May 7, 1866, George W. Coan (mission: 1849–74) describes a visit at a school in Geogtapa, which had over one hundred students of mixed sex.[111]

> Ten rules were imposed upon the scholars, among which were these,—that there should be no communication of any kind in school hours without permission; no loud study; no touching of the stove or paper windows; no chewing of gum or eating of raisins, etc. The children, as well as grown people, here, wear their hats in the house, but take off their shoes. Another rule was, that

the shoes should be arranged in perfect order, and always in place. The pupils were required also not to touch anything not belonging to them without the permission of the owner. They reported regularly every Saturday, in the presence of the visiting committee, which consisted of the parents invited to take turns in being present.

Thus, learning and discipline similar to what existed at the male and female seminaries was fostered in the village schools on a wider scale, and much of this was in turn further inculcated in the village Sabbath schools, many of which continued until World War I.[112] At these weekly schools, men and women, young and old, could attain basic biblical literacy as well as a foundation in moral living, while they were expected to submit to disciplinary rules similar to those used in the seminaries.[113]

Public Examinations and the Display of Education's Benefits

The male and eventually the female seminaries, as well as some village schools, held large public examinations at which students' knowledge was tested. Those who were successful enough in their studies received prizes, such as their own copies of the New Testament. Family and friends gathered at these celebratory events, where they heard speeches given by missionaries, native assistants, and students on moral reform and the values of education.

The female seminary had an end-of-year ceremony as early as 1845, to which parents were invited and after which many of the girls received copies of the New Testament, which they paid for with their earnings from extra needlework, as well as a copy of *The Dairyman's Daughter*, a book I discuss in chapter 5.[114] The female seminary had its first official public examinations in 1850.

At the close of the term, their parents and friends, with some of the leading Nestorians, were invited to the examinations. More than one hundred and sixty spectators, besides the pupils, were crowded into the large recitation room. This had been adorned with a profusion of roses, from the vineyard of Mar Yo[k]hannan, arranged in wreaths and bouquets, with festoons of sycamore leaves, and other devices. The people were delighted,—for, like other Persians, they are great admirers of flowers,—and many, on entering, involuntarily exclaimed, "Paradise! Paradise!"[115]

Fiske herself writes of the event:

The pupils were examined in ancient and modern Syriac, Bible history, geography, and natural philosophy. They sang two pieces which they had practiced for the occasion, and joined in several hymns, with the whole congregation.

More than twenty of the girls had prepared compositions to be read; but the day was too short for all.[116]

Exercises ran from 9:00 a.m. to noon. After this there was a large lunch.

> The exercises were pleasantly diversified by a plentiful collation under the arbor in the court behind the Seminary, where lambs roasted whole, in the native style, lettuce, cherries, pilav (a preparation of rice), and some cake, prepared by the pupils, were duly discussed. Many of the women had never before sat at the same table with men, and it was amusing to witness their awkward embarrassment. Some snatched the food from the table by stealth, and ate it behind their large veils, as though it were a thing forbidden.[117]

The sexes intermingled at such events, and thus the missionaries "disrupted traditional habits of collective life by promoting new kinds of social interchange between men and women."[118] At 2:00 p.m. the crowd returned to the schoolroom, which had been enlarged for the occasion. Examinations continued until 6:00 p.m., at which time Perkins gave a speech, the Neo-Aramaic original of which was later printed in a special July 1850 issue of *Rays of Light* dedicated to this event. In his speech, which addresses the assembled family and friends of the girls who studied at the school, Perkins defends female education and then suggests that the composition to follow, which was also given as a speech at the event, will demonstrate that women are able to write. What follows, a speech on solitude entitled "The Lost Soul," is a composition by Sanam, the daughter of the native assistant Priest Dunkha. I address the content of this speech in chapter 5, but here I would like to note one of the ironies of the mission's overall message: a young woman was giving a speech on solitude at a gathering of almost two hundred people. After the speeches Sanam, Sarah, and Moressa, young students at the female seminary, all received special diplomas. We are told that Hormizd, the aged and now blind supporter of the mission who had traveled from Geogtapa for the event, announced toward the end of the ceremonies that he wished that Joshua were there to stop the sun and lengthen such a fine day (Jo 10:13). Certain elders, taking Fidelia Fiske and her assistant Mary Susan Rice (mission: 1847–69) by the hand, apologized that they had not supported the school more, whereas numerous women from the nearby villages, inspired by the event, begged for copies of the mission's introductory spelling book.

Examination day at the female seminary in 1851 was no less grand an event than that of the previous year.

> At noon, on the second day, four hundred and fifty persons, including all the bishops, most of the prominent men of the plain of Oroomiah, and about one hundred and fifty Nestorian mothers, sat down to a simple repast, which had

been provided in the mission yard. In the afternoon addresses were made by different members of the mission and several of the bishops, on topics suited to the occasion; and then all dispersed to their homes, feeling deeply, and speaking earnestly of the advantages conferred on their people by this seminary, the only one of the kind in the whole kingdom of Persia.[119]

Sanam again gave a valedictory speech, which begins by pointing out that separation has been a part of creation since the time when the "fallen and unhappy couple" left the Garden of Eden; however, because the sword that blocked the return to Eden (Gn 3:24) was removed by the blood of Christ—a theme common in the Syriac tradition—we can at least, despite the bitterness of earthly departures, look forward to a sweet heavenly meeting again in time to come.[120] The speech as a whole consists of a series of expressions of gratitude addressed to the various members of the community, only some of whom were in attendance: living and deceased missionaries, the female leaders of the school, native teachers, priests, deacons, leaders of the "people" (*tayepa*), and parents. Finally, she addresses her fellow students from whom she will depart and thus returns to the topic raised at the beginning of the speech. The global perspective in which she understands the location and workings of the school are revealed when she addresses the absence of such institutions elsewhere.

> If on the wings of an eagle we should fly to the extreme north, we should find no such school as this, crowned with blessings, but should see our sisters groaning in bitterness, saying, "Not one ray from the divine sun rises on us in our misery." If we turn to the south, there we see the daughters of Arabia lamenting, "In all this desert, not one oasis yields the waters of life to quench our burning thirst." Eternity alone will suffice to praise Him who sent you, the only heralds of his grace, to us sinners. But our southern journey is not finished. From one end of Africa to the other our sisters lie wrapped in the shadows of death; and if we turn to the east, all the way to China, the daughters cry, "Wretched is our unhappy lot: no cloud of mercy, such as surrounds you, lights up the place of our abode." So on the west, as far as Constantinople, our companions in suffering have no school to sound in their ears the blessed name of Jesus. What are we, that the Lord should choose us from the midst of such darkness, and send you to us with the message of life? Let all nations, with wondering lips, praise the Almighty for his grace to us, so worthless.[121]

Sanam sets the school into a cosmic frame, sketching for the assembled audience a frozen image of the world at large, as if they could fly above it and see its various regions all at once. This capacity to imagine the world from above reflects the common use of maps and globes in missionary preaching and like the world exhibitions of the late nineteenth century demonstrates "the world conceived and grasped as though it were an exhibition."[122]

Public examinations were large social gatherings at which students demonstrated their learning and the audience was informed of the benefits the mission offered. Similar events occurred at the village schools, especially the larger ones such as at Geogtapa.[123] These events consisted of performance, competition, new types of interaction between the sexes, and the exaltation of evangelical virtues, while mission institutions were praised as worthy of future support. In the context of this new public conviviality, Christians celebrated themselves as Christians, moral exhortation demanded a new Christian way of life, the missionaries performed their roles as the paternal and maternal custodians of the Gospel, and members of the group were encouraged to interact and understand themselves as a nation.

The Concert of Prayer

> Dear sisters, we love the monthly concert day very much. Three hours on that day we meet together, and pray that God's kingdom may come in our midst, and among all the nations of the earth.
>
> —extract from an 1846 letter written by pupils at the female
> seminary to their benefactors in Massachusetts[124]

One of the most significant ritual gatherings at the American mission was the so-called concert of prayer, which was a public assembly on a designated day to pray for the conversion of the world. Ideally, this gathering would occur at the same time all over the world so that people could simultaneously and globally entreat God for the same favor. The concert, which was practiced both in the United States and at missions around the world, depended on the idea of "disinterested benevolence" of Samuel Hopkins (1721–1803), and its origins correspond with the rise of missions: if not all Christians could embark on mission, they could at least engage in mission prayer at home. Concerts also served as opportunities for fund-raising for foreign missions.

Just as the ritual of reading the daily newspaper, according to Benedict Anderson, helped to create a sense of empty homogenous time in which the nation could be imagined, the concert of prayer, in creating a sense of simultaneous action across the globe, may have had similar effects.[125] The focus of prayer was not that each and every individual in the world would convert to Christianity. Rather, the constituent units the East Syrians were asked to pray for were "nations," and they themselves were asked to do this as a "nation." Thus, the concert of prayer helped to cultivate a sense of national unity and the diversity of nations, thereby making it a ritual performance of a Christian theology of nations. From an experiential perspective, the concert linked

the visceral presence of the group to the abstract community of Christians—
and human beings more broadly—around the world, thus combining the socially real and transcendent. This resembles the connection made between
the local and the global in Sanam's 1851 valedictory speech, discussed above.
Furthermore, it is not unlike the kind of imagined community in which many
Christians had always understood themselves as participating—that is, the
"church" in the abstract or the "City of God." However, in this case the purpose of the gathering itself was to consider this broader community of human
beings and to pray for its simultaneous transformation.

The tract *The Conversion of the World; or, the Claims of Six Hundred Millions, and the Ability and Duty of the Churches Respecting Them* (1818) provides an argument for this increased interest in world mission. Its authors,
Samuel Newell (1784–1821) and Gordon Hall (1784–1826), members of the
first generation of American missionaries, both died from disease while on
mission in Bombay. One of the primary concerns in this tract is that Christianity's truth will appear to be in doubt so long as it is not spread around the
world, because although the Christian message is universal, Christians do not
do their best to disseminate it.[126] The Gospel does not rule the world, the tract
explains, because it has not been preached sufficiently. This failure to step
up to the challenge makes Christianity look hypocritical: "Until Christians
undertake in good earnest to evangelize the world, their creeds and their conduct will be contradictory, sinners will be quick to see it, and when they see
it, they will be hardened in unbelief."[127] Newell and Hall articulate a contradiction that was made apparent by the modern rationalization of the Gospel:
Christianity's universal message had to come to terms with Americans' growing awareness of the world.

*The Monthly Concert; with Facts and Reflections Suited to Awaken a Zeal
for the Conversion of the World* (1836) by Harvey Newcomb (1803–63), a Congregationalist minister and writer on missions, lays out the ideology and practice of the concert of prayer. Included in *The Monthly Concert* is a foldout map
of the world, upon which the degrees of global Christianization of the world
are marked in a color-coded system.[128] The book, which is a guide for putting
on monthly concerts, begins:

> The observance of the Monthly Concert of Prayer for the Conversion of the
> World is one of the most interesting features of the age. "If two of you shall
> *agree* on earth as touching any thing that they shall ask, it shall be done for
> them of my Father which is in heaven."—Mat. 18:19. In compliance with the
> condition of this promise, Christians, in the four quarters of the globe, meet
> on the first Monday of every month, (having agreed together as to the object of
> their petition,) to pray for the blessing of God upon the efforts of the church,

NO. 138.

THE
CONVERSION OF THE WORLD,
OR THE
CLAIMS OF
SIX HUNDRED MILLIONS,
AND THE
ABILITY AND DUTY OF THE CHURCHES
RESPECTING THEM.

PUBLISHED BY THE

AMERICAN TRACT SOCIETY,

AND SOLD AT THEIR DEPOSITORY, NO. 144 NASSAU-STREET, NEAR
THE CITY-HALL, NEW-YORK; AND BY AGENTS OF THE
SOCIETY, ITS BRANCHES, AND AUXILIARIES, IN
THE PRINCIPAL CITIES AND TOWNS
IN THE UNITED STATES.

Vol. 5.

G

FIGURE 8. *The Conversion of the World.* (American Tract Society.)

for the salvation of the world. This is a public and united acknowledgement that the vast system of benevolent operations of the present age is, of itself, perfectly impotent. It is looking to the Almighty Arm, which only is able to accomplish this great work. And it is a remarkable fact, that Christians feel a sense of dependence upon the Spirit of God, for success, just in proportion to their active efforts for the salvation of souls. A spirit of prayer, and a spirit of activity, accompany each other.[129]

Regarding the simultaneity of prayer, Newcomb later exclaims: "How touching the reflection, that at the same moment the Christian world, in Europe, Asia, Africa, and the isles of the sea, are bowed before the throne of grace, to plead for the special accomplishment of the promises relating to the universal reign of the Messiah."[130] What we see here is a kind of Christian imperialism *avant la lettre*. The same spirit of "expansive benevolence" that brought Christ to this world sends missions out to the heathens.

Newcomb describes preparation for the concert as requiring the labor not just of the minister but of the whole congregation. The requirements include right intention on the part of the participants, their regular attendance, acquainting themselves with the condition of the heathens and what efforts are aimed at their conversion (in part through reading travel memoirs), daily meditation on this condition and that of their mission, and a special daily prayer for them. The minister should offer a sermon on the Sabbath before the concert, which should take place on a Monday. To keep the ceremony interesting, the focus should be prayer, which is to be "simple, fervent, short."[131] The second chapter is on "Entire Consecration," which is "to lay ourselves out for doing *all we can to establish the reign of Christ upon earth*."[132] In a description of the absurdities and ignorance of heathenism, Newcomb describes the "horrid solemnities of Juggernaut," which is a European myth, going back to the late Middle Ages, holding that at a holy place in India fanatics cast themselves beneath the wheels of massive chariots in a sacred procession, a misunderstanding of practices in honor of Krishna at the Jagganath Temple at Puri in India.[133] Newcomb goes on to describe each of the "Miseries of the Heathen," which include their despotic governments, cruel religious customs, lack of "natural affection," barbaric wars, unrestrained indulgence of passions, and the degradations suffered by their women. Like Newell and Hall, Newcomb finally turns to statistics: he demonstrates the number of heathens in the world, summing things up when he points out that thirty-eight heathens perish "every minute!!!!!"[134] After asking "Can 30,000 missionaries be furnished?" he addresses the amount of money needed and what each American should give to the cause.[135] He then speculates how much it would cost to supply every family in the world with a Bible.[136] In the end he returns to the issue of the concert and how every New Year a concert should take place on the first Monday of January.[137]

Newcomb's book articulates the ideas behind the monthly and yearly concerts of prayer held at the mission in Urmia, and this is especially useful because the practice is often taken for granted in the mission sources. He explicitly links the concert to the project of foreign missions, and its use of numbers and statistics corresponds with the modern business accounting of the ABCFM. The map of the world and the expansionist rhetoric of the text are a synthesis of a Christian universalism as old as Matthew 28:19–20 ("Go ye therefore, and teach all nations") and the political and economic expansion of the nineteenth century. The whole world had become a potential field for mission, and its constituent parts were nations.

Concerts were held at the American mission every month from the early 1840s onward. The most important of these was the New Year's concert, which was usually held on the first Monday of January every year. This was a special concert because it began the year and therefore provided fodder for the missionaries' practice of fostering a greater awareness of the passage of calendrical time. Such an awareness was supposed to induce thoughts about mortality and in turn an increased sense of a need for salvation. In fact, the first full-fledged revival occurred at the mission not long after the New Year's concert of 1846.[138] Thomas Laurie notes, "Most of the revivals in Oroomiah commenced on the day of the monthly concert of prayer, and several on or immediately after the first Monday in January—a day specially set apart to prayer for missions."[139] Concerts were held in both Urmia and Geogtapa, at the retreat in Sire, and also in some villages, and eventually the New Year's concert became the "Week of Prayer."

Yonan of 'Ada composed an account of several monthly concerts that took place in Geogtapa in 1851 and 1852. At these concerts collections were first taken up for foreign missions. "One Sabbath last year [i.e., 1851] Mr. [Joseph G.] Cochran came to our village, and brought a missionary map, and talked about the state of different nations, and told us it was our duty, not only to pray for them, but to give them the words of God."[140] Money was not sought at first, and Yonan expresses the anxiety he and others associated with the mission felt about seeking cash gifts from the townspeople, who were poor. Later Perkins sent John, son of Hormizd, from Sire to take up a collection on the first Monday of the year, and a small amount was collected.

In Geogtapa concerts were held on Sabbath evenings (Sunday night) because on Mondays "the people are scattered for their business."[141] At the February 1852 concert, Yonan himself preached.

More people than usual assembled; and the church was so full that some stood up. I first pointed out the countries on the map, and spoke about Greenland, its inhabitants, and the work of God there; then about Africa, and its poor people; and the missionaries there; afterwards about the Sandwich Islands, their former state, their present change of condition, and how the people there give for the spread of the gospel.

The Sandwich Islands—that is, Hawaii—and the successful mission there was a popular topic at the mission, and there are several articles in *Rays of Light* describing this mission, including a long one translated by Yonan himself.[142] After Yonan preached, Bibles were distributed and the biblical basis of giving for foreign missions was demonstrated. The poor have always given for such causes, it was argued, just as the "poor widows in America, who were giving them preachers, books, and instruction for their children." For not only spiritual but also temporal blessings are promised to those who give. After the assistants John and Moses preached, the elders, such as Mar Elias, the bishop of the city, and Malik Agha Bey, its chief, were asked to profess their support for the effort.[143] According to Yonan, the event was a great success, with people exclaiming aloud their readiness to help. Over two hundred people had gathered to hear the preaching, engage in several group prayers, and then sing a Neo-Aramaic rendering of the "Missionary Hymn" of Reginald Heber (1783–1826), the Church of England's bishop of Calcutta:

> From Greenland's icy mountains,
> From India's coral strand,
> Where Afric's sunny fountains
> Roll down their golden sand;
> From many an ancient river,
> From many a palmy plain,
> They call us to deliver
> Their land from error's chain.
> . . . .
> Shall we whose souls are lighted
> With wisdom from on high;
> Shall we to man benighted
> The lamp of life deny?

The people enthusiastically made donations, some handing over small amounts of money, others cotton, which would later be sold. Although most "had not yet learned to lay by in store for the first of the month," some had saved for the event by working on traditional saints' days: "We have several days in the year in which, if we labor, we are blamed by our ignorant people, because they consider them saints' days. This month several had worked on these days, and got money for the concert. When asked by the ignorant in regard to it, they replied, 'It is better to labor for the spread of the gospel, than to be idle for Satan.'"[144] Thus, East Syrians were encouraged to profane sacred days and save up the proceeds of the extra labor done on those days. The need to proselytize the world was a lesson in bourgeois austerity.

The following month, March 1852, Stoddard came to Geogtapa to preach to a Sabbath crowd of over five hundred people (not including the children present). Many had to remain outside the church because of the size of the audience.

> Mr. Stoddard took India for his subject, because the people had expressed a desire to send their money there. He told us about the country, its size, its climate, and great population. He also told us of their cruel religion; how the people cut their bodies, and fill their mouths with mud; and many other such things. He gave us the number of their gods, and brought with him a picture of Juggernaut. And we understood from him how many roll hundreds of miles to perform a pilgrimage to it, often dying on the way. He also brought with him two idols, one from China and one from India. He took them in his hands, and spoke as if the idols themselves were speaking in this manner: "O Sons of Geog Tapa! Ye Nestorians! We are the gods of the people of China and India. They worship us. Do something for them, that they may turn from us. Help them. Let your hearts burn for them." We were thankful that day that our people could stand in Elijah's place, and laugh at idols.

After Stoddard, Mar Elias stood up to speak. He described the idolatry of antiquity and the prophets' endeavor to prevent the Israelites from such worship, concluding, "So we must labor for people worshipping vanity." Later that evening there was a smaller gathering for the concert. The church was still not large enough, and so they moved to Mar Elias's home. In taking up the collection, someone confronted Yonan, telling him that it was a shame for him to carry around a collection box. To these claims that perhaps suggested a similarity between his actions and those of the "Thieves of the Cross," the questionable holy beggars of Jilu, he responded, "I am not begging for myself; I am begging for Christ." That evening they received money, as well as eggs and yarn, which were soon sold.

The use of the Juggernaut in Stoddard's speech was a homiletical commonplace. Articles and references to India in *Rays of Light* suggest that India represented in mission preaching the extreme of benighted heathenism and idolatry. The Juggernaut appears in mission publications as a standard example of the inhumanity, even cruelty, of idolatry, as we saw in Newcomb's book.[145] It was representative because it combined the worship of a false God and the human subjection to objects even to the point of death, thus bringing together the missionaries' theological and epistemological concerns about fetishism. Stoddard employed the idols in his speech as a form of object lesson and simultaneously, through his personification of them, mocked the power idolaters supposedly attributed to them.[146]

The link between the concert and charitable giving for foreign missions is further demonstrated by the concerts held in Geogtapa and Urmia in April 1861. At Geogtapa on a Sunday afternoon, John "called for a volunteer laborer for the mountains, and appealed to the people for his support."[147] An audience member rose up to pledge support and this proved "infectious," with people one after another jumping up to make their pledges, "and soon the whole congregation was in a blaze of enthusiasm." The following day at Urmia the speakers told the audience what liberality they had seen the day before at Geogtapa. A great response ensued, with people giving "money, portions of their vineyards or their produce, or ornaments." Someone gave a small inheritance he had recently received. One man even gave the money he had been saving for a gravestone for his wife. Perhaps aware of the long-standing popularity of bridal imagery in the Syriac tradition, George Coan cunningly used in his preaching at the event the figure of the "bride" to describe the church, that people might contribute "for her 'shoes,' 'veil,' 'dress,' etc., until the 'church' . . . had a very comfortable outfit." In a letter dated May 10, 1861, Joseph P. Cochran describes how the giving increased at the following month's concert, and how at the concert at Sire, despite the debts due to the previous year's famine, $120 was pledged through subscription made with the pencils and paper that were at hand. "'A new source of delight,' they say, 'is this of giving, and one we have been strangers to till now.'"[148] This support for mountain missions by concert funds is attested as early as 1848: Deacon George, the so-called mountain evangelist, received support from the monthly concert contributions from Sire.[149]

A new, special weeklong concert of prayer after the New Year, the so-called week of prayer, which included fasting, was instituted in January 1861 and practiced in small and large towns alike, and even farther west in Gawar.[150] For the 1863 week of prayer, Perkins translated the list of topics of prayer for each day from a circular published by the Evangelical Alliance in London and published it in *Rays of Light* the preceding December. He writes, "A cloud of the precious incense of united prayer went up, during that week of privilege, from this beautiful Persian plain and the old Assyrian mountains, to call down blessings on these dark regions and on our perishing world. The idea of a *union in prayer* is peculiarly interesting to the pious Nestorians."[151] This focus on union is apparent in Samuel Rhea's description of the week of prayer in the quotation used above for one of the epigraphs of this chapter.

The week of prayer, like the concerts of prayer, had a global focus.[152] On Sunday, January 1, 1871, the first week after the mission was officially taken over by the Presbyterian Church, it began with an emphasis on the Gospels themselves as a basis of Christian faith. On Monday there was then a focus on gratitude and a renewal of commitment "and self-humbling for the globalization [*dunyayuta*] of the church, and for the sinners of the nations [*melate*] who have been awakened [*mar'uše*] to the judgments of God." Tuesday then consisted of "prayer for the nations, for kings, for all the people of the government, for soldiers and sailors, for all who have endured loss or suffering during this war [the Franco-Prussian War, 1870–71], and for the blessings of peace." The next day's prayer was for Christian children, for their households and teachers, for the children's "self commitment to God in their childhood and for the many works in the service of Christ." On Thursday prayer was for the baptism of the Holy Spirit to come upon those who "believe and call themselves Christians, and for a fellowship possessing love and a unity [*ḥdanayuta*] among all in every land that they might love our Lord Jesus loyally." The prayer on Friday was "for the dissemination of the word of God, for increase in faithful ambassadors for Christ, for the end of persecution on account of religion [*mazhab*], and for the removal of all hindrances from before the spread of the Gospel." On Saturday prayer was "for the Christian missionaries, and for the renewal of the Jews, and for keeping watch for the better day of our Lord, for a blessing upon Christian teachings, and the glorious arrival of our Lord Jesus Christ." Finally on Sunday, the last day, there was a renewed focus on the Gospels with an emphasis on faith, hope, and love. This same routine was repeated the following year, in 1872, and concerts would continue to play a role at the now Presbyterian mission through the end of the nineteenth century.[153]

Assistants' Meetings and the Formation of a Separate Church

The original intention of the American missionaries was to reform the Church of the East. They did not plan to create a separate Protestant church, which they eventually did but not without some controversy among the missionaries themselves.[154] A separate communion only began to take shape at the congregational level when some East Syrians were given permission to take part in American worship: the missionaries celebrated communion with East Syrians associated with the mission as early as September 1854.[155] By 1857 up to 200 East Syrians had joined in communion with the missionaries, each after close spiritual inspection.[156] At the end of 1862 there were 476 people in the communion.[157] There were usually special ceremonies for the induction of new members, and the mission kept an account of all who had been admitted.[158]

Parallel to this participation in the American communion, and yet more important for the creation of a formally distinct ecclesiastical structure, was the development of a network of assistants. By the late 1840s native assistants began to hold occasional meetings, which were both practical and ritual: they addressed the difficulties of spreading the Gospel and offered collective prayers for success. By 1850 the teachers of the village schools on the plain began to meet on the first Monday of each month, often the same day as the concert of prayer.[159] Regular meetings of native assistants began after an ad hoc two-day meeting of alumni of the male seminary following the monthly concert in November 1859.[160] All the living graduates of the male seminary, those who had completed its full course, were in attendance. Of the sixty-two present, fifty-six were in communion with the Americans, forty were preachers in their respective villages, and fifteen were part-time teachers and preachers.

> All personalities and unpleasant reminiscences, so far as there might have been any, were carefully avoided; and with all the ardor of youthful feeling and oriental temperament, the young men gave themselves up to the enjoyment of this intellectual and fraternal festival. Addresses on subjects assigned were committed, and pronounced with animation and propriety; and several topics for voluntary discussion and remark were taken up with promptness, and discussed with a courtesy and dignity of manner far exceeding our expectations.[161]

At the event, speeches were given on "pastoral labors and responsibility," especially the difficulties involved and possible ways to make such work easier. Pastor John of Geogtapa gave a speech on "his sad experience in attempting to carry on matters of trade in connection with pastoral and revival labors." There was a sermon on Romans 14:7 ("For none of us lives to himself alone and none of us dies to himself alone"), as well as "personal narratives and reports," not only on the assistants' work in evangelism but on their "personal piety and experience, their domestic relations, family devotions and the like." Some wept at reference to the name of the late David Stoddard, who had died on January 22, 1857. "The afternoon of the second day was devoted to the examination and ordination of six of the young men, as evangelists and pastors of their respective flocks."[162]

By the early 1860s an annual meeting of the mountain assistants was held at the mission station in Gawar, on the edge of Hakkari. Such meetings of assistants would continue through the 1860s, and Deacon Tamo, whom I address in more detail in chapter 6, played an important role at them.[163] At the 1862 meeting, attended by assistants from the various mountain districts from May 30 to June 2, several lectures were given on the assorted hindrances to, and needs of, the mission to the mountains. Each day began with devotional services, and the three days were concluded that Sunday night with a concert of prayer at which numerous offerings in support of mission work were made, including money amounting to fifty-two dollars as well as "a mare, an ox, a sheep, a goat, grain, jewelry, headdresses, etc."[164] The participants at the meeting came to the following conclusions: "1. We regard the duty of giving to support the gospel as binding as any other Christian duty. 2. We will hold regular monthly concerts for prayer and communicating missionary intelligence, and at such times the contribution box shall be circulated. 3. We will take up an annual collection in our congregations. 4. The proceeds of our contributions we will apply to the support of a mountain helper."[165] The assistants in the mountains were especially interested in forming a separate church because of the opposition they regularly met from within their own. Living in Ottoman territory, they thought that "the time had come for the evangelical portion to avail themselves of the protection granted them by the Sultan, and declare themselves a body distinct and separate from that old man of corruption with which they have long kept up a nominal alliance."[166] The sultan had recognized Armenian Protestants as a separate *millet*, or sanctioned religious community, by 1850. The group thus called for an application to be made to the Sublime Porte to be part of this recognized community, another example of how the meaning of the cognate Neo-Aramaic term *melat*, which I commonly gloss as "nation," was still in flux at this time: Syrians could be part of the "nation" (*melat*) of the Armenians.

The annual meeting of native assistants in October 1862 took important steps toward the development of a separate evangelical church. Already by this time the mission had begun to promote evangelism "societies" (*dastate*), each of which was a separate "assembly" (*jama'at*) with a pastor, directors, its own finances, and designated meeting times.[167] At the 1862 event, as was usual, missionaries and native assistants gave a series of speeches. The topics included the mission of the "Reformed Nestorian Church," the advantages of a *sunhados* (synod) or general council, and the adoption of a creed and church directory.[168] The use of the term *sunhados* was strategic: cognate with the English *synod*, it had a Classical Syriac pedigree going back to the church councils of the fourth and fifth centuries (as the word used for "presbytery," *knušya*, lit. "gathering," also had a history of prior usage). Deacon Isaac, the brother of the late patriarch, spoke on "national unity." It is likely that the article entitled "Unity" (*ḥdanayta*), in *Rays of Light* from the same month, is a printed version of this speech. It begins:

> Inasmuch as one nation [*melat*] is divided into various parts against one another and everyone works for his own advantage against the advantage of the collective [*jam'*] of the nation it is not possible for the affairs of the nation to be healthy. The nation is a body possessing many limbs, and as in a natural body every limb does its own business and helps the other limbs, and the body lives in good health, so a nation when all of its limbs are yoked in love lives a healthy life and grows and arrives at a state [*ahwal*] of prosperity. But how is a nation able to become one? Secular people [lit. "people of the world"] are not able to associate with one another [lit. "yoke themselves together"]: everyone loves himself and his own advantage, and he is content if a nation is lost provided his own business makes progress. It is necessary that true unity come about from the church, built upon sound doctrine, and it is rooted in love of Christ. Love of a savior who bought us by his blood binds [*aser*] hearts with bonds [*yesure*] stronger than fleshly kinship and worldly profits.[169]

The article then describes the church as the "center," the "magnet," and the "heart, beating, warm, and making the blood go to all the limbs." The author states that the community must put away its differences and work for "our nation" (*melatan*) and ends with what is clearly a translation of a common English expression: "United [lit. "yoked together"] we stand and divided we fall." According to the author, the "love of a savior" trumps family ("fleshly kinship") and wealth ("worldly profits") as a glue for social cohesion: intimacy with Christ creates social intimacy. In this text, composed at a formative moment in the history of the Syrian Evangelical Church, we witness a step in the process whereby the social was disembedded and named the nation. Within the prior tradition, a "body" and "limbs" referred to the church, the body of Christ. However, in this text the church is rendered only as a "heart," an essential part of the body but not the body itself. That role has been taken up by the nation.

The *melat*, or "nation," in this text does not refer to all Syriac Christians. Only in the twentieth century would notions of the nation be so broad as to embrace all Christians of the Syriac heritage. Rather, the "nation" here consists of all East Syrians, whether they be Old Church, Chaldean, Protestant, or the soon to develop Orthodox community. Therefore, a call for national unity in this case reflects an ecclesial base threatened by missionary divisions. This explains why the issue of national unity came to the fore specifically in discussions leading to the formation of a separate church and how such a unity was imagined as based upon the love of Christ. This author's response is a Protestant one: ecclesial identity is predicated upon love of Christ, which allows for a unity of the nation in one church. It is not a coincidence that it was at this time, the early 1860s, that the missionaries first expressed anxiety about the Russian Orthodox overtures to the East Syrians, an issue that would become acute by the end of the century.[170]

By the conclusion of the October 1862 meeting, a general synod (*sunhados*) had been formed.[171] Originally there was a plan to create a civil head of the community, and the British consul K. E. Abbott was even consulted regarding this. It was thought at the time that the community would eventually submit itself to this civil authority. The issue was deferred—each of the major missions had such civil authorities by the early twentieth century—and in the meantime a synod of twelve was formed, which was elected annually. This synod "adopted a complete confession, covenant and church directory, which is to be printed and circulated, and the signatures of all bishops and deacons in our communion, is to be obtained to it."[172] This volume was printed soon after as the *Book of Faith and Rules* (*Ktawa d-todita w-qanone*) (1862).[173] At the same time, it was determined that regional associations would meet quarterly or semiannually, especially for the plains of Urmia and Salmas, where the majority of the Reformed population lived.

The details pertaining to the formation of an autonomous church were further ironed out in February 1863.[174] At this next meeting the confession of faith and church directory, which were adopted at the fall meeting and had since been printed, were distributed as a manual for formal adoption. To this manual was added a number of the "resolutions" of Jonathan Edwards, which are published devotional demands that he put upon himself as a Christian, and a translation of the *Westminster Shorter Catechism*, the seventeenth-century document that summed up the Christian faith for many Protestants. Even despite these developments, the missionaries still considered themselves "as laboring in the old church, and in the hope of its rejuvenation."[175] The separate church would not officially come into being until 1871, the year at which the purview of this chapter ends, but by this time a notion of religion as a cognitive, faith-based commitment to a certain catechism and national identity as something embodied and irreducible and yet based upon a common ground in Christ had emerged.

Time as the Space of Sociality

In the prior chapter I addressed the "spatialization" of time in mission publications. There was concurrent with this what me might call the "temporalization" of space: for the social practices introduced at the mission required a disciplining of time through ritual. Not only did all of the formal social occasions discussed in this chapter occur at specific times, whether on specific days or at specific times of the day, but these events were often also in some way *about* time itself. Public examinations took place at the end of the school year, which consisted of a set of courses, as opposed to an informal curriculum containing a set of ideas to master. The concert of prayer was predicated upon a notion of simultaneous temporality: ideally, the world prayed all at once. Furthermore, the mission introduced the celebration of anniversaries, including birthdays, a practice that is different from the calendrical repetition of the East Syrian holy calendar, which included various irregular holy days.[176] The former are specifically about the passage of time, whereas past events in the latter are celebrated in a manner that invokes the saving power of Christ or of a saint as especially manifest on that particular day. Moreover, as was discussed in the previous chapter, the mission encouraged a respect for the Sabbath, which created a strict division of each week. The day of rest was for devotion and gathering in the church, and was thus an inversion of what was supposed to be the workaday week.

Modern time consciousness came about with emergent industrial capitalism, but simultaneously the rise of capitalist time discipline was accompanied by the Protestant ethic, which implanted in every Christian his or her "own interior moral time-piece."[177] Despite the bourgeois nature of their ideas of time (and money), the American missionaries' intention was not to create settings and events that would inculcate modern temporality or capitalist discipline. Rather, they were cultivating their own vernacular of Christianity. For example, although homogeneous, empty time was implicit in the temporality of the New Year's week of prayer, focusing on the passage of time and the turning of the New Year was an American evangelical tool to evoke thoughts of time and death. One publication of the American Tract Society characterizes the "closing of the year" as a time "proper for reflection. . . . It is a complete period. It is short enough to have its scenes remembered. It is long enough to take a startling portion from human life. It has something of the solemnity of the end of life. It is a miniature judgment-hour, when we may summon ourselves before conscience—receive its verdict, and if need be, repent and reform."[178] As was discussed in the previous chapter, *Rays of Light* often addressed the passage of time, in particular at the beginning of the New Year.

A rule of time was also applied in the management of the mission itself. The courtyard on the one-acre mission premises in Urmia had a clock above it, placed in the second-story window of one of the mission buildings.[179] This clock had been originally set up by David Stoddard for the male seminary when it was still in Urmia, because "he found it difficult to secure punctuality in the exercises of the seminary, and the religious service of the Sabbath, for want of a common standard of time."[180] Stoddard had at first set up several sundials, but eventually sent away for the clock, which was a gift from one of his brothers who was a merchant in Boston.[181] He then wrote to a watchmaker in Northampton for instructions so he could maintain it himself. This may have been the only openly displayed clock in Urmia at the time.

Building a Church, the Nation in Time

In this chapter I have emphasized the collective practices introduced by the missionaries, in contrast to the preceding chapter, where I outlined many of the terms and concepts we find in the mission literature. This has been for heuristic purposes. In reality it is difficult to separate practices from, for example, the intentions inspiring different social occasions and the ideas expressed at them. Such a distinction is even more difficult to maintain in what follows because I want to look at a public ceremony at which books were the centerpiece.

In 1867 a dedication ceremony was held for a new church built in Chahargushe, a village on the Urmia plain.[182] The new structure had a cornerstone repository wherein were placed several books as well as documents. The practice of including a cornerstone repository in a new building was common in the United States, and by the nineteenth century it was used not only for churches but for secular buildings as well. Today such a compartment is often called a "time capsule," revealing our own self-consciousness about the present and how it will be different from the future.

This public ritual event, the foundation and consecration of a church, took place in a town not known for its strong Protestant leanings. The anonymous author of the article describing the event was an East Syrian, perhaps the native assistant, Moses of Chahargushe.[183] A brief article in *Rays of Light* describes the ceremony and the contents of the repository.

> Some history [*tariḫe*, lit. "dates"] and events that occurred in this generation were placed with some books in a stone carved like a chest, which was placed in the foundation to be preserved for the generations to come, and as we ourselves desire to know the history preceding us, so those after us will desire to know the history [*tariḫ*] of our generation.

The article explains that several books were placed in the repository: an edition of the mission's bilingual Neo-Aramaic / Syriac Old Testament; one of the mission's editions of the New Testament; a calendar, which was probably the mission's 1868 calendar, printed in 1867; and a "book of confession" [*ktawa d-todita*], most likely the *Book of Faith and Rules* (*Ktawa d-todita w-qanone*) (1862).[184] Finally, there was also a "history of the church," which would be the *Short History of the Church of Our Lord Jesus Christ: From the Year 33 until the Present* (1856), which was a translation of *A Brief History of the Church of Christ*.[185] This work, originally composed in German by the German pietist Christian Gottlob Barth (1799–1862), employs an explicitly Protestant historical schema. The mission's version contains as appendixes a translation of "Missions of the Nestorian Christians in Central and Eastern Asia," which was published in the *Missionary Herald* in 1838, and a translation of an English rendering of the text from the famous Nestorian Stele erected in 781 in Xi'an fu, China.[186] This *Short History* combines Protestant and East Syrian history. However, its version of East Syrian history derives from European and American scholarship, even if some of it is ultimately based upon East Syrian sources.

Rays of Light provides a "portion of the history [*tariḥe*]" that was placed in the cornerstone repository.

> The name of our nation [*melatan*] is Nestorian Syrians. For a long period our nation preserved a healthy faith [*todita*], but after this a spiritual cancer began to work within it, the laxity of our priests increased, bad traits became abundant, our Scriptures were almost lost, errors from perverse churches filled our faith [*toditan*], our generations groped in the dark, and a small spark of truth remained, until the Lord with mercy sent American evangelists. With great risks and with much expense they came to us. The darkness, which was spread out over our nation, was enlightened by an increase of Scriptures through printing, by teaching our sons and daughters to read, and by the blessed evangelizing of free salvation in Christ.
>
> The church's name is St. George's. It was built in the Christian year 1867, the village is 33 houses, its people are poor, but everyone helped as he could. The foundation stone was [laid] on June 6. We began the building with prayer. On September 5 it was consecrated after it was completed. Evangelists, bishops, priests, deacons, and the nobles of the nation [*melat*] gathered for its consecration.
>
> The name of our king is Naser al-Din Shah; his capital Tehran; he began to rule in the place of his father, Muhammad Shah, in the year 1848.
>
> The costliness in our generation: wheat [went] from 5 qiran to 50 qiran. Three times locusts visited, there was famine, and due to the difficulty of our generation, there were parents who sold their children for bread. Also there were plagues: three times there was the powerful sickness of cholera, sweeping [people] away by the hundreds and by the thousands.
>
> In the pulling down and renewing of our church a stone came out. Upon it were these carvings in the ancient tongue of the Armenians. From its writing

until now [there have been] 639 years. The village was a small city in the past, and the name of a priest and of a deacon are carved upon the stone, and the name of the stone carver was Qazar.

The public depositing of this document into the corner of the new church was a self-conscious performance of the historicism attested in the document itself. The ceremony suggests an awareness of the linear movement of time and a concern for posterity that is fundamentally modern, whereas the noting of the past presence of Armenians in this location implies a thinking in terms of national groups. The church is *now* Syrian. Furthermore, the focus on the political and economic circumstances of the day and the implicit notion that society is in transformation suggest a naturalism and historicism concerned with the kind of "current events" discussed in *Rays of Light*.

The story told of the "nation" (*melat*) of "Nestorian Syrians" shows the extent to which an emergent national consciousness, or protonationalism, had already developed among the East Syrians in proximity to the mission by the late 1860s. "Nation" here is clearly distinguished from "religious confession" (*todita*). The fact that a *melat* can preserve or not preserve its *todita* and yet still remain a *melat* means that it can exist prior to or without that *todita*: it is a distinct entity, perhaps not yet with the precise meaning of "nation," but something more stable and grounded than religious identity or a religiosity that can increase or decrease over time. Furthermore, the idea that a *todita* can be lost or become corrupted reflects a Protestant view of history, and in the repository document the missionaries are cast as reforming heroes, whose arrival saved the "Nestorian Syrians" from their own decline and stagnation. That books were the primary implements at this ritual event further demonstrates its distinctly Protestant bent. However, it also exposes a contradiction in the missionaries' own rejection of what they deemed to be the fetishism of the indigenous East Syrian book culture, as discussed in chapter 2. Books could be material objects with more significance than their content for evangelicals, too. The 1867 event (and its recording in *Rays of Light*) not only reveals the close connection between a certain type of temporality and the nation, but it also illustrates how both came about simultaneously within a millennial project of reform, one that assumed an evangelical Protestant historiography.

Conclusion: The Protestant Missionary Engine of Sociality

I have aimed in this chapter to identify an emergence, a "structure of feeling," the first signs of a Syrian national consciousness, through an examination of the collective practices and the new forms of social interaction introduced by the American mission. The mission's project of religious, moral, and educational reform prompted the creation of a social matrix in which a new set of national practices, as well as affects and ideas, came about. The development of national consciousness was a slow and sometimes anomalous process, and it is difficult to consistently isolate the thing in itself in its gestation. Such an emergence has also been studied with great subtlety, for example, in queer theoretical historiography on the origins of the homo/heterosexual binary and even in the analysis of identities of American spiritualists in the late nineteenth century.[187] Just as the scholars working in these areas, I am looking at a process of self-discovery, a coming out, and the eventual sense of solidarity that can lead to further purifications, exclusions, and controversy.

One conclusion I would like to draw is about the Protestant basis of the new mode of sociality at the mission. By sociality I refer to collective social practices and correlative ideas about the social itself. As I suggested in the introduction, recent work on Christian mission, such as Webb Keane's *Christian Moderns* (2007), a book that has been a theoretical touchstone for my own work, overestimates the individualism (as opposed to relationalism) of Protestantism and its transformative potential. The "moral narrative of modernity" and the "semiotic ideology" Keane examines played a central role at the American mission in Urmia, but this was in conjunction with the introduction of new collective social practices and new ideas about the social itself. From its origins, Calvinism promoted the notion of the hidden, often unknown community, the true church, an idea that derives ultimately from Augustine's *City of God*. This notion of the church as a community, which depends on the biblical notion of the Israelites as the people of God, was certainly not new to the Church of the East. However, the Reformed Gospel, while maintaining a notion of the church community, could be simultaneously isolating.

The idea and practices of community that emerged from the missionary encounter were predicated upon the individualism so often associated with Protestantism. Protestant individualism contributed to the development of the idea of abstract community because it suggested that individuals were disaggregated from the variety of often hierarchical social relations that existed within the indigenous community. As we will see in chapters 5 through 7, the disaggregated were simultaneously bound together in new ways through new social practices and unprecedented calls for the unity of the "nation" (*melat*). A comparison of the tribe and the national community, two social congeries that differ in more than just size, may highlight what is new in the nation. National community, at least as it is imagined, is not simply an all-inclusive tribe, a supertribe that brings all tribes together as one. Although both the tribe and the nation rely heavily on the family, this smaller unit functions as a different kind of constituent part in each. In the former, the family is a sub-structure under the clan moving upward into the hierarchy of relations of the tribe. In the latter, the family is the only constituent unit above the individual, and the nation, when not thought of as a unity of individuals, is imagined as a collection of families (hence the importance of women from the perspective of republican motherhood). Furthermore, the tribe and the nation differ in that the "unity of the tribe (or, from another perspective, its boundaries) is only asserted on rare occasions."[188] Unity tends to come out in conflict only in the case of the tribe, whereas the nation is predicated upon the notion of its own unity.

5

Death, the Maiden, and Dreams of Revival

Everybody's got to walk this lonesome valley;
We've got to walk it by ourselves;
There's nobody else can walk it for us;
We've got to walk it by ourselves.
—traditional American Gospel folk song

From the day that Mr. Perkins came to our village, nearly twenty years ago, I have
known and felt myself a great sinner.
—an old woman on her sickbed, October 1856[1]

Try as the Bororo may to bring their system to full flowering with the aid of a deceptive
prosopopoeia, they will be unable, as other societies have also been unable, to smother
this truth: that the imagery with which a society pictures to itself the relations between
the dead and the living can always be broken down in terms of an attempt to hide, em-
bellish or justify, on the religious level, the relations prevailing, in that society among
the living.
—CLAUDE LÉVI-STRAUSS, *Tristes tropiques* (1955)[2]

There is something characteristically modern in the prevalent knowledge,
even among the biblically illiterate, of Psalm 23 ("The Lord is my shepherd").
It is one of the few portions of the Bible with which most Americans are
familiar. This psalm, which offers promise and consolation "though I may
walk through the valley of the shadow of death," is commonly part of funeral
services, as the Psalter in general has traditionally been employed as a tool
to help us "fear no evil." The first-person voice of the psalm is singular, and
the walk through the valley is a solitary trek. In *Pilgrim's Progress* (1678), a
popular work at the mission, Christian, the allegorical hero, passes through
this "valley of the shadow of death." However, he discovers that God is with us
even in the valley's darkness, as are others who fear him. In fact, these fellow
travelers will be our "company by and by."[3] As he walks through the valley,
Christian hears the voice of an unseen man reading Psalm 23, and from this
he knows that, although solitary, he is not alone.

The experience of death is an isolated one, and once life is complete, there
are no benefits the living can provide the dead nor the dead the living. This
is the message the American missionaries announced repeatedly and in different contexts to their East Syrian audience. Each person dies alone, and

after death there is an agonizing eternity prepared for those who have not been saved by faith in Christ. Nothing can be done for the dead. The hero of *Pilgrim's Progress* leaves his family behind and travels alone, and yet he receives armor upon his stay at "House Beautiful," an allegory for the Christian congregation. Moreover, the second part of *Pilgrim's Progress* describes the journeys of Christian's wife and children on the same road he has traveled. Thus, we are alone on our journey, but others travel along the same route. Implicit in the evangelical notion of personal salvation is a solitary sociality: the social is not rejected, but rather the links that exist among the living are transformed.

Furthermore, in this world, according to the theology of the missionaries, nothing can be *done* for our own salvation. A familiar problem in Reformed theology, it is by grace that one is saved, and one must have faith, which is an opening to God's graciousness rather than an actual act in itself, for grace to take its effect. Just as nothing can be done for those in the hereafter, so also nothing can be done for one another in this life. We can only exhort others and provide examples. Reformed theology rejects what it deems works righteousness—that is, the Protestant supposition, usually a distortion, holding that other forms of piety presuppose that one can do things to be saved in an exchange relationship with God. This rejection is part of the interiorization of religion commonly associated with Reformation thought and the concomitant disembedding and privatization of religion. Religion—or at least, true religion—begins to be understood primarily as an internal state, and this Protestant tendency is only a few steps away from the common secularist perspective that religion is, and should be, essentially private. Of course, what we often call "religion" is not private belief, but this is how it is conceptualized by many. The interiorization of religion correlates to the lonely, isolated self often taken to be an essential characteristic of modernity, a self thought to be bounded and ontologically closed to the disenchanted world around it and temporally limited by its future dissipation in death.

In this chapter I examine how the anxieties around death introduced by the missionaries were part of their larger project of cultivating an interiorized form of piety, one that correlates to the new forms of community imagined and practiced among the East Syrians under missionary influence, which I addressed in chapters 3 and 4, respectively. This shift occurred in tandem with a process whereby the solitary self was articulated and selves were imagined as existing outside of prior notions of community. The chapter consists of four parts. First I address the differences between the cultures of death of the East Syrians and the missionaries. Then I describe the process of conversion as it was understood and cultivated at the mission. Following this I turn to an analysis of the representation and imagery of death, particularly exemplary death, in the mission literature. After this I examine the early revivals experienced at and in the vicinity of the mission. East Syrians confirmed their belonging to the mission community through public conversion at these ritual events, at which the anxieties induced in them by the missionaries' Gospel were made manifest. I conclude by describing the life led by one East Syrian woman, Sanam, daughter of Priest Dunkha, and how the way her life was described after her death fit into the discourse of death and life this chapter describes.

Cultures of Death: Funereal Ritual, Mourning, and the Cult of the Dead

Unfortunately, death is not just a social construction. On account of this, all cultures have their particular ways of conceptualizing and dealing with it, and as Lévi-Strauss discusses in the chapter I quote from in one of this chapter's epigraphs, a culture's understanding of death and the rituals it develops around it can also tell us something about the ways the living are understood to relate to one another. In my analysis I want to find the right balance between treating death as an irreducible part of human life and remaining aware that "death" itself has its own discursive history in any given culture. Without emphasizing the constructedness of death, we risk treating it, for example, as a transhistorical, anomic phenomenon that all cultures accordingly must deal with because of its tendency to destroy meaning.[4] The problem with this approach is that it presupposes death to be ultimately the same object of fear and anxiety in all cultures, universalizing a particular understanding of the human body and soul and thereby assuming that each culture of death is built upon the same foundation. To put it simply, yes, we all die, but not all the same death.

The Americans and the East Syrians had different normative ways of understanding and dealing with death. The older, more stoic approach to death and mourning of the Puritans gave way in the early nineteenth century to a variety of reconceptualizations that eventually subverted the apparent hegemony of Christianity in this central part of human social life. The Puritans had lived and died according to an "evangelism of fear," in which death was a result of human depravity and the corpse represented our sinful nature.[5] Among the variety of new responses to death in the antebellum period, that of the American missionaries in Urmia was more conservative. Although they participated in the sentimentalization of death—for example, through the memorialization of the departed, especially the young—the Calvinist concern to trust in God and accept that mortality was our lot continued to guide their approach to death. The extended and intensified forms of mourning, typical of certain echelons of American society in the nineteenth century, and commonly held in contempt by certain cultural critics, were rejected by the missionaries. In a way, they were traditional Calvinists in a sentimental mode, and this distinguished them from the broader culture from which they came. Furthermore, as with the Second Great Awakening in general and the whole project of the ABCFM, the missionaries put more emphasis on free will (thus being more Arminian) than their predecessors: they hoped to communicate to their audience that all people had a choice to make to transform themselves. However, they had to make that choice at some point in life and not at the last minute.

Deathbed conversions are not part of the missionary literature, despite the central importance of the deathbed scene to their descriptions of the dying, which will be addressed below. Rather, the deathbed was an opportunity to perform one's salvation, like Socrates in the *Phaedo* demonstrating the truth of philosophy as he, untouched, accepts death. "During the climactic period before death the religious condition of the dying individual seemed to be particularly important. Yet of equal concern in many descriptions of these last moments were the physical characteristics and pathological symptoms manifested by the fading patient."[6] The deathbed scene had had a long history by the time it was taken up by the American missionaries. Death had become a focal point of the person, "the occasion when man was most able to reach an awareness of himself."[7] According to Philippe Ariès, "A formerly unknown relationship developed between the death of each individual and his awareness of being an individual."[8]

Despite the fact that they did not participate in the extremes of the funereal culture developing in the United States at the time, the missionaries nonetheless demonstrated the new emphasis on mourning and death considered typical of a nineteenth-century American culture in which mourning had become a "sentimental ritual."[9] Mourning—or more specifically, the correct practice of it—was an eminently Christian act, which itself could shape moral character.[10] "Mourning was regarded as the most sacred of social feelings because the heart softened by affliction turned with greater love not only to the departed loved one, but to all living members of the family, and finally to all mankind."[11] This ritual entailed a disciplined emotional self-expression, and yet truly deep grief demonstrated true gentility.[12]

The sentimentality the missionaries demonstrate regarding sublime landscapes, the Christian's role in the world, and almost everything else of import to them is most apparent when they address death. It is a commonplace in the scholarship on sentimentalism in nineteenth-century America to link it to the development of the marketplace and the increasingly impersonal nature of capitalist culture in an increasingly urbanized nation.[13] However, whether or not it can be explained as a response to consumer capitalism, this sentimentality, which is often discounted as mere kitsch, was an important affective trait of the Christianity and culture of the Americans who went to Iran, and corresponds with the renegotiation of gender roles at the mission, addressed in chapter 4.[14] The culture of death they introduced, as I show below, was central to the cultivation of a Reformed version of Christianity, and one of the foremost parts of their focus on death is the repeated representation of and attention to the death of young children. As Karen Sánchez-Eppler claims, "Dying is what children do most and do best in the literary and cultural imagination of nineteenth-century America."[15]

The tale of the Christian girl who provides a model for others by dying young yet converted to Christ's fold is almost as old as Christianity itself, going back to, for example, the martyrdom of Saint Perpetua at the turn of the third century. In its nineteenth-century Protestant instantiation, it is most commonly known from the story of Evangeline St. Clare, or "little Eva," from *Uncle Tom's Cabin* (1852), the pious young girl who preaches a loving Christianity until her premature death.[16] Such figures were common enough that Mark Twain satirizes them in *The Adventures of Huckleberry Finn* (1885) in the figure of Emmeline Grangerford, the morbidly obsessed obituary scrapbooker and death poetess, who herself dies young. Weak young females exemplify the lowliness of Christ, who "made himself of no reputation, and took upon him the form of a servant, and was made in the likeness of men" and "humbled himself, and became obedient unto death, even the death of the cross" (Phil 2:6–7). Incarnationally speaking, the *kenosis*, or self-emptying, of Christ allows for the other, weaker vessels of this world to bear the power of the Spirit, and therefore, sickly young women like Evangeline demonstrate the transformative power of the word made flesh. "In *Uncle Tom's Cabin*, death is the equivalent not of defeat but of victory; it brings an access of power, not a loss of it; it is not only the crowning achievement of life, it *is* life, and Stowe's entire presentation of little Eva is designed to dramatize this fact."[17]

Furthermore, Eva's death "explicitly illustrates the way the deathbed scene serves to pass on a moral responsibility to others."[18] In her Christ-like demise, she takes on the sins of slavery, while the focus on her meeting with the "bridegroom" reorients her sexual innocence to a higher plain. Her death is characterized as an almost angelic transformation, where the body of death is elided by spiritual performance. As Elisabeth Bronfen emphasizes, Eva's death points to the heavenly world to which she, unlike the other characters in the novel, will have access, while offering a glimpse at what the living can only know by inference from watching the dying.[19] As I argue below, the culture of death the American missionaries introduced, which was part of their evangelism of fear, held that the dead could only serve as exemplars for the living, while death itself, the great winnowing of good mortals from wicked, was solitary, stark, and determinative.

When we compare the American to the East Syrian culture of death, the basic contents of the two traditions are the same inasmuch as they are both Christian: human beings are mortal due to sin, and Christ's sacrifice on the cross is salvific for all humankind.[20] However, within the Classical Syriac liturgical and exegetical tradition, there are of course different emphases and nuances in this schema. For example, Death or *Sheol*, the term for the underworld deriving from the biblical tradition, is often personified as a contender with Christ for human souls, whereas our created, mortal, and therefore transitory state is often vividly described. For example, the following passage is from the burial service for priests:

> Mourn not, ye children of Adam, for Christ the King has lifted up your
> heads.
> Mourn not in the day of your death, O ye prudent ones, for death is but a
> sleep in which the righteous and wicked rest.
> It is the cup which justice mingled for the children of Adam, and all his
> children must drink of it.
> It is a bridge over which all generations must pass from this world to the next
> where no fear is.
> Behold how every man tastes the cup of death, and not one is free from its
> power and sovereignty.
> Where is Adam whom the Lord formed out of the dust, and called him His
> image, and made heaven and earth subject to him?[21]

After asking similar rhetorical questions about Abel, Seth, Noah, Shem, Abraham, Isaac, Moses, Joshua, David, Goliath, Samson, and others, the service continues:

> Where are the generations which have been since the beginning, and the
> nations from Adam until now?
> Behold all these, O ye prudent ones, and see to what the beauty of their
> persons is reduced.
> Ask of Sheol and she will tell you where they are: ask of the earth and she will
> show you the place of their burial.
> They all are embosomed in the ground, and there shall they remain till the
> resurrection day.[22]

Such biblically based language is common to Syriac liturgy, and a passage such as this gives a sense of the rhetoric of this poetic liturgical tradition.

Like adherents of other Christian traditions, the East Syrians hold that there will be a general resurrection at the end of time, when Christ will raise up all the dead from their graves. The common funeral liturgy begins: "Blessed is Christ who became a key and opened Sheol and will come and again open it on the day of resurrection."[23] One particularity of the Syriac tradition is its emphasis on what is commonly called the "Harrowing of Hell"—that is, Christ's descent to the underworld in the period between Good Friday and Easter Sunday to free the just who had preceded him, such as the patriarchs of the Old Testament.[24] Christ is commonly described as breaking down the doors of Sheol: "By death the Living One emptied Sheol. He tore it open and let entire throngs flee from it," writes Saint Ephrem (d. 373).[25]

We do not know the extent of popular knowledge in the nineteenth century of many of the traditions that descend from the Syriac church's distant past. The funeral liturgy, which preserved many elements of the tradition, seems to have been well known and commonly employed. However, what we are more certain of is practices: the East Syrian funeral service by the modern period consisted of four parts: "the ritual washing of the body, the vigil office of prayer in the house of the deceased, a solemn procession accompanied by chants from the house to the cemetery, and the actual burial."[26] The latter three of these had specific liturgical parts, some rather long. Surma Khanum provides a basic summary of funeral practices as she knew them. She describes the washing and shrouding of the dead and the formal procession on a bier to the church.

> The grave has been made ready and the service and burial will be concluded there, and afterwards all return to the house of the departed and will eat and go to their houses. The second day there will be a celebration for the departed, and his relations will distribute food to the poor before the door of the church. For three days the neighbours come to the house of mourning to condole, and on the third day the priest goes at four in the morning to the grave before celebrating *Qurbana*, with some of the women who are most nearly related to the departed, and will say some short prayers and will cense the grave. This resembles the visit of the women to our Lord's grave.[27]

Surma also describes the custom of placing lights on graves during Easter vigil, and during the same season using the greeting "Light to your departed." She adds that in some regions, such as Tkhuma, food was also put on graves and sometimes niches were built into their sides as places for a light or food.

Mourning for the East Syrians, especially at the funeral itself, was a public display, the necrotic equivalent of the festival, a time to let things hang out, even to the point of evoking tears that were not inclined to fall. The Americans characterized East Syrian rituals of mourning and the cult of the dead as excessive, inauthentic, and leaning toward paganism. "No reader of the Bible needs any description of Oriental mourning for the dead,"[28] writes Thomas Laurie in 1863, and then proudly provides several examples of how traditional mourning had been reformed by the presence of the mission.[29] Reflecting contemporary anxieties simultaneously expressed back home in the United States concerning the culture of mourning, the Americans complained about the excess of feeling displayed in East Syrian mourning: this excess was criticized as both uncontrolled and yet fake. In fact, the missionaries' anxieties about sincerity in mourning reflect a larger concern in contemporary American culture about trickery, confidence men, and the need for there to be a clear correspondence between outward signs and the inner heart.[30] This in turn corresponds with the missionaries' critique of ritualized reading and speech, as we saw in chapter 2, which for them was the same as Catholic mummery.

The East Syrian liturgical tradition had grown complex and diverse by the nineteenth century, and this was also true of the service for the dead. As in other Eastern churches, there was a variety of burial services, depending on the departed's position: there were different services for different levels of clergy, as well as for laity (males, females, or children), even for pilgrims and the rich. With liturgical specificity, the service for the deceased bride describes her approach to the heavenly bridegroom, whereas in a service for children, bereaved parents are told that as Isaac was to be sacrificed but in the end was saved, so shall the soul of their child.[31] Such a differentiation would have been anathema to the sensibility of the Americans, even if in practice they employed and benefited from local social distinctions in their engagements with the people of the region. For them, we are all equal in death. In contrast, in the East Syrian ritual description of the washing of the dead, we find the demand that we "know this, too, that in the rank in which he used to go to the altar while living, in that [rank] they shall let him enter the grave."[32] This East Syrian hierarchization of the dead corresponded with the system of favors, as practiced both in the church and in the tribal and village system. For total equals are limited in their ability to help one another, while difference allows for the possibility of exchange.

Although there was not a formal doctrine of purgatory, something that would be introduced by Rome to the Chaldean Church, the East Syrians did have a notion that the dead could benefit from the prayers and almsgiving of their relatives.[33] This idea that the living could help the dead resonates with the cult of the saints, which will be addressed in the following chapter: as we can help the dead, so some of the dead, the special ones, can help us. These relations with the dead were maintained through transactions of prayer and sacrifice (*qurbana*).

The East Syrian practice of exchange for the benefit of the dead and the American rejection of it are both apparent when the missionaries describe their conversations with the East Syrians about the ritual of making sacrifices for the dead. In 1841, after a session of Bible study, Deacon Badal asked Albert Holladay his opinion of the *qurbana*, the sacrifice for the dead, and whether it should be performed. This was already an issue that had been debated within the East Syrian tradition, and an explicit theology had been developed for it.[34] Holladay responded that Badal should look to Paul for the correct answer. Perkins had preached the night before on the doctrine of sacrifice as it appears in the Epistle to the Hebrews, a text that states that Christ's sacrifice is the end of all sacrifices (10:1–18). Holladay then explained that

they have fallen into a practice which is founded on the hope of effecting a change in the state of the dead who have died in sin. On particular occasions (sacramental occasions) they kill animals, as sheep or cattle, and having given a part of the flesh to the priest, distribute the rest among the poor; and they believe that the man who does this may thereby secure a place in paradise for his deceased father and mother.[35]

In this ritual, described by Holladay, we see the common and ancient Christian practice of giving to the poor in exchange for benefits in heaven, combined with a making of the "heave offering" (Hebr. *terumah*), a gift to the priests, from the Hebrew Bible. This social and religious exchange—a complex system linking the donor, the priest, the poor, the departed, and God—is precisely what the missionaries rejected as spiritually illegitimate, as I addressed in chapter 2. True religion does not consist in exchange.

After the conversation with Badal, Priest Dunkha remained when everyone else had left the room, and he cautiously confronted Holladay about the issue of sacrifice. After a long disclaimer in which he admitted that his people had a number of "unscriptural opinions, especially on this subject of sacrifice," and that he knew that the Americans were not there, like other (Catholic) missionaries, simply to make proselytes, "but to bring back the ignorant and sinful to the right way of the Lord," he told Holladay that he felt obliged to give him a warning. Using a Pauline theme himself (e.g., 1 Cor 4:10), Dunkha continued, "And now although you are wiser than I, I wish you to be very guarded, and use your influence with the other gentlemen [i.e., *sahabe*, the missionaries] that they should be very guarded, in speaking of the customs of the people, for all have not understanding, and they may think that you wish to abolish our customs and our way (i.e., sect [re-flects Neo-Aramaic *mazhab*])."[36] We saw already in chapter 2 the East Syrians' concern for the traditions of the "teachers" (*malpanas*) of the church, one of which was the idea of the efficacy of prayers for the dead.[37]

Holladay explained that the missionaries were obliged to preach only what they found in the Scriptures. Dunkha responded that this was fine, "But do not turn aside to preach about our peculiarities in things not spoken of or decidedly revealed." Holladay then went into further detail: the missionaries had no intention of interfering in the church or their forms of worship, but only aimed to turn people to what Scripture demands and forbids. The salva-tion of others is all they sought, and therefore, the practice of sacrifice was a problem: the Scripture teaches that "the soul which is lost, that is, which dies impenitent and unsanctified, is lost forever; and all hopes of a change in its condition are fallacious."[38] Dunkha assented to this.

Holladay's argument was one commonly used by the missionaries. For example, in 1843 an old man in the church at 'Ada suggested there were prob-lems in what Austin H. Wright was preaching.[39] "The priest and bishop saw at once that he thought I was attacking their fasts, forms, etc.; and they spoke earnestly, therefore, assuring him, and all others who thought like him, that our intention was not to destroy their fasts, etc., but only to prevent their trusting in them." The old man was of course correct: the missionaries may not have been arguing against certain practices, but they were subverting them nonetheless by suggesting that, being local customs not essential to Christianity, they were useless for personal salvation.

Compared to the East Syrian system, the stakes were higher in the Protes-tant schema of heaven and hell. The results of death were more stark and final, and in these two Christian cultures, "salvation" meant two different things. The winnowing of death, the separation of the wheat from the chaff, was cold and exact for the Americans. This created a greater focus on death itself, par-ticularly the moment of death, which provides an opportunity for the final performance of our Christian virtue and the recognition of the immortality offered by Christ. That moment was for the Americans an end point, a telos for our whole lives, providing direction for how we should act in the time we have remaining. For the East Syrians salvation was promised by Christ's sal-vific death, lived in the lives of the saints, ritually practiced at the Eucharistic service, and experienced at festival times. In contrast, salvation was uncertain for the Americans, and all the more so in their own eyes the salvation of the East Syrians, whose conversions they often did not deem authentic.

The Americans' stark view of death relates directly to their mourning practice, inasmuch as they introduced a system in which death is not to be mourned because we have hope that the departed will be saved. To mourn too much would suggest that the departed was a condemned sinner. In contrast to the East Syrian system, which seems to have treated life as a series of episodes of bounty and loss and the afterlife as more vague and at the same time dynamically related still to this world, the Americans saw this world as one great gift, even in bad times, for the undeserving, whose only hope in the face of eternal doom was to be saved through faith in Christ. Therefore, the only characteristic of the dead that could be focused on, aside from the eternity of their death itself, was their exemplary quality, which I address further below.

Death was a common occurrence at the mission, especially the death of the young due to cholera, measles, and other diseases.[40] Late January and early February of 1840 saw multiple deaths, particularly of children: Elias, the teenage brother of Priest Dunkha; the seventeen-month-old twins Judith Sabine and Mary Electra Grant, whose mother had died on January 14, 1839; eighteen-month-old Charles Stocking; nineteen-month-old Catherine Holladay; the not-yet-four-year-old William Riach Perkins; and later in January Dunkha's second wife, whom he had married only a few months before. On the same day that his child died in the dark early-morning hours of February 2, 1840, after two weeks of illness, Albert Holladay thought of the other mission children who had died in the past week and wrote: "The sudden and almost simultaneous removal of these little ones, whose smiling countenances and cheerful voices so often filled our hearts with hope and gladness, and imparted an air of cheerfulness to our dwellings, can not but be deeply felt, but we rejoice in the hope of their salvation."[41] On seeing how composed the Holladays were on his condolence visit the following week, Mar Elias commented: "Your custom is better than ours: you do not weep aloud and make a noise like our people."[42] Elias told Holladay how twelve members of his own family had died in one week. After recommending to his bereft family members that they praise God, he himself went off alone and wept. Elias then related the story of his dead brother, who, after being a regular wine drinker, had reformed himself, from which point onward he would admonish others neither to drink nor to lie, and would lend money without voucher. When Holladay asked whether his brother had feared death, Elias said that he did not, "but lay perfectly composed, looking up to heaven, until he died."[43] The story of Elias's brother gave Holladay hope for the East Syrians, even the unlettered ones, and this episode shows the link between the right relationship to death and moral reform.

Perkins's account of this difficult time attests to the kind of spiritual consolation employed at the mission to deal with such loss and also demonstrates the opportunities for the observation of character that such events provided the missionaries. When Dunkha told Perkins that his teenage brother, Elias, was not afraid to die, Perkins went and visited the boy, who was too weak to say anything but "By the strength of God I hope in Christ."[44] During this episode Perkins also observed Dunkha, whose "appearance was deeply interesting."

> He solemnly warned his family and others who were present, "to be also ready" and heed the voice of God in the scene before them. There was, in this instance, none of the noisy, frantic grief, which is often witnessed at the dying bed in these countries. There was deep sorrow, but also solemnity and still-ness. I never felt more grateful for the precious hopes and consolations of the gospel, than while standing by that death bed, and witnessing their soothing, sustaining influence on the afflicted priest.

It is clear that Dunkha had learned well from the missionaries: Elias's death was to serve as a moral lesson and not simply a source of uncontrolled and, to Perkins's sensibilities, excessive grief. Perkins writes, "I have never felt so much confidence in priest Dunk[h]a's piety, as I have, since observing the manner in which he has sustained this trying affliction." This observation corresponds with the idea expressed several times in Perkins's journal that "nothing, save the Holy Spirit, lays open the heart to religious influence, like affliction," and the suggestion that "the Lord is perhaps taking our treasures (our little children) to himself, that he may draw our hearts after them."[45] On the death of Dunkha's wife, Perkins told the priest that "it seemed that the Lord desired to have his whole heart, and is therefore taking from him his dearest earthly treasures, to draw his undivided affections up to himself, that the Lord is chastising him, that he may partake of his holiness."[46] In turn, East Syrians associated with the mission, as Perkins notes, would provide similar "sympathies" to the missionaries.[47] Amid these circumstances, after a discussion of East Syrian infant mortality, Perkins then describes "a long and serious conversation with priests Abraham and John, on the importance of habitual preparation for death."[48]

Conversion: Penitence, Awakening, and the Solitude of the Closet

The missionary focus on death was part of the rhetoric of reform. However, the significance of this death talk should not be linked to the missionaries' success in making formal converts, even in the later period, when from the 1860s onward, a separate indigenous evangelical church was created. The conversions that occurred at the mission are not demonstrative of its rate of growth. Rather, they are significant as manifestations of the tensions and anxieties that were promoted through the discourse of reform and experienced by those locals trying to find their place in the mission community. To treat the conversions simply as a sign of the mission's expansion is to employ the missionaries' understanding of such phenomena, and, furthermore, it implicitly diminishes the mission's historical significance because it is clear that the majority of the people who came into contact with it did not have such experiences, even if many important actors there did.[49]

If we take the American missionaries at their word, in the early period they did not want to "convert" people to a particular church. This is in accord with the general precaution with which we must approach the topic of conversion, which is not a simple and transparent term of analysis. It has a particular discursive history, and to apply it uncritically to transhistorically distinct phenomena can be misleading. Talal Asad recommends that "if one wishes to avoid the danger of confusing word with concept and concept with practice, it would be better to say that in studying conversion, one was dealing with the narratives by which people apprehended and described a radical change in the significance of their lives."[50] The standard terms in the sources, especially in the Neo-Aramaic, for what the missionaries wanted to bring about are *penitence* and *awakening*. This process is also regularly described as one of "enlightenment" in the basic meaning of the term: the introduction of light to benighted souls, just as the mission itself brought light to a benighted land. As we saw in chapter 3, light themes are common in the mission literature, such as in the title of *Rays of Light* itself.

The conversion experiences of East Syrians, which are especially common in accounts of revivals at the mission, may be understood as anxious and ritualized attempts at self-transformation from the status of "nominal Christians" to that of "true Christians." This was never fully successful in the eyes of the missionaries, who in their circumspect hesitation usually labeled converts as "hopefully pious." To be sure, relations with the mission could affect local Christians' standing in their own community, whether for better or for worse, but conversion in this case was not understood to be a move out of one social group into another, but rather from a tepid way of life to a more vibrant and authentic one. This was conversion without communal affiliation, except for with the church in the abstract, theological, and imagined sense. Furthermore, this transformation to what was understood to be an authentic Christian identity was linked to the mission's civilizational discourse: ultimately, this awakened Christian identity entailed demonstrating traits commonly associated later in the century with being modern, although *modern* itself is not a term used at the mission in the early decades.

In general, evangelical conversion consists of two parts: (1) the conviction of one's own sinful status combined with an awareness of the inability as a mere creature of God to help oneself, (2) followed by the acceptance of Christ as one's savior. The rhetoric of death is key to the first of these steps. The African American evangelist Jarena Lee (1783–?) describes her process of conviction (and conversion, and later, as a Methodist, sanctification) in her spiritual autobiography.

> Even the falling of the dead leaves from the forests, and the dried spires of the mown grass, showed me that I too must die, in like manner. But my case was awfully different from that of the grass of the field, or the wide spread decay of a thousand forests, as I felt within me a living principle, an immortal spirit, which cannot die, and must forever either enjoy the smiles of its Creator, or feel the pangs of ceaseless damnation.[51]

This awareness of one's mortality and the impending judgment was often linked to the rhetoric of fear. As mentioned above, fear is a common tool of exhortation in the American Calvinist tradition. The best-known example of this is Jonathan Edwards's famous sermon "Sinners in the Hands of an Angry God" (1741), in which Edwards expounds upon how, if not for God's forbearance, the sinner "would immediately sink and swiftly descend and plunge into the bottomless gulf."[52] To those who challenged the use of terror and "frightening poor innocent children with talk of hell fire and eternal damnation," Edwards responds, "To say anything to those who have never believed in the Lord Jesus Christ, to represent their case any otherwise than exceeding terrible, is not to preach the Word of God to 'em; for the Word of God reveals nothing but truth; but this is to delude them."[53] It is noteworthy that a corresponding language of fear had long been employed in Syriac literature to address matters of piety. As I pointed out in chapter 3, even the decision to label the first and apparently most important section of *Rays of Light* "Fear of God" (*deḥlat alaha*) was one of the missionaries' rare retrievals from the Syriac tradition. Such fear is fundamentally related to death: it is God who determines who will live and who will die in this world, and the status of each person in the next one.

In the early mission literature, the standard questions the readers are encouraged to ask are "What must I do to be saved?" and the so-called Great Question, "For what is a man profited, if he shall gain the whole world, and lose his own soul?" (Mt 16:26). Overtly, the missionaries were offering an answer to these questions, but implicitly, they were creating a context in which such questions were a concern in the first place. To be sure, the East Syrians already had certain Christian concerns about salvation, but the Syriac word *purqana*, which meant originally "removal" or "release" and then "forgiveness of sins," appears more often in the mission sources where it is used to translate "salvation" than it does in the indigenous tradition. Thus, members of the audience were burdened with an even greater concern for their own sinfulness and salvation.

To understand the conversion process at the mission further, we must be aware of the semiotic ideology implicit and explicit in the language introduced by the missionaries and in their own observation of possible converts. In chapter 3 I discussed the semiotics of the self introduced in the mission literature. This semiotics, a process of searching for signs that guide us to true faith and show us when we have found it, is an important part of the introspection of conversion. A number of the mission publications, such as the translated works of Isaac Watts (1674–1748) and Philip Doddridge (1702–51), were manuals for such self-analysis. The type of self-examination advocated by these works fits with already existing parts of East Syrian intellectual tradition. For example, the monastic tradition of the Church of the East had long posited an interiority requiring scrutiny through a system of semiosis. (It is worth noting that Wesleyanism has a shared genealogy with the East Syrian tradition in that John Wesley read the Pseudo-Macarian literature, enthusiastic spiritual texts from the Syriac cultural milieu.)[54]

Parallel to this interior semiosis of the self was the exterior observation of potential converts: the missionaries themselves closely scrutinized their subjects for signs of true Christianity. Such observation was a common practice at missions, as is attested in reference to an earlier mission to Native Americans in John Eliot's *Tears of Repentance; or, A Further Narrative of the Progress of the Gospel amongst the Indians in New England* (1653).[55] Signs included the more radical "tokens of God's presence," as Jonathan Edwards refers to fainting and various ecstatic acts, but more significantly they also included the subtle changes in character that would reveal that a true change had occurred in the subject's heart.[56] The American concern with correctly reading signs belongs to the general interest in authenticity that comes up in many conversionary discourses, but it also fits with the fear of artifice and trickery that was typical of American middle-class culture at the time.[57] The uncertainty of what is truly in another's heart often led to remarks by the missionaries about the "hopeful" state of someone, or that a particular East Syrian professed to be a Christian but still had not proved her- or himself transformed. This raises the issue of "passing": the precarious status many East Syrians held in the missionaries' eyes and possibly in their own, though the sources are limited for the latter, may have resulted in an anxiety to walk the walk and talk the talk. In fact, Calvinist uncertainty, the same uncertainty that, according to Max Weber's well-known thesis, served as a motor for the development of capitalism, in combination with the racialized aspects of the civilizational discourse the missionaries introduced, opened the door to an anxiety about identity, which was eventually alleviated by the irreducibility of new racialized national ideals, such as "Syrianness," which would eventually be labeled "Assyrianness" by the early twentieth century, as we will see in chapter 8. The lists extant in the mission archive of who may be regarded as "pious" point to the scrutiny the missionaries applied to their East Syrian audience.[58]

This observation both of the self by the East Syrian and of the East Syrian by the missionary was not acts oriented. Practices and habits were to be reformed, but ultimately, the missionaries were concerned with hearts more than deeds. It was assumed, for example, that the subject would not steal, and such bad habits were regularly disciplined.[59] One of the first traits noted by the missionaries on their arrival among the East Syrians was the absence of "auricular confession," a practice that was associated with Catholicism and that seemed to allow for absolution from sinful practices and thoughts by placing an intermediary between the Christian and God. Catholic confession—for example, as described by Vicente Rafael in his study of early colonial Philippine society—was a full accounting that led to a multiplication of narratives of sin, a Foucauldian proliferation of knowledge.[60] According to the American missionaries, the human being was far more corrupt than any list of sins could articulate, and furthermore, the prayer and penitence enjoined during auricular confession were from their perspective a form of exchange or works righteousness. Someone could sin and then take his or her punishment and be done with it. In contrast, for the missionaries the human being was fundamentally sinful, and this is why they had little interest in specific faults, transgressions, thoughts, or desires. The human being was wholly corrupt, and only through a personal recognition of this could one then be fully convicted, which would then create the space for true conversion. In both the Philippine and the Iranian contexts, the "speaking subject" was also "the subject of the statement," but at the American mission the speaking was more significantly done in private to oneself and the statement was always the same: I am a worthless sinner.

The privacy of conversion, the close relationship with and analysis of the self—a self that was in fact cultivated, even created, in this very process—is exemplified by the reliance on prayer closets at the mission, especially during times of revival. A prayer closet was a small room, a nook, or an actual closet in which a Christian could pray, a private space for the self and God alone. Although obviously cognate with a variety of Christian practices reaching into antiquity, the use of prayer closets became prevalent in the seventeenth century in England, whereupon it also became, like conversion itself, a standard motif in poetry and prose.[61]

Although other passages are commonly cited in reference to the use of the prayer closet, the biblical basis of this practice is found in Matthew 6:5–6 (King James Version):

> And when thou prayest, thou shalt not be as the hypocrites are: for they love to pray standing in the synagogues and in the corners of the streets, that they may be seen of men. Verily I say unto you, They have their reward. 6: But thou, when thou prayest, enter into thy closet, and when thou hast shut thy door, pray to thy Father which is in secret; and thy Father which seeth in secret shall reward thee openly.

This passage, which is part of the Sermon on the Mount, belongs to a general critique of ostentation and hypocrisy, but when read by later Christians, it became a programmatic rejection of exteriority and an embrace of what is in the heart as the essence of religion.

The prayer closet was a technology, a ritual space, that supported individualization and the cultivation of an interior self, and at the same time the interiorization of religion. "In both respects, the door of the prayer closet opens onto an incipiently modern figuration of selfhood, the work of the closet likewise hinging upon a more individuated self conceived to reside at an inward remove from outward deed and public expression."[62] In his study of the prayer closet in the early modern period, Richard Rambuss wants "to put forth the subjectifying apparatus of the prayer closet, and the culture of private devotion it comes to represent, as a node for another chapter in the history of the self and its passions taken up in medias res by Foucault at the Counter-Reformation confessional." Rambuss continues: "Closet devotion, in other words, is the technology by which the soul becomes a subject."[63]

The isolation of the prayer closet corresponds with the isolated state of the soul at death, which is also a reflection of the soul's essential isolation even in life. The social disaggregation of the prayer closet reflects our true state as solitary souls in this world and the next. Nothing can be done for the sinner in the afterlife, and life in this world is isolated, like a Christian in a prayer closet. Furthermore, death and the closet are also linked in that our creatureliness and future annihilation are the subjects of closet meditation. This new technology for the performance of the soul's solitude, a solitude that constitutes the psychic entity it isolates, has its predecessors in Syriac culture. By the nineteenth century, monastic isolation, a practice going back to late antiquity, was only just about to vanish from the Church of the East, after centuries of decline. However, it is striking that the term the missionaries used for "prayer closet," *kuḥta*, although commonly employed to refer to a pantry, is possibly cognate with the Classical Syriac *kurḥa*, which was often used in earlier periods for a hermit's cell (in contrast to *qelayta*, which referred to a cell in a cenobitic monastery).[64] In contrast to the apparent literalism on the part of Protestants in their reading of the dominical saying of Matthew 6:5–6, the classical Syriac tradition generally took the "closet" or "inner chamber" in this passage to be a reference to the heart of the human being.[65] Ironically, the East Syrian tradition maintained a more spiritualized reading of the biblical text.

Accounts of revivals at the mission in the 1840s and 1850s regularly mention prayer closets. In July 1851 David Stoddard, on returning to the mission after an absence of three years, reminisced: "On this stairway, how often have I stumbled over the pupils when unable to find a closet, they had kneeled here, under cover of the night, to pour out their souls to God? In this wood-house our students, straitened for places of retirement, divided the room by piles of wood into compartments, that each might find a little Bethel, where he could meet his Savior."[66] In the revival of 1850, young women at the female seminary spent up to five hours a day in their closets.[67] In his description of the layout of the female seminary, Thomas Laurie designates as closets several small rooms with windows in the building that served as both school and dormitory.[68] Laurie also claims that each dormitory room slept six to eight pupils and had two or more closets "designed especially, but not exclusively, for devotion."[69] However, any private space could serve as a closet: when asked by Fidelia Fiske whether she had a place for private devotion, Selby, an East Syrian teen, told her, "There is a deep hole under our house, like a cellar, and there I go every day to pray."[70]

Representations of the Dying

The cultivation of a solitary, mortal self reflected in the missionaries' moral exhortation and conversionary discourse and in their arguments for reforming East Syrian funereal culture, as well as in the ritual use of prayer closets, was further articulated by the numerous references to death in the mission literature and more significantly by the use of actual deaths at the mission, as well as literary ones, as exempla for the Christian life. Death was a central component of the missionaries' preaching and a common topic in the literature printed by the mission press, especially in *Rays of Light*. Death, the missionaries' audience was constantly reminded, is always near and could occur at any moment, and when it did, one had better be in the right state because the soul's status after death was eternal. The larger purpose of this message was to demonstrate the necessity of Christ for each person's salvation, but this demonstration created new needs for, and anxieties about, salvation itself. One of the primary purposes of the mission was to cultivate these concerns. For example, the emphasis on unilinear calendrical and clock time at the mission—both the idea of it and the organization of social life around it, as was addressed in chapters 3 and 4—was part of the broader moral exhortation about the brevity of life. Death's imminence and therefore the need for salvation were invoked with the regularity of a clock ticking.

Not only was death a common topic of preaching, but actual deaths were often turned to didactic purposes.[71] Perkins writes in 1844, "Sept. 10. I preached in the city today. I alluded particularly of the death of priest Abraham's mother, who was buried yesterday in the church-yard where we held our meeting, and whose new made grave was under our eyes. The audience was very attentive. Priest Abraham was with me, and spoke with much tenderness and feeling."[72] Implying that she had been affected by the evangelism of the mission, Perkins then describes Abraham's account of his mother's condition in the end, including her openness to death.[73] Accidental deaths offered particularly vivid occasions to expand upon the uncertainty of life. When a wall collapsed, burying several people and killing a woman and her child, William Stocking included the event in his preaching, whereas on another occasion, when a woman died after falling into an oven, it was put to similar use.[74] At times when cholera was especially virulent, it served as a tool for calls to repentance.[75]

Rays of Light often presents moral tales, some based on reality, others obviously fictitious, that conclude with someone dying either in a saved or a lost state.[76] Those who die in a state of sin, their "harvest is past," as one story puts it.[77] We are told in one article of a *saz* (a stringed instrument) player who died at a wedding: he would have been better off had he died at a prayer gathering.[78] Death appears homiletically in *Rays of Light* in articles on how there is nothing human beings can do about death because we are merely dust, or on human error and how the expulsion from the garden led to death.[79] The concern about imminent death, like death itself, could appear anywhere—even, for example, in an article on the human heart in the "Science" section of *Rays of Light*: after describing the human heart, its size, how often it beats, and how it does so our whole life long, the article states, "Why does it not cease like the work of the human being? Because the eyes of God are always gazing upon it, . . . and when he says stop, it will just stop."[80] An article on a disobedient child in the "Education" section of the paper tells how "a death sentence goes against him and he has no means of salvation."[81]

The most striking appearance of death in *Rays of Light* is in the long, sometimes highly rhetorical obituaries that frequently take up the whole or most of the "Fear of God" section of the paper. It is noteworthy that this was the front-page section and that it usually consisted of the moral exhortation typical of the mission. It was not uncommon for whole homilies to be reprinted in this section. *Rays of Light* often also has obituaries, sometimes with deathbed scenes, in the "Miscellanies" section and occasionally, from the early 1860s onward, in the "Youth" section. Versions of several of the longer obituaries printed in "Fear of God" appeared in English years later in *Nestorian Biography: Being Sketches of Pious Nestorians Who Have Died at Oroomiah, Persia, by Missionaries of the A.B.C.F.M.* (1857), whereas other obituary material in English was printed in the *Missionary Herald*.

The first appearance of an obituary in *Rays of Light* was in March 1850 (the first issue appeared in November 1849). In the "Fear of God" section, just after the opening article, "What Are the Signs of a True Christian?" the article entitled "Death" uses a recent death at the mission as a tool for instruction: "Many of the readers of this paper knew Moses, one of the boys of the school of Sire. Some days ago his health was agreeable like our own, but one day he became sick and his sickness became strong and grew until his mind was disturbed and his tongue was stuck, and the messenger of death stood at the gate."[82] The article explains that death can come at any time and that our wealth will be of no help to us when it does. The readers are asked to prepare themselves because death "will not let its hand up from you, even if you cry and beseech and beg him."[83]

After the brief piece of March 1850, long, sentimental obituaries began to appear in the "Fear of God" section until 1871, after which the paper is no longer extant until the 1890s. The first full obituary, which appeared in June 1850, is that of Martha, a late teen who, despite being blind, studied at the school in Geogtapa, and after being affected by the revival of 1846, died later in the summer of 1847.[84] Sarah, who died in June of 1846 and was the daughter of Priest Isho' (Jesus) of Gawar (d. 1846), a teacher at the male seminary (and brother of Deacon Tamo), is the subject of the next obituary, a long document published in October 1850.[85] That these long, pathetic life narratives with extensive deathbed scenes were published several years after the death of their subjects demonstrates their ultimately homiletical, as opposed to informational, purpose.

The repeated retelling of the death of George, the nephew of Priest Isho' and Deacon Tamo, who passed away at the age of seventeen in the midst of the revival of 1851, provides an example of the missionaries' willingness to recycle the news of people's deaths.[86] George's deathbed was observed by those around him: the young man dying in agonizing pain provided a spectacle of

truth, which was then mediated via several Neo-Aramaic and English publications. The March 1851 issue of *Rays of Light*, which contains his obituary,
even concludes with a song entitled "Remembrance of George of Gawar."

Preaching at George's funeral, Perkins claimed:

> I have been happy, during his sickness, to try to alleviate his bodily pains; but I
> have also been greatly refreshed in spirit; and I have been instructed, admon-
> ished, edified and comforted in watching the remarkable exercises of his mind,
> and the ardent longing of his soul after Christ and heaven. Since the death of
> Mrs. Grant, more than twelve years ago, I have been present at no so rapturous
> death-bed scene; nor have I ever beheld any more interesting or wonderful.[87]

The funeral was teary, and yet "the boisterous and loud lamentations for the
dead, which ordinarily characterize Nestorian funerals," were absent.[88]

George had left his home of Memekkan in Gawar in 1847 to study at the
male seminary. In 1849, on one of his later journeys between his mountain
home and Urmia, he and his three uncles, including Tamo, were beaten, almost killed, and even held for ransom because the patriarch had sent word
out that those who had joined the mission were personae non gratae.[89] The
various obituaries for George, who had been studying at the seminary in Sire
for four years at the time of his death, describe his formerly rugged mountain
demeanor and eventual transformation into a prayerful, pious young man,
who would shut himself away in his prayer closet sometimes for hours at
a stretch, even remaining there through the night. *Rays of Light* details the
various questions posed to him while he was dying. As was mentioned above,
the deathbed for Protestants, as it had been in different ways for others, had
become a proving ground, like the arena for early Christians, a stage upon
which they could perform and confirm the truth of Christianity. In the direct
dialogue quoted in *Rays of Light*, George bravely embraces death, provided it
is one in Christ, and thus he resembles the patient Evangeline St. Clare. Finally, he receives visions, which he narrates to those around him, of ascending
a mountain, like Moses, and yet unlike Moses, we are told, he directly apprehended the face of God. In a letter composed soon afterward, Joseph Cochran
cannot account for the "originality and sublimity" of his views on God and
the heavenly world "save on the supposition of a special illumination given
to departing spirits."[90] Also the inclusion in the text of George's vision of his
friend Michael, son of Dunkha, draws an intertext between this exemplum
and a prior one. Michael had died the previous year, and the narrative of his
death, written by his sister Sanam, had appeared in the November 1850 issue
of *Rays of Light*.[91]

In the years to follow, similar obituaries would often appear in "Fear of

God." For example, Maryam, the wife of Priest Aslan, a copyist at the mission, died in 1854, and her husband wrote a moving obituary for "Fear of God," including a drawn-out deathbed interview about her faith (later published in English in *Nestorian Biography*).[92] Many of the major figures at the mission, both missionaries and native assistants, received obituaries in *Rays of Light*, sometimes with similar dramatic deathbed scenes. These accounts are often the only text in the entire "Fear of God" section of the issue, and at times the section takes up much of the space for that issue. On my accounting, approximately one in four, possibly more, issues of *Rays of Light* up to 1871 had such material in the "Fear of God" section.[93]

The mission's representation of death had a disproportionate focus on the suffering and premature death of young Christians, especially girls and young women. This focus corresponds with some of the works most commonly translated at the mission, what we might call Christian novellas: Legh Richmond's *The Dairyman's Daughter* (1809; Neo-Aramaic: *The Daughter of Walbridge* [1845]) and *The Young Cottager* (1815; Neo-Aramaic: *Little Jane* [1850]), two similar stories about precociously pious Christian girls who die young.[94] Also published at the same time was Hannah More's *The Shepherd of Salisbury Plain* (1795–97; Neo-Aramaic: same title [1849]), a book related in genre, but about a pious and poor shepherd who recognizes his place in society and keeps it.[95] The two novellas by Richmond tell the standard tale of the Christian girl who, not unlike "little Eva" of *Uncle Tom's Cabin*, die young while confessing Christ. Such deaths are part of God's wise plan: as Thomas Laurie states with regard to the actual deaths of three young women at the mission in the late 1840s, "It is remarkable that three timid girls should have been chosen to lead the advance of a great multitude of Nestorians through the dark valley into the light. . . . Infinite Wisdom chose, through such weak and timorous ones, to glorify the power of Christ to bear his people through the last conflict into everlasting rest."[96] In reference to Jane, *The Young Cottager* even quotes from 1 Corinthians 1:27: "But God hath chosen the foolish things of the world to confound the wise," a common proof text for the paradoxical reversal of the incarnation and the power of the Gospel.[97]

Such Christian narrative literature was extremely popular throughout the nineteenth century. Millions of copies of *The Dairyman's Daughter* were printed in numerous languages, and it enjoyed a broad popular reception from England to the United States, through Europe, and to the missionary peripheries.[98] Elizabeth Walbridge, the heroine of *The Dairyman's Daughter*, is a model Christian, who realizes her sinful nature, converts to true Christianity, and then provides an example for others as she patiently endures sickness and eventually, after a brilliant deathbed performance, dies. The evangelical community fostered a "cult of Walbridge" in the early nineteenth century. Testimonials of the text's capacity to convert people were sought, and the "real" Elizabeth's grave on the Isle of Wight became a place of pilgrimage, while the chair that belonged to her was on display in New York City at the American Tract Society.[99] The mission press printed numerous books and tracts, Bible editions and hymns, but of these various genres, aside from the Bible, this Christian narrative literature, including *Pilgrim's Progress*, is referred to most often in the sources of the 1840s and 1850s. This is perhaps because the genre itself allowed for identification like no other. "Evangelicals believed a tract could effect the conversion of its reader, or in this case, its listener. It could transform a person reading a tract aloud into a minister exhorting the unconverted, and in the process, turn the confines of a private home into a sacred space."[100] This is all the more so with this narrative genre.

A number of interesting correspondences and changes can be seen in how this and other texts were rendered into Neo-Aramaic and how they would have been received in mid-nineteenth-century Iran. *The Dairyman's Daughter* shares many sentiments that we find in the missionaries' writings. The narrator's exclamations about the beauty and order of nature, its present fallen state, and its future restitution resemble the Romantic wonder, followed by a sense of tragic loss, expressed by Perkins in his memoir. The nostalgia for the late English feudal system of these novellas, which were "designed to convince the lower orders in society that their station was an appropriate, happy, and pious one," and reflected "a preindustrial world in which personal relationships rather than contracts ruled," corresponded with the socioeconomic system the missionaries found in Urmia.[101] This is obviously the case in *The Shepherd of Salisbury Plain*, the author of which, Hannah More (1745–1833), was a political and cultural reactionary.

An important aspect of *The Dairyman's Daughter* and these other tales is the observation that is part of their narrative structure: the author regularly observes Elizabeth's character, and this tendency in the text would only be further drawn out in a context where the indigenous strongly identify with the heroine and the missionaries map easily onto the position of the narrator, especially due to parallels in class and in the missionaries' self-perceived religious authority. However, this observation also turns back onto the narrator. He and the audience are compelled to look into themselves to examine how they can possibly imitate the example provided by Elizabeth.

Because of the more limited vocabulary of the Neo-Aramaic translation, the mission's version of *The Dairyman's Daughter* has an even greater focus on the condition of the self or soul (*ahwal d-gana*) and the state of one's heart (*ahwal d-lebba*).[102] The ongoing discussion of the condition or status of the heroine's soul aims to create an awareness in the audience of their own souls and the condition of each. The heroine's death in the book's final scene points forward to our own: how will we stand up to death? Reminiscent of the theatricality of the early Christian martyr acts, death became a spectacle both at and for the mission: it was understood that although one may die surrounded by family and friends, death is a solitary act that can only serve as an example for others.

It has been argued that books like *The Dairyman's Daughter* "presented a vision strikingly at odds with the individualism of liberal economic thought."[103] They "privileged the values of community and benevolence over the quest for personal gain."[104] Spiritual values are elevated over the temporal, and the social links of family and community are emphasized.[105] How does this focus on community relate to the isolation of the self in death that I am proposing is implicit in such texts? For, to have no relations with the dead, to have no effect on them nor to receive any benefits from them, reflects at the fundamental level an absence of relations with other human beings. However, inasmuch as death is a leveling, it also creates the possibility of community among Christians. All become equal as mortals and as Christians. The dead can serve only as models, just as we can only serve as models for one another in this life. In this way, in Richmond's *The Young Cottager*, another tale of a pious girl who dies young, also translated at the mission, the pastor-narrator describes taking children to a cemetery to have them memorize epitaphs: "Thus my churchyard became a book of instruction, and every gravestone a leaf of edification for my young disciples."[106] We cannot gain from one another through exchange, but only through example. This fits with the solitary sociality implicit in Christian's experience in *Pilgrim's Progress*, the new ideas and practices of community discussed in chapters 3 and 4, and the rejection of the idea that giving charity to the poor was beneficial, as we find in Perkins's tract against begging.[107]

In June of 1844 Perkins rode out to Geogtapa to spend the Sabbath and to investigate the new enthusiasm in the village, spurred on by the work of John of Geogtapa, Priest Abraham, and some graduates from the female seminary. He attended services and then visited the Sunday school, after which "a room full of villagers assembled in the same place, and listened with deep interest to the reading of the *Dairyman's Daughter*, which was read by John, Moses, and myself, in turn."[108] Perkins doubted "whether it was ever clothed in any garb in which its rare excellence can be better understood and felt than in this simple language, among this poor people." "Elizabeth Walbridge," Perkins explains, had "already become a familiar and favorite name among scores of them." "A great amount of light has been diffused there, and not without happy effects."

Perkins notes changes among the population: a concern for the Sabbath, an interest in preaching, a decline of intemperance, and even a decrease in theft. On another visit to Geogtapa, which was "becoming a kind of radiant centre," Perkins visited the house of Priest Abraham after a prayer meeting. "A number of persons came in, and the priest's daughter, Sarah, a girl of fourteen, who is a member of Miss Fisk[e]'s school, read to them from the *Dairyman's Daughter*. All present appeared to be deeply interested in what they heard. An aged uncle of priest Abraham expressed the hope that this Sarah, the reader, might become just such a girl as Elizabeth Walbridge."[109]

Priest John of Kosi was a diligent assistant to the mission, whose tale of moral reform and of giving up drink is the first life described in *Nestorian Biography*. When the priest died at Geogtapa on August 31, 1845, Perkins wrote in his journal that Priest John happened to stop by the mission one day just after *The Dairyman's Daughter* was printed. He picked up a copy and started reading, "and soon became so engrossed that he could not lay it down till he had finished it."[110] He was found weeping over the book and exclaimed, "This poor girl repented on hearing one sermon; and what will become of our girls, who hear so much truth and still do not repent?" David Stoddard mentions that, during the first full revival in 1846, John the native assistant named his newborn daughter Elizabeth after Elizabeth Walbridge (and Perkins years later positively compared the girl to her namesake).[111] Stoddard then notes that aside from the Bible, *The Dairyman's Daughter* was the most popular reading among the people.

When Sarah, daughter of Priest Isho', died in the early summer after the revival of 1846, *The Dairyman's Daughter* was read at prayers.

> This being the first death which has occurred among those who were hopefully born again during the past winter, it is calculated to produce a deep impression on them all, and especially on the members of the seminaries. At evening prayers I read the last part of *The Dairyman's Daughter*, and I have rarely seen the audience in a more tender and interesting state of feeling.[112]

In *Nestorian Biography* Sarah is compared to Elizabeth Walbridge,[113] whereas Thomas Laurie writes, "Her emaciated form, her hollow cough, her eye bright with unnatural luster, all told that she was passing away, but, combined with her sweet singing and heavenly spirit, led her companions sometimes to whisper, as she took her seat in the chapel, 'Have we not an Elizabeth Walbridge among us?'"[114]

After the death of Judith Grant Perkins (August 8, 1840–September 4, 1852), one of several of the Perkinses' young children to die at the mission, "little Judith" was transformed into a model of Christian virtue. She was named after Judith, founder of the female seminary and wife of Asahel Grant, who had died less than a year before little Judith was born and whom Justin Perkins had eulogized. (This eulogy was later published separately, as were others, such as Austin Wright's one for Martha Ann Rhea, wife of Samuel Rhea, who died in 1857.)[115] The "Fear of God" section of *Rays of Light* of September 1852, entitled "Judith, the Flower Withered (Is. 40:7)," describes her awareness of her impending death and how she suffered like an exemplary Christian. The article concludes: "Reader, do you not open your eyes to see death, how near it is, and do you not hear the voice from this dying girl which calls you to repent from sins and to prepare your soul to meet your predicament [*ahwal*]?"[116] Soon afterward an English volume was composed at the mission (possibly by Joseph G. Cochran) and sent to America for publication: *The Persian Flower: A Memoir of Judith Grant Perkins of Oroomiah, Persia* (1853), provides a pathetic, highly sentimental tale of a pious and sweet child who dies of cholera, bravely facing the death she prophetically foresees. Judith becomes an intertextual link of exemplarity when she is described as reading *Uncle Tom's Cabin* to her mother not long before her death.[117] She is then explicitly compared to "little Eva." (A copy of *Uncle Tom's Cabin* was sent to the mission on its publication because of Perkins's prior relationship to Henry Ward Beecher as his tutor.)[118] Later, we are told that, as with Elizabeth Walbridge, some East Syrians named their daughters Judith after her, and she is compared to little Jane, the "young cottager."[119] The exemplarity of death and the intertextuality between books and people led to the conflation of real and fictional lives, not unlike the "cult of Walbridge." In several mission publications, and even in mission letters, Judith Perkins is referred to simply as the "Persian Flower," the identity of the dead child being equated with the title of a book about her.[120]

The focus on the dead, especially on the exemplary death of leaders among the mission and the missionized community, on the one hand, and that of paradigmatic young Christians, particularly young women, on the other, provided a substitute for the cult of the saints the missionaries were interested in eradicating. The East Syrians traditionally would name children after saints, as is common in many Christian communities. As the missionaries note, the names *Jane*, *Elizabeth*, and *Judith* became popular. However, the use of these names is different from naming children after saints. A saint can offer help, but a dead young woman can only offer an example. The saints were to be imitated, but also, as God's favorites whom he endowed with power, they could spread their bounty upon the earth, even long after their deaths. In contrast, Elizabeth Walbridge and her ilk could only provide models of true piety, pointing to the signs of correct faith, but ultimately they could do nothing for others' salvation.

Awakenings

The pressing, even anxiety-inducing conversation about death and salvation cultivated by the missionaries helped set the affective tone for the various revivals that occurred at the mission and elsewhere in the 1840s and 1850s. These sometimes ecstatic, sometimes solemn events were regularly marked by a great concern about the finality and permanence of death. Revival, or awakening (*r'ašta*), as it was known in Neo-Aramaic, was a ritual and figurative goal of the mission. As discussed in chapter 3, the root *r-'-š* means more than just "to wake up," but has the sense of "to begin to feel," "to come to one's senses," even "to experience." The whole project of the mission was to "revive" or "awaken" (*mar'eš*) the "Nestorians" from the slumber into which their ancient church had fallen so that they could again, like their ancestors, spread Christianity across Asia. More specifically, "revival" was the ritual event that would demonstrate the presence of God and his Holy Spirit working again among the Nestorians.

The missionaries themselves would of course not refer to this as a ritual event. Aside from their general antipathy toward ritual as rote, heartless action, they specifically note in their descriptions of local revivals that these events were not stimulated by any particular change in routine. This served for them as further evidence that these revivals were instigated from on high. In contrast, I refer to revivals as ritual events because they followed certain unspoken scripts and were aimed at and cultivated by the mission, even if their specific outbreaks were not actively incited. The revivals both in Urmia and those extending out from there to Sire, Geogtapa, Ardishai, and into the mountains west of the plain tended to occur, at least in the early years, at the same time each year, beginning in January and running into February, sometimes even into the spring. The missionaries were not unaware of this calendrical correspondence. Moreover, knowing the history of their own churches, they were acquainted with such texts as Jonathan Edwards's "A Faithful Narrative of the Surprising Work of God" (1737), which gives a history of the revival in Northampton, Massachusetts, in 1734–35.[121] Such accounts provided a blueprint for what a revival should look like, and so it is not a coincidence that successful revivals among the Nestorians were compared to "genuine New England Revivals,"[122] or even that David Stoddard's published description of the first revival is titled *Narrative of the*

Late Revival among the Nestorians (1847), a gesture toward Edwards's and others' works.

One important aspect of revival was its affective and visceral physicality. The presence of the Spirit could cause people to fall down, cry, and shake. Such a physical response to the Spirit was expected but also needed to be controlled. Already in the eighteenth century during the First Great Awakening, in response to critics of the high emotionality of some participants of revival, supporters of the movement became conscious of the need to correctly interpret and sometimes limit this affective response and the physical display of conversion. Edwards, for example, in his *Some Thoughts Concerning the Present Revival of Religion in New-England* (1742), complains that critics judge these events a priori and should rather wait and see the results, whether they correspond with the word of God. He argues that the affections are an important part of religion, and responds to those who would make a clear distinction between the will, which they link to rationality, and the affections, which they deem primarily as bad. "True virtue or holiness" in fact has its seat in the human heart, and "it consists chiefly of holy affections."[123] However, Edwards admits that there are false affections in religion, and that some people are affected in different ways by the power of the Spirit. This is why it is necessary to apply semiology to its symptoms: ecstatic behavior could be a sign of the Spirit, but one needs to make further observations and should not assume that such behavior is necessary for everyone to be converted. Related to this concern about authentication, missionary accounts of the various revivals among the East Syrians often include analytical lists of the general qualities of emotion and feeling demonstrated during the events.[124]

To the missionaries' chagrin, in the early years the mission's audience remained lukewarm, only at times showing "interest." Before 1846 there were promising hints of the affective state the missionaries hoped for, but nothing like a revival: in early 1844 "the first indications of unusual seriousness appeared on the first Monday in January,"[125] the opening concert of prayer of the New Year.

> At the close of this meeting, the pupils in the Seminary and Girl's Boarding School were earnestly and affectionately addressed; they were reminded that the prayers of many Christians, far away, were ascending in their behalf; and they were solemnly urged to seek the pardoning love of Christ without delay. It was soon evident that God was giving efficacy to his truth; and the inquiry was heard, "What must I do to be saved?"[126]

The following year, after the massacres of 1844, as noted by the missionaries, there was even greater interest, and in Geogtapa in particular "some exhibited considerable 'tenderness of feeling.'"[127] As mentioned above, Perkins describes participating at this time in a public reading of *The Dairyman's Daughter*.

David Stoddard's letters attest to the missionaries' ongoing desire for revival as well as their frustration at its absence.[128] Even in late 1845, not long before the beginning of the first revival at the mission, during one of these periods of seriousness and solemnity, Stoddard had little expectation of what was about to occur. At the New Year's concert in January 1844, some "were permitted to enjoy a refreshing from the presence of the Lord," but no full revival.[129] The archive attests to these periods of *interest*, which is the term the missionaries used to refer to what looked like minor sparks that could lead to the fire of revival, but the flame did not take until January 1846. Despite claims about its spontaneous occurrence, Stoddard also seems to suggest that, at least at the male seminary, the revival may have been aided by the reorganization of the school and in particular Stoddard's and John of Geogtapa's project of selecting a different individual to pray over each day.[130]

On Monday, January 5, at the concert of prayer for the New Year, which was also an exercise for the beginning of the school year, two young women, Sarah (1831–46) and Sanam (d. 1865), both daughters of priests, showed an unusual interest. This was the same Sarah, the daughter of Priest Isho', who would die that year and be compared to Elizabeth Walbridge for both her piety and her premature death. Sanam, who has appeared already above and whom I will address again below, had grown up mostly around the mission.

> Miss Fiske went into her school, as usual, at nine o'clock, and, after telling her flock that many prayers were being offered for them that day in a distant land, led their morning devotions, and then sent them into another room to study with a native teacher. San[a]m and Sarah lingered behind the rest and as they drew near, she asked, "Did you not understand me?" They made no reply; and she saw they were weeping. "Have you had bad news?" Still no reply; but when they got near enough, they whispered, "May we have to-day to care for our souls?" and Sarah added, "Perhaps next year I shall not be here." There was no private room to give them, but they made a closet for themselves among the fuel in the wood cellar, and there spent that day looking unto Jesus; nor did they look in vain.[131]

Things remained calm until January 19, when "there were such unusual appearances of deep and tender interest, as led us to feel that the Holy Spirit had decidedly commenced his gracious work in the hearts of a considerable number."[132] This occurred simultaneously at both the male and female seminaries. "In the course of the day, five came to Miss Fisk[e] with the anxious inquiry, 'What shall I do to be saved?'"[133] As news of the revival spread, some mothers visited their daughters at the female seminary and entered their prayer closets with them to be instructed about the message of salvation their daughters had acquired and to pray with them.[134]

Despite their enthusiasm, the missionaries demonstrated early caution regarding the veracity of the revival. Perkins writes:

> The work has all the characteristics, so far as we can judge, of genuineness and thoroughness; quite as much so as any of the revivals which it has been my privilege to witness in America; and our knowledge of the superficial character of the people, in religious matters, leads us to exercise our utmost discrimination in relation to it.[135]

Stoddard similarly explains how the missionaries approached the revival with the "utmost caution . . . to prevent self-deception" because "the Nestorians" could "imagine themselves to have feelings and exercises to which they are strangers."[136] Elsewhere he states, "At least we need far more caution in regard to encouraging hopes than would be necessary in America."[137]

The revival was marked by a rampant tendency to pray, sometimes anywhere and everywhere. "The feeling in the seminary has increased with great rapidity. Many are beginning to pray in secret and to weep over their sins," writes Stoddard in his journal entry for January 22.[138] One young man "came into my study, trembling exceedingly, like a man in convulsions."[139] Stoddard spoke with him and then left him in the room to pray alone. The next morning he found the boy, who had formerly lived in William Stocking's household, still there praying, apparently having not slept at all. By January 25 Stoddard writes of John tripping over someone praying in the stairwell and of himself overhearing another praying in the wood house. At times of revival, prayer closets were in the highest demand. Even though many spaces were made accessible for the students to pray, "Such is the disposition to pray without ceasing, and so numerous are those who are awakened that individuals are often distressed because they can find no place in which to pour out their souls to God."[140] The excitement and the close quarters could lead to problems. The next day, on being told that some boys were "weeping violently in one of their rooms," Stoddard went to check on them. "I entered the room, and found fifteen or twenty boys lying on the floor, weeping, groaning, in broken sentences asking God for mercy, and presenting a scene of great confusion. Some of the older natives were standing around in silent wonder, thinking that an angel had visited the school."[141]

Stoddard "succeeded in checking this manifestation of feeling, and addressed those assembled on the nature of true repentance, and the danger to be apprehended from such disorder." He had the students promise that no more than two would pray together at once. Some students were unable to eat and sleep, and one came down with a violent fever, "induced, at least indirectly, by the intensity of his feelings."[142] In the spring, following the revival, the members of the male seminary left the city for Sire. Stoddard writes, "It is delightful, as I walk about the mountain, to find here and there, in some secluded spot, individuals wrestling with the angel of the covenant."[143]

At the female seminary, "We began to fear that some were affected merely by animal sympathy."[144] The "apparent depth and pungency of conviction on the part of a few" combined with the close quarters was deemed a danger. "To avoid, as far as possible, all spurious excitement, and to give to those interested a separate place of retirement, we appropriated every 'nook and corner' in our house, in addition to the premises allotted to the school, for their benefit." This had an immediate effect of distinguishing those who were "really awakened to a sense of their sins" from those who were "moved by a mere animal sympathy." As a preventative measure, the heads of the female seminary enforced strict rules about hours of sleep, lest the girls remain up all night in their religious enthusiasm.[145]

The extreme prayerfulness of some students was not only noted but closely observed.

> One of the girls, believing that she was still unrenewed, and greatly fearing permanent injury from mingling with the world at this time, has spent the whole day in earnest cries for mercy. Never have I listened to supplications that seemed more earnest and affecting, than I overheard from this girl of twelve or fourteen, after her companions had left, and where she supposed that no one but the infinite Searcher of hearts was near her.[146]

Stoddard describes the intensity of the experience of one of the native assistants:

> Yonan of Ada, particularly, lay tossing upon the floor the whole Thursday night, begging for mercy, and there was serious reason to apprehend that he would fall into a fit. The natural clearness of his mind and his familiarity with gospel truth, added to the continued warnings he had received, and his repeated attempts to stifle the convictions of his conscience, all now heaped fuel on the fire, and he seemed overcome with horror.

The following day Yonan "had his mouth filled with the praises of redeeming love."[147]

The missionaries' descriptions of these events are often rendered in a language of observation, especially with regard to the native assistants. For example, the accounts sometimes note how individual East Syrians were faring in the revival, whether they were affected, and whether it seemed authentic.[148] A number of East Syrians who would become important figures at the mission, as well as some who had already been working with Perkins and the other missionaries for years, experienced conversions during this first revival. When the brothers of Deacon Tamo came from the mountains at this time, one of them, we are told, threw his dagger to the ground after being prayed over, saying that it was of no use to him and exclaiming, "What shall I do to be saved?"[149] George, the "mountain deacon," whose career I address in the next chapter, also visited the mission for the first time during this revival and was touched by the enthusiasm.[150] Apparently, those who were associated with the mission longer or were more advanced in the mission school were more likely to be affected by the revival, even though the authenticity of the event was confirmed for the missionaries by the enthusiastic transformation of a number of illiterate young people who would not have had any "mercenary motives."[151]

If we understand revival and the public displays that attended it as an opportunity to form close social links with the mission or to confirm those that already existed, then it makes sense that both those with the deepest, longest-term commitments to the mission and the socially dislocated would equally participate in these events. For the former, the performance of ontological helplessness during periods of revival was a way to normalize prior connections to the mission. In regard to the latter, there were instances of conversion among refugees from Hakkari who had only recently found their way to Urmia.[152] Two young men from 'Ada, who had previously become Catholic, arrived at the mission and were "almost immediately under conviction of sin."[153] Stoddard "was still more interested, considering they had never been brought under the direct influence of the mission, till the past month, to see the amount of doctrinal knowledge which they possessed, and the depth and fulness of their religious experience."[154] The revival then spread to the East Syrian quarter of the city of Urmia and the village of Sire, where the health retreat was, while other outsiders, such as a local tailor, the mission printers, and George, the nephew of Tamo, were also brought into the fold.[155] Despite the collective enthusiasm of the revival, isolation and anxious engagement with death were central to the conversion experience advocated by the missionaries. Solitary meditation upon mortality was part of a performance of the type of self the missionaries were trying to foster, a self that when multiplied became a constituent unit in the new social forms emerging at the mission.

Deacon Isaac, who would years later speak on national unity and support the mission, was in a precarious position: as the brother of the patriarch and his informal liaison to the mission, it was difficult for him to join the Americans. His liminal social position was expressed in his ambivalent stance toward the salvation of which the Americans spoke. On February 13, 1846, in the midst of the revival, Isaac visited Stoddard, who asked him whether the events made him rejoice. He explained that he would be happy but that he felt like

> a man that stands on the shore of a lake, and seeing a beautiful country on the other is gladdened by the prospect, but has no means of reaching that beautiful country himself. . . . My heart is perfectly dead. You may cut and thrust me with a sword, but I am insensible to the stroke. And if you kindly pour ointment on my wounds, it is all the same. I choose sin. I love sin. The wild beasts in the mountains are enticed by the hunters, and seize the bait, not knowing what they do. But I take this world with my eyes open, knowing that I am choosing destruction and eating death.[156]

Isaac demonstrated his liminal position by rejecting the message of salvation while accepting its claims about mortality. He would come to terms with his status and join the mission years later, afterward serving it until his death in 1864.[157] In this case his ambivalence reveals the sociological relations that could structure conversions and the public ecstatic experience of revival.

The missionaries note their pleasant surprise at the absence of resistance from the East Syrian clergy, who even at times showed support.[158] They specifically compare the situation to that of the mission to the Armenians, which continued to experience resistance from the church hierarchy.[159] Stocking speculates why the clergy and other influential East Syrians did not oppose what was going on.[160] To begin with, the local governor, who was Kurdish, was in fact a relative of Badr Khan Bey, the Kurdish chief who was responsible for the massacres of East Syrians in Hakkari in 1844. In contrast, the East Syrian clergy had no civil authority, and the patriarch and his family were in a humiliating position: the patriarch himself was in exile in Mosul, and his family were divided among themselves. Furthermore, Stocking says that the many benefits the missionaries had brought over the years were admitted to be great and that the missionaries could always refer to the Bible as a common standard to justify the revival. Finally, he mentions that, aside from the general impression that the events were divinely inspired, several clergy members were converted early in the revival, thus setting an example for others. However, there was some resistance. Stoddard states that some people at Geogtapa were "ridiculing those who were earnestly seeking the salvation of their souls.

'Why all this ado?' say they. 'Must all that we have done for salvation, go for nothing? Have all our fathers gone to hell?'" a sentiment that reflects the simultaneously developing discourse on tradition.[161]

The enthusiasm of the revival was reawakened at each monthly concert into the spring, and it was on June 15 that Sarah, the daughter of Priest Isho', died. This also seemed to the missionaries to serve a purpose in the revival. For months afterward the missionaries noted the apparent results of this first revival, finding meaning in any noteworthy changes in the East Syrian community. According to a letter written by William Stocking on September 18, 1846, the power of grace was demonstrated at Geogtapa by the fact that theft had decreased; the Sabbath was observed, as if in New England; and the people felt a hunger for religious knowledge, as well as a more "scriptural observance" of the sacrament after much deliberation about whether they could "conscientiously administer the ordinance."[162] Two hundred of a village of about one thousand came to the prayer meetings and to hear preaching, a crowd that included the "hopefully pious," whereas Stocking later claimed that "while the prevailing sentiments of the people are decidedly evangelical, about seventy, including those who are connected with our seminaries, furnish decided evidence of regeneration, and exert a happy Christian influence over the whole place."[163] The prayerfulness of the young converts during the revival "strongly reminded" Stoddard "of the spirit of their fathers."[164] Perkins similarly noted that they were "not unworthy of their illustrious ancestry of missionary and martyr memory."[165] Signs of revival in Tergawar, a mountainous area west of the plain, were even compared to the famous Haystack Prayer Meeting, the founding event of the ABCFM, which took place in Williamstown, Massachusetts, in August 1806.[166]

Another revival did not occur until three years later, in 1849.[167] Again, it started after the New Year with a certain solemnity leading to an emotional crescendo that began in the middle of the month. The mission, the seminaries, and Geogtapa were especially affected. Perkins, in a letter dated to January 29, 1849, suggests that the timing the revival shared with the beginning of missionary preaching tours in Hakkari was not a coincidence and furthermore that the "persecutions of the Patriarch" suffered by East Syrians and the mission may have been spiritually beneficial.[168] At the male seminary, which had moved to Sire in June 1847, this revival was reinvigorated on February 1. When the students had gathered for their normal daily school exercises, "The young men seemed more like culprits, dragged to the block of execution, than like youth in pursuit of knowledge."[169] Several prayers were offered, "all of which seemed only to increase the agony and intensity of desire for the blessing of the Lord." Joseph Cochran suspended studies for the day and "ex-

horted the boys to repair to their closets, to implore relief and to ask pardon-
ing mercy from their grieved but compassionate Savior."

> The prayer closets attached to the seminary buildings, and all the unoccupied
> rooms, were immediately filled; and yet a majority of the pupils had no place
> to give vent to their burdened hearts. Hamis [Khamis], the brother of Deacon
> Tamo, proposed prayer in the yard, and there, on a wintry day, for nearly an
> hour, these youths were pouring forth their earnest prayers to heaven for par-
> don and salvation. It was a scene more solemn than language can describe;
> and it seemed to me more like the dread assizes of the judgment day, than any
> thing I had ever before seen.

On assessing these events several months later, Cochran was comfortable in
affirming the reality of this revival. Although "only those who endure to the
end, can be counted as genuine disciples," he states that of the forty-eight
students, seventeen became "hopeful converts." As in 1846, he provides the
criteria by which he judged the event genuine: (1) "the *remarkable pungency
of their convictions of sin*," (2) "*Their views of saving truth were very intelligent
and discriminating*," and (3) "*their all-absorbing interest in the one question of
salvation by Christ*." The students showed little interest in "earthly science,"
and even "the reading of the Old Testament in the ancient Syriac was regarded by many as too cold a service; and the request was often made to me,
that they might study the New Testament ever more."[170] In his own analysis,
Perkins notes the various characteristics of the revival, such as a developing
sense of one's own sinfulness, and describes among the students "an ardent
desire for the salvation of their friends and their perishing people."[171]

Yet again in 1850 a revival began in January at the male seminary at the
same time as similar events transpired in Urmia at the female seminary.[172] "At
the evening prayer-meeting [Sunday, January 13], Deacon Tamo spoke of the
uncertainty of life, and the need of preparation for death, alluding in his remarks to the death of two of our number during the past year, and the sickness
of many others. The congregation was moved, and wept freely and audibly."[173]
The whole congregation continued to weep and refused to leave. They demanded another prayer meeting. Perkins obliged them, but then became concerned when the weeping spread and became louder. He "requested all who
were so disposed to repair to their closets, and there unburden their hearts
before the mercy seat." The intense feeling increased over the next few days,
and similar events were reported in the female seminary and in Geogtapa. The
events were managed by the missionaries and their helpers through regular
preaching combined with an attempt to preserve at least some of the normal
school routine. Again, it is noted that no special prior instigations were imple-

mented, nor was there communication at first between the two seminaries, both of these facts taken as evidence that the event was divinely inspired.

Deacon Jeremiah came under conviction of sin. He had been a Catholic monk at the monastery of Rabban Hormizd in Alqosh in what is now northern Iraq and had come from Mosul with Perkins and William Stocking after their visit there. At a prayer meeting on the morning of January 22, he "stated his religious experience in a very affecting manner," which intrigued Perkins since it seemed to suggest that, because he was new to the mission, "a true work of grace is essentially the same, in all ages and in all lands!"[174] At the female seminary special hours of "social prayer" were instituted, which led to intense emotional outbreaks, with girls running to their prayer closets and also forming "little family prayer meetings" in their rooms.[175] George Coan describes his conversation with one young girl affected by this revival. When asked about hell, she responded, "I know I deserve to go there; and let God throw me into hell, if he will; only let me go out from my body; but I thought of my poor people, and said, 'Who will preach the gospel to them'; and so I was encouraged to go on."[176] Stocking describes the restlessness of the girls at the female seminary: when told that they should go to sleep, they responded, "We *have been* asleep for weeks—doing nothing for God—ruining souls—how can we sleep till we are forgiven?"[177] According to Coan, the great similarity the revival shared with those at home in America demonstrated that "the power of divine grace is the same, the world over."[178]

There were repeated revivals for years to come (1851, 1854, 1856, 1857, 1858, 1859, 1860, 1862, 1863, and 1864).[179] We also read of localized revivals in other cities on the plain as well as, for example, in Gawar in 1865.[180] Deaths during times of revival continued to be used for preaching. The cook at the male seminary became ill during the revival of 1856. "This sudden and alarming prostration was a voice which preached loudly to all on our premises to be ready for eternity, and especially as the poor man was himself unprepared to die." The day he died, the evening meeting "was one of the most solemn we have ever witnessed."[181] The following day was devoted to religious exercises integrated into a funeral.

Conclusion: A Pilgrim's Dream

In this chapter I have compared the East Syrian and American missionary cultures of death; addressed how conversion was conceived of as an interiorization of religion, especially through the technology of the prayer closet; described the representation of death employed in the missionaries' "evangelism of fear"; and finally provided an account of some of the early revivals at, or in the vicinity of, the mission. I begin these concluding remarks by describing a text composed by a young East Syrian woman, setting it within the context of her life of evangelical service to her people.

In the spring of 1850, Sanam, who had just completed her education at the female seminary, gave a valedictory address, which was later entitled "The Lost Soul" and published in the July 1850 issue of *Rays of Light*, where it is presented as an example of the benefits of female education.[182] In the previous chapter I described the speech she gave the following year on examination day. Sanam had originally composed this one, we are told, when, during the revival of 1850, the students at the female seminary were left to their own devices to compose what they liked, while their teachers were gone to an examination at the male seminary in nearby Sire. Sanam's 1850 speech begins with what seems to be a reference to the beginning of *Pilgrim's Progress*: "I have dreamed a dream, dear friends—may I relate it? In my dream I was wandering about, seeking for earthly pleasures, though my life was crowned with blessings more plentiful than the dew of the morning."[183] Sanam describes how her parents and teachers were unable to save her, despite their efforts at setting her on the right path. She details her own inner reflections and anxieties about salvation and the conversations she had with herself. This is followed by an account of her vision of "the Ancient of Days seated on his throne" (Dn 7:9).[184] The vision of the throne results in her judgment and condemnation for the many sins she has committed, all of which arise before her. She finds herself associated with Cain, Judas, Jeroboam, and Jezebel. Across an unbridgeable abyss she sees her companions who have already been saved. She then feels the fire and worm of rot that last for eternity.

> In my anguish I cried, "Roll on, ye eternal ages!" But why? They will be no nearer through. "O Lord, how long?" With an earthquake, that seemed to shake the very throne, came back the reply, "Forever! Forever!" I sank down in unutterable agony. Then I awoke, and lo, it was all a dream. The darkness of night was yet around me; a cold sweat covered me; and that word, "Forever!" still rang in my ears. Friends, this was a dream, and only a drop in the ocean, compared with the terrible reality. Let us pray we may be saved from it through Jesus Christ our Lord.[185]

According to Laurie's account of the public performance of this speech, "The large audience listened to these vivid delineations, part of the time, in breathless silence; and again the women beat on their breasts with half-suppressed cries of mercy."[186]

Sanam's composition is one young woman's rearticulation of the evangelism of fear the missionaries had fostered among the East Syrian population. Sanam had grown up at the mission and eventually served as a native assistant, spreading the Gospel to her people. Her father was Priest Dunkha, whose family was originally from the Tiyari tribal region of Hakkari.[187] After being pushed out of the Shemsdin district by local marauders, they settled in Memekkan in the Gawar valley. Life was rustic and rough. One of Dunkha's uncles died when a roof collapsed on his head after the buffalo, which had been sheltering in the house, got into a squabble and knocked down the posts that held up the ceiling. Dunkha's other uncle, Solomon, who was a learned priest, stayed with Perkins and Grant in 1835 during their first winter in Urmia. Solomon instructed his nephew, Dunkha, who then also became a priest.

Dunkha married and had at least two children, Sanam (d. 1865) and Michael (ca. 1836–50). In 1835–36 he went on a visit to Mar Bisho and met Priest Abraham of Geogtapa and another Syrian whom Perkins had sent into the mountains to find someone to help him in translating the Bible into the vernacular. Before this, Dunkha had been teaching on the Urmia plain at the school that Hormizd Muqdasi had already established at Geogtapa prior to the arrival of the missionaries.[188] After joining the mission, Dunkha served as a native assistant for several years.

Dunkha's first wife died in 1839 while still with the children in Memekkan, after which their father brought them to Urmia to study. His second wife, whom he had only recently married, died in 1840. Sanam and Michael both attended the mission schools. Sanam, who had already learned to read at the age of only five or six, first studied with Justin Perkins. Then she moved with her family to Sire, where she continued her studies of both English and Syriac with Albert Holladay. Eventually she returned to Urmia and entered the female seminary under the tutelage of Sarah Rice and then Fidelia Fiske. She underwent an evangelical conversion during the first revival in 1846 and was a friend and schoolmate of Sarah, the daughter of Priest Isho', who died that same year, and Moressa, later assistant and wife of Jacob Yauvre.[189]

In 1851 Sanam went to Gawar to serve as an aide to George Coan and Samuel Rhea at the outstation in Memekkan. In 1852 she married Joseph of Sire, who had completed his studies at the male seminary that same year.[190] The two settled in 1853 in Dizataka, in the Baranduz region, south of the Urmia plain, where they served the mission.[191] On April 20, 1856, someone tried to poison Sanam and her family.[192] Joseph returned home late that night and did not consume the food laced with arsenic. Sanam survived the poisoning, but her two children eventually died. According to the missionaries, when Joseph sought justice, the local governor, Asker Khan, despite an abundance of evidence, had Joseph's father beaten and Joseph himself expelled from Dizataka. Over the following years, Sanam and Joseph continued to serve the mission in different locales.

Sanam died on September 1, 1865.[193] Her body was brought from 'Alyabad in Baranduz, and she was buried at the mission cemetery in Sire next to her dead children. After describing how learned she was in Scripture, her inclinations toward prayer, and her virtues as a devoted wife and mother, the obituary in *Rays of Light* recounts her patient endurance of a slow, painful and feverous death. To her obituary there is appended a song entitled "My Sister Is Dead." Joseph remarried and was still alive in 1892.[194]

The example of Sanam's life demonstrates the multigenerational integration of one East Syrian family into the mission and the manner in which the new concern for death affected indigenous lives. Sanam was present at a number of the events discussed so far in this book, and participated in, and contributed to, the new culture of death, which in the end guided the representation of her own death and life. The evangelism of fear was an isolating Gospel, but it was conveyed through collective practices and its exhortation was directed at the East Syrians, not simply as individuals, but *as a community*. Death stands before each and every one of us, but at the mission this claim was part of an invigorating set of new presuppositions about community.

The prior East Syrian ethnoreligious identity was bound to village, tribal, and family affiliations, which entailed different degrees and types of social ties, and this scaled sociality corresponded with a particular set of precepts and practices pertaining to the dead. Diversity of social relations extended to the afterlife. In contrast, in the new Gospel only the individual soul and the emergent nation receive prominence after death, the former as potentially saved, the latter as a corporate continuity over time. The national community was construed as a congeries of isolatable selves that would persist. Without understanding this difference, we risk treating the nation as a secularized version of the prior ethnoreligious community. The evangelical Gospel heightened the theodical problem of death, and the continuity of the nation would eventually serve as a new response to this problem.

At the beginning of *The Elementary Forms of Religious Life*, a book that is also fundamentally about the sociological origins of the nation, Émile Durkheim famously suggests that humans are made up of two beings, the physical and the social.

> As a well-known formula has it, man is twofold. Within him are two beings: an individual being that originates in the organism and whose sphere of action is strictly limited by this fact; and a social being that represents within us the higher reality of the intellectual and moral order that we know through observation—by which I mean society.[195]

The "well-known formula" that Durkheim quotes is a notion, both Platonic and Christian, holding that the human being is duplex, *double* in the French, because he or she consists of both body and soul. Durkheim reconfigures this dichotomy, the former part as the "individual being," the latter as the "social being." This entails not simply the displacement of the traditional dichotomy, because the original referents, the body and the soul, remain. The individual is located in the body, whereas the soul, along with the moral and intellectual life that belong to it, is a real force that derives from society.[196] Religion for Durkheim is a functional equivalent of nationalism. The body of Christ is an unconscious prefiguration of the national body, whereas the latter is more easily observable and more manifestly observes itself.

As I demonstrated in chapters 3 and 4, the mission sources attest to new forms of interaction, especially in groups, combined with new ideas about the private self and the community. These new practices and ideas contributed to the creation of a new social formation, one that was more conscious of itself as a social entity and in which the members related to one another as equal constituents. The engine for this was Christian theology and its implicit notions of the social, but this naming of the social (which would eventually be "the nation"), performed at ritual occasions and in everyday life, disembedded sociality, constituting it as something that can be identified, discussed, and problematized. The soul—and the church and the whole apparatus of ecclesial identity, for that matter—eventually became superfluous within nationalist discourse because the nation as a collection of souls that individually belong to the social had become immortal.

Although he posits a discontinuity between religion and nationalism, as I discussed in the introduction, with regard to the theodical problem of death, Benedict Anderson suggests a similar functional equivalence between the two, using the example of tombs of unknown soldiers to demonstrate the affinity between nationalist and religious imaginings. The "dawn of the age of nationalism" coincided, according to him, with "the dusk of religious modes of thought."

> With the ebbing of religious belief, the suffering which belief in part composed did not disappear. Disintegration of paradise: nothing makes fatality more arbitrary. Absurdity of salvation: nothing makes another style of continuity more necessary. What then was required was a secular transformation of fatality into continuity, contingency into meaning. As we shall see, few things were (are) better suited to this end than an idea of nation.[197]

Implicit in Anderson's argument is that religion resolves the problem of death by holding out the possibility of paradise. However, subjective continuity after death has not always been a worry among all cultures (for example, ancient

Israel), even if Christianity, like certain other religious traditions, articulates death as a problem that it alone is able to resolve. The nation, Anderson suggests, provides an alternative resolution to this problem (although for some, including myself, communal continuity provides little consolation for the termination of our own subjectivity). The social being—that other half of the human being in Durkheim's formulation—continues. It is to the nation what the soul is to religion, that which can persist postmortem.

In Urmia the problem of death was exacerbated by the American mission, and the nation as immortal entity, a response to this problem of death, came about within Christian reform. The imagined community of the nation is not simply an abstraction, but a viscerally felt series of relations with friends and family, with neighbors, and even with imagined persons far off or long gone. Service, including death, for the nation is service for a parent, a child, or a friend, inasmuch as each member of the nation understands him- or herself as part of the whole. This felt link explains how the persistence of the nation is a consolation for death.

The privatization and individualization of death, the heightening of anxiety about death through an evangelism of fear, are part of an evangelical secularism that internalizes and constitutes religion as private: our own death, the death of each of us, is solely an individual concern. Such a secularism does not entail the total removal of everything commonly associated with religion. Rather, it is the relegation of the religious to specific spheres, in this case the Christian's heart. Death is privatized in modernity, and the living and the dead are not permitted to interact directly, except when the dead threaten to break through into this world by means of various hauntings.[198]

Nationalism may be characterized as a form of soteriology. However, it is not my argument that nationalism took the place of religion. Rather, religious and moral reform raised problems, including an anxiety about death, and nationalism responded to these problems, in the same way that the practices, affects, and ideas cultivated at the mission made it possible to imagine and even *feel* the nation. The dead and the living no longer have the same relationships for women like Sanam. No one can save anyone else. However, Sanam led a life of service for her people and was held up as a model, like Elizabeth Walbridge and the numerous other models that so easily proliferated at the mission due to Christianity's age-old Christo-mimetism. She and, as we shall see in the following chapter, the native assistants who traveled and preached among the East Syrians, helped to create an intracommunal conversation about death, salvation, community, and tradition. Although their motivation was evangelical, these missionaries addressed other East Syrians as their own people, and although the message was often of individual salvation, it was couched in a rhetoric of commonality, which was only a few steps away from the Assyrian national identity that would appear at the turn of the twentieth century. Women like Sanam were working for their "people" (*tayepa*) and unwittingly creating a "nation" (*melat*).

6

National Contestation and Evangelical Consciousness: The Journals of Native Assistants

It has ever been a matter of fond anticipation with us, as also with you, to see the Nestorians a *missionary people*, emulating the bright example of their ancestors.
—JUSTIN PERKINS, May 3, 1857[1]

Other nations, in former times, took our nation as an example; for our preachers used to go to India and China; but you now wonder at us.
—JOHN AND TAMO, native assistants, July 9, 1848[2]

To reignite an ancient fire that would burn its way across Asia as it had many centuries before was one of the stated goals of the American mission from the very beginning. The "Nestorians," nominal Christians who as orientals knew oriental ways, were to be missionized in order that they might wake up, become true Christians again, and convert others. In the preceding chapters a number of East Syrian men and women, some old, some teenagers, appeared as important members of the community that developed at the mission. Many of these "reformed Nestorians" accepted the Americans' Gospel as their own and preached and taught it in Urmia and in towns and villages on the plain. By the late 1840s, the troubles in Hakkari caused by the Kurdish emir Badr Khan Bey had subsided, and the mission began to send sorties of evangelists into the mountains. Native assistants performed much of this work, and some of the most fascinating evidence from the mission in the pre-1870 period is the first-person journal accounts from these preaching tours.

Native assistants, who almost always came from clerical families, performed several duties at the mission, including teaching, preaching, and working at the press. As we have seen, Justin Perkins would not have been able to learn Neo-Aramaic, create teaching tools, and establish a school so quickly at the mission without the help he received from members of the local clergy. Eventually some assistants would translate works from English on their own and make independent contributions to *Rays of Light*. Whereas some devoted the majority of their efforts to such scholarly work, others took time off to participate in occasional preaching tours.

Assistants who proselytized in the mountains included East Syrians from both the plain and the mountains. Those from the mountains are often portrayed as rough and rugged men who, though lacking in etiquette and education, were inspired by an authentic love of God. The exemplary rugged "mountain evangelist" is Deacon George. According to his obituary in the *Missionary Herald*, he was "a worldly, hardened, wicked man, and even a thief and an adulterer."[3] Originally from Haki, a village in Tergawar, a mountainous area on the Ottoman-Qajar frontier, George came to Urmia in the winter of 1846 to visit his eldest daughter, who was studying at the female seminary. "Hearing some of the girls of the school in a room weeping and praying, he burst in among them, and angrily broke out thus: '*What is the matter with you? Are your grandfathers all dead?*'"[4] The hard shell cracked within two days, and "the roaring lion was converted into a gentle lamb." Characters such as George represented for the missionaries the power of the Gospel to tame the uncivilized, as well as the absence of a need for deep book learning for one to become a true Christian. Recall the Christian novellas popular at the mission, such as Hannah More's *The Shepherd of Salisbury Plain*, which tells the tale of the luckless yet happy shepherd, the rustic bearer of true faith.

Things were of course more complex than this, and the mountain piety depicted in the sources was for the consumption of the American readers back home. In contrast to such representations, this chapter examines the firsthand accounts of native assistants who made preaching tours in the mountains. These journals, as well as several other documents I discuss, are important because they are some of the few pieces of early evidence for the experiences of local Christians associated with the mission. They attest to the kind of conversation Reformed East Syrians had with the audiences to whom they preached during their travels, as well as to an evangelical self-consciousness that is echoed in the reflective voice of early twentieth-century nationalist literature.

Yonan of Geogtapa and Khamis of Gawar

The first journal account I examine, which is only extant in an English translation, describes a journey through the mountains made by the two native assistants Yonan of Geogtapa and Khamis of Gawar. Yonan was born in about 1824 in Geogtapa.[5] His mother died when he was an infant, and he was raised by his grandmother, who lived with her brothers.[6] He shepherded as a youth, and had a sister, Rachel, who was later "under papal influence."[7] His great-uncle was Malik Agha Bey, the *malik* (chief) of Geogtapa, who was converted during the revival of 1849.[8] This village chief had supported the mission from early on and was memorialized by an obituary in *Rays of Light* when he died in 1863, after which Yonan himself became *malik* until his death (after 1897).[9]

Yonan was put under the tutelage of the mission by his uncle, and in his early teens he lived part of the time in David Stoddard's household.[10] He had a negative influence at the male seminary, we are told, until he was affected during the revival of 1846.[11] He completed his studies at the seminary in 1847.[12] (For a later picture of Yonan, see fig. 9, in chapter 7.)

From 1847 to 1860 (or 1848 to 1858), Yonan worked at the female seminary, where one of the subjects he taught was Classical Syriac.[13] In the early years he also made occasional preaching tours in the mountains. He was forced into marriage by his father in 1848–49, but happily the young woman was one of the first outside of the female seminary to receive "a second baptism."[14] By the end of 1853, Yonan, although still associated with the female seminary, had trouble teaching because of his eyesight.[15] However, while continuing to work there, he would return to Geogtapa on Sundays to minister.[16]

Khamis of Gawar was a priest and one of the brothers of Deacon Tamo, whom I will address below. Their family was from Memekkan, a village in Gawar, in the Nehil River valley, an elevated plain formed by the river as it comes down from the heights and meanders north until it becomes a tributary to the Greater Zab (which turns south into Mesopotamia). His family had lived in Gawar for two hundred years, but had originally come from Jilu.[17] Khamis came into contact with the mission when he descended from the mountains to Urmia at the time of the revival of 1846.[18] Tamo had already been an assistant at the male seminary, and Khamis, drawn in by the enthusiastic calls for repentance, told the missionaries that Gawar was ripe for revival. Khamis's wife, Nargis, who was a classmate of Sanam and Moressa, was also involved in mission preaching (and was the author of an extant homily on Hannah, the prophet Samuel's mother).[19] Khamis graduated from the male seminary in 1852, and then returned to work in the Gawar region, attending several mountain preaching tours through the 1850s.[20] In the 1850s and 1860s, he taught at the male seminary and at a school in Memekkan.[21] He continued to work in the mission community until his death sometime after 1892.

In late September and early October 1850, Yonan and Khamis made a trip by foot southwest across Hakkari. The ultimate goal of their journey was to visit three Tiyari girls Yonan had taught at the female seminary. Nazi, Helene, and Sarah had arrived in Urmia with their families after the violence caused by Badr Khan Bey had displaced many East Syrians from the mountains in 1843.[22] Sarah and Nazi were affected by the revival of 1846, Helene later in 1849.[23] Sarah in particular was known for her habit of continual prayer.[24] The three girls returned to the mountains in the spring of 1849, when their families were compelled to leave the plain because of a scarcity of food.[25] The missionaries wanted them to stay behind without their parents, but they de-

cided to go, and their parting, we are told, was long and tearful. A letter from
the girls, written by Nazi, was published in the August 1850 issue of *Rays
of Light*.[26] In it they express their love for their former teachers and school-
mates and their hope that they be remembered at the seminary. They pray as
well that the recipients of their letter "also remember our lost nation [*tayepan
tliqa*] . . . as you know well how foolish men are alert to guard the old law of
their fathers and do not receive the new word about Christ."[27]

On Saturday, September 21, 1850, Yonan and Khamis started their journey
from Memekkan. Leaving the valley, they traveled through the mountains
on a path, hemmed in on the northwest by Mount Jilo (Turk., Buzul Dağı),
with its high point of Reshko (Uludoruk Tepesi, 4,135 meters), and on the
southeast by the Sat Mountains (İkiyaka Dağları, 3,711 meters). These heights,
jagged and snow covered, are not only beautiful, but also served for centuries
as a natural barrier to the region, preventing would-be rulers from attempting
to impose their suzerainty.[28] The pair eventually entered the Ishtazin district
(or Little Jilu, as it was called).[29] The villagers of Bubawa assembled upon their
arrival. Illiterate children came running out bearing the books given to them
by the missionaries who had passed through previously. After preaching, the
two spent the night, and on the following day, the Sabbath, they visited the
village's derelict church, "which was a very fine one, and worthy of a large
assembly."[30] The villagers explained that no sacraments were administered
there nor prayers performed, "because they had no priests or teachers." They
complained that the missionaries had not yet set up a school in their village.

The two then ascended to the nearby village of Sarpel, where they were
hospitably received. The villagers listened attentively as Yonan and Khamis
preached from the Scripture in the churchyard for several hours. Some of
the locals even claimed that one of the assistants was a kinsman to them, the
other an old acquaintance. The account of their visit to this village contains
several motifs that are common in assistants' journals: the dereliction of the
local church, the absence of clergy, the ignorance of the villagers, the antipathy of a sinful few toward their preaching, and the local enthusiasm for the
missionary project. From there they hiked farther up the heights to Muspiran,
where, a couple of hours before sunset, villagers assembled on the roof of a
house to hear the missionaries preach from the New Testament. The view
from the heights at sunset would have been breathtaking, as the village offered a panoramic view of the surrounding mountains.[31] Khamis commenced
preaching but was interrupted by a man yelling from the street below, who
demanded that the two receive permission from the patriarch in Qudshanis
before coming to the village to preach. The audience were divided over this
issue. Khamis calmly invited the man to join them, to "listen to the gospel and

the words of God." Yonan challenged him to come up onto the roof to discuss matters: "He came to us, and spoke in favor of the Wednesday and Friday fasts and other national customs [a translation of *adate d-melat*?]."[32] In response, the two began to preach again and the man listened in silence, "and at length he received at our hands a copy of the New Testament, intended for the village." On seeing the two off, the villagers entreated them to send "a teacher or preacher to instruct them."

They spent that night in Ore (Mata d'Oryaye) in a house crowded with the people who had gathered to hear them preach. "We preached to them about sin and the torments of the lost; and they appeared to be filled with fear, 'What shall we do?' said they. 'We are so great sinners, we shall never behold the face of our Lord.' We told them, so far as we were able, what they should do." The assistants were pleased to find old friends and acquaintances in this village.

The next day was hot. The pair left the village, passed by another one because the locals were too shy to show themselves, and ascended the heights under the sweltering sun toward the village of Zir. On arriving, exhausted, they "sat down under an arbor of vines, where it was very cool." In response to the many curious villagers who were gathering around, they explained why they had come and then asked for "a book, from which to preach."

> They brought us one of the ancient books, thinking to try us; for some of them had said, "They cannot read the books of the melpanas [lit. "teachers"—i.e., fathers of the church], and they do not receive our ancient books; they have rejected them." Their deacon also came to us. My companion translated a portion of the book to him. In turn he requested the deacon to translate; but he was not able either to read or translate. He said he was afraid to read before us. The people said, "We have such a deacon! What shall we do?"

As we have seen, the American mission generally demonstrated a marked disinterest in "the books of the melpanas"—that is, the Classical Syriac literary tradition. However, in this anecdote, the native assistants trump the local deacon through an exhibition of their literate skills by reading a text from this tradition. Furthermore, the deacon's inability even to read the text aloud points to what the missionaries saw as the fetish nature of indigenous book learning: books, and not their contents, were all that mattered to these "nominal Christians," even though "the letter kills but the spirit gives life" (2 Cor 3:6).

After the deacon's poor performance, the local priest, afraid of being shamed, rejected an invitation for a meeting. So the assistants taught from the book that was offered to them and answered questions before an assembled crowd. The deacon then led them into the local church, in which, he explained, no services were held, but rather "every night the priest sent a boy to place a light in the church, that the patron saint might not be angry with them." In the church the assistants found dust-covered books. They then spent the rest of the day in the village preaching and conversing with the villagers, including its elders, about Scripture. Enticed by their learning, the deacon swore an oath that he would send his son to the school in Urmia.

The following day they arrived at a village in Jilu proper. They dined but did not preach there because the men were at work and the women were preparing for a festival. They then turned to the village of Mar Zay'a hoping to find a crowd before whom to preach. Mata d'Mar Zay'a, or the village of Saint Zay'a, was the religious center of Jilu and one of the most important holy sites in the wider region.[33] An account by a British visitor in 1899 describes the village church:

> It stands high, the old square stone walls bulging outward, and the porch, the paving of which has been worn into shiny and slippery hollows by the feet of countless worshippers, is so low, that you cannot enter without stooping. Though apparently a single building, it consists in reality of two churches, separated by a thick partition wall. The first, nearest to the entrance, stands on a lower level than the other, and is never used except on very special occasions. At its eastern end is the sacristy, where the communion bread is prepared, and the sanctuary, containing two ancient liturgies of enormous proportions. It is almost entirely dark, for it derives little benefit from the two small deep window slits which light the upper and larger building.[34]

The tomb of the saint stood before the sanctuary "beneath a canopy of embroideries."[35] Upon the tomb was an ancient manuscript of the Bible as well as three wrought metal crosses.

William A. Wigram, a member of the archbishop of Canterbury's Mission to the Assyrian Christians in the early twentieth century, describes the village's church as unique in character. The building itself, he states, was not noteworthy, "being a mere rectangular box of stone, with a roof vaulted within and flat without, and arranged according to the usual type of Nestorian building."[36] However, "for centuries" men from Jilu who traveled to foreign parts had given gifts to the church to fulfill vows taken on leaving. Furthermore, because the church contained what locals considered to be the handkerchief of the Prophet Muhammad, the structure was protected from the sporadic violence and looting that occurred in the region. By the time of Wigram's visit in the first decade of the twentieth century, the church was filled with paraphernalia representing the global links of this obscure mountain village.

The consequence is that the building contains such a collection of ex voto offerings as can hardly be matched in the world, reaching back for one is afraid to say how long. The most modern feature is a grand collection of American clocks, alarm and otherwise, that hang on a cord, touching one another, all across the church. Bells, usually of small size (for half a mule load or 125 lbs. is the strict limit of weight that can be transported in one mass), are hung everywhere; long strings of them decorating the curtain that veils the sanctuary. Vestments for the priests, of Russian cut and make, hang all along the walls, while ostrich eggs and coral speak of the connexion with Malabar. Finally, away at the back, and covered thick with dust, stand rows of "China jars," said to have been brought back thence when this Nestorian church had its bishops at Pekin [Beijing] and Singan [Xi'an] in the eighth century, and which connoisseurs would probably think cheap at their weight in gold.[37]

The abandoned building still stands in Hakkari today, but stripped of all its accoutrements. No Assyrians have lived in the region for almost a century. (The bishop of Jilu remains in Modesto, California, where he has been since his flight from Baghdad in 2003.)

The assistants had arrived at the holy site during a festival involving the local saint, who was celebrated throughout the region. Churches of Mar Zay'a could be found as far away as Geogtapa and Salmas, and he remains a popular saint among Assyrians today.[38] Participants in popular cults or revelers at a saint's festival are often unaware of the details narrated in literary texts about the saints they honor. Nonetheless, we can draw correlations between the sentiments the journal account attributes to those at the festival and certain themes in the Syriac life of Mar Zay'a, the published version of which is based upon a manuscript from Jilu.[39]

Although it is a much later text, probably from the Islamic period, *The Life of the Blessed Mar Zay'a* places the birth of its hero in the early fourth century.[40] He was born in the "promised land" (i.e., Palestine) to a family close to the king. Throughout the life, the author plays on Zay'a's name, which, we are told, derives from the fact that "accursed demons, wicked human beings, oppressive authorities are moved [*zāy'in*] by [the invocation of] his name," and even the "earth" was "moved by his radiance."[41] The text compares him to a sprout that gives forth fruit abundantly upon the face of the earth, and in celebration of his birth, his father "had a rather great drinking party, and killed ten fattened bulls, and forty fat male sheep, and there was great joy and pleasure and rejoicing, and they had a feast for seven days and seven nights."[42] Similar festivities are held at his baptism. When Zay'a is three, his father puts him in school, where he learns all of Scripture, but after two years he realizes the transitory nature of this world, whereupon he leads a life of ascetic renunciation and excels in "incorporeal contemplation."[43] Then, at the age of six (!), Zay'a leaves his family and goes to Jerusalem. He eventually becomes a priest and converts Tabor, the son of the king, who becomes his disciple. After traveling about and healing the illnesses of many people, the two make their way to Mosul (a city founded in the seventh century), where Zay'a converts the king, who kills those Jews who had previously maligned the saint. From Mosul the pair head north to Shosh (possibly 'Aqra),[44] where the saint heals lepers and slices up a serpent that the locals worship as a god out of fear of its daily consumption of humans. After years spent in different locales in the region just south of Hakkari, the two go to Jilu, where King Balaq rules. Zay'a and Tabor seek the king's aid in building a church. The king wonders at Zay'a's radiant countenance, and after the saint turns a flask of water into wine exclaims, "This is heavenly wine. It is not from a vine which is upon the earth."[45] The king offers his resources to build the church, and the saint, like Moses, causes a spring to gush forth with a blow from his staff (Nm 20:11). The church is completed, and, after the death of Tabor, whose festival day is in September, the saint continues to heal and protect the local population until his death at the age of 120, which he himself predicts. As his soul is escorted away by angels, the people of Jilu hold a procession with his remains and establish a three-day festival beginning on the first Wednesday of January. His bones, according to the text, continue to provide miraculous favors from their place in the church.

The Life of the Blessed Mar Zay'a is a legendary text, containing little, if any, historical information. Unlike many other saints, Zay'a does not meet adversity in the course of his life. He is never tempted or tested, nor do any of his adversaries ever pose a remarkable challenge to him. From start to finish, the Life is a story of abundance and divine graciousness. In the typical model of the late antique and medieval holy man, the saint's self-abnegation and abstemious lifestyle make him a conduit of earthly goods for the rest of humankind. Just as Christ sacrificed himself to conquer the devil and bring new life to this world, so also Zay'a led a life dedicated to God and by this bore fruit upon the earth.

Not only was the cult of Mar Zay'a popular in the wider region, but the saint appears in several books of charms as one of various powerful figures who can be invoked for aid. (See fig. 3, in chapter 1.) In one manuscript the saint is depicted upon a blue horse. In his hand he holds a spear with which he stabs the Angel of Death, who is depicted as a monster lying dead upon the ground with an ax still in his hand. The charm (herma) invoking the saint serves to protect those who employ it from the plague.[46] The appearance of the saint in these books of charms points to his popular appeal and demonstrates that the connection drawn between him and the staving off of plague in the *Life* was part of his popular reception. Yonan and Khamis had arrived at a renowned regional center of devotion, a place of healing where a powerful, and even wrathful, local saint held sway.

After the evening services at the local church, the assistants were unable to preach because "the people scattered to light their torches over the sepulchers of the dead, according to their custom, which they derive from Constantine."[47] Light from torches could be seen upon the mountains surrounding the site of the church. I described this custom of placing lights on graves, even constructing graves with niches for these lights, in the previous chapter. It is not clear what this reference to Constantine means, whether it represents a local tradition or is the assistants' interpretation of this practice. If the latter, placing the blame on Constantine for "pagan" habits would fit with the tendency among many Protestants to see the Constantinian age as one of Christian decline. In any case, specifying that this was a "custom" reflects the missionary tendency to relativize as cultural differences those Christian practices they found either useless or detrimental.

People began to gather, "among them a company with drums and other music, to kiss the cross, and gladden the heart of the patron saint of the church." When one of the musicians stopped playing and kissed the cross, the assistants declared, "These are customs of the heathen, not of Christians." They were told that the saint once killed the children of a musician who would not play for him, a claim other assistants' journals recount about other saints.[48] The revelers told Yonan and Khamis, "The saint appeared in a dream, and said, 'I will cause your herds to die, if you do away with my remembrance,'" and then they danced into the night.[49]

On the following day the assistants sought permission from the bishop to preach. They estimated the crowd at two thousand, with people attending from the various tribal areas of Hakkari as well as from Urmia. At the time for administering the sacrament, so many people went off to dance that there were not enough deacons to perform the service. The assistants' experience of the event was clearly guided by their Reformed, antiritual disposition down to the stereotyped anti-Catholic irritation at the ringing of bells (although in this case the bells were not large ones in a tower but small ones on strings): "We saw men who had come to the festival, kissing the door of the church, all its walls, and its hangings. And our heads ached from the ringing of the bells all day, asking for sons and other things from the saint. There were those, standing before the body and blood of Christ, armed with swords and staves." During the church service, the priest failed to explain the lection. After reading, he permitted one of the assistants to preach, but first put the liturgical book away lest he preach about the sacrament. The crowd listened, though begrudgingly: "With an apology, they desired I would not protract my speaking; because they were in haste to go to the dance," which continued from that morning until early the next day.

At noon the following day, a crowd had formed around the two as Khamis openly conversed with people. The assistants "were telling them that dancing and other things which they were doing, were sinful." This angered some, and the two were told, "If the heart of a man be good, no matter for his dancing and reveling. Paradise is really this, to join hands with women and dance." The ensuing quarrel was broken up, after which the dancers became even more rambunctious: people began to leap about and a lit-up chandelier was placed in the middle of the crowd, "that saints might be better pleased with them."

At another point the assistants assembled a number of people around themselves. The two were asked "if we were of their nation." Presumably "nation" is a translation of *melat* in the original text. "We told them, 'Yes, we are Syrians.' They said, 'You are welcome; talk.'" After they conversed for a long time, the assistants made some headway: "While speaking to them, some said, 'This world has become insignificant in our view from your words.' Some said, 'This dancing is nothing in our eyes now.' Others said, 'If you would teach us thus a few times, we trust we should repent.'" These same men invited the assistants to the Baz district to teach, especially because "devouring wolves (papists)" had entered the fold there. Then, while preaching, Yonan and Khamis again denied that fasting on Wednesdays and Fridays was obligatory.

The actual festival Yonan and Khamis attended does not correspond with the three-day fast of Mar Zay'a that took place on the Monday, Tuesday, and Wednesday after the second Sunday of the Nativity (January).[50] There was also a festival of the Holy Cross celebrated in September.[51] However, the lights placed on the graves suggest that perhaps they were there during a special commemoration for all the dead, mentioned by George Percy Badger (1815–88): "Once a year there is a kind of *agape* to commemorate the departed in all the mountain villages. This service generally takes place on some Saturday in the month of October, and for days previous such families as intend to contribute to the feast are busily engaged in preparing their offerings."[52] Badger describes how lambs and bread were brought to the churchyard, and after a Eucharistic service, the priest threw several locks of wool from the lambs into a censer to burn.

The following day, September 25, the two assistants moved on. They arrived at the village of Talana, but turned away because Ottoman soldiers were there collecting taxes and the chief told them to leave and come back to preach another time. In the next village they visited, someone complained,

"What have we done? From one side you are coming; from another the papists. We are not pleased with any of you."[53] Yonan took this as a sign that Satan too was working in the same field as they were. The two "made known to them that we were of their nation, and talked with them three hours or more." Again, "nation" probably represents *melat*. This successful preaching visit also offered them an opportunity to dispel the various errors spread by Catholic missionaries who had passed through the village. Next, after preaching in yet another village, they went to Nahra, a village by the riverside, where they preached to a small crowd, "because the people had gone out to guard their fields from the wild beasts." After this they came to Nirek, where Yonan's ancestors once lived. "Then you are our cousins; we are relatives; this village is your home," they said, offering hospitality and an opportunity to preach. In the house where they stayed, Khamis accosted an old man, bent over with age: "You are on the brink of hell. Repent." The man responded, "They do not give me needles and thread to mend my clothes. I cannot but revile. I am unable to repent."

The two then crossed over into the Baz district, first stopping at Orwantus. Before their arrival, a controversy had arisen in the village. A well-educated priest who had studied for several years in Rome had proselytized several families and a Catholic mass was performed in one of their homes. The patriarch had already informed the chief of the village that he would hold him responsible if anyone there became Catholic. So the chief threatened to beat the priest and expel those who followed him. In turn, the priest forged a document from the local pasha giving him permission to teach in the village. He later said he was going to make a visit to the patriarch himself, but in fact fled to Urmia. The villagers were anxious that they not be misled again and thereby displease the patriarch. The assistants were therefore compelled to preach under special conditions. "The arrangement with the head man of the village was this, that if we preached erroneously, or more than the Scriptures authorized, we were to be beaten with sticks; and he seated the priest one side of us, and the deacon the other, that they might see every verse that was read." The two local clergy, however, were unable to follow the Scripture and simply agreed that the assistants preached the truth. As a result, some of the locals complained that they had no way of discerning whether anyone who visited them actually spoke the truth.

The following day was again the Sabbath. After visiting the local church as well as receiving hospitality from a dejected local Catholic, the two attended the funeral of a young girl, where they preached both in her family home and at the graveyard. They then took turns preaching into the afternoon, with the chief orchestrating the affair by taking the Bible from the hand of one when he seemed exhausted and handing it to the other. The village had come under Catholic influence: the two were asked about "pictures," what harm they offered and why they were not useful for increasing the fear of God. "If you wish to fear God, look on these mountains. They are pictures which he has drawn, and more fearful than any that man can make," Yonan responded, advocating the natural theology taught at the mission, while Khamis argued that if people are willing to sin in broad daylight, a mere picture will do little to induce anyone to fear God. After they explained why priests were able to administer the sacrament but not forgive sin, the locals expressed concern—"What shall we do? We have sinned greatly against God. We desire to repent"—and they demanded that the assistants teach them, threatening that if they did not, they would turn to Catholicism.

On that same day, Yonan and Khamis left for Shwawuta in order to be able to preach there in front of a Sunday crowd. Before their arrival, the villagers, who had already learned of their approach, had resolved to beat them for teaching that the saints and the Virgin Mary were mere mortals. In response, they explained to the villagers that all people could become saints and that Christians were not obliged to pray to Mary, even if she was blessed, according to Scripture. The saints, the two explained, are with God in heaven. After demonstrating that the reports about them were false, they preached twice in the village, Khamis after the evening prayer, Yonan later at the priest's house. The priest was impressed by their capacity to preach after they successfully expounded on the topics he chose: the Samaritan woman (Jn 4:4–26), the image of the brazen serpent Moses set up in the wilderness (Nm 21:4–9), and lukewarm Christians (Rv 3:16), the last a surprising text because Revelation was not traditionally in the East Syrian New Testament.

On Monday morning, September 30, the two went to other villages in the Baz district and continued their preaching tour, addressing assembled crowds of fifty to sixty people at a time.[54] At one village they were asked to defend their position on penitence and confession, a demand that betrays local Catholic influence. In the village of Argeb, where they preached from a local New Testament manuscript, they lodged in the house of a priest who told them that the patriarch had said that missionaries should be banned from the village.

On October 2 they left Baz and headed southwest to Tkhuma, in the district of the same name. When accosted by a local priest about why they had opened no mission schools in the area, the assistants blamed the patriarch for obstructing such projects. After openly rejecting the patriarch's authority, the priest responded with an apocalyptic statement that reflects the mission's ideas of progress, education, and the millennium: "Mar Shimon [Shem'on] does not wish that the promise of the prophet may be fulfilled, that the knowledge of the Lord shall cover the whole earth; but he desires that all Tekhoma [Tkhuma] may remain in its ignorance, and Tiary [Tiyari] also."[55] Yonan and Khamis remained there that night and heard numerous complaints against the patriarch.

On the following day, October 3, they entered the Tiyari district. The heat and hard travel made them ill. In a valley, in a narrow rocky crevice, they found a house, whose owner invited them in, asking them to provide him with instruction. After they preached from the Gospels, informing him about repentance, he told them about the deaths in his family at the time of the massacres of East Syrians in 1843 and how he and his family had hidden themselves under a rock for a week with only one pomegranate to eat. The missionaries turned this into a lesson about God's salvation. The man had saved his body and now he had the opportunity to save his soul.

The next day they crossed the Great Zab River and preached that night in Lizan in the home of a local Tiyari chief, who was the attendant at the nearby church as well. There they also met a "Nazarite," who abstained from meat and a variety of foods and lived next to the church, isolated from others. Like the hypocritical Pharisees of the Gospels (Mt 23), his appearance was "deathlike," and despite his abstemiousness, "He would swallow oaths, lies, etc. with a sharp appetite." He challenged them because they did not have the patriarch's permission to travel and preach. They responded that their movements were under Christ's direction. Then they were shown "the place, where three thousand six hundred men were slain by the army of the enemy." The journal does not provide any details about what they saw, but according to Austen Henry Layard, who passed through Lizan in 1846, the site of the massacre was a macabre muddle of rocks, soil, bones, clothing, shoes, "skulls of all ages, from the child unborn to the toothless old man"—the detritus of mass slaughter.[56] Layard describes a precipice from which numerous East Syrians were thrown when the marauding Kurds tired of using their weapons. Asahel Grant, who also visited the spot, heard from locals that it had been used in the distant past for exposing the elderly.[57] The assistants rendered the location part of an evangelical object lesson: "This place preaches to you in one continued echo," to which the locals responded, "Yes, it is so. We were very wicked, destitute of friendship, and God has destroyed us." Such a response was not uncommon among East Syrians and reflects how the massacres of 1843 were treated as a sign of divine judgment.[58] The next day, October 5, they came to Ashita, where they hoped to stay with a priest at whose house Asahel Grant had stayed years before, but he was absent and a local deacon likened them to the "papists" he had already chased off.[59]

Finally the assistants arrived at the ultimate goal of their long trek: Nazi, Helene, and Sarah, the three Tiyari girls whom Yonan had taught in Urmia. On arriving, they discovered that the girls were no longer in their original village but had moved to separate locales. They pressed on to the village of Nazi, the oldest of the three, where they found that although she was absent, her beneficent influence could be felt. They preached several times from her own copy of the New Testament to an audience who were clearly "accustomed to the sound of the gospel."[60] The following day was the Sabbath. Exhausted after days of travel, Yonan and Khamis preached in the morning and then went to sleep, but they were woken up by a man enthusiastically chiding them that the Holy Spirit "comes to visit men on the Sabbath." They were delighted to see how Nazi had affected this village more than any priest could.

When Nazi arrived the following Monday, the two were impressed by the great respect the villagers showed her, even begging her pardon if one of them happened to swear an oath. After spending time with her, the two left on Tuesday, in part out of anxiety about the coming change of seasons and concerns about snow. "We longed to pray with our sister before we left; but the customs of the people would not allow us to do it." However, her mother, who also had spent time in Urmia and knew the different gender relations practiced at the mission, permitted her to accompany the assistants part of the way out of town. "We reached a mountain top; and there we all three knelt down and prayed. She wept, and so did we."

The assistants then went to see the other girls. Sarah, who had been forced to marry a "wicked man," was not permitted to see them. Helene, on meeting them, began to weep. They spent the night by her and preached. The next day they began the return journey to Urmia. Helene, again weeping, entreated them to ask all her friends in Urmia to pray for her. "We traveled till night; and, reaching no inhabited place, we slept in the open fields, in the midst of the falling snow, as we did also the succeeding night." Preaching along the road, they eventually arrived back in Urmia.

Native assistants made regional tours with the aim of spreading a more authentic Gospel, but in doing so, they cultivated new conversations about religion, culture, and national identity. Calling for Christian revival, they took a rhetorical position in which a stable national (*melat*) identity was implicit: their calls for conversion were founded on a premise of shared nationality, a presupposed underlying identity that remains static. The religious and ethical challenge of their preaching, their manner of relating to others as potential Christians, demanded the transformation of their audience and simultaneously interpellated them in a shared "Syrian" national discourse.

In their preaching, the assistants emphasized themes reminiscent of the missionary discourse. The rejection of "national custom" as a legitimate and authoritative practice essential to true Christianity was a common way of rhetorically separating out local religious practices deemed inappropriate by the missionaries. This was akin to the missionaries' rejection of the authority of the books of the "melpanas" (*malpane*), the teachers of the church, and part of a broader rejection of tradition deriving ultimately from Protestant anti-Catholicism. Such echoes of missionary discourse were common in the preaching tours of native assistants. Deacons Tamo and John went on a tour in the summer of 1848 to preach to the "Nestorian nation in the Mountains," an appellation attesting to the continuing *melat* bounds of the community.[61] As they left Urmia, the two preached to their traveling companions, who in turn replied that they did not understand, for "the missionaries have neither fasts nor the cross." The assistants explained that fasts are not in fact prescribed in the Holy Scriptures, but rather were established by "our fathers." "The fathers of the people in the New World have made some rules for themselves, which we do not observe. But there is no salvation in customs; salvation is alone in the blood of Christ." They then explained the meaning of the cross, which they opposed to the mere act of kissing it. "Even Judas kissed our Lord," they explained, thus demonstrating how meaningless such an act can be.[62] The rejection of custom and indigenous tradition was part of a critique of the supposed fetishism practiced by the Syrians. This denial of what was deemed to be an enthrallment to objects was a rejection of intermediaries—not just material intermediaries, such as fetish objects, but also human ones, such as priests and saints, both the living and the dead. All Syrians were equally sinners before God.

However, despite the missionary goal of eradicating certain practices, to relativize them by labeling them "custom" may have had an inverse effect: it could contribute to the process of traditionalization. In his journal entry for October 2, 1843, Austin Wright records a conversation that for him represents the "vanity" of the East Syrians' relation to their "ancient habit" and indicates how rich the field was for planting.

> Yesterday I was at Ardishai. One of the deacons of the village remarked that early in the morning he was going to a neighboring village, to make a sacrifice and read prayers for a man who had died a day or two before. I asked if they read the prayers for the dead or the living. The deacon replied, "For the dead." The Bishop—Mar Gabriel, who was standing by,—said, "Sahib, I think it is of no use to pray for the dead. They have gone." The deacon said, "I think so too." I then asked, "If you think so, why do you do it?" They replied, "It is the custom, and has been of old. If we do not do it now, the people reproach us, and ask why; they say, 'Are you going to change the customs of our fathers?'"[63]

This conversation, even if mediated through the missionary's journal and written for an American audience, points to the discourse of tradition that had already been developing, especially in response to the missionaries' attacks on "the customs of [the] fathers." For the missionaries to name certain practices "national customs" was to make them therefore unnecessary, but in the long run it could make them foundational to national identity. This is similar to the process whereby, as we will see in the following chapter, Syrians from different churches began to recognize the patriarch as a national leader. Contestation and the precariousness of practices perceived to be under attack resulted in self-conscious assertion.

Yonan and Khamis created a conversation about shared Syrianness during their visit to the regional holy site of Mar Zay'a, a place visited by Syrians from as far away as the Urmia plain. This particular place had a special significance for such a conversation: although it is not mentioned in their account, the Jilu territory and especially the holy site of Mar Zay'a were well known as the launching point to distant regions for temporary labor migrations.[64] Many of the various exotic treasures in the sanctuary were votive offerings from those who had traveled abroad and returned. By the 1840s members of the Jilu tribe, Jilwaye, had long been making seasonal migrations north to work in the Caucasus and south to work in the region around Mosul. Asahel Grant noted how because of this labor migration, the men in Jilu often knew much about the surrounding cultures and spoke various languages, a fact he employed to make a point about the usefulness of the "Mission to the Nestorians" for further missions to "rekindle the light of the gospel over all the central highlands of Asia."[65]

The labor migrations of the Jilwaye paralleled another form of migration, which would continue into the twentieth century: the movement of spiritual beggars, holy mendicants, from Jilu not only to the surrounding region but by the late nineteenth century all over the world.[66] I have already mentioned in passing these "thieves of the cross" (hačaqoge, from the Armenian), men from Jilu who traveled, perhaps at first to gather alms, but eventually with ornate stories about the persecuted Christians of the East and their need for financial support. According to tradition, Mar Zay'a himself commissioned this activity, blessing it and saying, "You should not work but you will eat," a saying that rhymes in Neo-Aramaic.[67] Eventually these men became an embarrassment of spiritual charlatanry to some members of the community, and an internal communal critique developed against them. Daniel Wolk has drawn a link between this communal self-criticism, which took place in the early twentieth century, and the development of nationalism in the community.[68] Already in

1862 Justin Perkins had published a tract on the evils of begging, and he himself criticized these scoundrels, who during his own lifetime were traveling as far as England and Germany.[69] Still later, in 1908, William A. Shedd of the American mission had to advise Robert Speer (1867–1947), secretary of the Board of Foreign Missions, in New York, "Always take it for granted, with no exception that a Jilu man is a beggar, a fraud, and to be calmly ordered out of your office."[70]

Despite its secluded location in the mountains, Mar Zay‘a was both a destination for Syrians from afar and the place of origin of those Jilwaye going abroad either for temporary labor or for plying their trade as religious mendicants. This was a cosmopolitan center of the church, similar to the patriarch's residence in Qudshanis, another place visited by Syrians from far and wide. Syrians of different tribal and nontribal backgrounds intermingled at the holy site, and therefore, it is appropriate that it was specifically in the account of their visit there that the assistants mention having a conversation with other Syrians *as Syrians*. However, that conversation, although based upon an existing transecclesial identity, cut across different boundaries than the prior identity did. Just as the two assistants' movement through Hakkari crossed tribal, linguistic, and geographic boundaries, so also their journey (and their travelogue) are part of a process of missionary effects that cut straight through the social hierarchy and epistemic scheme of the Church of the East. This journey occurred at the same time that, as I have noted, the border was being formulated between the Ottoman Empire and Qajar Iran, when the Ottomans were subjugating the historically intractable region of Hakkari. The movement of the assistants across this area and their conversation with other Syrians reflect notions of space and community that defy these new fast-growing boundaries but also differ from the ethnoreligious identity of the past. Yonan and Khamis were at Mar Zay‘a for religious purposes, but as Syrians.

Murad Khan and Moses

The second journal I examine describes a journey that began with a trip to Qudshanis in Hakkari to visit the patriarch. However, the assistants then traveled south and west of the East Syrian mountain homeland to regions that had become predominantly Catholic, but where the patriarch's nominal authority nevertheless remained in place. The purpose of this journey was ultimately to visit Bohtan, northwest of Hakkari. Bohtan is technically only the Bohtan River valley east of Siirt, but the toponym could include the region south of this, such as Gazarta and its surrounding districts. This was a region that had suffered much in recent years due to the Ottoman state's assertions of control and the violence of the local Kurdish emir, Badr Khan Bey. When they eventually arrived there, the two assistants heard many complaints about Ottoman oppression in the region.

The two assistants who made this journey were Deacons Murad Khan and Moses, both of whom continued their association with the mission until their deaths at the end of the nineteenth century. Murad Khan, who was born around 1800, had been a teacher at the female seminary.[71] He was one of the few educated members of the local clergy in Geogtapa before Perkins arrived.[72] In Sanam's commencement speech given at the seminary in 1851, discussed in chapter 4, he is referred to as the "master" who had given up his office in order to preach in Bohtan. In a reference to Acts 16:9, when in a vision Paul sees "a man of Macedonia pleading with him and saying, 'Come over to Macedonia and help us,'" Sanam says, "he was summoned by a voice, full of woe, of a Macedonian, to help."[73]

Moses (or Mosheil) of Geogtapa lived in the early years of the mission with the Holladays, like other young Syrians who lived in missionary homes.[74] He graduated from the male seminary in 1846.[75] He was a teacher in the village school at Sire and also had experience in itinerant preaching.[76] In 1850 he had traveled with Deacon Sayad to Mosul and then made a tour of Bohtan, where they were barred from certain villages.[77] In their letters from this trip, which were published in *Rays of Light*—one includes an exegesis of Acts 16:9—the two describe speaking with the local populace, "whether papists or from our nation [*melatan*]."[78] However, during their tours they often had difficulty communicating because of dialectical differences. In part of this journey, in which they aimed "to remove the people [*tayepa*] of the Syrians from under the rule of Satan," they were guided by Jeremiah, the Chaldean monk from Alqosh, who would have been proficient in a wider range of Aramaic dialects than the two assistants from Urmia spoke. Jeremiah had converted during the revival of January 1850. After going to Bohtan in the service of the mission, he asked that assistants be sent and also forwarded a petition making a similar request signed by a number of local chiefs.[79]

On November 10, 1851, Murad Khan and Moses left Urmia and traveled west preaching village by village through the mountains to Memekkan, where they stayed with Deacon Tamo.[80] As in similar accounts, Murad Khan, the narrator, describes reading and preaching from local copies of the Bible, as Perkins had done on his arrival in Iran. They also brought their own printed editions to the sometimes contentious settings where they were publicly challenged by local religious authorities. Not long after their arrival in the mountains, they went to Qudshanis in order to request a letter of commendation from the patriarch so that they could preach without obstruction in Bohtan.

> We were received with much kindness at the house of Mar Shimon [Shemʻon].
> We entered the hall of divan and kissed the hand of Mar Shimon. We delivered
> our letters to him and he directed us to sit down. He rose before the window
> & read the letters, but gave us no answer. On Saturday, we expected Dunkha,
> (his brother) to ask him to give us a letter; he said, "I will give them an answer."
> On Monday, we entered the Divan and spoke with him. We said, "We were
> sent to you, that you might give us a letter of commendation, to go to Bootan
> [Bohtan] to preach." He said, "To whom shall I write a letter? I have not seen
> the people of Bootan." We said, "We know the names of the principal men
> [raʾise]." He said, "It can not be." Deacon Kamo, and priest Hooreea [Ḥuriya],
> and priest Ablahad, contended with us about the cross and baptism and the
> sacrament. We replied to them meekly. Mar Shimon said nothing excepting
> this; said he, "all the gentlemen [sahabe—i.e., the missionaries] are good men."
> We rose and asked permission to depart, kissing his hand. He said, "Go in
> peace." On Friday, an earthquake occurred at Kochanis [Qudshanis], which
> shook Mar Shimon's house.[81]

This quotation is from the mission translation of the assistants' journal as preserved in the archive because the version of the text printed in the *Missionary Herald* is abbreviated: it leaves out the more contentious aspects of this episode, such as the debate, as well as the kissing of the patriarch's hand, a sign of fealty. The fact that they did not receive the patriarch's letter in the end and also that they were often in strongly Catholic areas may explain why so frequently throughout their journey they lodged and preached at the houses of *raʾise*, local chiefs, as opposed to with local clergy, who would have been hierarchically subject to the patriarch and perhaps also resistant to mere deacons lecturing them on theological matters. In any case, when challenged about whether they had obtained permission from the patriarch, they would at times simply lie, something else omitted from the *Missionary Herald*'s version.[82]

On leaving the patriarch, the two crossed over a snow-covered mountain and then followed the Great Zab River south along a road that was at points cut into cliffs. When their horse, weighed down with books, slipped, its shodden hooves gave off sparks against the rocks. "There was the roaring of the Zab; and there was the powerful rain; but I cannot describe the difficulty of the way, as it was." At one point, near where the Tal River runs into the Zab, the two became distressed. It was dark, but "looking up to the summit of a high cliff, we saw a light appearing like the light of the moon." They ascended the rock and found a cave with about fifteen men sitting around a fire. When they told the men, who turned out to be from the Tiyari and Dez tribes, that they had come from visiting the patriarch—but not that they had not received the documentation they had sought—"They quickly rose before us, and took our garments and dried them, while we rested." Taking these events as a divine sign and the fire as prepared for them by the Lord, they preached and then sang for the men.[83]

From Hakkari, Murad Khan and Moses continued south to 'Amadiya. Their journey in what is now northern Iraq was dangerous. The region was suffering from a food shortage, and even fodder for their horses was scarce. They came close to being robbed at an inn; at another point they were shadowed and then chased at night by an Arab horseman with a spear. They lingered for several days in a quarantine outside of Mosul, and were released only after reading aloud and singing for the Ottoman captain. They then went to the Monastery of Rabban Hormizd in Alqosh, which remains today an important Chaldean religious center. It served for centuries as an East Syrian monastery and following many years of abandonment was reoccupied by Chaldeans in the 1820s.[84] Their visit to the monastery attests to the dissimulation in which Murad Khan and Moses were willing to engage as well as how close they would bring themselves to Catholic cult. It also explains why the following passage too was excised from the English version in the *Missionary Herald*.

> We went to prayers with them. When the monks went out, we remained be-hind, with the monk Michael. We said to him, "We wish you to show us all the places here, for we have come from a distant land." So he lit a taper and showed us several places. We ourselves wondered, and he said, "Do you wish to see more?" We replied, "yes." So he showed us the tomb of Rabban Hor-mizd, and an iron ring to which he used to fasten his scalp. This we of course did not believe in our heart [*ina b-lebban la humenan*].[85]

The capacity to dissimulate requires the ability to maintain an outer face and an inner self. "Religion"—that is, what they truly believed—was in the assistants' hearts, whereas their ability to interact and even attend Catholic rituals suggests that the exterior was distinct from the inner self, or at least that they knew to dissimulate in the composition of their journal. Furthermore, if the two did not actually "believe," on what level were they relating to those around them? To be sure, they wished to convert others to their form of Christianity, and in this instance they were dissembling because they were guests in need of hospitality. However, their engagement with these other Syrians was not simply through subterfuge. They related to their hosts as members of a common people, even if they spoke a different dialect of Aramaic than they did.

A similar episode occurred in the 1848 preaching tour made by Tamo and John of Geogtapa. This passage, which was also removed from the account provided in the *Missionary Herald*, likewise depicts the assistants in proximity to practices that would have been too "papist" for American evangelical taste.

> We arose & went up to the church of Mar Abdisho on a mountain, & distant from the villages. We had heard from many men that there is a hole there, cut in a stone, through which men & women who want sons & daughters, pass, & many of them are held fast by the stone. I however embraced the stone, I was not held by it. We reached the door of the yard & knocked. No one opened to us. The church has a woman to do service in it, & she is there, day & night, summer & winter. Just then she had gone to bring wood from the mountain. We waited until she came; we then entered the church & prayed. Afterwards she went and shook a string in our behalf, on which bells were hung & asked the Saint that our pilgrimage might be acceptable. Upon leaving the church we went to her room, & talked with her long about salvation by the blood of Christ, & how the saints—even that one whom she was serving—were saved by him, if they believed in him. We also prayed with her, offering our prayer wholly in the name of Christ. We preached to her from Hebrews 11th about faith, & taught her many other things. She swore often, & we reproved her sharply, & she was pleased with our words. When we were in the church, she said, "What have you brought to throw upon the grave of Mar Abdisho, that I may guide you to it." We replied, "We have hope in nothing save in the re-demption of the blood of Christ, but for yourself we will give a handkerchief for your head," for she was poor. We went to the grave. She said, "Do you see how Mar Abdisho has become a stone?" We replied, "That stone on his grave was so cut by men." For it was in the shape of a man. We remained with her until noon.[86]

The church they visited was that of Mar 'Abdisho' and Mar Qardagh near the village of Bet 'Aziza in the Tal district in central Hakkari.[87] The shrine was part of a then defunct monastic complex. Sterile women could purportedly be rendered fertile at this site, which also enjoyed a high reputation among the Muslim Kurdish population of the region.[88] As we find in Murad Khan's jour-nal account, this episode demonstrates how dangerously close some assistants were willing to get to the cult of the saints and also how they justified this proximity by both practicing dissimulation and using a utilitarian critique borrowed from the missionaries.

Upon finally arriving in Mosul, Murad Khan and Moses stayed with W. Frederic Williams of the short-lived ABCFM "Assyrian Mission." In order to acquire a travel document for Bohtan, they visited Christian ('Isa) Rassam (1808–72), a Chaldean convert to Anglicanism who served as the British vice consul in Mosul. He was the brother of the renowned archaeologist-diplomat Hormuzd Rassam (1826–1910). (A third brother, Mansur, shows up later in this same journal petitioning the local Ottoman governor to send the assistants protection at Gazarta.)[89] Moses had met Christian Rassam the year before when he had helped him and Deacon Sayad through the city quarantine, and Rassam regularly provided help to the American missionaries in the region.[90] When Murad Khan and Moses met with him, the consul took out a copy of the *Ḥudra*, an East Syrian liturgical collection, and after the three read Classical Syriac hymns together, he gave them passports. The *Missionary Herald* also excised from its account this episode of reading Classical Syriac poetry with a well-known Episcopalian, who was the brother-in-law of George Percy Badger, the aggressive advocate for an Anglican mission to the "Nestorians" and polemicist against "dissenting" churches.

The two left Mosul and traveled north. In the town of Naherwan, after preaching at the local church, the *ra'is*, Shem'on, brought them a copy of the *Warda*, a collection of hymns, many of which are attributed to Gewargis Warda ("George the Rose"), the liturgical poet of the thirteenth century. In the crowded yard in front of the church, they preached from the section of the book on Lazarus. "In the evening the people of four nations [*melate*] assembled at the house of the Rais, Nestorians, Armenians, Jacobites, and Kleebai [*qlibe*], or 'fallers away,' as the papists are there called, about twenty persons."[91] The people requested that the two deacons sing, and so again they opened the *Warda* to a passage on the rich man and Lazarus and they sang and explained the text. The following day they were treated to pilav and coffee before leaving. The two then continued on, passing through Gazarta on the Tigris.

In the Tigris River valley near the monastery of Mar Akha (Aḥḥa), the Assyrian Mission in Mosul had an outstation run by Dwight Marsh (1823–96).[92] Deacon Isaiah, who, like his former companion Jeremiah, had been a monk at the Chaldean monastery of Alqosh, joined the American effort after a visit to Urmia and received proceeds from the monthly concert in Urmia for his work in Bohtan.[93] The monastery of Mar Akha, also called Zarnuka, was named after Mar Akha the Egyptian, a mythical fourth-century companion of Mar Awgen, who, according to tradition, had brought monasticism to the region from Egypt.[94] It was the sister monastery to that of Mar John the Egyptian, mentioned in chapter 1.

The assistants' nemesis in the area was the priest, Gabriel of Mar Akha (d. 1859). Gabriel was not Chaldean, but at times supported Catholic efforts. He obstructed the assistants where he could. This is possibly the same Gabriel who copied a manuscript produced at Mar Akha in the 1830s, which includes hagiographies of Mar Akha and Mar John, as well as a life of the Virgin Mary.[95] Gabriel is described by mission sources as a "soothsayer" who "carries on a lucrative trade in 'charms,' which he sells to Nestorians, Armenians, Koords and Yezidees."[96] The missionaries thought that he was opposed to the true Gospel because it would hurt his business. "Many think he can make any woman love any man, or make a barren woman fruitful, or protect stray cattle, sheep or donkeys, by shutting the mouths of wild animals."[97] A holy man and ecclesiastic, one with mixed allegiances socially and spiritually, Gabriel exemplified the Americans' anxiety about intermediaries: magic, the cult of the saints, and priesthood are attested in his person and his piety. Despite his obstreperousness, Gabriel gave George Coan and Samuel Rhea a teary welcome not long later in 1853, particularly because they brought letters from Deacon Isaac, his nephew who had gone to the male seminary at Sire to study.[98]

The assistants' visit to the region and the adversity they met among its mixed population point to both the limits of the East Syrian world and the ethnic boundaries within which the East Syrians associated with the American mission worked. In Bohtan they interacted with Catholics (Chaldeans), Catholic sympathizers, "Nestorians," evangelical sympathizers, non-"Nestorian" Syriac Christians (West Syrians, or "Jacobites"), and Armenians. Furthermore, the limits of their dialect of Aramaic were pushed: at Khanduk they met a former West Syrian monk who was working with the mission and Mr. Marsh. They were only able to communicate with him in Classical Syriac: "We conversed in the ancient language [*b-lešana d-ktawa*, lit. "in the language of the book"] and prayed together."[99]

During their travels the two assistants regularly demonstrated their expertise in Scripture and tradition, sometimes in public disputes. They also met the same concern for the precise wording of the biblical text that Perkins found in his initial travels. At one village they preached from the Psalter, extemporaneously translating the text into the vernacular "as at Urmia." The local priest lit a candle and checked each verse as they read, in the end exclaiming loudly to the congregation, "Whoever says these men are not of us, is accursed. I have looked into the book and not even one dot have they omitted." They then received communion from him.

In Shakh, a village in Bohtan, the assistants proved their versatility in the Bible and the East Syrian tradition. Upholding tradition, a local priest argued with the two: "We will do as our fathers and grandfathers did." In response, the assistants recalled the story of Abraham's rejection of the practice of his father, Terah. The priest was ashamed by the people's acceptance of the strangers' words, at which point "a man of the company requested of us permission to smoke his pipe in the time of fast." The two "asked for the old book of canons [*sunhados*], and looked out and read the place where it said, 'This fast is optional with every individual.'" The man then happily puffed upon his pipe.

In the village of Mar Isaac, Murad Khan was approached by a man named Anias, who asked for a rule for fasting that would make it possible for him to follow the assistants' message of repentance. According to the account, the man had prided himself on his abstinence since youth. Murad Khan told him, "Still you lack something that you may be righteous. Now you have fasted the fast of seven weeks. Rise up, go and enter the cave of some rock. See no mortal; drink no water, as the tradition runs of the saint Mar Akha himself. Do not break your fast for a whole year! May hap you will be a perfect man!"[100] Anias was then shamed into total silence at his own inability to recite the Lord's Prayer. In this anecdote Murad Khan employed his knowledge of Scripture (cf. Lk 18:18–23) and the tradition to make an evangelical reductio ad absurdum. If fasting is good, then one should simply stop eating.

At another town, Hassan, after being accosted by a Chaldean deacon, whom they trumped with their learning, the two had to contend with mendicants from Jilu, "thieves of the cross," who maligned them, saying, "These fellows have become English. They have no fasts." After the *ra'is* rebuked these men from Jilu, the assistants sent a letter to Shakh suggesting that these beggars "were unworthy applicants for charity." These conflicts, especially those with Priest Gabriel, combined with the fact that Murad Khan and Moses lacked a letter of introduction from the patriarch, resulted in the two being barred from certain villages.

This second journal account attests to a number of the same issues as the first one. Native assistants took up the missionary discourse of reform, creating a shared ethnic conversation among "Syrians" through proselytism and moral exhortation. Furthermore, such first-person accounts are evidence for the development of an evangelical literary self-consciousness, a textual reflection upon the self and its relationship to the world. Real events are described, but the literary recounting of them includes information about an inner self, one that at times must engage in religious dissimulation to fit into its environment. This inner self may not have seemed sufficiently evangelical to the Americans, and the mission's expurgation of the account points to the anxiety felt about the success of "oriental" conversions. Nevertheless, the irreducible subjects and objects of conversion in this account, whether it was successful or failed, are "Syrian": the substrate of the person, the entity that exists before and after or even without a religious transformation, is part of the "nation" (*melat*) of the Syrians.

At several points in their journey, Moses and Murad Khan were accused of not belonging to the community of those they were addressing. While still in Hakkari, they stopped at the village of Gundikta and were reproached by an intoxicated priest who refused them hospitality, accusing them of aligning themselves with the "English."[101] This accusation was common. Not only were the assistants regularly accused of working with the English—that is, the Americans—but they were accused of becoming English themselves. At one point later in their journey, they were asked by "papists," "Are you Americans?" To which they replied, "We are Christians."[102] In another instance, when Priest Gabriel denied them permission to preach after mass, one of the two simply started to do so anyway. Relying upon the Arabic word *din*, which has a long history of functioning like our term *religion*, Gabriel stood up and said, "You are not of us; you are Protestants; your religion [*dinokon*] is corrupt."[103] At another encounter, Gabriel attempted to bar them from entering the church, exclaiming, "You are not of my community [*melati*]." When they challenged him, he explained, "You are Protestants; you are English; you are deceivers."[104]

Such episodes are obvious examples of the conflation that could occur between the English and Americans, but such a conflation was made possible by the prior imbrication of ethnoreligious identities in the Near East. Such views of religion and nationality would continue into the next century, as is attested in the story of the Christian man who, when accused of murder, demanded to be under American consular jurisdiction because "my mother was an Assyrian . . . my father . . . was of the Armenian sect, . . . but I myself belong to the sect of the Americans"—that is, he had joined the Presbyterian Church.[105] He seems to have thought that becoming a Christian made him American and therefore exempt from Iranian law. Such an approach of course was also guided by European and American actions in the region. The concessions the Ottoman Empire made to European states, allowing them to take responsibility for respective religious communities, suggested that, for example, to be Catholic was to be French and to be Protestant was to be English, and therefore American. In contrast, for Syrians like Moses and Murad Khan, and eventually many in the environs of the mission in Urmia, religion was successfully internalized such that it was distinguished from national identity. At least within the circumscribed limits of Christianity—for conversion to Islam was beyond the pale—Syrians could embrace a variety of religious identities and remain Syrian. Such an ecumenical approach to Syrianness existed previously in nuce among East Syrians, West Syrians, and Catholic Uniates, but this expanded and was actively endorsed within the Protestant context of the mission.

Deacon Tamo's Imprisonment

Deacon Tamo has appeared several times already in this book, and his brother Khamis was addressed above. Like Khamis, he was from Memekkan in Gawar and began to work with the mission by the mid-1840s. His yearlong imprisonment (1852–53) on a charge of murder provides a different perspective on the native assistants' labors in the mountains as well as on their own evangelical discipleship and self-consciousness.

Tamo's initial work with the mission lasted only a few weeks, after which he left due to some perceived slight and traveled to Beirut and then Jerusalem. He returned to the mission only after being entreated not to travel to Russia to evangelize. David Stoddard describes his conversion during the revival of 1846: "At last, in agony of spirit and choked by emotion, he cried out, 'Lost, lost, lost!'"[106] That same year Tamo joined Austin Wright and Edward Breath on a journey to meet with Badr Khan Bey.[107] He seems to have played a key role in persuading the mission to establish the station in Gawar, which was maintained through the 1850s.[108] One of the most important biographical facts about him is avoided in missionary publications, where he appears often: the manuscript of the journal of the preaching tour made by Tamo and John in 1848, quoted above, states in reference to Catholicism, "Deacon Tamo told them that he had grown up under this doctrine, and even Deacon Tamo was once in a Papal school at Elkosh, near Mosul."[109] In other words, he had traveled from his home in Gawar prior to his encounter with the American mission and studied at the Chaldean monastery in Alqosh. This explains how he was able later to produce a version of the Gospels in the Mosul dialect.[110] He also had made a pilgrimage to Jerusalem before his encounter with the mission.[111] Therefore, although the mission sources often cast him as a rugged mountain Nestorian, before joining the Americans, Tamo had traveled and studied widely.

Another noteworthy silence in the sources about Tamo is the dearth of information regarding his later life. In 1862 he was still supporting the American mission in the mountains.[112] We are told in a later source that he died on May 10, 1873, and that "he was a very learned and famous person among this nation [*melat*]."[113] However, the petition from a number of East Syrians to the archbishop of Canterbury in 1868, a document that provided motivation for the subsequent establishment of the Anglican mission and specifically discounts the benefits of the American one, was signed by both Tamo and Khamis. This is all the more striking because one of the three primary signatories of the petition was Bishop Sliwa of Gawar (d. ca. 1888), who, as we will see, was hostile toward Tamo when he was working with the American mission.

(Sliwa's *natar kursya*—that is, his nephew-successor who would inherit his name and his office—was later educated at an Anglican mission school.)[114]

Tamo had already begun making preaching tours from Memekkan in 1847. When the locals were unable to understand the dialect of Neo-Aramaic he spoke, he preached in Classical Syriac, perhaps a token of his Catholic education (he proctored Syriac exams at Sire).[115] By the time of his imprisonment in the summer of 1852, he had a long record of trouble with the ecclesiastical and local political authorities. An attempt made on his life in August 1848 was attributed to the patriarch, with whom he later enjoyed an audience in the company of William Stocking and other native assistants.[116] The local Ottoman officials had their eye on him for some time, and his preaching continually vexed Bishop Sliwa.[117] The founding of the mission station in Gawar in November 1851 heightened these local tensions.[118] The station was at first in Tamo's house, and the circumstances were tight for the missionaries and their families, who had to share the space with Tamo's livestock, which had to be kept inside for fear of theft. In response to Tamo's support for the station, the chief men of the town held a council to which Tamo and his brothers were not invited, and this group agreed to stay aloof from the mission, which was already suffering extortion from the local authorities.[119] In early 1852 Bishop Sliwa held a several-day wedding celebration in the Gawar village of Bashirga for another of his nephews.[120] Tamo was invited and seated next to the bishop. He was asked to preach at the event and did so several times each day. He persisted in this even after annoyed guests demanded that he stop. Before the wedding had ended and everyone had returned to their respective villages, a meeting was held with the bishop presiding and it was decided that a complaint would be sent to the Ottoman official in nearby Diza asking that the "English" be expelled from Gawar.

Tamo continued his work unmolested until one night in mid-July 1852 when an Ottoman soldier arrived in Memekkan.[121] The young man, who was of East Syrian background and from Mosul, had originally joined the military to flee from the potential penalty he would have to pay for a death he had accidentally caused. He had visited the mission the previous year on his way to Jilu. That night he slept with his mare, along with others, outside the door of the mission, which was at that time still simply Tamo's house. Dogs barked, shots were fired, and someone hidden in the darkness threw stones at the village shepherd. In the middle of this confused night, the young man was shot, and although most people remained inside, hiding in fear, some came to his aid, including Tamo. The sources mention Kurdish thieves, but it is possible that the young soldier was killed as part of a blood feud for the earlier manslaughter for which he was responsible. Soon after this, the Ottoman authorities in Diza brought many of the senior men of Gawar in for questioning. Two weeks later, twelve men, including Deacon Tamo and his brothers Isho' and Zay'a, were arrested and detained in Diza. Seven were eventually released, but the other five, including Tamo and his brothers, were insulted, roughed up, and thrown into prison in Bashkala, the residence of the pasha, north on the way to Van.

George Coan, one of the missionaries in Gawar, found Colonel Williams of the commission for the determination of the Persian-Ottoman border and brought him to the pasha in Bashkala. Williams tried to negotiate not only for the freedom of the prisoners, but also for the "right of Deacon Tamo to put up a house without orders from his superiors."[122] Williams was able to provide some comforts to the prisoners, such as food, and eventually left for Van to make further entreaty, and Coan left for Gawar, where he found additional attacks had occurred against the mission community. In all of this, Coan held Bishop Sliwa personally responsible, as well as some local Kurds who with Sliwa held seats in the local council. It is clear that the missionaries' attempt to build a house for themselves and Tamo's efforts to aid them were a source of conflict, and we should recall that it was the house Asahel Grant built in the mountains only a few years before that was in part a cause, or at least a pretext, for Kurdish raids in the area.[123]

Colonel Williams had several audiences with Muhammad, the pasha of Van, eventually negotiating the release of the prisoners and obtaining permission for the mission and its companions to construct a residence for the winter, but not a school without permission from Constantinople.[124] Once Colonel Williams was gone from Van, the prisoners were brought from Bashkala, interrogated, and made to swear their innocence. Tamo was supposed to be released, but when he acknowledged that the murder had occurred in front of his own home, he was fined and given a sentence of three years. Soon the missionaries began to suspect that the patriarch was somehow involved in the affair, as he had been of late receiving greater recognition from the Ottoman authorities. It was said that when the father of one of the prisoners had sought help from the patriarch, he responded that because the young man had become English, he should seek aid from the English.

Affairs stalled. For months Muhammad Pasha awaited word from Constantinople, while building in Memekkan, although officially permitted, was delayed.[125] When work was done, it was done poorly through forced labor.[126] Tamo received guests regularly, including his brother Khamis, to whom the pasha complained that Tamo had brought the English to the country. "Such is the Turkish toleration, when administered by a genuine Turk," wrote Samuel Rhea, in a snide reference to the contemporary *tanzimat* ("reorganization") reforms promulgated by the Ottomans. Petitions continued to be sent to the capital, and only with the aid of the well-known British ambassador, Stratford Canning (1786–1880), was Tamo's release finally secured in September 1853.[127]

The episode of his imprisonment served as a kiln to fire Tamo's evangelical self-consciousness. We have two letters he wrote from prison, both printed in *Rays of Light*. In the first, published in September 1852, Tamo describes the joy he felt upon receiving news from his village and his sadness in learning that a number of people in the village were ill.[128] He prays that they will improve and also that the "work of God may make progress [*ate la-qamu(hy)*]." He points out that he has often preached that Christians "suffer" (*ke qabli ḥašša*, lit. "receive suffering" or "passion"), and therefore he is thankful that he has been judged worthy by God to be in prison. His imprisonment is not so bad: he is comfortable and only has a few lice. His children, who had brought letters to him, had departed a few days before, and being left alone saddened him. However, not long after they had gone, he was told that Colonel Williams had come, which made him rejoice again. Williams met with the pasha's head guard (who held Tamo's money for him for safekeeping) and when permitted to visit told Tamo how he had met with the pasha, who had sent to Constantinople an inquiry seeking a response about what to do. Tamo expresses the hope that Coan and Rhea were continuing their work, and that his household did not mind their presence. He asks his brothers Khamis, Isho', and Zay'a to take care of the household, and compares his situation to that of Joseph in Egypt: it began as bitter but ended sweet. He sends his regards to everyone in Urmia and accepts that it could be God's will that he die in prison.

In this letter Tamo embraces martyrological suffering and suggests that his travails are part of God's plan, "what is pleasing to God" (*rezayeh d-alaha*). In contrast, the preface to the letter in *Rays of Light* plays down the notion that he was persecuted for his religion. Whereas Tamo thought that he was accused because he was preaching the "teaching of the Messiah" (*yulpana d-mšiḥa*), the article explains that there is a "custom" (*'adat*) in the region of taking revenge on a village where a murder has occurred.[129] In contrast, Colonel Williams's labors on Tamo's behalf are cited as a sign that God is at work in the affair. For Tamo the events are the age-old phenomenon of Christian martyrdom, which would have been familiar to anyone versed in the East Syrian tradition, but *Rays of Light* renders this in more orientalist and colonial terms: the problem has to do with the local culture. It is something that can in fact be fixed, a notion contrary to Tamo's much older Christian idea that the world is a dark place that hates and at times persecutes Christians. Furthermore, by employing a martyrological paradigm, he implies his own salvation: he had only been in prison for so long, and the authority that martyrdom offered him may have been awkward for Perkins and the other missionaries, who often refused to vet the authenticity of Syrians' religious claims.

The second letter from Tamo, addressed to his "beloved friend" David Stoddard, was published in *Rays of Light* in March 1853, in the "Evangelism" section of the paper.[130] Tamo begins by acknowledging the receipt of a letter from Stoddard. He was overjoyed to read the "many encouraging words, that is, that righteous people of the past received prison [sentences] and tortures, like Joseph, Jeremiah, Daniel, Shadrach, Meshach, Abednago, Peter, Silas [Acts 15:22], and John. Our beloved savior even received such sufferings upon himself." Tamo then humbly retreats from any self-comparison to the righteous of the biblical past:

> Those encouragements were pleasant and delightful for me, which were written about the righteous of the past, but I do not deserve to complain about justice because I have greatly angered that one who is just and true. However, still in his great grace he certainly receives those who have angered his justice, and [his grace] persuades and reconciles justice by establishing the law of that one who is Lord of All, by giving a great, rather abundant price to redeem the guilty from under the sword of the executioner. Moreover, [his grace] buys those for whom there is a price greater than frightening death with a greater price, more than all arithmetic is able to provide an account for, and [his grace] sets them along with their sons at a meal prepared from the foods of kings and dresses them in garments which shine like the luminous sun, etc.

In this letter Tamo moves away from the language of martyrdom and the righteousness it implies to focus on the need, in any circumstances, for grace. He then provides an account of the evangelical conversion he experienced during the revival of 1846 and the intimacy he shared at the time with Stoddard.[131]

> I remember that day in the small upper room when you and I alone prayed that prayer full of weeping and joy; I know that without a doubt it was received by the Lord, the one who hears all the prayers of his servants, for the good and the benefit of myself, foolish and poor, that I might take by the hand the one who is the head of the faith [*todita*] of the Christians and the believers, with a true heart and a pure intention, with the power of that one who in honor and in glory is together with the Father and the Son. From that time until now many times I slipped and fell due to failures in divine duties, also due to the power of innate sin which has clung and stuck like a cancer in my limbs. Moreover, I intended to flee from that one who saved me from heavy and harmful oppressions, in order that I might not be subject to that one who subjects all, but still he did not let me go, although I was unwilling. Still in my wretchedness and my injury in this intention of mine he made me a sign [*ešarat*, Ar. *išara*]. I saw in my limb[s] another one, which was my old nature.

It still drew me to that previous will of mine and many times it still suited my heart. This was more so, although the previous one was for my good and that other one was for my injury and destruction. However much he pointed out humility to me I hardened myself [or, my soul] to that which opposed it, although it was loftier and more powerful than all.

The sinful self uncertain of its own salvation and stuck in a loop of self-conscious meditation upon and conflict with its sinful nature derives from a specifically Protestant reading of the Pauline corpus, including Romans 7, a passage underlying Tamo's description of his own experience. Tamo then fits his recent suffering into a narrative of God's pedagogical chastisement, repeatedly using the Arabic-derived Neo-Aramaic word ta'lamta in a manner that suggests an evangelical version of a traditional Syriac Christian notion of divine pedagogy.[132]

> After this he intended to instruct me, but first with only small instructions that I might not deny him. After the one or two small instructions that he instructed me and [still] I did not guard myself, he drew back his powerful hand and he instructed me with a very forceful instruction, such an instruction that a man who was a soldier of the king would come before the door of our house and be killed by thieves; it happened thus; and this was set in the mouth of everyone that I certainly was the killer of that man. He transmitted me into the hand of oppressors, so that they cast chains upon my neck and chains upon my feet and transferred me from Bashkala to Van, with great torment and pummeling, and in Van put me in prison a long time. He knew that this instruction was not complete: he instructed me with another instruction more harsh, so that there might be an instruction upon the instruction, that is, he instructed me with a harsh and forceful illness; a prisoner and a foreigner, and ill, I was so ill that from morning until evening I was lying down [lit. "fallen"] and I had no aid. After this I lay down from evening until morning. At first I was shaking with a fever for one or two hours late in the day. Occasionally before the lamp I was shaking, and in no way at all was I able to warm myself. This occurred for about two hours. After this I had a fever until the morning, and I had no rest at all, there was no one there to have pity [lit. "ignite the heart"] upon me, and raise me up and sit me down except that one who had given me instruction.

The letter concludes with the long prayer Tamo says he made at the time followed by greetings to members of the mission, especially Perkins, whose daughter Judith's death (on September 4, 1852), he states, had caused him to suffer much even though he also rejoiced in her future salvation.

Instead of martyrdom, Tamo's imprisonment is rendered in this second letter as an instruction, a further attempt by God to bring Tamo closer to himself, and not as proof of Tamo's own salvation. The conflict described in Tamo's heart reflects the need for complete inner transformation demanded by the missionaries. What is the difference between evangelical conversion and other forms of Christian conversion? In Classical Syriac the standard verb for "convert" is *ettalmadh*, "to become a disciple or student," in contrast to the evangelical emphasis on penitence (Neo-Aramaic *tyawuta*). In classical texts conversions usually occur quickly and the template story is that of the saint. The virtuous or sinful prior life of the tale's protagonist is followed by that of her or his perfect life after conversion. In contrast, Tamo's second letter shows the extended process of evangelical conversion and the possibility of its failure. Such a failure resulted from both the intensified doubt of Reformed theology and the immobility of national identity. True religion required evangelical conversion, a spiritual transformation that could fail, whereas national identity was irreducible. Tamo would remain a Syrian whether he was saved or not.

The interiorization of evangelical piety and its abstract notion of belief were inverse complements to a national, often racialized, substrate of Syrianness. One could never know what was in another's heart, and racial difference, including the tendency of all Syrians to be liars, as the missionaries thought, made their conversions less reliable. The Syrians could always just be "passing." Religion in this case functions to mark national difference, in contrast to early Christianity, where conversion was from ethnic particularity to a higher, abstract plain of peoplehood, from pagan or Jewish difference to the new universal people of God. In the case of the mission to the Syrians, evangelical conversion stimulated the articulation of national identity, which produced a contradiction: a national substrate was marked and its essential place at the core of the person made conversion more difficult. The missionaries' wariness of accepting indigenous Christians' conversions could result, as in the case of Tamo, in the process of conversion being drawn out ad infinitum. Tamo's problem is like that expressed by Sanam in her meditation on her lost soul: there is always doubt, and at the mission that doubt was based upon and revealed national difference.

Conclusion: Priest Jacob Dilakoff, the Syrian Missionary Hero

Through the nineteenth century and into the early twentieth, East Syrians associated with the American mission traveled as missionaries beyond Urmia. Hakkari remained a focus of missionary activity: the mission even printed up a special booklet of rules for native assistants who preached in the mountains.[133] However, Syrian missionaries eventually traveled across Iran and even, in the case of Isaac Duman, as far as Japan. These missionary tours traversed a discursive landscape of universal religion and national particularity: Christianity was to be preached to every living soul, but often in a form of address aimed at each individual nation, whether the missionary's own or the Japanese. National identity, which was spoken about in increasingly hardened culturalist and even biological, racialized terms by the late nineteenth century, was an irreducible factor in human society and therefore an important part of Christian reform.

In concluding this chapter, I would like to move ahead several decades and discuss a memoir composed by an East Syrian who went through the mission school system in the mid-nineteenth century before becoming a missionary abroad. In 1904 in the volume *Three Missionary Heroes*, the American Presbyterian Mission Press in Urmia published a memoir by Jacob Dilakoff (ca. 1832–98), an East Syrian from the Urmia plain who spent much of his life preaching in various parts of the Russian Empire.[134]

In the preface to Dilakoff's memoir, Benjamin Labaree, who served at the mission from 1893 until his murder in 1904, claims that Dilakoff had visited him in America in 1892, when he came to find a school for his son, who would eventually attend the recently founded evangelical Moody Institute in Chicago. Labaree states that Dilakoff's memoir "would serve as a reminder to the nation [*melat*] of the Syrians of this honorable man who had been an apostle of the Gospel from them in benighted lands."[135] Labaree hopes the work might serve as an example because Dilakoff's story was reminiscent of the ancestors of the Syrians who "went to regions much further east to lay a foundation for the church of Christ . . . that this nation might again be as before a tower of light in this generation."

After acknowledging Labaree for requesting the work and entreating God for help in an endeavor that would be for his glory, Dilakoff states, "As I understand it, every Christian who gazes upon the journey of his past life sees how wondrous are the counsels of the Lord unto him."[136] As in *Pilgrim's Progress*, time is conceived of as the space through which life is a journey. Dilakoff sees himself as having enjoyed particularly wondrous attention from the Lord over the sixty years of this journey. At seven years old he was orphaned and at ten adopted by relatives. While attending a mission village school, he worked as a shepherd in the summers. This would have been in the early 1840s. "In the fourteenth year of my life I awoke to the wretchedness of my lost state [*mar'ešli l-šaqiyuta d-ahwali tliqta*]." He became more and more aware of his sinful nature and eventually wanted to commit suicide. Unable to kill himself, he thought to try to incite Muslims to do it for him. Later, Dilakoff ran away from home to join the mission, but his brother caught him and compelled him to return home by taking away his shoes. He eventu-

ally entered the mission school and graduated from the male seminary in
1858.[137] His autobiography then describes his missionary travails in Russia,
which later led him to Vladivostok. This long text offers us a self-conscious
account of one missionary life and serves as an excellent example of the literary interiority evangelicalism fostered as well as the theology of nations implicit in Dilakoff's work. His autobiography demonstrates the inculcation of
evangelical values, including the demand for introspection, self-analysis, and
the interiorization of religion.

Dilakoff's colorful career as a missionary attests to the capacity of a
national self-understanding to emerge within evangelical piety and the agency
that piety offered those immersed in it. In an extant letter to Labaree written in Boston on July 4, 1892, Dilakoff describes his long-held desire to see
"this blessed land of freedom [azaduta]" and expresses thanks to God and his
"American friends" for the hospitality he has received, while acknowledging
all the service America has done for the enlightenment of the world.[138] However, he then claims that he was woken in the night by shooting and cannon
fire due to Independence Day celebrations and complains about the amount
of money spent on these festivities. Revealing the degree to which he had
absorbed the missionaries' ethic of frugality, he asks rhetorically if the Bosto-
nians spend as much money to recognize the freedom Christ provided from
Satan's rule. Comparing Easter Sunday to the American day of independence,
he states, using a Classical Syriac expression, that "since the beginning of creation [šurraya d-brita] until its consummation no day has been or will be such."

Ironically, Dilakoff's critique of the commemoration of a foundational
event in American history reflects the same argument the missionaries used
against the East Syrian liturgical calendar: aside from the Sunday of Christ's
resurrection, all days existed in a secular time that extended back to the beginning of the world and forward to its conclusion. For Dilakoff all nations
required the work of reform. Thus, evangelical piety promoted a nationalizing discourse of religion, one in which national identities were articulated
through the ethical exhortation of reform. Universal mission and national
identities were not in contradiction, but complemented each other as parts of
a Christian theology of nations. As we will see in the following chapter, this
was all the more so by the late nineteenth century, when the proliferation of
foreign missions and liberalizing trends in American Protestantism further
contributed to the emergence of a distinct national identity among the Syrians, one that included a literary subjectivity akin to what we find in Dilakoff's memoir and in the writings of the native assistants from decades earlier.

7

Continuity and Change in the Late Nineteenth Century:
New Institutions, Missionary Competition,
and the First Generation of Nationalists

I think there are various signs of a new national spirit among the Syrians. Neither the
Catholics nor the Russians can give this spirit free play and our people are the ones
most affected by it.

—WILLIAM A. SHEDD, November 1, 1908

The preceding chapters examined the social and theological matrix for the
emergence of nationalism among the East Syrians by focusing on the history
of the American mission before 1871. On December 27, 1870, the ABCFM
"Mission to the Nestorians" was transferred to the Presbyterian Church, becoming part of its broader "Mission to Persia." By the late nineteenth century,
the focus of the American mission had shifted away from the millennialism
of early evangelicalism to the worldly and progressive Social Gospel. At the
same time, the Americans were no longer the only substantial actors in the
missionary field in Urmia. By the 1890s Catholic (French Lazarist), Anglican,
Lutheran (German, Swedish, and American), Baptist (American), and Orthodox (Russian) missions, several of which to differing degrees had already
been working in Urmia, asserted themselves in the region. At the turn of the
twentieth century, the national consciousness that was already apparent by
the 1860s had further emerged, and explicit claims of nationality were being
made, especially among the second and third generation of Syrians associated
with the American mission.

In this chapter I first describe institutional and intellectual developments
at the American mission in the late nineteenth and early twentieth centuries. After this I provide a brief account of the other missions working in
Urmia by the end of the nineteenth century. One of my arguments is that the
intensification and proliferation of missionary work in the late nineteenth
century created a pluralism in which a secularized national discourse further
emerged. "Syrian" became a distinctly national identity, one imagined as sep-
arable from religion. Related to this development was the politicking in which
some clergy engaged, including the patriarch, who began to act as a *national*
representative of the community, despite his distance from Urmia and his

weak political (and military) position. Over time he was drawn into the role
he would eventually play—and be expected to play—as ethnarch of the Assyrians in the aftermath of World War I. The back-and-forth maneuvering of
some clergy and church members led to a failed attempt at mass conversion,
for what seem to be primarily political purposes, to Orthodoxy in 1897, the
same year that we have evidence for the first explicit claims that the Syrians
were descendants of the ancient Assyrians. Moreover, in reaction to Orthodox
and Catholic missionary success, an indigenous movement developed, which
aimed at defending the ecclesial authority of the patriarch in Urmia. Members
of this movement, many of whom received their education at the American
mission, were disproportionately the first nationalists. Finally I describe the
founding of the first nationalist organization and the creation of the nationalist newspaper, the *Star*, in 1906.

The American Mission: Continuity and Change

The fifty-year jubilee celebrations at the American mission provide a snapshot
of the mission before the tumultuous 1890s, a period of cholera epidemics,
strident competition with other missions, and the birth of an explicit nation-
alist discourse.[1] The celebrations were held in two parts: in 1884 Perkins's arrival in Iran was commemorated at the annual meeting of the West Persia
Mission, the new broader Presbyterian mission comprising both Tabriz and
Urmia; and in July 1885 a celebration was thrown by the Syrian Evangelical
Church. The Synod of New York sent as its special delegate to the events Rev.
Dr. Henry A. Nelson (1820–1906), editor of the Presbyterian monthly *The
Church at Home and Abroad*.[2] Nelson bore a special letter of introduction
from Mirza Malkam Khan (1833–1908), the contemporary Persian ambas-
sador to Great Britain and a major advocate of reform in late nineteenth-
century Iran.[3] He also carried a special letter from the local governor endorsing the mission and its educational work.

At the 1884 celebration, held in English, lectures were given on the history,
success, and promise of the American mission. The July 1885 one, in Neo-
Aramaic, included a communal feast. "A large booth furnished accommoda-
tions for the fourteen or fifteen hundred people assembled. Syriac mottoes
were put over the platform, 'Jubilee 1835–1885.' 'Praise God, for His mercy
endureth forever.' 'And ye shall sanctify the fiftieth year, it shall be a jubilee
unto you.' A young Eastern Syrian presided at the organ, and a choir of college boys, under Mr. Oldfather's direction, led the singing."[4] Dinner was provided for several hundred people, including the many Syrians from abroad
wearing European attire. Old alumni and alumnae from the male and female

seminaries attended, including one considered the first student at the female seminary, Selby of Marbisho (b. ca. 1836), who had been brought as a girl to study at the seminary by her uncle Mar Yokhannan of Gawilan.[5] Armenians and Jews also attended; "posters showed where the delegates from the different villages were to sit, and the dinner was cooked out under the trees in great kettles holding from half a barrel to two barrels."[6] Tickets, which were also distributed beforehand, were on sale at the July 15 and 16 celebration, and although the demand was greater than expected, the missionaries were impressed at the propriety maintained throughout. Women lodged at Urmia College, the new name for the male seminary, which had been moved back into the city from Sire, and the overflow of people resulted in many men remaining outside through the night.

The two days of festivities included a program of religious exercises and lectures. After an opening lecture by a native assistant, John H. Shedd (mission: 1859–95), employing specially prepared colored diagrams, spoke about the history of the mission. Lectures by native assistants included such topics as "Eminent Nestorians Who Have Labored in the Gospel" and "Annals of Educational Work." Three alumnae of the female seminary alternated in giving a paper on female education since the time of Judith Grant, the seminary's founder. Papers were also given on the printing press, the distribution of Bibles, and past revivals. This last topic deeply affected the crowd. On the following day, Thursday, July 16, lectures addressed the mission's medical work, its trials and persecution, and "Changes, Good and Bad, in the Moral and Social Developments of the Nation during the Fifty Years Past." The services were concluded with a sermon by Malik Yonan, the same Yonan whose 1850 journey with Khamis I addressed in chapter 6. By then he had long been the *malik*, or chief, of Geogtapa. The city governor was unable to attend because of Eid ul-Fitr, the feast celebrating the end of Ramadan, but the regional bureaucrat responsible for the Christian community was there and, so we are told, was shocked to see hundreds of women with books in hand reading and singing aloud.

Through the end of the nineteenth century and into the following one, the American mission in Urmia changed in many ways, but most of the institutions, practices, and beliefs that we find in the 1834–70 period persisted. Justin Perkins died on December 31, 1869, not long after his arrival back in the United States, and the following year the mission was officially handed over from the ABCFM to the care of the Board of Foreign Missions of the Presbyterian Church.[7] The Urmia mission had already changed its name from the "Mission to the Nestorians" to the "Mission to Persia,"[8] reflecting a changing of the guard at the mission and a swinging of the pendulum back in the direction of the position contentiously advocated by James L. Merrick (1803–66) in the 1840s that the mission should focus on a larger community than just the East Syrians.[9] Although the mission in Urmia and those mission stations under it continued to focus on evangelizing the East Syrians, with the accession to the Presbyterian Church, the mission now had links to a wider missionary network in Iran. The intended audience was larger and included the Jews and Armenians of the plain, and even Muslims. Said Kurdistani (1863–1942), who became a missionary physician, was celebrated as a successful case of Muslim conversion, whereas the story of Mirza Ibrahim (d. 1893), a Muslim convert who died in jail after confessing Christ, combined a traditional tale of martyrdom with modern ideas about the need for religious liberty and tolerance.[10]

The Urmia mission maintained close contacts with the mission in Tabriz, which was founded in 1873 and became the bureaucratic center for the Presbyterian mission.[11] By 1883 the organization of the Presbyterian mission had become too complex, especially in a country as large and difficult to travel through as Iran: the field was divided into the East and West Persia Missions, the latter consisting of Urmia and Tabriz.[12] The link to Tabriz was important because it connected the missionary community in Urmia to the city that at the turn of the twentieth century was the center of political reform and burgeoning Iranian nationalism. Through the mission network, native assistants from the East Syrian community even engaged in mission work outside of Urmia among other ethnic groups.

In 1884 a mission station was established in Heftdewan in Salmas, the plain north of Urmia, where the Christian population was predominantly Chaldean or Armenian.[13] There were several outstations in Salmas—for example, in Ula, a village that retained members of the Church of the East—and in the larger town of Khoy. The mountain mission continued in Hakkari as well as in Bohtan to the east and Berwar to the south. In the 1880s a station was established in Tiyari, and the mission enjoyed the favor of the local chief, Petros.[14] The mountains remained the object of considerable missionary hope and frustration, as they had been since the origins of the mission, while the Ottoman authorities continued to obstruct efforts in evangelism there—for example, shutting down several of the mission's schools in Gawar in 1888.[15] Native assistants continued to make mountain preaching tours, those who were members of the college typically during the off-season or even during winter break.[16] Like the earlier short-lived "Assyrian Mission," a mission opened in 1889 at Mosul aimed at both Arabic- and Aramaic-speaking Christians of the plain and the mountains to the north.[17]

The accession to the Presbyterian Church required some adjustments.

Both the male seminary and publication of *Rays of Light* were suspended briefly in the 1870s.[18] The funding of the mission came from the Board of Foreign Missions, but it also continued to rely on private donations, which were particularly helpful for the development of the hospital and medical school linked to it.[19] Despite this funding, the missionaries demonstrated an increased emphasis on Syrian self-reliance in the 1870s. The rhetorical linking of reform and self-support, which was also a financial preference of the board, corresponded with the effort since the early 1860s to create an autonomous evangelical church. The salaries of pastors were to be based upon local tithes, and the members of each community were to support their own schools.[20]

The Syrian Evangelical Church was organized already in the early 1870s into three conferences or presbyteries (*knušye*), which would meet each year in the fall and the spring.[21] These presbyteries, based upon traditional geographical divisions, were each named after one of the three main rivers of the plain: the City, the Nazlu Chai, and the Baranduz. Local women's synods were organized in the same way.[22] To the south, in the region around Mosul, there was the Tigris presbytery, and to the east that of Gawar. The church kept membership rolls, which were regularly checked, updated, and purged.[23] The broader church authority was the general synod. Its yearly meetings included discussion of the long-term obstructions and temporary setbacks to evangelizing the "nation."[24] The synod, or general assembly (*knušya*), had as its executive committees a board of education and an "evangelistic board." The former, organized in 1877, received funds directly from the mission, which it then allocated to schools on the plain.[25]

The number of members of the mission, the evangelical church, and students at mission schools continued to increase through the late nineteenth century. The *1895 Annual Report* states that there were 59 persons in the missionary staff, including "four lady physicians."[26] There were 96 mission outstations, 121 native preachers, 119 congregations, and 38 organized churches. By 1895 Urmia College had 110 students, and the female seminary, now Fiske Seminary, 200. The village schools, of which there were almost 100, had over 2,200 students.[27] That same year the Syrian Evangelical Church had 2,800 members. The number of officially enrolled members always remained low relative to the broader population, in part because the rolls were strictly enforced.

The male seminary, which Perkins commenced in a room with a handful of students in 1836, had already expanded by the time of the Presbyterian accession in 1870. By the mid-1870s Greek and Hebrew were added to the curriculum, which also included examinations in Classical Syriac, Neo-Aramaic, Armenian, Persian, Ottoman and Azeri Turkish, English, mathematics, sacred and political geography, and theology, including exegesis and homiletics.[28] In 1879 the male seminary was moved back to Urmia from Sire, where it had been relocated in 1847, and it was reorganized that same year as a "Young Men's College or Training School, together with a residence."[29] Its initial endowment of five thousand dollars was provided from the estate of Henry Marquand (1819–1902), the well-known art collector and philanthropist from New York.[30] A further portion of the college's funding came from an annual gift of two thousand dollars from "a gentleman in Philadelphia."[31]

In addition to medical training, the seminary began in the 1870s to offer a separate degree, something like a certificate, in theology, and in the fall of 1887 an industrial branch was added, which began with carpentry but was eventually expanded to include other crafts such as ironworking, a trade from which Christians were traditionally excluded.[32] As stated in the *1889 Annual Report*, the purpose of the college was:

1. To furnish teachers and preachers for the native church and for mission work. This is essential to the permanence of the church and to the evangelization of a vast region in Persia and Koordistan, and to some extent in Russia and the farther East.
2. To educate young men to be physicians, for whom there is a great opening.
3. To furnish leaders of their people in every capacity in which they can be useful.[33]

Regular meetings of alumni of the male seminary, a practice that went back to 1859, continued, and this association contributed to the development of national ideas and institutions. Regarding the meeting of 1892, we are told, "The alumni meeting held at the close of the collegiate year is always a breezy occasion, at which the literary, social, and spiritual interests of the nation are pretty freely discussed."[34] At the meeting of 1896, "Topics of national interest were discussed. Among those present were the Rev. Mr. Neesan of the Anglican Mission, and a prominent Catholic priest, both being old pupils in the school."[35] The alumni association was an incipient form of the national committee that was organized only a few years later.[36]

Like the male seminary, the female seminary continued its work through the end of the nineteenth century, though also with occasional stoppages. For much of 1887, the seminary was closed due to a lack of funds.[37] However, in 1888 it reopened with new buildings and its new name: the Fiske Seminary, after Fidelia Fiske.[38] In the early 1890s, a kindergarten was introduced to help support students who had children.[39] Like the other institutions, it received direct gifts from abroad, such as a new organ donated by a society of women in the United States.[40] Aside from scriptural study and secular learning, there was also a focus, as in the college, on industrial education.[41] In the 1890s sewing machines were introduced.[42] In 1893, of the 194 students at varying levels from kindergarten to the seminary proper, 83 were boarders.[43] The girls were encouraged to be self-sufficient: they were expected to make their own clothes, cook their own meals, and keep their rooms in order, while upper-school girls were responsible for teaching their juniors. There were triennial alumnae meetings for the female seminary similar to those of the college.[44] Aside from the numerous village schools, there was also an experiment in developing local high schools, which were to serve as intermediate institutions between the village schools and the college. In the late 1870s, there was one in Urmia, one south of the lake in Sulduz, and a third in the mountains.[45]

The communal assemblies and events I described in chapter 4 continued to take place through the end of the nineteenth century. School examinations remain the topic of articles in *Rays of Light*.[46] There were regular prayer meetings; monthly concerts; weeks of prayer, especially in January after the New Year; and on occasion revivals, such as in 1890 and 1891. (The college's new buildings even had prayer closets built into the basement.)[47] A special day of prayer for colleges was also observed.[48] In the 1890s the mission ran a weeklong summer camp, which included lectures and group prayers.[49] Within the Syrian Evangelical Church, a group was founded in 1890 called the Young Men's Band (or Board), which, along with other indigenously organized groups, aimed to reform and missionize their own people.[50] The mission often participated in current American religious trends: the Young People's Society of Christian Endeavor, a nondenominational Protestant group founded in 1881 by Francis Edward Clark, was an early form of youth ministry, popular in the late nineteenth and early twentieth centuries in the United States as well as around the world. Christian Endeavor groups were organized at the mission by the turn of the twentieth century, even in the mountains of Hakkari.[51]

Ideological continuity with the ABCFM mission is apparent in the ongoing missionary concern for the elevation of women. Some female native assistants held positions at the mission specifically designated for work among women.[52] By the 1890s the improvement of women's lives and prospects at the mission was referred to as "Woman's Work for Women," also the name of the monthly magazine published by the Woman's Foreign Missionary Society of the Presbyterian Church.[53] The Persian mission was covered in the United States in the Presbyterian women's magazine *Woman's Work for Women*, and through its female reading public and church auxiliary organizations, funds were donated to the mission—for example, the hundred dollars donated by a society of women in Stockton, California, to build a church on the plain of Urmia.[54]

The mission had always offered medical attention to the local population, as medical care had long been a missionizing tool. Medical classes were taught at the college already by the 1870s.[55] These classes were formally organized when the college began to offer a medical degree, and students engaged in medical observation at the Westminster Hospital, built in 1882 (and named after the church in Buffalo, New York, which provided funds).[56] Graduates of the medical school would serve at the hospital, and several alumni became medical missionaries in other parts of Iran.[57] One early graduate served as a doctor in the Qajar army.[58] Built in 1891, the Howard Annex, which took its name from Mrs. George Howard of Buffalo, New York, who funded the structure with a gift of two thousand dollars, was specifically for the care of female patients.[59] Its head doctor was Emma T. Miller (Woman's Medical College of Chicago, 1890; mission: 1891–1909). When the hospital was closed, patients could also visit the local dispensary.[60] In the 1890s the mission dedicated further resources to Salmas, and accordingly Westminster opened a branch on the plain to the north.[61]

By the 1890s hundreds of patients were treated in the hospital each year, and thousands received some form of care from the mission's medical department as a whole.[62] Despite temporary closures of the hospital due to a lack of funds, the mission became a regional center for medical care, especially during cholera outbreaks.[63] As at other missions, the hospital also provided opportunities to preach to patients. Here the medical body was linked to the evangelical body of sin: "Dissolute and reckless men have been brought to confess that their afflictions were consequences of their evil ways, and declared that by the blessing of God their sufferings had become the occasion of their visiting Oroomiah and learning the way of Life."[64]

The hospital as well as medical education were under the direction of Dr. Joseph P. Cochran (1855–1905), son of missionaries Joseph G. Cochran (mission: 1847–71) and Deborah (Plumb) Cochran (mission: 1847–71). His wife, Katherine (Hale) Cochran (1853–95), helped at the hospital and also proselytized there, reading Scripture to patients.[65] Cochran was born in Urmia but went to the United States in 1868 to study, graduating from New York Medical College in 1876. He and Katherine arrived in Urmia in 1878, and his medical practice, combined with his long connections to the region through his parents' prior residence there, gave him clout typical only of local elites. In 1880 Kurdish leader Shaykh Ubaydullah (d. 1883), who attempted to form his own realm in Hakkari and the neighboring areas of the Ottoman Empire, invaded Qajar territory. Cochran maintained contact with the shaykh during his incursion, and this helped to ameliorate the situation for the local population.[66] Supposedly thousands of mourners from Urmia and beyond came to pay their respects upon Cochran's death in 1905.[67]

The mission had a close working and financial relationship with the orphanage in Geogtapa, which was directed by Khenanisho' Abraham, or Khenanisho' "of the Orphanage."[68] He had finished his studies at the male seminary in 1853 and then worked at the female seminary for several years. He was the son of Priest Abraham of Geogtapa (d. 1871), the native assistant who had worked with Perkins.[69] Khenanisho' had gone to England in 1875, and again in 1878, to raise funds for orphans left behind after famine.[70] He established the orphanage in 1880 and returned to England in 1884 to seek further funds. By the 1890s it was home to fifty to sixty children at any given time and was funded by evangelical Christians in England, in particular Henry Tasker of Hants, part of the renowned engineering and later transport company, Taskers of Andover.[71] Khenanisho''s second wife, Esther (the first, Asle, died on a tour of the mountains in 1889), helped administer the orphanage and took charge of it after he died in 1904/5.[72] Born in Marbisho in 1870, she underwent an evangelical conversion at thirteen and moved to Urmia, where she studied at the female seminary and then in 1887 began teaching there for two years. She and Khenanisho' married in 1890. She traveled to England in 1892 to learn how to better manage the orphanage, and visited again in 1906.[73]

Syrians had been traveling outside of Urmia and Hakkari, especially in the Caucasus, to find work long before the arrival of the missionaries. The movement of Syrian men into Russia was thought to be a regular source of instability: it was never certain whether they would return, and Tbilisi and cities in the north were places where morals could be corrupted.[74] Moreover, in the late nineteenth century, Syrians began to study abroad, Chaldeans in Rome, Old Church in England, and evangelicals in the United States. Already by the early 1890s, study abroad had become a controversial topic within the evangelical church. There was a concern that young men who went abroad to study returned expecting to receive high salaries.

> The rush to America is not surprising. From out of conditions akin to serfdom under Mohammedan masters, these Christian young men of Persia have opened their eyes to larger possibilities for themselves. The Gospel has been to them as the leaven of a new manhood. Education in missionary schools has awakened in them the consciousness of new powers. They have seen some of their own number getting a higher education in the colleges and seminaries of the West, and attaining to enviable positions of usefulness, reputation, and worldly comfort. So it has come about that few of the licentiates are willing to remain at home and minister to humble congregations on meager salaries.

There is danger that churches will become pastorless, and the higher schools
be left without teachers. The movement is not wholly to be derided, however.
It is an almost inevitable outcome of missionary training, the key which has
unlocked the mental fetters of ages.[75]

As this statement attests, the missionaries were often aware of the contradictions their presence created. The American Gospel liberated but in doing so
also disaggregated and secularized. In response to this problem, the synod of
the evangelical church decided that men studying abroad would not be given
special positions upon their return.

From its inception, the mission was visited by various local Qajar officials
and royalty, as well as by European diplomats who happened to be in the area.
Such visits continued in the late nineteenth century as the mission became
a fixture in the region. Those in attendance at the college's public examinations in 1882 included the governor, who was Crown Prince Mozaffar ad-Din
(1853–1907); Capt. Wagner of the Austrian officers corps, who were responsible for modernizing the Qajar army; and a number of army officers from
Tehran and Hamadan.[76] The crown prince again attended the commencement
ceremonies in 1890.[77] The presence of such visitors shows the college's affinities with the Qajars' project of reform and modernization. By the late nineteenth century, Urmia was no longer in a distant corner of the globe, and the
mission enjoyed several distinguished guests from even farther afield. In 1890
L. D. Wishard, secretary of the YMCA, visited Urmia during his worldwide
tour.[78] Robert Speer, director of the board and an important figure in the later
modernist/fundamentalist dispute in the church, visited during his 1896–97
tour of Asia. (He composed a biography of Dr. Joseph P. Cochran, published
in 1911, and later helped organize relief for the Syrian community during and
after World War I.)[79]

The Mission Press under the Presbyterians

Many of the publications of the press in the post-1870 period reflect concerns consistent with those of the earlier mission. They include Bibles; biblical
commentaries and reference works; church rules and confessions for the now
autonomous evangelical church; devotional works; a Sunday school quarterly; works on mathematics, science, geography, history, and medicine; and
spelling primers. Among these was an 1882 translation of Joseph C. Martin-
dale's *First Lessons in Natural Philosophy for Beginners* (1881), an introduction
to physics and mechanics.[80] There was also a turn to individual biography:
memorials of great missionaries, both from the local mission and elsewhere;

a collection of biographies of eminent men; and a 1907 Horatio Alger–like collection of stories of poor boys who had become famous, such as George Washington, Jacob Riis, John Bunyan, Christopher Columbus, and Dwight Moody.[81] Historical volumes consisted of a survey of church history, a volume on the early revivals at the mission, a history of Babylon, and a history of the kings of Iran.[82] *Rays of Light* continued publication, albeit at varying rates. Publication was disrupted in the period of sluggish work at the mission after the transition to the Presbyterian Board, but in 1878 it became semimonthly.[83] It is not extant from 1871 until 1892, and when it does reappear, it has changed in significant ways.

In the 1890s the paper, again a monthly, regularly begins with "Seasonal News," which consists of local news pertaining to the mission; the schools; public health, such as problems with cholera; recent revivals; examinations in the schools; and synod meetings. The section on "Gospel Preaching" (*Karozuta*) has long homilies, often by the missionaries, but also translations of, for example, sermons by the well-known London Baptist preacher Charles Spurgeon (1834–92). The "Evangelism" section focuses on foreign missionary work and provides geographical and demographic information on different regions of the world. "World" and "Foreign News" describe events beyond the Urmia region but with a strong emphasis on Europe, and occasionally there is an "Iran News" section. The paper continues to contain obituaries, some short, others rhetorical paeans to those who loved and benefited their "nation." Among the miscellaneous articles on science, geography, history, ethics, health, and hygiene, the paper ran series of articles over several months on, for example, the lives of John Wesley and Abraham Lincoln.[84] At times there are longer pieces on the finances and size of the mission and its schools, and in 1895 there was an addendum to the paper detailing the events of that year's general synod meeting. Moreover, *Rays of Light* began to encourage charitable giving to the community by listing the names of those who made donations for the mission's projects.

By the turn of the twentieth century, editorship had passed over into Syrian hands—namely, Mirza Shmuel (Samuel) Badal Hangaldi (1865–1908). Badal was born in Geogtapa and attended a mission school in the city.[85] In 1882 he entered the college in Urmia, where he received a theological degree. He taught in village schools and also helped in Khenanisho''s orphanage in Geogtapa. At this time he began to work with Khenanisho' on *The Book of Excerpts from Forty Years of "Rays of Light"* (1895).[86] This encyclopedic work in Neo-Aramaic treats, among other things, religion, biology, history, education, health, and the lives of those associated with the mission. In 1891 Badal went for three years to the United States, where he received a degree from Drew

Theological Seminary (now Drew University) in Madison, New Jersey. In part due to poor health, he returned home in 1894 and in 1895 became "proof reader" for *Rays of Light*, a position he held until his death, while also engaging in translation work.[87] He maintained active membership in the evangelical church and yet was also an important promoter of national sentiment across religious confessions. Under his editorship, more explicitly nationalist ideas were expressed in *Rays of Light*: in 1897 the paper claimed that its aim was the unification and education of the "nation" and that articles appearing therein should come from all members of the nation, regardless of confessional distinction.[88]

Christian Liberalism and the Theology of Nations

Despite continuities, the ideology of the mission changed with the times. Progressive ideas, which went hand in hand with the Social Gospel, were creeping in by the end of the nineteenth century.[89] The mission's contemporary priorities are apparent in the division of annual reports under three rubrics: evangelistic, educational, and medical. The use of the language of progress and enlightenment increased among the missionaries, whereas the millennialism of the earlier mission either disappeared or at times was reconfigured with a this-worldly understanding of the end-time, the millennium albeit in a bourgeois mode:

> In general it may be said of Persia that an awakening has begun. The third visit of the Shah to Europe has taken place, and now he is showing himself the foremost man in Persia in desiring reforms and progress. Concessions and proclamations announce the dawn of a new era. Banks have been opened in the capital at Tabriz. The Karun River is being made a highway of commerce from the south into the heart of the country. Railways are projected, mines and manufactories are opened, and highways are built. There are more signs of progress in the two years past than in a thousand years before. These signs of the times render certain the incoming of English and American capital and enterprise. They also render our mission stations strategic points for the great campaign of evangelization on the broad field of Western Asia. Nearly twenty degrees of longitude must be crossed before our missions in Persia can clasp hands with the China missions. We must ever have an eye on this great field and estimate the work of the year, not only as so much done, but as far more a preparation for the great work yet to do. The day of opportunity is at hand.[90]

Along with such breathless descriptions of the opening up of Persia, mission reports continued to describe "oriental despotism," but now in the vernacular of political liberalism.[91] "Progress" (*mantayta*) in Iran became a common topic of conversation at the mission.[92] These shifts also affected the message of reform, even if the object of that reform remained the Syrian nation and the primary means was still the Gospel.[93] As in the United States, temperance remained a major focus of moral reform into the twentieth century, but a greater focus on health and hygiene displaced the earlier ubiquity of the language of sin. The concern to improve the lives of Christians, long part of missionary discourse, became something more overtly material: the missionaries accepted the desire for this-worldly prosperity despite the ambivalence they expressed about such nonspiritual concerns.[94]

By the early twentieth century, mission work was being recast as a program of social uplift and utility. In a chapter on "American Missions and Social Reforms in Persia" in his 1908 Twenty Years in Persia, John G. Wishard (1863–1940), director of the Presbyterian Mission Hospital in Tehran, describes how the school in Urmia "has raised hundreds of Nestorian families from a condition of serfdom to respectable citizenship."[95] Mission education, which he compares to the public education system in the United States, allows for a mixing of the different groups of people in Persia: "In a land saturated with race-prejudice and hatred, who can measure the good that is to come from the association of all classes in these schools?"[96] Wishard demonstrates the same evangelical concern for women and the sentimental warmth they were understood to help cultivate as we find at the very beginning of the American mission in the 1830s. He even repeats the same cliché about the absence of a word for "home," which we find in earlier sources, except this time it is stated about the Persian language instead of Neo-Aramaic.[97] He identifies the mission's goal as the implementation of social reforms (and not political ones), and he addresses women, children, the insane, lepers, and animals as groups whose lives these reforms will alleviate.[98]

The mission ideology at this time was a Christian liberalism in tune with a Christian theology of nations. This is well attested in William Ambrose Shedd's Islam and the Oriental Churches: Their Historical Relations (1904), which began as a series of lectures Shedd gave at Princeton Theological Seminary during a visit to the United States in 1902–3. Shedd, son of the missionaries John H. Shedd (mission: 1859–95) and Sarah Jane (Dawes) Shedd (mission: 1859–96), served at the mission from 1892 until his death in 1918. Born at the mission in 1865, he spent his youth moving back and forth between the United States and Iran (and was a first cousin to Charles G. Dawes [1865–1951], vice president under Calvin Coolidge). In 1885, at the age of twenty, he returned to the United States, finished college, and then attended Princeton Theological Seminary from 1889 to 1892. After ordination, he returned to Urmia, where he eventually served as president of the college.

Shedd's volume is dedicated to Benjamin Woods Labaree, a member of the mission who was murdered in Salmas on March 9, 1904. Labaree, son of missionary Benjamin Labaree (b. 1834; mission: 1860–1906), had served since 1893. His death became a local cause célèbre, and the US Department of State involved itself in the affair, which put Urmia officials and their practices under the scrutiny of the authorities in Tabriz. Shedd's dedication is fitting because Labaree's murder and its aftermath represented for the missionaries what was wrong with Persia: hatred, intolerance, and a slow and corrupt government.

This historical essay renders the story of the relationship between Islam and the Eastern churches in liberal terms: "religious freedom," "freedom of worship," "religious equality," and "toleration" are its concerns. Shedd states that Islam is not necessarily an intolerant religion, but Islamic civilization, being based on prior civilizations of Western Asia, lacks innovation. He makes intriguing comments about the inculturation of Syriac Christianity and notes the "inseparable relation between religious and national movements."[99]

> Missions have for their primary and unalterable aim the making known to the individual the gospel of Christ in order that he individually may come into living fellowship with God the Father of all through Christ the Son. This aim is inevitably bound up in the conception of religion embodied in Christianity and emphasized by the Protestant Reformation. All other results of Christian missions depend upon the realization of this aim. The method to accomplish other changes is first to change the individual. At the same time, in order to be a permanent and effective force Christianity must lay hold of the nation and must itself be so organized in its outward form and in its intellectual character as to become an integral part of the life of the nation.[100]

Success, he claims, depends on "moral and intellectual leadership."[101] The Greek Church Fathers not only created an intellectual culture, but "they bound up with Christianity the destinies of the Greek race. . . . The same service was done with equal effectiveness and without the aid of political bonds by the Syrian Fathers of Edessa." These Syriac Church Fathers successfully created a national culture, as did the Armenian Fathers, in contrast to the "transitoriness among the Arabs, Persians, and Turks."[102] This is why Christianity was able to persist. "Christian schools, the Bible and other Christian literature in the vernacular, the creation of a truly national culture, are indispensable to the conquest of the nations."[103]

Shedd's discussion of Islam and the history of different churches reflects a new type of approach to other religious traditions. Less openly polemical, it engaged in comparison through a reserved historicism. The curriculum at the college included a similar comparative study of religion, which aimed to demonstrate the superiority of Christianity over Zoroastrianism, Buddhism, and especially Islam.[104] Despite its sectarian intentions, such study was part of a "World Religions" discourse, which in turn contributed to further development of the secular concept of religion at the mission.[105]

At the end of his volume, Shedd raises the issue of the relationship of mission to the Eastern churches. He states that there are three different approaches: absorption (Catholic), support of indigenous institutions (Anglican), or American reform.[106] Shedd notes an absence of national ambitions among Syrians as opposed to Armenians, but by this he does not refer to a lack of nationality (for this would counter his whole argument).[107] Rather, he means the absence of explicitly nationalist political claims, which had in fact developed among the Armenians by the turn of the twentieth century. After raising the question "What is the character of the Christianity that shall win the victory for the faith?"[108] he draws a link between the spread of commerce and that of Christianity. The two stand to benefit from each other.[109] "Why should not men go out into the great roads of trade and the great marts of commerce to build up the kingdom of God, as the Empire of Britain has been built up by merchants?"[110]

Shedd's work bears witness to a Christian liberalism and theology of nations that would lead indirectly to the death of Howard Baskerville in Tabriz in 1909. Born in Nebraska in 1885 to a family of Presbyterian ministers, Baskerville graduated from Princeton in 1907, after studying jurisprudence and constitutional government with Woodrow Wilson, president of the university at the time.[111] He soon after joined the West Persia Mission in Tabriz. By April 1909 he had resigned from the mission to help lead forces fighting on the constitutionalist side against the royalists supporting Muhammad Ali Shah. When the American consul attempted to dissuade him from his revolutionary activity, he responded, "I am an American citizen and proud of it, but I am also a human being."[112] On the night of April 19, he was shot dead by a sniper and since then has often been cited as an example of the constitutional democratic values shared by Americans and Iranians.[113] He remains a known figure in Iran today, an example of a good American, worthy of street and school names.

The story of Baskerville and his "sacrifice" for Iranian freedom, as it is usually told, has been sanitized of the Christian motivation behind his political acts. Although his actions were not endorsed by the mission, they derived from a logic the missionaries shared, the same Christian logic lying behind Wilsonian internationalism: there is a common humanity it behooves us to serve, and this humanity is organized into the constituent units of nations. This culturalist and racialized Christian discourse of nations does not conceive of nations as particularistic entities in contradiction with the claims of a universal humanity, but rather as essential parts of humanity that need to be organized individually for freedom. These ideas go back to earlier liberal notions more obviously marked as Christian, such as the abolitionist politics of the antebellum period, the only contemporary American political issue addressed in mission publications for the East Syrian audience. This is why it is important that we qualify claims that shifts in the audience of the missions "resulted in Presbyterian schools . . . altering their priorities over time from evangelizing to modernizing Iranians."[114] Missions did change over time from the millennialist evangelicalism of the early nineteenth century to a progressive Social Gospel with an explicit focus on modernizing and civilizing. However, the shift from the former to the latter was not necessarily a de-Christianization of mission. Rather, there was a continuity between the former and the latter in their shared republican Christian concern for freedom and their rejection of what was understood as all forms of tyranny, whether mental (as manifested in the supposed fetishism of the indigenous culture) or political (as imagined in the critique of oriental despotism). To highlight how the liberal political concerns of the mission had evolved by the end of the nineteenth century, we need only look across the border to the west at the missionary agitation for political rights among Armenians within the Ottoman Empire by the 1870s.[115] It was for the same Christian politics that William Shedd would die in 1918: he remained committed to the East Syrian community and tried to help as many as possible during the turmoil of World War I and its aftermath. He formally gave up his position at the mission in 1918 to become the local American consul and died of cholera during the mass exodus of East Syrians from Urmia not long after.

Baskerville was inspired by a progressive Christianity, but it is important to observe the continuities between the later history of the mission and its early decades. The continuity between the period of millennial revivalism of the early mission and the end of the century, when progressive Christianity became prevalent and the nationalist movement began, was not just ideological but also social. The gap of time between Perkins's arrival in the 1830s and the beginnings of an explicitly nationalist discourse in the 1890s was not insurmountable for the long-lived. A number of early students and assistants from the mission lived into the 1890s. Take, for instance, the native assistants whose preaching tours I examined in the previous chapter: Yonan, by the 1890s chief (*malik*) of Geogtapa, was seventy-four years old in 1897; Khamis lived into the 1890s; and Murad Khan died in 1897.[116] Moses of Geogtapa was living in New York in 1892, but, we are told, wanting to return.[117] Murad Khan had left the Syrian Evangelical Church and rejoined the Church of the East,

MALEK YONAN.

FIGURE 9. Malik (Malek) Yonan in 1897 in *Persian Women* (1898) by his son Isaac Malek Yonan.

and Malik Yonan at points had supported the arrival of Anglican missionaries, but all continued their association with the American mission. Another example of social continuity between these apparently disparate periods in the mission's history is provided by an evangelical couple, Osha'na Saro and his wife, Sarah, sister of Khenanisho' "of the Orphanage." Both were born around 1825 and spent their lives in service to the mission until they died at approximately ninety years old in the winter of 1914–15.[118]

The Pluralization of Missions

The later nineteenth century witnessed a proliferation of foreign missions, with the result that by the turn of the twentieth century, Urmia had become a dense and competitive missionary field. However, it is important to emphasize that many of those who worked with the Anglican, Orthodox, Lutheran, Baptist, and even Catholic missions in the 1890s were often originally educated at the American one.

THE CHALDEAN CHURCH AND CATHOLIC MISSIONS

The major missionary competitor of the Americans from the beginning of their residence in Urmia until the end of the nineteenth century was the Catholic Church.[119] Already by the time of Perkins's arrival in Iran, large parts of the Church of the East had become Chaldean (Catholic Uniate). The membership of the Chaldean Church doubled in the second half of the nineteenth century, from approximately 50,000 to 100,000. By the eve of World War I, its population almost matched that of the Church of the East (Qudshanis patriarchate), which was at most 120,000.[120] The 'Amid (Diyarbakır) patriarchate had come to an end in 1830, and the Chaldean Church under Yokhannan VIII Hormizd (1830–37) consisted of the dioceses of 'Amid, Mardin, Se'ert (Siirt), Gazarta, Mosul, 'Amadiya, Karka d-Beth Slokh (Kirkuk), and Salmas. Chaldeans were predominant in the regions south and west of the central Church of the East lands of Hakkari and Urmia, and also north of Urmia in Salmas. Through the end of the nineteenth century, they made a concerted effort to take the lead in Gazarta, 'Amadiya, and 'Aqra, which remained heavily Old Church.[121] By the mid-nineteenth century, missions were sent into Hakkari, a region in which Catholic influence had historically been minimal.[122] Despite the church's overarching control, the Chaldean patriarchs in the nineteenth century were often in conflict with Catholic missionaries and the Vatican, and this led to a politicking and negotiation similar to that practiced by the East Syrian clergy.[123]

The largest Catholic missions in the region were the Dominican mission in Mosul and the Lazarist mission in Salmas and Urmia. The Dominican mission at Mosul was founded in the mid-eighteenth century by Italian Dominicans, but handed over to French Dominicans in 1856. The mission had a press that printed Arabic and Classical Syriac works, primarily of a liturgical and devotional nature, as well as works for clerical education.[124] Neo-Aramaic literature composed in the region shows evidence of Catholic influence. Mariology, not historically a strong part of East Syrian tradition, increased, whereas in the works of Damyanos of Alqosh, *On the Torments of Hell* (1855) and *On the Delights of the Kingdom* (1856), Catholic notions of the afterlife are rendered in Neo-Aramaic verse.[125] Damyanos worked as a translator for the church, and his vision of heaven and hell reflects the seventeenth-century Catholic works he translated. By the late nineteenth century, Catholic influence had seeped from Alqosh into the mountains. Even the poetry of Yonan of Tkhuma, a mountain scribe and poet known as the last monk of the Church of the East, demonstrates Catholic notions, even if he never abandoned the church of the patriarch.[126]

Catholic missionary work in Salmas and Urmia had a more immediate effect upon that area in which Assyrian nationalism first emerged. In 1839 Eugene Boré (1809–78) founded a controversial and relatively unsuccessful school on the Urmia plain in the large village of Ardishai, which already had a Chaldean population.[127] French Lazarists (also known as Vincentians or the Congregation of the Mission) became interested at the same time, but they met local resistance, as well as obstruction from the Russian ambassador, who was reputed to be a Protestant. They were able to establish themselves in Urmia in 1843, building a church dedicated to Mary, the "Mother of God," a title disputed between the Church of the East and the Chaldeans. (The rejection of this title was foundational to the split between the Church of the East and the Syrian Orthodox in the fifth century.) These Catholic efforts had a slow start, were underfunded, and lacked the organization and demographic reach the Americans enjoyed.[128] However, in time the Lazarist mission's influence grew. One significant institution was the Lazarist seminary, founded in 1846 in Khosrowa, a town in Salmas, and by the mid-nineteenth century, Chaldeans were studying in Rome at the Propaganda Fide, the primary center for Catholic missionary study and training. Some even remained in Rome, thus following in the footsteps of the great Maronite Syriacist and orientalist J. S. Assemani (1687–1768). In 1896 the Lazarists in Urmia began the monthly publication *Voice of Truth* (*Qala d-šrara*), which served as the Catholic equivalent of *Rays of Light* but had a stronger focus on history, biblical learning, and philology.

As Heleen Murre-van den Berg states, "The Jesuit order and the Lazarist congregation, however different in many respects, may both serve as examples of a new type of Roman Catholic missions that in method and focus was rather similar to that of the Protestants."[129] If the Americans were fighting a Reformation battle in their mission, as is attested in their virulent and anxious anti-Catholicism, so the Catholic missionaries were engaged in a nineteenth-century Counter-Reformation. This is exemplified in the translation work of Priest Joseph Gabriel (Guriel) (ca. 1815–85), who was educated in Khosrowa, where he was born, and later at the Propaganda.[130] Gabriel published a translation of the *Doctrina Christiana* into the Urmia dialect in 1861. This 1589 lay catechetical work by Jesuit Robert Bellarmine (1542–1621), which had already been printed in Syriac in Rome in 1633 and in the Salmas dialect in 1841, was a popular text for Catholic missions.[131] Basing his work on an earlier 1715 version, Gabriel also translated Thomas à Kempis's *De imitatione Christi* into Syriac (1857), another popular Catholic work aimed at a nonclerical audience.[132]

The most important representative of what we might call this *Devotio moderna Syriaca* was Paul Bedjan (1838–1920).[133] Born in Khosrowa to a wealthy Chaldean family and educated there at the Lazarist seminary, at the age of seventeen he went to Paris and entered the Lazarist order. After ordination to the priesthood in 1861, he returned to Khosrowa. For the next nineteen years he worked as a missionary in both Salmas and Urmia until his transfer in 1880 to Paris, after which he never returned to Iran. Bedjan's works remain today an important source for the study of Syriac literature. Aside from the numerous Classical Syriac texts he published, his Neo-Aramaic works were composed for missionary schools and lay devotion.

THE ARCHBISHOP OF CANTERBURY'S MISSION
TO THE ASSYRIAN CHRISTIANS

The Anglican mission had an impact in Urmia by the turn of the twentieth century, but it arrived on the scene late.[134] The Church of England had already had contacts with the East Syrians for decades: there were expeditions, for example, by the Society for Promoting Christian Knowledge and the Society for the Propagation of the Gospel, including the 1842–44 tour of the region by George Percy Badger (1815–88), after which he composed *The Nestorians and Their Rituals* (1852). Attempts to create a mission were stop-and-go, and in addition to several East Syrians traveling on their own to England to seek aid for their people, a formal petition was sent to the archbishop of Canterbury in 1868, signed by a large number of clergy, including some associated with the American mission. The archbishop of Canterbury's Mission to the Assyrian Christians was finally founded in 1886. This mission, which was Anglo-Catholic and Puseyite, was aimed not at converting the East Syrians, but rather at strengthening the indigenous church against the American "dissenting" churches on the one side and Roman Catholicism on the other.

In scale the Anglican mission was relatively small. Arthur J. Maclean (1858–1943) and William Henry Browne (1847–1910) immediately began setting up schools upon their arrival. When A. H. Lang arrived in 1887, Browne went to the mountains, where he became close with the patriarch and his family, even living in their household for some time. He spent many years in the mountains, working as a tutor to the patriarch's niece, Surma Khanum, who would become de facto leader of the church for a time after the murder of the patriarch in 1920, even participating in the Assyrian delegation to the League of Nations. Photos of Browne, who died in 1910 still in his mountain retreat, show that he had embraced a Syrian appearance and "gone native." In fact, when she was thirteen and he was in his fifties, Browne asked the patriarch's permission to marry Surma, but his suit was rejected.[135]

The Americans watched warily as the Anglican emissaries passed through and as the mission finally found its footing in the late 1880s.[136] "Anglican ritualists" were "trying to prejudice the people of the old Nestorian Church against any further evangelistic work."[137] By 1889 they had already led many astray by teaching "loose morals."[138] The mission grew quickly, boasting almost forty schools by the 1890s. Maclean was initially responsible for the press, which began production in 1889, but by 1892 he had returned home (where he would write an important grammar and dictionary of Neo-Aramaic). Under his and his successors' guidance, the press printed numerous liturgical, historical, and educational works, most notably Old Church liturgical texts, which created some controversy.[139] Their "heretical" (i.e., "Nestorian") content shocked some Anglicans, whereas Old Church members were disturbed by their expurgation. Despite its size relative to the American mission, the Anglican mission had significant influence in the 1890s, especially in promoting the autonomy of the Old Church. However, by the turn of the twentieth century, its importance declined as the Orthodox mission was established. In 1903 the Anglicans moved to Van and three years later to Bebadi, a village near 'Amadiya.

An important figure in the early national movement associated with the Anglicans was Yaroo M. Neesan (1853–1937).[140] Neesan was from the mountains but as a boy, in 1864, was driven by Kurdish raids with his family to Mergawar, on the southwest frontier of Urmia. He attended an American village school and then the male seminary, from which he graduated in 1875.[141] While a student, he participated in preaching tours. He later taught in Tabriz and

Maragheh. In 1882 he went with Isaac Duman of Digala to New York, where the two entered the Episcopal fold. They studied at St. Stephen's College, Annandale, New York, and then General Theological Seminary. For several years Neesan lectured for money on Persian themes and the oppression of his people, while also showing and selling manuscripts. After becoming a naturalized US citizen, he returned to Iran, whereupon he became an important member of the Anglican mission, despite early concerns within parts of the Episcopal hierarchy that his presence would contradict their claim that their mission did not aim to proselytize. Although he was committed to the Anglican mission, he was elected president of the male seminary alumni association in 1897, which demonstrates the ecumenism of the organization.[142]

THE ORTHODOX MISSION

In the nineteenth century the Russians increasingly projected their imperial power south through the Caucasus and into Iran, while East Syrian laborers traveled north to Tbilisi and elsewhere.[143] The Syrian community attracted the attention of the Orthodox Church as early as the 1850s.[144] In 1862 Archimandrite Sophoniah went on a fact-finding mission that resulted in an extant document assessing the size and organization of the East Syrian community at that time.[145] Although there may have been some earlier missionary excursions in the region, the Orthodox mission in Urmia did not get under way until 1897 after an episode that would have repercussions within the whole Syrian community on the plain.

In 1897 Mar Yonan, the bishop of Sepurghan, the last Old Church bishop of the plain, put together a formal petition endorsing the Orthodox Church and then traveled from village to village on the plain seeking signatures.[146] The petition was signed by ten thousand people, perhaps more. Mar Yonan traveled to Saint Petersburg to deliver this document, and in the early spring of 1898 he and those with him formally rejoined the Orthodox Church in Alexander Nevsky Cathedral through the rites of receiving heretics back into the church. When he returned to Urmia accompanied by Orthodox emissaries, thousands of Syrians came out in support of the Orthodox communion. An Orthodox mission was founded in 1898, and by 1900 an ecclesial infrastructure of churches and schools had been established. This was the heyday of the Orthodox mission. In 1904 it began to publish its own periodical, the bilingual Russian and Neo-Aramaic *Orthodox Urmia* (*Urmi Artadoksayta*), which was produced until 1915.[147]

The missionary sources regularly accuse the Syrians of making "worldly" decisions or acting for pecuniary purposes, and such claims should certainly

not be taken uncritically. However, Russian political expansion over the preceding century suggested that the Russians would be the major players in
the region and that this role would grow. "They expect redress of wrongs,
protection from the oppressions of their landlords, from the exactions of Persian officials, and the fanaticism of the Mohammedan priests and populace,"
claimed Samuel G. Wilson, an American missionary in Tabriz at the time.[148]
One source alleges that Yonan had specifically promised that the Russians
would free the Syrians from the temporal yoke of Islam.[149] In addition to
the mission, Russian imperial power soon expanded farther in the region. The
Anglo-Russian Pact of 1907 established the northwest of Iran as part of the
Russian zone of influence; in 1909 the Russians occupied Tabriz and the following year Khoy and Urmia, where they would remain until World War I.

The majority of East Syrians to convert to Orthodoxy were from the Old
Church, but those under the influence of the Roman Catholic and Anglican
missions also converted. The Anglicans, who favored the autonomy of Eastern churches, supported this movement. To the great chagrin of the Americans, even many from the evangelical church converted. As we will see below,
by the early years of the twentieth century, national sentiment was fully developed among many Syrians. The ease with which so many joined the Orthodox Church demonstrates how mutable religious identity could be in the
current social and political context. Religion had become sufficiently distinct
from national identity that it could be taken off and replaced like a shirt, but
the body—to maintain the metaphor—remained Syrian.

OTHER MISSIONS: GERMAN AND SWEDISH LUTHERANS AND BAPTISTS

In 1875 Pera Yokhannan, who was born in Ardishai, had started theological
studies at the Hermannsburg Mission, which was established in the city of the
same name in Lower Saxony in 1849.[150] He returned in 1880 and with financial support from the mission began to preach and set up schools.[151] Swedish
Lutheran missionaries arrived from Russia in the mid-1880s.[152] Luther Pera
(b. 1882), Pera Yokhannan's son, also studied theology in Hermannsburg, after
which he returned in 1904. He worked with other East Syrians to reorganize
the Church of the East in response to the movement for unification with the
Orthodox Church.[153] Furthermore, by the late nineteenth century, German
business interests in Iran had increased, and German missionary organizations
were sending evangelists and establishing orphanages. However, after a period
of patriarchal endorsement, the Lutherans lost much of their church property
due to the mass conversion to the Orthodox Church, mentioned above.

In 1887 Deacon Khenanisho' Moratkhan (d. 1901), possibly the son of the native assistant Murad Khan, came to the United States seeking American Swedish Lutheran support for schools in Urmia.[154] He had already, after studying in London, visited Sweden, where he received financial support from the Lutheran community there.[155] Like the Anglicans with whom he studied, the Lutherans did not aim to bring him over to their church. He remained a deacon in the Church of the East. His son, Joseph Khenanisho' (d. 1909), studied at Augustana College and Theological Seminary in Rock Island, Illinois, and then returned to the mission field after his 1902 ordination. In fact, several other Syrians at the American mission received an education and ordination at Augustana, as well as at other Lutheran institutions abroad.

Baptists are attested in Urmia in the early 1880s.[156] Yonan H. Shahbaz (1870–1936), author of *The Rage of Islam* (1918), an account of the destruction of the community in Urmia, originally attended the American school, as did other Baptist converts. Inspired by the preaching of Charles Spurgeon, which he would have read in translation in *Rays of Light*, he traveled to London, but arrived there after Spurgeon's death. He continued on to New York, where he was welcomed into Baptist circles and baptized on September 26, 1892.[157] He then returned to Urmia with his American wife for mission work. There are also references to other smaller sects such as the Plymouth Brethren making their way to Urmia.

Melat Nationalism and the Patriarchal Church Committee

The Church of the East was struggling by the turn of the twentieth century. Its clergy were often uneducated, and observers at the time noted the shortage of priests.[158] This insecurity increased with the expansion of foreign missions. The patriarch, who for years had allowed himself to be courted by foreign churches, was anxious to maintain authority over his flock. Shem'on XVII Abraham (1820–61), who went into exile in the 1840s due to Kurdish raids, competed with the American mission and the Chaldean patriarchate in the south. Shem'on XVIII Rubil (1861–1903) had even more forces to balance: pressure came from the Ottoman state to the west and Russian and Catholic missions to the east. The division of the Syrian community into several churches had unforeseen and problematic consequences. For example, Presbyterians permitted divorce, and more than once there were public disputes after Syrian men converted and divorced their wives whom they had married in the Old Church.[159] Furthermore, by this time each major community (Orthodox, Old Church, Presbyterian, Catholic) had its own civil authority or representative (*melat bašı*, Turk. "nation head") before the local Qajar governor.[160]

In response to the sense that the community was fracturing into various *melats*, the concern for the "unity" (*ḥdayuta*) of the "nation," which was apparent already by the 1860s, became more prominent in the pages of *Rays of Light*. An 1895 article by Elisha' Adam, a teacher at the mission in Salmas, bemoans the "tribalism" (*qabilayuta*) within the nation.[161] Among the Syrians, there are "various tribes of religion [*mazhab*]." This problem derives from the fact that all Syrians have the "freedom" (*azaduta*) to choose their own "confession" (*todita*). "National love" has dissipated, and falling away from the shared unity of their ancestors and the teachers of the past, the Syrians have lost the "name of our nation."

> Nationally [*umtana'it*] all of us are Syrians without a difference; we will not be able to deny this. However, in religion [*mazhab*] we are free; in matters of religion the duty of every one of us is to take up the Gospel to gaze at it. It demonstrates the path of salvation and the pure elements of religion. Everyone who walks by it will not stumble. It is an enlightening lamp for our road of life. Take it in your hands and administer the matters of religion.

In lieu of *melat*, the more common term in previous protonationalist literature, Adam uses *umta*, which derives from Classical Syriac and is cognate with the Arabic *umma*, which denotes the broader community of Muslim believers, a supranational Islamic commonwealth. However, his argument is at base a Protestant one: Christians may differ but they are all the same inasmuch as they share Scripture, which each person is obliged to read. Adam calls on Syrians to reject religious dispute, which "loosens the bond of unity [*yesura d-ḥdayuta*]." For it is because of their "unity" and "love" that Europeans and Americans are so "prosperous" (or "advanced") (*mantyane*). Adam then demonstrates the nationalizing cosmopolitanism typical of the mission when he claims, "If we are sons of God then we should love his family, and if we are sons of a nation, let us love our brothers." Finally the article ends, "Then let us all be yoked to one another in this entreaty; let us seek from our heavenly father that he send to us a Holy Spirit to bind us with a mighty bond [*yesura*] of unity and love for one another unto the end."

A growing focus on the nation as a social entity coincided with these calls for unity. In *Rays of Light* from these years, there is an increased prevalence of sociological terms, such as *band* or *society* (*dasta*, originally from the Persian word for "hand"), *community* or *social group* (*šotaputa*), and *assembly* (*knušya*, *jama'at*, the former from Classical Syriac, the latter Arabic).[162] To express the idea of the social, terms were developed from *šotaputa*, a borrowing from the Classical Syriac *šawtaphuta*, which historically denoted "communion," especially in the Eucharist, or "participation," including "sexual intercourse" and the "sharing" of divine and human natures in Christ. Also at this time Classical Syriac *umtha* ("nation") and *'amma* ("people") often replaced the Neo-Aramaic *melat* and *tayepa*, whereas *progress* (*mantayta*), *benefit* (*payda*), and *awakening* (*mar'ašta*), terms we saw in the pre-1870 mission publications, remained common but with a less explicitly Christian connotation.[163]

A series of 1892 articles on "Humanity" (*Našuta*) explains that even the virtue of self-reliance requires "community" (*šotaputa*).[164] However, "community" should not cancel out "individuality."

> The existence of community [*šotaputa*] is by necessity required for the health and blessing of individual [*tak*] human beings. However, it is necessary that individuality [*lḥudayuta*] not be sacrificed for the sake of unity [*ḥdayuta*]. . . . The unity of the community is not like that of the ocean or like a flock of sheep, but the yoking of rational entities to one another by their own free will for the purpose of the good of all.[165]

This preservation of individual identities resembles the analogy to the montage discussed in the introduction. Furthermore, one must be "free," which entails not "political freedom" (*azaduta poliṭiqayta*) but a "personal freedom" (*parṣopayta*). Bodily slavery is not as bad as a slavery of the mind, which limits our "power of thought."

At the same time that focus on the social unity of the nation increased, national and individual reform remained regular topics and yet also with a less explicitly Christian tone. An 1895 article, "Self Help," begins with the cliché "God helps those who help themselves."[166] It then describes the work one must do in order to improve him- or herself. The article continues:

> What is necessary for progress? It is neither wealth nor a big family. The things necessary for progress are in everyone's power. They are not only given to some. I will recall here some of the things that are necessary: diligence, patience, centralization of labors and aims, attention to details, and good character.

The article then quotes numerous sayings from figures as diverse as Confucius, Charles Dickens, and Michelangelo. Finally the personal virtues the article advocates are demonstrated through biblical examples. Another 1895 article describes Frederick Douglass, the hero of the abolitionist movement, as having similar virtues: "force of character, diligence, patience."[167]

Syrians began to identify the cause of national unity with the patriarch, as is apparent in an 1895 article in *Rays of Light* on the "unity of the nation" by Abraham Morhatch, an evangelist and early nationalist writer. Morhatch points out what soon became obvious to many: the missions had come to help the nation, but in doing so, they had divided it.[168] According to Morhatch, unity is an essential sign of nationality, and therefore religious divisions threaten the existence of the nation. He acknowledges the difficulty of bringing the different groups together and also notes how the missionary encounter has created new and paradoxical circumstances:

> Was it not better for all of us that we distinguished religion [*mazhab*] from nationality [*melatuta*]? It is not necessary that the members [lit. "sons"] of one nation should simply believe in one rule. Faith forms confession [*todita*], not nation. As soon as our men learned to distinguish national business from religious business we did not fear to say that [the nation] is making a step towards unity [*ḥdayuta*].

The missions caused division but also made it possible to think about nationality as distinct from religion, which is ultimately the way back to unity, according to Morhatch. He notes how the recent death of the patriarch's brother, Deacon Jesse, brought people together regardless of confession, which in turn points to the benefits of the patriarchate: "The patriarch is the patriarch of the nation, therefore of all of us." Morhatch, who spent many years in the United States, indicates that there are nations that have many "religious sects" (*mazhabe*) in them. He suggests that a "society" (*dasta*) be established for dealing with problems of unity. He then turns to an issue that became a focus of burgeoning nationalist discourse: orthography. "We should lament and cry for the daughter of our people. Until now they are so distant from one another that even their spellings do not correspond." The missions had different printing presses with different approaches to printing the vernacular, and Morhatch calls for a unified Neo-Aramaic lexicon, grammar, and orthography. He ends with a prayer that God help the nation, thus revealing the sacral aspect of his national concern.

The American missionaries themselves had focused on the patriarch since their first attempts to cross the mountains in the 1830s and their subsequent struggles with him in the 1840s. In the early 1890s they were frightened that he might be drawn over to the Catholic cause.[169] In 1892 Frederick G. Coan (mission: 1885–1924) made a trip to the mountains with the aim of convincing the patriarch to reject Catholic advances.[170] The patriarch's control over Urmia, always tenuous, was even weaker by the late nineteenth century. The clergy were split among the different missions, and some of the dioceses had lapsed with their episcopal lines.[171] The 1897 accession to the Orthodox Church and the rapid success of the Orthodox mission contributed to the sense that the patriarch and the Old Church were under siege. With Yonan of Sepurghan's defection, there were no longer Old Church bishops on the plain.

In 1898, in the face of the crisis caused by this Orthodox expansion, Syrians in Urmia created the Patriarchal Church Committee (*motwa*), established with the patriarch's imprimatur. The majority of its members were Syrians associated with the American mission. The purpose was to help guide the church in Urmia and to prevent further attrition due to Orthodox proselytizing. The sense of crisis was further increased by the events across the border in the Ottoman Empire. The era of Sultan Abdul Hamid II (1876–1909) was characterized by the sultan's attempt to dismantle the earlier *tanzimat* reforms and the increased violence suffered by Armenians and some Syrians. In 1900 the *motwa*, consisting of Syrians primarily with a Protestant education, sent a petition to Mar Khenanisho', the metropolitan in Shemsdin, who was responsible for ordaining patriarchs and other high clergy, asking that he ordain a bishop for the plain.[172] This group, along with others, then undertook to pay this new bishop a salary.

Osha'na-khan Badal, or Dr. Osha'na (d. 1911), was selected as chairman of the committee, and Nestorius George Malik its secretary. Dr. Osha'na was born in Gulpashan, attended the college, and was one of the first three students to receive its medical diploma.[173] He became an assistant to Dr. Cochran at the hospital and then went to Edinburgh in 1886 for a supplementary medical course. He was actively engaged in the alumni association of the college and the general synod of the evangelical church, and wrote for *Rays of Light* and the *Star*, and support for his candidacy in the National Assembly in Tehran came from the so-called progressives (*šuwšaṭaye*). According to his obituary, his lifelong goal was that the church and the nation be one and that the nation follow the religion of its ancestors. Malik, an 1888 graduate of the male seminary, had been sent by his father, George David Malik, to Norway to study with Lutherans.[174] Others who served on the committee included Ezra and Isho', the two sons of the native assistant Khamis of Memekkan.[175]

The group immediately set up a fund, which was managed by Khenanisho' Moratkhan, whom I mentioned above. They had several formal meetings during the summer of 1900 at which they determined their theology and church practice: although they maintained certain traditions of the Old Church, their emphasis on the sole reliance on Scripture and its literal meaning and their streamlining of the traditions—for example, on fasting—reflect their Protestant education and background. As they continued their meetings through the fall and into the following year, they addressed the establishment of schools. By 1901, this led to the creation of so-called national schools, institutions some had already demanded for several years.[176] When disputes arose over property allegedly usurped by the Orthodox mission, the committee sent two representatives, Dr. Osha'na and David George Malik, Nestorius's

THE PATRIARCHAL CHURCH COMMITTEE,
Urmia, Persia.

FIGURE 10. The Patriarchal Church Committee. David George Malik stands in the back row, second from the right. (G. D. Malech, *History of the Syrian Nation and the Old Evangelical-Apostolic Church of the East*, 1910.)

brother, to Tabriz to represent the case of the Old Church.[177] The wrangling in court continued for several years.

Local Urmia affairs were then drawn into wider political developments, while the growing awareness of events not only from the broader region but from around the world, often addressed in *Rays of Light*, contributed to an emerging national consciousness in Urmia. In a letter from Frederick Coan to Robert Speer, dated February 4, 1907, Coan describes the Japanese victory in the Russo-Japanese War (1904–5) as an inspiration for the Syrians, who by now had begun to understand themselves as orientals vis-à-vis Europe and the United States: "Of course the papers exaggerate it and are not accurate, but something has happened to this whole east ever since Japan licked that great cumbersome bear, and it has aroused their pride and touched them deeply to know that after all they too are men and can do things once they are given a chance."[178] Events closer to home also would have had an impact. The Committee of Union and Progress was formally organized in the Ottoman Empire in 1906, and by 1908 the Young Turk Revolution compelled the sultan to reinstitute the constitution he had previously suspended.

More significantly, many of the most important events in the Iranian Con-

stitutional Revolution of 1905–7 took place in nearby Tabriz and were witnessed by many Syrians and missionaries. In early 1906 the Shah Mozaffar-al-
Din Shah (1896–1907) yielded to public protests, and the process of forming
an Iranian parliament began. The first meeting took place the following fall.
That winter and into the spring of 1906, Robert Labaree reports, "in nearly
every village where we had a congregation there was a very genuine and
heartening awakening of the church, and in many places a very deep work of
grace in the whole community."[179] The following summer the Syrian nationalist biweekly, the *Star* (*Kokhwa*), began publication. The *Star* immediately
promoted the National Society (*šotaputa umtanayta*) for the Aid of the Poor,
an organization founded that same year.[180] Its different "chapters" (*dastate*)
were based upon the rules established by its "committee" (*motwa*), which had
members "from the whole nation."[181] Information both on this benevolent
society for Syrians and on its organization and finances is common in the
Star. The language of self-reliance used to describe the society echoes that
used by the American mission decades before: the Syrians needed to learn to
take care of themselves, both individually and as a nation.

By the following year, the Syrians had organized their own National Assembly. The first issue of the second year of the *Star*, June 24, 1907, begins with
the happy announcement of the founding of the "National Union."[182] "Long
live the National Committee!" is the byline of the article describing the assembly, which would be fractured by an Orthodox attempt to assert control.[183]
Though organized primarily by evangelicals and members of the Old Church
educated by the American mission, the inauguration was ecumenical: the first
Chaldean bishop of Urmia, Thomas Audo (or Odo, the modern rendering of
'Abda) (ordained 1892), "spoke eloquently about the goals of the gathering
of this assembly, which were first to establish a committee or general council of the nation to look into corporate [lit. "bodily"] matters and concerning the common good of the nation [*umta*] and not after our own personal
benefit. . . . He had a pleasant effect upon the heart of all of the audience." The
officers of the National Assembly as of June 15, 1907, were divided according
to the synods of the Syrian Evangelical Church.[184] On the following day five
representatives from each of the four major religious communities (Catholic,
Old Church, Orthodox, and Presbyterian) were selected for the Committee of
Union (*motwa d-ḥuyyada*).[185] The patriarch was in communication with the
committee and appointed his own deputy in 1908.[186]

The following year, after the founding of the National Union, a more actively nationalist organization was founded: the Syrian Union (*ḥuyyada suryaya*). In September 1908 a meeting was held at Isaac Malek (Malik) Yonan's
home at the college to determine the rules for the new society. Born in 1869

and educated at Louisville Theological Seminary (Presbyterian) after his education at the mission, Malek Yonan was the youngest son of the native assistant Malik Yonan.[187] In the 1890s he wrote on national issues, showing a concern for the relationship between the nation and the evangelical and "Nestorian" churches.[188] The group of youth who met at Malek Yonan's home to found the Syrian Union were "awakened," according to the *Star*, to the dangers to themselves and the nation.[189] For some time they had been discussing the nation's problems, such as "selfishness" (lit. "I-ness"), the "impurity of women," and a lack of literate culture. At this meeting they established a formal organization with the explicit goal of helping to unite the nation. The leader of this group, Malek Yonan, was that same month the director at a meeting of the general synod of the evangelical church. In fact, the report he wrote of this event is printed in the *Star* just after the article describing the new Syrian Union.

The missionaries took note of the developing national sentiments and institutions. They themselves recognized the overlap between Syrians associated with their mission and those involved in national organizing. "Another interesting combination is the Motwa or Committee who have organized themselves to save the ragged remnant of Nestorianism. The strange fact and anomaly is that most of those who are on the committee have been educated by us and quite a number have at times been helpers," Frederick Coan wrote.[190] A letter from William Shedd to Robert Speer dated November 1, 1908, offers the missionaries' perspective on these events. Shedd argues that the existence of a separate evangelical church has not served to build up a common evangelical community and that there is now a need to unite against the Catholics. The Gospel has been harmed, he admits, by the divisions caused by the missions, including the American one. He then continues:

> I think there are various signs of a new national spirit among the Syrians. Neither the Catholics nor the Russians can give this spirit free play and our people are the ones most affected by it. I hope this will infuse a new spirit of independence in our people. It may also lead to some newer identification of our church with the national church. Here in the city the experiment is being made of establishing a "national" school without foreign help. Our church joins in & also the Nestorians, and they hope to force the various free lances into adhesion. The station is cordially cooperating with this. I have long urged the people to do this kind of thing. Altogether I have a little hope, but not very much. More & more am I impressed with the moral degeneration of the Syrians. I don't mean merely the low moral standard of honesty etc., common to all here; but the actual degeneration of the past few generations, resulting from the changed conditions of new temptations of the new age. One demoralizing

influence has been the missions; and we must be very careful lest our influence, because of ill adjusted education, wrong use of money, and ignorance of
actual conditions, be demoralizing instead of elevating. It is hard to keep up a
spirit of high moral effort, because there is nothing of the sort in the country.
Among Moslems, Armenians, Russians, etc., there is a spirit of progress but
not much care for morals. Bad government is opposed, and ignorance is opposed, because they are the cause of poverty & want, and not because they
are wrong.[191]

Shedd's tone resembles that of Stoddard almost sixty years before when he
hesitantly described the spirit of revival among the Syrians. However, whatever diffidence they showed, the American missionaries generally supported
the committee, whose proceedings were printed at the mission press.[192] Of
greater relevance was their decision to print the *Star*, which began publication in 1906.

The *Star* (*Kokhwa*)

In the midst of the Iranian Constitutional Revolution, on June 21, 1906, the
first biweekly issue of the *Star* (*Kokhwa*) appeared. The first Syrian nationalist
newspaper, its motto was "A Small Star Alone in the Firmament" (perhaps
reflecting Dn 12:3, which would give to it a millenarian connotation).[193] This
organ of Syrian nationalism was founded and printed at the American mission press. The mission had already done some printing work for nonmission
business, such as for the Patriarchal Committee. In 1906 the missionaries also
expressed a desire to expand the work of the press, taking on extra projects
that would allay some of their debts.[194] The *1908 Annual Report* claims:

> In June a year ago about nine or ten young men of Urumia formed a partner-
> ship company to publish a national paper. This group contains some of the
> most wide-awake, progressive young men of our Syrian people. Arrangement
> was made with them to print their paper, named *The Star*, on our press, and
> the contract provided that they were to furnish their paper, pay the wages of
> the printers, and pay a small monthly rental. . . . Such a paper aroused con-
> siderable interest among the Syrians, and many, especially in America, not
> only subscribed but also sent in contributions to help on the national cause.
> They find at the close of their year that it is not a profitable business; but, not
> discouraged, they have increased their paper to twelve pages. Their constitu-
> ency is much the same as ours, but we find so far that our list of subscribers
> is affected very little, although it may be too soon to decide that point yet.[195]

Again, it is clear from this passage that the missionaries were aware of the
ideological and social links between the mission and the early nationalists.

The background of the original editorial board and staff of the *Star* demonstrates both its ecumenical aims and its Protestant leanings. Most of the men were members of the Syrian Evangelical Church, whereas Paul Shem'on Malik of Geogtapa worked with the Anglican mission but wrote for *Rays of Light*.[196] Two members, Shem'on Ganji and Lazar Pera, both evangelical, were raised in the orphanage of Khenanisho' in Geogtapa.[197] Another orphan, Priest Isaac Yokhannan of Digala, though educated by the Americans and in the evangelical church, had also spent time in the United States studying at Augustana Lutheran Seminary and returned as a Lutheran missionary.[198] In general, most of these men had received an American mission education. Several had also gone to the United States for further study. Often their families were long associated with the American mission. They also were commonly teachers or preachers for the mission and already wrote for *Rays of Light*. These men were members of the college's alumni association, and several demonstrated an interest in liberal and humane studies. Despite their national concerns, some of them also worked as missionaries elsewhere, a sign of their interest in the universality of the Christian message.

The editor of the *Star* for most of its run from 1906 to 1918 was John Mushe (Moses) (1874 [or 1872]–1918) from Geogtapa.[199] He attended the mission school in his hometown and then completed his education at the college in Urmia. From 1894 to 1901, he was in the United States, where he studied at Colgate College.[200] Upon returning, he was made an administrator for the village schools of the plain. His future wife, Suraya Khan Pera, whom he married in 1904, was from Tbilisi, where she had completed her education in Russian. While working simultaneously on *Rays of Light*, he was the founding editor of the *Star* in 1906, for which he contributed a large portion of the articles. That same year he spoke at the general synod of the church.[201] In 1912 he published a grammar of Neo-Aramaic, a volume aimed at an indigenous audience yet employing contemporary Western grammatical and rhetorical categories.[202] In 1918 he also published a book on Old Testament history.[203]

Although the early nationalist movement, like the patriarchal movement from which it descended, consisted primarily of evangelicals, Old Church Syrians, and Lutherans who had an American mission education, there were some exceptional Catholic and Orthodox figures. The most important Catholic was Thomas Audo (1854–1918), the Chaldean Metropolitan of Urmia and Salmas. He and other Chaldeans studied at the Propaganda in the 1860s and 1870s, and it is possible that their nationalist ideas were spurred on by their residence in Rome during the period of the unification of Italy and the Risorgimento. Those Syrians who received an Orthodox education or were members of the Orthodox Church did not belong to the first generation of nationalist thinkers of the 1890s. The most significant Orthodox Syrian among the early nationalists was Benjamin Arsanis (1884–1957), whom, along with Audo, I discuss further in the following chapter.

The content and format of the *Star* in its early years would have been familiar to contemporary readers of *Rays of Light*. The paper covers perceived national issues, such as health; education; morality, including modesty in female dress; and the need for Syrian self-reliance (as opposed to relying on the support of missionaries). It includes long-format articles explaining what a nation is and what the Syrian nation needs to do to improve itself. The paper also contains poetry on national and religious themes, sometimes one and the same, such as the poetic prayer, printed appropriately two weeks before Christmas, asking Jesus to help the "infant" journal.[204]

Christian holidays, especially Easter and Christmas, are addressed in innovative ways in the *Star*. The paper takes an ecumenical perspective and, for example, in 1910 describes Christmas as a holiday about the birth of a universal humanity.[205] Christianity is generally treated as a liberal, cosmopolitan religion, one presumably shared by all Syrians, in contrast to the various "religious" (*mazhabaye*) differences that exist between them, which are characterized as "tribalism" (*qabilayuta*).[206] In fact, the purportedly Bible-based Christianity of the *Star* resembles what we find in the extant documents of the earlier Patriarchal Committee.[207]

As in *Rays of Light*, news is divided between local and foreign. The former, which addresses events in Urmia and its immediate vicinity, has subsections for marriage notices and obituaries, which at times describe the dead as models for, or great lovers of, the nation. Foreign news covers events in the rest of Iran, such as Tehran and Tabriz, but the bulk of it pertains to Europe, although China and other regions are occasionally discussed as well. There are also long essays on famous figures, such as Joan of Arc, Napoleon, and Tolstoy. Some issues contain a "News from the Border" section, on the Qajar-Ottoman border zone, which was becoming increasingly impermeable and violent by the turn of the twentieth century.

I addressed the opening pages of the first issue of the *Star* in the introduction. The stated aim of the paper was to help provide a "bond" for the nation. The *Star* treats the nation as an object of reform while addressing it as a subject of action. Service to the nation is an important issue: one article claims, "Love of homeland [*watan*] or nationalism [*umtanayuta*] establishes the homeland or nation [*umta*] as first in our lives. . . . The true nationalist does not at all ask, 'What is better for me?,' but always asks, 'What is better for my nation [*melat*]?'"[208] Numerous articles in the *Star* provide advice for how to "lift up" or "elevate" the nation. One on Syrian unity explains that "in the history of every nation two things are essential: self reliance and work for progress or advancement [*šuwšaṭa yan 'zalta laqa(d)ma*]."[209] (The Classical Syriac term *šuwšaṭa* became the standard word for "progress.") Every nation that has such goals "will make progress." Two particular areas where the Syrians need to "wake up" regarding their "present condition" are economic self-sufficiency and the establishment of their own schools.[210]

Many articles address the condition of the nation, including its history and progress. In a 1906 article, "The Means of Elevating the Nation," Dr. Joseph Y. Yauvre (d. 1915) of Tabriz, one of the sons of the missionary couple Jacob and Moressa Yauvre and a graduate of the male seminary and the medical school, focuses first on business and the need to develop commerce within the nation.[211] He then argues that religious differences among Syrians do not necessarily conflict with "nationality" (*umtanayuta*) and that everyone should accept the patriarch as the "head of the nation" (*reš umta*). Moreover, for the sake of the nation's "progress" (*mantayta*), Syrians need an awareness of "economy," a "science" (*'ilm*) essential for knowing how to live and spend. Syrians should be generous in helping one another but not "crazy." Finally, Yauvre refers to the need to systematize language. The article ends with a prayer for the long life of the Shah.

Economic concerns in general are common in the *Star*: the paper discusses current economic conditions as well as commercial issues. In a final brief section, current exchange rates are listed. Technological and demographic information—for example, on bridges, trains, the telegraph, and the size of different populations—is often provided, and this is at times linked to market concerns. Syrian immigrant communities, such as those in the Caucasus, Yonkers, and Chicago, are the topic of numerous articles, which provide demographic and economic information, and the poverty of the community in Urmia and abroad is a subject of ongoing discussion.[212] The nation's progress is identified with helping its poor and avoiding extravagances.[213] Articles appear on the groups and societies working to improve the "present societal conditions of our nation and our country," such as the National Society for the Aid to the Poor.[214] The finances of the National Society are detailed, and those who donated funds are honored by having their names listed.

In conjunction with its economic outlook, the *Star* attests to a philosophy of sociality and a concern for the affective bonds that make up the nation. An article by Dr. Osha'na, "The Condition and Quality of the Nation," is striking both for the content of its argument and for the language it uses.[215] The author employs numerous Classical Syriac terms, but these are often followed by the Neo-Aramaic equivalents provided in parentheses. The article begins by enthusiastically referring to "this feeling that is stirring in the hearts of the sons of the nation (*umta*)." Dr. Osha'na wants to "write some ideas which I am moved to write."

First he describes the *Star* as a body and delineates a basic physical science of bodies, one reflecting a combination of nineteenth-century atomism with the basic Greek philosophical physics the Syriac tradition had inherited from antiquity. Bodies can be simple or compound, but all require "tightening forces," or "bonds" (*yesure*), for their "atoms." In a statement suggesting an awareness of the dialectical relationship between the nation and its media, he claims that the *Star* is an offspring of the nation, but also can help to beget it. For "the nation, like a body, is formed from parts and members. When this is accepted, then also this body will need elements that bond atoms to one another," some of which are the following: (1) "natural love of kinship," as animals have; (2) "love of homeland" (both the Syriac-derived *bet ma'mra*, and the Arabic *watan* are used); (3) "love of the guardian power of our homeland or love of our king, etc."; (4) "personal love for ourselves and for sons of our nation [*umta*]"; which in turn points to the final love: (5) "love for God, that one who is all in all." According to Dr. Osha'na, creation teaches us that God has made certain laws, and "so we are in need of such a bond that will bind all of the atoms or members [*haddame*] of the body, the nation, with one another, [the nation] which is the body, the progenitor of *The Star*, the 'only begotten son' as it is called by many, and I will call it the 'firstborn son' [Col 1:15]." In this analogy the *Star* is to the nation as Christ is to God the Father, and yet the nation is also the body of Christ with its "members." Finally (6) Dr. Osha'na describes the Syrians' need for a book of laws, "common and not particular, national and not confessional [*umtanaya w-la toditanaya*]," one "received by a united nation [*umta huyyedta*], sufficient for all."

An article from June 3, 1909, by Pera Mirza, a member of the Syrian Evangelical Church, entitled "Social [or "Communal"] Life," relies on a neologistic adjective, *šotapaye*, to express the "social" or "communal" in its title.[216] The article begins with a general statement about the sociality of the world:

> Love for community is one of the natural drives in creation. The gathering of birds in roosts, animals in flocks, and insects in swarms demonstrates love for community. There is no condition more wretched for a human being than the condition of solitude. The circumstance of solitude is chosen by poets and singers of love songs as a circumstance more bitter and painful than all. When they have wanted to draw a picture of life forsaken and forgotten in order to awaken hardened imaginations and to soften sympathy they have taken the story of solitary life, life cut off from community.[217]

The article divides "community" into two types. The former, which is "temporal," has specific aims, whether they be business or education. The latter, which is "established by God," is the community of spouses, parents, and children, as well as "the community of the nation, which is considered one family, etc." The author then provides examples of ways by which "our national communities" (*šotapuyatan umtanaye*) can be strengthened. The initial requirement for him is the recognition of the "foundational elements of national community [*šotaputa umtanayta*]." The first of these is familial love, which entails educating the young. The second is love of "religion" (*mazhab*), which among other things consists of God's laws. "Religion," however, should not be confused with "tribalism" (*qabilayuta*). The third element is love of "nation" (*melat*), which is particularly necessary for "the progress [*mantayta*] of the community."

In a subsequent article, Mirza discusses the means of strengthening community.[218] The first is made manifest in the "law of equality": despite differences in conditions, each member should have a voice equal to that of his companions in the community. This allows each person to live up to his or her God-given potential, which also requires freedom (*azaduta*) and education. The second is "perfection of character in individual members," and the third is a life "sacrificed or lived for others." Hierarchy damages community, but ethical action aimed at others, including a conquering of the self, improves it. He concludes with a martyrological claim: "That person who establishes his life as a sacrifice for others deserves a most radiant crown."

In addition to the problem of social cohesion, some articles in the *Star* address the relationship between religion and nationality. In "The Nation," Yonan Abraham (d. 1915), an associate of the mission and secretary of the National Society for the Aid of the Poor, expands on the distinction between the two:

> It is a great joy and immense pleasure in the heart of every Syrian in Urmia that it is now apparent that the Syrians have arrived at a point where they distinguish between religion [*mazhab*] and nation [*umta*]. Confession [*todita*] for every person is between himself and his God, as he learns it in his own "tribe." Being that the meaning of "nation" is that number of men and women together with children who reside in one country, speak one language, and are united by their customs [*'adatay*] and by their labors with one another, by this meaning we are able to call ourselves a nation [*melat*].[219]

The 1907 article then describes the problem of "tribalism" and claims, "We have become a laughing stock among other nations." The example of the Spanish-American War is given. During the war, contrary to the fears of some, American Catholics did not support Catholic Spain. It turned out that "Americanism was not against Catholicism, nor also was Catholicism against Americanism." Likewise, the National Assembly in Iran declared that there should be no difference in justice between religious communities. Abraham pleads that the existing differences among the various Syrian communities be transcended and then thanks "the leaders of the various missions who have helped to cause a unity to take hold within our nation, and who without a doubt will be greatly pleased by our progress." In the end he prays that God will give wisdom to those chosen to establish new rules for the nation "upon a strong foundation of unity."

Despite this distinction between religion and nationality, a common shared Christianity is assumed for all Syrians in the pages of the *Star*. At times broad religious themes are addressed as if they were nonsectarian. For example, the observance of Sunday as the Sabbath was an important part of American missionary reform from early on, but it is treated in one article as if it were something "beyond dispute" (*d-la heč drašta*).[220] The author laments that people have the "habit [*ʿadat*] of going to the city for business or for work on Sunday." To be sure, Sunday observance has "spiritual benefits," but it is also "one of the great secrets of progress and growth of Christian workers." Our ancestors observed it as "holy" (*qaddiša*), but "also if it is not in our heart that we observe Sunday from our love for our religion [*mazhaban*] and our God, nevertheless it is necessary and beneficial nationally and socially [*mare payda umtana'it w-šotapa'it*] that it be for us a day of rest."

What was also shared among confessions was a support for the patriarch. The *Star* backed the work of the Patriarchal Committee, even though its editorial board was dominated by evangelicals. In the local news section in 1909 we read:

> With great sympathy all of us are delighted about the great awakening [*rʾašta*] and the zealous return of our Nestorian brothers to the patriarch Mar Shemʿon. Among all the renewals and changes that have occurred for the elevation of the ancient religion [*mazhab*] of our ancestors and for bringing it to its prior form that better known and practical one is the gathering of a tithe. It was for some years that this work was abandoned. Its beginning now proves that love of the elements of the old religion still remains. This love and zeal are not only within the Nestorians alone, but also within many others. Whatever confession [*todita*] to which they may belong, zeal for the old church has nevertheless pressed a seal on their heart and they will not abandon it.[221]

Another article declares that a nation is "a community [*šotaputa*] or a people bound [*ʾsira*] to one another by a political bond [*yesura*] and which has its own head and government," and the "head of the Syrian religion and nation" is the patriarch.[222]

The several instances that we have seen so far of the metaphorical use of Christian motifs and themes in the *Star* are part of a broader integration of Classical Syriac terms and ideas into the new nationalist culture. One simple example of this is the appropriation of the Classical Syriac word, *ḥuyyadha*, for national "unity": the term was most commonly used in the classical language for both the unity of human and divine natures in Christ and the unity of the three persons of the trinity. Such appropriations can be at times surprising in their audacity. In describing the need for a building for national affairs, one article describes the Israelites' tabernacle in the wilderness and the subsequent Temple in Jerusalem.[223] It then paraphrases Matthew 8:20, replacing the role of Jesus ("the Son of Man") in the original verse with the "people" and their "leaders": "Foxes have holes and birds of the heavens places to rest, but the people of the Syrians do not have a place to rest, in which their leaders [*rešanu(hy)*] may place their heads [*rešay*]."[224] In the end the article claims that the hope of the *Star* is "that this nation will wake from its sleep." This innovative gloss on Matthew 8:20 reveals how the social body was imagined through and took on the features of the body of Christ.

According to a 1909 article, the spirit of Easter and Christ's power are apparent in the return to life that occurs around us in springtime,

> whereas we learn from year to year how effective in waking us up from national unconsciousness are those lessons of the rising and resurrection of nature all around, oh Lord. We are afraid that we are still in an unconsciousness and mortal state with the result that many Easters will not wake us up.... Would that this Easter would wake us up and suddenly we would be resurrected from these national sins.[225]

The resurrection of Christ at Easter and evangelical awakening are analogized to the natural world, which in turn is likened to the nation, dormant in a winter of unconsciousness.

Conclusion: Mission Diversity, Secularized Discourse, and the Theology of Nations

By the end of the nineteenth century, many East Syrians were confronted in their travels and their interactions with foreigners with the ideas of nationality that had been spreading around the world from Europe and the United States. Even many of those who had remained in Urmia were more cosmopolitan by the end of the century, even if they had not gone to the United

States or Rome to study. Armenian nationalism, which had developed in more distant locales, was conspicuous in the region by the 1890s, whereas Tabriz was a center of revolutionary thought in Iran. East Syrians had longtime links in Georgia and other parts of the Caucasus, and the Russian presence there provided them with yet another model of a growing nationalism. This acquaintance with global affairs, whether learned locally or acquired abroad, helped ground ideas and practices that had already been developing for decades within the context of the American mission. Furthermore, the business and commercial concerns of some of the earliest national thinkers point to the bourgeois background of Syrian national thought: further integration into the world economy contributed to specific local ideological shifts.[226] However, it is important to see how this national consciousness and nationalist discourse derived, as I have emphasized in this book, from the missionary encounter itself, and not simply from the existence of the new professional class cultivated by the missions.[227]

The proliferation of missions in the late nineteenth century contributed to the further differentiation of religious and national identity among the East Syrians. Pluralization, the growing heterogeneity of the religious world in modern society, is a common explanation for secularization. It maintains that the plausibility of religious worldviews declines as the number of worldviews one can choose from increases.[228] One obvious problem with such an argument is that it ignores the heterogeneity of the premodern world. A qualifying variant of this argument suggests the development of a secularized discourse within modern democratic culture.[229] Jeffrey Stout makes such an argument when he describes secularization as part of the process of "exchanging reasons in public settings" in a pluralistic context. Stout claims, "The mark of secularization, as I use the term, is rather the fact that participants in a given discursive practice are not in a position to take for granted that their interlocutors are making the same religious assumptions they are."[230] What can be presupposed in any public conversation decreases. The issue, then, is not belief but discursive practice, the kinds of arguments people can make. This does not necessitate a disenchanted world or an absence of belief in God, especially in a context such as Urmia, where the plurality within the community was one of Christian denominations. Out of the internal diversity provoked by the variety of missions, the prior American missionary notion of "true religion" resulted in demands for the removal of "religion" from national debate, aside from those aspects of it that were shared by all, such as the Bible. In this way, Protestant presuppositions about religion were taken for granted in secular national political culture.

The splintering of the community due to foreign missions created a context where demands for national unity flourished in the new Christian public sphere produced by the various mission presses. However, it would be misleading to refer to this as the "reunification" of the *melat*: the new calls for unity implied a new type of community.[231] The distinction between religion and nationality, an idea promoted by the Americans and socially instantiated in the new sectarian context, became a rallying cry of nationalists. This early nationalism, even after the formation of the Syrian Union and the emphatically nationalist *Star*, did not move into making territorial claims. Early Syrian nationalism remained what we might call a "millet nationalism." It was only in the future exile after 1918, in the era of the League of Nations, that a nationalism demanding land appeared, and this would have been incompatible with the Qajar and Ottoman pluralism of the status quo ante, if changes in Iran and especially Turkey had not followed a similar logic. Turkish nationalism eventually rejected all forms of non-Turkish identity, whereas Iranian nationalism, always more cosmopolitan, allowed for the inclusion of ethnic others, some of whom later received "protected" status in the Islamic Republic of Iran.

The American missionaries themselves were aware of how missionary competition had an acid effect upon religious identity. The *1899 Annual Report* worries:

> Events in Urumia have proven the spiritual destitution of those who are least willing to acknowledge it. Any hesitation to join the Russian cause by enlightened persons outside the Evangelical Church seems to be entirely from worldly wisdom, and not from principle. The long years of mission work have unsettled many and freed them from superstition, without establishing their faith. To such it has been a savour of death unto death. The widespread hypocrisy involved in making religious professions for the sake of gain, has eaten out the vitals of the nation, and hence the perversion to the Russian Church from purely political motives. Not a few of those trained in our schools are included among these.[232]

The missions helped to create the context for nationalist thought to thrive, but the primary argument of this book has been that the ideas and practices of nationhood had already come about at the antebellum American mission.

This is apparent from a perusal of the *Star*, a paper containing many ideas reminiscent of what we find in *Rays of Light* decades before, from the calls for self-support to the expressed need for every nation to have its own schools.[233] Just as the missionaries had worried in the 1860s about the detrimental role they played in creating a relation of dependence with the Syrians, so now critiques developed of the excessive reliance on the missions, however much gratitude was thought owed to them.[234] Even the language of national awakening is one that echoes similar claims about awakening in earlier missionary literature.[235] Many of the ideas about sociality and the terms I discussed in chapters 3 and 4, such as *benefit*, *time*, and *condition*, are also apparent in the *Star*, but in a more developed form, whereas the self-consciousness of evangelical culture and the concern for an exchange-free relationship with God have now been transformed into a reflective national consciousness and a concern for religious freedom, confessional autonomy, and market culture. The romantic, sentimental self of evangelical revivalism has been transformed into an at times poetic self, anxious about the nation and yearning for communal awakening.

In the late nineteenth century, the shift to an explicitly Christian theology of nations put a new emphasis on a theological concern that was attested at the mission from the beginning: the earliest nationalists were not only disproportionately linked to the American mission, but they were also engaged in mission work, often to non-Syrian, even Muslim, communities. These Christian nationalist cosmopolitans demonstrated a strong concern, even love, for their own "people," while simultaneously performing a Christian universalism in their careers as preachers. Each mission had its impact on the development of Syrian nationalism. The Catholics and the Anglicans stressed theological differences, the former attempting to transform the East Syrians into Chaldeans and the latter aiming to help them remain "Nestorian" but without the heretical aspects of "Nestorianism." The Americans, even after the development of a separate evangelical church and the accession to the Presbyterian mission, tended to emphasize issues of education and affect over confessional clarity, and it was in this private sphere of the self, the family, the congregation, the school, and the prayer circle that the nation was born and in the public sphere of missionary debate that it came to maturity.

8

Retrieving the Ruins of Nineveh:
Language Reform, Orientalizing Autoethnography,
and the Demand for National Literature

Probably such persons do not understand that the substance and stability of a nation
depends in general upon the substance and stability of its language: without language
there is no nation, and when language dies and goes, so also that nation will sink and
be mixed with other nations.
—*Star*, November 24, 1912[1]

Language therefore became a zone over which the nation first had to declare its sovereignty and then had to transform in order to make it adequate for the modern world.
—PARTHA CHATTERJEE, *The Nation and Its Fragments* (1993)[2]

The name *Assyrian* as used for the contemporary ethnoreligious community
of Assyrians is an "invented tradition," a retrieval of an ancient appellation
that had fallen into disuse for over two thousand years. Invented traditions
"are responses to novel situations which take the form of reference to old
situations, or which establish their own past by quasi-obligatory repetition."[3]
The use of *Assyrian* derives from Western sources, not from a continuity of
identity between the ancient Assyrians and the modern ones. European and
American missionaries, diplomats, and archaeologists used the terms *Chaldean* and *Assyrian* to refer to the region, as well as to the Christian communities of upper Mesopotamia and even of Urmia, and this usage eventually
led to the appropriation of the name by the East Syrian community itself.
One of the goals of this book has been to try to understand how it is that
this retrieval was possible, why the East Syrians took up an Assyrian national
appellation and identity. Such an inquiry may be divided into two different
approaches. The first, which is what I have focused on through most of the
book, is to study the transformations within the community that allowed for
nationalist claims to be made and for renaming to occur. To point out that
the name derives primarily from Western sources does not explain why it is
that it was happily taken up by so many. The underlying social and ideological mechanics that would allow for this process of cultural appropriation and
renegotiation have required close examination. The East Syrians' engagement
with Western scholarship occurred primarily through their contact with mis-

sionaries, whose projects of moral and religious reform helped to create a discursive framework within which Assyrian nationalist claims emerged. I turn now to the second approach, which is to analyze the reception of the name *Assyrian* within the East Syrian community and its links to contemporary debates about culture and nationality.

In this chapter I discuss how the East Syrian encounter with Western archaeology and orientalism in the late nineteenth century contributed to the development of Assyrianism, the political and cultural philosophy that holds that the "Nestorians," and even all Syriac Christians, are descendants of the Assyrians of the ancient Near East. The reception of the name *Assyrian* is an instance of autoethnography, a response to missionaries' introduction of orientalist forms of knowledge, as well as information about local archaeology. By "autoethnography," I mean the practice commonly found in colonial settings of indigenous populations taking on a name and identity based upon the ethnographic discourse of the colonial authority, or "partly collaborating with and appropriating the idioms of the conqueror."[4] In response to what they learned from missionaries, the East Syrians engaged in an autoethnographic self-identification as an ancient nation. Mission publications reproduced ancient "oriental" history, themes, and motifs and thereby mediated actual Near Eastern material through an imagined Orient, and this European notion of the ancient Orient served as a template for an innovative East Syrian self-imag(in)ing. A significant portion of this chapter describes early nationalist dialogue concerning language, history, and literature. For it was in these intellectual fields that Assyrian identity first developed its imaginary potential for the community.

The phenomenon I am examining is common in the development of modern ethnoreligious and national identities, especially in the Middle East. The retrieval of Assyrian identity is comparable to the recasting of ancient Phoenicia whereby it has become a part of Lebanese and Maronite identity since the nineteenth century.[5] Similarly, modern Coptic Christian identity has articulated links to Pharaonic Egypt, and Iranian nationalism, especially before the Islamic Revolution, underlined links to the pre-Islamic past. The Canaanite movement reimagined Jews as ancient residents of the land of Israel, and Zionism has often conceived of centuries of diasporic history as an aberration and not essential to Jewish identity. Likewise, Greek nationalism attempted to reinvent classical Athens, thus downplaying most of Greek history. The pan-Turkism of the late nineteenth and early twentieth centuries highlighted the shared nomadic origins of the various Turkic peoples now spread across Asia. Even Saddam Hussein, no friend to modern Assyrians, emphasized his connections as the president of Iraq to ancient Mesopotamian kings. Nationalism always retrieves the past, but the Middle East has a lot of well-attested past to retrieve, and, moreover, has for centuries been imagined as an ancient land.

The Retrieval of the Name *Assyria*

For the sake of simplicity, I have throughout this book preferred *Syrian* to *Assyrian* because this is the term used in Neo-Aramaic sources from the nineteenth century, even if nineteenth-century Syrians are the progenitors of the modern Assyrians. The question of the actual biological descent of modern Assyrians from the Assyrians of antiquity is of no interest to me. This issue, which has produced some scholarly debate, even forays into physiognomy and popular genetics, is not relevant to cultural history. Furthermore, it is for me ethically moot because it centers around an issue of origins that should be politically irrelevant: whether or not the modern Assyrians are descendants of the ancient ones should not determine the recognition of what this community has suffered in the past century and a half nor whether this community should be respected and in some cases receive communal rights.[6]

Several scholars have already addressed the controversial topic of the origin of the name *Assyrian* as it is used by contemporary Assyrians.[7] Nationalists tend to take a primordialist position, holding that the Assyrian nation has existed continuously since antiquity and that this identity has been rediscovered in the modern period. Critiques of this position tend toward what scholars of nationalism since the 1980s have termed "constructivism": the idea that the "nation" is a modern invention, a projection of institutions and identities into an imagined past.

In his 1993 "historical-onomastical" analysis of the modern retrieval of the term *Assyrian*, Wolfhart Heinrichs focuses "on the various acceptions of the name 'Assyrian' during the course of history as well as on the various other names applied to the people presently carrying that name."[8] In looking at the origins of "Assyrianism," Heinrichs begins with the following questions: "When was this idea born and why? Which factors contributed to the adoption of the self-designation 'Assyrians'? And what function was it meant to fulfill?"[9] Assyrianism was born in Urmia, and both the name itself and the people's onomastic history offered the preconditions of this renaming. "The self-designation of the Eastern Syrians as well as the Syrians in general had been, throughout many centuries, the term *sūryāyē* ('Syrians')."[10] A degraded form of this name, *sūrāyē*, was not uncommon, and this term, the singular of which is *sūrāyā*, allowed some to make the link to *Assyrian*. "They de-

clared the form *sūrāyā* to be a truncated *asūrāyā* and started to write the word
sūrāyā with an initial *ālaph*, put under a cancellation line (*linea occultans*)—a
common orthographic convention in Neo-Syriac to indicate an etymological
sound no longer spoken." The earliest reference Heinrichs finds for this practice is in an article in *Rays of Light* from 1897 by the prolific nationalist writer
Mirza Mesroph Khan Karam (1862–1943), but below I address an earlier and,
for the purposes of my argument about the orientalist background to this
practice, more important example from 1895.

After providing an etymological history of *sūryāyā* (plural, *sūryāyē*),
showing how it was that the Aramaic-speaking Christians of upper Mesopotamia and beyond took up this name for themselves in late antiquity, Heinrichs points out that Attūr/Āthūr, the Aramaic form of *Assyria*, continued to
be used into the Middle Ages for the area surrounding the Assyrian capital
of Nineveh. The remains of Nineveh were across the Tigris from Mosul, a
city founded in the period after the Arab conquest, and so Christians in this
region were at times referred to by the geographical appellation, *ātōrāyē*, but
without the notion of descent from the actual Assyrians. Compounded with
this usage is the continuity of referring to the area by outsiders as Assyria—
for example, *Asorestan* in Middle Persian and *Assyria* in Greek.

Heinrichs notes that on account of this, *Asori* became the term for "Syrians" in Armenian. This may have had some effect upon the development
of Assyrianism when many East Syrian workers settled in Tbilisi and other
parts of the Caucasus in the early and mid-nineteenth century. East Syrians
would have become acquainted with the name there, and "once this name
had been generally accepted, it was sure to become well known also in Urmia,
because of the many seasonal workers who went back and forth between the
Urmia region and Tiflis [Tbilisi]."[11] The Armenian form would have eased
the shift from *sūrāyā* to *asūrāyā* and finally to *ātōrāyā*. "What we have here,
then, is an outside designation of the Eastern Syrians, which was, however,
known to them and reminded them phonetically of the name 'Assyrian.'" Add
to this both the usage of the Latin *Assyrii* and *Chaldaei* in the Roman Curia,
which led to the eventual naming of the "Nestorian" Uniates as Chaldeans,
who were recognized by the Sublime Porte as a *millet* in 1845, and also the
naming of the Anglican mission to the area as "to the Assyrian Christians."
Heinrichs emphasizes that *Assyrian* in this usage had a vague geographical
sense and "was introduced for practical reasons and had no historical claims
attached to it."[12] For example, a scribe from the Mosul region writing in West
Syrian script in 1826 identified himself as Behnam *Ātōrāyā* ("the Assyrian").[13]
However, due to the "hypnotic power of names," it was eventually linked to

historical claims. Another factor Heinrichs singles out for these developments is the terms used in publications in the West produced not only by East Syrians but also by members of various Syrian Christian communities: in order to avoid confusion with "Syria," the geographical and political unit, *Assyrian* was on occasion used in English, whereas in the original languages, Aramaic, Arabic, and Turkish, "Syrian" was retained.

Heinrichs's article demonstrates how it was plausible that *Assyrian* could be taken up as a name, but the actual process, he admits, was complex. Along with a reference to the archaeological interest in ancient Assyria due to the work of Austin Henry Layard and others in the region, Heinrichs suggests that the name was useful for those intellectuals "aiming to replace the traditional idea of the *millat* [*millet*] (the internally autonomous religious community recognized by the Islamic state) by the concept of the *umta*, 'nation,' which would heal the political disunion of the Eastern Syrians caused by the *millat* system."[14] This is of course true, but I have devoted most of this book to revealing where these intellectuals, who were predominantly educated at the American mission, developed their ideas and how it was that they and other members of the community made the transition to such nationalist thinking. Heinrichs clearly demonstrates the onomastic process, but the *social* one goes back several decades earlier than the growing prominence of *Assyrian* as a national title for the community in the early twentieth century.

In contrast to those who would claim that the use of *Assyrian* and *Chaldean* is a completely modern invention, one synthesis position holds that some Syriac Christians in late antiquity and after "Assyrianized"—that is, they engaged in autoethnography, locating themselves and parts of their tradition in an imagined Assyrian past they found in the Bible.[15] This compromise position obviously would not please a strict nationalist, but it does acknowledge an earlier interest in Assyria within the tradition while positing Assyrian identity as new. Such a prior tradition of Assyrianizing helps to explain those few premodern references to Assyria in some Classical Syriac sources.[16] These references to Assyria or Assyrians in the tradition are in fact used by Assyrian nationalists today to defend the historical links they envision, but ultimately for my argument they do not matter. Even if some trace of the name continued in regular use among some East Syrians, hypothetically for centuries— and this does not seem to be the case—the communal renaming that we see from the turn of the twentieth century onward needs to be explained. A seventeenth-century reference to someone as an "Assyrian" or a similar reference to a group of Christians near Mosul in the eighteenth century are exceptions: the rule was that this was not the name used by members of the East

Syrian Christian community, nor does it reflect their own self-understanding until the early twentieth century.[17] As most of this book has argued, national identity consists of far more than the names people call themselves.

Austin Henry Layard and Hormuzd Rassam

It was in the late 1890s that the Syrians began to consider the "Assyrians" as their progenitors. However, a number of important developments preceded this. In Europe and the United States, the nineteenth century saw a turn to the past both in the development of modern academic historiography and in the popular interest in history among the increasingly nationalist reading public. From the late 1840s onward, an interest in certain sectors of the Euro-American public in the archaeological discoveries of the ancient Near East led to a cultural fad of "Assyrian chic," which would only be displaced later by the far more virulent "Egyptomania" of the early twentieth century.[18] This trend had already begun before the important archaeological discoveries of midcentury: for example, Edwin Atherstone (1788–1872) began his massive thirty-book poem *The Fall of Nineveh* by the 1820s. Assyrian chic, which required several decades to take hold in the United States, was heavily fueled by the early discoveries of Austen Henry Layard (1817–94).[19] Not long after Layard led an expedition at the ruins of Nineveh, he published *Nineveh and Its Remains: With an Account of a Visit to the Chaldaean Christians of Kurdistan, and the Yezidis, or Devil-Worshippers; and an Inquiry into the Manners and Arts of the Ancient Assyrians* (2 vols., 1848–49). In this work Layard draws connections between the ancient Chaldean and Assyrian populations and the Christians of the region, as well as those he met on a tour of the mountains of Hakkari. Though he hedges about the exact name to give them—acknowledging, for example, that *Chaldean* was probably introduced by the Catholics—in the end he treats the Syrian Christians as the remnants of an ancient race, the original inhabitants of the region: "As the only remnant of a great nation, every one must feel an interest in their history and condition; and our sympathies cannot but be excited in favor of a long persecuted people, who have merited the title of 'the Protestants of Asia.'"[20] (His own Huguenot background perhaps made this final missionary cliché poignant for him.)

The link Layard draws between the Syrians and ancient races was already in the air. Early at the American mission Asahel Grant famously concluded that the East Syrians were the descendants of the Lost Tribes of Israel. This was generally rejected by contemporaries, including Justin Perkins himself, despite Grant's long-winded attempt to prove his thesis in his book *The Nesto-*

rians; or, The Lost Tribes: Containing Evidence of Their Identity; an Account of Their Manners, Customs, and Ceremonies; Together with Sketches of Travels in Ancient Assyria, Armenia, Media, and Mesopotamia; and Illustrations of Scripture Prophecy (New York, 1841).[21] Horatio Southgate (1812–94), an Episcopalian missionary from the United States, traveled through the region in the 1830s and identified the Syrians with the Chaldeans and then emphasized, against Asahel Grant, that they were "descendants of the Assyrians and not of the Jews."[22] However, Layard's work was not like these other lone voices in learned tomes or travelogues: he wrote a best seller.

The archaeology of the ancient Near East was a component of European national discourses in the nineteenth century. Layard's excavations at Nineveh were immediately celebrated, and upon his return he was exalted as a national hero.[23] *Nineveh and Its Remains* sold in the thousands, going through several printings, and his later volumes, including the breathtaking *Illustrations of the Monuments of Nineveh* (1849), sustained his fame. This was the heyday of the British Museum, and archaeology was part of the public conversation about cultural, material, and moral progress in Britain. Ancient Assyria was understood to be one of the acmes of ancient civilization as well as a precursor to the eminent European cultures of the modern age. Furthermore, the birth of modern archaeology functioned to confirm for many the historicity of the Bible: the Assyrians of Scripture were vividly attested by the grandeur of Layard's discoveries.

An important aid in Layard's work, someone who may have pushed him further in drawing connections between the Syrians and ancient peoples, was Hormuzd Rassam (1826–1910), a local Chaldean from Mosul who served as Layard's aide and then, after leading his own excavations, eventually became a well-known British diplomat.[24] Already on a visit to England in 1848, Rassam passed himself off as a descendant of the ancient Assyrians.[25] Later in his colorful career, he published *Asshur and the Land of Nimrod* (1897), in which he claims that, with the exception of some Armenians and members of the Greek church, all the Christians of the region, including the Syrian Orthodox, share "the same Chaldean or Assyrian origin."[26]

The popularity of Assyria in the late nineteenth century explains why when the Anglicans sent a mission to Urmia, it was called the archbishop of Canterbury's Mission to the Assyrian Christians. The missionaries did not see themselves as necessarily working with actual Assyrians and were concerned to downplay the historical implications of the name.[27] However, as Heinrichs points out, the "hypnotic power of names" is compelling: in his account of traveling through the region in 1876 on a mission for the archbishop of Canterbury, Edward L. Cutts blithely refers to "Assyrian Christians," even labeling the Syrian Orthodox (West Syrians) as "Assyrian Monophysites."[28] Although he treats these "Assyrians" as a race, he does not show the concern for their supposed ancient Near Eastern origins that would become so common just a few years later.[29]

Ancient Near Eastern and Oriental Studies at the American Mission

The American missionaries arrived self-consciously aware of the ancient history of the land in which they were to be stationed. They often remarked upon the antiquity of sites and noted those where famous events took place, such as Urmia as the possible birthplace of Zoroaster.[30] These Christian Romantics asserted the antiquity of Persia and the entire East, and often thought they saw connections between the practices and customs of the people around them and those of the Bible, suggesting continuity between the ancient and the contemporary. All of this is typical of nineteenth-century orientalism and need not give us pause. Biblical archaeology was beginning at this time, and just as the ruins of the Near East confirmed biblical historicity, the people in the region were treated as ethnographic verification thereof. The Near East was understood, in a sense, to have more history than other places, and for visitors this history was always present and tangible inasmuch as the region was thought to have remained, despite the centuries, as it had been.

In the spring of 1849, Justin Perkins, William R. Stocking, and Mar Yokhannan along with other native assistants made a trip to Mosul, where they visited the excavation site at Nineveh and met with Hormuzd Rassam.[31] In his account Perkins demonstrates interest in the current work of archaeologist Henry Rawlinson (1810–95), like Layard, a preeminent figure in early Assyriology. Perkins's description of this trip refers repeatedly to Xenophon's fourth-century-BCE *Anabasis*, a Classical Greek work that was a standard local reference for Europeans and Americans in the region in the nineteenth and early twentieth centuries.[32] During their journey, the Great Zab River inspired contemplation of the biblical past: "Our thoughts naturally dwelt on sacred as well as classic themes, in this venerable region; and as we sat down under our tents, on the banks of the Zab, toward evening, we remembered the plaintive strain of the captive Jews sitting by the rivers of Babylon." Perkins describes how Deacon Tamo then read Psalm 137 ("By the rivers of Babylon") and "artlessly remarked" that the Kurds mockingly demand that the local Christians and Jews sing them their songs.[33] Such a focus on biblical themes explains Perkins's interest during the journey in Nebi Yunus, the shrine of the prophet Jonah near the dig site at Nineveh.

At Amherst, Perkins had studied Hebrew with Moses Stuart (1780–1852), an important early figure in American oriental studies, many of whose students became the founding members of the American Oriental Society in 1842.[34] Perkins himself, a member of the society, published on Classical Syriac texts in its journal in the 1850s and 1860s,[35] and David T. Stoddard published a Neo-Aramaic grammar there in 1856.[36] Their orientalist work often had a practical aim: the missionaries produced a grammar of Classical Syriac in 1858 and a grammar of Modern Persian in 1861, both in Neo-Aramaic and therefore for the local audience.[37] The missionaries also served as intermediaries of orientalia to Europe and the United States. Perkins would on occasion send manuscripts to Europe as well as to the United States, including to his alma mater, Amherst, as did James L. Merrick, a controversial early member of the mission.[38] Missionary Austin Hazen Wright (mission: 1840–65) helped broker the transfer of the Nimrud slabs to Dartmouth, and in the 1840s and 1850s Edward Breath was the treasurer of the "Nineveh Enterprise," an organization for bringing antiquities to the United States.[39]

Perkins's interest in archaeology and the ancient Near East is apparent in the mission publications.[40] His visit along with others to the "wonders" of Nineveh is described briefly in the first issue of *Rays of Light*.[41] In 1852 the "Science" section of *Rays of Light* had a long article on "Babylon, the Famous City," describing the city's majesty; its kings, including its mythical founder, Nimrod; the exile of Israel there; how "God awakened [*mureʿsle*] the spirit of Cyrus"; the sack of the city by the Medes and Persians; Belshazzar's feast; the liberation of "the people of God" (*tayepa d-alaha*); and the career of the prophet Daniel.[42] "Chaldeans" are mentioned in the article in the earlier biblical sense as "soothsayers" and "magicians." Also in 1852 a "Science" article discusses the purpose of the pyramids of Egypt, comparing them to those in Mexico, and explains how such structures represent worldly vanity, and an article on the palace at Susa, the capital of the kings of Persia at the time of Daniel, describes the discovery of its ruins and the grave of Daniel maintained there.[43] In 1859 there was a series of articles on Jonah, the biblical prophet who was sent to Nineveh. One article describes the city and its location vis-à-vis modern Mosul (whereas in another the author offers a naturalistic reading of the tale of the prophet by providing an account of his own firsthand knowledge of whales).[44] This awareness of the ruins of Nineveh was prevalent enough that it could be used in moral discourse: in a February 1862 article on the "Strength of the Church" in the "Fear of God" section, the fallen state of ancient cultures, such as Nineveh, is contrasted to the staying power of the church.[45]

From early on, the missionaries were interested in teaching geography, and they typically preferred the ancient geography of the region over the contemporary geographies of Qajar Iran or the Ottoman Empire. An early tool Perkins used at the male seminary was "Peter Parley's" popular *Universal History on the Basis of Geography* (1837), where a student could learn about the ancient Near East, such as that "Ashur, the grandson of Noah, was the first ruler of Assyria."[46] In 1853 the press published Austin H. Wright's question-and-answer-format geography textbook. Joseph G. Cochran's biblical geography, published in 1856, was based upon *An Historical Text Book and Atlas of Biblical Geography* (1854) by Lyman Coleman (1786–1882), a work that includes discussion of Layard's work (similar geographies were published in 1859 and 1885).[47] Perkins's last publication before leaving the mission was an extensive commentary on the Book of Daniel (1869), a "book full of wonders," according to the preface.[48] Perkins explains that the Book of Daniel is important "especially for Nestorian readers who reside in a land very close to the land where Daniel lived and speak a language so close to that language in which Daniel prophesied."[49] He includes a prayer that in their belief and religious zeal they might be like Daniel.[50] Perkins suggests that like the Book of Ezra, much of which is written in Aramaic ("Chaldean"), the Book of Daniel demonstrates "true knowledge of the ancient history of the nation [*melat*] of the Chaldeans, their various ways and habits."[51]

After an early attempt at establishing a mission in Mosul (1841–44), Perkins's visit to the region in 1849 was a preliminary move in establishing the "Assyria Mission," which covered the region from Mosul northwest to Diyarbakır and "was so named for geographical reasons."[52] This mission operated from the early 1850s until it was closed down and its field was joined to the Eastern Turkey mission in 1860. As with the later Anglican mission, the naming of this one demonstrates the link the missionaries drew, especially after Layard's discoveries, between this region and historical Assyria. Henry Lobdell (1827–55), who served (and died) in this mission, showed an interest in local archaeology, concerning which he was in correspondence with Perkins.[53] By the time of the Urmia mission's accession to the Presbyterian Church in 1870, *Assyria* had become a standard term for this part of the mission field.[54]

In contrast to this focus on biblical history and the archaeology of the Near East, the primary understanding of East Syrian history that the missionaries brought with them, aside from tales of malignant Nestorian heresy, was that of the once great missionary church whose enthusiasm for Christ had spread the Gospel as far as China. Exemplary of this for the missionaries was the famous Nestorian Stele, a large stone inscribed with Chinese and Syriac, discovered in Xi'an in 1625.[55] Through Jesuit channels, this monument, dated to 781 CE, was already an object of great curiosity and excitement in Europe in the seventeenth century. It was J. S. Assemani in the eighteenth century who integrated it into Nestorian history. By the mid-nineteenth century, despite its long-held Catholic pedigree, the stone was taken as a sign of proto-Protestantism in distant China.[56] As we have already seen in Rufus Anderson's instructions to Perkins upon his departure for Iran, one of the mission's goals was to revive this ancient missionary spirit, to subvert Islam, and ultimately to convert Asia, and this understanding of the evangelism of the Nestorian past would persist in missionary discourse into the twentieth century.[57] Related to this was the notion that the ancient Syrians developed the first schools of higher learning, even the first universities, in the Middle East, in Edessa and Nisibis.[58] The focus on the ancient learning of the East Syrians both justified the schools established by the missionaries and strengthened the link between the East Syrian past and a missionary present.

This link to the ancient church was further maintained and eventually developed by Perkins's decision to print the vernacular Aramaic of Urmia in Classical Syriac script. Contrary to what the missionaries thought, Neo-Aramaic does not derive from Classical Syriac. It is not a degraded remnant of a classical language, but a later dialect of a language with a complex dialectical history. The decision to employ Classical Syriac orthography for the modern language corresponded well with the narrative of decline the missionaries introduced when they addressed the history of the Church of the East. However, this decision led to new emphases and the creation of new links between the contemporary language and that of the past. It also contributed to the contestations about orthography that were so important in early Syrian national discourse, as we will see below, as well as to a general sense among the Syrians that in comparison to their ancestors, they were now in decline.

An area of oriental studies that eventually flourished at the mission was the collecting and copying of Classical Syriac manuscripts. By the late nineteenth century, the American mission had developed a small business in copying and selling manuscripts to Western scholars.[59] Despite an evangelical emphasis on the vernacular, by the 1880s, in part due to the encouragement of John H. Shedd, the copying of manuscripts for and at the mission was common, and the scribe of many of these was Osha'na Saro, mentioned in the previous chapter.[60] He prepared the catalog of the mission's Classical Syriac manuscript collection, which was printed in 1898 (an important document because the library was lost during the catastrophe of 1918).[61] Many of the manuscripts in the mission's library were copied by scribes from Mazra'a, Osha'na's village in Hakkari, and this points to the ongoing connections between the scribal community there and the mission.[62] The village was a center of mountain evangelism, and David of Mazra'a, a scribe of many manuscripts held in the mission collection, attended the male seminary.[63]

By the late nineteenth century, historical interests at the mission had further developed. Already in 1882 students at the college were taking exams in the "Ancient History of the East."[64] *Rays of Light* is not extant from 1871 until 1892. The 1892 edition, however, shows important developments: this year witnessed a series of long articles, including a special April supplement, on Chaldea, Assyria, and Babylon. These articles provide an up-to-date précis of where ancient Near Eastern history and archaeology stood by the 1890s, detailing the geography and political and cultural history of Mesopotamia. Intriguingly, that same year several articles appeared on the biblical prophet Daniel, playing up his oriental provenance. Furthermore, in the 1890s the mission published several volumes that addressed the ancient Near East: a "History of Babylon," which is unfortunately no longer extant; an 1892 translation of *Outlines of the World's History, Ancient, Mediaeval and Modern, with Special Relation to the History of Civilization and the Progress of Mankind* (1874) by William Swinton (1833–92), which is a school textbook that includes a section on the Assyrians and Babylonians (the maps for which were seized by Turkish authorities because the name *Armenia* appeared on them); and in 1896 a book of biblical geography, including material on the ancient Near East.[65] Aside from ancient Near Eastern history, *Rays of Light* also published in the 1890s a series of articles on the history of the Church of the East as it had been reconstructed by the end of the nineteenth century. The apparent increase in interest in ancient history at the mission was no coincidence and may reflect competition with other missions, such as the Anglicans. William A. Shedd warned that the Americans were "losing in some measure an influence of the highest importance in not making more use of the past as an incentive to present achievement."[66] After mentioning the Syrian history of martyrs, he noted that "the history of one's own nation is a book of God to him."

Baba of Kosi and the Debate about the National Language

In the form of Neo-Aramaic printed at the mission, there were a number of orthographic inconsistencies and ambiguities because in developing a system for printing the vernacular, Perkins relied on Classical Syriac, a wholly different dialect of Aramaic from the language spoken in Urmia. Furthermore, his assistants in this project were often from the mountains, whereas it was the language of the plain that they were trying to render in written form. This led to exceptions and obscurities. Some of these problems were addressed in the early years of printing as the orthography was slowly systematized: the diverse variations in spelling we find in the early tracts printed at the mission gave way to a standardized form. In the following decades, orthography, in addition to lexicography, developed further.

By the 1860s an interest in language, especially that of the Bible, is apparent in *Rays of Light*. Several articles address foreign or anomalous words in Scripture, and there are also articles on language in general.[67] Furthermore, in some issues, questions were printed and readers' responses would then be published in a later issue.[68] These trivia questions generally concerned scriptural knowledge or biblical figures. However, in April 1866, pointing ahead to interests in the indigenous tradition and the identity of the Syrians that would arise later, a question was asked about Saint Ephrem and another on whether the "nation" should be called "Syrian" or "Nestorian."[69] In the same issue in 1866, a young man, Baba of Kosi (d. 1906), sent in a learned response to several of these trivia questions.[70] Baba, who graduated from the male seminary in 1863, was possibly the nephew of Priest John of Kosi, an early assistant in translation work at the mission and principal of the male seminary until his death in 1845.[71] After graduating, Baba preached and also worked as a teacher in the college.[72]

In 1886 the mission began its production of a fully revised version of its translation of the Bible with the printing of a new translation of Genesis.[73] In this version more Classical Syriac words were used in order to make the text more accessible to the wider Neo-Aramaic-speaking audience, such as those mountain Nestorians who were not accustomed to those aspects of the Urmia dialect in the earlier version.[74] The full translation was printed in New York in 1893.[75] Benjamin Labaree (mission: 1860–1906) led this project in which several native assistants, including Baba of Kosi, participated. At this time Baba was also working on a lexicon of the modern language. He traveled as far as the United States in an attempt to have it published (we know he was there in 1892), but his plan never came to fruition.

An 1892 letter from Baba to John H. Shedd, which was published in *Rays of Light*, points to important developments in the conversation at the mission and among Syrians about their language and its relationship to the nation.[76] Writing from England, Baba begins with a description of his visit to the Christian community in Salisbury, where he had lectured on missionary activity in Iran. When he arrived back in London, he found the July edition of *Rays of Light* and an article by Moses Duman (1872–1918), an evangelical missionary pastor. He agrees with Duman that every nation must stand on its own. "The Syrians, sons of my nation [*bnay melati*, or "my compatriots"] rely on foreigners as if upon crutches and they will fall if these are removed." For "a nation without its own potential will not make progress." Further employing the language of national self-help, Baba discusses the needs of Syrian youth who go abroad. He then turns to the issue of language:

> Concerning the idea of reforming [*turraṣa*] the language I have this briefly [to say]: to judge the language by one dialect or spoken form [*mamla*] is not right. Let us not think that the speech [*mamla*] of Kosi or of Digala ought to dominate over the whole. Rather, let us take hold of the language in a general manner, also too in a manner that it may increase thoughtfully in meaning. Those who go in their own furrow reject that of others. The speech of Gulpashan I do not believe is so florid and blossoming such that it is worthy of so much honor.

Regarding orthography, Baba suggests that it be based upon the language itself and its own sounds, not foreign ones, and that in general speech should be more learned and pleasant. He then argues against the archaizing practice of prefixing the letter *mim* to certain verbs where it has been lost in the spoken language. After this he addresses the ethical aspect of speech:

> It is a duty of all Syrians to reform the character that it be ethical, humble, possessing of culture [*adab*] and modest both in speech and in honoring one another, and to cast off sport, which reduces thought, and envy, which destroys the intention to have good and lofty discourse. Let us all remember that rotten discourses destroy good thoughts. Moreover, let us reform our language in both its content [*ḥabre*] and mode of expression [*memre*], and also by a spelling method [*huggaya*] that, inasmuch as possible, is grammatical and based upon rules.
>
> There is not any nation [*melat*] advanced in knowledge and in reputation whose tongue is not revered and possessing of lofty discourses. That one whose life until now has made derisive words, having become a flower in the alley, let him be a person noble in speech. There is no person low or high in rank in London who does not speak an honorific word in conversation, sir is sir, monsieur monsieur, gospodar [Russian, "Mr."] gospodar.

Baba then describes visiting the church of the famous preacher Charles Spurgeon and afterward Hyde Park, where he heard numerous speeches on a variety of topics. He ends with advice:

> Leave the furrow you have had until now; let it not fill up your time. Employ new paths, my brothers, my compatriots [*bnay melati*, lit. "sons of my nation"]. May the Lord bless all of us that all of us, our power and our potential, may be sanctified unto him; also may he give us humility, as well as tenderness of heart, character, and tongue.

Baba's letter points to the close links the Syrians had begun to draw between the reform of language, both in printing and in speech, and the ethical reform of the nation.

Such links were further articulated in 1897 in a number of articles on language and orthography in *Rays of Light*. First there was an article, "The Quiddity of Human Speech," written by Isaac Malek Yonan in America.[77] In this piece, he responds to a series of articles by Oshaʿna Saro that appeared in *Rays of Light* in 1896, but acknowledges that he offers a critical perspective not as a linguist but as a believer. The orthodox view, he suggests, is that language was given to Adam by God, whereas the modern view is that it derives from a system of signs and imitations of sounds in nature, a view that, according to him, is heretical (and that is found in the works of Max Müller and Charles Darwin, both popular authors at the time). Malek Yonan's article attests to a tension within the community between traditional and modern understandings of language.

That same year Baba of Kosi's work on the modern Aramaic lexicon inspired an ongoing technical debate about orthography and language.[78] In "A Call for Help for the Syrian Nation," Priest Jacob Yauvre describes orthographic problems and the need for systematic rules now that Baba of Kosi was producing his lexicon. In a response to this article, Baba demands more precision from Yauvre, that he justify his call for consistent rules. Yauvre died that year and thus never responded. However, not long afterward Dr. Oshaʿna-khan Badal pointed out that there was a variety of dialects even on the plain and that a lexicon was first needed before the orthography could be unified. William Shedd also responded to Yauvre in an article on "Spelling": it is true, he admits, what Yauvre points out about problems in the system created by Perkins and his assistants, yet there will always be variations in how the spoken language is written.

In another article Priest Benjamin of Digala suggests that the orthography be reformed by returning to that of the Classical Syriac authors such as Ephrem, Narsai, Jacob of Sarug, and Bar Hebraeus. It is noteworthy that he includes the latter two West Syrian authors in this list. Benjamin criticizes the early Neo-Aramaic compositions of Syrians associated with the mission and mentions the orthographic work of Arthur J. Maclean, the Anglican missionary who at that time, with the aid of several Syrians, was producing a lexicon that would appear in 1901.[79] What motivated Maclean was the variety of spellings among the American, Lazarist, and Anglican missions. Benjamin then recommends the use of Classical Syriac words where they exist in place of the foreign words (Persian, Arabic, Kurdish, Azeri Turkish, and even English) that were prevalent in the language. He also suggests the indigenizing of foreign words through the addition of the Classical suffix -*uta*. Benjamin offers several recommendations, all aimed at making the orthography correspond better to the way the language actually sounded—that is, rendering the spelling more phonetic. Thus, he supports a purifying and classicizing of the language combined with a practical phonetic approach. According to him, this approach to language corresponds with a specific temporality: "The people of the mountains, who have remained one hundred years behind the people of Urmia, should not wait for us, who have cultivated our language, to adapt ourselves to them. They must follow us!"[80]

The next article in this public conversation was by Priest Osha'na Isho' "of the College." He addresses further problems in orthography and challenges Benjamin's argument: if spelling is going to be phonetic, should different dialects have different spellings? Next, other Syrians from abroad made their contributions to this debate: in a letter written from America, Jesse Malek Yonan, another son of Malik Yonan, suggests that the work of the missionaries and assistants of the past must be recognized and appreciated, but contemporary needs must guide the language, even if this means including foreign technical expressions (e.g., *sayqologiya* and *baysikel*).[81] Those who are opposed to Baba's lexical work, he argues, are against the education of the nation, free thought, and free expression. In a subsequent article on improving orthography, Priest Moses Duman, writing from his missionary post in Kermanshah, claims:[82]

> The Syrian language is a pearl, which lights up in the darkness of the age. It is the oldest language in the world. Adam spoke it and Eve taught it to their children. We Syrians are not only Adam's descendants, but we speak also his language. In this language the savior of the world heralded salvation. Some of his original sayings were kept in all the translations of the Holy Scriptures, as in Mt 27:46 (Mk 15:34), Mk 8:34 [a typo that should read 7:34], 5:41. Jesus Christ spoke Chaldean.

By "Chaldean," he means "Aramaic," and the passages he cites are those in the Gospels where Jesus is quoted speaking Aramaic. Duman then admits the distinction between the new and classical forms of the language, and suggests that foreign words be removed from the new language and replaced with classical ones. However, if indigenous, nonforeign words exist in the new language, they should not be replaced by classical words. Furthermore, the classical orthographic rules should be maintained, and, as much as possible, the new language should be subject to the spelling of the old. He also advocates the removal of silent letters (equivalent to the *gh* in the English *eight*) as well as a number of other specific reforms.

In no other year did *Rays of Light* have so many articles on language as in 1897, although it remained an important topic.[83] In 1898 Baba of Kosi published a long article, "Language and Spelling,"[84] in which he begins by emphasizing the ephemerality of spoken language. Spoken dialects, he argues, have changed, as we can see from old vernacular manuscripts from Alqosh. Furthermore, the vernacular (*swada*) has died out because farmers and workers only need a simple language, with words such as for "work," "eat," and "drink." Although this vernacular has been intermingled with Turkish, Arabic, and Kurdish, printing now preserves and again unites the language. Baba describes the establishment of the press by Perkins and the prayerful gathering on its first day of production. He claims that as the press began to print over the next decade, the language became more "clean, polished, and pure," no longer "the body of Jacob with the smell of Esau." Not long after this article appeared, on May 13, a group gathered at the college to address the complex issues of dialectical variation, dependence on the classical language, and orthography.[85] Also in 1898 the Committee for the Reform of Spelling (*Motwa d-ʿal turraṣa d-huggaya*), a group of Syrians charged with addressing the orthographic problems that had developed, especially on account of the diversity among the different mission printing presses, decided on the heated and problematic issue of prefixing the letter *mim* to certain words.[86] The compromise position, which held that the letter should be maintained if it clarified ambiguities in form—a pragmatic approach—was offered up to the public, who were asked to write to *Rays of Light* with their opinion. The following year another article by Priest David Benjamin of Digala on raising up the Syrian people and their language points toward what was to come.[87] Benjamin claims that although the people and their language are "Syrian," "we are the descendants of Nebuchadnezzar and Laban. There is no other people who are so ancient and can write the language of their forbearers." Benjamin, a Chaldean, then states that all the church confessions should be respected, although they should not be permitted to divide the people.

By the late 1890s language had become an important object of national reform. In the debate about language, men with national inclinations, most of whom were associated with the American mission, performed their concern for the nation in the growing Syrian Christian public sphere. The topics addressed in *Rays of Light* were also spoken about at public assemblies. For example, Baba of Kosi gave a lecture on the Syrian language at the annual meeting of alumni of the male seminary in 1897.[88] In contrast to the indigenous tradition's approach to language, which Isaac Malek Yonan alluded to in the article mentioned above, language in this debate was treated like the nation itself: it was a living organism that had its own evolution and that was now in decline and in need of renewal.[89]

Chaldean Interest in Language

As I mentioned in the preceding chapter, in the nineteenth century, Chaldean clergy began to travel regularly to Rome, where they studied at the Propaganda Fide. Several of these men became prolific authors, producing historical, grammatical, theological, and polemical works in Arabic, Classical Syriac, and Neo-Aramaic. In this learned literature, there developed a focus on, and linking of historical origins to, the ancient Near East.

In 1860 Priest Joseph Gabriel from Khosrowa, also mentioned in the preceding chapter, published a grammar of Classical Syriac, *Elementa linguae chaldaicae*, which also includes a chronology of the patriarchs of the "nation [*umtha*] of the Chaldeans."[90] In the introduction Gabriel states that the Chaldean language (*chaldaica lingua*), despite being "foremost—even mother—of all languages," has a variety of names due to its widespread use in diverse locales.[91] As evidence of Aramaic's priority, he cites statements from the great West Syrian and East Syrian medieval synthesizers, Bar Hebraeus (d. 1286) and ʿAbdishoʿ bar Brikha (d. 1318), who themselves rely on sources from a debate going back to late antiquity. At the end of the introduction, Gabriel makes an important claim for the priority of Chaldean learning and implies the equivalence between "Chaldean" and "Assyrian":

> All the wisdom of the other nations drew its origin from the Chaldeans, and all the sciences flow from the East into the remaining regions of the world: as the Latins from the Greeks, so the Greeks and the others received all the sciences which they later cultivated, first from the Chaldeans, or Assyrians, which means the same thing.[92]

Gabriel's emphasis on the antiquity of the Chaldeans and the connection he draws between them and the Assyrians is, although in part dependent upon earlier European scholarly discussions, an early step in the inventive process of identifying historical links, which came to the fore later in the nineteenth century.

Parallel to this linking of Aramaic, ancient Chaldeans and Assyrians, and the modern Syrian community is the new emphasis on Aramaic as the language of Jesus. Into the modern period, Aramaic and Hebrew were not clearly distinguished by European Christian scholars.[93] Aramaic was commonly referred to as "Chaldean" until the eighteenth century, thus confusing it with the ancient astronomers of the same name in Latin. However, in 1798 Raimundo Diosdado Caballero (1740–1829 or 1830) argued that Syriac was the language of Jesus. In the nineteenth century, Aramaic and its dialects were differentiated and systematically studied. Gustaf Dalman's *Grammatik des jüdisch-palästinensischen Aramäisch* (Leipzig, 1894) presented a "scientific" approach to the specific dialect that Jesus would have spoken. By the late 1890s, several works had appeared on the original language of Jesus, and Aramaic had become the focus of much scholarship.

Abba Jeremiah Maqdasi (1847–1929), another Chaldean who had studied at Rome, draws this connection between Jesus and Aramaic in his Syriac grammar, which was published at the Dominican monastery at Mosul in 1889.[94] In the preface to this work, composed in a poor Syriac that declines into Neo-Aramaicisms, Maqdasi addresses those who have shown a renewed interest in the "Chaldean language."

> On the one hand, its value is known by the fact that the Son of God, when he came to his own, sanctified it and elevated it with divine speech. He spoke it everyday with Mary his blessed mother and with his holy apostles and the rest of the Jews, his compatriots [lit. "sons of his race"]. Furthermore, individual parts of the Holy Scriptures are written in it, as is not hidden from the literate. On the other hand, its benefit is known by the fact that many teachers, skilled in divine and human science, have written with it materials of various sorts, belonging to theoretical and practical theology, philosophy, physics, the ecclesial and civic histories, religious [*tawditanaye*] teachings and polemics, and the interpretation of texts, and the teachings of the fear of God, and [there are] also the poems of every sort found in it.
>
> Therefore, let the sons of our nation [*umthan*], especially the ecclesiastics, be warned lest they ignore the study of this language of the Lord, which is valuable, beneficial, and necessary for them, that they may be able to fulfill easily the prayers of the liturgy and the rest of the ecclesial services as is fitting and right for the majesty of our God, worthy of worship, to whom be glory and honor forever and ever. Amen.[95]

Although there were hints at such a linkage in the past, Maqdisi's emphasis on Aramaic as the language of Jesus is an important new step in the Syrian relationship to the language: language is now essential to a nation (*umtha*), and in this case it is sacralized by its role in the history of the church.

That Aramaic was the language of Jesus is mentioned by the American missionaries as well, and it seems to have become common knowledge.[96] In fact, in 1897, the same year so many articles on language appeared in *Rays of Light*, the periodical had two articles on the life of Christ and one on "Which Language Christ Spoke."[97] The latter also describes the work of Agnes Smith-Lewis (1843–1926), who, with her twin sister, Margaret Dunlop Gibson (1843–1920), became famous in the late nineteenth century for traveling in 1892 to Saint Catherine's Monastery in Sinai and "discovering" the oldest Syriac manuscript of the Gospels.[98] Nineteenth-century scholarship on the life of

Jesus has been linked to the emergence of national identities in Europe, and this is no less the case here: an interest in the language of Jesus correlates to the emergence of a national discourse on language among the Syrians.[99] Increasing emphasis on Aramaic as the language of Jesus and the introduction of this point of information into discussions of language reform were part of the sacralization of emergent national identity. That Jesus spoke the Syrians' language in particular served as an argument for the sacrality of their nation.

An important characteristic of the Catholic circles in Urmia was the degree to which they promoted biblical learning and East Syrian church history in the Lazarist periodical *Voice of Truth*. In its second year of publication (June 1898–May 1899), the paper focused on complex issues in the history of the text of the Old Testament / Hebrew Bible. There were articles on Hebrew, its writing system, the *targumim* (Jewish Aramaic translations of Scripture), the Septuagint and later Greek versions, Syriac translations, the Vulgate, and the various other translations and modern editions of the text. The article on the "Chaldean" language—that is, Aramaic—begins by discussing its relevance to the biblical text, but then devotes space to the debate about whether Hebrew or Aramaic was the first language before the multiplication of languages at Babel.[100] The article cites and quotes several Classical Syriac authors and ultimately supports the position that God spoke Aramaic with Adam and Eve in the Garden.

The Syria/Assyria Switch and the Retrieval of the Ancient Orient

By the end of the 1890s, Syrian authors were making explicit links between themselves and the ancient Assyrians. This connection to ancient Assyria was made linguistically possible by the reception of European scholarly speculation about the relationship between the names *Assyria* and *Syria*. In 1895 an article appeared in *Rays of Light* entitled "The Syrian Language," which, as its preface notes, was translated from Rubens Duval's *Traité de grammaire syriaque* (Paris, 1881). It begins:

> The word "Suryaya" comes from the ancient language of the Greeks. It was taken from the name of the land, Syria, which comes from Assyria (that is, Ator). This name was assigned to refer to the western part of the empire of the Assyrians [*atoraye*]. Within the Old Testament this land is called Aram. This name also embraces the inhabitants of Mesopotamia, those who spoke the same language and were worshippers of idols, like the Arameans. So Jews of Palestine applied the name "Aramean" to pagan nations [*melate*]. In this way this name was transferred to Syria.[101]

This paraphrase from Duval expresses an idea that was soon taken up by local Syrian writers. Mirza Mesroph Khan Karam (1862–1943), who was associated with the American mission, made this connection based upon supposed sound shifts in an 1897 article in *Rays of Light*: "The Kingdom of the <u>Assyrians</u> or the <u>(As)Syrians</u> according to the Biblical History and the Antiquities of Nineveh [*malkuta d-'atoraye yan d-(')suraye men haqiyat qaddišta w-'antike d-ninwe*]."[102] Further mission publications made it easier to establish this connection: for example, in 1904 the Anglican mission published a Neo-Aramaic translation of the *Histories* of Herodotus, who also draws a link between Syrians and Assyrians.[103]

The shift between "Assyrian" and "Syrian" contributed to a new interest in the culture and history of the ancient Assyrians. Deacon Augustine Thomas, a Chaldean from Khosrawa (Khosrawabad), a village on the Urmia plain, wrote a series of articles for *Voice of Truth* in 1898–1900 addressing ancient Near Eastern archaeology and mythology.[104] Thomas begins with a description of the tale of Shamiram, or Semiramis, her more widely known Greek name, the wife of Ninos, the mythical founder of Nineveh. His account is at times taken verbatim from the first-century-BCE Classical Greek author Diodorus Siculus ("of Sicily"). There are also articles on ancient Near Eastern kings, on the Assyrians and the Babylonians, and finally on the discovery of Babylon.[105] The borrowing of the story of Semiramis from Diodorus Siculus, as in the general use of biblical, classical, and archeological learning in these articles, is an example of the distant mediation of ancient Near Eastern sources through the Western missions. Diodorus's *Bibliotheca historica* is a world history that includes the mythical tales of various non-Greek peoples. The story of Semiramis and her husband, Ninos, the eponymous founder of Nineveh, has an originally Eastern provenance, but the remaining sources for this are thin. More significantly, Semiramis was a character in classical and later medieval European literature, and she became especially popular in later European arts, where she was a common heroine of opera, being the focus of a number of pieces in the early nineteenth century, culminating in Rossini's *Semiramide* in 1823.[106] Edgar Degas incorporated recent archaeological knowledge into his *Semiramis Constructing a City* (ca. 1860–62), a painting possibly influenced by Rossini's opera.[107] At the turn of the twentieth century, Semiramis continued to be the topic of poems and plays as well. The name *Shamiram* seems to be an attempt to re-Semiticize the Greek name. For the actual person, disputed among Assyriologists to be the historical figure behind the various Greek fables, is the ninth-century BCE Assyrian woman Sammuramat.

As was typical of the nineteenth century, an interest in language and names was not simply a linguistic curiosity: language, history, and nationality were closely linked realms of knowledge, three points in the triangle of the nationalist intellectual imagination. Therefore, the history of language was implicitly the history of a nation. This tripartite connection is apparent in "The Preservation of the Syrian Nation and Its Language," Mirza Mesroph's article in *Voice of Truth* in 1898, which I quoted in the introduction.[108] In this article praising the mission papers for the benefits they have conferred on the Syrian language, Mesroph demands that readers understand the ancient Near Eastern as well as ecclesial history of the Syrians, even asking that they visit the ruins of Nineveh.

The works of Thomas Audo, Chaldean archbishop of Urmia, expand upon the Syrians' possible descent from ancient Near Eastern predecessors. Audo was born in Alqosh to a distinguished Chaldean family.[109] His uncle, the patriarch Joseph Audo, took him to Rome to study at the Propaganda. He was eventually ordained archbishop of Urmia in 1892, an office he held until he was killed during the assault on the city in 1918. In 1895 he published a Neo-Aramaic translation of *Kalila wa-Dimna*, an influential piece of medieval Arabic prose, also extant in Syriac, based originally on the *Panchatantra*, a much earlier Sanskrit collection of animal fables. The Syriac version had been edited and published by the prolific British orientalist William Wright (1830–89) in 1884. Audo's work on this translation indicates his Catholic humanist training and his own interest in creating a Neo-Aramaic literary education.

Audo's national interests are apparent in his most important work, *The Treasury of the Syrian Language* (*Simtha d-lešana suryaya*) (Mosul, 1897–1901), a Classical Syriac dictionary that remains useful for scholars today. In the preface Audo describes the history of the Syrian language and people, while giving them pride of place as the inventors of writing.

> That one who discovered the art of writing in the world rendered unto the human race [*gensa*] a great favor on account of which he is worthy of continual praise and unceasing thanks. In spite of this, behold, hidden is the name of the one who brought forth this art of much value and first introduced it into the world. Nor is it known at what time this was, but certainly it is known which nation [*umtha*] before all first began to write and which race [*šarbtha*] taught writing to the rest of the nations. We shall say then that the Syrian nation has this cause for pride over all the previously known nations [*'amme*].[110]

According to Audo, all European writing comes from the Romans, who learned to write from the Greeks, who, in turn, however cultured they were, learned to write from the Syrians through the Phoenicians. Audo describes the Greek mythological figure Cadmus, who according to tradition was the Phoenician who introduced the alphabet to the Greeks (e.g., Herodotus, *Histories*, 5.58). However, the Phoenicians learned the alphabet from "the Eastern Syrians such as the Babylonians and Assyrians," who also transmitted it to the "Hebrews and Jews." Audo then describes the proliferation of scripts and the development of Syriac printing in the West and among the missions. After addressing the complex development of the Syriac vocalization system, he describes the loss of the name *Aramaic*, which was covered up by the name *Syrian*.

> It is not hidden from the knowledgeable that the Syrian language was once the language of a great and strong people [*'amma*], who abided in a great portion of the lands of the East, that is, Syria, Mesopotamia, Assyria, the land of Shinar, and the surrounding area. All of these lands, as it is revealed by the books of the Old Testament, were called by the Jews Aram. Because Aram the son of Shem ruled over them and settled his descendants there, therefore the Syrian language is only called Aramaic in the Old Testament, and this is its true and earlier name, as it seems to us.[111]

The name *Syrian*, he explains, derives from Greek and Latin usage, and it was employed for Aramaic because of the early spread of Christianity in that part of "Beth Aram" called "Syria."

> After the Aramaic race [*šarbtha*] clung as a group to Christ before all and embraced his teaching then the name "Aramaic" was concealed from it little by little. The entire nation in all its tribes and shoots was called "Syrian" and its language was named "Syrian" until today.

The conversion to Christianity also led to the loss of indigenous literature, and therefore, according to Audo, the Syrians must learn about their pre-Christian past, including "their ancestors, their kings, and their habits," from other nations.[112]

> However, if [the nation] wants to understand these things, it needs to search closely the works of foreigners, especially the Jews and the Greeks. If not for the works of these [peoples], we would not know anything of the conditions of the earlier Aramaeans and the lands in which they resided until the revelation of Christ.

Audo thus establishes a legitimation for the reception of orientalist art, ideas, and historiography. The Aramaic past must be retrieved from others. In the rest of this introduction, he addresses the Eastern and Western dialects; different periods in the language's history, including first-century Palestine and the language spoken by Jesus, Mary, and the Apostles; the decline after the

"Syrian nation [*umtha*]" became subject to Muslims; a number of technical linguistic issues; and his sources. Regarding foreignisms, he demands of
the reader: "Let your speech be clear, pure, and polished [*šaphya w-dakhya
wa-mriqa*],"[113] the same phrase Baba of Kosi used in Neo-Aramaic in *Rays of
Light* in 1898 for the result of the missionary reforms in orthography (*ṣepye
dekye mriqe*).[114] Intriguingly, the same terms are used in the Classical Syriac
tradition to describe the qualities of the soul in its ideal state. Traditional
devotional characteristics of the soul, such as that it be pure, have been transmitted to the language of the nation.

In 1905 Audo published a grammar of Neo-Aramaic (Urmia, 1905; 2nd
ed. 1911), in which he places the decline of the Aramaic dialects and their corruption with foreign words after the Muslim conquest, thus synchronizing
the loss of political autonomy with the corruption of the language.[115] In "The
Remnant of the Chaldean Nation," an essay in his *Selected Readings* (1906), he
describes the ancient Chaldean, Babylonian, and Assyrian kingdoms and how
they were swallowed up by other nations.[116] The only *remnant*, a term con-
noting the biblical narrative of Israel's exile and redemption, consists of the
East Syrian "nation" (*melat*) and the Kurds in the mountains, who, although
Persianized, maintain "the nature, blood, and character of the Assyrians."[117]
He describes the elevated culture of the Assyrians, and then continues: "We
too, the East Syrians, descend from the aforementioned Assyrians, we are
children of the Assyrians or Ashur son of Shem and on account of this we
are also Semites. We have preserved until today the language of our ancestors
with of course some changes which have entered it."[118] He next takes up the
by then common argument that the loss of the initial vowel and letter *aleph*
in "Assyrian" resulted in the name "Syrian." "If we are Assyrians [*atoraye*] by
nature, why are we called and call ourselves Syrians? Some learned men of
Europe think that Syria comes from Assyria [*ator*] or Ashur."[119] Finally, he
notes that some scholars think the name *Syrian* was only taken up when the
East Syrians became Christians. The first Christians, converted by apostles
from Palestine, which is in Syria, changed their name to "Syrian" because they
loved their "religion" (*todita*) so much.

In an early contribution to the *Star*, Audo claims that the Syrian "nation"
(*melat*) was the first to become Christian, after which it sent apostles across
the globe.[120] Everywhere Europeans have conquered with their weapons and
wealth, the Syrians, he adds, preceded them with the cross, their faith, and the
holiness of their way of life. Echoing a Protestant theme, the nation, according
to Audo, lost its way, and therefore God sent missionaries to help reform it.
This has been successful, and "the nation in general advanced in education
and learning and in temporal condition," but its progress has been hindered

"because strength is in unity." Audo compares the nation to a cluster of grapes and laments its divisions: the "common good" (*ṭota gowanayta*) should trump the "particular" (*dilanayta*). Referring to the paper's motto, he suggests that with the *Star*, "the nation is beginning again, although very small and little, to appear in the firmament." He ends with the Pauline motif of the new man and old, the Adam we are to take off and the Christ we are to put on (Rom 6:6, Eph 4:22–24, Col 3:9–10). Thus he employs the clothing metaphor that is so common in Classical Syriac literature, although using it to describe a new form of community within the nation as opposed to individual Christian redemption or Christ's Incarnation.

Oriental Middlemen

The ancient Orient was not only of growing bookish interest to East Syrians. By the end of the nineteenth century, some, especially those who went through the American mission schools, often traveled in England and the United States, presenting themselves as authentic "orientals" and giving lectures on "oriental" themes. Many of these Syrians who traveled abroad, particularly to the United States, became important intermediaries in the West for the representation of "Persia" and the "Orient." Exemplary of this was Abraham Yohannan (1853–1925), who attended and taught at the Urmia College and eventually traveled to New York, became an Episcopalian, and did his doctoral studies at Columbia under R. J. H. Gottheil (1862–1936), the orientalist and Zionist leader, and A. V. Williams Jackson (1862–1937), the well-known scholar of pre-Islamic Iran. While he served at Columbia as an instructor in oriental languages, his letters from New York were published in *Rays of Light*, and through him historical lectures by Jackson were translated and published, along with descriptions of his work, in 1907.[121] His reputation in Iran was such that a personal bio piece on him was written in the *Star* in 1911.[122] Whereas Yohannan served as a cultural intermediary at the height of the American academy, his position at Columbia was precarious, thus demonstrating the difficulty Syrians had passing in white society. Despite Jackson's continued support for Yohannan, the president of the university was opposed to his receiving a full position, and Yohannan himself had to solicit his own salary from outside benefactors.[123]

An early instance of this performance of "oriental" expertise by those self-consciously acting as "orientals" can be seen in Jacob and Moressa Yauvre's tour of England in 1879–81, during which they made public appearances at church and missionary institutions. Jacob would often speak in his native language while Moressa translated for him. Their appearance in their native clothing was so striking to audiences that when they visited a home for the blind, Jacob described his appearance to those who were unable to see them and allowed them to feel the shape of his hat.[124] As with their appearance, so also the very sound of their language: Jacob was asked to pray in Aramaic in public assembly.[125] One of their hosts in Manchester requested from Jacob: "Say in your own language that work of the Lord's: 'I am the light of the world,' as well as other words of the Lord."

> When I had spoken he would say, "I feel that I am hearing my savior speak, for He spoke in that language." He introduced us at a meeting by saying, "If you wish to see Isaac and Rebecca, here they are." Then he added that we had received Christianity when their ancestors were savages, and had kept our faith under all manner of persecution.[126]

This orientalizing, in which Jacob and Moressa willingly participated, was not uncommon when East Syrians traveled, and later some would openly advertise their exoticism while abroad.

Such self-representations should be understood not only within the context of the general orientalist culture of the United States and Europe in the late nineteenth century, but also next to the romantic reception of the "Nestorians" in the latter half of the century as wild mountain Christians, such as in works of fiction like Annie Webb's *Julamerk: A Tale of the Nestorians* (1849), based upon Asahel Grant's *The Nestorians; or, The Lost Tribes*.[127] Westerners wrote numerous memoirs and travelogues about the region by the turn of the twentieth century, and we know that some of these works were read by Syrians themselves. For example, in 1899 Isaac Malek Yonan returned from the United States with copies of George Hughes Hepworth's *Through Armenia on Horseback* (1898) and Samuel G. Wilson's *Persian Life and Customs, with Scenes and Incidents of Residence and Travel in the Land of the Lion and the Sun* (1895; 2nd ed. 1896).[128] By the 1890s some Syrian travelers composed books on the Orient, usually during their stays in the United States, and these works shed further light on the process of auto-orientalizing that contributed to the development of Assyrian nationalism.

In his book *Modern Persia* (1898), Moshe G. Daniel, who graduated from the college in Urmia in 1882 and then, after working at the mission for several years, attended McCormick Seminary in Chicago, provides a survey of the geography and cultural life of Iran. Daniel rejects the title *Nestorian* and identifies the Syrians as originally *Assyrians*: "The true origin of the Nestorians was in the old Assyrian nation. The Assyrians were descendents of Arphaxad, the son of Shem."[129] He continues, "They originally dwelt in or near the cradle of mankind, in eastern Mesopotamia, Assyria and Syria. At times their empire extended nearly to Babylon and Nineveh, and the great empire of Assyria was established."[130] He further claims that "Assyrian" was the first language.[131] Daniel's description of the Schools of Edessa and Nisibis reflects the missionaries' historiography of these institutions, and he even offers to sell manuscripts to any reader who is interested, a common practice of Syrians in the West.[132] When he describes the missionary past of the "Assyrians," telling of how they traveled in sandals with staffs spreading Christianity across Central Asia and even Africa, he is simply exaggerating the tales told to the Syrians by the American missionaries.[133]

Such ethnographic works were often composed by colorful characters themselves, such as Isaac Adams (1872–1942), who wrote two works on Persia (1898, 1900), both of which include self-aggrandizing personal memoirs. Later, in 1910, after participating in a prior settlement in Canada, he led a group of Syrian immigrants to Turlock, California, where he worked as a real estate broker for immigrants, and in 1924 founded the nondenominational Assyrian Evangelical Church. This is someone who benefited from his place betwixt and between, and part of this intermediary status was his role as a mediator of the Orient. This role is best exemplified in a photograph printed in both of his books: it shows him and his three brothers, each dressed in a different ethnic garb, Adams in "high-class costume" and his brothers respectively as a "Mohammadan priest," a Kurd, and a "common" Persian. Joseph Khenanisho', the son of Khenanisho' Moratkhan, possibly a third-generation associate of the American mission, includes two portraits of himself with his family in his popular ethnographic survey, which contains stories from ancient Persian history, primarily depending on Herodotus, as well as romantic Persian tales: one portrait in formal Western attire, the other in "Persian costume."[134] This dual portraiture conveying the variability of the oriental had precedents: Hormuzd Rassam had dual occidental/oriental portraits painted of himself in 1851.[135] Such an ability to take on and off cultural appearance along with clothing suggests a self-consciousness about the role these oriental middlemen played as intermediaries between oriental and white culture.

Language and History

Reform of the national language was a common theme in the *Star*, as it had been in *Rays of Light* in the 1890s. Language reform was treated as a fundamental part of national reform, and connections were commonly drawn between language and nationality, as when a 1907 article includes a false etymology for the word *melat* ("nation"): "The term 'nation' [*melat*] is without a doubt from 'word' [*meltha*], that is, 'word' [*hemezman*, the Neo-Aramaic equivalent to the Classical Syriac, *meltha*], and its meaning is a community which has one speech or common language for all. By this meaning the Syrian or Chaldean people, which are today in the East, are a nation."[136]

A 1909 article on "how to teach our own language" was written "because we are awakening to the deficiency of the spoken tongue in the schools."[137] Another article begins by claiming, "The expression 'unity' [*huyyada*] is sweet to the palate of the members of the Adamic race."[138] People have a basic tendency "to bring all divisions and groups under the rules of unification [*methaydanuta*]," and "that period of the height of progress was when they were subject to unity [*hdayuta*]. The perfection and harmony [*harmoniya*] of a nation's language are significant of its culture [*marduta*]." Other nations have found such a unity in their print orthography, and the Syrians must do the same. The author calls for an "assembly of learned men and grammarians from all of the (mission) presses" to come together and agree upon shared rules for the language. The Committee on Spelling (*Motwa d-huggaya*) started its work not much later.[139] A 1913 article on the failure of Syrians to study their own language declares, "If we make the claim that we are a nation, we must not be ashamed of our mother tongue!"[140]

Along with the reform of the national language, the *Star* demanded a new national historiography as well as national poetry. In an enthusiastic letter about the new publication, Mirza Mesroph Khan Karam describes the *Star* as "an 'only begotten' [*ihidaya*] of literate culture [*seprayuta*] in the holy tongue of our Syrian mother."[141] In this paper "a spirit of love for the nation will be awakened [*mur'ešta*] in all of the Syrians." He rejects confessional titles for the Syrians and then claims: "All of us Syrians are the sons of one nation. Death is necessary for that Syrian who denies his Syrian mother." He then suggests three things the paper must do to fulfill its goal: (1) avoid "religious" (*mazhabaye*) disputes and teach that all Syrians are Christian and each is "free" (*azad*) to act according to his own conscience; (2) devote space to the history of "our ancestors," which will be pleasing "to every single Syrian who has sympathy [*sumpatiya*] with his Syrian mother"; and (3) include "national-ist" (*umtanaye*) poems written "to awaken [*l-mar'uše*] the enthusiasm of every member of the nation [*bar umta*], just as all educated nations [*melate mare marduta*] do."[142]

National historiography required the identification of the true nature or origin of the nation, which remained a contested issue (as it is even today) during all the years of the *Star*'s publication. Some contributors supported what would become the Assyrian thesis, whereas others tried to maintain an ecclesial basis for the history of the nation (*melat*). For example, the editors

seem to reply to Mesroph's call for historical writing when, after acknowledging the need for a "history of the Syrian nation," they claim: "The history of
our nation is ecclesial," not a history of kings and locations.[143] "Rather, it is a
history of evangelism in the eastern region where the Syrians arrived." The
possibility of national history based upon the history of the ancient Near East
is impossible: "We will not be able to call the history of the Assyrians, Babylonians, and Chaldeans the history of our nation [melat] because although
without a doubt we are descended from these kingdoms there is nevertheless
no path remaining by which we may go and arrive at such and such a generation and recount that we are descended from there." The Syrians derive their
origin from the kingdoms of Nebuchadnezzar and Belshazzar, but over the
centuries the various nations have intermingled. What remains of their lost
history, particularly in the libraries of Europe, is "clerical and fragmented,
not national [umtanayta] and political." The author, presumably the paper's
editor, John Mushe, suggests that it is better to write about renowned Syrian
authors. After this, a long article, "History of the Nation [melat]," provides
an account of the life of the East Syrian patriarch Timothy I (d. 823), thereby
implying the earlier meaning of "melat" as church community, although in
this case that community included members of the "Nestorian" and various
mission churches.[144] The idea of church community had been infected by the
notion of nationality.

Such church historical approaches were maintained despite the rising
popularity of the Assyrian thesis. A 1907 article, which describes the Anglican
mission's recent publication of a large Neo-Aramaic history of the Church of
the East, expresses the desire to "awaken the Syrians zealous and full of love
for the nation [melat] and for learning to a book about their nation."[145] In 1910,
in response to an exhibit at the Metropolitan Museum of Art in New York, the
Star ran a long article on the Nestorian Stele from Xi'an.[146] The monument, it
argues, is evidence for how widely missionaries from the Syrian nation traveled in the past. (The stele later remained an object of interest to Assyrian
nationalists: Benjamin Arsanis published a short work on it in 1951.)[147]

Despite resistance from some at the newspaper, the ancient Near East continued to receive attention. In 1908 George David Malik published an article
about two books he had been working on for seven years.[148] One was a history of Iran and the other a history of the Syrian "nation" (umta). The latter
treated the nation's chronology, language, the "homeland" (bet ma'mra) of the
Syrians, the Assyrian and Babylonian kingdom, the reception of Christianity,
church history, missions to other nations, martyrs, "the whole ecclesial and
national system . . . from the Flood to Christ and from Christ to the present."
Malik laments the decline of the Syrian nation since the fourteenth century,

and declares his motive for writing to be his love for it: "Now let it be known to my beloved brothers, sons of our nation (*bnay umtan*), that by the command of no man at all nor as a hireling, but on my own I awakened to this need and deficiency we suffer in" historiography. Malik's work, and that of his son, David, were transitional and representative of what was to come, and are therefore addressed further in the epilogue.

Freydun Abraham (1891–1926), or as he is more commonly known, Freydun Atoraya ("the Assyrian"), was an important proponent of the Assyrian thesis, and remains today a romantic figure lionized by some Assyrians as a national hero and martyr. Atoraya was born in an Urmia village but grew up in Tbilisi. He studied medicine in Harput (near modern Elazığ), a center of Armenian and Syrian Orthodox (West Syrian) nationalist sentiment until the violent destruction of the communities there in 1915, the same year he graduated.

In Harput he would have known Ashur (Abraham) Yusuf (1858–1915), who, after receiving a mission education at Aintab (Gaziantep), served as professor at Euphrates College in Harput until his murder during the genocide.[149] He was a Protestant of West Syrian background. His *Guide to the Assyrians* (*Muršid-i Asuriyun*), a periodical in Syro-Ottoman (Ottoman in Syriac script), promoted ancient Assyrian origins for Syrian Christians.[150] However, members of the Church of the East do not seem to have had subscriptions to it, nor did it make calls for unity among the various Syrian peoples.[151] In this period West Syrians like Yusuf and Naum Faiq (Palak) (1868–1930), who worked in Diyarbakır but emigrated to the United States in 1912, promoted the idea of Assyrian descent, but this was not part of a nationalism outside the bounds of liberal Ottomanism, nor was such a shared Assyrian descent used as an argument for working with other Syriac Christians.[152] The connection was perhaps drawn because in a heavily Armenian context, *Asori*, the Armenian term for "Syrian," evoked the name of the ancient "Assyrians."[153] Benjamin Trigona-Harany, one of the only scholars to actually examine the Syro-Ottoman sources, suggests that "although they both described the origins of the Süryânî [Syrian Orthodox] to be Assyrian, there is no indication that, during the period in question, either man could be considered an Assyrian nationalist."[154] Until 1914 their hopes remained with the late Ottoman Committee of Union and Progress (CUP), as were the hopes of many Armenian nationalists.

Atoraya perhaps also studied in Russia. In 1917 he, along with Benjamin Arsanis and Baba Bet Parhad, founded the Assyrian Socialist Party, the first Assyrian political party. He was arrested by Soviet authorities in 1924 because of his nationalist organizing and poisoned in prison in 1926. The song he wrote, "Oh Eagle of Tkhuma," which has become a national anthem of sorts for many Assyrians, describes the flight of an eagle over the territories of "ancient Assyria." Its focus is at first on the mountains, which the missionaries had already long romanticized, and later the poet asks the eagle to "visit the bold, warlike man who has sacrificed his life" for Assyria.[155] Atoraya's self-understanding as a revolutionary is apparent in an extant portrait photograph: unlike the tribesmen of the mountains he heralded in song, he was a slender man with round wire-frame glasses, leaning his head forward with his right fist on his temple in the typical pose of a "serious" thinker and revolutionary.

At just twenty years old, Freydun Atoraya wrote an assertive piece for the April 24, 1911, issue of the *Star*: "Who Are the Syrians? How Is Our Nation to Be Raised Up?"[156]

> In the past years many Syrians have spoken about the nation [*umta*] and the weakening of tribalism. Sometimes in the pages of *The Star* and other papers the name of our ancestors the Assyrians has been recalled. . . . However, until now in almost no book at all of the Syrians, except for the *Selected Readings* of the honorable Mar Thomas Audo and in the pages of *Voice of Truth*, is it recalled who the Syrians are and from where they have come.
>
> The national sentiment [*umtanayuta*] of a nation [*melat*] increases and makes progress when the youth knows the history of his nation [*umteh*] and remembers the deeds of his forefathers or also is awake and sees the indignities suffered due to other nations. There are two primary goals in projects of awakening: one is to learn the history of our nation [*umtan*] and the other is to see the indignities of our nation. The second goal is being fulfilled little by little, but the first is rarely remembered in our writing or in our newspapers. Therefore, before we can be nationalists [*umtanaye*] that more necessary task for us is that we learn the history of our Syrian—Assyrian—nation.
>
> Now let us return to the purpose of our speech and tell in brief who we are:
>
> The Syrians are the children of Ashur or Ator, the second son of Shem, who about 8000 years before Christ came to the upper portion of Mesopotamia and near the Tigris river founded for himself a city, which he called Ashur. That country which was conquered by him he called by his own name Assyria [*atoriya*], his first god he called Ashur, and so all of his tribe was also called by this same name "Assyrian" [*atoraya*].

Over several centuries the power of this tribe expanded into the regions once ruled by Chaldeans and Babylonians until the time of Tiglatpileser I, the first king of the Assyrians. Then various kings such as Sargon, Sennacherib, and Ashurbanipal ruled until the fall of Nineveh in the late seventh century BCE. After this the "name of the Assyrians" was forgotten, and the people were scattered and made subject to other peoples. Only a remnant remained that did not intermingle with other nations. "This small portion of our Assyrian nation [*umta*]" became Christian and suffered persecution but maintained their national identity and now live in Urmia and in the mountains of Hakkari. "First of all, a great part of European scholars and also Mar Thomas Audo think that from our name 'Assyrian' [*atoraya*] the first *aleph* has been lost and the *tau* has been softened to a *samket*, as in the mountains they say *alahusa* instead of *alahuta* ["divinity"]." The second reason for this name change is that the Assyrians, when they converted to Christianity, out of shame did not want to be called by the name of their ancestors who were not Christian. Other evidence he then provides is the etymological connections between Aramaic and Assyrian names and then the fact that Armenians and Persians call the Syrians "Asori." He concludes with the suggestion that once the Syrians know the history of their own people, "national sentiment [*umtanayuta*] will enter our heart on its own."

This epic national myth, the synthesis and extrapolation of what was only hinted at before, was not immediately accepted. It does not appear often in the *Star*. Freydun Atoraya is important not only because he is an early advocate of Assyrianism but also because of the new tone and significance he brought to such claims. Speculation about ancient Near Eastern origins had gone on for over a decade. However, this tended to be in learned discussions, and a nationalist logic had not been applied to such discussions. Esoteric discussion about the pedigree of the Syrians, especially in Catholic publications, was different from what Atoraya propounded. He combined this speculation with the nationalist politics of the *Star* and the American mission community, and this resulted in a powerful political myth, one appropriate to the new political party he would help establish.

Literature of the (As)Syrians

The national reform of language and the demand for an authentic history of the nation went hand in hand with calls for a national literature. By the late nineteenth century, European scholars were writing histories of Syriac literature, often heavily dependent upon Assemani's eighteenth-century work of patristic scholarship. The Anglican mission and the Dominican mission in Mosul produced large annotated surveys of Classical Syriac literature in 1898 and 1901–2, respectively.[157] The former relied on local Urmia resources, including Thomas Audo's library and the archive at the American mission.[158]

The preface of the latter states that the Chaldean patriarch knows "the blessing of how at this time the old age of our Aramaic language is, behold, becoming young, and its dead state has begun to be resurrected through the care of locals and foreigners."[159] It continues:

> For in every place, behold, its difficulties are carefully investigated and its praiseworthy gems are examined by everyone because European teachers ardently desire its antiquities like those thirsting for a drink of cold water, and Aramaic students after casting afar their prior negligence investigate with care its buried treasures.

We are told of the patriarch's "great love for this language" and "attested concern for the education [mardutha] of our nation [umthan] in all types of learning."[160] Echoing Baba of Kosi and Thomas Audo, the preface holds that a "pure," "polished" form of Aramaic was preserved in Urfa (ancient Edessa) until the time of Christianization, when neglect of pagan works led to the disappearance of all pre-Christian literature. This also explains, we are told, the generally religious nature of Aramaic literature. The editor of the collection, Jacques Eugène (Ya'kob Awgen) Manna (1867–1928), thanks the Dominicans who are engaged in works "for the progress [šuwšaṭa] of learning and the good of the eastern nations [emwatha]."[161] Citing the great French orientalist Ernest Renan (1823–92), he claims, "All the writers of the first generations of Christianity who became famous among the Syrians were Chaldean, that is, from Babylon, Assyria, and Mesopotamia."[162]

Such anthologies of Classical Syriac authors, though produced in part with a Catholic and Anglo-Catholic concern for patristic authorities, represent a growing humanism among the Syrians, a humanism that understood the greatness of a nation to be represented by its literature. Such a concern for Syriac literature is exemplified in the massive corpus of texts edited by the Chaldean Paul Bedjan, who was discussed in the preceding chapter, including his seven-volume *Acta Sanctorum et Martyrum* (1890–97) and his five-volume collected works of the West Syrian poet Jacob of Sarug (1905–10). Although he operated within a Catholic milieu, his work, especially his focus on West Syrian texts and authors, attests to the further development of an ecumenical field of Syriac literature, as do the contemporary anthologies mentioned above. In his Neo-Aramaic *Vies des saints* (1912), he even claims that he wrote about the lives of the "Chaldean and Persian martyrs . . . that everybody might know these Fathers of ours as well as the glory of our nation [melatan]."[163]

The *Star* maintains an interest in literature as part of humane edification as well as national culture. Corresponding with both of these is the ongoing focus on education (*marduta*), which according to one article is defined by the cultivation of language, knowledge ('ilm), imagination, and character.[164]

Humane studies included literature beyond the Aramaic corpus, such as the
Persian poet Omar Khayyam, who was extremely popular in English at the
time.[165] Abraham Morhatch wrote on modern Persian literature for the *Star*,
and Mirza Mesroph, who called early on for the publishing of national poetry,
wrote about and also translated the Persian poet Hafez.[166] Linking the reform
of the nation to what we might call literary patriarchy, the *Star* even printed
translations of Mark Twain's "Woman, God Bless Her" and Washington Ir-
ving's "The Wife."[167] In the "Syrianism" (*Suryayuta*) section of the *Star*, which
began to appear in 1914, Freydun Atoraya published a letter addressed to
the "Sons of Assyria" on the absence of the study of literature at the mission
schools, and a long poem by him, "The Prayer of the Nation," appeared in the
same section in 1917.[168] Within this context in which demands for a national
literature were being made, there developed an interest in theater.[169] Plays
by standard Western playwrights such as Shakespeare and Molière were performed, but also original pieces were produced in which the basic concerns
of the community were addressed, such as their relationship to missionaries
and the Orthodox Church, the need to work and avoid the habit of drinking,
and the defense of the community against Kurdish raids.

In 1910 Syrian youth in Tbilisi "awakened to a national need and decided
to work with all their power to found a society by the name of the Dramatic
Society [*Šotaputa dramaṭiqayta*] of Assyrians in Tbilisi."[170] Freydun Atoraya
wrote a play, *Grief*, which was performed on May 2, 1911. A strong advocate of
national literature, within a few years he was leading the Dramatic Society.[171]
In 1914 the troupe performed a production of the play *Shamiram*, which included the characters Sargon, Sennacherib, Nimrod, and Ninos, for an audience consisting of members of the different Syrian *melats* in Delgosha, the
new higher-end Syrian neighborhood of Urmia.[172] All the proceeds went to
the printing board of the *Star*. The play, which had martial themes, excited
the crowd: "Syrian blood was boiling and the youth shouted, 'Long live Syrianism [*suryayuta*]!'" A few weeks later the troupe performed in Gulpashan
and Geogtapa.[173] Drama was especially popular among nationalist thinkers.
After fitting literature into the broader category of art or craft, the 1914 article,
"What Is Literature?" describes the different parts of literature, putting drama
in the "highest class of all human writings."[174] The same article mentions a
production of *The Merchant of Venice* put on by the printing board of the *Star*.

The founding of the Society of Syrian Literary Culture was announced in
the *Star* on May 10, 1912.[175] The society (*dasta*) had precedents, such as the
Society for the Literature of the English Language, which was a circle of cosmopolitans rather than literati. In January 1907 this society met at Yonan Abraham's home, where Dr. Agajan Sargis gave a lecture on dentistry and Freder-

ick Coan addressed Iran's contemporary needs.[176] The purpose of the Society of Syrian Literary Culture was "to increase enthusiasm for the nation and to expand authorship in the spoken language." The director of the organization, which met weekly to discuss these issues, was Benjamin Arsanis (1884–1957) of Digala.[177] Arsanis had studied at the newly established Orthodox school in Urmia and then went to Russia, where he studied history. He was of the same family as Mirza Joseph Khan Arsanis, who helped Mar Yonan in gathering signatures for the petition to the Orthodox in 1897.[178] Upon his return to Urmia, he taught again at his alma mater until the Orthodox mission was closed in 1918. Arsanis supported early efforts to develop Syrian printing houses, founding a newspaper, *Thoughts of Rising* (*Ḥuššawe d-denḥa*), in 1913.[179]

In 1912 the Society of Syrian Literary Culture published its bylaws at the American mission press.[180] These bylaws address the structure of the society (*šotaputa*) or group (*dasta*) and the payment of dues. Both sexes were welcome to join, and members (*haddame*) were free (*azad*) to leave when they liked. Benjamin Arsanis, who would within only a few years embrace the ethnonym *Assyrian* in lieu of *Syrian*, composed this document, the prologue of which explains the civilizational need for literate culture, its benefits, and the current condition of the Syrians without it. The term Arsanis uses, *saprayuta*, is cognate with *seprayuta*, the term translated as "literature" above, but it is an abstract noun built upon an agentive form—a *sapra*, traditionally a "scribe" or "learned, bookish person"—but here Arsanis's use of *saprayuta* suggests something rather like "literary culture," which is how I translate the term.

> After many generations passed and many great changes took place in nature and in human life, many nations [*melate*] then arose and with the weapons of their mind fought with all the various natural and human injustices and conquered all ignorant enemies, both the outer and inner ones, and overthrew those mighty walls of solid fortifications and prisons, which have surrounded and limited their minds and imaginations with so much severity. By the force of their strong hands they cut the chains from their arms and cast the fetters of ignorance from their feet and demonstrated the great and wondrous signs of the mind. Then they resembled complete [*kamil*, or "adult"] human beings. Now the descendants of those nations have chosen the sweet national [*umtanaye*] fruits and they are given rest under the cool and pleasant shadows of the trees which their fathers planted. May there be honor and glory to their name, because they demonstrated to humanity by their example and by their works the perfect [*kamil*] paths of the mind and ethical freedom.

Arsanis's description of human mental emancipation with its metaphors of masculine violence expresses notions of Enlightenment and national prosperity not uncommon in the early twentieth century. He then turns to the fallen state of the Syrian nation, even referencing the "Thieves of the Cross," that group of religious hucksters that had long been a concern to the missionaries and more recently an embarrassment to members of the Syrian community.

> However, despite all this light and culture [*marduta*] our Syrian nation [*mel-atan*] still declines into the sleep of ignorance, and the heavy rock of careless-ness for injustice [or: with injustice] has pressed the breast of our nation and it soon will hand itself over to death if we, its children, do not stand and turn this great rock from off its breast. Stop a moment and see what our nation is now! It long ago lost the likeness of humanity. It does not have love for its members nor its members for it. It does not have culture for it to be reckoned in the line of humanity, perfect [*kamil*] in mind. It does not have the pru-dence to conquer the cruelty of nature and it does not have order of life for its members to take as a life example and to let go of their corrupt and loathsome characters. We have become the laughingstock of nations: our great class is the Thieves of the Cross [*hačaqoge*], and our youth are menial laborers and our students are without potential, because we do not have literary culture [*saprayuta*], and that nation which does not have literary culture and books of learning has died.

The term *marduta*, translated here as "culture," also connotes "education." It is the Classical Syriac word used for "education" in *Rays of Light*. Arsanis de-scribes the cultural reform he envisions the society offering the nation in the traditional Syriac language of clothing metaphors, although in the tradition, such language is used to refer to the incarnation in Christ or the transforma-tion of the Christian at baptism, not the revival of a nation and the perfection of the human being through enlightened national consciousness.

> But now the whole aim and purpose of this Society of Syrian Literary Culture is to pass on to its brothers the path of perfection [*kamiluta*] of the mind and the free power of ethics. The aim of [the members of the Society of] Syrian Lit-erary Culture is that their nation, wretched and poor in mind, may come upon culture [*marduta*] and they may teach it the meaning of life that its members may be a sacrifice for their nation [*umtay*] so that perhaps in this way our na-tion [*melatan*] may strip off from itself the clothes of strange ugliness, put on the garb of humanity and education, be armed with the weapons of mind, and resemble the complete [*kamil*] person. The society of literary culture wants to establish in its nation [*melatuh*] men [who are] writers, historians, poets, perhaps also philosophers, so that they may purify with their speeches and their essays the Syrian nation and others in the path of the mind and that all of its thinkers may be learned and equal with those of other educated nations. It also wants to demonstrate ways to acquire lawfully and to set up the partner-

ship of commerce [*qamayrsyon*] (trade [*tajiruta*]), farming, and industry, and to give great prizes to literate youths for their speeches, deep in imagination and possessing character, perhaps that in this way it might produce books and foster literate culture [*saprayuta*]. In this way it also wants [the nation] to have its own schools so that from them youths possessing capacity of character may go forth, as well as scientists [*'ilmdare*], teachers, and professors, who may by the power of their imaginations shake the bricks of the ignorance, which for so many generations has limited the mind of our nation with strange, ugly injustice.

However, national reform, Arsanis then explains, requires not just learning and schools, but also public literary culture and moral reform, which will allow human beings to find the perfection built into them because they are created in the likeness of God, who stands outside the world as the "king of nature."

The aim of the [Society of] Syrian Literary Culture is that there be printing houses, complete [*kamil*] newspapers, book publishers, theaters, reading houses (reading rooms), newspapers [*jurnale*], so that our brothers may not be in the streets and idlehouses, their mouths open before the sun and learning unpleasant words, slander, and quarreling. The [Society of] Syrian Literary Culture seeks to awaken its nation [*melatuh*] from its sleep of lethargy and to get it thinking about its wretched condition so that in the end it might have a likeness [*dumya*] [Gn 1:26] of complete men, and the likeness of man is the king of nature.

The "likeness" that is lost echoes the "likeness" of God that human beings lost when they were expelled from the Garden. However, in this case it is a likeness of the human being itself, a hypostatized and ideal man. Arsanis completes his account of the self-activation of secular culture by borrowing the passage in Genesis in which God breathes life into the human being:

The Society of Syrian Literary Culture invites all the members of its nation [*umtuh*], small and great, to join with one another, to teach one another the paths of life, and to breathe into the nostril of their nation [*umtay*] new life [Gn 2:7], so that in the end they not turn red with shame before the generations [*ojage*] to come. It also invites everyone who has love and ethical responsibility for his nation [*melatuh(y)*] low in education and in imagination. It invites all the youths who secretly weep about that unfortunate illness which has struck their Syrian nation, buffeted by ignorance. Honored Syrians, it is indeed a shame for us that, while foreigners work on our behalf in the path of mercy, we ourselves, however, hate one another; while sitting in our own house we do not work on behalf of our needy brothers, who are of our own blood and flesh.

This document reveals the degree of secularity that Syrian nationalism had reached by 1912: God is no longer imminent, but rather stands above nature, whereas it is the human being who is both subject and object of his or her own activity. Human beings can make themselves "perfect" (*kamil*).

The *Star* discontinued publication in November 1914 as a result of the war. It was revived in March 1917, but this only lasted through January 1918. The second edition after its return begins with a discussion by the editor about the ongoing dispute concerning the "pedigree of our nation."[181] He explains that articles from different perspectives on the Assyrian issue will be published. Two weeks later an essay appeared by Dr. Theodore Mar Yoseph, an associate of the American mission, entitled "Syrians, Not Assyrians."[182] He acknowledges that the Syrians may have Assyrian blood, but this is mixed up, he adds, with the blood of a number of races. He argues that there is no historicity to the practice of calling themselves *Assyrian*, as opposed to *Syrian*, a title that links them to the Syrian Orthodox community. His rejection of the ethnonym *Assyrian* is based upon a nationalist logic.

Mar Yoseph's article provoked extended essays, entitled "Assyrians, Not Syrians or Chaldeans," by Benjamin Arsanis and Dr. Baba Parhad.[183] Bemoaning the absence of a name, which thus means "we are not a nation at all," Arsanis compares the community to "inhabitants of the jungle who live in the world yet do not think about a name." He laments confessional divisions ("We are like a drop of water but divided into many parts"). However, ruins such as those of Nineveh point to a true identity. Arsanis employs his own knowledge of ancient Near Eastern history to reject other possible titles, such as *Aramaean* or *Syro-Chaldean*. He concludes by explaining the shift from *Assyrian* to *Syrian* and how by a return to their original name the community will enjoy "unity" (*ḥuyyada*). He concludes: "When we had substance [*ituta*] we called ourselves Assyrians, but now growing weak and dying we are named by this name of ruin, that is, Syrians." Arsanis's use of the word *ituta* may be read as another instance of the transferal of traditionally theological terms to a national ontology: *ituta*, literally "being" or "existence," is used most commonly in the classical tradition for the divine essence.

The article by Dr. Baba Parhad in the following issue makes several arguments for the name *Assyrian*, legitimating his argument, like Arsanis, by citing "the learned men of Europe and America."[184] One striking aspect of the article is his use of the apostle Paul: Parhad begins by distinguishing nation (*melat*), country (*atra*), and subject of a government (*ra'yat d-hukma*) from one another. He suggests that if the apostle Paul were asked about these three things, he would say that his country was Tarsus and his nation was

Jewish, but that he was a subject of Caesar. Parhad would doubtless say that Paul's religion is Christianity, but in this secular national argument, he does not feel the need to refer to religion. Rather, the Jews, the "nation" par excellence in Syriac tradition, serve for him as a model for thinking about Assyrian nationality.

Conclusion: Auto-Orientalism and the National Imagination

Assyrianizing, the tendency to imaginatively link the East Syrian and even broader Syriac communities to ancient Assyria, increased in the post–World War I period, and it persists in the community today. This retrieval of the Assyrian past is not unlike that of the Aryanizing of the Indian past among Indian thinkers working within the framework of European orientalism.[185] European civilizational dichotomies, such as that of Aryans and Semites, were generative as they were taken up around the world in diverse ways. Orientalist discourse is complex, contradictory, and heterogeneous. Ancient Assyria was both embraced and excluded in the civilizational discourse of the Western missions. Whereas Assyria was the ancient enemy of Israel and inferior to Greece, it was also a great civilization, a mighty predecessor of the civilizations to come. This ambivalence is consonant with the racialized relativity of the Syrians in the eyes of the missionaries: they were not Muslims and were at least nominally Christians, some even hopeful ones, and yet they were not white Americans.

Assyrianizing was a form of auto-orientalism, an assertion within a discursive field in which the Syrians had long been interpellated. Western intellectual fields, such as the archaeology and history of the ancient Near East, offered spaces for the articulation of Assyrian identity. However, it is important to emphasize that the appropriation of, for example, archaeology for national purposes was not the abuse of a Western rational and scientific discipline. For this "device of modernity . . . developed as an organized discipline in Europe at the time when the emerging nation-states were in need of proving their perceived antiquity with physical proofs."[186] It came about as a "response to the need to produce the national archaeological record." The national imagination, already activated for some time at the American mission, settled, at least for some within the community, upon the magnificent ruins of ancient Assyria and led to the rearticulation of stories of the greatness of Assyrian civilization. The same can be said for the early nationalists' interest in philology and their sense that the nation needed to foster literary culture. Language and literature had long been important areas for the articulation of national discourse. However, in the case of Assyrian nationalism, the focus on the essential importance of the true name of the nation resembled a much older concern for names within the theological tradition, even if in the tradition God's "borrowed" (metaphorical) and essential names are the focus, whereas in this case it is the name of the nation.[187]

Epilogue

Mirza David George Malik (1861–1931) and the Engaged Ambivalence of Poetry in Exile

Poetry can be an introspective and personal literary genre, especially in the modern period. To conclude this study, I would like to examine a short collection of poems published in Chicago in October 1916, *The Throne of Saliq: The Condition of Syrianism in the Era of the Incarnation of Our Lord, with Poems on Various Themes*. It will offer a vivid glance at the romance of Assyrian nationalism and the interpersonal, even visceral, level on which it affected people's lives. National identity is an abstraction, but it is also deeply sentimental and affective, providing a way of life, of seeing the world, and of telling our own stories.

The author of this Neo-Aramaic volume, Mirza David George Malik, attended American mission schools, including the college in Urmia, and then received a degree in history from Saint Petersburg University.[1] Upon returning from his studies abroad, Malik served as a secretary on the Patriarchal Church Committee, cofounded by his younger brother Nestorius George Malik. In June 1907 he was selected to be a Presbyterian member of the National Union.[2]

Malik's father, Deacon George David Malik (1837–1909), came from the line of *maliks* (chiefs) of the town of Sepurghan.[3] He was the younger brother of Moressa, who was the schoolmate of Sanam and wife of Jacob Yauvre.[4] He graduated from the male seminary in Sire in 1853 (or 1855) and then, after working as a missionary preacher both on the plain and elsewhere in Iran, taught at the college for eight years, serving as an instructor in oriental languages until 1891. This was despite his opposition to the evangelical church's attempt to appropriate local church properties in his home village. During his peripatetic years, he visited the ruins of Babylon and Nineveh and also traveled to India. Drawn into Lutheran circles, he spent time abroad in Sweden and Norway, where he sent his son Nestorius for a theological education. In his later years in Delgosha, he served as a member of the National Committee.

A polyglot of the various languages of the region, George composed several works, including a history of his own people and church, a history of Iran, an anthology of Iranian poets, a grammar, a lexicon, and a translation of the councils of the Church of the East into the vernacular. In 1909 he set out for the United States to publish an English version of his book, "History of the Church of the East" (*Tašʿita d-ʿedta d-madenḥa*). He died in transit between Tabriz and Julfa, but his son Nestorius, who accompanied him on the trip, carried out the project and the book was published in 1910 as *History of the Syrian Nation and the Old Evangelical-Apostolic Church of the East*, a volume that identifies Aramaeans, Chaldeans, Assyrians, and Syrians as one "nation" sharing one language. It is the first of such large histories of the nation, and others would soon follow. Nestorius had already traveled to the United States before, working for the Christian Aid Society of Syrian Youth in Chicago in 1907.[5] Sarah, one of the four sisters of Nestorius and David, left for America in 1909 to acquire a prosthetic leg and eventually settled in Chicago, as did David's son Samuel in 1912 after completing his education in Urmia.

David himself left for the United States not much later, just before a period of turmoil in his homeland:[6] in November 1914, at the beginning of World War I, Russia declared war on the Ottoman Empire. By December the Turks invaded the area of northwestern Iran that had been occupied by the Russians since 1907. The subsequent Russian flight, accompanied by much of the Christian population, was followed in the early months of 1915 by massacres and the destruction of dozens of Christian villages. There was a back-and-forth campaign, simultaneous with the destruction of Christian villages in the mountains of Hakkari and the displacement of much of the tribal population of the mountains. In January 1915 in Urmia, in the midst of upheaval, Malik's mother Rachel died.[7] In the late winter of 1915, the Armenian population of Anatolia, which had suffered greatly in 1894–96 and 1909, was almost completely eradicated by murder and forced expulsion.[8] The Armenian genocide affected the Syriac communities to the west of Hakkari in Ottoman territories, and along with the Armenians, many Syriac Christians in what is now Turkey were expelled or killed.[9] These events are referred to by Christians in the Syriac church tradition as the *Sayfa* (*Seyfo*), "(the year of) the sword."

After its title page, *The Throne of Saliq* reproduces a portrait of the East Syrian patriarch, Shemʿon XXI Benyamin, a handsome man, born in 1887, who had taken this office in 1903 after the death of his predecessor. The title essay, "The Throne of Saliq" (or, "The Patriarchal Seat of Seleucia"), begins by describing the original lands of the Syrians before they were settled by

Persians, Greeks, and Arabs, after which, Malik claims, the Syrians still maintained their own language and "customs" ('adate). These lands consist of those "between the Persian Gulf and the Zagros Mountains (Kurdistan) in the east, the edges of the Mediterranean Sea in the west, the desert of Arabia in the south, and the mountains of Armenia in the north."[10] The term he uses for "homeland," bet ma'mra, which may be translated more literally as "dwelling place," is uncommon enough that in the glossary at the back of the book he provides a more easily recognizable Neo-Aramaic equivalent, the originally Arabic word watan, which had earlier meant "place to reside, settlement" but by the early twentieth century had taken on the nationalist meaning of "homeland," as it is also used today in several modern languages (e.g., Turkish vatan).

According to Malik, King Abgar, the first-century ruler of the small kingdom of Syrians at Urhay (Edessa, modern Urfa, in southeastern Turkey), wrote a letter inviting Jesus to visit his city and heal him from the illness he suffered. Jesus promised to send one of his disciples after his resurrection, and so Addai and Thomas visited Urhay and healed the king, and as a result the first political "authority" (hukma) to receive Christianity was "that one of us Syrians."[11] However, this small kingdom was destroyed, and the Syrians became "subject" (ra'yat) to the Roman and Persian kingdoms, while some "tribes" (aširat) maintained their political autonomy.

With the subsequent spread of Christianity to all lands and "nations" (melate), centers of "secular authority" (hukma 'almanaya) also became religious centers: Jerusalem, Antioch, Alexandria, Rome, Byzantium, and Seleucia (Saliq), the last being the capital of the Persians and the only one outside of the Roman Empire. These patriarchates endured persecution until Constantine gave his famous firman, or royal decree, of 313 concerning the "freedom" (azaduta) of Christians. Western Christians were not only saved from persecution, "but they also took primary position in secular authority [hukma 'almanaya]."[12] According to Malik, in the late second century, the Syrian patriarchs began to send missionaries into Central and East Asia, while persecutions worsened in the Persian Empire in the post-Constantinian period. Malik describes the successes of later patriarchs, even while being persecuted, and their devotion to learning and the Gospel at a time when Western churches were immersed in theological disputes.

So people will now ask, Malik admits, why God would allow this renowned church to fall into its present "condition" (ahwal). In the "temporal conditions [ahwalate] and worldly authority" that have come about such that the patriarch and his people have had to hide themselves away, the Lord will protect and save them, just as he did Elijah, and in these circumstances they fulfill the dominical command: "Take up your cross and follow me" (Mk 8:34–35). The Church of the East can boast, Malik concludes, that it "goes in the footsteps of its Lord" because of the nineteen hundred years of persecution it has endured, and he hopes that the Lord will continue to preserve the throne of Saliq "as a monument [*yagara*, or "heap"] of truth for the sons of the East." This last line would again send the reader to the book's glossary. *Yagara*, a word that would not have been familiar to many, is glossed there as *qayemta* ("column," "pillar") and *quḥa* ("heap," "pile"). Literally meaning "heap," *yagara* derives its meaning of "memorial to a compact" from the "heap of witness" set up by Jacob and his father-in-law Laban at Genesis 31:47 (where the ancient Aramaic word is *yaghra*). Laban and Jacob had been at odds, and when peace was finally made between the two, they set up a "heap" as a memorial. The patriarchal office for Malik serves as an ongoing memorial to the pact between God and the Syrians. Malik would have known Genesis 31:47 as evidence within the Hebrew Bible for Aramaic being spoken in ancient Mesopotamia. An article in a 1909 issue of the *Star* discusses precisely this, and therefore, integral to Malik's understanding of this pact between God and the Syrians is the antiquity of the Aramaic language itself.[13]

The few scholars acquainted with the history of Syriac Christianity would recognize the historical conflations and schematizations Malik proffers in his account. For example, the Abgar legend and the story of the conversion of the kingdom of Edessa are extant in the Syriac tradition from antiquity. Such a national narrative of "Syrian" history had begun to be produced by missionaries and Syrians themselves, including Malik's father, by the turn of the twentieth century. Furthermore, several of the terms Malik uses are anachronisms. "Subjects" (*ra'yat*) and "tribes" (*aširat*) are the two major distinctions of the East Syrian population in Malik's own day, not in the Middle Ages. A *firman* was the standard term for a royal decree of the Ottoman sultan, and, as we have seen, *melat* (pl. *melate*), cognate with the Turkish *millet*, was the term for religious community within the Qajar and Ottoman Empires as well as a more recently christened Neo-Aramaic term for "nation." Finally, the "homeland" Malik attributes to the Syrians extends through the whole Fertile Crescent and seems to represent the full extent of the Neo-Assyrian Empire (tenth to seventh centuries BCE). Thus, we have in Malik's historical account a mélange of ancient Assyrian, early Syriac Christian, medieval, and late Ottoman and Qajar history.

In the last paragraph of his introduction, Malik offers a martyrological interpretation of the history of the Church of the East, one that fits with the church's traditional self-understanding. As he correctly notes, the East Syrians never enjoyed a Constantinian revolution, and the genre of martyrology continued to be a tool for viewing the church's relationship to the world through the Middle Ages, just as martyrdom itself continued to be an option for imagining relations between the church and the political authority. By Malik's day, East Syrian writers had begun to systematize the history of the Church of the East, rendering it in national terms and casting modern political events in a traditional martyrological framework: church history was becoming the history of a nation, and martyrs of the past the martyrs of that nation.

The remainder of *The Throne of Saliq* is a collection of poems, which are composed in rhyming stanzas. They have a traditional Aramaic meter, which means that each line may contain only a certain number of full vowels. The first, "Lamentation and Entreaty," describes, and at times is written from the perspective of, a woman in a hospital, dreaming of her distant homeland. The poem is written in the voice of Malik's sister Sarah, who was in the United States for medical treatment, and yet in the end it analogizes her as well as their mother to the nation. The combination of viscerality and abstraction points to the intimate social relations within which Assyrian national consciousness could be articulated.

1. In the hospital like a prisoner
Guarded by guards on every side,
Without people who know her, an exile she
Remains alone weak hidden.

2. There is no comfort nor sleep.
From the force of the illness, she, my soul, is enervated,
By night, by day buried in thought
That there is no hope at all for happiness.

3. Whenever asleep
By the wing of imagination she has passed over the sea
To a distant land where there is healing,
The worn out body arriving there.

4. When the sun rises at the beginning of day,
When looking out at the mountain and the sea
A pleasant wind, behold, is blowing;
To every living thing it gives a portion.

5. From the top of the mountains covered with snow,
From the valleys newly clad with colors,
From the clothes of the meadow and all the flowers,
And with green and the scent of pastures,

6. Nature produces an apothecary
From its diverse and pleasant species.
For every illness there are medicines,
With no payment at all required from those who seek them.

Within his splendor in the heavens, God guides human life (stanza 7), and the contemplation of this provides pleasant distraction from pain (8–9), as the mind remains in control (10).

11. Suddenly, behold, remembering
That I am sojourning far from that land,
At present I am in the homeland [*bet ma'mra*]
Trusting firmly in hope.

The "I" here, as in the poem as a whole, is feminine, a grammatical distinction that is marked in Neo-Aramaic but not in English. The only explicit possible speaker so far in the poem is the "my soul" (*gani*) in the second stanza, which is a feminine noun in Neo-Aramaic. However, the several references to a medical context and nostalgia for home suggest that the subject of the poem is Malik's sister Sarah, and it is she who is speaking (and yet there is a double meaning: "my soul" can also mean "my beloved," used of various loved ones, like its Turkish cognate *canım*, a usage that reintroduces the author's voice). The subsequent stanzas describe the healing the narrator receives upon meeting her parents again (12), and her friends and kin (13), and yet in a moment all is transformed and she is unable to track their faces (14), everything is lost (15), and only destruction of homes and bodies remains (16). Everything is burned and drenched with blood (17), young women's adornments are scattered about (18), and various creatures come: spiderwebs fill skulls of children and adults, a mad hyena after the snowfall searches for the bones of the slaughtered (19), the remains putrefy and are covered with insects, and there is no one to bury the dead nor any doctor to treat the wounded (20–22). The homeland that once gave joy to broken hearts is now an image of hell (23). The poem then introduces explicitly national themes:

24. The vineyard, the field, behold, are desolate,
There is no human being to reside within them,
Also no bird to sing bitterly,
To give speeches about the ruin of the nation [*umta*].

25. Four-cornered gardens shaped by walls,
Between their trees roses are planted,
Adorned with red and blue hues,
They have been changed to a cemetery for the martyrs [*sahde*].

The land becomes overgrown, and the survivors are imprisoned without visitors (26). The speaker's mind reels in contemplating all this (27). She trembles and finds no consolation (28). Her tongue is unable to lament, she has no place to reside, nor can she drive scavenging animals away from the corpses (29).

> 30. There is neither writer nor scribe
> To write a few lines for remembrance
> That children of the future may know the grave
> Of those who bore witness [shedlun] to the truth with their blood.

> 31. In this such a rotten state [ahwal]
> Cut off from hope on every side
> Behold, I desire to meet death
> To unite with those who have departed for eternity.

She is unable to move, nor can she understand the speech around her (32). She is happy for a moment, but "Perhaps the dream was empty; / It is taken out of memories" (33). She then sees herself on an operating table and yet the anesthesia does not help her forget the violence at home (34–35). She feels exiled, like "roses" from their "gardener," and unable to rejoice (36–37).

> 38. Like a miscarriage that has not seen the light
> —It separates from the womb and goes to the grave—
> So for me in the morning time
> A bitter cup is prepared.

> 39. The longing in my heart is not for adornment
> Nor for blessings from the wealth of sin.
> Surrounded by darkness in clothes of mourning,
> I arrive at the graves of those fallen in the massacre.

> 40. I kneel and pray at the resting place
> For the souls that have departed with cries of "alas."
> Groaning before the torturous pains
> I do not cease from giving praises.

> 41. With a sweet voice in sadness
> I cry and sing bitterly.
> I soothe my mother with poems,
> Lamentations for the shattered state of my people.

> 42. For the deceased in the sweet homeland [watan]
> Having let flow ample tears,
> Death is a crown for me,
> I who shall be buried with my loved ones.

The poem then becomes a petition. The poet asks God to save the "oppressed people" (*'amma ṭlima*) and to have mercy on the "children of the church" (43). (Malik's glossary explains that the Classical Syriac *'amma* is equivalent to the Neo-Aramaic *tayepa*.) Borrowing from traditional imagery, in which the church is a ship at sea (44) and Christ is imagined as a doctor, the poem continues:

> 45. Have mercy on everyone, Just Doctor,
> Guide our nation [*umtan*] to the port of salvation.
> You alone are the one who is able:
> To our sickness give healing.

> 46. Our patriarch, the successor of [Shem'on; i.e., Simon] Peter,
> The Shem'on of our time, the bishop,
> From the wicked and the plunderer
> Save him as from the persecutor.

> 47. The throne of Saliq, pillar [*yagar*] of truth,
> Giver of light to the sons of the East,
> By the blood of its martyrs from generation to generation
> Was a source of glory for the church of Christ.

Various patriarchs have received a martyr's crown (48), but it is hoped that God will help the current patriarch and send an angel to protect him (49–50). The narrator then seeks help from God for herself, especially in illness (51). Then, more clearly in the voice of Malik's sister Sarah, the poem refers to Rachel, Malik's (and Sarah's) mother, and likens her to the biblical matriarch Rachel through a reference ("Ramah") that intertextually recalls the slaughter of the innocents in the Gospel of Matthew (Mt 2:16–18):

> 52. Son of the Creator, Emmanuel,
> Good hope of the sons of the world,
> The debts and sins of your servant Rachel,
> Her faults and transgression forgive.

> 53. Upon the day of your arrival for the resurrection
> Render us worthy, daughter and mother,
> That along with your dwellers of the kingdom on high
> We ourselves though weak may receive a portion.

> 54. The prophets and the just, the sons of the Old Testament,
> Like Jeremiah and Rachel of Ramah [cf. Jer 3:15],
> Let flow tears while thinking
> About their loved ones who went to the slaughter.

The matriarch Rachel weeping prefiguratively at the infanticide perpetrated by Herod serves as a model for the poet's mother weeping for her own dead as well as for the nation at large. Through this figure Malik renders his mother the mother of all Syrians who have suffered. Finally, the poet addresses his sister directly and suggests that her pain, sorrow, and exile are the nation's in microcosm:

> 55. The daughter of Ashur is a type for you:
> Although your wounds are very great
> Go in the tracks of your ancestors;
> Certainly you will receive your petitions.
>
> 56. Expect the commander and lord of the cherubs.
> Not by word, but by good deeds
> That one will save you from enemies.
> From the coin of sin do not expect blessings.

In the glossary Malik explains that Ashur is "the son of Shem, the son of Noah, from whom comes our name: *Atoraye, Ašoraye, Asoraye, Suraye*," implying in this list the false etymological connection between *Syrian* and *Assyrian* that had become popular among other Syrian nationalists.

Through the voice of his sister alone in a foreign hospital, Malik's poem laments the loss of the nation, combining an awareness of its fallen state and a pious entreaty that it may be raised up again. He incorporates into this the ancient and ecclesial history that had become better known to the East Syrians by the turn of the twentieth century due to the numerous mission publications that focused on such material. The book's long historical introduction and the inclusion of historical figures in the glossary confirm that this historicist approach would not have been obvious to some readers of the poem.

The first-person voice of the poem, its focus on the experience of the individual self and its authorial subjectivity, in this case Malik's sister's subjective experience of surgery abroad, combined with her fantasies, memories, and nightmares of home, is reminiscent of the evangelical personal narratives introduced by the American missionaries in the mid-nineteenth century. Its sentiments, such as the sense of loss and fallenness, echo the affect cultivated at the American mission for decades.

The national longing and isolation evoked in the poem are not desacralized: the nation and the church are linked, and for Malik it is the patriarch who serves as both a temporal and religious leader. The poet's use of terms borrowed from Classical Syriac, the language most East Syrians would have

known only from the liturgy, creates a sense of pious solemnity or perhaps
what would have seemed at the time to be an odd mix of the archaic and the
contemporary. His work is an early instance of a trend in Neo-Aramaic composition toward purifying the language of what were perceived to be foreign
words and often replacing them with Classical Syriac vocabulary, while simultaneously employing standard Classical Syriac theological motifs, albeit in a
nationalist register. Such a classicizing, common in other nationalist movements' relationship to language, such as in the promotion of *katharevousa* in
modern Greece, created a nostalgic link to the nation's imagined past.

Other poems in *The Throne of Saliq* are no less melancholy than "Lam-
entation and Entreaty." "On the Festival of Christmas, the Year 1916: For the
Syrians of Iran and Kurdistan" describes the Syrians as present-day martyrs,
while self-consciously calling attention to their memorialization. "King of
Kings: Nicholas II—May He Live Forever" is dedicated to the czar whom
Malik hoped would aid the Syrians (but who was instead executed less than
two years later). "Metrical Letter from America to Urmia," dated "Chicago,
October 8, 1913," describes the difficult life of poor immigrants and contrasts
it to the ease of the privileged. The poem compares America to Babylon and
ancient Rome, referring to it as a prison and a place of enslavement. The comparison relies on imagery from the book of Revelation, a biblical book the
American missionaries pushed the East Syrians to study. The poet then gazes
upon the world and responds with uncertainty:

9. What is the cause and the power
That make this orb to turn?
From the doctor and the eloquent one
There is no answer to the question.

10. Whether by the creator or by fate
Or even nature with its silent material,
What has held the balance
Which is so far from justice?

11. While thinking about the forgotten past
Looking also at the future of imprisonment
There is not a light in the hard present
Able to reveal the hidden mystery.

12. It is not possible for them to arrive at the truth,
The living ones under the sun and the moon,
They are filled with silence and wonder,
Accompanied by work, patience, and hope.

Nature itself has substance in Malik's poetry, and God is more distant from his creation than he is in the indigenous theological tradition. However, according to the "Metrical Letter," the church service, which is performed in a sacred language, offers an opportunity for transcendence:

> 29. Our hope is for the hidden creator,
> Who was pierced by the cross,
> That he may make our meeting swift;
> Let us hear the mystery before his altar

> 30. In that holy language
> Which the Son of Man spoke.
> Out of his love he received suffering
> For the salvation of human beings.

The "hidden creator" (*baroya gniza*) reflects traditional East Syrian theological language, but that the creator should be the one crucified blurs boundaries between the Father and the Son in a way that would have troubled the fathers of the church. Another innovation is the notion that the Aramaic of the Eucharistic service was sanctified by Jesus. Aside from the church service, the poet then claims, the only consolation in his lonely exile is the presence of his sister.

Finally, the last poem in this volume, "True Love," dated "Sepurghan, 1891," is an extended piece of romantic pastoral poetry, perhaps inspired by Malik's first wife, Farangis, whom he married in 1890 (and who died at twenty-three in 1900). The poem begins by describing nature robed in the power of the sun at dawn, the blossoming of springtime, and the innate procreative urge of all living beings. This description is contrary to the tendency in the indigenous Syriac tradition of treating nature primarily as an instrument by which we may infer the existence of God the creator. The poet compares nature's bounty to a wedding feast, a table "arranged by the mother of the world for everyone. / All of them invited, from little to great, / Are urgent to worship beauty" (11).

> 12. It is the source of all delight.
> Beyond it there is no flavor.
> Blessed is he in this world
> Who has a portion in it.

The author then sees his beloved:

> 14. Among the trees, under the shade
> One appears like a pillar

Vowed by a great people,
Established as a memorial to heroes.

15. Not distinguishing the vision from the truth,
In this corporeal form in which there is wonder
She is a being or a radiant beam
Or an angel, the daughter of light,

16. Or a Siren who upon lakes,
Queen of beauty and poetry,
With a sweet voice in anthems
Is inviting everyone to bondage.

The poet describes the features of her beauty, comparing them to the parts of nature. He likens her to an object of reverence, even a pagan idol, or the morning star for Zoroastrian priests, "a place of worship [*masgada*] of love for the lover" (38), "a rose of Shiraz, redolent in gardens, / Standing alone among lilies" (39). At the end of the poem he turns to the question of the afterlife, the transmigration of souls, and the resurrection of the dead: each offers an opportunity for lovers to be together again.

57. Let us hope in the great Lord,
The creator of nature, as well as of love:
Seeking with a pure intention
We shall certainly taste from the honey.

58. Also we shall hear the sound of a bell
Which will announce to us, "Stand in line!
A lover and a flower—
It is a command that they be a married couple."

59. The lake of Urmia and Mt. Honeybee,
Which exist since eternity,
They are for us as a testimony
That we will be faithful even after death.

The poem ends with the certainty of both love and nature. The former is as stable as a national monument ("like a pillar / Vowed by a great people"), whereas the latter exists forever and therefore outside of the traditional Christian scheme of creation, which has a beginning and an end. (That Lake Urmia is today drying up and much of Mount Zanbil, the "Mt. Honeybee" of the poem, has been demolished and pushed into the lake would, sadly, challenge Malik's claims.) God's role in this poem is distant: our own transcendence is at times a possibility, and yet God's absence is ever present.

The theological disposition in Malik's poem corresponds with what

Charles Taylor calls "secularity 3." In *A Secular Age*, Taylor begins his project of historicizing the secular by distinguishing between three different types of secularity: secularity 1 he defines as the retreat of religion from the political, scientific, aesthetic, and economic realms; secularity 2 is the decline of religious belief and practice; secularity 3, which is of foremost concern to him, entails a shift in the "conditions of belief" such that belief in God is no longer unproblematic but simply an option, one existing in a precarious epistemological world. Belief is a possibility, and in his book Taylor provides what Talal Asad terms "an account of historical remaking in which the choice of belief and unbelief come to have an equal and equally protected status in the liberal-democratic state."[14] We live within an "immanent frame," stuck between narratives of both closure and immanence and our yearning for a lost transcendence.[15]

Assyrian nationalism did not lead to strong calls for a separation of church and state (Taylor's secularity 1) nor a necessary turning away from God and the church (Taylor's secularity 2). These are of course attested. Some Assyrians have preferred secular regimes in the Middle East, and some prioritize ethnicity over church affiliation in their identity. However, the Church of the East never had a state from which to be separated, and Assyrian nationalism has at times heightened the focus on and support for the church and the patriarch. This nationalism, however, came about within secularity 3. We find in Malik's poetry evidence of it, attestation of a grasping for transcendence, the "fullness," as Taylor puts it, toward which all humans aspire, whereas the object, while grasped at, remains unstable and fleeting. For Malik, this elusive object can be found in memory, in nature, in love, or in the church service performed "In that holy language / Which the Son of Man spoke." Malik does not make an "assertion of the self-sufficiency of the secular and the exclusion of religion."[16] In his poetry he performs the ambivalence of a modern self, one aware of various truths and unable to cleave to one. In fact, at times his work possibly betrays the influence of the *Rubaiyat* of Omar Khayyam, most likely Edward FitzGerald's loose translation, which had become a sensation by the turn of the century. His willingness to engage in nihilistic thinking, doubting divine providence, while yet affirming Christian beliefs, is nevertheless fundamentally modern. The cultural conditions of belief had shifted for his community such that one could think to say that perhaps there is no God. This is a modern development, a shift toward a secular form of culture, in which belief now exists in a framework where it must be defended. Malik's ambivalence becomes even more noteworthy if we consider how he devoted much of his life to his church and to the nation, two entities that were not absolutely distinct for him. The protection of the former for him was essential for the preservation of the latter, and his secular sensibility appears in the ir-reducibility of national identity in his work.

Less than two years after the publication of *The Throne of Saliq*, on March 3, 1918, the Patriarch Shem'on XXI Benyamin was assassinated with his retinue by Simko Shikak, a Kurdish *agha* (lord) who led a revolt against the Iranian state in northwestern Iran. His successor, Shem'on XX Paul, would fare even worse: born in 1885, he died in 1920 during the exodus of thousands of Assyrians from Iran to British Mandate Iraq. Becoming ill in transit with the other refugees, he died at a monastery belonging to the Syrian Orthodox, historically the theological adversaries of his church, and was buried in an Armenian cemetery in Baghdad. He was in turn succeeded by an eleven-year-old boy. The difficult career of the patriarchs in the early twentieth century may be read as a synecdoche for the Assyrian community: they suffered violence, expulsion, and exile.

After the Bolshevik Revolution, Russian forces were withdrawn from the area south of the Caucasus. The Iranian National Assembly considered rec-ommending a mass flight with the Russian army, but the Allies encouraged the leaders of the community to remain.[17] Many Syrians, especially the already dislocated Hakkari tribesmen, who had at that point been fighting for some time, fought on. They lost, and execution, rape, and plundering followed. In July 1918 Malik, his brother Nestorius, and their families were forced to flee Urmia along with most of the Christian population. They ended up in Hamadan, but Malik's wife Eve died in flight. Many communal leaders were murdered at this time. Thomas Audo, the Chaldean archbishop of Urmia and imaginative nationalist, was mistreated, shot in the face, thrown back in jail after hasty treatment, and died of infection.[18] John Mushe, already ill from typhus, was murdered in his home in front of his family. Those who were nei-ther slaughtered nor died on the road were scattered across the region, some only after several years finding stable homes again in exile in Iraq, elsewhere in Iran, Syria, India, Chicago, New York, and California. It was at this time that the American mission came to its de facto end. William A. Shedd (1865–1918) quit his position at the mission that year in order to help the suffering Syrian population as a US political consul.[19] He and his wife, Mary Lewis Shedd, eventually fled the city with the Christian population, and he died of cholera on the road (and was later buried in Tabriz).

In 1920 Malik's family went to Baghdad, and Nestorius eventually went to America to serve as a priest in Chicago and then in Turlock, California. Ma-lik went in 1921, with his fourteen-year-old son Joel, to Gardanne, outside of Aix-en-Provence, where he wrote, among other works, his massive 1,290-page unpublished manuscript "History of Assyria from the Beginning to the Present."[20] In this work his earlier hesitant use of *Syrian* instead of *Assyrian* was gone: by the 1920s scattered in diaspora, East Syrians took up the appellation *Assyrian* even more stridently. Malik's signature to a nationalist poem about exile in a 1928 publication includes the title "Assyrian teacher."[21]

Malik was loath to join his brother in America in part because of his distrust of Americans and their missionaries. However, as he wrote: "I thought, while our country is in ruins, we ourselves expelled without a homeland, and there being no hope that my son Samuel would return from America, that I might see him one more time before I die; I decided that if America is Hell I will go and let me burn in it provided that I see my firstborn son, the sweet remembrance of his mother."[22] By the late 1920s, Malik was in Chicago again, attempting to publish more of his by then extensive corpus, which included poetry (some in Azeri Turkish), plays, a work on Mongol history, a history of his family, and his "History of Assyria," as well as *The Story of Shamiram, Queen of Assyria*, and a romance, *The Story of Asle and Karam*. A family member recalled that all he did at the time, living in the home of his sister Sarah, was drink tea, smoke, and write. In 1931 his only other published book appeared in Chicago, a miscellaneous collection, which includes an essay on the history of the patriarchate, poems on heroes and martyrs of the Assyrian nation, and selections from some of his later writings. That same year, he returned to the Middle East and died not long after he arrived in Baghdad, where he was buried, like many Assyrians, a stranger in a strange land.

*

Syrian identity and the national organizations that had formed by World War I continued to reflect a *millet* (*melat*) nationalism: there is little evidence that Assyrians, even once they referred to themselves as Assyrians, saw all Syriac Christians as part of their community. This was to change after the genocide and displacement of much of the Assyrian population (1916–20). Assyrians sought a homeland at the Paris Peace Conference of 1919, at which new universal claims were made: "The idea of an Assyro-Chaldean nation uniting all peoples of Syriac origin first appeared publicly during the peace conference debates. It was put forward by an Assyro-Chaldean delegation from Paris which does not seem to have had any official contacts with the Syriac Catholic or Syriac Orthodox delegations."[23] However, their petitions ultimately failed, and national recognition was left out of the Treaties of Sèvres (1920) and Lausanne (1923).[24] A national myth has formed around the figure of Agha Petros (1880–1932) and his role at this time. Originally from the lower Baz, he studied at the American mission but eventually became a leader in the local community.[25] He commanded the Assyrians on the Russian side against the

Ottomans during the war and, at Lausanne, attempted to negotiate a resettlement in Hakkari. He died an exile in Toulouse.

After the traumatic displacement of the genocide, the nationalist literary culture that had spread early in the twentieth century continued to grow in various parts of the Assyrian diaspora. In the 1920s nationalist authors were writing in south India, Iraq, and several American cities. Soon the existence of formal nationalist organizations and periodicals became a normal part of life in the Assyrian diaspora. An explicit territorial nationalism also developed, while ideas about Assyrian history and culture were further articulated in these diasporic settings. Maronites, Syrian Orthodox, and East Syrians in New York intermingled in circles adjacent to the Pen League, that group of Lebanese writers who helped to found Arab literary modernism and nationalism, such as Ameen Rihani (1876–1940) and Khalil Gibran (1883–1931). Syriac Christians, both Syrian Orthodox and Church of the East, with their own local incipient nationalisms, came together and a broader nation was imagined.[26] For example, West and East Syrians in New York worked on the *Union* (*Ḥuyyada*), the monthly paper of the Assyro-Chaldean Union of America (1921–22).

Assyrians continued to suffer displacement even after World War I, such as during the Simele massacre in fledgling Iraq in 1933. In contrast, a vibrant cultural and artistic nationalism flourished in Iran in the 1950s and 1960s. Within the ambience of the anticolonial and revolutionary enthusiasm of 1968, the Assyrian Universal Alliance (*ḥuyyada*) was founded in Pou, France. The organization's founding document declares "Assyrian" the "singular name for all the members of our nation [*umtan*]," and then lists each of the various churches of the Syriac heritage.[27] The Assyrian Democratic Movement, which I mentioned in the prelude to this book, was founded in 1979 in Iraq. More recently in Iraq, many Assyrians and Chaldeans have been displaced or killed, as have so many Iraqis, due to the civil war and ongoing instability caused by the American invasion of 2003, whereas Christians continue to enjoy some autonomy in Iraqi Kurdistan. There the Chaldo-Assyrian nationalism promoted since the 1920s has been expanded into a Chaldean-Assyrian-Syriac (Syrian Orthodox) identity in this polity independent of the strictures of Arab nationalism.

Assyrian identity so affected the Church of the East that the church itself was eventually renamed the "Assyrian Church of the East." Contemporary Assyrian national identity includes the celebration of the first of Nisan as the Assyrian New Year, and this has been rerendered by some as the ancient Assyrian Akitu festival at which celebrants dress in faux ancient Assyrian garb, including fake long beards. At times Assyrian nationalists even

FIGURE 11. An Assyrianizing advertisement for the new Syriac Press, a Chaldo-Assyrian printing company founded by Samuel A. Jacobs, a Presbyterian originally from Urmia. (Columbia University Rare Books and Manuscripts.)

engage in esoteric readings of Scripture, such as the interpretation of God's self-revelation in Exodus 3:14 ("I am who I am"; Hebr. *ehyeh asher ehyeh*) as a hidden revelation of the ancient Assyrian divinity Ashur (the Hebrew relative pronoun *asher* resembles the name *Ashur*). It is even argued that the Bible is a "biased" document, a piece of anti-Assyrian propaganda. Reflecting

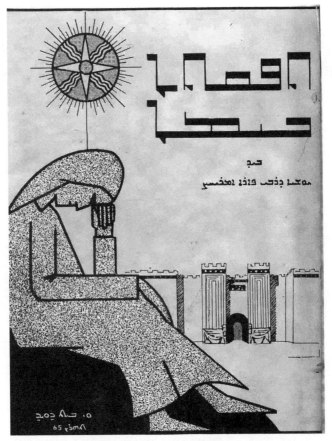

FIGURE 12. *The Meeting with Mother* (*Tpaqta b-yema*), a collection of poems printed in Tehran in 1965 by Yoshiya Amrikhas (b. 1900), son of Pera Amrikhas (1872–1945), who taught at the Urmia College and wrote for *Rays of Light* and the *Star*.

the value put on modern science, nationalist literature treats the ancient Assyrians, especially their great rulers, such as Ashurbanipal, as foundational
figures in the history of the sciences.[28] Furthermore, by a figure resembling
the common personification of "Mother India" as mother goddess for the
Indian nation, a "matriotic" nationalism has been articulated whereby the
anthropomorphized Assyria is a mother of the nation, as is the great queen
Shamiram.[29] The Chaldean Syriac Assyrian Popular Council, a political party
in Kurdistan, has even named its television station, Ishtar TV, after the ancient
Near Eastern goddess. Part of this national imagination, especially in recent
years, has entailed a conflation of the violence of World War I and before:
Assyrian nationalist historiography tends to characterize the massacres of
West Syrians in Ottoman territories and the violence suffered in Hakkari and

Urmia during World War I as all part of the same lachrymose history, which even extends back to the sack of Nineveh in 612 BCE.[30]

The history of Assyrian nationalism from the 1920s onward needs to be written. Moreover, the Russian and Caucasian background for early Assyrian nationalism requires study, as do the links to Armenian nationalism, which preceded it.[31] In contrast to the Assyrians, Chaldeans, who are members of the worldwide Catholic Church and often identify as Christian Arabs, wear their ancient pedigree more lightly. Their story is a different but interrelated one of displacement and ethnic minoritization.[32] In Europe a strong Aramaean identity has developed in more recent decades, and this is often in conflict with an Assyrian one, whereas the online virtual spaces in which many identities are now fostered have also been fecund for Assyrian identity.[33]

One of the consequences of the engagement with foreign missions was the fracture of the East Syrian community into several churches, which led to the emergence of nationalism and ongoing attempts to compartmentalize "religion." This has resulted in a series of ongoing conflicts and contradictions within the various churches of the Syriac tradition (such that even my referring to the "Syriac tradition" can be taken by some nationalists as a loaded political statement). However, both because of its failure to attain a state and due to its own internal contradictions, this nationalism has remained fractured and unstable. There remains a congeries of contested names for the different communities and great confusion for those who unknowingly venture into this field.[34] The contours of *millet* nationalism can still be traced within the several contemporary Syriac nationalisms, because without a national homeland and without robust transdenominational political organizations, this creative and modern identity often relies upon the formal and informal social institutions of the different Syriac churches to anchor itself in a global sea of nations.

Notes

Prelude

1. The video of Juliana Jendo's "Alap Bet" can be found on YouTube.
2. Wenger, *We Have a Religion*, 10. Cf. Hamilakis, *Nation and Its Ruins*, 22–23.

Note on Transliteration and Names

1. E.g., Joseph, *Modern Assyrians*, 1–32.

Introduction

1. [Jacobs], *Reviving a Famous Ancient Language*, 7. (For the cover of this publication, see fig. 11 in the epilogue.) For a similar, contemporary poem by Naum Faiq, see Butts, "Assyrian Christians."

2. *K* 1, no. 1 (June 21, 1906): 1. See also De Kelaita, "On the Road to Nineveh," 6–30, esp. 8–11.

3. *K* 1, no. 1 (June 21, 1906): 2.

4. *K* 1, no. 1 (June 21, 1906): 3.

5. *QŠ* 2, no. 10 (Mar. 1899): 385–86.

6. Anatolia: Salt, *Imperialism, Evangelism, and the Ottoman Armenians*; Kieser, *Der verpasste Friede*; and Kieser, "Ottoman Urfa and Its Missionaries." Syria: Masters, "Competing for Aleppo's Souls"; and Masters, *Christians and Jews*. Lebanon: Makdisi, *Artillery of Heaven*; and Makdisi, *Culture of Sectarianism*. Egypt: Sharkey, *American Evangelicals in Egypt*; and Sedra, *From Mission to Modernity*. In general, see Murre-van den Berg, "Study of Western Mission in the Middle East"; Khalaf, *Cultural Resistance*, 105–96; Doğan and Sharkey, *American Missionaries and the Middle East*; Tamcke and Marten, *Christian Witness between Continuity and New Beginnings*; Tejirian and Spector Simon, *Altruism and Imperialism*; Tejirian and Spector Simon, *Conflict, Conquest, and Conversion*; Murre-van den Berg, *New Faith in Ancient Lands*; and Kawerau, *Amerika und die Orientalischen Kirchen*.

7. Robson, *Colonialism and Christianity in Mandate Palestine*; and Sharkey, *American Evangelicals in Egypt*.

8. Marr, *Cultural Roots of American Islamicism*; Kidd, *American Christians and Islam*; Kieser, *Nearest East*; and Makdisi, *Faith Misplaced*.

9. Chakrabarty, "Difference-Deferral of a Colonial Modernity," 81, quoted in Mitchell, *Questions of Modernity*, xvi.

10. There are, however, numerous articles by Heleen Murre-van den Berg, as well as several general works on the modern history of the Assyrians: Joseph, *Modern Assyrians*; Wilmshurst, *Martyred Church*; and Baum and Winkler, *Church of the East*. Gordon Taylor, *Fever and Thirst*, treats the idiosyncratic Asahel Grant. There are two historical monographs: Coakley, *Church of the East*, which is a detailed, narrative history of the Anglican mission, and O'Flynn, "Western Christian Presence in the Caucasus and Qajar Persia," which treats all missions up to 1870, including the early Scottish and German missions. See also Hellot, "Western Missionaries"; and Elder, *History of the Iran Mission*.

11. E.g., Bastian, "Sociétés Protestantes et rupture révolutionnaire."

12. *ZB* 46, no. 9 (Sept. 1898): 65.

13. Wolk, "Emergence of Assyrian Ethnonationalism."

14. In general, see Murray, *Symbols*.

15. Murray, *Symbols*, 246.

16. Murray, *Symbols*, 226.

17. Murray, *Symbols*, 77.

18. Charles Taylor, *Secular Age*, 54-61. See also comments in Charles Taylor, "Western Secularity," 32.

19. Most other work begins where my study leaves off. See, for example, the list of interrelated factors in Al-Rasheed, *Iraqi Assyrian Christians*, 26-27.

20. E.g., Dubuisson, *Western Construction of Religion*; J. Z. Smith, "Religion, Religions, Religious"; Chidester, *Savage Systems*; and Chidester, "Colonialism."

21. Masuzawa, *Invention of World Religions*.

22. Kippenberg, *Discovering Religious History in the Modern Age*.

23. Anidjar, "Idea of an Anthropology of Christianity," 373.

24. See comments on postsecularity in Dressler and Mandair, *Secularism and Religion-Making*, 3-24.

25. Asad, *Formations of the Secular*, 25.

26. Asad, *Genealogies of Religion*, 27-54.

27. Dressler and Mandair, *Secularism and Religion-Making*.

28. Lorenzen, "Who Invented Hinduism?"

29. E.g., Dalmia, *Nationalization of Hindu Traditions*.

30. Dressler, *Writing Religion*. See also Dressler, "Religio-secular Metamorphoses."

31. E.g., Palmié, *Wizards and Scientists*.

32. E.g., Becker, "Martyrdom, Religious Difference, and 'Fear.'"

33. Asad, *Genealogies of Religion*, 207.

34. Charles Taylor, *Secular Age*, 26-29.

35. Asad, *Formations of the Secular*, 191-92.

36. E.g., Mahmood, *Politics of Piety*.

37. E.g., Hauerwas, *State of the University*.

38. E.g., Hutchison, *Errand to the World*, 8.

39. Cameron, *Christianity and the Rhetoric of Empire*, 120-54; and Peter Brown, *Rise of Western Christendom*, 54-92. On the "saeculum" in Augustinian thought, see Markus, *Christianity and the Secular*.

40. MacCormack, *Religion in the Andes*, 205-48.

41. See comments, e.g., in Khalaf, *Cultural Resistance*, 118, 134.

42. For a more recent discussion, see Stroumsa, *End of Sacrifice*.

43. See the discussion in Casanova, *Public Religions in the Modern World*, 1-66.

44. Rufus Anderson, *Foreign Missions*, 96; on this text, see Harris, *Nothing but Christ*, 158-59. In general, see Hutchison, *Errand to the World*, 62-90.

45. Rufus Anderson, *Foreign Missions*, 99.

46. See comments in Khalaf, *Cultural Resistance*, 139, 149-50.

47. Harris, *Nothing but Christ*, 77-95.

48. Harris, *Nothing but Christ*, 162-63.

49. See Murre-van den Berg, introduction to *New Faith in Ancient Lands*, 13-17, on the opposition between converting and civilizing.

50. Murre-van den Berg, introduction to *New Faith in Ancient Lands*, 8. See also Makdisi, "Reclaiming the Land of the Bible," 707.

51. Murre-van den Berg, introduction to *New Faith in Ancient Lands*, 15n25; and Doğan and Sharkey, *American Missionaries and the Middle East*, xxviii.

52. Modern, *Secularism in Antebellum America*.

53. It seems that *secularism* and its cognates have begun in recent years to function as a stand-in for the term *modernity* and its cognates, and the former seems to be hitting contradictions and limits similar to the latter.

54. Ussama Makdisi uses the expression "evangelical modernity" to refer to the modernizing effects of missions in the absence of a colonial authority—i.e., as opposed to "colonial modernity." Makdisi, "Reclaiming the Land of the Bible," 680-713, esp. 681-84.

55. Van der Veer, *Imperial Encounters*, 7; Stanley, "Christian Missions and the Enlightenment"; and Walls, "Eighteenth-Century Protestant Missionary Awakening."

56. The mediation of modernity through colonialism is a common topic in the historiography of the Middle East—e.g., Abi-Mershed, *Apostles of Modernity*.

57. Stanley, "Christian Missions, Antislavery and the Claims of Humanity."

58. R. Pierce Beaver, *To Advance the Gospel*, 65-66, quoted in Walls, "American Dimension in the History of the Missionary Movement," 3-4.

59. Kedourie, "'Minorities,'" 289.

60. Makdisi, *Artillery of Heaven*; Khalaf, *Cultural Resistance*; Merguerian, "'Missions in Eden'"; and Kieser, "Muslim Heterodoxy and Protestant Utopia."

61. To state that there is one Christianity is a theological claim going back to the second century CE. The recent literature on the anthropology of Christianity attempts to treat this vast religious tradition as having common themes and tensions—e.g., Cannell, *Anthropology of Christianity*; the University of California Press's Anthropology of Christianity series, edited by Joel Robbins; and Robbins, "What Is a Christian?" Of course, technically there are always those forms of Christianity that can be excluded from any definition we provide, as Robbins notes (194). Christian philosophers of mission have had to work through this problem in order to find a unity, one that allows for Christianity's "infinite translatability." Walls, *Missionary Movement in Christian History*, 22. One way to conceptualize Christianity without being trapped in the limiting intellectual box of "religion" is as a discursive tradition, which would be to borrow from Talal Asad's influential approach to the study of Islam (which relies heavily on a reading of Alasdair MacIntyre). (See Ovamir Anjum, "Islam as a Discursive Tradition.") However, such a simple application of Asad's thinking on Islam to Christianity can be misleading, and has been criticized: Anidjar, "Idea of an Anthropology of Christianity," esp. 386-92.

62. See Charles Taylor's use of Norbert Elias's notion of the "civilizing process" in *Secular Age*, 137-42.

63. Charles Taylor, *Secular Age*, e.g., 151–58 passim.

64. Keane, *Christian Moderns*, 5.

65. Rublack, "Grapho-Relics," 144.

66. Yelle, *Language of Disenchantment*, 3–32.

67. Charles Taylor, *Secular Age*, 37–41; and Charles Taylor, "Western Secularity," 39–42.

68. E.g., Charles Taylor, *Secular Age*, 73–87.

69. Sedra, *From Mission to Modernity*; and Sengupta, *Pedagogy for Religion*.

70. Makdisi, "Ottoman Orientalism."

71. Fahmy, *All the Pasha's Men*.

72. E.g., Keddie, *Qajar Iran*; Lambton, *Qajar Persia*; and Ringer, *Education, Religion, and the Discourse of Cultural Reform*.

73. Zaman, *Ulama in Contemporary Islam*, 62.

74. E.g., Robbins, *Becoming Sinners*, 293, contrasts relationalism to individualism and, quoting Louis Dumont, refers to Christianity as "nonsocial."

75. Asad, *Formations of the Secular*, 194.

76. E.g., Anthony D. Smith, *Ethnic Origins of Nations*.

77. Karpat, *Inquiry into the Social Foundations of Nationalism*.

78. Masters, *Christians and Jews*, 61.

79. Masters, *Christians and Jews*, 11.

80. Makdisi, *Culture of Sectarianism*.

81. Benedict Anderson, *Imagined Communities*, 7.

82. Benedict Anderson, *Imagined Communities*, 6 (my emphasis).

83. Benedict Anderson, *Imagined Communities*, 12.

84. Benedict Anderson, *Imagined Communities*, 12.

85. Benedict Anderson, *Imagined Communities*, 14.

86. Keane, *Christian Moderns*, 2.

87. Benedict Anderson, *Imagined Communities*, 22.

88. Benedict Anderson, *Imagined Communities*, 24.

89. Benedict Anderson, *Imagined Communities*, 24.

90. Charles Taylor, *Modern Social Imaginaries*, 98.

91. Benedict Anderson, *Imagined Communities*, 26.

92. Benedict Anderson, *Imagined Communities*, 35.

93. On continuity, see most recently Anthony D. Smith, *Chosen Peoples*.

94. Charles Taylor, *Modern Social Imaginaries*, 99.

95. Van der Veer, *Imperial Encounters*, 28.

96. Van der Veer, *Imperial Encounters*, 43.

97. Van der Veer, *Imperial Encounters*, 53.

98. Goswami, "Rethinking the Modular Nation Form," 773n8.

99. Asad, *Formations of the Secular*, 190–91.

100. Charles Taylor, "Why We Need a Radical Redefinition of Secularism," 43.

101. Comaroff and Comaroff, *Of Revelation and Revolution*, 1:6.

102. Mehta, *Liberalism and Empire*.

103. Carey, *Empires of Religion*, 12.

104. See Robert, *Converting Colonialism*, 1–6, for a summary of the scholarly debate. For an example of the revisionist model, see Porter, "Religion and Empire." The revisionist position of Andrew Porter and Brian Stanley is discussed and challenged in Copland, "Christianity as an

Arm of Empire." See also Stuart, "Introduction: 'Mission and Empire'"; and Etherington, *"Missions and Empire* Revisited." I borrow here from the title of Beidelman's *Colonial Evangelism.*

105. Makdisi, "Reclaiming the Land of the Bible," 682.

106. Chatterjee, *Nation and Its Fragments,* 75.

107. For an attempt to amend the modularity argument, see Goswami, "Rethinking the Modular Nation Form."

108. *AR 1845,* 115.

109. This is how my work differs most from the Comaroffs' two-volume study of missionaries in Southern Africa, *Of Revelation and Revolution* (1991–97): religious discourse is of central importance to my project and in fact remains the focus of analysis. For similar criticisms, see Robbins, "Continuity Thinking and the Problem of Christian Culture"; and Peterson, "Conversion and the Alignments of Colonial Culture." On Raymond Williams's notion of "structures of feeling," see chap. 4.

110. Yelle, *Language of Disenchantment,* 137–60.

111. Fessenden, *Culture and Redemption,* 42.

112. On the late creation of the term *ethnicity,* see Prentiss, *Religion and the Creation of Race and Ethnicity,* 6–7.

113. Van der Veer, *Imperial Encounters,* 30–54.

114. Figueira, *Aryans, Jews, Brahmins.*

115. Bhatia, "Devotional Tradition and National Culture."

116. Charles Taylor, *Secular Age,* 454.

117. E.g., Catherine Hall, *Civilizing Subjects.*

118. Van der Veer, *Imperial Encounters,* 8.

119. Van der Veer, *Imperial Encounters,* 8.

Chapter 1

1. *ZB* 1, no. 2 (Dec. 1849): 14–15. This chapter has benefited from my reading of Wolk, "Preserving a Name in a Restless Land."

2. The document, several manuscript versions of which are attested, had already been published in Rome in the eighteenth century by the Maronite scholar J. S. Assemani, whose work Perkins in fact owned, but in this case seems to ignore. Below I quote from Assemani's Syriac original (*Bibliotheca Orientalis* 3.2.589–99). See most recently Murre-van den Berg, "Church of the East in the Sixteenth to the Eighteenth Century," esp. 309–13.

3. For dating, see Murre-van den Berg, "Patriarchs of the Church of the East."

4. Assemani, *Bibliotheca Orientalis* 3.1.598.

5. Justin Perkins, *Residence,* 170.

6. See Wallis Budge, *Monks of Kûblâi Khân,* for a translation of his memoir.

7. Ho, *Graves of Tarim,* 188–91.

8. Berthaud, "La vie rurale dans quelques villages chrétiens."

9. Justin Perkins, *Residence,* 177. Cf. Joseph P. Thompson, *Memoir,* 127–33.

10. Berthaud, "La vie rurale dans quelques villages chrétiens," 300.

11. Wilmshurst, *Ecclesiastical Organisation,* 339.

12. Lambton, *Qajar Persia,* 111. Cf. Justin Perkins, *Residence,* 148, 150.

13. Justin Perkins, *Residence,* 129.

14. Chevalier, *Les montagnards chrétiens,* 26n1.

15. Chevalier, *Les montagnards chrétiens*, 190, 125, respectively.

16. Chevalier, *Les montagnards chrétiens*, 193.

17. See the collection of figures, for example, in Murre-van den Berg, *From a Spoken to a Written Language*, 38-42.

18. Chevalier, *Les montagnards chrétiens*, 49.

19. Berthaud, "La vie rurale dans quelques villages chrétiens," 302.

20. E.g., Braude and Lewis, *Christians and Jews*, 15.

21. Nikitine, "La vie domestique des Assyro-Chaldéens," 359. For *headman*, see Maclean, *Dictionary*, 126.

22. Chevalier, *Les montagnards chrétiens*, 91-97.

23. Coakley, "Assyrian Christians in English Fiction."

24. See, e.g., Atesh, "Empires at the Margin."

25. Chevalier, *Les montagnards chrétiens*, 97-98; see p. 54 for the possible "Nestorian" origins of some Kurdish tribes.

26. Chevalier, *Les montagnards chrétiens*, 149-50.

27. Chevalier, *Les montagnards chrétiens*, 212.

28. Chevalier, *Les montagnards chrétiens*, 164n1; in general, 164-75.

29. Chevalier, *Les montagnards chrétiens*, 177. Cf. Gordon Taylor, *Fever and Thirst*, 69-71.

30. Chevalier, *Les montagnards chrétiens*, 209.

31. Chevalier, *Les montagnards chrétiens*, 219-20.

32. Chevalier, *Les montagnards chrétiens*, 99-100.

33. E.g., Chevalier, *Les montagnards chrétiens*, 205.

34. Chevalier, *Les montagnards chrétiens*, 180-88.

35. Murre-van den Berg, "Classical Syriac," 345.

36. Murre-van den Berg, *From a Spoken to a Written Language*, 87-91; and Murre-van den Berg, "Classical Syriac," 344.

37. Murre-van den Berg, "Let Us Partake," 151-52.

38. Murre-van den Berg, "Classical Syriac," 344.

39. Murre-van den Berg, *From a Spoken to a Written Language*, 31-42.

40. Trigona-Harany, *Ottoman Süryânî*, 102. See his discussion of new *millets*, 77-111.

41. See several essays in Braude and Lewis, *Christians and Jews in the Ottoman Empire*, vol. 1. Also, Karpat, *Inquiry into the Social Foundations of Nationalism*.

42. Chevalier, *Les montagnards chrétiens*, 61.

43. Compare, e.g., Chevalier, *Les montagnards chrétiens*, 196-200; Nikitine, "La vie domestique des Assyro-Chaldéens," 363; and Joseph, *Modern Assyrians*, 71-72, 76-78.

44. Van Bruinessen, *Agha, Shaikh, and State*, 177-80; Joseph, *Modern Assyrians*, 72-85; and Wilmshurst, *Martyred Church*, 373-75.

45. Chevalier, *Les montagnards chrétiens*, 60.

46. Cf. van Bruinessen, "Kurdish Tribes and the State of Iran."

47. Masters, *Christians and Jews*, 133.

48. Masters, *Christians and Jews*, 5-6. On the *dhimmi* system in general, see 18-26.

49. Masters, *Christians and Jews*, 132.

50. MacEvitt, *Crusades*, 21.

51. MacEvitt, *Crusades*, 25.

52. MacEvitt, *Crusades*, 101.

53. Makdisi, *Artillery of Heaven*, 34.

54. Abrahamian, *History of Modern Iran*, 33.

55. Makdisi, *Artillery of Heaven*, 47.

56. E.g., Murre-van den Berg, "Apostasy"; and Wolk, "Migration and the Transformation of Assyrian Stereotypes."

57. Murre-van den Berg, "Apostasy."

58. Murre-van den Berg, "Apostasy," 238–40, 237, respectively.

59. Murre-van den Berg, "Apostasy," 235.

60. Murre-van den Berg, "Apostasy," 230–31.

61. Murre-van den Berg, "Apostasy," 239–40.

62. Becker, "Martyrdom, Religious Difference, and 'Fear.'"

63. On patriarchal lines, see Murre-van den Berg, "Patriarchs of the Church of the East."

64. Wilmshurst, *Martyred Church*, 376–783.

65. Chevalier, *Les montagnards chrétiens*, 229.

66. Chevalier, *Les montagnards chrétiens*, 211.

67. Chevalier, *Les montagnards chrétiens*, 224.

68. Chevalier, *Les montagnards chrétiens*, 227–28.

69. Chevalier, *Les montagnards chrétiens*, 234; Wilmshurst, *Ecclesiastical Organisation*, 365; and Wilmshurst, *Martyred Church*, 396.

70. Chevalier, *Les montagnards chrétiens*, 236.

71. On weapons in general among the East Syrians, see Dalyan, "Robbery, Blood Feud, and Gunpowder."

72. Chevalier, *Les montagnards chrétiens*, 240.

73. Chevalier, *Les montagnards chrétiens*, 241–42.

74. Macuch, *Geschichte*, 42–44; and Teule, "Joseph II, Patriarch of the Chaldeans (1676–1713/4)." See also comments in Murre-van den Berg, "Classical Syriac," 341. On study at Muslim schools, see Murre-van den Berg, "Apostasy," 233.

75. Chevalier, *Les montagnards chrétiens*, 243n5.

76. Wilmshurst, *Ecclesiastical Organisation*, 276–78.

77. Becker, "Doctoring the Past in the Present."

78. Wilmshurst, *Ecclesiastical Organisation*, 13–14.

79. Murre-van den Berg, "I the Weak Scribe," 16.

80. Murre-van den Berg, "I the Weak Scribe," 17–18.

81. Murre-van den Berg, "I the Weak Scribe," 19–20.

82. E.g., *MH* 1:398; and Chevalier, *Les montagnards chrétiens*, 227n1.

83. Murre-van den Berg, "Classical Syriac," 337–39, 342; and Murre-van den Berg, "'Let Us Partake,'" 146.

84. Murre-van den Berg, "Classical Syriac," 343.

85. Mengozzi, *Religious Poetry*, v–xxiv (translation); Murre-van den Berg, "'Let Us Partake,'" 147–50; and Murre-van den Berg, "Classical Syriac," 340, 346–47.

86. Murre-van den Berg, "Neo-Aramaic Gospel Lectionary."

87. Murre-van den Berg, "Syrian Awakening," 509–12.

88. Murre-van den Berg, "Generous Devotion."

89. Cf. Murre-van den Berg, "I the Weak Scribe," 20–25.

90. De Mauroy, "Lieux de culte."

91. Wigram and Wigram, *Cradle of Mankind*, 291.

92. Witakowski, "Magi in Syriac Tradition."

93. Wigram, *Cradle of Mankind*, 264; and Chevalier, *Les montagnards chrétiens*, 225n3.

94. Chevalier, *Les montagnards chrétiens*, 107; Wilmshurst, *Ecclesiastical Organisation*, 303–4, 369; and Chevalier, *Les montagnards chrétiens*, 113.

95. Wilmshurst, *Ecclesiastical Organisation*, 217–18, 241.

96. Chevalier, *Les montagnards chrétiens*, 257.

97. Wilmshurst, *Ecclesiastical Organisation*, 70, 72.

98. On this church, see de Mauroy, "Lieux de culte," 321–23; and Wilmshurst, *Ecclesiastical Organisation*, 324, 334, 353, 354.

99. Justin Perkins, *Residence*, 380.

100. De Mauroy, "Lieux de culte," 321, describes a *qorban* there on Aug. 24, 1971.

101. *MH* 1:520–21.

102. Laurie, *Dr. Grant*, 340; and Chevalier, *Les montagnards chrétiens*, 122.

103. Cf. Bruce Grant, "Shrines and Sovereigns."

104. Bigelow, *Sharing the Sacred*, 22.

105. Bigelow, *Sharing the Sacred*, 21.

106. *MH* 2:477–78.

107. Joseph P. Thompson, *Memoir*, 130–31.

108. *MH* 1:145, 1:147.

109. Chevalier, *Les montagnards chrétiens*, 109.

110. Cutts, *Christians under the Crescent*, 209.

111. Surma, *Assyrian Church Customs*, 27–28.

112. E.g., *MH* 1:157.

113. Surma, *Assyrian Church Customs*, 18.

114. Gollancz, *Book of Protection*; Bcheiry, "Syriac Manuscripts in New York Public Library"; Balicka-Witakowska, "Illustrating Charms"; and Teule, Kessel, and Sado, "Mikhail Sado Collection of Syriac Manuscripts in St. Petersburg," MSS 1, 5, 6, 11, 14, 20, 26.

115. For numerous examples, see Nikitine, "Superstitions des Chaldéens du plateau d'Ourmiah."

116. Keane, *Christian Moderns*, 47–55.

117. See similar comments on feminism: Mahmood, "Feminist Theory, Embodiment, and the Docile Agent," 203. See also Asad, *Genealogies of Religion*, 16.

118. For a broader frame for this issue, see Mahmood, "Religious Freedom, the Minority Question, and Geopolitics in the Middle East."

119. Kantorowicz, *King's Two Bodies*.

120. Asad, *Formations of the Secular*, e.g., 190–92.

121. Chakrabarty, *Provincializing Europe*, 15–16.

122. Nongbri, "Dislodging 'Embedded' Religion."

123. Masuzawa, *In Search of Dreamtime*, 43.

124. Asad, *Formations of the Secular*, 30.

Chapter 2

1. Justin Perkins, *Residence*, 170.

2. Wilmshurst, *Ecclesiastical Organisation*, 318–19.

3. Pratt, *Imperial Eyes*, 7–8.

4. Justin Perkins, *Residence*, 491.

5. Charles Samuel Stewart, *Journal of a Residence in the Sandwich Islands*.

6. Letter to Rufus Anderson, Jan. 15, 1842, Papers of the ABCFM, reel 553, doc. 77 (underlining in the original).

7. Justin Perkins, *Residence*, 84.

8. *MH* 2:13.

9. *MH* 1:23 (emphasis in the original).

10. Ameer, "Yankees and Nestorians," 203.

11. *MH* 1:62, 1:63, 1:238, 1:496, 1:551, 1:557.

12. *MH* 1:503.

13. *ZB* 1, no. 1 (Nov. 1849): 8.

14. *ZB* 2, no. 4 (Feb. 1851): 127–29.

15. *ZB* 2, no. 5 (Mar. 1851): 136.

16. Letter to Rufus Anderson, Mar. 23, 1842, Papers of the ABCFM, reel 553, doc. 79.

17. Letter to Rufus Anderson, Apr. 19, 1842, Papers of the ABCFM, reel 553, doc. 84.

18. Letter to Rufus Anderson, Apr. 19, 1842, Papers of the ABCFM, reel 553, doc. 84.

19. Letter to Rufus Anderson, Aug. 9, 1841, from Albert Holladay et al., Papers of the ABCFM, reel 553, doc. 48.

20. Letter to William J. Armstrong, Jan. 24, 1843, Papers of the ABCFM, reel 553, doc. 99.

21. Letter to Rufus Anderson, June 15, 1842, Papers of the ABCFM, reel 553, doc. 87.

22. Letter to Rufus Anderson, Oct. 7, 1842, Papers of the ABCFM, reel 553, doc. 95.

23. Letter to Rufus Anderson, Dec. 2, 1842, Papers of the ABCFM, reel 553, doc. 98. See Justin Perkins, *Residence*, after p. 172, for the image of Yohannan he did publish.

24. Letter to Rufus Anderson, Feb. 17, 1843, Papers of the ABCFM, reel 553, doc. 102.

25. Letter to Rufus Anderson, Feb. 17, 1843, Papers of the ABCFM, reel 553, doc. 102.

26. Letter to Rufus Anderson, Feb. 18, 1843, Papers of the ABCFM, reel 553, doc. 105 (underlining in the original).

27. Cf. Justin Perkins, *Residence*, 438, for the expression "Magnus Apollo."

28. Letter to Rufus Anderson, Feb. 17, 1843, Papers of the ABCFM, reel 553, doc. 102.

29. Letter to William J. Armstrong, Apr. 3, 1843, Papers of the ABCFM, reel 553, doc. 104.

30. E.g., Justin Perkins, *Missionary Life in Persia*, 57–59.

31. Berthaud, "La vie rurale dans quelques villages chrétiens," 299.

32. Pratt, *Imperial Eyes*, 9.

33. Justin Perkins, *Residence*, 17, 254, 499.

34. His son's biography provides a handy chronology: Henry Martyn Perkins, *Life*.

35. Henry Martyn Perkins, *Life*, 9.

36. Henry Martyn Perkins, *Life*, 10.

37. Henry Martyn Perkins, *Life*, 10.

38. Henry Martyn Perkins, *Life*, 11–12.

39. For the millennialism of this period in American missions to the Middle East, see, e.g., Marr, *Cultural Roots of American Islamicism*, 82–133.

40. Amanat, "*Mujtahids* and Missionaries." The story of Martyn and British/Iranian relations at the time is told in several articles by Nile Green—e.g., "Madrasas of Oxford."

41. Coakley, *Church of the East and the Church of England*, 11–97.

42. Justin Perkins, *Residence*, 33.

43. Justin Perkins, *Residence*, 28 (emphasis in the original).

44. Justin Perkins, *Residence*, 29 (emphasis in the original).

45. Justin Perkins, *Residence*, 30.

46. Justin Perkins, *Residence*, 31 (emphasis in the original).

47. Justin Perkins, *Residence*, 33 (emphasis in the original).

48. Murre-van den Berg, "'Simply by Giving to Them Macaroni . . .'"

49. E.g., Joseph P. Thompson, *Memoir*, 99–106.

50. Philips, *Protestant America and the Pagan World*, 20–31.

51. Keane, *Christian Moderns*, 6.

52. *MH* 1:28.

53. On the city in the mid-twentieth century, see Berthaud, "La vie rurale," 299. For clergy on the plain, see Wilmshurst, *Martyred Church*, 396.

54. Justin Perkins, *Residence*, 171.

55. Justin Perkins, *Residence*, 171–72.

56. Eli Smith and H. G. O. Dwight, *Missionary Researches in Armenia*, 342–411, esp. 370–85.

57. Justin Perkins, *Residence*, 173.

58. Justin Perkins, *Residence*, 173n*.

59. Justin Perkins, *Residence*, 173–74.

60. Justin Perkins, *Residence*, 175–76 (emphasis in the original).

61. Justin Perkins, *Residence*, 177.

62. Justin Perkins, *Residence*, 179; and Wilmshurst, *Ecclesiastical Organisation* 320, 335.

63. Wilmshurst, *Martyred Church*, 383.

64. Wilmshurst, *Ecclesiastical Organisation*, 32.

65. For Perkins's poor understanding of the situation, see Justin Perkins, *Residence*, 199.

66. Justin Perkins, *Residence*, 180–82.

67. Justin Perkins, *Residence*, 28, 163–64, 32.

68. Justin Perkins, *Residence*, 279.

69. Justin Perkins, *Residence*, 20.

70. Justin Perkins, *Residence*, 209.

71. Justin Perkins, *Residence*, 14.

72. Justin Perkins, *Residence*, 15–16.

73. Justin Perkins, *Residence*, 16, 185.

74. Justin Perkins, *Residence*, 16.

75. Justin Perkins, *Residence*, 89–91.

76. Justin Perkins, *Residence*, 50.

77. Justin Perkins, *Residence*, 94, 231, 126–27, 159.

78. *MH* 1:427, 2:44.

79. *MH* 2:38.

80. E.g., *MH* 2:38, 2:43, 3:269.

81. Justin Perkins, *Residence*, 422–23.

82. Justin Perkins, *Residence*, 446–47; cf. Malick #2.

83. *MH* 1:406.

84. Justin Perkins, *Residence*, 272–73.

85. Justin Perkins, *Residence*, 273.

86. Reinders, *Borrowed Gods and Foreign Bodies*, 100–112.

87. *ZB* 2, no. 12 (Oct. 1851): 189.

88. *ZB* 3, no. 4 (Feb. 1852): 223–24.

89. Modern, *Secularism in Antebellum America*, 106, cf. 57.

90. Justin Perkins, *Residence*, 329–30.

91. Biography in Malick #129, 295–96.

92. Justin Perkins, *Residence*, 182.

93. [Missionaries of the ABCFM], *Nestorian Biography*, 177–200, is the primary source. See Murre-van den Berg, "Missionaries' Assistants," 4.

94. Malick #129, 290; and Macuch, *Geschichte*, 158–59.

95. Justin Perkins, *Residence*, 185.

96. Justin Perkins, *Residence*, 232. See also [Missionaries of the ABCFM], *Nestorian Biography*, 189.

97. Murre-van den Berg, "Missionaries' Assistants," 13–15.

98. Becker, *Fear of God*, esp. 22–40.

99. Justin Perkins, *Residence*, 183.

100. *MH* 1:23; cf. Justin Perkins, *Residence*, 183.

101. See, for example, the discussion in Becker, "Polishing the Mirror," 2:907–8.

102. Rubenstein, *Strange Wonder*, 7–12.

103. Justin Perkins, *Residence*, 211.

104. Justin Perkins, *Residence*, 211–12.

105. Justin Perkins, *Residence*, 334.

106. Justin Perkins, *Residence*, 335 (emphasis in the original).

107. Justin Perkins, *Residence*, 257; cf. *AR 1837*, 66.

108. Justin Perkins, *Residence*, 257.

109. Isho'dad, *Commentaries*, 2:99 (translation: 1:58–59).

110. For the former, see Brock, *Luminous Eye*, 46–51.

111. *MH* 1:284.

112. *MH* 1:408.

113. Justin Perkins, *Residence*, 317.

114. *ZB* 1, no. 7 (May 1850): 53.

115. Justin Perkins, *Residence*, 318.

116. Papers of the ABCFM, reel 553, doc. 123.

117. *ZB* 1, no. 6 (Apr. 1850): 44–45.

118. Justin Perkins, *Residence*, 329 (emphasis in the original).

119. Pietz, "Problem of the Fetish, I," 11.

120. Pietz, "Problem of the Fetish, I," 14.

121. Pietz, "Problem of the Fetish, I," 15.

122. [Missionaries of the ABCFM], *Nestorian Biography*, 188.

123. Justin Perkins, *Residence*, 456 (emphasis in the original).

124. Malick #1.

125. Murre-van den Berg, "Missionaries' Assistants," 10–11; Eli Smith and H. G. O. Dwight, *Missionary Researches*, 370; Hornus, "Un rapport du consul de France à Erzeroum" (1971), 144–46; and Malick #129, 305–6.

126. Malick #129, 302.

127. Wilmshurst, *Ecclesiastical Organisation*, 319.

128. De Mauroy, "Lieux de culte," 344–45.

129. Keane, *Christian Moderns*, 23–25.

130. Keane, *Christian Moderns*, 224.

131. Hutchison, *Errand to the World*, 49–51.

132. E.g., Justin Perkins, *Residence*, 225, 227, 505.

133. *MH* 1:24.

134. *MH* 1:23.

135. E.g., "harvest" in Justin Perkins, *Residence*, 73, 199, 209, 212, 245, 287, 374–75, 432.

136. Thomas, *Entangled Objects*, 28.

137. Meyer, "Religious Revelation, Secrecy and the Limits of Visual Representation," esp. 435–37; Meyer, *Aesthetic Formations*, 11–14; and Zito, "Culture." See also Meyer and Moors, *Religion, Media, and the Public Sphere*, 1–25.

138. Modern, *Secularism in Antebellum America*, 60.

139. Meyer, *Aesthetic Formations*, 2.

140. Meyer, *Aesthetic Formations*, 14.

141. Stolow, "Religion and/as Media," 122. See also Zito, "Culture," 70–71.

142. Stolow, *Orthodox by Design*, 23.

143. Warner, *Letters of the Republic*, 5–7; and Yelle, *Language of Disenchantment*, 15, 31.

144. Warner, *Letters of the Republic*, 71.

145. Warner, *Letters of the Republic*, 4.

Chapter 3

1. Justin Perkins, *Residence*, 497 (emphasis in the original).

2. Wosh, *Spreading the Word*.

3. Candy Gunther Brown, *Word in the World*, esp. 9–15.

4. For a list of all publications with descriptions, see Malick, *American Mission Press*.

5. Coakley, *Typography of Syriac*, 198–215.

6. Malick, *American Mission Press*, 8–25.

7. Murre-van den Berg, *From a Spoken to a Written Language*.

8. Murre-van den Berg, "Missionaries' Assistants."

9. Malick, *American Mission Press*, 115–17, brings together the numbers from the annual reports.

10. Malick #43.

11. Unfortunately, the paper is not extant between Dec. 1871 and 1892, and many issues are missing from the period 1856–71.

12. *ZB* 14, no. 5 (May 1864): 39.

13. Becker, "Martyrdom, Religious Difference, and 'Fear.'"

14. *ZB* 3, no. 10 (Aug. 1852): 274.

15. E.g., *ZB* 2, no. 8 (June 1851): 155.

16. *ZB* 19, no. 4 (Apr. 1869): 30.

17. *ZB* 1, no. 1 (Nov. 1849): 1; translated in Murre-van den Berg, *From a Spoken to a Written Language*, 381–83.

18. *ZB* 1, no. 1 (Nov. 1849): 2; translated in Murre-van den Berg, *From a Spoken to a Written Language*, 385. Cf. Assemani, *Bibliotheca Orientalis*, 3.2 (chap. 15).

19. *ZB* 1, no. 1 (Nov. 1849): 4–5; translated in Murre-van den Berg, *From a Spoken to a Written Language*, 385–87.

20. *ZB* 1, no. 3 (Jan. 1850): 19–20.

21. Masters, *Christians and Jews*, 61.

22. Konortas, "From Tā'ife to Millet."

23. Masters, *Christians and Jews*, 63.

24. *ZB* 1, no. 4 (Feb. 1850): 26.

25. *ZB* 2, no. 4 (Feb. 1851): 123.

26. *ZB* 3, no. 3 (Jan. 1852): 216 (reads: 116); *ZB* 3, no. 4 (Feb. 1852): 223; and *ZB* 3, no. 12 (Oct. 1852): 290.

27. E.g., Kashani-Sabet, *Frontier Fictions*, 101–43.

28. *ZB* 2, no. 5 (Mar. 1851): 137.

29. *ZB* 2, no. 5 (Mar. 1851): 137.

30. *ZB* 2, no. 2 (Dec. 1850): 113.

31. *ZB* 3, no. 9 (July 1852): 263–64.

32. Wolk, "Expressions Concerning the Heart (*Libbā*)."

33. E.g., *ZB* 13, no. 10 (Oct. 1863): 74–75.

34. *ZB* 1, no. 4 (Feb. 1850): 27.

35. *ZB* 1, no. 4 (Feb. 1850): 29.

36. *ZB* 3, no. 8 (June 1851): 155.

37. E.g., *ZB* 3, no. 5 (Mar. 1852): 228.

38. Malick #18c (dated 1843), 10; see also p. 17 (separate 1844 edition missing from Malick).

39. Malick #16, 2; printed in Murre-van den Berg, *From a Spoken to a Written Language*, 365.

40. *ZB* 1, no. 5 (Mar. 1850): 34 (reads: 50).

41. Malick #8, 9ff. and passim.

42. Malick #55.

43. Malick #17, 6–12.

44. Malick #17, 8.

45. Malick #17, 10–11.

46. *ZB* 1, no. 1 (Nov. 1849): 3.

47. *ZB* 1, no. 2 (Dec. 1849): 9.

48. *ZB* 3, no. 2 (Dec. 1851): 203–4.

49. *ZB* 3, no. 3 (Jan. 1852): 212.

50. Malick #12, 1.

51. *ZB* 1, no. 1 (Nov. 1849): 3.

52. *ZB* 3, no. 10 (Aug. 1852): 268.

53. *ZB* 2, no. 2 (Dec. 1850): 113.

54. *ZB* 10, no. 7 (Mar. 1859): 246.

55. *ZB* 1, no. 1 (Nov. 1849): 6.

56. *ZB* 3, no. 10 (Aug. 1852): 269.

57. *ZB* 3, no. 11 (Sept. 1852): 278; *ZB* 3, no. 10 (Aug. 1852): 267.

58. *ZB* 3, no. 3 (Jan. 1852): 214.

59. *ZB* 14, no. 3 (Mar. 1864): 17; *ZB* 15, no. 8 (Aug. 1865): 64; *ZB* 17, no. 3 (Mar. 1867): 18; and *ZB* 19, no. 11 (reads: 19, no. 10) (Nov. 1869): 89.

60. Cf. Tsereteli, "Velar Spirant ġ," 36–37.

61. *ZB* 1, no. 8 (June 1850): 59.

62. Macuch and Panoussi, *Neusyrische Chrestomathie*, 126.

63. E.g., David, *First English-Chaldean Dictionary*, 126–27.

64. *ZB* 3, no. 3 (Jan. 1852): 215.

65. Asad, "Thinking about Religion, Belief, and Politics," 54, including n. 35.

66. Malick #18c, 11.

67. Malick #18c, 30, 20, and passim.

68. Malick #18c, 5, 7, respectively.

69. Malick #18c, 8.

70. Malick #18c, 17.

71. Malick #18c, 5.

72. For several usages in one article, see *ZB* 3, no. 4 (Feb. 1852) (reads: Jan. 1852): 219–22.

73. *ZB* 1, no. 1 (Nov. 1849): 8.

74. *ZB* 3, no. 12 (Oct. 1852): 290.

75. *ZB* 3, no. 2 (Dec. 1851): 208; and *ZB* 3, no. 6 (Apr. 1852): 240.

76. *ZB* 3, no. 6 (Apr. 1852): 238.

77. Malick #75, 27; and *ZB* 3, no. 1 (Nov. 1851): 197.

78. *ZB* 3, no. 5 (Mar. 1852): 227.

79. *ZB* 3, no. 1 (Nov. 1851): 197.

80. *ZB* 1, no. 8 (June 1850): 61.

81. *ZB* 2, no. 3 (Jan. 1851): 118.

82. Malick #10/#18e, 1.

83. Malick #10/#18e, 7.

84. Malick #10/#18e, 12.

85. Malick #10/#18e, 13.

86. Wendy Brown, *Regulating Aversion*, 150–51.

87. Keane, *Christian Moderns*, 104.

88. E.g., *MH* 1:194.

89. *MH* 1:499.

90. E.g., *MH* 1:195.

91. Malick #15/#18d. See also, e.g., *MH* 1:438.

92. *MH* 1:342.

93. Malick #15/#18d, 8–9.

94. Malick #15/#18d, 12.

95. Malick #15/#18d, 37.

96. Malick #15/#18d, 40.

97. *MH* 1:199.

98. This tract in addition to three others was translated into Classical Syriac by Deacon Joseph (cf. Perkins, *Residence*, 336–37) and presented as a gift to William R. Stocking in 1844. It was copied by a young Osha'na Saro, who will appear in chapters 8 and 9. Harvard Syriac 9 (formerly: Houghton Syriac 9).

99. Malick #15/#18d, 25.

100. *ZB* 12, no. 12 (Dec. 1862): 99.

101. Justin Perkins, "Our Country's Sin," 9; and *MH* 2:303–7.

102. *ZB* 2, no. 3 (Jan. 1851): 119–20.

103. *ZB* 14, no. 5 (May 1864): 39.

104. E.g., *ZB* 1, no. 1 (Nov. 1849): 2.

105. E.g., *ZB* 11, no. 4 (Apr. 1861): 25–26.

106. Malick #12.

107. *ZB* 1, no. 10 (Aug. 1850): 79–80.

108. *ZB* 2, no. 7 (May 1851), 152–53.

109. *ZB* 2, no. 12 (Oct. 1851): 190.

110. *ZB* 2, no. 9 (July 1851): 165.

111. *ZB* 2, no. 12 (Oct. 1851): 188.

112. Sivasundaram, *Nature and the Godly Empire*, 20.

113. Elshakry, "Knowledge in Motion," 708.

114. Sivasundaram, *Nature and the Godly Empire*, 8.

115. *ZB* 1, no. 6 (Apr. 1850): 45.

116. *ZB* 1, no. 6 (Apr. 1850): 46.

117. *ZB* 1, no. 2 (Dec. 1849): 12.

118. *ZB* 2, no. 7 (May 1851): 151–53.

119. *ZB* 3, no. 2 (Dec. 1851): 206–7.

120. *ZB* 3, no. 2 (Dec. 1851): 207.

121. *ZB* 3, no. 2 (Dec. 1851): 208.

122. *ZB* 1, no. 8 (June 1850): 61.

123. *ZB* 3, no. 11 (Sept. 1852): 278.

124. *ZB* 14, no. 8 (Aug. 1864): 43.

125. Malick #31 and #32.

126. *MH* 2:79–80. Cf. *MH* 2:104.

127. Malick #31, 1–2.

128. Malick #31, 2.

129. *ZB* 2, no. 2 (Dec. 1850): 111.

130. *ZB* 2, no. 2 (Dec. 1850): 112.

131. *ZB* 2, no. 2 (Dec. 1850): 112.

132. Malick #77.

133. Malick #77, g–d.

134. Malick #77, 1, 34.

135. Malick #77, 2.

136. Becker, "Doctoring the Past in the Present."

137. Malick #77, 5, 14.

138. Malick #77, 7–8.

139. Malick #77, 21–22.

140. Malick #77, 25.

141. See also Malick #77, 141.

142. Nanni, *Colonisation of Time*, 42–50.

143. *ZB* 14, no. 1 (Jan. 1864); *ZB* 16, no. 1 (Jan. 1866); *ZB* 17, no. 1 (Jan. 1867); *ZB* 19, no. 1 (Jan. 1869); *ZB* 20, no. 1 (Jan. 1870); and *ZB* 21, no. 1 (Jan. 1871).

144. *ZB* 14, no. 1 (Jan. 1864): 1–2, 8. Cf. Malick #91, 15.

145. *ZB* 11, no. 2 (Feb. 1861) through 1865; quotation from *ZB* 11, no. 2 (Feb. 1861): 13.

146. *ZB* 1, no. 5 (Mar. 1850): 56.

147. *ZB* 13, no. 4 (Apr. 1863): 31–32.

148. *ZB* 2, no. 6 (Apr. 1851): 139–40.

149. *ZB* 13, no. 3 (Mar. 1863): 24.

150. Meyer, *Translating the Devil*, 31–32.

151. *ZB* 13, no. 7 (July 1863): 49.

152. Malick #10/#18e, 23–24.

153. Malick #46.

154. *MH* 3:371.

155. *ZB* 3, no. 8 (June 1852): 252–55 passim.

156. *ZB* 2, no. 11 (Sept. 1851): 181.

157. *ZB* 2, no. 9 (July 1851): 163.

158. *ZB* 2, no. 8 (June 1851): 162.

159. Malick #70.

160. Malick #70, 2.

161. Mehta, *Liberalism and Empire*.

162. Mill, *On Liberty*, 74.

163. Murre-van den Berg, "'I the Weak Scribe,'" 24–25.

Chapter 4

1. *MH* 3:372–73.

2. Ameer, "Yankees and Nestorians," 302 (app. F).

3. For a source treating many of the events to follow, see Joseph P. Thompson, *Memoir*, 169–77.

4. Murre-van den berg, "American Board," 122–23.

5. Murre-van den berg, "American Board," 127–28.

6. Gordon Taylor, *Fever and Thirst*, 312.

7. Gordon Taylor, *Fever and Thirst*, 25.

8. Murre-van den berg, "American Board," 123–26.

9. Murre-van den berg, "American Board," 128–34. See also Marr, *Cultural Roots of American Islamicism*, 120–26.

10. E.g., Porterfield, *Mary Lyon*, 157.

11. Robert, *American Women in Mission*, 109.

12. *AR 1851*, 87–88; and *AR 1852*, 89–90.

13. For full numbers, see Malick, *American Mission Press*, 115–17. See also Laurie, *Woman and Her Saviour*, 297.

14. *MH* 1:244.

15. Walls, "American Dimension," 14 (emphasis in the original).

16. *MH* 2:23; *Missionary Herald* 34 (1838): 135, 192; *Missionary Herald* 49 (1853): 95; and Laurie, *Woman and Her Saviour*, 211.

17. *MH* 1:65, 1:466.

18. *MH* 3:121.

19. Meyer, *Aesthetic Formations*, 5.

20. Simmel, *Sociology*, 41.

21. Simmel, *Sociology*, 43.

22. Simmel, *Sociology*, 42.

23. Simmel, *Sociology*, 43.

24. Simmel, *Sociology*, 52.

25. Simmel, *Sociology*, 10.

26. Simmel, *Sociology*, 10–11.

27. Simmel, *Sociology*, 32–33.

28. Scott, "Evidence of Experience."

29. Williams, *Marxism and Literature*, 126.

30. Williams, *Marxism and Literature*, 128.

31. Williams, *Marxism and Literature*, 129.

32. Williams, *Marxism and Literature*, 130.

33. Williams, *Marxism and Literature*, 130–31.

34. Williams, *Marxism and Literature*, 131.

35. Williams, *Marxism and Literature*, 132.

36. Williams, *Marxism and Literature*, 133–34.

37. Elisha, *Moral Ambition*, 20.

38. Elisha, *Moral Ambition*, 18.

39. Elisha, *Moral Ambition*, 18–19.

40. *ZB* 20, no. 12 (Dec. 1870): 90.

41. *ZB* 4, no. 13 (Jan. 1853): 33; see also *ZB* 3, no. 15 (Mar. 1852): 228; and *ZB* 19, no. 11 (Jan. 1869): 1.

42. Douglas, *Feminization of American Culture*.

43. Murre-van den Berg, "'Dear Mother of My Soul,'" 40–41.

44. Murre-van den Berg, "'Inheritance with Sarah,'" 200–201.

45. Murre-van den Berg, "'Dear Mother of My Soul,'" 45.

46. Malick #99; see Murre-van den Berg, "'Good and Blessed Father.'"

47. Bielo, *Words upon the Word*, 74.

48. Bielo, *Words upon the Word*, 75.

49. Bielo, *Words upon the Word*, 76.

50. Bielo, *Words upon the Word*, 77.

51. Harding, *Book of Jerry Falwell*, 12, 34, 36–37.

52. Calvin, *On the Christian Faith*, 124.

53. E.g., Murre-van den Berg, "Nineteenth-Century Protestant Missions and Middle Eastern Women," 107.

54. For a brief summary of Elias's work, see Goudsblom and Mennell, *Norbert Elias Reader*, 40–45.

55. Fiske, *Faith Working by Love*, 145.

56. Fiske, *Faith Working by Love*, 145–46.

57. Fiske, *Faith Working by Love*, 146.

58. *MH* 1:497.

59. On these institutions in the early period, see Ameer, "Yankees and Nestorians," as well as Ameer, "Curriculum and Literacy"; on the last of these, see Justin Perkins, *Residence*, 404, and the discussion in Ameer, "Yankees and Nestorians," 106–12.

60. Justin Perkins, *Residence*, 250; and Ameer, "Yankees and Nestorians," 120.

61. Mitchell, *Colonising Egypt*, 69–71; Sedra, *From Mission to Modernity*; Khalaf, *Cultural Resistance*, 186–88; and Sivasundaram, *Nature and the Godly Empire*, 66–74.

62. Sedra, *From Mission to Modernity*, 23, 30, respectively.

63. Sedra, *From Mission to Modernity*, 14.

64. Justin Perkins, *Residence*, 249.

65. Ameer, "Yankees and Nestorians," 120.

66. *MH* 1:465.

67. Kieschnick, *Impact of Buddhism*, 222–47.

68. Foucault, *Discipline and Punish*, 165.

69. [Missionaries of the ABCFM], *Nestorian Biography*, 8–9.

70. *AR 1844*, 144.

71. Ameer, "Yankees and Nestorians," 145–47.

72. On the Darwin controversy, see, e.g., Elshakry, "Gospel of Science."

73. Sengupta, *Pedagogy for Religion*, 44.

74. Fiske, *Faith Working by Love*, 289.

75. Pruitt, *Looking-Glass for Ladies*, 104–13; Porterfield, *Mary Lyon*, 68–86; Robert, *American Women in Mission*, 109–14; and Ameer, "Fidelia Fiske: Missionary in Urmia." In general, see Murre-van den Berg, "Nineteenth-Century Protestant Missions and Middle Eastern Women"; and Reeves-Ellington, "Women, Protestant Missions, and American Cultural Expansion." For

useful parallels in the Balkans, see Reeves-Ellington, "Gender, Conversion, and Social Transformation"; Reeves-Ellington, "Women, Gender, and Missionary Education"; and Reeves-Ellington, "Vision of Mount Holyoke in the Ottoman Balkans."

76. Porterfield, *Mary Lyon*, 5.

77. Burton, *Burdens of History*, 42.

78. Burton, *Burdens of History*, 43.

79. Pruitt, *Looking-Glass for Ladies*, 4, 68–86; cf. Burton, *Burdens of History*, 63–66.

80. Pruitt, *Looking-Glass for Ladies*, 3.

81. Fiske, *Faith Working by Love*, 275 (letter of Fidelia Fiske and Mary Susan Rice to ABCFM, Sept. 15, 1853, ABCFM archive 5:58, reprinted in Ameer, "Yankees and Nestorians," 281).

82. *MH* 1:544; and *AR 1844*, 144.

83. Letter of Fidelia Fiske and Mary Susan Rice to ABCFM, Sept. 15, 1853, ABCFM archive 5:58, reprinted in Ameer, "Yankees and Nestorians," 282; see also Robert, *American Women in Mission*, 112–13.

84. Fiske, *Faith Working by Love*, 128; and *MH* 1:543.

85. Laurie, *Woman and Her Saviour*, 61.

86. Fiske, *Faith Working by Love*, 128–30; and Laurie, *Woman and Her Saviour*, 22–23.

87. Fiske, *Faith Working by Love*, 134.

88. *MH* 1:545–46.

89. *MH* 3:474.

90. Fiske, *Faith Working by Love*, 123, 125; Ameer, "Yankees and Nestorians," 279–80; and Laurie, *Woman and Her Saviour*, 13–26 (chap. 1, "Woman without the Gospel").

91. Murre-van den Berg, "'Inheritance with Sarah,'" 192.

92. Murre-van den Berg, "'Inheritance with Sarah,'" 200–201.

93. Murre-van den Berg, "'Inheritance with Sarah,'" 206.

94. Porterfield, *Mary Lyon*, 12.

95. Robert, *American Women in Mission*, 110.

96. Murre-van den Berg, "'Inheritance with Sarah,'" 204–5.

97. Fiske, *Faith Working by Love*, 303–4.

98. Justin Perkins, *Residence*, 235.

99. Malick #61.

100. E.g., Laurie, *Woman and Her Saviour*, 14–15.

101. Malick #80.

102. *ZB* 43, no. 12 (Dec. 1892): 91; and *AR 1893*, 177.

103. See Murre-van den Berg, "Nineteenth-Century Protestant Missions and Middle Eastern Women"; Okkenhaug, "Introduction: Gender and Missions in the Middle East," which focuses on women's transnational vocations and their role as agents of social welfare; and Reeves-Ellington, "Women, Protestant Missions, and American Cultural Expansion."

104. Laurie, *Woman and Her Saviour*, 234.

105. Letter of Fidelia Fiske and Mary Susan Rice to ABCFM, Sept. 15, 1853, ABCFM archive 5:58, reprinted in Ameer, "Yankees and Nestorians," 278.

106. Ameer, "Yankees and Nestorians," 199.

107. Ameer, "Yankees and Nestorians," 202; cf. *MH* 1:244–45.

108. *MH* 2:510.

109. *MH* 2:82.

110. *MH* 2:82.

111. *MH* 3:460.

112. Ameer, "Yankees and Nestorians," 217.

113. *MH* 2:360–66.

114. Fiske, *Faith Working by Love*, 157–58.

115. Laurie, *Woman and Her Saviour*, 223–24.

116. Fiske, *Faith Working by Love*, 239.

117. Laurie, *Woman and Her Saviour*, 224.

118. Porterfield, *Mary Lyon*, 74.

119. *MH* 2:320.

120. *ZB* 2, no. 10 (Aug. 1851): 171.

121. Laurie, *Woman and Her Saviour*, 228–29, translation of *ZB* 2, no. 10 (Aug. 1851): 173.

122. Mitchell, *Colonising Egypt*, 13.

123. Laurie, *Woman and Her Saviour*, 231–36.

124. *MH* 1:620.

125. Benedict Anderson, *Imagined Communities*, 35.

126. Newell and Hall, *Conversion of the World*, 3.

127. Newell and Hall, *Conversion of the World*, 13.

128. Newcomb, *Monthly Concert*, 107.

129. Newcomb, *Monthly Concert*, 5–6.

130. Newcomb, *Monthly Concert*, 7.

131. Newcomb, *Monthly Concert*, 20.

132. Newcomb, *Monthly Concert*, 25 (emphasis in the original).

133. Newcomb, *Monthly Concert*, 39.

134. Newcomb, *Monthly Concert*, 63.

135. Newcomb, *Monthly Concert*, 74.

136. Newcomb, *Monthly Concert*, 88.

137. Newcomb, *Monthly Concert*, 105.

138. Stoddard, *Narrative*; for "interest" before 1846, see Joseph P. Thompson, *Memoir*, 153–55.

139. Laurie, *Woman and Her Saviour*, 189.

140. *MH* 2:366.

141. *MH* 2:367.

142. *ZB* 21, no. 9 (Sept. 1871): 65–71.

143. Cf. Laurie, *Woman and Her Saviour*, 231–36, for Malik Agha Bey as chief.

144. *MH* 2:368. Until indicated otherwise, the quotations and information that follow are from this page.

145. *ZB* 14, no. 1 (Jan. 1864): 5–6.

146. On the use of the object lesson in a mission context, see Sengupta, *Pedagogy for Religion*, 61–80.

147. *MH* 3:292.

148. *MH* 3:294.

149. *MH* 2:131.

150. *MH* 3:288, 3:321, 3:455, 3:479.

151. *MH* 3:343; and *ZB* 13, no. 12 (Dec. 1863): 89 (emphasis in the original).

152. *ZB* 21, no. 1 (Jan. 1871): 2.

153. *ZB* 21, no. 12 (Dec. 1871): 89–90.

154. Murre-van den Berg, *From a Spoken to a Written Language*, 66–68; and Speer, "Hakim Sahib," 29–30.

155. Laurie, *Woman and Her Saviour*, 293ff.

156. *MH* 3:147–48.

157. *AR 1863*, 89.

158. *MH* 3:235, 3:251, respectively.

159. *MH* 2:319.

160. *MH* 3:261–62, 3:256.

161. *MH* 3:261.

162. *MH* 3:262.

163. E.g., in 1865, *MH* 3:431.

164. *MH* 3:332–33; cf. *AR 1862*, 112, 114.

165. *MH* 3:332.

166. *MH* 3:333; cf. *AR 1863*, 91.

167. *ZB* 12, no. 1 (Jan. 1862): 1–2.

168. *MH* 3:338; and *AR 1863*, 92.

169. *ZB* 12, no. 10 (Oct. 1862): 31.

170. *MH* 3:337–38.

171. On the need for each church to have a synod, see *ZB* 12, no. 10 (Oct. 1862): 32.

172. *MH* 3:338.

173. Malick #73.

174. *MH* 3:345–47.

175. *MH* 3:346; also quoted in Malick #73, 67.

176. E.g., Laurie, *Woman and Her Saviour*, 95. See *ZB* 17, no. 4 (Apr. 1867): 31–32, on the special birthday celebration for Justin Perkins.

177. E. P. Thompson, "Time, Work-Discipline, and Industrial Capitalism," 87. For the focus on practices, see Nanni, *Colonisation of Time*.

178. [Brainerd], *New Year*, 1–2.

179. Laurie, *Woman and Her Saviour*, 36 (see image on p. 131).

180. Joseph P. Thompson, *Memoir*, 180.

181. Laurie, *Woman and Her Saviour*, 36.

182. *ZB* 19, no. 4 (Apr. 1869): 30.

183. *ZB* 20, no. 2 (Feb. 1870): 16–17.

184. Malick #36 or #60; #27, #45, or #67; #91; and #73.

185. Malick #48. On this text in Barth's oeuvre, see Schnur, *Weltreiche und Wahrheitszeugen*, 80–81.

186. *MH* 1:125–37; and Keevak, *Story of a Stele*.

187. E.g., McGarry, *Ghost of Future Pasts*.

188. Van Bruinessen, *Agha, Shaikh, and State*, 59.

Chapter 5

1. *MH* 3:114.

2. Levi-Strauss, *Tristes tropiques*, 231.

3. Bunyan, *Pilgrim's Progress*, 110.

4. E.g., Berger, *Sacred Canopy*, 43–44.

5. Laderman, *Sacred Remains*, 52–55.

6. Laderman, *Sacred Remains*, 28.

7. Ariès, *Western Attitudes toward Death*, 46.

8. Ariès, *Western Attitudes toward Death*, 51.

9. See chapter title of Halttunen, *Confidence Men and Painted Women*, 124–52.

10. Halttunen, *Confidence Men and Painted Women*, 129; and Schofield, "Fashion of Mourning," 161.

11. Hattunen, *Confidence Men and Painted Women*, 131–32.

12. Hattunen, *Confidence Men and Painted Women*, 134, 144, respectively.

13. Douglas, *Feminization of American Culture*, 11–12.

14. For a response to Douglas, see Tompkins, *Sensational Designs*, 122–46.

15. Sánchez-Eppler, "Then When We Clutch Hardest," 64.

16. Cf. Tompkins, *Sensational Designs*, 122–46.

17. Tompkins, *Sensational Designs*, 127.

18. Bronfen, *Over Her Dead Body*, 90.

19. Bronfen, *Over Her Dead Body*, 90–92.

20. The publication of Nicholas Al-Jeloo's work promises to shed light on East Syrian funerary culture and its possible relationship to that of the missionaries. See Al-Jeloo, "Evidence in Stone and Wood."

21. Badger, *Nestorians and Their Rituals*, 2:319.

22. Badger, *Nestorians and Their Rituals*, 2:320.

23. Ephrem, *Opera omnia*, 6:300.

24. Buchan, *"Blessed Is He Who Has Brought Adam from Sheol."*

25. Ephrem the Syrian, *Hymns on Nativity*, 4:38 (translation in Ephrem, *Hymns*, 92).

26. Macomber, "Funeral Liturgy of the Chaldean Church," 19.

27. Surma, *Assyrian Church Customs*, 19.

28. Laurie, *Woman and Her Saviour*, 273.

29. Laurie, *Woman and Her Saviour*, 273ff.

30. Halttunen, *Confidence Men and Painted Women*.

31. Isaac Hollister Hall, "Specimens from the Nestorian Burial Service."

32. Isaac Hollister Hall, "Nestorian Ritual of the Washing of the Dead," 85.

33. E.g., Badger, *Nestorians and Their Rituals*, 2:130–39, 2:177.

34. Isaac Hollister Hall, "Specimens from the Nestorian Burial Service," 198–99.

35. *MH* 1:342.

36. *MH* 1:342.

37. *MH* 1:408.

38. *MH* 1:343.

39. *MH* 1:460.

40. See the list of American graves at Sire (Mount Seir) drawn up by Gordon Taylor, http://feverandthirst.com/graves.php, as an addendum to his book *Fever and Thirst*.

41. *MH* 1:286.

42. *MH* 1:287. Thomas Laurie even compares dead missionary children to the ointment poured out upon Jesus at Bethany (Mk 14:1–9). Laurie, *Woman and Her Saviour*, 278.

43. *MH* 1:288.

44. *MH* 1:275.

45. *MH* 1:276, 1:277, respectively.

46. *MH* 1:279.

47. *MH* 1:276.

48. *MH* 1:277.

49. See comments in Viswanathan, *Outside the Fold*, 42, and Sharkey, *American Evangelicals in Egypt*, 15 and 15n72.

50. Asad, "Comments on Conversion," 266.

51. Griffith, "Life and Religious Experience of Jarena Lee," 202.

52. Edwards, "Sinners in the Hands of an Angry God," 96.

53. Edwards, "Some Thoughts Concerning the Present Revival of Religion in New England," 100, 99, respectively.

54. E.g., Ware, preface to Pseudo-Macarius, *Fifty Spiritual Homilies*, xi.

55. On Eliot, see Makdisi, *Artillery of Heaven*, 19–31.

56. Edwards, "Some Thoughts Concerning the Present Revival of Religion in New England," 101.

57. Halttunen, *Confidence Men and Painted Women*; van der Veer, *Conversion to Modernities*, 10; and Asad, "Comments on Conversion."

58. Papers of the ABCFM, reel 555, docs. 47 and 48.

59. Fiske, *Faith Working by Love*, 128–30.

60. Rafael, *Contracting Colonialism*, 102–7.

61. Rambuss, *Closet Devotions*, 103–35.

62. Rambuss, *Closet Devotions*, 105–6.

63. Rambuss, *Closet Devotions*, 109; see also p. 8.

64. Nikitine, "La vie domestique des Assyro-Chaldéens," 363; and Fränkel, *Die aramäischen Fremdwörter*, 39–40.

65. Brock, *Syriac Fathers*, 3; see index under Matthew 6:6 for examples.

66. *MH* 2:318.

67. *MH* 2:225.

68. Laurie, *Woman and Her Saviour*, 39.

69. Laurie, *Woman and Her Saviour*, 40.

70. Laurie, *Woman and Her Saviour*, 101.

71. Khalaf, *Cultural Resistance*, 192–94.

72. *MH* 1:495.

73. *MH* 1:495–96.

74. *MH* 1:242–43, 2:142.

75. *MH* 2:480–81.

76. *ZB* 1, no. 2 (Dec. 1849): 10.

77. *ZB* 3, no. 3 (Jan. 1852): 211–13.

78. *ZB* 2, no. 2 (Dec. 1850): 114.

79. *ZB* 1, no. 6 (Apr. 1850): 42; and *ZB* 2, no. 2 (Dec. 1850): 107–8.

80. *ZB* 4, no. 3 (Feb. 1853): 38.

81. *ZB* 4, no. 1 (Nov. 1852): 4.

82. *ZB* 1, no. 5 (Mar. 1850): 34 (reads: 50).

83. *ZB* 1, no. 5 (Mar. 1850): 35. Cf. *MH* 2:216: George Coan's letter of Feb. 21, 1850.

84. *ZB* 1, no. 8 (June 1850): 57–59. Cf. [Missionaries of the ABCFM], *Nestorian Biography*, 43–51.

85. *ZB* 1, no. 12 (Oct. 1850): 91–94. Cf. [Missionaries of the ABCFM], *Nestorian Biography*, 25–40. See also Macuch, *Geschichte*, 158.

86. *MH* 2:287–94; *ZB* 2, no. 5 (Mar. 1851): 131–34; and [Missionaries of the ABCFM], *Nestorian Biography*, 127–50.

87. *MH* 2:292.

88. *MH* 2:289.

89. [Missionaries of the ABCFM], *Nestorian Biography*, 128–33.

90. *MH* 2:294.

91. His death was announced in July: *ZB* 1, no. 9 (July 1850): 74.

92. *ZB* 5, no. 2 (Feb. 1854): 209; and [Missionaries of the ABCFM], *Nestorian Biography*, 221–30. For Aslan as copyist, see Wilmshurst, *Ecclesiastical Organisation*, 338.

93. *Rays of Light* is not extant from 1871 to 1892, but obituary material from this period is preserved in Malick #129.

94. Malick #25 and #35.

95. Malick #33.

96. Laurie, *Woman and Her Saviour*, 136.

97. Richmond, *Young Cottager*, 23.

98. On the *Dairyman's Daughter*, see Roberts, "Locating Popular Religion."

99. Roberts, "Locating Popular Religion," 261–66.

100. Roberts, "Locating Popular Religion," 234.

101. Schantz, "Religious Tracts," 432, 442.

102. Malick #25, 12, 16, 17, 19, 24, 36, 65, 67, 73, 75, 81.

103. Schantz, "Religious Tracts," 433.

104. Schantz, "Religious Tracts," 454.

105. Schantz, "Religious Tracts," 462–66.

106. Richmond, *Young Cottager*, 8.

107. Malick #76.

108. *MH* 1:567.

109. *MH* 1:574.

110. *MH* 1:576; and [Missionaries of the ABCFM], *Nestorian Biography*, 18.

111. *MH* 1:592, 3:452.

112. *MH* 1:621.

113. [Missionaries of the ABCFM], *Nestorian Biography*, 32.

114. Laurie, *Woman and Her Saviour*, 130.

115. Justin Perkins, "A Sermon Delivered to the Members of the Nestorian Mission"; and Wright, *Looking unto Jesus*.

116. *ZB* 3, no. 11 (Sept. 1852): 279.

117. [Cochran?], *Persian Flower*, 33.

118. Henry Martyn Perkins, *Life of Reverend Justin Perkins*, 10, 35.

119. [Cochran?], *Persian Flower*, 170.

120. Henry Martyn Perkins, *Life of Reverend Justin Perkins*, 86; and [Missionaries of the ABCFM], *Nestorian Biography*, 242.

121. Edwards, "Faithful Narrative of the Surprizing Work of God."

122. *MH* 2:18.

123. Edwards, "Some Thoughts Concerning the Present Revival," 95.

124. E.g., *MH* 2:217.

125. *MH* 1:495.

126. *MH* 1:495.

127. *MH* 1:564. See *MH* 1:562 for a link to massacres.

128. E.g., Joseph P. Thompson, *Memoir*, 164–65.

129. *AR 1844*, 140.

130. *MH* 1:583, 1:584, respectively.

131. Laurie, *Woman and Her Saviour*, 115–16. See also *MH* 1:579–80; Stoddard, *Narrative*, 88; and [Missionaries of the ABCFM], *Nestorian Biography*, 30–31.

132. *MH* 1:580.

133. *MH* 1:580.

134. *MH* 1:581.

135. *MH* 1:579.

136. *MH* 1:585.

137. *MH* 1:590.

138. *MH* 1:586.

139. *MH* 1:587.

140. *MH* 1:589.

141. *MH* 1:589.

142. *MH* 1:595, 1:593, respectively.

143. *MH* 1:618.

144. *MH* 1:580.

145. *MH* 1:608.

146. *MH* 1:605–6.

147. Stoddard, *Narrative*, 10.

148. *MH* 1:582, 1:588, 1:594, 1:600–601, 1:604.

149. *MH* 1:608.

150. *MH* 1:602, 1:604.

151. *MH* 1:596, 1:599.

152. *MH* 1:608–9.

153. Stoddard, *Narrative*, 12.

154. *MH* 1:588.

155. *MH* 1:582, 1:590; and [Missionaries of the ABCFM], *Nestorian Biography*, 55–64.

156. *MH* 1:591–92.

157. See his obituaries in *MH* 3:400–401 and *ZB* 14, no. 10 (Oct. 1864): 57–61.

158. E.g., *MH* 1:598.

159. *MH* 1:600, 1:620.

160. *MH* 1:600.

161. *MH* 1:602.

162. *MH* 2:18.

163. *MH* 2:19.

164. *MH* 1:593.

165. *MH* 1:599.

166. *MH* 1:633–34.

167. *MH* 2:132–41, 2:146–48, 2:158–59.

168. *MH* 2:134.

169. *MH* 2:146.

170. *MH* 2:147 (emphasis in the original).

171. *MH* 2:140.

172. *MH* 2:210–29.

173. *MH* 2:210.

174. *MH* 2:213.

175. *MH* 2:226–27.

176. *MH* 2:215–16.

177. *MH* 2:225 (emphasis in the original).

178. *MH* 2:214.

179. E.g., revival of 1854: Rufus Anderson, *History*, 2:118; revival of 1856: *MH* 3:72–75, and Rufus Anderson, *History*, 2:125; revival of 1857: *MH* 3:132–34; revival of 1858: Rufus Anderson, *History*, 2:135; revival of 1859: *MH* 3:232–34, and Rufus Anderson, *History*, 2:139, which says this is the tenth; revival of 1860: *MH* 3:251; revival of 1862: *MH* 3:320–21, and Rufus Anderson, *History*, 2:145; revivals of 1863 and 1864: Rufus Anderson, *History*, 2:145.

180. *MH* 3:446–48.

181. *MH* 3:74.

182. It was later published in English in Laurie, *Woman and Her Saviour*, 245–51.

183. Laurie, *Woman and Her Saviour*, 245–46.

184. Laurie, *Woman and Her Saviour*, 248.

185. Laurie, *Woman and Her Saviour*, 250–51.

186. Laurie, *Woman and Her Saviour*, 251.

187. *ZB* 15, no. 12 (Dec. 1865): 89–91; and [Missionaries of the ABCFM], *Nestorian Biography*, 101–24. This Sanam is not to be confused with the Sanam who was born in 1824 and died in 1863: *ZB* 13, no. 4 (Apr. 1863): 25–27.

188. [Missionaries of the ABCFM], *Nestorian Biography*, 185.

189. For a letter from Sanam to Fiske, see Laurie, *Woman and Her Saviour*, 148–49.

190. *ZB* 43, no. 7 (July 1892): 52.

191. *MH* 2:462.

192. *MH* 3:78–79, 3:91–92; and Laurie, *Woman and Her Saviour*, 165.

193. Malick #129, 305; cf. *MH* 3:446.

194. Malick #129, 305; and *ZB* 43, no. 7 (July 1892): 52.

195. Durkheim, *Elementary Forms*, 18.

196. E.g., Durkheim, *Elementary Forms*, 193.

197. Benedict Anderson, *Imagined Communities*, 11.

198. E.g., McGarry, *Ghost of Future Pasts*.

Chapter 6

1. *MH* 3:149.

2. *MH* 2:101.

3. *MH* 3:80. For another example, see Marogen (Mar Awgen) the Pipemaker, in [Missionaries of the ABCFM], *Nestorian Biography*, 267–84.

4. *MH* 3:81.

5. Malek Yonan, *Persian Women*, 210; seventy-four years old in 1897. He is easy to confuse with Yonan of 'Ada in the sources.

6. Malek Yonan, *Persian Women*, 211.

7. Laurie, *Woman and Her Saviour*, 107.

8. *MH* 2:145.

9. *ZB* 13, no. 12 (Dec. 1863): 91; and *MH* 3:365.

10. Joseph P. Thompson, *Memoir*, 142.

11. Laurie, *Woman and Her Saviour*, 106; and Joseph P. Thompson, *Memoir*, 195.

12. *ZB* 43, no. 7 (July 1892): 52.

13. Malek Yonan, *Persian Women*, 215; and Laurie, *Woman and Her Saviour*, 63, 106.

14. Fiske, *Faith Working by Love*, 214–15.

15. *MH* 2:488.

16. Laurie, *Woman and Her Saviour*, 106–12.

17. *MH* 3:206.

18. *MH* 2:13–14.

19. Laurie, *Woman and Her Saviour*, 205; *ZB* 3, no. 4 (Feb. 1852): 219–23; and Laurie, *Woman and Her Saviour*, 257–62.

20. *ZB* 43, no. 7 (July 1892): 52.

21. *MH* 2:146; *ZB* 4, no. 4 (Mar. 1853): 54; and *MH* 2:351, 3:512–13, 3:26.

22. Laurie, *Woman and Her Saviour*, 191–204; and Papers of the ABCFM, reel 555, docs. 65–67, 69.

23. Laurie, *Woman and Her Saviour*, 192.

24. Laurie, *Woman and Her Saviour*, 192–93.

25. Laurie, *Woman and Her Saviour*, 194–95.

26. *ZB* 1, no. 10 (Aug. 1850): 81–82.

27. *ZB* 1, no. 10 (Aug. 1850): 82.

28. Chevalier, *Les montagnards chrétiens*, 22.

29. Chevalier, *Les montagnards chrétiens*, 18–19 (and 18n2 on the pair of mountains), 95.

30. *MH* 2:272.

31. See image of Zirani in Percy, *Highlands of Asiatic Turkey*, 196.

32. *MH* 2:273–74. Until indicated otherwise, the quotations and information that follow are from these pages.

33. Chevalier, *Les montagnards chrétiens*, 257; and Fiey, "Proto-histoire," 456–59. For some of the other visits, see *MH* 1:387–89, 2:44–45, 2:325.

34. Percy, *Highlands of Asiatic Turkey*, 199–201.

35. Percy, *Highlands of Asiatic Turkey*, 201.

36. Wigram and Wigram, *Cradle of Mankind*, 171.

37. Wigram and Wigram, *Cradle of Mankind*, 172.

38. De Mauroy, "Lieux de culte," 333–34. See also Wilmshurst, *Ecclesiastical Organisation*, 334.

39. Bedjan, *Acta*, 1:ix.

40. Bedjan, *Acta*, 1:398.

41. Bedjan, *Acta*, 1:399.

42. Bedjan, *Acta*, 1:400.

43. Bedjan, *Acta*, 1:402.

44. Fiey, "Proto-histoire," 456.

45. Bedjan, *Acta*, 1:418.

46. MS NYPL Syriac MS 3; and Bcheiry, "Syriac Manuscripts in the New York Public Library," 150.

47. *MH* 2:274.

48. Papers of the ABCFM, reel 555, doc. 64, 14.

49. *MH* 2:274. Until indicated otherwise, the quotations and information that follow are from this page.

50. Badger, *Nestorians and Their Rituals*, 2:188.

51. Badger, *Nestorians and Their Rituals*, 2:132. Cf. Maclean and Browne, *Catholicos of the East*, 335.

52. Badger, *Nestorians and Their Rituals*, 1:229.

53. *MH* 2:275–77. Until indicated otherwise, the quotations and information that follow are from these pages.

54. Papers of the ABCFM, reel 556, doc. 144, 14.

55. *MH* 2:278.

56. Layard, *Nineveh*, 1:188–90. See also Laurie, *Dr. Grant*, 361–62.

57. Asahel Grant, *Nestorians*, 64.

58. Cf. *MH* 2:8.

59. Papers of the ABCFM, reel 556, doc. 144, 15.

60. *MH* 2:279. Until indicated otherwise, the quotations and information that follow are from these pages.

61. *MH* 2:99.

62. Papers of the ABCFM, reel 555, doc. 64, 1.

63. *MH* 1:502–3.

64. For a basic history and an introduction to their dialect, see Fox, *Neo-Aramaic Dialect of Jilu.*

65. *MH* 1:389.

66. MacDonald, "Beggar Chiefs."

67. Fox, *Neo-Aramaic Dialect of Jilu*, 122–23.

68. Wolk, "Emergence of Assyrian Ethnonationalism."

69. Malick #76; and Henry Martyn Perkins, *Life of Reverend Justin Perkins*, 67–68.

70. PCUSA-BFM 203 (274), doc. #4 (Feb. 5, 1908) (underlining in the original).

71. Macuch, *Geschichte*, 146 (*ZB* 1897); and *MH* 2:332.

72. *K* 10, no. 4 (May 10, 1917): 29.

73. *ZB* 2, no. 10 (Aug. 1851): 171.

74. *MH* 1:149.

75. *ZB* 43, no. 7 (July 1892): 52.

76. *MH* 2:270.

77. *ZB* 1, no. 12 (Oct. 1850): 97–98; *ZB* 2, no. 3 (Jan. 1851): 122; and *ZB* 2, no. 5 (Mar. 1851): 136–37. Cf. *MH* 2:280–81 on their visit in Dec. of 1850 to Mosul from Mr. Marsh; Sayad and Moses went to Bohtan in the winter of 1850–51. Papers of the ABCFM, reel 556, doc. 144, 1.

78. *ZB* 1, no. 12 (Oct. 1850): 97–98; and *ZB* 2, no. 5 (Mar. 1851): 137.

79. *MH* 2:269–71; and Papers of the ABCFM, reel 556, doc. 144, 2–3.

80. *ZB* 3, no. 7 (May 1852): 243–49; and Papers of the ABCFM, reel 555, doc. 71. Abbreviated version: *MH* 2:370–77. Quotations are from the missionaries' translation, but I provide the Aramaic from the original text as printed in *ZB*. Dates are Old Style (Julian calendar).

81. Papers of the ABCFM, reel 555, doc. 71, 1–2.

82. Cf. *ZB* 3, no. 7 (May 1852): 246 and *MH* 2:374.

83. Papers of the ABCFM, reel 555, doc. 71, 2–3.

84. Wilmshurst, *Martyred Church*, 358–59, 384.

85. Based on Papers of the ABCFM, reel 555, doc. 71, 5, but fitted to the Aramaic in *ZB* 3, no. 7 (May 1852): 244.

86. Papers of the ABCFM, reel 555, doc. 64, 11–12.

87. Wilmshurst, *Ecclesiastical Organisation*, 299.

88. Wigram and Wigram, *Cradle of Mankind*, 306–7; Warkworth, *Notes from a Diary in Asiatic Turkey*, 164; Maclean and Browne, *Catholicos of the East*, 303–4; Chevalier, *Les montagnards chrétiens*, 258; and Wilmshurst, *Ecclesiastical Organisation*, 299.

89. *ZB* 3, no. 7 (May 1852): 247; and Papers of the ABCFM, reel 555, doc. 71, 16.

90. *ZB* 2, no. 3 (Jan. 1851): 122.

91. Papers of the ABCFM, reel 555, doc. 71, 7–8.

92. Cf. *ZB* 3, no. 4 (Feb. 1852): 226.

93. *MH* 2:270.

94. Wilmshurst, *Ecclesiastical Organisation*, 115–16; and Fiey, *Nisibe*, 194–97.

95. Wilmshurst, *Ecclesiastical Organisation*, 116n380; and Mingana, *Catalogue*, 502 A and E (I. colls. 924–28).

96. *MH* 2:373.

97. *MH* 3:107.

98. *MH* 2:470, 3:255.

99. Papers of the ABCFM, reel 555, doc. 71, 9–14. Until indicated otherwise, the quotations and information that follow are from these pages.

100. *MH* 2:375 changes *may hap* to *peradventure*.

101. *ZB* 3, no. 7 (May 1852): 244; and *MH* 2:371.

102. *ZB* 3, no. 7 (May 1852): 245; and *MH* 2:372.

103. *ZB* 3, no. 7 (May 1852): 245; and *MH* 2:373.

104. *ZB* 3, no. 7 (May 1852): 247; and *MH* 2:375.

105. Zirinsky, "American Presbyterian Missionaries," 11n15.

106. Papers of the ABCFM, reel 556, doc. 200, 1–2. See also *MH* 1:588–89.

107. *MH* 1:622.

108. *MH* 2:13.

109. Papers of the ABCFM, reel 555, doc. 64, 10–11.

110. *AR 1871*, 49.

111. *MH* 1:588.

112. *MH* 3:332.

113. Malick #129, 305.

114. Coakley, *Church of the East*, 55–58, 109.

115. *MH* 2:49, 2:172.

116. *MH* 2:108, 2:322. Cf. *MH* 2:122–26; and Papers of the ABCFM, reel 555, doc. 33.

117. *MH* 2:198.

118. *MH* 2:333.

119. *MH* 2:343.

120. *MH* 2:349–50. For more on the wedding, see Marsh, *Tennesseean in Persia*, 97, and 95–107 for this early problem period in general.

121. Aug. 12, 1852, *MH* 2:393 (Papers of the ABCFM, reel 55, doc. 141); for the whole story, see Marsh, *Tennesseean in Persia*, 112–40.

122. *MH* 2:396.

123. Gordon Taylor, *Fever and Thirst*, 316.

124. *MH* 2:399–402.

125. *MH* 2:405–7.

126. *MH* 2:407–8.

127. *MH* 2:412–15, 2:419–22, 2:424–25, 2:457–58; and Papers of the ABCFM, reel 555, docs. 141, 146, 148.

128. *ZB* 3, no. 11 (Sept. 1852): 81.

129. *ZB* 3, no. 11 (Sept. 1852): 80.

130. *ZB* 4, no. 4 (Feb. 1853): 57–60. Translation my own. For the translation by David Stoddard, see Papers of the ABCFM, reel 556, doc. 200, 5–8.

131. See also Laurie, *Woman and Her Saviour*, 120.

132. Becker, *Fear of God*, 22–40.

133. Malick #168.

134. Malick #144; and Macuch, *Geschichte*, 151–52 (*ZB* 1899). Cf. Labaree, "Modern Apostle."

135. Malick #144, 216.

136. Malick #144, 217.

137. *ZB* 43, no. 7 (July 1892): 52.

138. Rosenberg, *Lehrbuch*, 62–64 (German translation: 92–93).

Chapter 7

1. Samuel G. Wilson, *Persia: Western Mission*, 43–53. See also *AR 1885*, 68, 71; and *AR 1886*, 78.

2. Cf. Malek Yonan, *Persian Women*, 220–22.

3. Ringer, *Education, Religion, and the Discourse of Cultural Reform*, 214–21.

4. Samuel G. Wilson, *Persia: Western Mission*, 49.

5. Samuel G. Wilson, *Persia: Western Mission*, 53; Speer, "Hakim Sahib," 137; and Laurie, *Woman and Her Saviour*, 51–52, 240–42.

6. Samuel G. Wilson, *Persia: Western Mission*, 50.

7. Elder, *History of the Iran Mission*, 23.

8. *AR 1869*, 41.

9. Murre-van den Berg, *From a Spoken to a Written Language*, 69; and Murre-van den Berg, "American Board and the Eastern Churches."

10. J. Christy Wilson, "Persian Apostle—Dr. Sa'eed Kurdistani"; Malek Yonan, *Beloved Physician*; cf. *AR 1893*, 171; and Samuel G. Wilson, *Persia: Western Mission*, 31–38.

11. *AR 1880*, 41.

12. *AR 1883*, 54.

13. *AR 1885*, 67; and *AR 1895*, 160–61.

14. *AR 1883*, 58; *AR 1888*, 82; and *AR 1889*, 74.

15. E.g., *AR 1895*, 154–55; and *AR 1889*, 81.

16. E.g., *AR 1885*, 67.

17. E.g., *AR 1895*, 161–63.

18. *AR 1873*, 54; and *AR 1875*, 39.

19. *AR 1885*, 72.

20. *AR 1872*, 59; and *AR 1877*, 40, 42.

21. *AR 1871*, 46; *ZB* 46, no. 1 (Jan. 1895): addendum, which includes a synod meeting program with a list of presbyteries.

22. E.g., *ZB* 49, no. 11 (Nov. 1898): 81.

23. *AR 1890*, 164; and *AR 1891*, 165.

24. *AR 1893*, 168–70; e.g., *ZB* 49, no. 12 (Dec. 1898): 94.

25. *AR 1879*, 45; and *AR 1878*, 47.

26. *AR 1895*, 149. The statistics vary in the different sources.

27. *AR 1895*, 149, 154. For a full chart of statistics, see Malick, *American Mission Press*, 115–17.

28. *AR 1876*, 40.

29. *AR 1880*, 40.

30. Samuel G. Wilson, *Persia: Western Mission*, 75.

31. *AR 1890*, 168.

32. Samuel G. Wilson, *Persia: Western Mission*, 75; *AR 1889*, 80; and *AR 1894*, 184.

33. *AR 1889*, 79.

34. *AR 1893*, 174.

35. *AR 1897*, 162.

36. See also Rosenberg, *Lehrbuch*, 146–50.

37. *AR 1886*, 81.

38. *AR 1889*, 80.

39. *AR 1892*, 205.

40. *AR 1893*, 175.

41. *AR 1894*, 184–85.

42. *AR 1893*, 176.

43. *AR 1894*, 184–85, 193; and *AR 1895*, 154.

44. *AR 1893*, 175.

45. *AR 1878*, 47; and *AR 1879*, 45.

46. *ZB* 49, no. 12 (Jan. 1898): 90.

47. Samuel G. Wilson, *Persia: Western Mission*, 62ff., 70, 76.

48. *AR 1880*, 41.

49. *AR 1896*, 190.

50. *AR 1891*, 166; *AR 1893*, 170–72; *AR 1894*, 186; and Samuel G. Wilson, *Persia: Western Mission*, 69.

51. *AR 1905*, 290.

52. *AR 1893*, 176.

53. *AR 1895*, 156–58.

54. *Woman's Work for Women* 10 (1895): 380; and *AR 1889*, 79.

55. *AR 1876*, 42.

56. *AR 1883*, 60; *AR 1884*, 64; *AR 1894*, 187–88; Samuel G. Wilson, *Persia: Western Mission*, 74–75; and Elder, *History*, 21.

57. *AR 1876*, 42; *AR 1877*, 40; *AR 1883*, 62; *AR 1884*, 66; and *AR 1889*, 82.

58. *AR 1883*, 63.

59. *AR 1891*, 172; and *AR 1892*, 206.

60. *AR 1895*, 156.

61. *AR 1885*, 72; and *AR 1895*, 161.

62. E.g., *AR 1894*, 187–88.

63. *AR 1895*, 155.

64. *AR 1886*, 82.

65. *AR 1884*, 64; and *AR 1887*, 77.

66. Speer, "Hakim Sahib," 74–101; see also *AR 1881*, 44–46.

67. Speer, "Hakim Sahib," 287–94.

68. *ZB* 43, no. 7 (July 1892): 52; Macuch, *Geschichte*, 161 (*ZB* 1905), 169 (*ZB* 1908); *AR 1883*, 56; *AR 1884*, 64; *AR 1889*, 89; and Holme, *Oldest Christian Church*, 79–82. (See p. 107 for a list of trustees of the orphanage in Geogtapa, which include members of the American mission.)

69. Malick #129, 304.

70. Coakley, *Church of the East*, 378n132; see also 69–70.

71. Samuel G. Wilson, *Persia: Western Mission*, 56.

72. Malick #129, 316; and Holme, *Oldest Christian Church*, 84–90.

73. *K* 1, no. 7 (Oct. 10, 1906): 53.

74. *AR 1875*, 39; *AR 1886*, 86; *AR 1887*, 76; and *AR 1889*, 88.

75. *AR 1893*, 169. See also *AR 1894*, 182; and *AR 1894*, 184.

76. *AR 1882*, 53.

77. Samuel G. Wilson, *Persia: Western Mission*, 76.

78. Samuel G. Wilson, *Persia: Western Mission*, 76.

79. Speer, *"Hakim Sahib."*

80. Malick #113.

81. Malick #143, #149, and #144; #145; #148.

82. Malick #139, #146, #181, and #151.

83. *AR 1879*, 46.

84. These appear in 1895 and 1898, respectively.

85. Sarmas, *History*, 1:225; and Macuch, *Geschichte*, 215, 169 (*ZB* 1908).

86. Malick #129.

87. *AR 1895*, 156.

88. Macuch, *Geschichte*, 138–39.

89. Hutchison, *Errand to the World*, 102–11.

90. *AR 1890*, 163–64. See also *AR 1873*, 56.

91. E.g., *AR 1871*, 51, 52, 53; *AR 1875*, 41, 42; *AR 1882*, 58; *AR 1883*, 64; and *AR 1894*, 180. Cf. Mary Lewis Shedd, *Measure of a Man*, 81.

92. E.g., *ZB* 43, no. 7 (July 1892): 56.

93. *AR 1889*, 77.

94. *AR 1890*, 164–66.

95. Wishard, *Twenty Years in Persia*, 238.

96. Wishard, *Twenty Years in Persia*, 240.

97. Wishard, *Twenty Years in Persia*, 241–42.

98. Wishard, *Twenty Years in Persia*, 246.

99. William Ambrose Shedd, *Islam and the Oriental Churches*, 185.

100. William Ambrose Shedd, *Islam and the Oriental Churches*, 185–86.

101. William Ambrose Shedd, *Islam and the Oriental Churches*, 186.

102. William Ambrose Shedd, *Islam and the Oriental Churches*, 186–87.

103. William Ambrose Shedd, *Islam and the Oriental Churches*, 187.

104. *PMR* 33 (Oct. 1882): 344–45; and *AR 1888*, 78.

105. Masuzawa, *Invention of World Religions*.

106. William Ambrose Shedd, *Islam and the Oriental Churches*, 212–14.

107. William Ambrose Shedd, *Islam and the Oriental Churches*, 216.

108. William Ambrose Shedd, *Islam and the Oriental Churches*, 218.

109. William Ambrose Shedd, *Islam and the Oriental Churches*, 219.

110. William Ambrose Shedd, *Islam and the Oriental Churches*, 219–20.

111. Kinzer, *Reset*, 2; and Tejirian and Simon, *Conflict, Conquest, and Conversion*, 165–66.

112. Kinzer, *Reset*, 4.

113. Farnaz Calafi, Ali Dadpay, and Pouyan Mashayekh, "Iran's Yankee Hero," *New York Times*, Apr. 18, 2009; and Kinzer, *Reset*, 106.

114. Rostam-Kolayi, "From Evangelizing to Modernizing Iranians," 215.

115. Kieser, "Muslim Heterodoxy and Protestant Utopia."

116. Malek Yonan, *Persian Women*, 210, 222; and Macuch, *Geschichte*, 146 (*ZB* 1897).

117. *ZB* 43, no. 7 (July 1892): 52.

118. Macuch, *Geschichte*, 181 (*ZB* 1915).

119. Macuch, *Geschichte*, 189–201; Murre-van den Berg, *From a Spoken to a Written Language*, 53–60; and O'Flynn, "Western Christian Presence in the Caucasus and Qajar Persia," 186–228.

120. Wilmshurst, *Martyred Church*, 400–401.

121. Wilmshurst, *Martyred Church*, 390, 399–400.

122. Wilmshurst, *Martyred Church*, 391–93.

123. Wilmshurst, *Martyred Church*, 383–89; and Murre-van den Berg, *From a Spoken to a Written Language*, 56.

124. Coakley and Taylor, "Syriac Books Printed at the Dominican Press."

125. Mengozzi, *Religious Poetry*, 35–65 (translation: 42–78).

126. Mengozzi, *Religious Poetry* (translation), xiv.

127. Murre-van den Berg, *From a Spoken to a Written Language*, 54–55.

128. Babakhan, "Protestantisme et Catholicisme chez le Peuple Nestorien." Cf. Murre-van den Berg, *From a Spoken to a Written Language*, 59.

129. Murre-van den Berg, *New Faith in Ancient Lands*, 6.

130. Macuch, *Geschichte*, 399–400. He died in 1890, according to Oussani, "Modern Chaldeans," 90–91.

131. Coakley, *Typography of Syriac*, 196; Coakley, "Edward Breath and the Typography of Syriac," 43; and Guriel, *Doctrinae Christianae rudimenta*.

132. Macuch, *Geschichte*, 29.

133. Murre-van den Berg, "Paul Bedjan, Missionary for Life."

134. Coakley, *Church of the East*; and Wilmshurst, *Martyred Church*, 372–73, 375–76, 382.

135. Wilmshurst, *Martyred Church*, 376.

136. *AR 1883*, 58; *AR 1886*, 81, 87; *AR 1887*, 79; *AR 1888*, 78; and *AR 1893*, 167.

137. *AR 1889*, 77.

138. *AR 1890*, 164.

139. E.g., Coakley, *Church of the East*, 210–11.

140. Coakley, "Yaroo M. Neesan."

141. *ZB* 43, no. 7 (July 1892): 52.

142. Macuch, *Geschichte*, 143 (*ZB* 1897).

143. Murre-van den Berg, *From a Spoken to a Written Language*, 72–74; and Heyer, "Die russisch-orthodoxe Mission in Urmia."

144. Wilmshurst, *Martyred Church*, 380–83.

145. Sado, "Nestorians of Urmia in the Early 1860's."

146. Samuel G. Wilson, "Conversion of the Nestorians of Persia to the Russian Church"; Coakley, *Church of the East*, 218–21; Wilmshurst, *Martyred Church*, 380–383; and Malech, *History of the Syrian Nation*, 340–42.

147. Yonan, *Journalismus bei den Assyrern*, 24–25.

148. Samuel G. Wilson, "Conversion of the Nestorians," 751.

149. Malech, *History of the Syrian Nation*, 340.

150. Martin Tamcke has produced several articles on this mission—e.g., Tamcke, "Die Hermannsburger Mission in Persien."

151. E.g., *AR 1886*, 81, 87.

152. *AR 1889*, 84.

153. Tamcke, "Nestorianisch, syrisch oder assyrisch?" 162.

154. Johnston, *Augustana Synod*, 85–86; Malech, *History of the Syrian Nation*, 358; and Coakley, *Church of the East*, 66, 282.

155. Malech, *History of the Syrian Nation*, 376–77.

156. E.g., *AR 1882*, 56.

157. Shahbaz, *Rage of Islam*, x.

158. E.g., *AR 1885*, 68.

159. E.g., *K* 2, no. 15 (Feb. 10, 1908): 169–77.

160. Cf. Naby, "Assyrians of Iran," 246.

161. *ZB* 46, no. 6 (June 1895): 45.

162. *ZB* 46, no. 8 (Aug. 1895): 60.

163. E.g., *ZB* 46, no. 3 (Mar. 1895): 15.

164. *ZB* 43, no. 4 (Apr. 1892): 28; *ZB* 43, no. 5 (May 1892): 36; *ZB* 43, no. 6 (June 1892): 45; and *ZB* 43, no. 7 (July 1892): 52.

165. *ZB* 43, no. 6 (June 1892): 45.

166. Addendum to *ZB* 46, no. 4 (Apr. 1895): 9–12.

167. *ZB* 46, no. 6 (June 1895): 46.

168. *ZB* 46, no. 3 (Mar. 1895): 19.

169. For his relation with Catholics, see Coakley, *Church of the East*, 170–78, 258–66.

170. *AR 1893*, 172–74; Coakley, *Church of the East*, 176–77; and Wilmshurst, *Martyred Church*, 392.

171. Wilmshurst, *Martyred Church*, 396–97.

172. Malech, *History of the Syrian Nation*, 353.

173. *AR 1886*, 82; *AR 1887*, 78; *AR 1889*, 82; obituary: *K* 5, no. 15 (Feb. 10, 1911): 175–77. Cf. Macuch, *Geschichte*, 176.

174. His diploma appears in Malech, *History of the Syrian Nation*, 383. The scribe was Moses of Geogtapa.

175. Malech, *History of the Syrian Nation*, 371.

176. Coakley, *Church of the East*, 241–42; and Macuch, *Geschichte*, 140 (*ZB* 1897).

177. Malech, *History of the Syrian Nation*, 361.

178. PCUSA-BFM 202 (274), doc. 3 (Feb. 4, 1907).

179. PCUSA-BFM 201 (274), doc. 33 (Apr. 3, 1906).

180. *K* 1, no. 4 (Aug. 24, 1906): 25; and *K* 1, no. 11 (Dec. 10, 1906): 86–87.

181. *K* 1, no. 14 (Jan. 24, 1907): 109.

182. *K* 2, no. 1 (June 24, 1907): 1, 2–4.

183. On these events, see Naby, "Assyrians of Iran."

184. *K* 2, no. 2 (July 10, 1907): 16–17.

185. *K* 2, no. 2 (July 10, 1907): 17–18.

186. Coakley, *Church of the East*, 286; and *K* 2, no. 2 (July 10, 1907): 14.

187. Malek Yonan, *Persian Women*, 221.

188. Macuch, *Geschichte*, 142–43 (*ZB* 1897).

189. *K* 3, no. 10 (Nov. 24, 1908): 111–13.

190. F. G. Coan, quoted in *AR 1902*, 234.

191. PCUSA-BFM 203 (274), doc. 61 (Nov. 1, 1908).

192. *Report of the National Committee Meeting*, Malick #131, 92–93.

193. See Murre-van den Berg, *From a Spoken to a Written Language*, 75n147, for speculation about the origin of the title *Star*.

194. PCUSA-BFM 206 (274), "Minutes of the Annual Meeting of the West Persia Mission," 1906.

195. *AR 1908*, 360, quoted in Malick, *American Mission Press*, 100.

196. E.g., Macuch, *Geschichte*, 161, 162 (*ZB* 1906).

197. For an image of the two, see Holme, *Oldest Christian Church*, after p. 40.

198. *K* 2, no. 15 (Feb. 10, 1908): 170; and Macuch, *Geschichte*, 161 (*ZB* 1905).

199. Biographical information from preface to Mushie, *Outlines* (reprint of Malick #153). The Neo-Aramaic version is more detailed.

200. Sarmas, *History*, 1:227; and Macuch, *Geschichte*, 217–18. Cf. Murre-van den Berg, *From a Spoken to a Written Language*, 110n133.

201. *K* 1, no. 8 (Oct. 24, 1906): 62.

202. Malick #153.

203. Macuch and Panoussi, *Neusyrische Chrestomathie*, 27–28.

204. *K* 1, no. 12 (Dec. 12, 1906): 92.

205. *K* 5, no. 12 (Dec. 24, 1910): 134–35.

206. *K* 1, no. 18 (Mar. 24, 1907): 137–38.

207. Malech, *History of the Syrian Nation*, 351–61.

208. *K* 3, no. 20 (Apr. 24, 1909): 230.

209. *K* 3, no. 13 (Jan. 10, 1909): 148.

210. *K* 3, no. 14 (Jan. 24, 1909): 159.

211. *K* 1, no. 3 (Aug. 10, 1906): 18–19.

212. E.g., *K* 4, no. 15 (Feb. 10, 1910): 170–71.

213. *K* 1, no. 14 (Jan. 24, 1907): 107–8.

214. *K* 1, no. 14 (Jan. 24, 1907): 105.

215. *K* 1, no. 15 (Feb. 10, 1907): 114.

216. *K* 3, no. 22 (June 3, 1909): 253–56. On Pera Mirza, see, e.g., *K* 4, no. 8 (Oct. 24, 1909): 89, and possibly *ZB* 43, no. 7 (July 1892): 52.

217. *K* 3, no. 22 (June 3, 1909): 253–55.

218. *K* 4, no. 1 (June 24, 1909): 2–4.

219. *K* 1, no. 13 (Jan. 10, 1907): 100–101.

220. *K* 2, no. 2 (July 10, 1907): 14–15.

221. *K* 3, no. 15 (Feb. 10, 1909): 176.

222. *K* 1, no. 21 (May 10, 1907): 162.

223. *K* 1, no. 20 (Apr. 24, 1907): 156–58.

224. *K* 1, no. 20 (Apr. 24, 1907): 157. Cf. Macuch and Panoussi, *Neusyrische Chrestomathie*, 7, for a later parallel.

225. *K* 3, no. 18 (Mar. 24, 1909): 205.

226. Ernest Gellner's argument in *Nations and Nationalism* becomes relevant at this point. Cf. De Kelaita, "On the Road to Nineveh."

227. See discussion of class in Ishaya, "Ethnicity, Class, and Politics."

228. E.g., Berger and Luckmann, "Secularization and Pluralism."

229. Stout, *Democracy and Tradition*, 93–100.

230. Stout, *Democracy and Tradition*, 97.

231. Naby, "Assyrian of Iran."

232. *AR 1899*, 195.

233. *ZB* 13, no. 11 (Nov. 1863): 83–84.

234. *K* 1, no. 23 (June 10, 1907): 178–79.

235. *K* 1, no. 23 (June 10, 1907): 180–81.

Chapter 8

1. *K* 7, no. 10 (Nov. 24, 1912): 109.

2. Chatterjee, *Nation and Its Fragments*, 7.

3. Hobsbawm, "Introduction: Inventing Traditions," 2.

4. Pratt, *Imperial Eyes*, 9.

5. Jackson, "Phoenicians and Assyrians versus the Roving Nomad."

6. E.g., Odisho, "Ethnic, Linguistic and Cultural Identity"; Parpola, "Assyrians after Assyria"; Frye, "Reply to John Joseph"; and Frye, "Assyria and Syria." See the works of John Joseph in n. 15 below.

7. Fiey, "Comment l'Occident en vint à parler de 'Chaldéens'?"; Fiey, "'Assyriens' ou Araméens?"; Macuch, "Assyrians in Iran"; Coakley, "Assyrians or Arameans?"; Murre-van den Berg, *From a Spoken to a Written Language*, 35–38; Joseph, *Modern Assyrians*, 1–32; and Chevalier, *Les montagnards chrétiens*, 296–99.

8. Heinrichs, "Modern Assyrians," 99. See also Butts, "Assyrian Christians"; and Messo, "Origin of the Terms 'Syria(n)' & Sūryoyo."

9. Heinrichs, "Modern Assyrians," 101.

10. Heinrichs, "Modern Assyrians," 102.

11. Heinrichs, "Modern Assyrians," 107.

12. Heinrichs, "Modern Assyrians," 108.

13. Malick #133, MS 64.

14. Heinrichs, "Modern Assyrians," 109–10.

15. Joseph, *Modern Assyrians*, 22–25; Joseph, "Assyria and Syria: Synonyms?"; and Joseph, "Bible and the Assyrians." See also del Río Sánchez, "Aramaean Speakers of Iraq."

16. Becker, "Ancient Near East in the Late Antique Near East."

17. See Chevalier, *Les montagnards chrétiens*, 297–98, for such exceptions.

18. E.g., McCall, "Rediscovery and Aftermath"; and Bohrer, *Orientalism and Visual Culture*.

19. Holloway, "Nineveh Sails for the New World."

20. Layard, *Nineveh and Its Remains*, 1:224. He had drawn this connection even before his excavations: "An Inquiry into the Origin, History, Language, and Doctrines of the Chaldean or Nestorian Tribes of Kurdistan," BL MSS ADD 39061, 39062, 39063 (cited in Coakley, *Church of the East*, 367); see also Joseph, *Modern Assyrians*, 17–18.

21. Cf. Holme, *Oldest Christian Church*, which follows suit.

22. Joseph, *Modern Assyrians*, 5. On Southgate, see Marr, *Cultural Roots of American Islamicism*, 126–31.

23. Malley, "Austen Henry Layard and the Periodical Press."

24. Damrosch, *Buried Book*, 81–150.

25. Coakley, *Church of the East*, 44, 375n90.

26. Rassam, *Asshur and the Land of Nimrod*, 167.

27. Maclean and Browne, *Catholicos of the East*, 8–9.

28. Cutts, *Christians under the Crescent*, 107.

29. E.g., Cutts, *Christians under the Crescent*, 168–69.

30. E.g., Justin Perkins, *Residence*, 146.

31. Justin Perkins, "Journal of a Tour," 112–14.

32. Rood, *The Sea! The Sea!*

33. Justin Perkins, "Journal of a Tour," 108–9.

34. Foster, "On the Formal Study of Near Eastern Languages in America," 16–17.

35. Justin Perkins and Theodore Dwight Woolsey, "Notice of a Life of Alexander the Great"; and Justin Perkins, "Revelation of the Blessed Apostle Paul."

36. Stoddard, "Grammar of the Modern Syriac Language" (cf. Malick #53).

37. Malick #59, #72. See also Malick #62: conjugational booklet on Neo-Aramaic verbs.

38. Clemons, "Syriac Studies in the United States," 80, 83; and Henry Martyn Perkins, *Life of Reverend Justin Perkins*, 51.

39. Richardson, *Letters from a Distant Shore*, 20 and 20n50.

40. On archaeology in general, see *ZB* 4, no. 12 (Nov. 1853): 183–84.

41. *ZB* 1, no. 1 (Nov. 1849): 6; printed and translated in Murre-van den Berg, *From a Spoken to a Written Language*, 388–89.

42. *ZB* 3, no. 3 (Jan. 1852): 215–16.

43. *ZB* 3, no. 9 (July 1852): 264 (reads: 962); and *ZB* 3, no. 10 (Aug. 1852): 270–71.

44. *ZB* 10, no. 5 (Jan. 1859): 232, on Mosul; for illustration, see *ZB* 10, no. 7 (Mar. 1859): 249.

45. *ZB* 12, no. 2 (reads: 11, no. 2) (Feb. 1862): 9–10.

46. Justin Perkins, *Residence*, 329.

47. Malick #38, #52, #66, #116; also see Malick #101 (1872).

48. Malick #95, g (preface).

49. Malick #95, d (preface).

50. Malick #95, w (preface).

51. Malick #95, h.

52. Rufus Anderson, *History of the Missions*, 2:83.

53. Tyler, *Memoir of Rev. Henry Lobdell*, 204–5.

54. *AR 1871*, 45; see also *AR 1889*, 74.

55. Keevak, *Story of a Stele*.

56. Keevak, *Story of a Stele*, 102–11.

57. Justin Perkins, *Residence*, 30; and John Stewart, *Nestorian Missionary Enterprise*.

58. On these institutions, see Becker, *Fear of God*.

59. Coakley, "Manuscripts for Sale: Urmia."

60. Wilmshurst, *Ecclesiastical Organisation*, 298, 337. Cf. Macuch, *Geschichte*, 101 and 101n63; and Sarmas, *History*, 2:257–68.

61. Malick #133.

62. Wilmshurst, *Ecclesiastical Organisation*, 337.

63. E.g., *AR 1890*, 171; and Wilmshurst, *Ecclesiastical Organisation*, 297–98, 337.

64. *PMR* 33 (Oct. 1882): 344.

65. Malick #181 (before 1896), #123, #130.

66. Quoted in Malick, "Modern Assyrian Hymns," 227.

67. *ZB* 15, no. 5 (May 1865): 33–37; *ZB* 15, no. 7 (July 1865): 49–50; *ZB* 16, no. 9 (Sept. 1866): 57; and *ZB* 14, no. 12 (Dec. 1864): 74–75.

68. *ZB* 16, no. 2 (Feb. 1866): 15–16; and *ZB* 16, no. 3 (Mar. 1866): 24.

69. *ZB* 16, no. 4 (Apr. 1866): 32.

70. *ZB* 16, no. 4 (Apr. 1866): 31–32.

71. *K* 1, no. 6 (Sept. 24, 1906): 46; *ZB* 43, no. 7 (July 1892): 52; Macuch, *Geschichte*, 216; Murre-van den Berg, "Missionaries' Assistants," 10–11; Sarmas, *History*, 3:199–200; and Wilmshurst, *Ecclesiastical Organisation*, 330. See [Missionaries of the ABCFM], *Nestorian Biography*, 9–10, for his birth and possible family connection to Yohannan.

72. *ZB* 20, no. 2 (Feb. 1870): 16, "The Truant Youth," is by him.

73. Malick #118.

74. Murre-van den Berg, *From a Spoken to a Written Language*, 108–9.

75. Malick #126.

76. *ZB* 43, no. 12 (Jan. 1892): supplement, 1.

77. Macuch, *Geschichte*, 140 (*ZB* 1897).

78. Murre-van den Berg, *From a Spoken to a Written Language*, 188. The articles from 1897 are summarized in Macuch, *Geschichte*, 74–83, 138–46.

79. Maclean, *Dictionary of the Dialects of Vernacular Syriac*.

80. Macuch, *Geschichte*, 78–79 (*ZB* 1897).

81. Macuch, *Geschichte*, 80–81.

82. Macuch, *Geschichte*, 144 (*ZB* 1897); and Macuch, *Geschichte*, 81.

83. E.g., Macuch, *Geschichte*, 86 (*ZB* 1907).

84. *ZB* 49, no. 4 (Apr. 1898): 29–31. Cf. Macuch, *Geschichte*, 83–84, 148.

85. Macuch, *Geschichte*, 84–85 (*ZB* 1898).

86. *ZB* 49, no. 7 (July 1898): 49.

87. Macuch, *Geschichte*, 150 (*ZB* 1899).

88. Macuch, *Geschichte*, 143 (*ZB* 1897).

89. Elshakry, "Knowledge in Motion," 713–20.

90. Guriel, *Elementa linguae chaldaicae*, 3; cf. 5.

91. Guriel, *Elementa linguae chaldaicae*, 5–6.

92. Guriel, *Elementa linguae chaldaicae*, 7.

93. Schweitzer, *Quest of the Historical Jesus*, 270–75.

94. Coakley and Taylor, "Syriac Books Printed at the Dominican Press," 90 (#31); and Macuch, *Geschichte*, 408–9.

95. Maqdasi, *Grammaire chaldéenne*, preface.

96. *AR 1890*, 169.

97. Macuch, *Geschichte*, 140, 146 (*ZB* 1897).

98. Soskice, *Sisters of Sinai*.

99. For example, Moxnes, *Jesus and the Rise of Nationalism*.

100. *QŠ* 2, no. 3 (Aug. 1898): 247–49.

101. *ZB* 46, no. 11 (Nov. 1895): addendum, 14.

102. Macuch, *Geschichte*, 142. Underlining added.

103. Coakley, "Archbishop of Canterbury's Assyrian Mission Press," #42. Herodotus, *Histories*, 7.63, links Syria and Assyria; however, see Joseph, *Modern Assyrians*, 21.

104. Macuch, *Geschichte*, 228–29; and Wilmshurst, *Ecclesiastical Organisation*, 337–38. His village is not to be confused with the village of a similar name in Salmas.

105. *QŠ* 2, no. 1 (June 1898): 215–16; *QŠ* 2, no. 2 (July 1898): 233–35; *QŠ* 2, no. 3 (Aug. 1898): 258–59, 259–61; *QŠ* 2, no. 5 (Oct. 1898): 293–95, also 197–99, 582–84 (Macuch, *Geschichte*, 199–200).

106. Asher-Greve, "From 'Semiramis of Babylon' to 'Semiramis of Hammersmith,'" 323–73.

107. Bohrer, "Inventing Assyria," 255–56.

108. *QŠ* 2, no. 10 (Mar. 1899): 385–86.

109. Macuch, *Geschichte*, 211–13.

110. Audo, *Treasure*, 1:5.

111. Audo, *Treasure*, 1:9.

112. Audo, *Treasure*, 1:10.

113. Audo, *Treasure*, 1:14.

114. *ZB* 49, no. 4 (Apr. 1898): 30.

115. Selection in Sarmas, *History*, 3:35–36; and Macuch, *Geschichte*, 87–88.

116. Sarmas, *History*, 3:66–69.

117. Sarmas, *History*, 3:67.

118. Sarmas, *History*, 3:68.

119. Sarmas, *History*, 3:69.

120. *K* 1, no. 4 (Aug. 24, 1906): 27–28.

121. *ZB* 46, no. 6 (1895): 41; Macuch, *Geschichte*, 154, 158, 163, 177 (*ZB* 1903–11); and Macuch, *Geschichte*, 160–61, 165, 166, 167, 168, 169 (*ZB* 1905–7).

122. *K* 5, no. 23 (June 10, 1911): 268–69.

123. Columbia University Archives, Central Files, folder for Abraham Yohannan (box 664, folder 29).

124. Baaba, *Assyrian Odyssey*, 43–44.

125. Baaba, *Assyrian Odyssey*, 48, 58.

126. Baaba, *Assyrian Odyssey*, 50.

127. Coakley, "Assyrian Christians in English Fiction," 18–19.

128. Collected Letters of Louise Wilbur Shedd (in Presbyterian Historical Society, Shedd Family Papers, pt. 2): 1899–1900: Oct. 14, 1899, 120ff.

129. Daniel, *Modern Persia*, 170.

130. Daniel, *Modern Persia*, 171.

131. Daniel, *Modern Persia*, 171.

132. Daniel, *Modern Persia*, 183. Cf. Coakley, "Manuscripts for Sale."

133. Daniel, *Modern Persia*, 184–86.

134. Knanishu, *About Persia and Its People*.

135. See images in Reade, "Hormuzd Rassam and His Discoveries."

136. *K* 1, no. 21 (May 10, 1907): 161.

137. *K* 4, no. 9 (Nov. 10, 1909): 100.

138. *K* 4, no. 10 (Nov. 24, 1909): 113.

139. E.g., *K* 7, no. 5 (Aug. 24, 1912): 55.

140. *K* 7, no. 13 (Jan. 10, 1913): 147.

141. *K* 1, no. 5 (Sept. 10, 1906): 36.

142. *K* 1, no. 5 (Sept. 10, 1906): 37.

143. *K* 1, no. 7 (Oct. 10, 1906): 49.

144. *K* 1, no. 7 (Oct. 10, 1906): 50–51; continued in *K* 1, no. 8 (Oct. 24, 1906): 58–61.

145. *K* 2, no. 4 (Aug. 10, 1907): 42–43.

146. *K* 4, no. 16 (Feb. 24, 1910): 182–85.

147. Arsanis, *Works*, 211–39.

148. *K* 2, no. 14 (Jan. 24, 1908): 158–59.

149. Trigona-Harany, *Ottoman Süryânî*, 49–58. On the cultural context of Harput, see Akopian, "*Babylon*."

150. See the image of a cover page in Donabed, *Remnants of Heroes*, 116.

151. Trigona-Harany, *Ottoman Süryânî*, 145.

152. Trigona-Harany, *Ottoman Süryânî*, 41–44, 208, 212.

153. Trigona-Harany, *Ottoman Süryânî*, 124.

154. Trigona-Harany, *Ottoman Süryânî*, 4.

155. For one version, see Sarmas, *History*, 3:310.

156. *K* 5, no. 20 (Apr. 24, 1911): 233–35.

157. Coakley, "Archbishop of Canterbury's Assyrian Mission Press," #31; and Coakley and Taylor, "Syriac Books Printed at the Dominican Press," 102 (#59).

158. *Book of Crumbs*, 3.

159. Manna, *Morceaux choisis*, I.b.

160. Manna, *Morceaux choisis*, I.g.

161. Manna, *Morceaux choisis*, I.d.

162. Manna, *Morceaux choisis*, I.z–ḥ.

163. Murre-van den Berg, *From a Spoken to a Written Language*, 314.

164. *K* 1, no. 6 (Sept. 24, 1906): 43–44.

165. *K* 1, no. 9 (Nov. 10, 1906): 66–68.

166. *K* 5, no. 20 (Apr. 11, 1911): 230–33; *K* 7, no. 1 (June 24, 1912): 7; and *K* 7, no. 2 (July 10, 1912): 14.

167. *K* 3, no. 10 (Nov. 24, 1908): 110–11; and *K* 4, no. 12 (Dec. 24, 1909): 134–37.

168. *K* 9, no. 8 (Oct. 24, 1914): 59; and *K* 10, no. 2 (Apr. 10, 1917): 11.

169. Naby, "Theater, Language and Inter-ethnic Exchange."

170. *K* 7, no. 2 (July 10, 1912): 18.

171. Macuch, *Geschichte*, 389–90.

172. *K* 9, no. 1 (June 24, 1914): 2.

173. *K* 9, no. 2 (July 10, 1914): 15.

174. *K* 8, no. 15 (Feb. 10, 1914): 172.

175. *K* 6, no. 21 (May 10, 1912): 245.

176. *K* 1, no. 14 (Jan. 24, 1907): 111. Cf. *K* 2, no. 2 (July 10, 1907): 15–16.

177. Macuch, *Geschichte*, 279–81; and Arsanis, *Works*, 11–26.

178. Samuel G. Wilson, "Conversion of the Nestorians," 746.

179. *K* 7, no. 19 (Apr. 10, 1913): 218–19.

180. Malick #154.

181. *K* 10, no. 2 (Apr. 10, 1917): 9.

182. *K* 10, no. 3 (Apr. 25, 1917): 20–21. Cf. Macuch, *Geschichte*, 173–74 (*ZB* 1910).

183. *K* 10, no. 4 (May 10, 1917): 27; and *K* 10, no. 5 (May 25, 1917): 37, 40.

184. *K* 10, no. 6 (June 10, 1917): 44.

185. Figueira, *Aryans, Jews, Brahmins*.

186. Hamilakis, *Nation and Its Ruins*, 14.

187. E.g., Brock, *Luminous Eye*, 60–66.

Epilogue

1. Baaba, "Preservers of Language and Literature." Some of the biographical information provided here derives from unpublished work by David Malick.

2. *K* 2, no. 2 (July 10, 1907): 17.

3. Malech, *History of the Syrian Nation*, xi–xiii, 338; *K* 4, no. 2 (July 10, 1909): 20–21; *ZB* 43, no. 7 (July 1892): 52; and Macuch, *Geschichte*, 211.

4. Malech, *History of the Syrian Nation*, 336.

5. *K* 2, no. 1 (June 24, 1907): 6.

6. The poem "Metrical Letter from America" is dated Oct. 8, 1913. Malik, *Throne of Saliq*, 55.

7. For a local account of Sepurghan in the winter of 1915, see *K* 10, no. 15 (Nov. 10, 1917): 115.

8. Suny, "Explaining Genocide," discusses the genocide as well as the development of Armenian nationalism.

9. On the destruction of the Assyrian Christian communities in Hakkari and Urmia, see Yonan, *Ein vergessener Holocaust*. On the genocide of the Syriac communities farther west in Turkey, see de Courtois, *Forgotten Genocide*, and Gaunt, *Massacres, Resistance, Protectors*. See also Joseph, *Modern Assyrians*, 131–49. For the possible connections between violence during World War I and the missionaries, see Hellot, "Western Missionaries."

10. Malik, *Throne of Saliq*, 1.

11. Malik, *Throne of Saliq*, 6.

12. Malik, *Throne of Saliq*, 9.

13. *K* 3, no. 13 (Jan. 10, 1909): 146–48.

14. Asad, "Thinking about Religion, Belief, and Politics," 36.

15. Taylor, *Secular Age*, 542–44.

16. Taylor, "Western Secularity," 34.

17. Naayem, *Shall This Nation Die?*, 280.

18. Naayem, *Shall This Nation Die?*, 304, 309–14.

19. Zirinsky, "American Presbyterian Missionaries."

20. Facsimiles of "History of Assyria from the Beginning to the Present" are available in three volumes at Lulu.com.

21. *Ḥuyyada umtanaya* 11 (June 25, 1928): 2.

22. Baaba, "Preservers of Language and Literature," 61 (my translation).

23. De Courtois, *Forgotten Genocide*, 217.

24. Joseph, *Modern Assyrians*, 151–73.

25. PCUSA-BFM 204 (274), "Bimonthly Letter Urumia Station" (June 5, 1909).

26. Trigona-Harany, *Ottoman Süryânî*, 18, 147.

27. Macuch and Panoussi, *Neusyrische Chrestomathie*, 1.

28. Macuch and Panoussi, *Neusyrische Chrestomathie*, 4, 5, 9.

29. Macuch and Panoussi, *Neusyrische Chrestomathie*, 6–7, 5. On a similar figure in Iran, see Tavakoli-Targhi, *Refashioning Iran*, 113–34;

30. Cf. Trigona-Harany, *Ottoman Süryânî*, 20.

31. Cf. Naby, "Les Assyriens d' Union Soviétique"; Laing-Marshall, "Modern Assyrian Identity"; and Zubaida, "Contested Nations."

32. Hanoosh, "Chaldeans in America"; and Hanoosh, "Politics of Minority Chaldeans."

33. Atto, *Hostages in the Homeland*; and Fattah, "Negotiating Nationhood."

34. Makko, "Historical Roots of Contemporary Controversies"; and Wolk, "Church Colony vs. Congregation."

Bibliography

Journals

International Journal of Middle East Studies. (*IJMES*)
Journal of Assyrian Academic Studies. (*JAAS*)
Journal of the American Oriental Society. (*JAOS*)
Parole de l'Orient. (*PO*)

Primary Sources

ARCHIVES

Archives of the American Board of Commissioners for Foreign Missions (**ABCFM**). Houghton Library, Harvard University, Cambridge, MA. Microfilm.
Presbyterian Church in the USA. Board of Foreign Missions. (**PCUSA-BFM**). Presbyterian Historical Society, Philadelphia.

AMERICAN MISSION TRACTS AND BOOKS

Malick, David G. *The American Mission Press: A Preliminary Bibliography.* Atour, 2008. www .lulu.com. (**Malick #**)

PERIODICALS

Annual Report of the American Board of Commissioners for Foreign Missions. Boston, 1833–69. (*AR*)
Annual Report of the Board of Foreign Missions of the Presbyterian Church. New York, 1871–1923. (*AR*)
Ḥuyyada umtanaya.
Missionary Herald (*MH*). Material from the *Missionary Herald* collected in *The Missionary Herald: Reports from Northern Iraq, 1833–1870*, edited by Kamal Salibi and Yusuf K. Khoury. 3 vols. Amman: Royal Institute for Inter-faith Studies, 1997.
New York Times.

Presbyterian Monthly Review. (**PMR**)
Rays of Light (*Zahrire d-bahra*). (**ZB**)
Star (*Kokhwa*). (**K**)
Voice of Truth (*Qala d-šrara*). (**QŠ**)
Woman's Work for Women.

OTHER SOURCES

Anderson, Rufus. *Foreign Missions: Their Relations and Claims.* New York: Charles Scribner, 1869.

———. *History of the Missions of the American Board of Commissioners for Foreign Missions to the Oriental Churches.* 2 vols. Boston: Congregational Publishing Society, 1872, 1884.

Arsanis, Benjamin. *Works* [*Syame mardutaye w-tašʿitaye*]. Edited by Youel A. Baaba. Alamo, CA: Youel A. Baaba Library, 2008.

Assemani, J. S. *Bibliotheca Orientalis Clementino-Vaticana, in qua manuscriptos codices syriacos recensuit.* 3 vols. Rome, 1719-28.

Audo, Thomas. *Treasure of the Syriac Language* [*Simtha d-lešana suryaya*]. 2 vols. Beirut: Catholic Press, 1897.

Baaba, Youel A., ed. *An Assyrian Odyssey.* Alamo, CA: Youel A. Baaba Library, 1998.

Badger, George Percy. *Nestorians and Their Rituals; With the Narrative of a Mission to Mesopotamia and Coordistan in 1842-1844, and of a Late Visit to Those Countries in 1850; also Researches into the Present Condition of the Syrian Jacobites, Papal Syrians, and Chaldeans, and an Inquiry into the Religious Tenets of the Yeseedees.* 2 vols. London: Joseph Masters, 1852.

Beaver, R. Pierce, ed. *To Advance the Gospel: Selections from the Writing of Rufus Anderson.* Grand Rapids, MI: Eerdmans, 1967.

Bedjan, Paul, ed. *Acta martyrum et sanctorum syriace.* 7 vols. Leipzig and Paris: O. Harrassowtiz, 1890-97.

Book of Crumbs [*Kthabhona d-partuthe*]. Urmia, Iran: Archbishop of Canterbury's Mission, 1898.

[Brainerd, Thomas.] *The New Year.* Tract 437. New York: American Tract Society, before 1843.

Brock, Sebastian P., trans. and ed. *The Syriac Fathers on Prayer and the Spiritual Life.* Kalamazoo, MI: Cistercian, 1987.

Bunyan, John. *The Pilgrim's Progress.* London: Penguin Books, 1986.

Calvin, John. *On the Christian Faith: Selections from the Institutes, Commentaries, and Tracts,* edited by John T. McNeil. New York: Bobbs Merrill, 1967.

[Cochran, Joseph G.?]. *The Persian Flower: A Memoir of Judith Grant Perkins of Oroomiah, Persia.* Boston: John P. Jewett, 1853.

Cutts, Edward Lews. *Christians under the Crescent in Asia.* London: Society for Promoting Christian Knowledge, 1877.

Daniel, Mooshie G. *Modern Persia.* Toronto: Henderson, 1898.

Edwards, Jonathan. "A Faithful Narrative of the Surprizing Work of God in the Conversion of Many Hundred Souls in Northhampton." In *A Jonathan Edwards Reader,* edited by Jane E. Smith, Harry S. Stout, and Kenneth P. Minkema, 57-87.

———. "Sinners in the Hands of an Angry God." In *A Jonathan Edwards Reader,* edited by Jane E. Smith, Harry S. Stout, and Kenneth P. Minkema, 89-105.

———. "Some Thoughts Concerning the Present Revival of Religion in New England." In *American Religions,* edited by R. Marie Griffith, 92-102.

Elder, John. *History of the Iran Mission*. Tehran: Literature Committee of the Church Council of Iran, 1960.

Ephrem [Ephraem Syrus]. *Opera omnia*. 6 vols. Edited by J. S. Assemani. Rome: Vatican, 1732–46.

Ephrem the Syrian. *Hymns*. Translated by Kathleen E. McVey. New York: Paulist Press, 1989.

Fiske, D. T. *Faith Working by Love: As Exemplified in the Life of Fidelia Fiske*. Boston: Congregational Publishing Society, 1868.

Gollancz, Hermann, ed. and trans. *The Book of Protection, Being a Collection of Charms*. London: Henry Frowde; Oxford: Oxford University Press, 1912.

Grant, Asahel. *The Nestorians; or, The Lost Tribes*. New York: Harper, 1841.

Griffith, R. Marie, ed. *American Religions: A Documentary History*. New York: Oxford University Press, 2008.

———, ed. "The Life and Religious Experience of Jarena Lee." In *American Religions*, edited by R. Marie Griffith, 197–213.

Guriel, Joseph. *Doctrinae Christianae rudimenta in vernaculam Chaldaeorum linguam Urmiensis provinciae translata*. Rome: Propaganda Fide, 1861.

———. *Elementa linguae chaldaicae*. Rome: Propaganda Fide, 1860.

Holme, Henry. *The Oldest Christian Church, Supplying the Missing Link of Centuries: A Historic Revelation from the Assyrian Mountains of Adiabene, the Gozan of Scripture*. London: Marshall Brothers, 1897.

Isho'dad of Merv. *The Commentaries of Isho'dad of Merv*. 5 vols. Horae Semiticae, nos. 5–7, 10, 11. Edited and translated by Margaret Dunlop Gibson. Cambridge: Cambridge University Press, 1911–16.

[Jacobs, Samuel A.]. *Reviving a Famous Ancient Language: Linotype Syriac Faces; Estrangela, Nestorian, Jacobite*. New York: Syriac Press, 1920.

Johnston, Lawrence Albert. *The Augustana Synod: A Brief Review of Its History, 1860–1910*. Rock Island, IL: Augustana Book Concern, 1910.

Knanishu, Joseph. *About Persia and Its People: A Description of Their Manners, Customs, and Home Life, Including Engagements, Marriages, Modes of Traveling, Forms of Punishments, Superstitions, Etc*. Rock Island, IL: Lutheran Augustana, 1899.

Labaree, Benjamin. "A Modern Apostle." In *The Church at Home and Abroad*. Vol. 10, 313–14. Philadelphia: Presbyterian Board of Publication and Sabbath-School Work, 1891.

Laurie, Thomas. *Dr. Grant and the Mountain Nestorians*. Boston: Gould and Lincoln, 1853.

———. *Woman and Her Saviour in Persia*. Boston: Gould and Lincoln, 1863.

Layard, Austen Henry. *Nineveh and Its Remains*. 2 vols. London: George P. Putnam, 1852.

Maclean, Arthur John, and William Henry Browne. *The Catholicos of the East and His People*. London: Society for Promoting Christian Knowledge, 1892.

Macuch, Rudolf, and Estiphan Panoussi. *Neusyrische Chrestomathie*. Wiesbaden, Germany: Otto Harrassowitz, 1974.

Malech, George David. *History of the Syrian Nation and the Old Evangelical-Apostolic Church of the East: From Remote Antiquity to the Present Time*. Minneapolis: Augsburg Publishing House, 1910.

Malek Yonan, Isaac. *The Beloved Physician of Teheran: The Miracle of the Conversion of Dr. Sa'eed*. Nashville: Cokesbury Press, 1934.

———. *Persian Women*. Nashville: Cumberland Presbyterian, 1898.

Malik, Dawid Gewargis. *The Throne of Saliq: The Condition of Assyrianism in the Era of the Incarnation of Our Lord [*Kursya d-saleq: Ahwal d-suryayuta b-zona d-metbarnašuta d-maran*]. Chicago: Assyrian Messenger Press, 1916.

Manna, Jacques Eugène. *Morceaux choisis de littérature araméenne*. Mosul, Iraq: Dominican Press, 1901–2.

Maqdasi, Jeremiah Timothy. *Grammaire chaldéenne*. Mosul: Dominican Press, 1889.

Marsh, Dwight W. *The Tennesseean in Persia and Kurdistan*. Philadelphia: Presbyterian Board, 1869.

Mengozzi, Alessandro, ed. *Religious Poetry in Vernacular Syriac from Northern Iraq (17th–20th Centuries): An Anthology*. Corpus Scriptorum Christianorum Orientalium 627–28. Louvain, Belgium: Peeters, 2011.

Mill, John Stuart. *On Liberty*. Indianapolis: Hackett, 1978.

Mingana, Alphonse. *Catalogue of the Mingana Collection of Manuscripts*. 3 vols. Cambridge: Heffer and Sons, 1933.

[Missionaries of the ABCFM]. *Nestorian Biography; Being Sketches of Pious Nestorians who Have Died at Oroomiah, Persia*. Boston: Massachusetts Sabbath School Society, 1857.

Mushie, Yohannan. *Outlines of the Spoken Syrian Language: Part One*. Reprint, Chicago: Assyrian Language and Culture Classes, 1982.

Newcomb, Harvey. *The Monthly Concert; with Facts and Reflections Suited to Awaken a Zeal for the Conversion of the World*. Pittsburgh: Luke Loomis, 1836.

Newell, Samuel, and Gordon Hall. *The Conversion of the World; or, the Claims of Six Hundred Millions, and the Ability and Duty of the Churches Respecting Them*. Andover, MA: printed for the ABCFM by Flagg & Gould, 1818.

Percy, Earl [Henry Algernon George]. *Highlands of Asiatic Turkey*. London: Edward Arnold, 1901.

Perkins, Henry Martyn. *Life of Reverend Justin Perkins, D.D., Pioneer Missionary to Persia*. New York: Fleming H. Revell, 1887.

Perkins, Justin. "Journal of a Tour from Oroomiah to Mosul through the Koordish Mountains and a Visit to the Ruins of Nineveh." *JAOS* 2 (1851): 69–123.

———. *Missionary Life in Persia*. Boston: American Tract Society, 1861.

———. "Our Country's Sin." In *American Slavery, in Connection with American Christianity*, 3–25. New York: H. B. Knight, 1854.

———. *A Residence of Eight Years in Persia among the Nestorian Christians*. Andover, MA: Allen, Morrill, and Wadwell; New York: M. W. Dodd, 1843.

———. "The Revelation of the Blessed Apostle Paul Translated from an Ancient Syriac Manuscript." *JAOS* 8 (1866): 183–212.

———. "A Sermon Delivered to the Members of the Nestorian Mission, January 17, 1839, at the Funeral of Mrs. Judith S. Grant, Who Died at Ooroomiah, Persia, Jan. 14, 1839." In H. G. O. Dwight, *Memoir of Mrs. Elizabeth B. Dwight: Including an Account of the Plague of 1837; With a Sketch of the Life of Mrs. Judith S. Grant, Missionary to Persia*, 290–313. New York: M. W. Dodd, 1840.

Perkins, Justin, and Theodore Dwight Woolsey. "Notice of a Life of Alexander the Great." *JAOS* 4 (1854): 357–440.

Rassam, Hormuzd. *Asshur and the Land of Nimrod*. New York: Eaton & Mains, 1897.

Richardson, E. Allen, ed. *Letters from a Distant Shore: The Journal of Sarah Ann Breath*. Piscataway, NJ: Gorgias, 2008.

Richmond, Legh. *The Young Cottager*. London: Nelson, 1876.

Rosenberg, Isaak. *Lehrbuch der Neusyrischen Schrift- und Umgangssprache*. Vienna: A. Hartleben, 1903.

Shahbaz, Yonan H. *The Rage of Islam: An Account of the Massacre of Christians by the Turks in Persia*. Rev. ed. Philadelphia: Judson, 1918.

Shedd, Mary Lewis. *The Measure of a Man: The Life of William Ambrose Shedd, Missionary to Persia*. New York: George H. Doran, 1922.

Shedd, William Ambrose. *Islam and the Oriental Churches: Their Historical Relations*. Philadelphia: Presbyterian Board of Publication and Sabbath-School Work, 1904.

Smith, Eli, and H. G. O. Dwight. *Missionary Researches in Armenia: Including a Journey through Asia Minor, and into Georgia and Persia, with a Visit to the Nestorian and Chaldean Christians of Oormia and Salmas*. London: George Wightman, 1834.

Smith, Jane E., Harry S. Stout, and Kenneth P. Minkema, eds. *A Jonathan Edwards Reader*. New Haven, CT: Yale University Press, 1995.

Speer, Robert E. *"The Hakim Sahib," The Foreign Doctor: A Biography of Joseph P. Cochran, M.D., of Persia*. New York: Fleming H. Revell, 1911.

Stewart, John. *Nestorian Missionary Enterprise: The Story of a Church on Fire*. Edinburgh: T&T Clark, 1928.

Stoddard, David T. "Grammar of the Modern Syriac Language, as Spoken in Oroomiah, Persia, and in Koordistan." *JAOS* 5 (1855): 1–180.

———. *Narrative of the Late Revival among the Nestorians: Read at Oroomiah, Persia, at the Anniversary of the Mission, Held Simultaneously with the Meeting of the American Board of Commissioners for Foreign Missions, September 1846*. Boston: ABCFM, 1847.

Surma d-Bait Mar Shimun. *Assyrian Church Customs and the Murder of Mar Shimun*. London, 1920. Assyrian International News Agency (www.aina.org).

Thompson, Joseph P. *A Memoir of Rev. David Tappan Stoddard: Missionary to the Nestorians*. New York: Sheldon, Blakeman, 1858.

Tyler, W. S. *Memoir of Rev. Henry Lobdell, M.D.* Boston: American Tract Society, 1859.

Wallis Budge, E. A., trans. *The Monks of Kûblâi Khân, Emperor of China*. London: Religious Tract Society, 1928.

Warkworth, Lord [Henry Algernon George Percy]. *Notes from a Diary in Asiatic Turkey*. London: E. Arnold, 1898.

Wigram, W. A., and E. T. A. Wigram. *The Cradle of Mankind: Life in Eastern Kurdistan*. 2nd ed. London: A. & C. Black, 1922.

Wilson, J. Christy. "A Persian Apostle—Dr. Sa'eed Kurdistani." *Moslem World* 33, no. 2 (Apr. 1943): 129–39.

Wilson, Samuel G. "Conversion of the Nestorians of Persia to the Russian Church." *Missionary Review of the World* 12 (1899): 745–52.

———. *Persia: Western Mission*. Philadelphia: Presbyterian Board of Publication and Sabbath-School Work, 1896.

Wishard, John G. *Twenty Years in Persia: A Narrative of Life under the Last Three Shahs*. New York: Fleming H. Revell, 1908.

Wright, Austin H. *Looking unto Jesus: A Sermon Occasioned by the Death of Mrs. Martha Ann Rhea Preached at Oroomiah, Persia, October 11, 1857*. Boston: T. R. Marvin & Son, 1858.

SECONDARY LITERATURE

Abi-Mershed, Osama W. *Apostles of Modernity: Saint-Simonians and the Civilizing Mission in Algeria*. Stanford, CA: Stanford University Press, 2010.

Abrahamian, Ervand. *A History of Modern Iran*. Cambridge: Cambridge University Press, 2008.

Akopian, Arman, "*Babylon*, an Armenian-Language Syriac Periodical: Some Remarks on Milieu, Structure and Language." *Journal of the Canadian Society for Syriac Studies* 10 (2010): 83–98.

Al-Jeloo, Nicholas. "Evidence in Stone and Wood: The Assyrian/Syriac History and Heritage of the Urmia Region in Iran, as Reconstructed from Epigraphic Evidence." *PO* 35 (2010): 39–63.

Al-Rasheed, Madawi. *Iraqi Assyrian Christians in London: The Construction of Ethnicity*. Lewiston, NY: E. Mellen Press, 1998.

Amanat, Abbas. "*Mujtahids* and Missionaries: Shī'ī Responses to Christian Polemics in the Early Qajar Period." In Gleave, *Religion and Society in Qajar Iran*, 247–69.

Ameer, John P. "Curriculum and Literacy in the Urmia Mission Schools." *JAAS* 24, no. 1 (2010): 8–18.

———. "Fidelia Fiske: Missionary in Urmia." *JAAS* 21, no. 2 (2007): 41–56.

———. "Yankees and Nestorians: The Establishment of American Schools among the Nestorians of Iran and Turkey, 1834–1850." PhD diss., Harvard University, 1992.

Anderson, Benedict. *Imagined Communities: Reflections on the Origins and Spread of Nations.* Rev. ed. London: Verso, 1991.

Anidjar, Gil. "The Idea of an Anthropology of Christianity." *Interventions* 11, no. 3 (2009): 367–93.

Anjum, Ovamir. "Islam as a Discursive Tradition: Talal Asad and His Interlocutors." *Comparative Studies of Asia, Africa, and the Middle East* 27, no. 3 (2007): 656–72.

Ariès, Philippe. *Western Attitudes toward Death: From the Middle Ages to the Present*. Translated by Patricia M. Ranum. Baltimore: Johns Hopkins University Press, 1974.

Asad, Talal. "Comments on Conversion." In *Conversion to Modernities*, edited by Peter van der Veer, 263–73.

———. *Formations of the Secular: Christianity, Islam, Modernity*. Stanford, CA: Stanford University Press, 2003.

———. *Genealogies of Religion: Discipline and Reasons of Power in Christianity and Islam*. Baltimore: Johns Hopkins University Press, 1993.

———. "Thinking about Religion, Belief, and Politics." In *The Cambridge Companion to Religious Studies*, edited by Robert A. Orsi, 36–57. Cambridge: Cambridge University Press, 2012.

Asher-Greve, Julia M. "From 'Semiramis of Babylon' to 'Semiramis of Hammersmith.'" In *Orientalism, Assyriology and the Bible*, edited by Steven W. Holloway, 322–73.

Atesh, Sabri. "Empires at the Margin: Towards a History of the Ottoman-Iranian Borderland and the Borderland Peoples, 1843–1881." PhD diss., New York University, 2006.

Atto, Naures. *Hostages in the Homeland, Orphans in the Diaspora: Identity Discourses among the Assyrian/Syriac Elites in the European Diaspora*. Leiden, Netherlands: Leiden University Press, 2011.

Baaba, Youel A. "The Preservers of Language and Literature" [*Naṭore d-lešana w-seprayuta*]. *JAAS* 20, no. 2 (2006): 59–68.

Babakhan, J. "Protestantisme et Catholicisme chez le Peuple Nestorien: Une Revue Néo-Syriaque à Ourmiah (Perse)." *Revue de l'Orient Chrétien* 4 (1899): 428–43.

Balicka-Witakowska, Ewa. "Illustrating Charms: A Syrian Manuscript with Magic Drawings in the Collection of the British Library." In Kiraz, *Malphono w-Rabo d-Malphone*, 779–808.

Bastian, Jean-Pierre. "Sociétés Protestantes et rupture révolutionnaire au Mexique, 1872–1911." *Social Sciences and Missions* 20 (2007): 63–81.

Baum, Wilhelm, and Dietmar W. Winkler. *The Church of the East: A Concise History*. Translated by Miranda G. Henry. New York: RoutledgeCurzon, 2003.

Bcheiry, Iskandar. "Syriac Manuscripts in the New York Public Library." *Hugoye* 11 (2008): 141–59.

Becker, Adam H. "The Ancient Near East in the Late Antique Near East: Syriac Christian Appropriation of the Biblical Past." In *Antiquity in Antiquity: Jewish and Christian Pasts in the Greco-Roman World*, edited by Gregg Gardner and Kevin Osterloh, 394–415. Tübingen, Germany: Mohr Siebeck, 2008.

———. "Doctoring the Past in the Present: E. A. Wallis Budge, the Discourse on Magic, and the Colonization of Iraq." *History of Religions* 44, no. 3 (2005): 175–215.

———. *Fear of God and the Beginning of Wisdom: The School of Nisibis and the Development of Scholastic Culture in Late Antique Mesopotamia*. Philadelphia: University of Pennsylvania Press, 2006.

———. "Martyrdom, Religious Difference, and 'Fear' as a Category of Piety in the Sasanian Empire: The Case of the *Martyrdoms of Gregory and of Yazdpaneh*." *Journal of Late Antiquity* 2, no. 2 (Fall 2009): 300–336.

———. "Polishing the Mirror: Some Thoughts on Syriac Sources and Early Judaism." In *Envisioning Judaism: Studies in Honor of Peter Schäfer on the Occasion of his Seventieth Birthday*. Vol. 2, edited by Ra'anan S. Boustan et al., 897–916. Tübingen, Germany: Mohr Siebeck, 2013.

Beidelman, Thomas O. *Colonial Evangelism: A Socio-historical Study of an East African Mission at the Grassroots*. Bloomington: Indiana University Press, 1982.

Berger, Peter L. *The Sacred Canopy: Elements of a Sociological Theory of Religion*. Garden City, NY: Doubleday, 1967.

Berger, Peter L., and Thomas Luckmann. "Secularization and Pluralism." In *International Yearbook for the Sociology of Religion*. Vol. 2, 73–86. Cologne: Westdeutscher Verlag, 1966.

Berthaud, Edmond. "La vie rurale dans quelques villages chrétiens de l'Azerbaïjan occidental." *Revue de géographie de Lyon* 43, no. 3 (1968): 291–331.

Bhatia, Varuni. "Devotional Tradition and National Culture: Recovering Gaudiya Vaishnavism in Colonial Bengal." PhD diss., Columbia University, 2009.

Bielo, James S. *Words upon the Word: An Ethnography of Evangelical Group Bible Study*. New York: New York University Press, 2009.

Bigelow, Anna. *Sharing the Sacred: Practicing Pluralism in Muslim North India*. Oxford: Oxford University Press, 2010.

Bohrer, Frederick N. "Inventing Assyria: Exoticism and Reception in Nineteenth-Century England and France." In *Orientalism, Assyriology and the Bible*, edited by Steven W. Holloway, 222–66.

———. *Orientalism and Visual Culture: Imagining Mesopotamia in Nineteenth-Century Europe*. Cambridge: Cambridge University Press, 2003.

Braude, Benjamin, and Bernard Lewis, eds. *Christians and Jews in the Ottoman Empire: The Functioning of a Plural Society*. Vol. 1, *The Central Lands*. New York: Holmes & Meier, 1982.

Brock, Sebastian P. *The Luminous Eye: The Spiritual World Vision of St. Ephrem*. Kalamazoo, MI: Cistercian, 1992.

Bronfen, Elisabeth. *Over Her Dead Body: Death, Femininity and the Aesthetic*. Manchester, UK: Manchester University Press, 1992.

Brown, Candy Gunther. *The Word in the World: Evangelical Writing, Publishing, and Reading in America, 1789–1880*. Chapel Hill: University of North Carolina Press, 2004.

Brown, Peter. *The Rise of Western Christendom*. 2nd ed. Oxford: Blackwell, 2003.

Brown, Wendy. *Regulating Aversion: Tolerance in the Age of Identity and Empire*. Princeton, NJ: Princeton University Press, 2006.

Buchan, Thomas. *"Blessed Is He Who Has Brought Adam from Sheol": Christ's Descent to the Dead in the Theology of St. Ephrem the Syrian*. Piscataway, NJ: Gorgias, 2004.

Burton, Antoinette. *Burdens of History: British Feminists, Indian Women, and Imperial Culture, 1865–1915*. Chapel Hill: University of North Carolina Press, 1994.

Butts, Aaron. "Assyrian Christians." In *A Companion to Assyria*, edited by Eckart Frahm. Oxford: Wiley-Blackwell, forthcoming.

Cameron, Averil. *Christianity and the Rhetoric of Empire: The Development of Christian Discourse*. Berkeley: University of California Press, 1991.

Cannell, Fenella, ed. *The Anthropology of Christianity*. Durham, NC: Duke University Press, 2006.

Carey, Hilary M., ed. *Empires of Religion*. London: Palgrave Macmillan, 2008.

Casanova, José. *Public Religions in the Modern World*. Chicago: University of Chicago Press, 1994.

Chakrabarty, Dipesh. "The Difference-Deferral of a Colonial Modernity: Public Debates on Domesticity in British Bengal." In *Subaltern Studies VIII*, edited by David Arnold and David Hardiman, 56–88. New Delhi: Oxford University Press, 1994.

———. *Provincializing Europe: Postcolonial Thought and Historical Difference*. Princeton, NJ: Princeton University Press, 2000.

Chatterjee, Partha. *The Nation and Its Fragments: Colonial and Postcolonial Histories*. Princeton, NJ: Princeton University Press, 1993.

Chevalier, Michel. *Les montagnards chrétiens du Hakkâri et du Kurdistan septentrional*. Paris: Publications du Département de Géographie de l'Université de Paris–Sorbonne, 1985.

Chidester, David. "Colonialism." In *Guide to the Study of Religion*, edited by Will Braun and Russell McCutcheon, 423–37. New York: Continuum, 2000.

———. *Savage Systems: Colonialism and Comparative Religion in Southern Africa*. Charlottesville: University of Virginia Press, 1996.

Clemons, Jack T. "Syriac Studies in the United States: 1783–1900." *Aram* 5 (1993): 75–86.

Coakley, James F. "The Archbishop of Canterbury's Assyrian Mission Press: A Bibliography." *Journal of Semitic Studies* 30, no. 1 (1985): 35–73.

———. "Assyrian Christians in English Fiction, 1849–1967." *JAAS* 23, no. 2 (2009): 18–25.

———. "Assyrians or Arameans? In Memoriam J. M. Fiey." Unpublished manuscript, 2011, reproduction of typed text.

———. *The Church of the East and the Church of England: A History of the Archbishop of Canterbury's Assyrian Mission*. Oxford: Oxford University Press, 1992.

———. "Edward Breath and the Typography of Syriac." *Harvard Library Bulletin* 6, no. 4 (1995): 41–64.

———. "Manuscripts for Sale: Urmia, 1890–2." *JAAS* 20, no. 2 (2006): 3–17.

———. *The Typography of Syriac: A Historical Catalogue of Printing Types, 1537–1958*. London: Oak Knoll, British Library, 2006.

———. "Yaroo M. Neesan, 'A Missionary to His Own People.'" In "A Festschrift for Dr. Sebastian P. Brock," special issue, *Aram* 5 (1993): 87–100.

Coakley, James F., and David G. K. Taylor. "Syriac Books Printed at the Dominican Press, Mosul." In Kiraz, *Malphono w-Rabo d-Malphone*, 71–110.

Comaroff, Jean, and John Comaroff. *Of Revelation and Revolution*. 2 vols. Chicago: University of Chicago Press, 1991–97.

Copland, Ian. "Christianity as an Arm of Empire: The Ambiguous Case of India under the Company, c. 1813–1858." *Historical Journal* 49, no. 4 (2006): 1025–54.

Dalmia, Vasudha. *The Nationalization of Hindu Traditions: Bhāratendu Hariśchandra and Nineteenth-Century Banaras*. Oxford: Oxford University Press, 1997.

Dalyan, Murat Gökhan. "Robbery, Blood Feud, and Gunpowder in Nestorian Community." *Asian Social Science* 7 (2011): 81–87.

Damrosch, David. *The Buried Book: The Loss and Rediscovery of the Great Epic of Gilgamesh*. New York: Henry Holt, 2006.

David, Samuel. *The First English-Chaldean Dictionary*. Chicago, 1924.

de Courtois, Sébastien. *The Forgotten Genocide: Eastern Christians, the Last Arameans*. Translated by Vincent Aurora. Piscataway, NJ: Gorgias, 2004.

De Kelaita, Robert William. "On the Road to Nineveh: A Brief History of Assyrian Nationalism, 1892–1990." *JAAS* 8, no. 1 (1994): 6–30.

del Río Sánchez, Francisco. "The Aramaean Speakers of Iraq in the Arabic Sources." In *Eastern Crossroads: Essays on Medieval Christian Legacy*, edited by Juan Pedro Monferrer-Sala, 359–66. Piscataway, NJ: Gorgias, 2007.

de Mauroy, Hubert. "Lieux de culte, anciens et actuels, des églises 'syriennes orientales' dans le diocèse d'Ourmiah-Salmas en Iran (Azerbaïdjan occidental)." *PO* 3, no. 2 (1972): 313–51.

Doğan, Mehmet Ali, and Heather J. Sharkey, eds. *American Missionaries and the Middle East: Foundational Encounters*. Salt Lake City: University of Utah Press, 2011.

Donabed, Sargon. *Remnants of Heroes: The Assyrian Experience*. Chicago: Assyrian Academic Society, 2003.

Douglas, Ann. *The Feminization of American Culture*. New York: Avon Books, 1977.

Dressler, Markus. "Religio-secular Metamorphoses: The Re-making of Turkish Alevism." *Journal of the American Academy of Religion* 76, no. 2 (2008): 280–311.

——. *Writing Religion: The Making of Turkish Alevi Islam*. Oxford: Oxford University Press, 2013.

Dressler, Markus, and Arvind-Pal S. Mandair, eds. *Secularism and Religion-Making*. Oxford: Oxford University Press, 2011.

Dubuisson, Daniel. *The Western Construction of Religion: Myths, Knowledge, and Ideology*. Translated by William Sayers. Baltimore: Johns Hopkins University Press, 2003.

Durkheim, Émile. *The Elementary Forms of Religious Life*. Translated by Carol Cosman. Oxford: Oxford University Press, 2001.

Elisha, Omri. *Moral Ambition: Mobilization and Social Outreach in Evangelical Megachurches*. Berkeley: University of California Press, 2011.

Elshakry, Marwa. "The Gospel of Science and American Evangelism in Late Ottoman Beirut." *Past and Present* 196 (2007): 173–214.

——. "Knowledge in Motion: The Cultural Politics of Modern Science Translation in Arabic." *Isis* 99 (2008): 701–30.

Etherington, Norman. "*Missions and Empire* Revisited." *Social Sciences and Missions* 24 (2011): 171–89.

Fahmy, Khaled. *All the Pasha's Men: Mehmed Ali, the Army, and the Making of Modern Egypt*. Cairo: American University in Cairo Press, 2002.

Fattah, Hala. "Negotiating Nationhood on the Net: The Case of the Turcomans and Assyrians of Iraq." In *Native on the Net: Indigenous and Diasporic Peoples in the Virtual Age*, edited by Kyra Landzelius, 186–201. New York: Routledge, 2006.

Fessenden, Tracy. *Culture and Redemption: Religion, the Secular, and American Literature*. Princeton, NJ: Princeton University Press, 2007.

Fiey, Jean Maurice. "'Assyriens' ou Araméens?" *L'orient syrien* 10 (1965): 141–60.

——. "Comment l'Occident en vint à parler de 'Chaldéens'?" *Bulletin of the John Rylands University Library of Manchester* 78, no. 3 (1996): 163–70.

——. *Nisibe: Métropole syriaque orientale et ses suffragants des origins à nos jours*. CSCO 388. Louvain, Belgium: Secretariat of the CSCO, 1977.

——. "Proto-histoire chrétienne du Hakkâri turc." *L'Orient Syrien* 9 (1964): 443–72.

Figueira, Dorothy M. *Aryans, Jews, Brahmins: Theorizing Authority through Myths of Identity*. Albany: SUNY Press, 2002.

Foster, Benjamin R. "On the Formal Study of Near Eastern Languages in America, 1770–1930." In *U.S.-Middle East Historical Encounters: A Critical Survey*, edited by Abbas Amanat and Magnus T. Bernhardsson, 10–44. Gainesville: University Press of Florida, 2007.

Foucault, Michel. *Discipline and Punish: The Birth of the Prison*. Translated by Alan Sheridan. New York: Vintage, 1977.

Fox, Samuel Ethan. *The Neo-Aramaic Dialect of Jilu*. Wiesbaden, Germany: Harrassowitz, 1997.

Fränkel, Sigmund. *Die aramäischen Fremdwörter im Arabischen*. Leiden, Netherlands: Brill, 1886.

Frye, Richard N. "Assyria and Syria: Synonyms." *Journal of Near Eastern Studies* 51 (1992): 281–85.

——. "Reply to John Joseph." *JAAS* 13, no. 1 (1999): 69–70.

Gaunt, David. *Massacres, Resistance, Protectors: Muslim-Christian Relations in Eastern Anatolia during World War I*. Piscataway, NJ: Gorgias, 2006.

Gellner, Ernest. *Nations and Nationalism*. 2nd ed. Ithaca, NY: Cornell University Press, 2006.

Gleave, Robert, ed. *Religion and Society in Qajar Iran*. London: RoutledgeCurzon, 2005.

Goswami, Manu. "Rethinking the Modular Nation Form: Toward a Sociohistorical Conception of Nationalism." *Comparative Studies in Society and History* 44 (2002): 770–99.

Goudsblom, Johan, and Stephen Mennell, eds. *The Norbert Elias Reader*. Oxford: Blackwell, 1998.

Grant, Bruce. "Shrines and Sovereigns: Life, Death, and Religion in Rural Azerbaijan." *Comparative Studies in Society and History* 53 (2011): 654–81.

Green, Nile. "The Madrasas of Oxford: Iranian Interactions with the English Universities in the Early Nineteenth Century." *Iranian Studies* 44 (2011): 807–29.

Hall, Catherine. *Civilizing Subjects: Metropole and Colony in the English Imagination*. Oxford: Polity Press, 2002.

Hall, Isaac Hollister. "The Nestorian Ritual of the Washing of the Dead." *Hebraica* 4, no. 2 (1888): 82–86.

——. "Specimens from the Nestorian Burial Service." *Hebraica* 4, no. 4 (1888): 193–200.

Halttunen, Karen. *Confidence Men and Painted Women: A Study of Middle-Class Culture in America, 1830–1870*. New Haven, CT: Yale University Press, 1982.

Hamilakis, Yannis. *The Nation and Its Ruins: Antiquity, Archaeology, and National Imagination in Greece*. Oxford: Oxford University Press, 2007.

Hanoosh, Yasmeen. "Chaldeans in America: The Shifting Spaces of an Iraqi Minority's Discourses." *Journal of Associated Graduates in Near Eastern Studies* 11 (2006): 43–57.

——. "The Politics of Minority Chaldeans between Iraq and America." PhD diss., University of Michigan, 2008.

Harding, Susan. *The Book of Jerry Falwell: Fundamentalist Language and Politics*. Princeton, NJ: Princeton University Press, 2001.

Harris, Paul William. *Nothing but Christ: Rufus Anderson and the Ideology of Protestant Foreign Missions*. Oxford: Oxford University Press, 1999.

Hauerwas, Stanley. *The State of the University: Academic Knowledges and Knowledge of God*. Oxford: Blackwell, 2007.

Heinrichs, Wolfhart. "The Modern Assyrians—Name and Nation." In *Semitica: Serta philologica Constantino Tseretli dicata*, edited by Riccardo Contini, 99–114. Turin: Silvio Zamorani, 1993.

Hellot, Florence. "The Western Missionaries in Azerbaijani Society (1835–1914)." In Gleave, *Religion and Society in Qajar Iran*, 270–92.

Heyer, Friedrich. "Die russisch-orthodoxe Mission in Urmia und anderswo." In *Syriaca: Zur Geschichte, Theologie, Liturgie und Gegenwartslage der syrischen Kirchen*. Vol. 2, *Deutsches Syrologen-Symposium (Juli 2000, Wittenberg)*, edited by Martin Tamcke, 439–47. Studien zur Orientalischen Kirchengeschichte 17. Münster: LIT, 2002.

Ho, Engseng. *The Graves of Tarim: Genealogy and Mobility across the Indian Ocean*. Berkeley: University of California Press, 2006.

Hobsbawm, Eric. "Introduction: Inventing Traditions." In *The Invention of Tradition*, edited by Eric Hobsbawm and Terence Ranger, 1–14. Cambridge: Cambridge University Press, 1983.

Holloway, Steven W. "Nineveh Sails for the New World: Assyria Envisioned by Nineteenth-Century America." *Iraq* 66 (2004): 243–56.

———, ed. *Orientalism, Assyriology and the Bible*. Sheffield, UK: Sheffield Phoenix, 2006.

Hornus, Jean-Michel. "Un rapport du consul de France à Erzeroum sur la situation des chrétiens en Perse au milieu du XIX siècle." *Proche-Orient Chrétien* 21 (1971): 3–29, 127–51, 289–315; 22 (1972): 18–46, 288–304.

Hutchison, William R. *Errand to the World: American Protestant Thought and Foreign Missions*. Chicago: University of Chicago Press, 1987.

Ishaya, Arianne. "Ethnicity, Class, and Politics: Assyrians in the History of Azerbayjan, 1800–1918." *JAAS* 4 (1990): 3–17.

Jackson, Samuel. "Phoenicians and Assyrians versus the Roving Nomad: Western Imperialism, Western Scholarship and Modern Identity." In *Gilgameš and the World of Assyria*, edited by Joseph Azize and Noel Weeks, 207–23. Louvain, Belgium: Peeters, 2007.

Joseph, John. "Assyria and Syria: Synonyms?" *JAAS* 11, no. 2 (1997): 37–43.

———. "The Bible and the Assyrians: It Kept Their Memory Alive." *JAAS* 12, no. 1 (1998): 70–76.

———. *The Modern Assyrians of the Middle East*. Leiden, Netherlands: Brill, 2000.

Kantorowicz, Ernst H. *The King's Two Bodies: A Study in Mediaeval Political Theology*. Princeton, NJ: Princeton University Press, 1957.

Karpat, Kemal. *An Inquiry into the Social Foundations of Nationalism in the Ottoman State: From Social Estates to Classes, From Millets to Nations*. Princeton, NJ: Center of International Studies, 1973.

Kashani-Sabet, Firoozeh. *Frontier Fictions: Shaping the Iranian Nation, 1804–1946*. Princeton, NJ: Princeton University Press, 1999.

Kawerau, Peter. *Amerika und die Orientalischen Kirchen: Ursprung und Anfang der Amerikanischen Mission unter den Nationalkirchen Westasiens*. 2 vols. Berlin: De Gruyter, 1958.

Keane, Webb. *Christian Moderns: Freedom and Fetish in the Mission Encounter*. Berkeley: University of California Press, 2007.

Keddie, Nikki R. *Qajar Iran and the Rise of Reza Khan, 1796–1925*. Costa Mesa, CA: Mazda, 1999.

Kedourie, Elie. "'Minorities.'" In *The Chatham House Version and Other Middle-Eastern Studies*, 286–316. New ed. Hanover, NH: University Press of New England, 1984.

Keevak, Michael. *The Story of a Stele: China's Nestorian Monument and Its Reception in the West, 1625–1916*. Hong Kong: Hong Kong University Press, 2008.

Khalaf, Samir. *Cultural Resistance: Global and Local Encounters in the Middle East*. London: Saqi, 2001.

Kidd, Thomas. *American Christians and Islam: Evangelical Culture and Muslims from the Colonial Period to the Age of Terrorism*. Princeton, NJ: Princeton University Press, 2009.

Kieschnick, John. *The Impact of Buddhism on Chinese Material Culture.* Princeton, NJ: Princeton University Press, 2003.

Kieser, Hans-Lukas. *Der verpasste Friede: Mission, Ethnie und Staat in den Ostprovinzen der Türkei, 1839–1938.* Zurich: Chronos, 2000.

———. "Muslim Heterodoxy and Protestant Utopia. The Interactions between Alevis and Missionaries in Ottoman Anatolia." *Die Welt des Islams* 41 (2001): 89–111.

———. *Nearest East: American Millennialism and Mission to the Middle East.* Philadelphia: Temple University Press, 2010.

———. "Ottoman Urfa and Its Missionaries." In *Historic Armenian Cities and Provinces.* Vol. 6, *Armenian Tigranakert/Diarbekir and Edessa/Urfa,* edited by Richard G. Hovannisian, 399–466. Costa Mesa, CA: Mazda Press, 2006.

Kinzer, Stephen. *Reset: Iran, Turkey, and America's Future.* New York: Henry Holt, 2010.

Kippenberg, Hans G. *Discovering Religious History in the Modern Age.* Translated by Barbara Harshav. Princeton, NJ: Princeton University Press, 2002.

Kiraz, George A., ed. *Malphono w-Rabo d-Malphone: Studies in Honor of Sebastian P. Brock.* Piscataway, NJ: Gorgias, 2008.

Konortas, Paraskevas. "From Tầ'ife to Millet: Ottoman Terms for the Ottoman Greek Orthodox Community." In *Ottoman Greeks in the Age of Nationalism: Politics, Economy, and Society in the Nineteenth Century,* edited by Dimitri Gondicas and Charles Issawi, 169–79. Princeton, NJ: Darwin Press, 1999.

Laderman, Gary. *The Sacred Remains: American Attitudes toward Death, 1799–1883.* New Haven, CT: Yale University Press, 1996.

Laing-Marshall, Andrea. "Modern Assyrian Identity and the Church of the East: An Exploration of Their Relationship and the Rise of Assyrian Nationalism from the World Wars to 1980." MA thesis, University of Toronto, 2001.

Lambton, Ann K. S. *Qajar Persia.* London: I. B. Tauris, 1987.

Levi-Strauss, Claude. *Tristes tropiques.* Translated by John Russell. London: Hutchinson, 1961.

Lorenzen, David. "Who Invented Hinduism?" *Comparative Studies in Society and History* (1999): 630–59.

MacCormack, Sabine. *Religion in the Andes: Vision and Imagination in Early Colonial Peru.* Princeton, NJ: Princeton University Press, 1993.

MacDonald, Andrew. "The Beggar Chiefs of St. Zaia: Nestorian 'Great Deceivers' in South Africa and the Benevolent Empire, c. 1860–1940s." *Past and Present,* forthcoming.

MacEvitt, Christopher. *The Crusades and the Christian World of the East: Rough Tolerance.* Philadelphia: University of Pennsylvania Press, 2007.

Maclean, Arthur J. *Dictionary of the Dialects of Verbacular Syriac.* Oxford: Oxford University Press, 1901.

Macomber, William. "The Funeral Liturgy of the Chaldean Church." *Concilium* 2 (1968): 19–22.

Macuch, Rudolf. "Assyrians in Iran. i. The Assyrian Community (Āšūrīān) in Iran." In *Encyclopædia Iranica,* edited by Ehsan Yarshater. Vol. 2.5, 817–22. London: Routledge, 1987.

———. *Geschichte der spät- und neusyrischen Literatur.* Berlin: de Gruyter, 1976.

Mahmood, Saba. "Feminist Theory, Embodiment, and the Docile Agent: Some Reflections on the Egyptian Islamic Revival." *Cultural Anthropology* 16 (2001): 202–36.

———. *Politics of Piety: The Islamic Revival and the Feminist Subject.* Princeton, NJ: Princeton University Press, 2005.

———. "Religious Freedom, the Minority Question, and Geopolitics in the Middle East." *Comparative Studies in Society and History* 54, no. 2 (2012): 418–46.

Makdisi, Ussama. *Artillery of Heaven: American Missionaries and the Failed Conversion of the Middle East*. Ithaca, NY: Cornell University Press, 2007.

——. *The Culture of Sectarianism: Community, History, and Violence in Nineteenth-Century Ottoman Lebanon*. Berkeley: University of California Press, 2000.

——. *Faith Misplaced: The Broken Promise of U.S.-Arab Relations, 1820–2001*. Philadelphia: Public Affairs, 2010.

——. "Ottoman Orientalism." *American Historical Review* 107 (2002): 768–96.

——. "Reclaiming the Land of the Bible: Missionaries, Secularism, and Evangelical Modernity." *American Historical Review* 102, no. 3 (1997): 680–713.

Makko, Aryo. "The Historical Roots of Contemporary Controversies: National Revival and the Assyrian 'Concept of Unity.'" *JAAS* 24, no. 1 (2010): 1–29.

Malick, David G. "Modern Assyrian Hymns: The Introduction of the Vernacular in the Liturgical Services of the Church of the East." *Aram* 21 (2009): 215–49.

Malley, Shawn. "Austen Henry Layard and the Periodical Press: Middle Eastern Archaeology and the Excavation of Cultural Identity in Mid-Nineteenth Century Britain." *Victorian Review* 22, no. 2 (1996): 152–70.

Markus, Robert. *Christianity and the Secular*. Notre Dame, IN: University of Notre Dame Press, 2006.

Marr, Timothy. *The Cultural Roots of American Islamicism*. Cambridge: Cambridge University Press, 2006.

Masters, Bruce. *Christians and Jews in the Ottoman Arab World: The Roots of Sectarianism*. Cambridge: Cambridge University Press, 2001.

——. "Competing for Aleppo's Souls: The Roman Catholic and Protestant Missions in the Ottoman Period." *Archaeology and History in Lebanon* 22 (2005): 34–50.

Masuzawa, Tomoko. *In Search of Dreamtime: The Quest for the Origin of Religion*. Chicago: University of Chicago Press, 1993.

——. *The Invention of World Religions: Or, How European Universalism Was Preserved in the Language of Pluralism*. Chicago: University of Chicago Press, 2005.

McCall, Henrietta. "Rediscovery and Aftermath." In *The Legacy of Mesopotamia*, edited by Stephanie Dalley et al., 183–213. Oxford: Oxford University Press, 1998.

McGarry, Molly. *Ghost of Future Pasts: Spiritualism and the Cultural Politics of Nineteenth-Century America*. Chicago: University of Chicago Press, 2008.

Mehta, Uday Singh. *Liberalism and Empire: A Study of Nineteenth-Century British Liberal Thought*. Chicago: University of Chicago Press, 1999.

Merguerian, Barbara J. "'Missions in Eden': Shaping an Educational and Social Program for the Armenians in Eastern Turkey (1855–1895)." In Murre-van den Berg, *New Faith in Ancient Lands*, 241–61.

Messo, Johnny. "The Origin of the Terms 'Syria(n)' & Sūryoyo Once Again." *PO* 36 (2011): 111–25.

Meyer, Birgit, ed. *Aesthetic Formations: Media, Religion, and the Senses*. New York: Palgrave Macmillan, 2009.

——. "Religious Revelation, Secrecy and the Limits of Visual Representation." *Anthropological Theory* 6 (2006): 431–53.

——. *Translating the Devil: Religion and Modernity among the Ewe in Ghana*. Edinburgh: Edinburgh University Press, 1999.

Meyer, Birgit, and Annelies Moors, eds. *Religion, Media, and the Public Sphere*. Bloomington: Indiana University Press, 2006.

Mitchell, Timothy. *Colonising Egypt*. Berkeley: University of California Press, 1991.

———, ed. *Questions of Modernity*. Minneapolis: University of Minnesota Press, 2000.

Modern, John Lardas. *Secularism in Antebellum America*. Chicago: University of Chicago Press, 2011.

Moxnes, Halvor. *Jesus and the Rise of Nationalism: A New Quest for the Nineteenth Century Historical Jesus*. London: I. B. Tauris, 2012.

Murray, Robert. *Symbols of Church and Kingdom: A Study in Early Syriac Tradition*. London: Cambridge University Press, 1975.

Murre-van den Berg, Heleen L. "The American Board and the Eastern Churches: The 'Nestorian Mission.'" Orientalia Christiana Periodica 65 (1999): 117–38.

———. "Apostasy or 'a House Built on Sand': Jews, Muslims and Christians in East-Syrian Texts (1500–1850)." In *Contacts and Controversies between Muslims, Jews and Christians in the Ottoman Empire and Pre-modern Iran*, edited by Camilla Adang and Sabine Schmidtke, 223–43. Istanbuler Texte und Studien Bd. 2. Würzburg, Germany: Ergon-Verlag, 2010.

———. "The Church of the East in the Sixteenth to the Eighteenth Century: World Church or Ethnic Community?" In *Redefining Christian Identity: Cultural Interaction in the Middle East since the Rise of Islam*, edited by J. J. Van Ginkel, H. L. Murre-van den Berg, and T. M. Van Lint, 301–20. Orientalia Lovaniensia Analecta 134. Louvain, Belgium: Peeters, 2005.

———. "Classical Syriac, Neo-Aramaic, and Arabic in the Church of the East and the Chaldean Church between 1500 and 1800." In *Aramaic in Its Historical and Linguistic Setting*, edited by Holger Gzella and Margaretha L. Folmer, 335–52. Wiesbaden, Germany: Harrassowitz, 2008.

———. "'Dear Mother of My Soul': Fidelia Fiske and the Role of Women Missionaries in Mid-Nineteenth Century Iran." *Exchange* 30, no. 1 (2001): 33–48.

———. *From a Spoken to a Written Language: The Introduction and Development of Literary Urmia Aramaic in the Nineteenth Century*. Leiden, Netherlands: Brill, 1999.

———. "Generous Devotion: Women in the Church of the East between 1550 and 1850." *Hugoye* 7 (2004): 11–54.

———. "A 'Good and Blessed Father': Yonan of Ada on Justin Perkins, Urmia (Iran), 1870." In *Protestant Missions and Local Encounters in the Nineteenth and Twentieth Centuries: Unto the Ends of the World*, edited by Hilde Nielssen, Inger Marie Okkenhaug, and Karina Hestad Skeie, 187–206. Leiden, Netherlands: Brill, 2011.

———. "'An Inheritance with Sarah': Women in the Church of the East (1500–1850)." *Internationale Kirchliche Zeitschrift* 100 (2010): 190–208.

———. "'I the Weak Scribe': Scribes in the Church of the East in the Ottoman Period." *Journal of Eastern Christian Studies* 58, nos. 1–2 (2005): 9–26.

———. "'Let Us Partake, All Who Believe in Christ': Liturgy in the Church of the East between 1500 and 1850." In *Christliche Gotteslehre im Orient seit dem Aufkommen des Islams bis zur Gegenwart*, edited by Martin Tamcke, 139–53. Beiruter Texte und Studien 126. Beirut: Orient-Institut Beirut, 2008.

———. "The Missionaries' Assistants: The Role of Assyrians in the Development of Written Urmia Aramaic." *JAAS* 10, no. 2 (1996): 3–17.

———. "A Neo-Aramaic Gospel Lectionary Translation by Israel of Alqosh (Ms. Syr 147, Houghton Library, Harvard University, 1769/70)." In *Loquentes linguis: Studi linguistici e orientali in onore di Fabrizio A. Pennacchietti = Linguistic and Oriental Studies in Honour of Fabrizio A. Pennacchietti = Lingvistikaj kaj orientaj studoj honore al Fabrizio A. Pennacchietti*, edited by Pier Giorgio Borbone, Alessandro Mengozzi, and Mauro Mauro, 523–33. Wiesbaden, Germany: Otto Harrassowitz, 2006.

———, ed. *New Faith in Ancient Lands: Western Mission in the Middle East in the Nineteenth and Early Twentieth Centuries.* Leiden, Netherlands: Brill, 2006.

———. "Nineteenth-Century Protestant Missions and Middle Eastern Women: An Overview." In *Gender, Religion and Change in the Middle East,* edited by Inger Marie Okkenhaug and Ingvild Flaskerud, 103–22. Oxford: Berg, 2005.

———. "The Patriarchs of the Church of the East from the Fifteenth to Eighteenth Centuries." *Hugoye* 2, no. 2 (1999): 235–64.

———. "Paul Bedjan, Missionary for Life (1838–1920)." In *Homilies of Mar Jacob of Sarug,* edited by Paul Bedjan, vol. 6, 339–69. Piscataway, NJ: Gorgias, 2006.

———. "'Simply by Giving to Them Macaroni . . .': Anti–Roman Catholic Polemics in Early Protestant Missions in the Middle East (1820–1860)." In *Christian Witness between Continuity and New Beginnings: Modern Historical Missions in the Middle East,* edited by Martin Tamcke and Michael Marten, 63–80. Berlin, LIT Verlag, 2006.

———. "The Study of Western Mission in the Middle East (1820–1920): An Annotated Bibliography." In *The Social Dimension of Christian Missions in the Middle East: Historical Studies of the 19th and 20th Centuries,* edited by Norbert Friedrich, Uwe Kaminsky, and Roland Löffler, 35–53. Stuttgart: Franz Steiner, 2010.

———. "A Syrian Awakening: Alqosh and Urmia as Centers of Neo-Syriac Writing." In *Symposium Syriacum VII: Uppsala University, Department of Asian and African Languages, 11–14 August 1996,* edited by René Lavenant, 499–515. Orientalia Christiana Analecta 256. Roma: Pontificio Istituto Orientale, 1998.

Naayem, Joseph. *Shall This Nation Die?* New York: Chaldean Rescue, 1921.

Naby, Eden. "The Assyrian of Iran: Reunification of a 'Millat,' 1906–1914." *IJMES* 8, no. 2 (1977): 237–49.

———. "Les Assyriens d'Union Soviétique." *Cahier du monde russe et soviétique* 16 (1975): 445–57.

———. "Theater, Language and Inter-ethnic Exchange: Assyrian Performance before World War I." *Iranian Studies* 40, no. 4 (2007): 501–10.

Nanni, Giordano. *The Colonisation of Time: Ritual, Routine and Resistance in the British Empire.* Manchester, UK: Manchester University Press, 2012.

Nikitine, Basile. "La vie domestique des Assyro-Chaldéens du plateau d'Ourmiah." *L'ethnographie* 11–12 (1925): 356–80.

———. "Superstitions des Chaldéens du plateau d'Ourmiah." *Revue d'ethnographie et des traditions populaires* 3 (1923): 149–81.

Nongbri, Brent. "Dislodging 'Embedded' Religion: A Brief Note on a Scholarly Trope." *Numen* 55 (2008): 440–60.

Odisho, Edward Y. "The Ethnic, Linguistic and Cultural Identity of Modern Assyrians." In *Mythology and Mythologies: Methodological Approaches to Intercultural Influences,* edited by R. M. Whiting, 137–48. Helsinki: Neo-Assyrian Text Corpus Project, 2001.

O'Flynn, Thomas. "The Western Christian Presence in the Caucasus and Qajar Persia, 1802–70." PhD diss., University of Oxford, 2003.

Okkenhaug, Inger Marie. "Introduction: Gender and Missions in the Middle East." *Social Sciences and Missions* 23 (2010):1–6.

Oussani, Gabriel. "The Modern Chaldeans and Nestorians, and the Study of Syriac among Them." *JAOS* 22 (1901): 79–96.

Palmié, Stephen. *Wizards and Scientists: Explorations in Afro-Cuban Modernity and Tradition.* Durham, NC: Duke University Press, 2002.

Parpola, Simo. "Assyrians after Assyria." *JAAS* 13, no. 2 (1999): 1–16.

Peterson, Derek R. "Conversion and the Alignments of Colonial Culture." *Social Sciences and Missions* 24 (2011): 207–32.

Philips, Clifton Jackson, *Protestant America and the Pagan World: The First Half Century of the American Board of Commissioners for Foreign Missions, 1810–1850.* Cambridge, MA: East Asian Research Center and Harvard University Press, 1969.

Pietz, William. "The Problem of the Fetish, I." *Res: Journal of Anthropology and Aesthetics* 9 (1985): 5–17.

Porter, Andrew. "Religion and Empire: British Expansion in the Long Nineteenth Century, 1780–1914." *Journal of Imperial and Commonwealth History* 20, no. 3 (1992): 370–90.

Porterfield, Amanda. *Mary Lyon and the Mount Holyoke Missionaries.* Oxford: Oxford University Press, 1997.

Pratt, Mary Louise. *Imperial Eyes: Travel Writing and Transculturation.* 2nd ed. London: Routledge, 2008.

Prentiss, Craig R., ed. *Religion and the Creation of Race and Ethnicity: An Introduction.* New York: New York University Press, 2003.

Pruitt, Lisa Joy. *A Looking-Glass for Ladies: American Protestant Women and the Orient in the Nineteenth Century.* Macon, GA: Mercer University Press, 2005.

Rafael, Vincente L. *Contracting Colonialism: Translation and Christian Conversion in Tagalog Society under Early Spanish Rule.* Ithaca, NY: Cornell University Press, 1993.

Rambuss, Richard. *Closet Devotions.* Durham, NC: Duke University Press, 1998.

Reade, Julian. "Hormuzd Rassam and His Discoveries." *Iraq* 55 (1993): 39–62.

Reeves-Ellington, Barbara. "Gender, Conversion, and Social Transformation: The American Discourse of Domesticity and the Origins of the Bulgarian Women's Movement, 1864–1876." In *Converting Cultures: Religion, Ideology, and Transformations of Modernity*, edited by Dennis Washburn and A. Kevin Reinhert, 115–40. Leiden, Netherlands: Brill, 2007.

——. "A Vision of Mount Holyoke in the Ottoman Balkans: American Cultural Transfer, Bulgarian Nation-Building, and Women's Educational Reform, 1858–1870." *Gender & History* 16, no. 1 (2004): 146–71.

——. "Women, Gender, and Missionary Education: Ottoman Empire." In *The Encyclopedia of Women and Islamic Cultures.* Vol. 4, edited by Suad Joseph, 285–87. Leiden, Netherlands: Brill, 2007.

——. "Women, Protestant Missions, and American Cultural Expansion, 1800–1938: A Historiographical Sketch." *Social Sciences and Missions* 24 (2011): 190–206.

Reinders, Eric. *Borrowed Gods and Foreign Bodies: Christian Missionaries Imagine Chinese Religion.* Berkeley: University of California Press, 2004.

Ringer, Monica M. *Education, Religion, and the Discourse of Cultural Reform in Qajar Iran.* Costa Mesa, CA: Mazda, 2001.

Robbins, Joel. *Becoming Sinners: Christianity and Moral Torment in a Papua New Guinea Society.* Berkeley: University of California Press, 2004.

——. "Continuity Thinking and the Problem of Christian Culture: Belief, Time, and the Anthropology of Christianity." *Current Anthropology* 48, no. 1 (2007): 5–38.

——. "What Is a Christian? Notes Toward an Anthropology of Christianity." *Religion* 33, no. 3 (2003): 191–99.

Robert, Dana L. *American Women in Mission: A Social History of Their Thought and Practice.* Macon, GA: Mercer University Press, 1997.

———, ed. *Converting Colonialism: Visions and Realities in Mission History, 1706–1914.* Grand Rapids, MI: Eerdmans, 2008.

Roberts, Kyle B. "Locating Popular Religion in the Evangelical Tract: The Roots and Routes of *The Dairyman's Daughter.*" *Early American Studies* 4 (2006): 233–70.

Robson, Laura. *Colonialism and Christianity in Mandate Palestine.* Austin: University of Texas Press, 2011.

Rood, Tim. *The Sea! The Sea! The Shout of the Ten Thousand in the Modern Imagination.* London: Duckworth, 2004.

Rostam-Kolayi, Jasamin. "From Evangelizing to Modernizing Iranians: The American Presbyterian Mission and Its Iranian Students." *Iranian Studies* 41, no. 2 (2008): 213–40.

Rubenstein, Mary-Jane. *Strange Wonder: The Closure of Metaphysics and the Opening of Awe.* New York: Columbia University Press, 2008.

Rublack, Ulinka. "Grapho-Relics: Lutheranism and the Materialization of the Word." *Past and Present* 5 (2005): 144–66.

Sado, Stephan. "Nestorians of Urmia in the Early 1860's: A Look at Russian Sources." *JAAS* 6, no. 2 (1992): 49–59.

Salt, Jeremy. *Imperialism, Evangelism, and the Ottoman Armenians, 1878–1896.* London: Frank Cass, 1993.

Sánchez-Eppler, Karen. "Then When We Clutch Hardest: On the Death of a Child and the Replication of an Image." In *Sentimental Men: Masculinity and the Politics of Affect in American Culture*, edited by Mary Chapman and Glenn Hendler, 64–85. Berkeley: University of California Press, 1999.

Sarmas, Pera. *History of Assyrian Literature* [*Tašʿita d-seprayuta atorêta*]. 3 vols. Tehran: Assyrian Youth Cultural Society, 1962–70.

Schantz, Mark S. "Religious Tracts, Evangelical Reform, and the Market Revolution in Antebellum America." *Journal of the Early Republic* 17 (1997): 425–66.

Schnur, Jan Carsten. *Weltreiche und Wahrheitszeugen: Geschichtsbilder der protestantischen Erweckungsbewegung in Deutschland, 1815–1848.* Göttingen, Germany: Vandenhoeck & Ruprecht, 2011.

Schofield, Ann. "The Fashion of Mourning." In *Representations of Death in Nineteenth-Century US Writing and Culture*, edited by Lucy E. Frank, 157–71. Aldershot, UK: Ashgate, 2007.

Schweitzer, Albert. *The Quest of the Historical Jesus.* Translated by W. Montgomery. New York: Macmillan, 1956.

Scott, Joan W. "The Evidence of Experience." *Critical Inquiry* 17 (1991): 773–97.

Sedra, Paul. *From Mission to Modernity: Evangelicals, Reformers, and Education in Nineteenth-Century Egypt.* London: I. B. Tauris, 2011.

Sengupta, Parna. *Pedagogy for Religion: Missionary Education and the Fashioning of Hindus and Muslims in Bengal.* Berkeley: University of California Press, 2011.

Sharkey, Heather J. *American Evangelicals in Egypt: Missionary Encounters in an Age of Empire.* Princeton, NJ: Princeton University Press, 2008.

Simmel, Georg. *The Sociology of Georg Simmel.* Edited and translated by Kurt Wolff. New York: Free Press, 1950.

Sivasundaram, Sujit. *Nature and the Godly Empire: Science and Evangelical Mission in the Pacific, 1795–1850.* Cambridge: Cambridge University Press, 2005.

Smith, Anthony D. *Chosen Peoples: Sacred Sources of National Identity.* Oxford: Oxford University Press, 2003.

———. *The Ethnic Origins of Nations*. Oxford: Blackwell, 1988.

Smith, J. Z. "Religion, Religions, Religious." In *Critical Terms for Religious Studies*, edited by Mark Taylor, 269–84. Chicago: University of Chicago Press, 1998.

Soskice, Janet. *The Sisters of Sinai: How Two Lady Adventurers Discovered the Hidden Gospels*. New York: Alfred A. Knopf, 2009.

Stanley, Brian. "Christian Missions and the Enlightenment: A Reevaluation." In *Christian Mission and the Enlightenment*, edited by Brian Stanley, 1–21. Grand Rapids, MI: Eerdmans, 2001.

———. "Christian Missions, Antislavery and the Claims of Humanity, c. 1813–1873." In *The Cambridge History of Christianity: World Christianities, c. 1815–c. 1914*. Vol. 8, edited by Sheridan Gilley and Brian Stanley, 443–57. Cambridge: Cambridge University Press, 2006.

Stewart, Charles Samuel. *Journal of a Residence in the Sandwich Islands*. New York: John P. Haven, 1828.

Stolow, Jeremy. *Orthodox by Design: Judaism, Print Politics, and the Artscroll Revolution*. Berkeley: University of California Press, 2010.

———. "Religion and/as Media." *Theory, Culture and Society* 22 (2005): 119–45.

Stout, Jeffrey. *Democracy and Tradition*. Princeton, NJ: Princeton University Press, 2005.

Stroumsa, Guy G. *The End of Sacrifice: Religious Transformations in Late Antiquity*. Translated by Susan Emanuel. Chicago: University of Chicago Press, 2009.

Stuart, John. "Introduction: 'Mission and Empire.'" *Social Sciences and Missions* 21 (2008): 1–5.

Suny, Ronald Grigor. "Explaining Genocide: The Fate of the Armenians in the Late Ottoman Empire." In *Removing Peoples: Forced Removal in the Modern World*, edited by Richard Bessel and Claudia B. Haake, 209–53. Oxford: Oxford University Press, 2009.

Tamcke, Martin. "Die Hermannsburger Mission in Persien." In *Zu Geschichte, Theologie, Liturgie und Gegenwartslage der syrischen Kirchen, Ausgewählte Vorträge des deutschen Syrologen-Symposiums vom 2.–4. Oktober 1998 in Hermannsburg*, edited by Martin Tamcke and Andreas Heinz, 231–74. Münster: LIT, 2000.

———. "Nestorianisch, syrisch oder assyrisch? Beobachtungen zum Selbstverständnis der lutherischen Nestorianer in der Periode von 1875–1915." In *Hermeneutik und Exegese: Verstehenslehre und Verstehensdeutung im regionalen System koexistierender Religionsgemeinschaften im Orient, Leucorea-Konferenz 2005*, edited by Ute Pietruschka, 159–69. Hallesche Beiträge zur Orientwissenschaft 43. Halle an der Salle, Germany: Martin-Luther-Universität Halle-Wittenberg, 2009.

Tamcke, Martin, and Michael Marten, eds. *Christian Witness between Continuity and New Beginnings: Modern Historical Missions in the Middle East*. Berlin, LIT Verlag, 2006.

Tavakoli-Targhi, Mohamad. *Refashioning Iran: Orientalism, Occidentalism, and Historiography*. New York: Palgrave Macmillan, 2001.

Taylor, Charles. *Modern Social Imaginaries*. Durham, NC: Duke University Press, 2004.

———. *A Secular Age*. Cambridge, MA: Belknap Press of Harvard University Press, 2007.

———. "Western Secularity." In *Rethinking Secularism*, edited by Craig Calhoun, Mark Juergensmeyer, and Jonathan VanAntwerpen, 31–53. Oxford: Oxford University Press, 2011.

———. "Why We Need a Radical Redefinition of Secularism." In *The Power of Religion in the Public Sphere*, edited by Eduarto Mendieta and Jonathan VanAntwerpen, 34–59. New York: Columbia University Press, 2011.

Taylor, Gordon. *Fever and Thirst: A Missionary Doctor amid the Christian Tribes of Kurdistan*. Chicago: Academy, 2005.

Tejirian, Eleanor H., and Reeva Spector Simon, eds. *Altruism and Imperialism: Western Cultural and Religious Missions in the Middle East*. Middle East Institute, Columbia University, Occasional Papers 4. New York: Middle East Institute, 2002.

———. *Conflict, Conquest, and Conversion: Two Thousand Years of Christian Missions in the Middle East*. New York: Columbia University Press, 2012.

Teule, Herman. "Joseph II, Patriarch of the Chaldeans (1676–1713/4), and the Book of the Magnet. First Soundings." In *Studies on the Christian Arabic Heritage*, edited by Rifaat Ebied and Herman Teule, 221–41. Eastern Christian Studies, no. 5. Louvain, Belgium: Peeters, 2004.

Teule, Herman, Grigory Kessel, and Stephen Sado. "The Mikhail Sado Collection of Syriac Manuscripts in St. Petersburg." In *Eastern Christians and Their Written Heritage: Manuscripts, Scribes and Context*, edited by J. P. Monferrer-Sala, H. G. B. Teule, and S. Torallas Tovar, 43–76. Louvain, Belgium: Peeters, 2012.

Thomas, Nicholas. *Entangled Objects: Exchange, Material Culture, and Colonialism in the Pacific*. Cambridge, MA: Harvard University Press, 1991.

Thompson, E. P. "Time, Work-Discipline, and Industrial Capitalism." *Past and Present* 38 (1967): 56–97.

Tompkins, Jane. *Sensational Designs: The Cultural Work of American Fiction, 1790–1860*. New York: Oxford University Press, 1985.

Trigona-Harany, Benjamin. *The Ottoman Süryânî from 1908 to 1914*. Piscataway, NJ: Gorgias, 2009.

Tsereteli, Konstantin. "The Velar Spirant ġ in Modern East Aramaic Dialects." In *Studies in Neo-Aramaic*, edited by Wolfhart Heinrichs, 35–42. Atlanta: Scholars Press, 1990.

van Bruinessen, Martin. *Agha, Shaikh, and State: The Social and Political Structures of Kurdistan*. London: Zed Books, 1992.

———. "Kurdish Tribes and the State of Iran: the Case of Simko's Revolt." In *The Conflict of Tribe and State in Iran and Afghanistan*, edited by Richard Tapper, 364–400. London: Croom Helm, 1983.

van der Veer, Peter, ed. *Conversion to Modernities: The Globalization of Christianity*. New York: Routledge, 1996.

———. *Imperial Encounters: Religion and Modernity in India and Britain*. Princeton, NJ: Princeton University Press, 2001.

Viswanathan, Gauri. *Outside the Fold: Conversion, Modernity, and Belief*. Princeton, NJ: Princeton University Press, 1998.

Walls, Andrew F. "The American Dimension in the History of the Missionary Movement." In *Earthen Vessels: American Evangelicals and Foreign Missions, 1880–1980*, edited by Joel A. Carpenter and Wilbert R. Shenk, 1–25. Grand Rapids, MI: Eerdmans, 1990.

———. "The Eighteenth-Century Protestant Missionary Awakening in Its European Context." In *Christian Mission and the Enlightenment*, edited by Brian Stanley, 22–44. Grand Rapids, MI: Eerdmans, 2001.

———. *The Missionary Movement in Christian History: Studies in the Transmission of Faith*. New York: Orbis Books, 1996.

Ware, Kallistos. Preface to Pseudo-Macarius, *The Fifty Spiritual Homilies and the Great Letter*, translated by George A. Maloney, S.J., xi–xviii. Mahwah, NJ: Paulist Press, 1992.

Warner, Michael. *The Letters of the Republic: Publication and the Public Sphere in Eighteenth-Century America*. Cambridge, MA: Harvard University Press, 1990.

Wenger, Tisa. *We Have a Religion: The 1920s Pueblo Indian Dance Controversy and American Religious Freedom*. Chapel Hill: University of North Carolina Press, 2009.

Williams, Raymond. *Marxism and Literature*. Oxford: Oxford University Press, 1977.

Wilmshurst, David. *The Ecclesiastical Organisation of the Church of the East, 1318–1913.* Louvain, Belgium: Peeters, 2000.

———. *The Martyred Church: A History of the Church of the East.* London: East and West, 2011.

Witakowski, Witold. "The Magi in Syriac Tradition." In Kiraz, *Malphono w-Rabo d-Malphone,* 809–43.

Wolk, Daniel P. "Church Colony vs. Congregation: A Struggle for Control of the Church of the East in Chicago during the 1940s." *JAAS* 22, no. 1 (2008): 1–48.

———. "The Emergence of Assyrian Ethnonationalism: The Discourse against the *Hāčāqoḡē* ('Thieves of the Cross')." Unpublished manuscript, 2010, Microsoft Word file.

———. "Expressions Concerning the Heart (*Libbā*) in Northeastern Neo-Aramaic in Relation to a Classical Syriac Model of the Temperaments." In *Culture, Body, and Language: Conceptualisations of the Heart and Other Internal Body Organs across Languages and Cultures,* edited by F. Sharifian, René Dirven, Ning Yu, and Susanne Niemeier, 267–317. Berlin and New York: Mouton de Gruyter, 2008.

———. "Migration and the Transformation of Assyrian Stereotypes of Jews: A Conceptual, Historical Approach." Unpublished manuscript, 2010, Microsoft Word file.

———. "Preserving a Name in a Restless Land: The Assyrian Community in Chicago." Unpublished manuscript, 2010, Microsoft Word file.

Wosh, Peter J. *Spreading the Word: The Bible Business in Nineteenth-Century America.* Ithaca, NY: Cornell University Press, 1994.

Yelle, Robert A. *The Language of Disenchantment: Protestant Literalism and Colonial Discourse in British India.* Oxford: Oxford University Press, 2013.

Yonan, Gabriele. *Ein vergessener Holocaust: Die Vernichtung der christlichen Assyrer in der Türkei.* Göttingen and Vienna: Pogrom, 1989.

———. *Journalismus bei den Assyrern: Ein Überblick von seinen Anfängen bis zur Gegenwart.* Berlin: Zentralverband der Assyrischen Vereinigungen in Deutschland und Mitteleuropa, 1985.

Zaman, Muhammad Qasim. *The Ulama in Contemporary Islam: Custodians of Change.* Princeton, NJ: Princeton University Press, 2002.

Zirinsky, Michael. "American Presbyterian Missionaries at Urmia during the Great War." *JAAS* 12, no. 1 (1998): 6–27.

Zito, Angela. "Culture." In *Keywords in Religion, Media, and Culture,* edited by David Morgan, 69–82. New York: Routledge, 2008.

Zubaida, Sami. "Contested Nations: Iraq and the Assyrians." *Nations and Nationalism* 6 (2000): 363–82.

Index